EUROPE & THE MEDITERRANEAN

Turn to the page shown for the start of each country

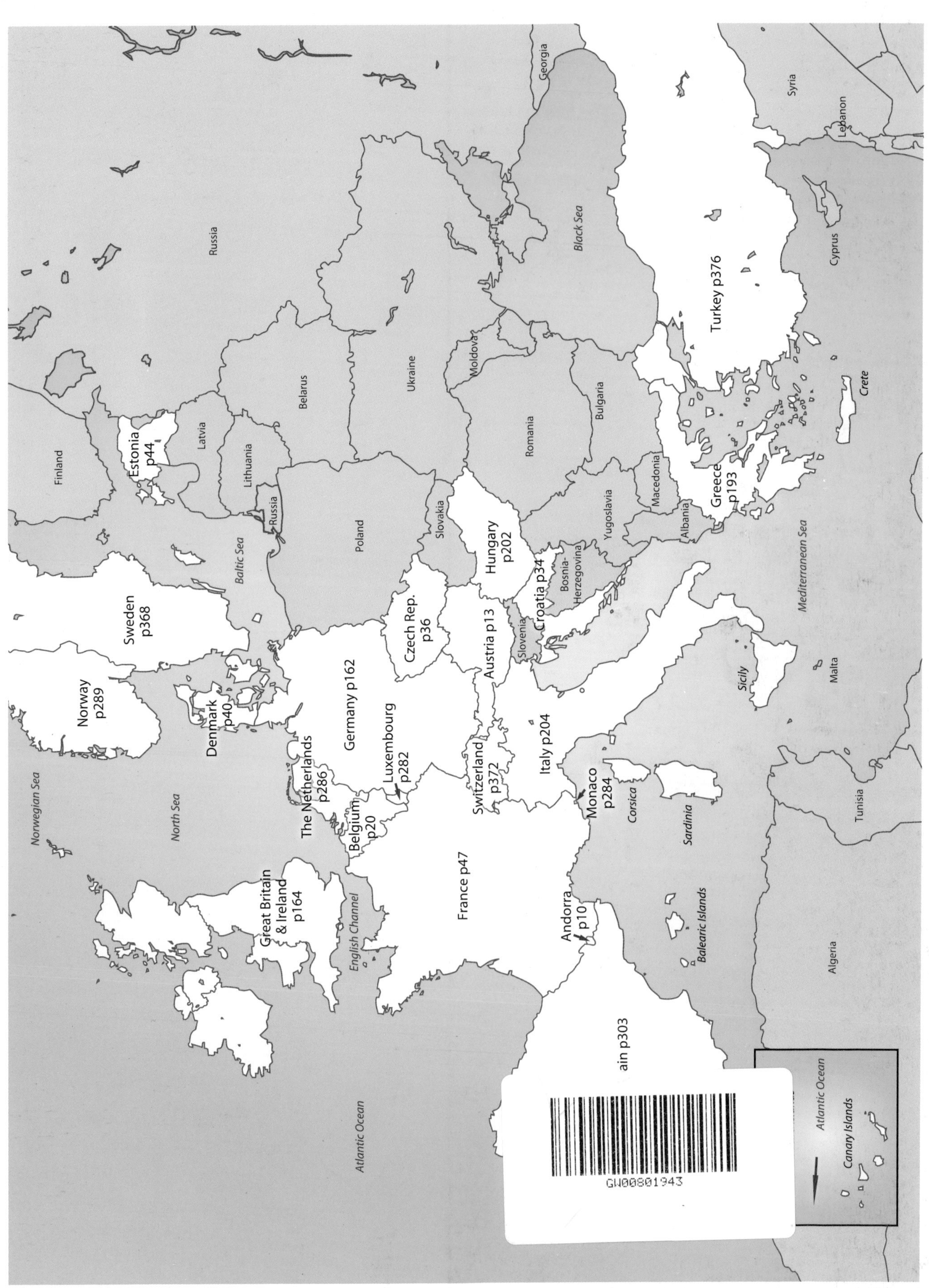

CONTENTS / SOMMAIRE / INHALT

Countries / Pays / Länder

Mini Listings / Mini Listing / Mini-Auflistung

ILISER CE GUIDE / BENUTZERHINWEISE

un hôtel dans un

d'Europe en page 2
que vous souhaitez

du pays désiré, où les
r ordre alphabétique
a ville.

à la première page du
rouverez une carte.
ue hôtel est marqué
ou un point violet
ial) avec un chiffre
à laquelle l'hôtel est

un hôtel dont vous
ez vous à l'index aux

liste des hôtels
isés par leurs
iple Centre thermal,

e divisent en trois

ffrant une prestation
u'un vaste choix de

itels de charme):
phère plus intime et

lôtes): établissements
es propriétaires et ne
ner

otre choix, veuillez
nt. Les tarifs indiqués
e l'impression mais il
es vérifier auprès de
avant de réserver.
onner Condé Nast
ence lors de votre

cevoir des lettres de
s chambres réservées
Les lecteurs doivent
e réservation auprès
r téléphone, courrier
ssent un contrat légal
nes circonstances, un
cturer une chambre
ésente pas à l'hôtel
nulation.

t être obtenus en
ectement Condé Nast
3 3597. Vous pouvez
le commande fournis
s 421 (anglais), 423
und). Vous pouvez
les sur Internet
shop

Wenn Sie ein Hotel an einem bestimmten Ort suchen:

- Blättern Sie zur Europakarte auf Seite 2, um das Land zu finden, in dem sich das gewünschte Hotel befindet.
- Blättern Sie zu dem relevanten Land - hier finden Sie alle Hotels alphabetisch nach Region und/oder Ortsnamen aufgelistet.
- Alternativ dazu blättern Sie zu der Titelseite des gewünschten Landes – hier finden Sie eine Karte. Die Lage eines jeden Hotels ist mit einem roten Punkt (Hotel) oder einem violetten Punkt (Kurhotel/Spa) auf der Karte markiert und mit einer Zahl versehen, die mit der Seitenzahl des Hoteleintrags übereinstimmt.

Wenn Sie ein Hotel suchen, dessen Namen Sie bereits kennen, hilft Ihnen das Inhaltsverzeichnis auf den Seiten 412 - 415.

Das Inhaltsverzeichnis listet die Hotels auch nach ihren besonderen Einrichtungen auf, wie z.B. Kureinrichtungen, Golfplatz etc.

Alle Empfehlungen sind nach drei Kategorien geordnet:

- **Hotels**: Häuser, die ein hohes Niveau und eine große Auswahl an Service und Einrichtungen bieten
- **Charming Hotels**: kleinere Hotels mit einer heimeligen und familiären Atmosphäre
- **Guest Houses (Pensionen)**: werden normalerweise vom Eigentümer geführt; es wird nur Frühstück serviert

Wenn Sie Ihre Wahl getroffen haben, wenden Sie sich bitte direkt an das Hotel. Die Preise hatten zur Zeit der Drucklegung ihre Gültigkeit. Bitte denken Sie daran, bei jeder Buchung zu erwähnen, dass Sie sich auf Condé Nast Johansens beziehen.

Manchmal erhalten wir Briefe von Gästen, die für stornierte Zimmer eine Hotelrechnung erhalten. Die Leser sollten sich darüber im klaren sein, dass sie bei einer Reservierung per Telefon, E-Mail oder auch schriftlich, einen rechtsgültigen Vertrag mit dem Hotel eingehen. Ein Hotelier kann unter bestimmten Umständen, auch bei rechtzeitiger Stornierung, eine Gebühr verlangen.

Alle Hotelführer sind im Buchhandel erhältlich oder direkt von Condé Nast Johansens unter der Telefonnummer +44 20 7538 3597. Alternativ können auch die Bestellformulare auf Seite 421 (Englisch), Seite 423 (Französisch) und Seite 425 (Deutsch) verwendet werden. Die Guides können auch über das Internet unter www.johansens.com/bookshop bestellt werden.

Introduction / Einführung

Andrew Warren, Managing Director, Condé Nast Johansens Ltd.

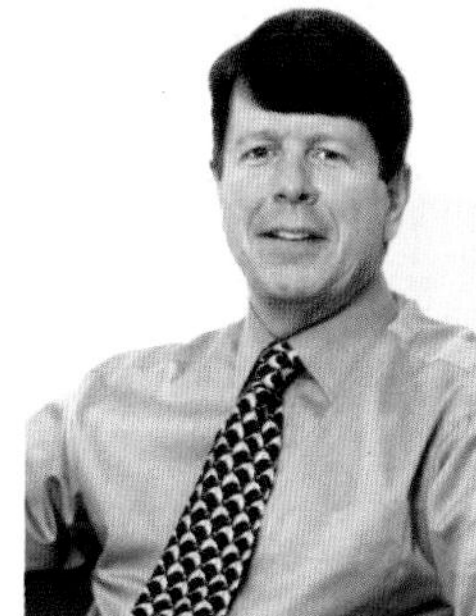

There has been no better time to travel and stay throughout Europe & The Mediterranean.

A more unsettled world has meant that travellers have stayed closer to home, creating an opportunity to rediscover the wonderful hospitality and welcome offered within their own country.

As you will see, our team of Regional Inspectors have once again been very busy and this edition of our Guide is a treasure trove of fabulous places including, for the first time, a stunning array of dedicated spa hotels.

Please let us know of your experiences at our Recommendations, there are "Guest Survey Forms" at the back of this Guide and on our website www.johansens.com where you can take advantage of some very attractive "Special Offers".

Above all, please remember to mention Condé Nast Johansens when you make an enquiry or reservation and again when you arrive. You will be especially welcome.

Il n'y a jamais eu de meilleur moment pour voyager et passer des vacances en Europe et au bord de la Méditerrannée.

Un monde plus incertain signifie que les voyageurs restent plus près de chez eux, ayant ainsi l'occasion de redécouvrir la merveilleuse hospitalité et l'accueil de leur propre pays.

Comme vous pouvez le voir, notre équipe d'Inspecteurs Régionaux a été très active et cette édition de notre Guide est une mine d'or d'endroits fantastiques y compris, pour la première fois, une collection incroyable d'hôtels centres thermaux.

Partagez vos expériences avec nous dans nos Recommandations; des « Enquêtes de satisfaction » pour nos hôtes sont au dos de ce Guide et sur notre site Internet www.johansens.com, où vous pouvez bénéficier d'offres spéciales.

N'oubliez pas de mentionner Condé Nast Johansens lors de votre réservation et à votre arrivée. L'accueil que vous recevrez n'en sera que plus chaleureux.

Es gab nie einen besseren Zeitpunkt, innerhalb Europas und des Mittelmeerraumes zu verreisen.

Unsere so unsicher gewordene Welt hat dazu geführt, dass man oftmals auf Fernreisen verzichtet und seinen Urlaub viel eher im näheren Umkreis verbringt. So bekommt man die Möglichkeit, die wunderbare Gastfreundschaft und Herzlichkeit auch im eigenen Land mit ganz neuen Augen zu betrachten.

Wie Sie sehen, war unser Team aus Regionalen Inspektoren auch dieses Jahr wieder vollauf beschäftigt, und diese Ausgabe ist eine wahre Schatztruhe, die traumhafte Urlaubsorte und zum ersten Mal auch eine eindrucksvolle Auswahl an Kurhotels bietet.

Bitte zögern Sie nicht, uns von Ihren Erfahrungen zu berichten. Am Ende dieses Guides finden Sie „Gastberichte" und auf unserer Internetseite www.johansens.com können Sie aus einer Reihe von interessanten „Special Offers" auswählen.

Und denken Sie daran, bei Ihrer Buchung und noch einmal bei der Ankunft im Hotel Condé Nast Johansens zu erwähnen – Sie werden besonders herzlich willkommen geheissen.

Andrew Warren

The Condé Nast Johansens Promise

Condé Nast Johansens is the most comprehensive illustrated reference to annually inspected, independently owned hotels throughout Great Britain, Europe and North America.

It is our objective to maintain the trust of Guide users by recommending through annual inspection a careful choice of accommodation offering quality, excellence and value for money.

Our team of over 50 dedicated Regional Inspectors have visited almost 3000 hotels, country houses, inns and resorts throughout 39 countries to select only the very best for recommendation in the 2004 editions of our Guides.

No hotel can appear in our Guides unless they meet our exacting standards.

L'Engagement de Condé Nast Johansens

Condé Nast Johansens est la référence de guides illustrés la plus complète en matière d'hôtels indépendants, inspectés annuellement en Grande-Bretagne, Europe et Amérique du Nord.

C'est notre objectif de maintenir la confiance de nos lecteurs en continuant à recommander, par le biais de nos inspections annuelles, une sélection d'établissements offrant qualité, excellence et un bon rapport qualité-prix.

Notre équipe de plus de 50 inspecteurs régionaux a visité près de 3000 hôtels, country houses, inns et resorts dans plus de 39 pays, pour ne sélectionner que le meilleur en recommandation dans les éditions 2004 de nos Guides.

Aucun hôtel ne peut apparaître dans nos Guides sans répondre exactement à nos standards.

Das Condé Nast Johansens Versprechen

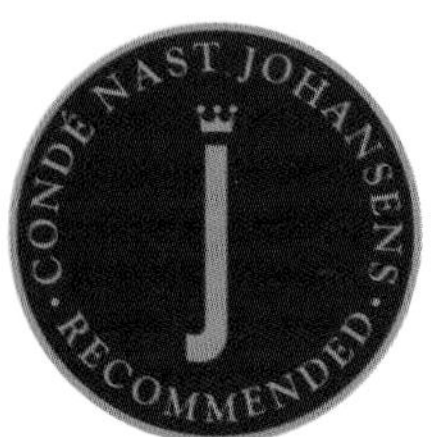

Condé Nast Johansens ist das umfangreichste illustrierte Nachschlagewerk für jährlich inspizierte, privat geführte Hotels in ganz Großbritannien, Europa und Nordamerika.

Unser Ziel ist es, das Vertrauen unserer Leser zu erhalten, indem wir durch jährliche Inspektion eine sorgfältige Auswahl der Häuser treffen, die höchste Qualität bei einem hervorragenden Preis-Leistungs-Verhältnis bieten.

Unser Team aus über 50 regionalen Inspektoren besuchte an die 3000 Hotels, Landhäuser, Inns und Resorts in 39 Ländern, um nur die besten Häuser für eine Empfehlung in unseren Guides für 2004 auszuwählen. Jedes in unseren Guides erscheinende Hotel muss unsere extrem hohen Anforderungen erfüllen.

HILDON
NATURAL MINERAL WATER
ESTABLISHED
1989
WELL... DE GUSTIBUS
NON EST DISPUTANDUM
HILDON
AN ENGLISH
NATURAL MINERAL WATER
OF EXCEPTIONAL TASTE
DELIGHTFULLY STILL
Hildon Ltd., Broughton, Hampshire SO20 8DQ, ☏01794-301 747
GENTLY CARBONATED
Hildon Ltd., Broughton, Hampshire SO20 8DQ, UK ☏ +44 (0)1794 - 301 747, Fax +44 (0)1794 - 301 718
e-mail: hildon@hildon.com – www.hildon.com

Condé Nast Johansens

Condé Nast Johansens Ltd, 6-8 Old Bond Street, London W1S 4PH
Tel: +44 (0)20 7499 9080 Fax: +44 (0)20 7152 3565
Find Condé Nast Johansens on the Internet at: **www.johansens.com**
E-Mail: info@johansens.com

Publishing Director:	Charlotte Evans
European Publishing Executive:	Claire Gorman
Manager, France:	Stéphanie Martinez
Inspectors:	Ana María Brebner
	Suzanne Flanders
	Gianna Illari
	Tunde Longmore
	Barbara Marcotulli
	Renzo Miracco
	Murat Özgüç
	Seamus Shortt
	Agnes Szent-Ivanyi Exton
	Danielle Taljaardt
	Christopher Terleski
Production Manager:	Kevin Bradbrook
Production Controller:	Laura Kerry
Senior Designer:	Michael Tompsett
Editorial Manager:	Stephanie Cook
Copywriters:	Clare Barker
	Sasha Creed
	Norman Flack
	Debra Giles
	Rozanne Paragon
	Leonora Sandwell
Sales and Marketing Director:	Tim Sinclair
Promotions & Events Manager:	Adam Crabtree
Client Services Director:	Fiona Patrick
P.A. to Managing Director :	Siobhan Smith
Managing Director:	Andrew Warren

Condé Nast Johansens Ltd. is part of The Condé Nast Publications Ltd.

ISBN 1 903665 15 9

Printed in England by St Ives plc
Colour origination by Graphic Facilities

Distributed in the UK and Europe by Portfolio, Greenford (bookstores). In North America by Whitehurst & Clarke, New York (direct sales) and Hunter Publishing, New Jersey (bookstores). In Australia and New Zealand by Bookwise International, Wingfield, South Australia.

WWW.JOHANSENS.COM

Visit the Condé Nast Johansens website to:

- Print out detailed **road maps**
- See up-to-date accommodation **Special Offers**
- Access each **recommended hotel's own website**
- Find details of places to visit nearby - **historic houses, castles, gardens, museums and galleries**

Condé Nast Johansens Home Page

Users can log in as an Online Member to receive regular e-mail updates, complete guest survey reports and create their own Personal Portfolio of favourite recommended hotels

Example of Recommended Hotel's Web Entry

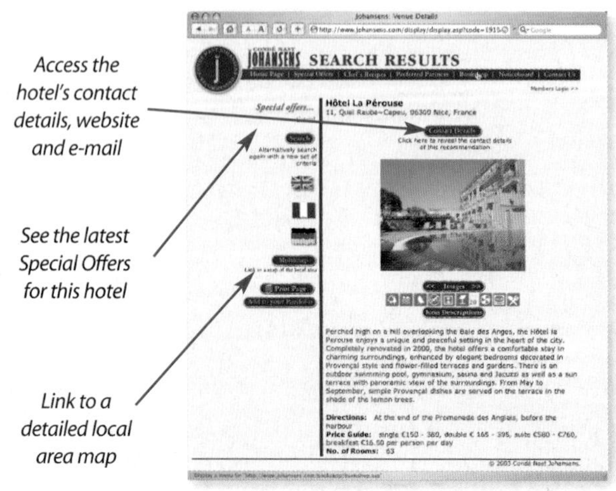

2003 Awards For Excellence

The winners of the Condé Nast Johansens 2003 Awards for Excellence

The winners of the Condé Nast Johansens 2003 Awards for Excellence

The Condé Nast Johansens 2003 Awards for Excellence were presented at the Condé Nast Johansens Annual Dinner held at The Dorchester on November 11th, 2002. Awards were made to those properties worldwide that represented the finest standards and best value for money in luxury independent travel. An important source of information for these awards was the feedback provided by guests who completed Johansens Guest Survey forms. Guest Survey forms can be found on pages 422 (English), 424 (French) and 426 (German).

Les vainqueurs des Conde Nast Johansens 2003 Awards for Excellence

Les Condé Nast Johansens 2003 Awards for Excellence ont été remis lors du Gala annuel de Condé Nast Johansens à l'hôtel Dorchester le 11 novembre 2002. Ces prix ont été créés afin de rétribuer les établissements qui, à travers le monde, offrent les meilleurs standards et rapport qualité prix dans l'hôtellerie de luxe indépendante. Une source d'information et de sélection importante pour ces prix provient des questionnaires de satisfaction renvoyés par les clients. Les questionnaires de satisfaction sont disponibles page 422 (en anglais), page 424 (en français) et page 426 (en allemand).

Die Gewinner der Condé Nast Johansens 2003 Awards for Excellence

Die Condé Nast Johansens 2003 Awards for Excellence wurden am 11. November 2002 beim jährlichen Condé Nast Johansens Dinner im Londoner Hotel The Dorchester präsentiert. Auszeichnungen erhielten diejenigen Häuser weltweit, die höchste Qualität und das beste Preis-Leistungs-Verhältnis bei privaten Luxusreisen bieten konnten. Eine äußerst wichtige Informationsquelle bei der Entscheidung für diese Auszeichnungen waren die Kommentare derjenigen Gäste, die unsere Johansens-Gastberichte ausgefüllt haben. Formulare für Gastberichte finden Sie auf den Seiten 422 (Englisch), 424 (Französisch) und 426 (Deutsch).

Most Excellent European City Hotel Award

Hôtel Plaza Athénée – Paris, France, p113

"This elegant hotel has become renowned for its luxury and charm."

« Cet hôtel élégant doit sa renommée à son luxe et son charme. »

„Dieses elegante Hotel ist bekannt für seinen Luxus und Charme."

2003 Awards For Excellence

The winners of the Condé Nast Johansens 2003 Awards for Excellence

Most Excellent European Countryside Hotel Award

READ'S – Mallorca, Balearic Islands, Spain, p331

"This 500-year old manor house has beautiful interiors and an outstanding new spa."

« Ce manoir vieux de 500 ans a de splendides intérieurs et un spa tout nouveau. »

„Dieses 500 Jahre alte Landhaus besitzt ein wundervolles Interieur und ein fantastisches neues Spa."

Most Excellent European Waterside Hotel Award

HOTEL PUNTA EST – Liguria, Italy, p224

"A magnificent 18th-century villa nestled in olive groves and overlooking the sea."

« Une magnifique villa du XVIIIe siècle nichée dans les oliveraies et surplombant la mer. »

„Eine herrliche Villa aus dem 18. Jahrhundert inmitten von Olivenhainen mit Blick aufs Meer."

European Best Value for Money Award

HOTEL GIORGIONE – Venice, Italy, p276

"Romantic and stylish with modern comforts but all of its original charm."

« Romantique et chic avec tout le confort moderne et tout son charme original. »

„Romantisch und elegant mit modernem Komfort und ursprünglichem Charme."

The following award winners are featured within Condé Nast Johansens 2004 Guides to Hotels – Great Britain & Ireland, Country Houses – Great Britain & Ireland, Hotels – North America. See page 8 for details of these Guides.

Les Prix d'Excellence ci-dessous sont présentés dans les Guides 2004 Condé Nast Johansens: Hotels – Great Britain & Ireland, Country Houses – Great Britain & Ireland, Hotels – North America. Voir page 8 pour plus de détails sur ces guides.

Die folgenden Preisträger werden in diesen Condé Nast Johansens 2004 Guides vorgestellt: Hotels – Great Britain & Ireland, Country Houses – Great Britain & Ireland, Hotels – North America. Siehe Seite 8 für Einzelheiten zu diesen Hotelführern.

Most Excellent Country Hotel Award
Dromoland Castle – Co. Clare, Ireland

Most Excellent London Hotel Award
One Aldwych – London, England

Most Excellent Value for Money Award
Hassop Hall – Derbyshire, England

Most Excellent Service Award
Kinfauns Castle – Perth, Scotland

Most Excellent Restaurant Award
Percy's Country House Hotel & Restaurant – Devon, England

Most Excellent Spa Award
Danesfield House – Buckinghamshire, England

Most Excellent Country House Award
La Sablonnerie – Sark, Channel Islands

Most Excellent Traditional Inn Award
The Lamb Inn – Oxfordshire, England

Most Excellent Coastal Hotel Award
The White Horse – Norfolk, England

North America & Caribbean: Most Outstanding Hotel
Sutton Place Hotel – Illinois, USA

North America & Caribbean: Most Outstanding Inn
Fairview Inn – Mississippi, USA

North America & Caribbean: Most Outstanding Resort
Curtain Bluff – Antigua, Caribbean

North America & Caribbean: Special Award for Excellence
Vista Verde Guest Ranch – Colorado, USA

Knight Frank Award for Excellence and Innovation
Martin & Joy Cummings - Amberley Castle, England

Condé Nast Johansens Guides

Recommending only the finest hotels in the world

As well as this Guide Condé Nast Johansens also publishes the following titles:
En plus de ce Guide, Condé Nast Johansens publie également les titres suivants:
Außer diesem Guide veröffentlicht Condé Nast Johansens auch folgende Titel:

Recommended Hotels, Great Britain & Ireland

411 unique and luxurious hotels, town houses, castles and manor houses chosen for their superior standards and individual character.

411 hôtels luxueux et uniques, hôtels particuliers, châteaux et manoirs sélectionnés pour leurs standards supérieurs et leur caractère individuel.

411 einzigartige luxuriöse Hotels, Stadthäuser, Schlösser und Landsitze, ausgewählt aufgrund ihres extrem hohen Niveaus und individuellen Charakters.

Recommended Country Houses, Small Hotels & Inns, Great Britain & Ireland

255 smaller more rural properties, ideal for short breaks or more intimate stays.

255 établissements plus petits et le plus souvent à la campagne. Idéal pour des courts séjours ou des escapades romantiques.

255 kleinere und eher ländliche Häuser, ideal für Kurztrips oder ein romantisches Wochenende zu zweit.

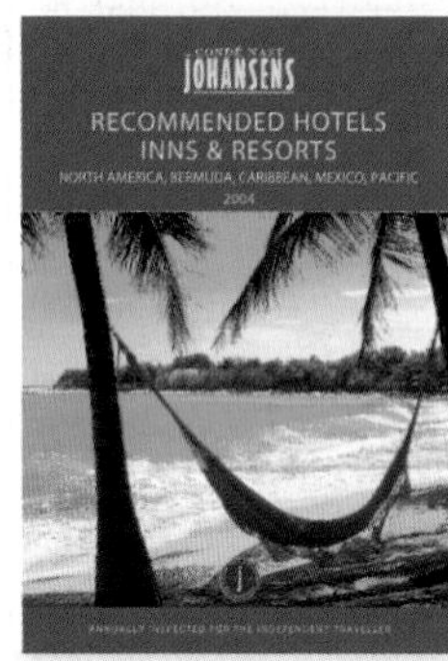

Recommended Hotels, Inns & Resorts, North America, Bermuda, Caribbean, Mexico, Pacific

200 properties including many hidden properties from across the region.

200 établissements dont de nombreux joyaux cachés à travers les régions.

200 Häuser, darunter zahlreiche Geheimtipps in der gesamten Region.

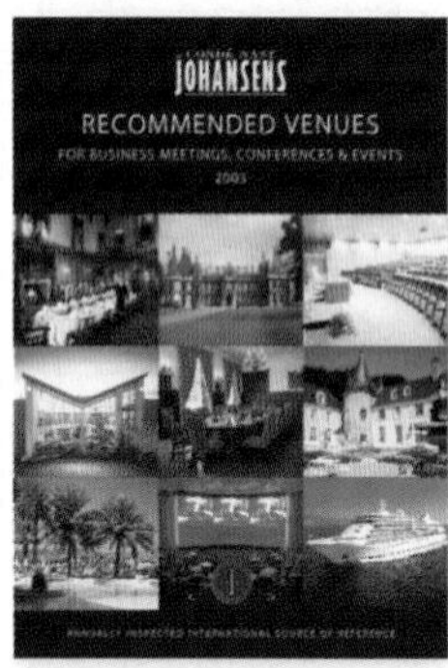

Recommended Venues for Business Meetings, Conferences and Events, Great Britain & Europe

230 venues that cater specifically for a business audience.

230 lieux de conférences s'adressant spécifiquement à une clientèle d'affaire.

230 Häuser, die speziell auf Geschäftskunden ausgerichtet sind.

To order any Guides please complete the order form on page 421 or call FREEPHONE 0800 269 397

Pour commander les Guides, merci de compléter le bon de commande situé en page 423 ou appelez +44 208 655 7810

Um die Hotelguides zu bestellen, füllen Sie bitte das Bestellformular auf Seite 426 aus oder bestellen Sie direkt unter der Nummer +44 208 655 7810

Andorra

Hotel location shown in red (hotel) or purple (spa hotel) with page number

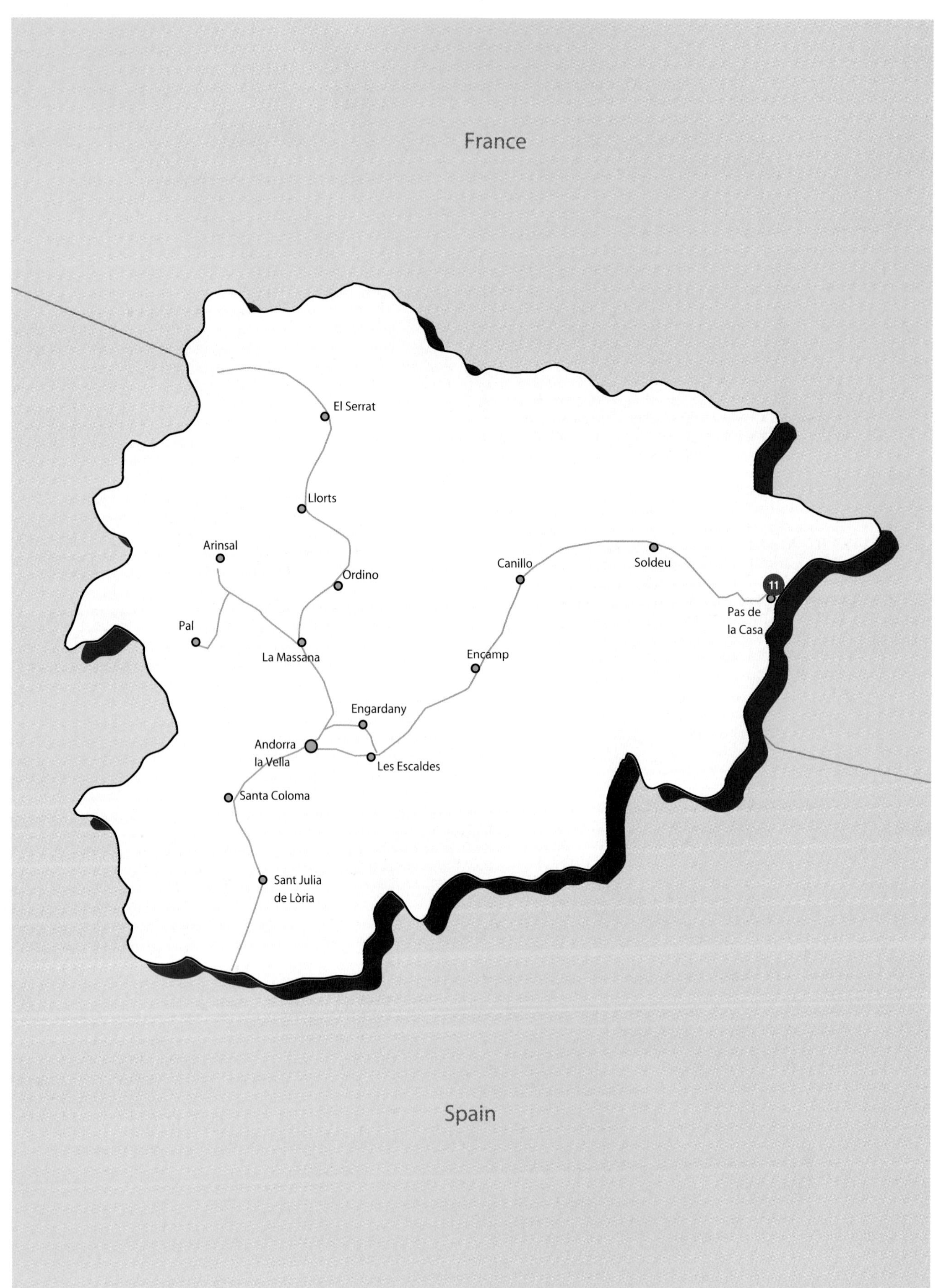

Font d'Argent Hotel Ski & Resort

C/ Bearn 20, 22, 24, Pas de la Casa, Andorra

Situated in the centre of Pas de la Casa and only 100m from the ski slopes, Hotel Font d'Argent is a most relaxing retreat in the heart of the Pyrenees. An excellent buffet and à la carte menu, freshly prepared in a show kitchen, are served in the Tristaina restaurant, whilst the Bar-Coctelería is the ideal place to relax with friends and sample some of the best cocktails around. Guests can enjoy the SPA area with Jacuzzis, saunas, solarium and a massage and treatment room.

Situé au centre de Pas de la Casa et à 100 m des pistes, Hôtel Font d'Argent est un retrait relaxant au cœur des Pyrénées. Un buffet excellent et menu à la carte sont préparés dans une cuisine cuisine de démonstration et servis dans le restaurant Tristaina, alors que le Bar-Coctelería est l'endroit idéal où se détendre avec des amis et déguster des meilleurs cocktails qui existent. Les hôtes peuvent profiter du SPA, qui dispose de jacuzzis, saunas, solarium et une salle de massages et traitements.

Das im Zentrum von Pas de la Casa gelegene und nur 100m von den Skipisten entfernte Hotel Font d'Argent ist eine Oase der Entspannung im Herzen der Pyrenäen. Ein hervorragendes Buffet und à la carte Menü wird in einer Schauküche zubereitet und im Tristaina serviert, und die Bar-Coctelería ist der ideale Ort, um sich mit Freunden zu treffen und die legendären Cocktails zu probieren. Der SPA-Bereich bietet Whirlpools, Saunen, Solarium und einen Massage- und Behandlungsraum.

Our inspector loved: *The warm welcome from the staff - everyone is made to feel like "the" special guest.*

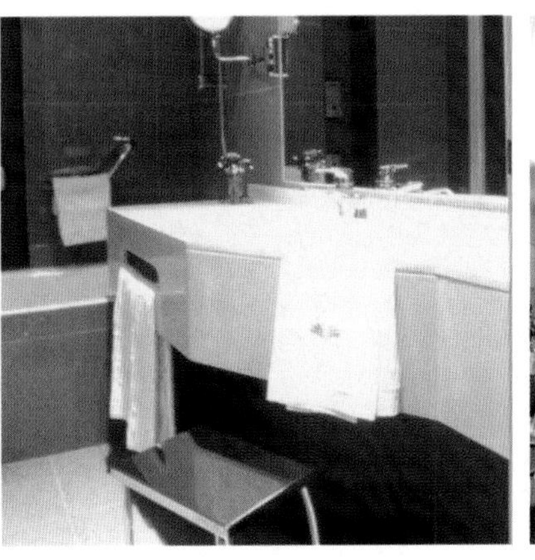

Directions: Enter Pas de la Casa > second turning on the right.

Web: www.johansens.com/fontdargent
E-mail: hotelfontdargent@hotelfontdargent.com
Tel: +376 739 739
Fax: +376 739 800

Soldeu
Pas de la Casa
Andorra de la Vella

Price Guide:
single €35–51
double/twin €51–79

Austria

Hotel location shown in red (hotel) or purple (spa hotel) with page number

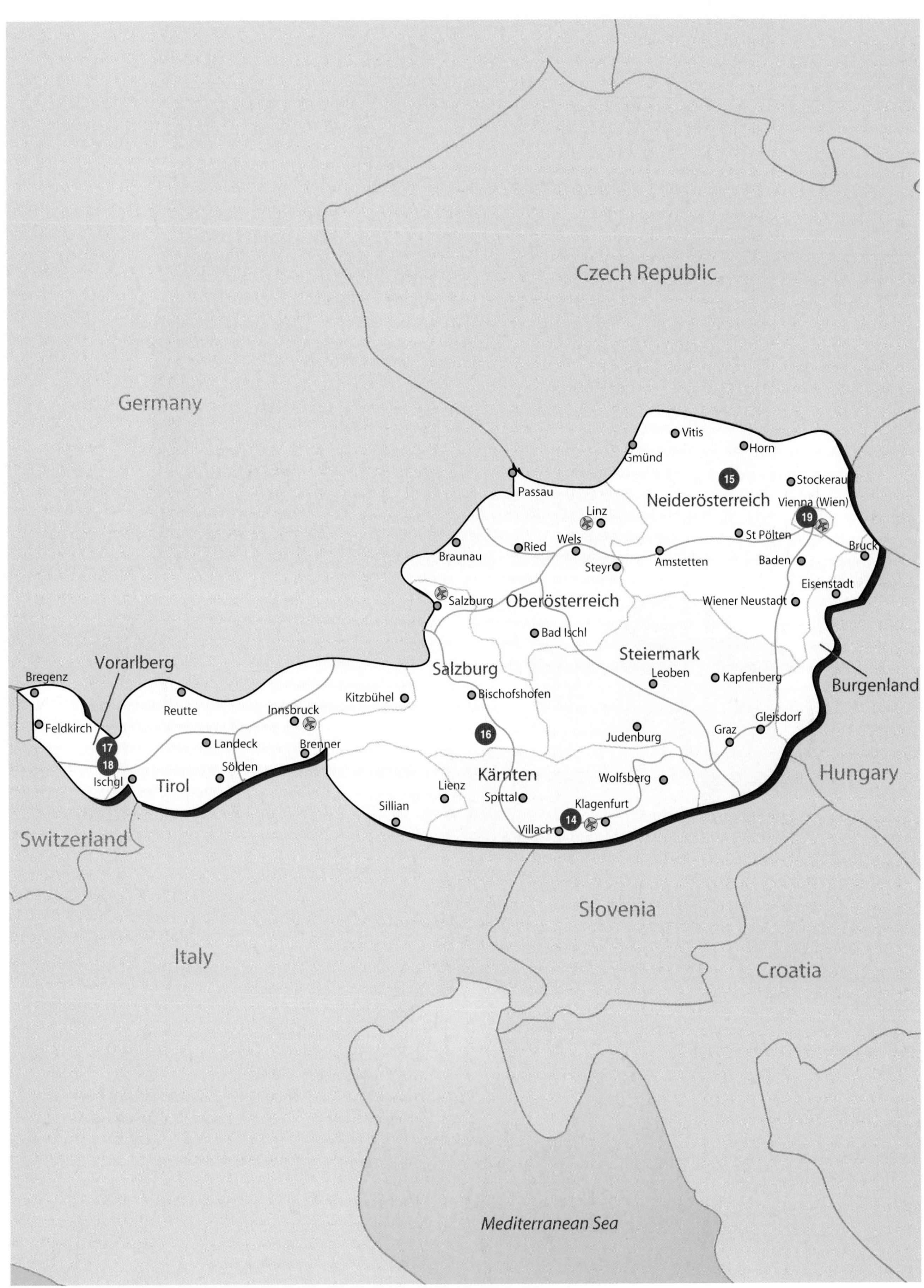

AUSTRIA / KÄRNTEN (VELDEN)

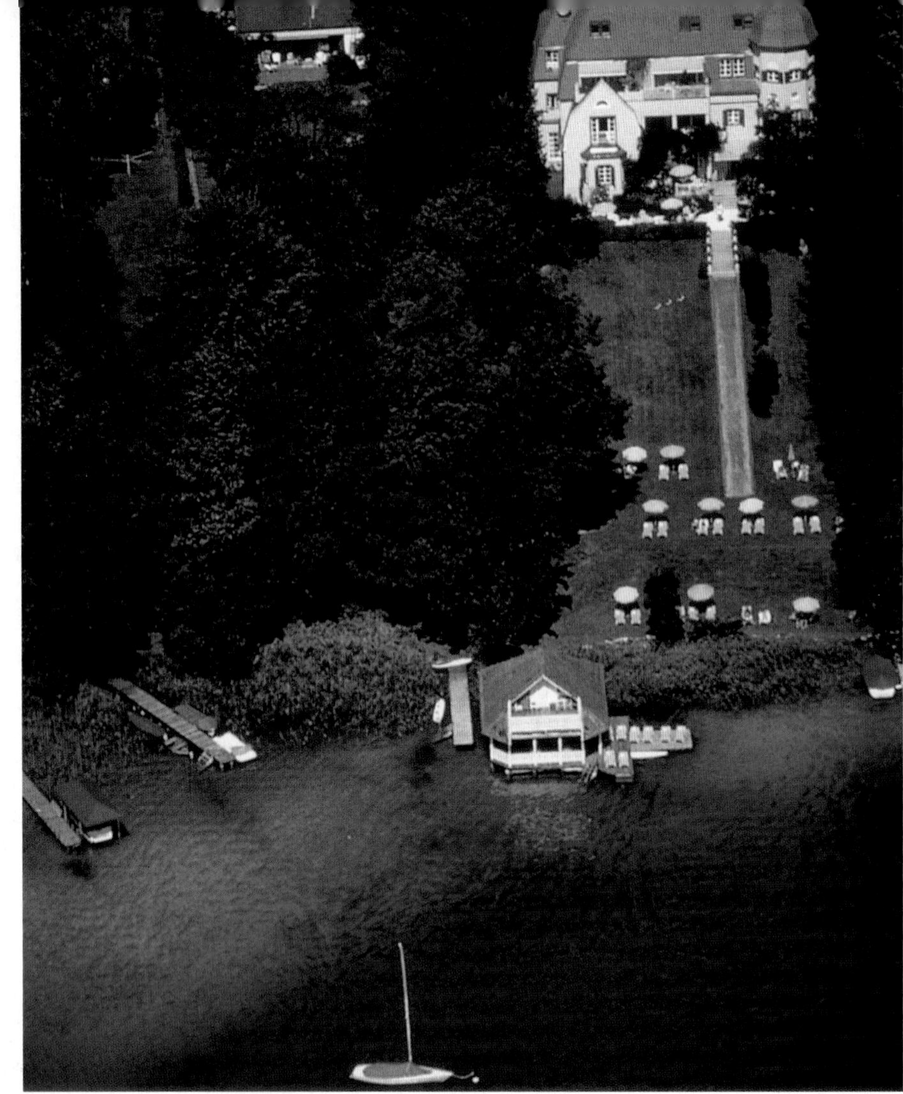

Seeschlössl Velden

KLAGENFURTER STRASSE 34, 9220 VELDEN, AUSTRIA

Directions: Near Velden town centre.

Web: www.johansens.com/seeschlosslvelden
E-mail: seeschloessl@aon.at
Tel: +43 4274 2824
Fax: +43 4274 2824 44

Price Guide:
single/double €120–260
suite €260

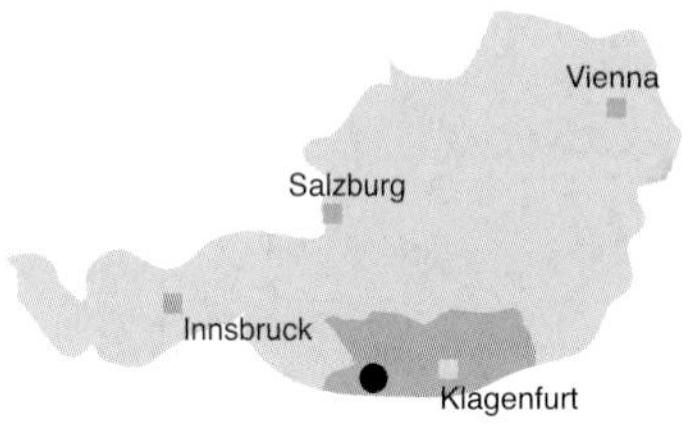

With its own private water front and pier, and shielded by a thick wall of imposing trees, this friendly secluded hotel is a mere 5 minutes from Velden's bustling town centre. The public rooms are luxuriously appointed with their panelled walls, polished wooden floors and delightful rustic furnishings. This high level of comfort extends to the bedrooms – all individually designed – some of which have scenic views over the waterfront.

Bénéficiant de son propre quai d'amarrage et entouré d'un mur épais de superbes arbres, cet hôtel sympathique est très calme, tout en étant à 5 minutes du centre bruyant de Velden. Les pièces communes sont luxueusement décorées avec des murs en lambris, des parquets polis et un ameublement délicieusement rustique. Le haut niveau de confort s'étend aux chambres – toutes individuellement décorées – dont certaines ont une vue scénique sur le bord de l'eau.

Dieses freundliche Hotel, durch hohe Bäume von der Außenwelt abgeschirmt und mit eigenem Steg und Anlegestelle, ist nur 5 Minuten vom geschäftigen Stadtzentrum von Velden entfernt. Die Aufenthaltsräume sind luxuriös mit holzverkleideten Wänden, polierten Holzböden und bezaubernden rustikalen Möbeln ausgestattet. Auch die individuell gestalteten Schlafzimmer sind luxuriös und komfortabel, und einige bieten herrliche Blicke auf den See.

Our inspector loved: *The very warm and distinctive welcome.*

Hotel Schloss Dürnstein

3601 DÜRNSTEIN, AUSTRIA

Built by the nobility 350 ago, and privately restored for nearly 30 years, Schloss Dürnstein is a jewel in the heart of the much praised Wachau region. This stylish and elegant 5-star hotel with its enchanting atmosphere and charm is a perfect retreat for the discerning guest. Each reception room and bedroom is furnished with priceless antiques and equipped with all modern comforts. Excellent facilities for conferences, presentations, weddings and family festivities are available.

Construit par la noblesse il y a 350 ans et restauré depuis presque 30 ans, Schloss Dürnstein est un joyau au sein la très appréciée région de Wachau. Cet élégant hôtel 5 étoiles est, grâce à son atmosphère enchanteresse et son charme, une retraite parfaite pour les hôtes les plus raffinés. Chaque salle de réception et chaque chambre est meublée avec des antiquités sans prix et équipée du confort le plus moderne. L'hôtel dispose de salles de conférence et de réunion, et organise réceptions de mariage et familiales.

Vor 350 Jahren von Aristokraten erbaut und in fast 30jähriger privater Initiative restauriert, ist Schloss Dürnstein heute ein Kleinod im Herzen der vielgepriesenen Wachau. Das stilvolle und elegante 5-Sterne Hotel besitzt eine charmante, zauberhafte Atmosphäre, und ist der ideale Ort für den anspruchsvollen Gast. Die Empfangsräume und Gästezimmer sind mit wertvollen Antiquitäten geschmückt und bieten jeglichen modernen Komfort. Hervorragende Einrichtungen für Tagungen, Präsentationen, Hochzeiten und Familienfeiern sind vorhanden.

Our inspector loved: *Sipping a glass of wine on the terrace overlooking the Danube River.*

Directions: In the centre of Dürnstein.

Web: www.johansens.com/schlossdurnstein
E-mail: hotel@schloss.at
Tel: +43 2711 212
Fax: +43 2711 21230

Price Guide:
single €146–164
double/twin €186
suite €290–355

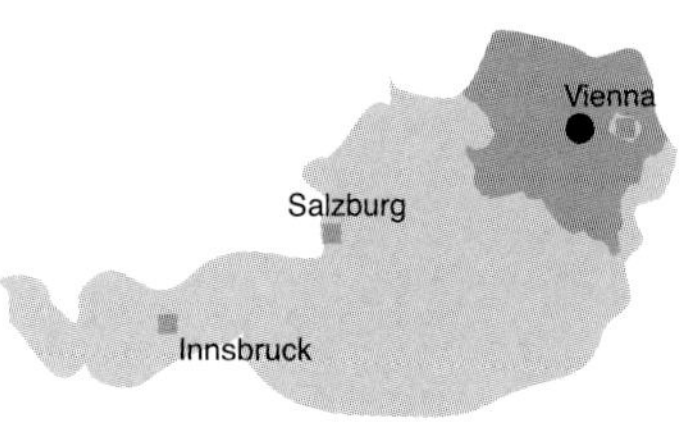

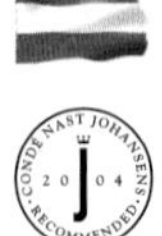

AUSTRIA / SALZBURG (BAD GASTEIN)

ALPINE SPA HOTEL**** HAUS HIRT

AN DER KAISERPROMENADE 14, 5640 BAD GASTEIN, AUSTRIA

Directions: Signposted from town centre.

Web: www.johansens.com/spahaushirt
E-mail: info@haus-hirt.com
Tel: +43 64 34 27 97
Fax: +43 64 34 27 97 48

Price Guide:
single €72–120
double €88–218

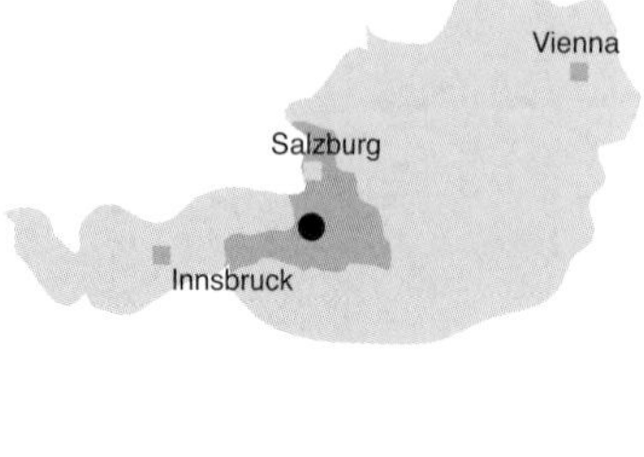

With awe-inspiring views over the Gastein Valley and the mountains beyond, and set in a glorious parkland garden, the Haus Hirt is one of Austria's finest rural hideaways. The Haus, built in the 1930s as a private villa, has hosted famous persons such as the writers Thomas Mann and Stefan Zweig. Relaxation is guaranteed – the Alpine SPA offers hot springs, an Aveda spa, panorama pool, manager antistress, ayurveda and yoga. Fresh and clean mountain air. Great mountain sports and superb skiing with the Haus Hirt guides!

Avec ses vues impressionnantes sur la Vallée Gastein et les montagnes, le Haus Hirt, au coeur d'un parc magnifique, est l'un des refuges le plus raffinés d'Autriche. Le Haus, construit dans les années 1930 en tant que villa privée, a accueilli de nombreuses personnalités tels que les écrivains Thomas Mann et Stefan Zweig. Une totale relaxation est garantie – "l'Alpine SPA" propose spa thermal, un spa Aveda, centre de santé, piscine avec vue panoramique, programmes manager-antistress, ayurveda et yoga. L'air pur, tous sports de montagne et une région de ski de rêve - toutes avec nos guides!.

Das Haus Hirt, in den 30er Jahren als Privatvilla erbaut und inmitten eines Parks gelegen, zählt mit seiner atemberaubenden Aussicht auf das Gasteiner Tal und die Berge zu den besten Landhotels in Österreich und beherbergte bereits Persönlichkeiten wie Thomas Mann und Stefan Zweig. Erholung wird garantiert: Alpine SPA mit heißen Quellen, Aveda-Spa, Beauty- und Gesundheitsfarm, Panoramapool, Manager-Antistress, Ayurveda und Yoga, sowie klare Bergluft, hervorragende Bergsportmöglichkeiten und ein Traumskigebiet, das mit den Hotelguides erkundet werden kann.

Our inspector loved: *The warm and friendly hospitality as well as the spa.*

Sporthotel Kristiania

OMESBERG 331, 6764 LECH AM ARLBERG, AUSTRIA

Set amidst the most stunning scenery – snow-clad mountains, pine forests and the picturesque mountain hamlet – this enchanting chalet-hotel offers winter sports in a warm and friendly ambience. The bedrooms, furnished with deep-pile rugs, modern chairs and local antiques, are simply a delight. Impeccable service and creative cuisine in the restaurant, with its fine modern art collection adorning the pine walls, is a great retreat after a long day on the piste. Open from 1st December until 15th April (end of season).

Ce charmant hôtel positionné de façon merveilleuse est entouré de montagnes enneigées, de forêts de pins et d'un hameau pittoresque de montagne. Le chalet offre aux fanatiques de sports d'hiver une ambiance chaleureuse et accueillante. Les chambres, meublées avec d'épais tapis, des chaises modernes et des antiquités locales, sont un vrai plaisir. Le restaurant offre un service impeccable et une cuisine créative et présente une collection d'art moderne raffinée sur ses murs en pin, créant un havre excellent après une longue journée sur les pistes. Ouvert le 1 décembre jusqu'au 15 avril.

Schneebedeckte Berge, Kiefernwälder und ein malerisches kleines Bergdorf bilden die Umgebung dieses zauberhaften, freundlichen Chalethotels – ein wahres Paradies für Wintersportler. Die herrlichen Zimmer sind mit flauschigen Teppichen, modernen Sesseln und regionalen Antiquitäten ausgestattet. Das Restaurant, in dem auch eine Sammlung moderner Kunst zu bestaunen ist, bietet kreative Küche und perfekten Service – genau das richtige nach einem langen Tag auf der Piste! Geöffnet vom 1. Dezember bis zum 15. April (Saisonende).

***Our inspector loved:** The hotel's fantastic location for skiing and shopping alike. A must for enthusiasts of either!*

Directions: Arlberg tunnel > hotel is on the left just before Lech village.

Web: www.johansens.com/sporthotelkristiania
E-mail: kristiania@lech.at
Tel: +43 5583 25 610
Fax: +43 5583 3550

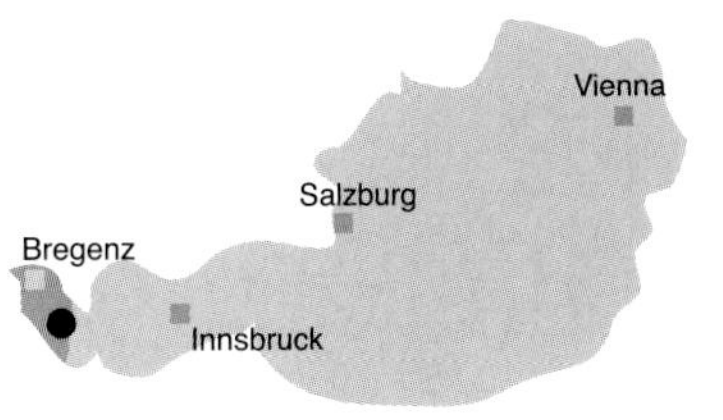

Price Guide:
single €140–350
double/twin/suites €280–1,500

THURNHERS ALPENHOF

The Leading Small Hotels of the World

6763 ZÜRS – ARLBERG, AUSTRIA

Situated high up in the Alps, Thurnhers is a luxury family-owned chalet hotel exclusively dedicated to winter sports enthusiasts. The interior is well designed, and the owner's interest in antiques is reflected in the plethora of knick-knacks that abound. The atmosphere is very convivial, with visitors mingling in the piano bar before dining in the restaurant. Other facilities include an indoor pool, sauna, steam room and solarium. The hotel has its own sports and facility instructor (certified skiing instructor).

Situé dans les Hautes Alpes, le Thurnhers Alpenhof est un chalet luxueux consacre exclusivement aux fanatiques du sport d'hiver. L'intérieur est fort bien décoré et l'intérêt du propriétaire pour les antiquités se manifeste par le bric-à-brac environnant. L'atmosphère y est fort conviviale, et les clients pourront s'installer au piano bar avant de dîner au restaurant. D'autres équipements incluent une piscine couverte, un sauna, un bain turc et un solarium. L'hôtel a son propre moniteur de ski agréé.

Der Thurnhers Alpenhof liegt wie der Name schon sagt, hoch in den Alpen, ein luxuriöses Chalet-Hotel, das völlig auf Wintersport eingestellt ist. Die Räume sind mit viel Liebe eingerichtet, und das Interesse der Besitzer an Antiquitäten wird anhand der Vielzahl von Kleinigkeiten deutlich. Die Atmosphäre ist sehr herzlich, und die Gäste treffen sich in der Pianobar, bevor sie sich im Restaurant verwöhnen lassen. Zur Entspannung gibt es ein Hallenbad, Sauna, Dampfbad und Solarium. Ein hauseigener Sport- und Freizeitbetreuer (staatl. gepr. Skilehrer) steht zur Verfügung.

Our inspector loved: *The distinctive flair of this sumptuous hotel.*

Directions: Follow signs to Zürs/Arlberg.

Web: www.johansens.com/thunrnhersalpenhof
E-mail: mail@thurnhers-alpenhof.at
Tel: +43 5583 2191
Fax: +43 5583 3330

Price Guide:
single €240–307
double/twin €448–584
suite €532–1,366

Grand Hotel Wien

KÄRNTNER RING 9, 1010 VIENNA, AUSTRIA

Originally built in 1870 as the first Grand Hotel in Vienna, this 5-star de luxe hotel has been completely reconstructed to combine the highest standards of modern amenities with the traditional flair of the Hotel. The Grand Hotel Wien offers 205 luxuriously furnished and decorated rooms and suites. Enjoy unforgettable culinary moments at the French gourmet restaurant Le Ciel, whilst overlooking the city or experience the most traditional Japanese cuisine in the gourmet restaurant, Unkai.

Construit en 1870 comme premier Grand Hotel à Vienne, cet hôtel de luxe 5 étoiles a été complètement rénové, tout en gardant son ambiance "Belle Epoque." Le Grand Hotel offre 205 chambres et suites luxueuses. Passez des moments inoubliables culinairement dans notre restaurant français à 2 toques Le Ciel avec sa vue splendide sur la ville ou au restaurant Unkai où l'art culinare japonais doit être savouré.

Ursprünglich 1870 als erstes Grand Hotel Wiens erbaut, wurde dieses 5-Sterne Deluxe-Hotel im klassisch traditionellen Stil mit modernster Technik wiederhergestellt. Das Grand Hotel Wien bietet 205 luxuriös ausgestattete Zimmer und Suiten. Unvergessliche kulinarische Erlebnisse können Sie im französischen 2-Hauben Restaurant Le Ciel mit einzigartigen Blick über die Dächer Wiens oder im japanischen Spezialitätenrestaurant Unkai genießen.

Our inspector loved: *The distinct Viennese atmosphere.*

Directions: On the Kärntner Ring, beside the Staatsoper.

Web: www.johansens.com/grandhotelwien
E-mail: sales@grandhotelwien.com
Tel: +43 1 515 80 0
Fax: +43 1 515 13 13

Price Guide:
single €300–380
double/twin €370–450
suites €660–3,500

Belgium

Hotel location shown in red (hotel) or purple (spa hotel) with page number

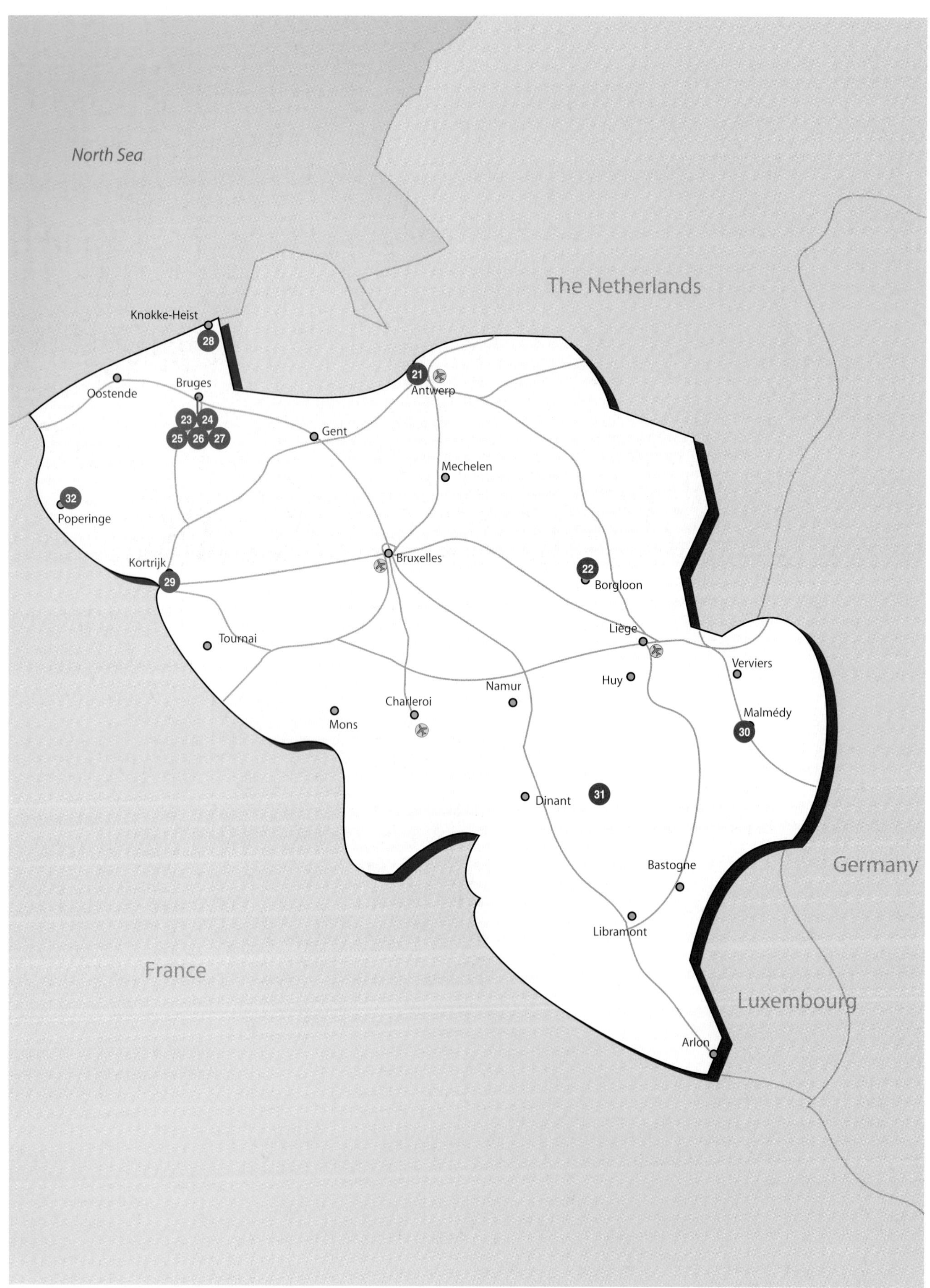

Firean Hotel

KAREL OOMSSTRAAT 6, 2018 ANTWERP, BELGIUM

Set in a quiet residential street minutes away from the centre of picturesque Antwerp, this art deco hotel is a genuine original. Ideally suited for the traveller weary of homogeneous hotel chains, its suave style is all-pervasive, from the stunning entrance right through to the Tiffany enamel and glass in the bedrooms. Renowned for the courtesy of its staff, the Firean's restaurant combines excellent service with the finest of cuisine.

Situé dans une rue résidentielle calme à quelques minutes du centre de la pittoresque ville d'Anvers, cet hôtel art déco est très original. Situé idéalement pour le voyageur lassé des chaînes d'hôtels, son style est suave et partout présent, de l'entrée étonnante à l'émail de Tiffany et aux glaces des chambres. Renommé pour la courtoisie de son personnel, le restaurant du Firean combine un excellent service avec une cuisine raffinée.

In einer ruhigen Straße, nur wenige Minuten vom Zentrum des malerischen Antwerpen entfernt, liegt dieses Art-Deco-Hotel, ideal für die Reisenden geeignet, die eintönigen Hotelketten entgehen wollen. Das stilvolle Ambiente reicht von dem beeindruckenden Eingang bis hin zu den Tiffany-Emaille- und Glaseinrichtungen in den Zimmern. Das hoteleigene Restaurant verbindet exzellenten Service mit köstlicher Küche.

Our inspector loved: *The art deco gates towards the dining area.*

Directions: From A14 > E17, exit 5.

Web: www.johansens.com/firean
E-mail: info@hotelfirean.com
Tel: +32 3 237 02 60
Fax: +32 3 238 11 68

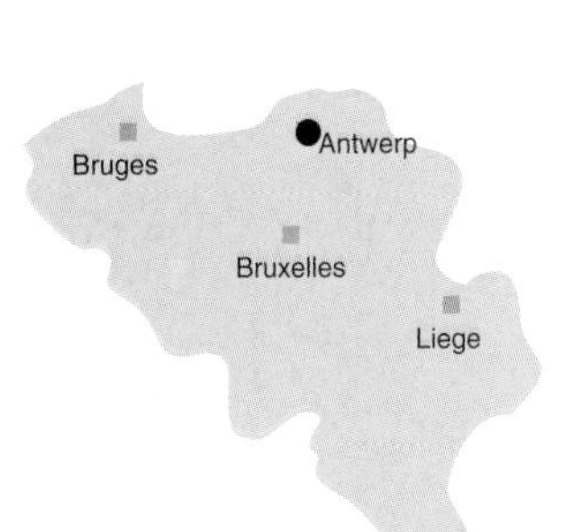

Price Guide:
single €136–141
double/twin €158–169
junior suite €213-229

Kasteel van Rullingen

RULLINGEN 1, 3840 BORGLOON, BELGIUM

Directions: Brussels (Zaventen Airport) > E40 towards St Truiden - Borgloon. Airport transfer can be arranged by the hotel.

Web: www.johansens.com/rullingen
E-mail: info@rullingen.com
Tel: +32 12 74 31 46
Fax: +32 12 74 54 86

Price Guide:
(room only)
single €86.76-114.03
double €96.68-123.95
suite €148.74-223.10

The ancient headquarters of the Counts of Loon, Rullingen Castle looks back on an eventful past. The 16 luxurious en-suite bedrooms and suites offer all modern amenities. Delicious classical Belgian cuisine is served in the à la carte restaurant, whilst the Orangerie bar is a popular venue to relax with a drink. Conference or banqueting facilities for up to 220 are available. Guests can enjoy relaxing walks or bicycle tours or play tennis and squash, whilst a 9 to 18-hole golf course is 15 minutes away.

L'ancien siège des comptes de Loon, le château de Rullingen a un passé mouvementé. Les 16 chambres attenantes et suites luxueuses offrent toutes les facilités modernes. Une cuisine délicieuse de tradition belgique est servie dans le restaurant à la carte, alors que le bar l'Orangerie est un endroit populaire où se détendre avec un verre. Des facilités de conférences et de banquets pour jusqu'à 220 personnes sont disponibles. Les hôtes peuvent faire une promenade relaxante, faire un tour en vélo ou jouer au tennis et squash, tandis que un parcours de golf de 9 à 18 trous est à 15 minutes à pied.

Dieser ehemalige Hauptsitz der Grafen von Loon blickt auf eine erlebnisreiche Vergangenheit zurück. Die 16 luxuriösen Zimmer und Suiten bieten jeglichen modernen Komfort. Köstliche klassische belgische Küche wird im à la carte Restaurant serviert, und die Orangerie ist der ideale Ort für einen Drink. Konferenz- oder Banketteinrichtungen für bis zu 220 Personen sind vorhanden. Man kann spazieren gehen, Fahrrad fahren, Tennis und Squash spielen, außerdem liegt ein 9- bis 18-Loch-Golfplatz 15 Minuten entfernt.

Our inspector loved: *The sterling silver collection and the beautiful handmade silk rugs.*

DIE SWAENE

1 STEENHOUWERSDIJK, 8000 BRUGES, BELGIUM

Overlooking one of Bruges' picturesque canals, this luxurious hotel offers a relaxing and romantic ambience. Each of the bedrooms is individually decorated and the hotel's candle-lit restaurant serves cuisine created from regional and organic ingredients. The 18th-century lounge, the former meeting room for the Tailors Guild, features fine tapestries and the 15th-century attic room is ideal for conferences accommodating up to 25 delegates. To relax, guests may use the hotel's indoor swimming pool, sauna and cold bath. Alternatively, drinks can be taken in the cosy bar.

Donnant sur un canal pittoresque, cet hôtel luxueux propose une ambiance romantique et relaxante. Chacune des chambres est décorée de façon unique et le restaurant éclairé à la bougie, sert des plats aux ingrédients régionaux. Le salon, datant du XVIIIe siècle et orné de tapisseries, est l'ancienne salle de réunion pour la guilde de tailleurs. La mansarde date du XVe siècle et offre un endroit idéal pour des conférences pour jusqu'à 25 délégués. Pour se détendre, les hôtes peuvent profiter de la piscine intérieure, la sauna et les bains froids ou prendre un verre dans le bar intime.

Dieses Luxushotel mit Blick auf einen der malerischen Kanäle Brügges besitzt ein entspanntes, romantisches Ambiente. Alle Zimmer sind unterschiedlich gestaltet, und im kerzenbeleuchteten Restaurant kann man Köstlichkeiten aus regionalen und biologisch angebauten Zutaten genießen. Im Aufenthaltsraum aus dem 18. Jahrhundert – dem einstigen Versammlungssaal der Schneidergilde – findet man edle Wandteppiche. Der Speicher aus dem 15. Jahrhundert ist ideal für Konferenzen für bis zu 25 Personen. Entspannung findet man im Hallenbad, der Sauna und dem Kaltbad oder bei einem Drink in der gemütlichen Bar.

Our inspector loved: The altar reception desk and tapestries in the lounge.

Directions: Take the E40 to Bruges in the direction of Ostend. Brussels (Zaventem) is the nearest airport.

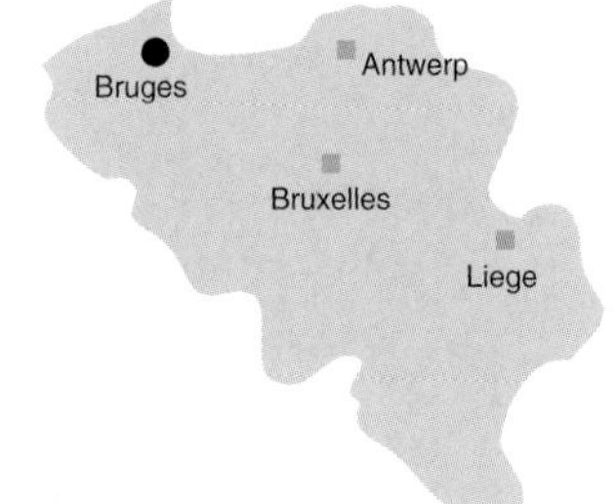

Web: www.johansens.com/swaene
E-mail: info@dieswaene-hotel.com
Tel: +32 50 34 27 98
Fax: +32 50 33 66 74

Price Guide:
single €160
double €185-295
suite €350-460

Hotel de Tuilerieën

DYVER 7, 8000 BRUGES, BELGIUM

This elegant 15th-century mansion has recently been converted into a most luxurious small hotel. Great care has been taken to create an extremely stylish interior without sacrificing the integrity of the building's age and character. All the expectations of modern conveniences are met and surpassed, and the stunning location alongside the picturesque canal is only enhanced by the dramatic interiors and Starck designed bathrooms.

Cette élégante maison de maître du XVe siècle a récemment été convertie en un petit hôtel des plus élégants. Un soin particulier a été apporté afin de créer un intérieur raffiné et cossu sans sacrifier au caractère et style d'époque du bâtiment. Toutes les facilités modernes sont présentes, et la situation privilégiée le long d'un canal pittoresque n'en est que mise en valeur par les spectaculaires intérieurs et les salles de bain dessinées par Starck.

Dieses elegante Haus aus dem 15. Jahrhundert wurde kürzlich in ein luxuriöses kleines Hotel umgewandelt, wobei sorgfältig darauf geachtet wurde, dass das stilvolle neue Interieur den Charakter und das Alter des Gebäudes nicht verfälscht. Jeglicher moderner Komfort wird geboten, und das dramatische Décor und die von Starck gestalteten Bäder werden durch die herrliche Lage des Hotels an einem malerischen Kanal perfekt ergänzt.

Our inspector loved: *The hotel's perfect situation and its stylish yet classical décor.*

Directions: E40 from Brussels > A17 from Courthai.

Web: www.johansens.com/hoteltuilerieen
E-mail: info@hoteltuilerieen.com
Tel: +32 50 34 36 91
Fax: +32 50 34 04 00

Price Guide:
single €233-286
double €259-352
junior suite €390-456

Hotel Montanus

NIEUWE GENTWEG 78, 8000 BRUGES, BELGIUM

Within historic Bruges the Montanus Hotel offers an air of cool modernity for business and leisure travellers alike. Bedrooms are simple and paintings by contemporary local artists adorn the walls. An excellent hot and cold breakfast buffet is served in the airy, well-designed breakfast room and a small, cosy bar and comfortable lounge offer guests plenty of books and magazines to read. Outside are attractive patio gardens, and further afield, the city's many museums and art galleries can be explored.

Dans le cadre historique de Bruges, cet hôtel se distingue par un style moderne élégant qui convient aussi bien aux voyageurs d'affaires qu'aux touristes. Dans les chambres sobres, les murs sont ornés de tableaux peints par des artistes locaux contemporains. Un excellent buffet composé de plats chauds et froids est servi à l'heure du petit déjeuner, dans la salle à manger attrayante. Dans le petit bar intime et le salon confortable, livres et revues invitent à la lecture. Dehors, vous attendent un joli jardin et les nombreux musées et galeries d'art de la ville.

Mitten im historischen Brügge gelegen, bietet das Montanus Hotel ein modernes Ambiente für Touristen und Geschäftsreisende. Die Zimmer sind einfach gehalten, und Gemälde zeitgenössischer einheimischer Künstler zieren die Wände. Ein ausgezeichnetes warmes und kaltes Frühstücksbuffet wird in einem luftigen, hübsch gestalteten Saal serviert, und eine gemütliche kleine Bar und bequeme Lounge bieten zahlreiche Bücher und Magazine. Draußen gibt es einen hübschen Innenhof und Garten, und zahlreiche Museen und Galerien liegen in der Nähe.

Our inspector loved: *The simple yet very tasteful décor as well as the big fluffy towels and bathrobes.*

Directions: From Brussels (Airport Zaventen) take the E40 to Bruges > exit 8 > follow N31 > Hotel Montanus is in the centre of Bruges.

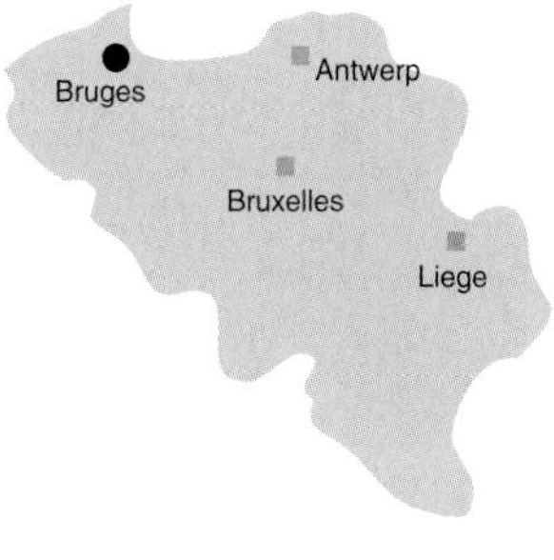

Web: www.johansens.com/montanus
E-mail: info@montanus.be
Tel: +32 50 33 11 76
Fax: +32 50 34 09 38

Price Guide:
single €120–225
double/twin €135–235
suites €230–265

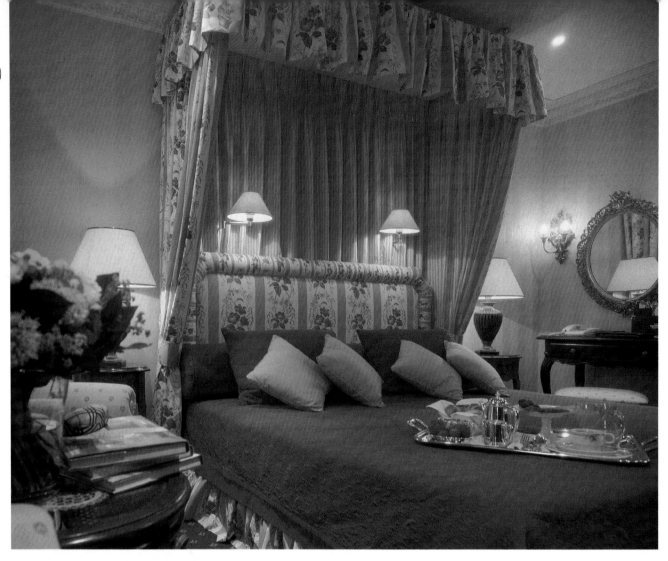

Hotel Prinsenhof

ONTVANGERSSTRAAT 9, 8000 BRUGES, BELGIUM

This elegant 20th-century Flemish mansion, hidden down a quiet side street, is a superb and welcoming hideaway just minutes from the pulsating heart of Bruges. Renovated with great flair, the Burgundy-style interior, rich with chandeliers, antiques and moulded ceilings, has an air of opulence, which extends into the charming breakfast room, where an excellent buffet is served. The bedrooms are furnished in traditional style and provide thoughtful extras including exceptional robes in the en-suite bathrooms. Member of "Relais du Silence".

Cet élégant manoir flamand du XXe siècle, caché au fond d'une rue calme, est une étape accueillante à quelques minutes du centre animé de Bruges. Récemment renovée avec beaucoup de goût, la décoration intérieure, qui foisonne de chandelliers, de plafonds à moulures et d'antiquités dégage une atmosphère d'opulence, qui s'étend à la salle du petit déjeuner où un délicieux buffet est servi le matin. Les chambres sont décorées avec soin dans un style traditionnel et proposent des petits plus tels que des peignoirs dans les salles de bains. Membre de "Relais du Silence".

Dieses elegante flämische Haus aus dem 20. Jahrhundert liegt in einer ruhigen Seitenstraße, nur wenige Minuten vom pulsierenden Herzen Brügges entfernt. Das Hotel wurde herrlich renoviert, und das Interieur im Burgunder Stil vermittelt mit seinen Lüstern, verzierten Decken und Antiquitäten ein Gefühl von Opulenz, das sich bis zum Frühstücksraum erstreckt, in dem morgens ein Buffet serviert wird. Die exquisiten Zimmer haben eigene Bäder, sind traditionell gestaltet und bieten Extras wie herrlich luxuriöse Bademäntel. Mitglied der "Relais du Silence".

Our inspector loved: *The classic décor and personable staff.*

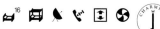

Directions: E40 exit 8 marked "Brugge" > follow N31 > in the centre of Bruges.

Web: www.johansens.com/prinsenhof
E-mail: info@prinsenhof.be
Tel: +32 50 34 26 90
Fax: +32 50 34 23 21

Price Guide:
single €128–278
double/twin €135–225
suite €285

Walburg Hotel

BOOMGAARDSTRAAT 13-15, 8000 BRUGES, BELGIUM

Located in a 19th-century neoclassic city castle, this splendid hotel in the heart of Bruges has undergone a 3-year refurbishment programme to provide all modern conveniences in a quiet and intimate setting. The bedrooms and luxury suites are spacious and elegant, each with its own marble bathroom. A wide selection of freshly prepared delicacies is served in the restaurant, whilst the cosy bar is the perfect place to unwind. City Hall and Belfry are only 100m away, and numerous other attractions are within easy walking distance.

Situé dans un château urbain néoclassique datant du XIXe siècle, ce splendide hôtel au cœur de Bruges a subi un programme de remise à neuf durant 3 ans pour offrir tout le confort moderne dans un endroit calme et accueillant. Les chambres et les suites luxueuses sont spacieuses et élégantes; chacune a sa propre salle de bains en marbre. Une grande sélection de mets délicats tout frais est servie dans le restaurant, alors que le bar intime est l'endroit idéal pour se dérouler. L'hôtel de ville et Beffroi ne sont qu'à 100m et de nombreuses attractions sont d'accès facile à pied.

Dieses Hotel in einem neoklassizistischen Stadtschloss aus dem 19. Jahrhundert wurde 3 Jahre lang renoviert und bietet nun jeglichen modernen Komfort in ruhiger und familiärer Atmosphäre. Die Zimmer und Luxussuiten sind geräumig und elegant und haben eigene Marmorbäder. Frisch zubereitete Köstlichkeiten werden im Restaurant serviert, und die gemütliche Bar ist der ideale Ort, um zu entspannen. Das Rathaus und Belfried sind nur 100m entfernt, und zahlreiche andere Sehenswürdigkeiten liegen in nächster Nähe.

Our inspector loved: *The impressive coach entrance and high ceilings in the hallway and bedrooms.*

Directions: Located in the city centre.

Web: www.johansens.com/walburg
E-mail: hotelwalburg@skynet.be
Tel: +32 50 34 94 14
Fax: +32 50 33 68 84

Price Guide:
single €130-180
double €150-200
suite 230-250

BELGIUM (KNOKKE~HEIST)

Romantik Hotel Manoir du Dragon

ALBERTLAAN 73, 8300 KNOKKE~HEIST, BELGIUM

Directions: Follow signs to centre of Knokke-Heist > signposted.

Web: www.johansens.com/dudragon
E-mail: manoirdudragon@pandora.be
Tel: +32 50 63 05 80
Fax: +32 50 63 05 90

Price Guide:
rooms €190–250
suite €300–450

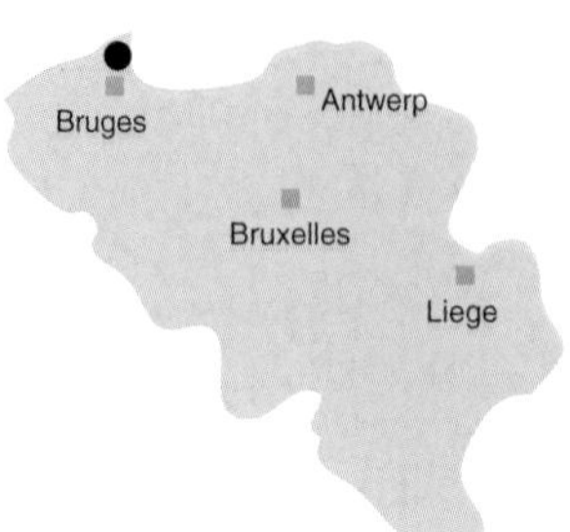

Overlooking the Royal Zoute Golf, this romantic hotel has a wonderful atmosphere complemented by individually decorated bedrooms and suites, offering an unequalled comfort with terraces, air conditioning, Jacuzzi baths, bathrobes and slippers and fresh flowers. In summer, a gastronomic buffet breakfast is served in the garden. The hotel is ideally located for walking and cycling tours, and a beach, shops and art galleries are within easy reach. 3 golf clubs are within 15km. Bruges is 18km away and Damme, a pretty 16th-century village, is 12km.

Cet hôtel romantique, situé aux bords du Royal Zoute Golf, se caractérise par une ambiance de charme et de distinction. Ses chambres et suites luxueuses offrent un confort inégalé: terrasses, climatisation, bain jacuzzi, fleurs fraîches, peignoir et pantoufles de bain ainsi que les petits déjeuners gastronomiques servis au jardin en été. Une situation centrale idéale pour des promenades à pied ou a bicyclettes, le sport, les boutiques, restaurants et les galéries d'art. 3 clubs de golf se trouvent à moins de 15 km de l,hôtel. Bruges est à 18 km et Damme, une ville jolie datant du XVIe siècle, à 12 km.

Dieses romantische Hotel mit Blick auf den Royal Zoute Golfplatz besitzt eine wundervolle Atmosphäre. Die Zimmer und Suiten sind unterschiedlich gestaltet und bieten unvergleichlichen Komfort, mit Terrasse, Klimaanlage, Jacuzzibad, Bademänteln, Pantoffeln und frischen Blumen. Im Sommer wird im Garten ein Gourmetfrühstück serviert. Das Hotel liegt ideal für Wanderungen und Fahrradtouren, und ein Strand, Geschäfte und Kunstgalerien liegen ganz in der Nähe. 3 Golfclubs befinden sich im Umkreis von 15km. Brügge ist 18km und Damme, ein hübsches Städtchen aus dem 16. Jahrhundert, 12km entfernt.

Our inspector loved: *The stylish bedrooms.*

Hotel Damier

GROTE MARKT 41, 8500 KORTRIJK, BELGIUM

This exquisite Rococo building is right in the town centre and ideally located for sightseeing, shopping and visiting the city museums. The hotel is one of the oldest in Belgium and is charmingly appointed with period features, elegant bedrooms and marble bathrooms. Its previous guests include Margaret Thatcher and President George Bush, who would have sampled the hotel's legendary silver service that takes place during functions in the dining room.

Ce immeuble raffiné de style rococo est situé en plein centre de ville, dans une location idéale pour visiter la ville et ses musées, et pour faire du shopping. Cet hôtel, l'un des plus vieux de Belgique, est aménagé de manière charmante avec des décors d'époque, de chambres élégantes et des salles de bain en marbre. Parmi ses hôtes précédents, on trouve Margaret Thatcher et le Président George Bush, qui ont pu apprécier le célèbre service stylé des grandes fonctions qui se tiennent dans la salle à manger.

Dieses bezaubernde Rokoko-Gebäude ist eines der ältesten Hotels in Belgien und liegt mitten im Stadtzentrum - ideal für Stadtbesichtigungen, Einkäufe und Museumsbesuche. Es ist liebevoll eingerichtet, die Zimmer sind elegant, die Bäder in Marmor gehalten. Zu den Gästen zählten bereits Margaret Thatcher und Präsident George Bush, die sicherlich in den Genuss des legendären "Silbernen Service" kamen, der während feierlicher Anlässe im Speisesaal stattfindet.

Our inspector loved: *The wonderful service of this outstanding, first-rate hotel.*

Directions: 42km from Bruges – take E403 from Bruges to Kortrijk.

Web: www.johansens.com/damier
E-mail: info@hoteldamier.be
Tel: +32 56 22 15 47
Fax: +32 56 22 86 31

Price Guide:
single €119–180
double €139–195
suites €199–359

HOSTELLERIE TRÔS MARETS

ROUTE DES TRÔS MARETS, 4960 MALMÉDY, BELGIUM

Set at the foot of the Hautes Fagnes National Park and offering a panoramic view across the surrounding valleys, the Trôs Marets is the epitome of modern style and comfort. The elegant furnishings immediately catch the eye, but the spectacular views from the lounge and dining room are undoubtedly the hotel's chief attraction. In addition to an alfresco terrace, there is an outstanding restaurant, where succulent dishes are complemented by fine wines.

Hostellerie située au pied du Parc Naturel des Hautes Fagnes avec vue panoramique sur les vallées avoisinantes, le Trôs Marets est l'incarnation même du style moderne et du confort. Les meubles élégants attirent le regard, et les vues spectaculaires du salon et de la salle à manger forment indubitablement la principale attraction de l'hôtel. Outre la terrace alfresco, l'établissement a un restaurant exceptionnel, où des plats délicieux sont agrémentés de vins fins.

Das Trôs Marets, am Fuße des Nationalparks Hautes Fagnes gelegen und mit Panoramablick auf die umliegenden Täler, ist die Verkörperung modernen Stils und Komforts. Die elegante Einrichtung sticht sofort ins Auge, doch die Trumpfkarte des Hotels sind zweifellos die spektakulären Aussichten vom Aufenthaltsraum und Speisesaal. Neben einer Sonnenterrasse gibt es ein exquisites Restaurant, das mit köstlichen Speisen und erlesenen Weinen für das leibliche Wohl sorgt.

Our inspector loved: *The serene setting in the scenic National Park.*

Directions: Liège > E40 > Malmédy > Eupean 6 km.

Web: www.johansens.com/trosmarets
E-mail: info@trosmarets.be
Tel: +32 80 33 79 17
Fax: +32 80 33 79 10

Price Guide:
double/twin €97–210
suite €225–459

CHÂTEAU D'HASSONVILLE

ROUTE D'HASSONVILLE 105, 6900 MARCHE~EN~FAMENNE, BELGIUM

This turretted 17th-century château, set in 140 acres of magnificent parkland, has the heady atmosphere of a fairy tale. With peacocks on the lawn and sparkling chandeliers in the opulent salons and breathtaking views, the chateau extends a luxurious, yet homely welcome to its guests. Enjoy a stroll through the park, or simply relax in front of an open fire, basking in the quiet grandeur of antiques and gilt-framed paintings. The restaurant serves delicious award-winning cuisine and fine wines from the superb cellar.

Entouré d'un superbe parc de 55 hectares, ce château à tourelles du XVIIe siècle baigne dans une atmosphère féerique. Les paons sur la pelouse et les lustres scintillants des salons opulents donnent un cachet unique à ce château luxueux qui réserve un accueil cordial et des vues sensationnelles à ses visiteurs. Pour se détendre, rien ne vaut une promenade dans le parc ou une rêverie au coin du feu, dans un décor somptueux de meubles anciens et de beaux tableaux. Le restaurant sert une cuisine primée savoureuse et d'excellents vins de sa cave impressionnante.

Dieses Schloss aus dem 17. Jahrhundert ist von 55ha Park umgeben und besitzt eine märchenhafte Atmosphäre. Mit Pfauen auf dem Rasen, glänzenden Kronleuchtern in den opulenten Salons und atemberaubenden Aussichten bietet das Schloss seinen Gästen einen luxuriösen und doch heimeligen Empfang. Genießen Sie einen Spaziergang durch den Park, oder entspannen Sie sich vor dem Kamin, umgeben von feinen Antiquitäten und goldgerahmten Gemälden. Das Restaurant serviert köstliche, mit Preisen ausgezeichnete Küche und erlesenste Weine.

Our inspector loved: *The enviable location on the outskirts of town.*

Directions: Brussels - Luxembourg > exit 18 Marche > N4 > exit km98 > Aye.

Web: www.johansens.com/chateaudhassonville
E-mail: info@hassonville.be
Tel: +32 84 31 10 25
Fax: +32 84 31 60 27

Bruges
Antwerp
Bruxelles
Liege

Price Guide:
single €115–165
double/twin €130–180
suite €280

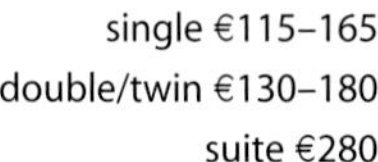

Hotel Recour

GUIDO GEZELLESTRAAT 7, 8970 POPERINGE, BELGIUM

Directions: A25 from Lille - Dunkerque (gate 13). From Brussels E40 > E17-A19. Hotel Recour is a 5-minute drive from Ypres.

Web: www.johansens.com/hotelrecour
E-mail: info@pegasusrecour.be
Tel: +32 57 33 57 25
Fax: +32 57 33 54 25

Price Guide:
single €125-200
double €125-250
suites €325

This 18th-century residential home, located in the heart of hop country, is only 100 metres from Poperinge town market square. The original luxury and opulence has been restored and now features magnificent pieces of furniture and exquisite details. Each of the 8 beautiful, individually furnished en suite bedrooms has every modern amenity including DVD players and internet access. The hotel's restaurant, Pegasus, serves sumptuous meals influenced by Mediterranean cuisine, created from the freshest ingredients. There are also 2 conference rooms with state-of-the-art equipment available.

Situé au coeur de la culture du houblon, cette maison datant du XVIIIe siècle est à 100 mètres de la place du marché de Poperinge. Le luxe original ayant été restauré, aujourd'hui l'hôtel est orné de meubles magnifiques et de détails exquis. Chacune des 8 chambres salle de bains attenante est meublée de manière individuelle, et est munie de tout équipement, incluant DVD et Internet. Pegasus, le restaurant de l'hôtel, sert des plats délicieux, influencés par la cuisine méditerranéenne et crées avec les ingrédients les plus frais. Il y a 2 salles de conférences du dernier cri disponibles.

Diese Residenz aus dem 18. Jahrhundert befindet sich mitten im Hopfenanbaugebiet, nur 100 Meter vom Marktplatz der Stadt Poperinge entfernt. Die einstige luxuriöse Pracht des Hotels zeigt sich am herrlichen Mobiliar und exquisiten Details. Jedes der 8 unterschiedlich eingerichteten hübschen Zimmer hat ein eigenes Bad und bietet jeden modernen Komfort wie z.B. DVD-Player und Internetanschluss. Im Hotelrestaurant Pegasus werden frisch zubereitete, mediterran geprägte Speisen serviert. Es stehen 2 Konferenzräume mit hochmoderner Ausstattung zur Verfügung.

Our inspector loved: *The exquisite bathrooms in this old residence.*

    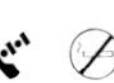  

Croatia

Hotel location shown in red (hotel) or purple (spa hotel) with page number

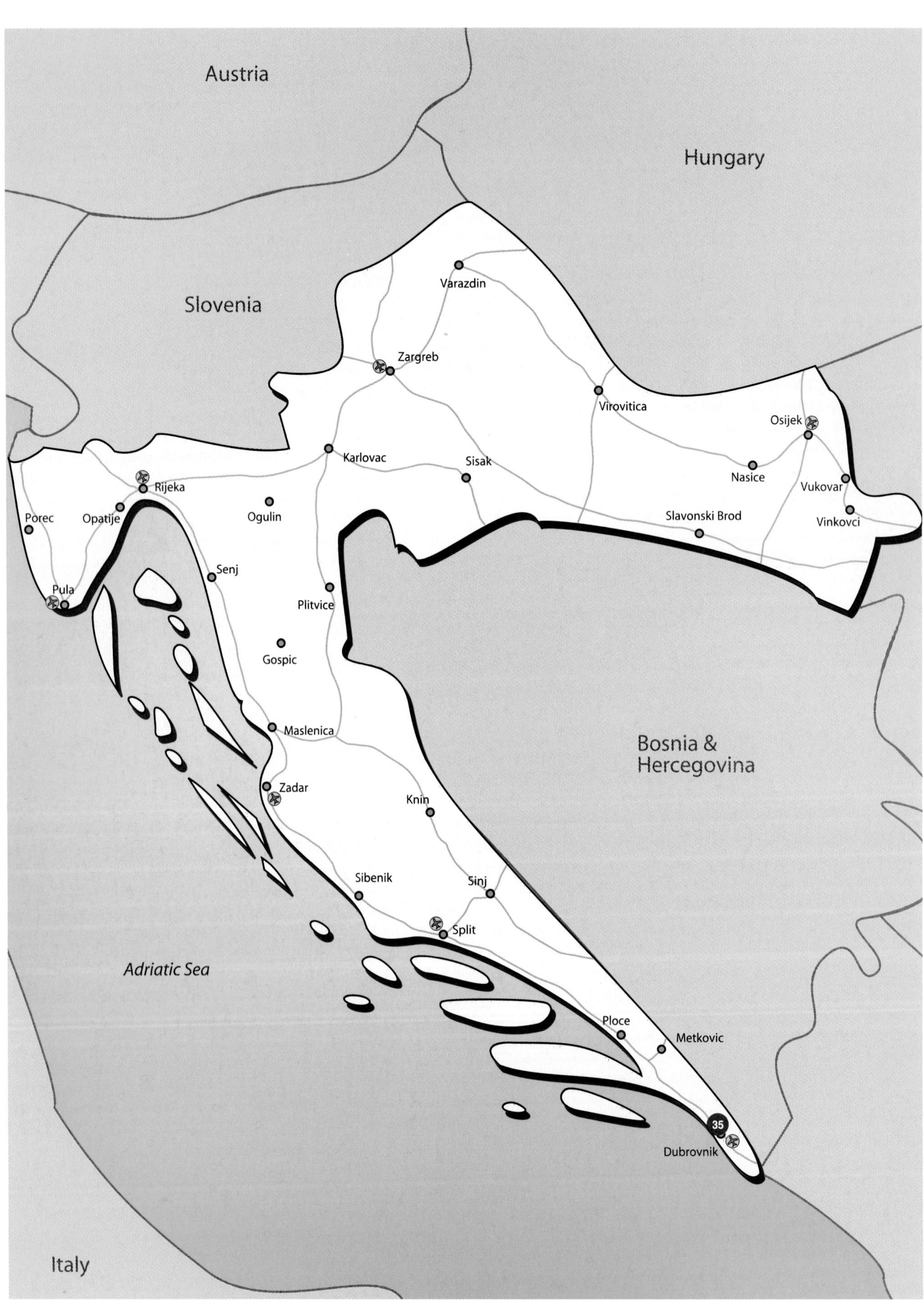

The Pucic Palace

ULICA OD PUCA 1, 20000 DUBROVNIK, CROATIA

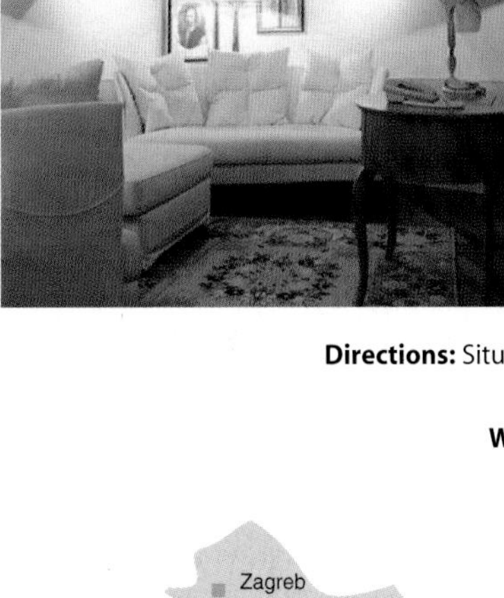

Situated in the centre of Dubrovnik, this historic building was considered the finest noble house of its time and is now an intimate and welcoming hotel, whose natural stone façade entices guests into its warm ambience. Antique furnishings are excellently combined with modern amenities. Classic and contemporary artwork adorns the walls and dark wooden floors and hand-woven rugs line the floor. Guests have a choice of 3 restaurants: Café Royal, a Parisian-style café, Defne, which serves Mediterranean cuisine and Razonoda wine bar.

Situé au centre de Dubrovnik, ce monument historique, autrefois considéré comme l'une des maisons les plus nobles, est maintenant un hôtel intime et accueillant, dont les façades en vraie pierre attirent ses hôtes dans son ambiance chaleureuse. Des antiquités sont gracieusement mélangées aux équipements modernes, œuvres d'art classiques et modernes ornent les murs et des tapis tissés àmain recouvrent le sol. Les hôtes ont le choix entre 3 restaurants: Café Royal, un café de style parisien, Defne qui sert une cuisine méditerranéenne et le bar à vins Razonoda.

Dieses im Zentrum Dubrovniks gelegene historische Gebäude war einst das edelste Haus seiner Zeit und ist heute ein familiäres Hotel, das seinen Gästen hinter der Fassade aus Naturstein einen herzlichen Empfang bereitet. Antiquitäten verbinden sich aufs Beste mit modernen Einrichtungen, klassische und zeitgenössische Kunstwerke zieren die Wände und dunkles Holz und handgewebte Teppiche bedecken den Fußboden. Man hat die Wahl zwischen 3 Restaurants, dem Café Royal im Pariser Stil, Defne, in dem Mittelmeerküche serviert wird, und der Razonoda-Weinbar.

Our inspector loved: *The wonderful blend of old and new.*

Directions: Situated in the centre of Gundulic Square.

Web: www.johansens.com/pucicpalace
E-mail: info@thepucicpalace.com
Tel: +385 20 324 111
Fax: +385 20 324 667

Price Guide: (excluding VAT)
single €195-295
double €265-565
suite €750-950

Czech Republic

Hotel location shown in red (hotel) or purple (spa hotel) with page number

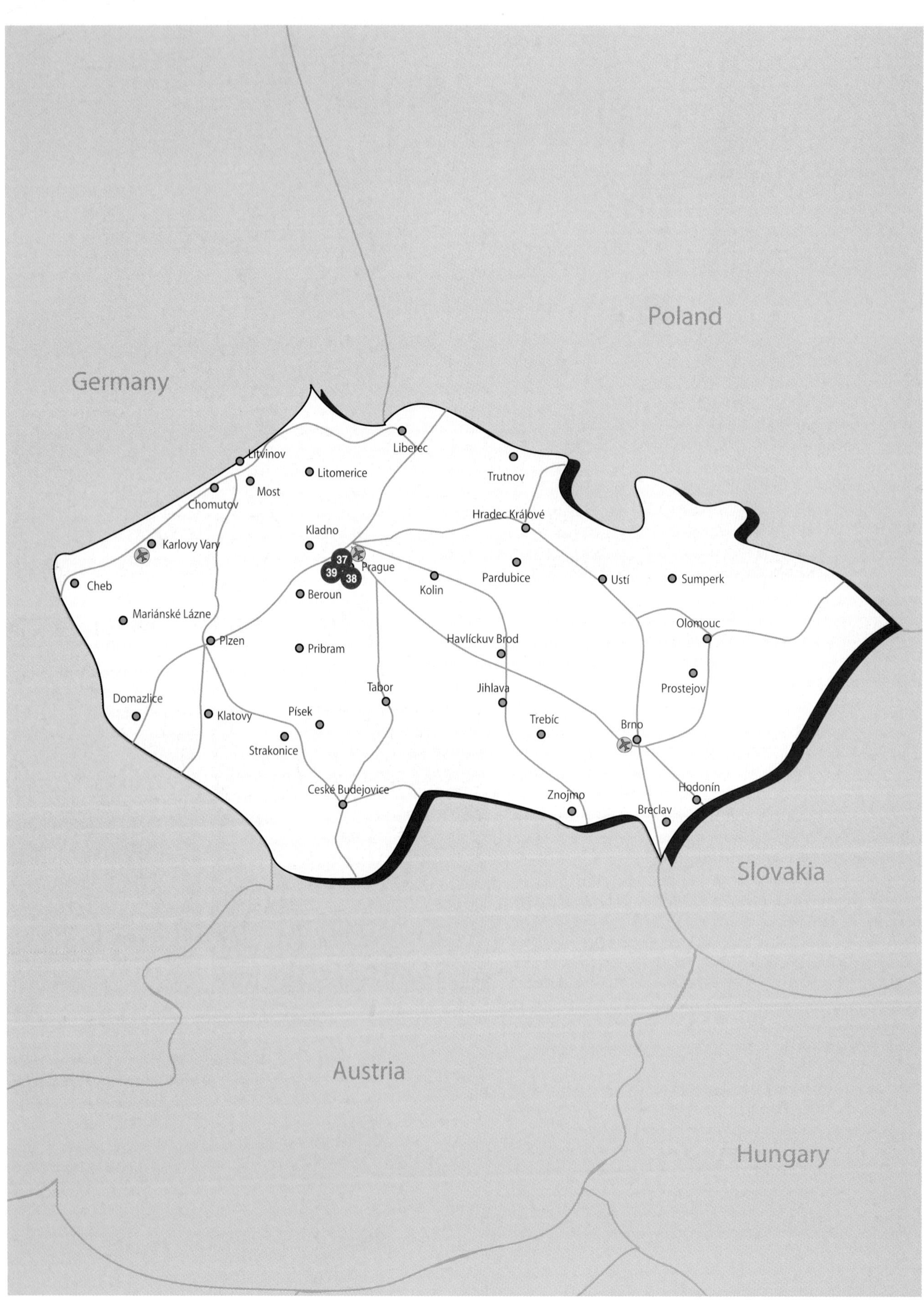

Art Hotel Praha

NAD KRÁLOVSKOU OBOROU 53, 170 00 PRAGUE 7, CZECH REPUBLIC

Displaying wonderful Czech modern art, created by some of the country's most celebrated painters, this contemporary hotel is located close to the city centre in a quiet neighbourhood of residential mansions and foreign embassies. Each of the de luxe 22 bedrooms and 2 attic suites features sophisticated, stylish décor with uniquely designed bathrooms. The suites have a fully-equipped kitchen. Many rooms overlook Stromovka park, whilst nearby Letná park offers an excellent view of Prague.

Montrant une belle collection d'art moderne tchèque, créée par des artistes les plus célébrés dans le pays, cet hôtel contemporain est situé au centre de la ville dans un quartier calme d'hôtels particuliers et d'ambassades étrangères. Chacune des 22 chambres luxueuses et les 2 suites mansardes a un décor sophistiqué et une salle de bain décorée de façon unique. Les suites ont une cuisine tout équipée. Plusieurs chambres donnent sur le parc Stromovka, alors que le parc Letnà, qui est tout proche,offre des vues imprenables de Prague.

Dieses zeitgenössische Hotel befindet sich im Stadtzentrum in ruhiger Lage umgeben von Wohnhäusern und Botschaften. Hier kann man eine Vielfalt herrlicher moderner tschechischer Werke einiger der besten Maler des Landes bewundern. Die luxuriösen 22 Zimmer und 2 Suiten im Dachgeschoss sind alle exquisit eingerichtet und haben einzigartig gestaltete Bäder. Die Suiten bieten zudem voll ausgestattete Küchen. Viele Zimmer blicken auf den Stromovka-Park, und vom nahegelegenen Letná-Park hat man eine traumhafte Sicht auf Prag.

Our inspector loved: *The modern, stylish design in a quiet residential area.*

Directions: The hotel is 12km from Prague Ruzyne Airport.

Web: www.johansens.com/arthotel
E-mail: booking@arthotel.cz
Tel: +420 2 331 01 331
Fax: +420 2 331 01 311

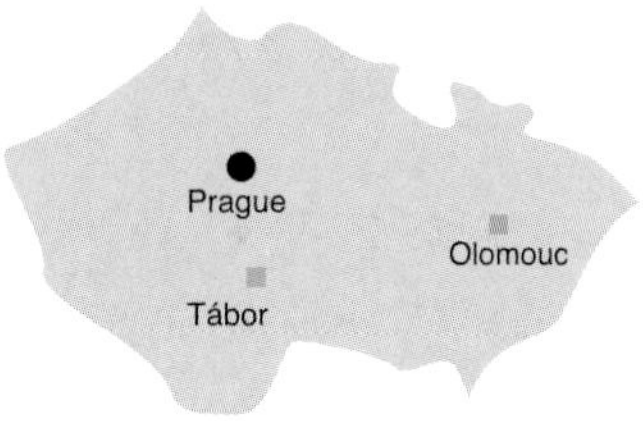

Prague
Olomouc
Tábor

Price Guide:
single €120
double €140
suite €170

Hotel Hoffmeister

POD BRUSKOU 7, KLÁROV, 11800 PRAGUE 1, CZECH REPUBLIC

Located just below Prague's enchanting castle and commanding stunning views of the river, the Hoffmeister subtly blends the old and the new. An intriguing collection of paintings and portraits is one of the most interesting features, although visitors are equally impressed by the terrace café and the charming cellar bar. The chef serves a fascinating combination of local and international cuisine, complemented by delicious wines.

Situé juste au dessous du château enchanteur de Prague et proposant des vues époustouflantes sur la rivière, le Hoffmeister mélange l'ancien et le moderne de façon subtile. Une collection intrigante de peintures et de portraits est un des points clefs de l'hôtel, bien que les visiteurs seront également impressionnés par le café terrace et le charmant bar en sous sol. Le chef sert une combinaison fascinante de cuisine locale et internationale, agrémentée de vins délicieux.

Direkt unterhalb der zauberhaften Prager Burg gelegen und mit traumhaften Aussichten über den Fluss, bietet das Hoffmeister eine perfekte Mischung aus Alt und Neu. Eines der interessantesten Merkmale des Hotels ist eine einzigartige Sammlung von Gemälden und Portraits. Das Terrassencafé und die charmante Kellerbar servieren eine köstliche Mischung aus einheimischen und internationalen Speisen, die durch erlesene Weine ergänzt werden.

Our inspector loved: *The unique touches given to this hotel, including the owner's father's paintings of 20th-century European and American personalities.*

Directions: The hotel is situated in the centre of the city.

Web: www.johansens.com/hoffmeister
E-mail: hotel@hoffmeister.cz
Tel: +420 251 017 111
Fax: +420 251 017 100

Price Guide:
single €165-220
double/twin €225-310
suite €275-430

Romantik Hotel U Raka

CERNÍNSKÁ 10/93, 11800 PRAGUE 1, CZECH REPUBLIC

Located on the castle hill in the Hradcany area, this enchanting hotel in the centre of Prague is an oasis of peace and seclusion – the ideal place for those who wish to escape the hustle and bustle of modern life, withdraw with a book and discover the city on a leisurely walk. With its cosy bedrooms and warming fireplaces, the atmosphere is more that of a private home than a hotel. The hotel serves snacks and drinks, whilst for dinner guests will find numerous restaurants in the vicinity.

Situé sur la colline du château dans le quartier de Hradcany, cet hôtel enchanteur du centre de Prague est un havre de paix et d'isolement -- l'endroit idéal pour ceux qui veulent échapper au tourbillon de la vie moderne, se retirer avec un livre et découvrir la ville au rythme d'une promenade. Avec ses chambres douillettes et de chaleureux coins cheminée, l'atmosphère ressemble plus à celle d'une maison privée que d'un hôtel. L'hôtel sert des en-cas et boissons, alors que pour le dîner les hôtes pourront faire leur choix parmi les nombreux restaurants du voisinage.

Dieses zauberhafte, auf dem Schlosshügel nahe des Hradschin gelegene Hotel ist eine wahre Oase der Ruhe und Abgeschiedenheit – der ideale Ort, um der Hektik des Alltags zu entfliehen, sich mit einem Buch zurückzuziehen und gemächliche Spaziergänge zu unternehmen. Mit seinen gemütlichen Zimmern und wärmenden Kaminen erinnert die Atmosphäre eher an ein Privathaus als an ein Hotel. Kleine Mahlzeiten und Getränke werden hier serviert, und zahlreiche Restaurants befinden sich in der Nähe.

Our inspector loved: *The romantic garden of this small hotel hidden in the heart of Prague.*

Directions: In the centre of the city, close to Prague Castle.

Web: www.johansens.com/uraka
E-mail: uraka@login.cz
Tel: +420 2205 111 00
Fax: +420 2333 580 41

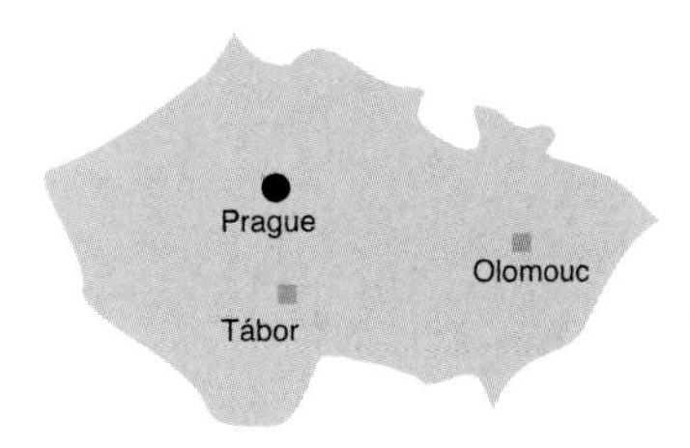

Price Guide:
single €185-210
double €205-230
suite €240-260

Denmark

Hotel location shown in red (hotel) or purple (spa hotel) with page number

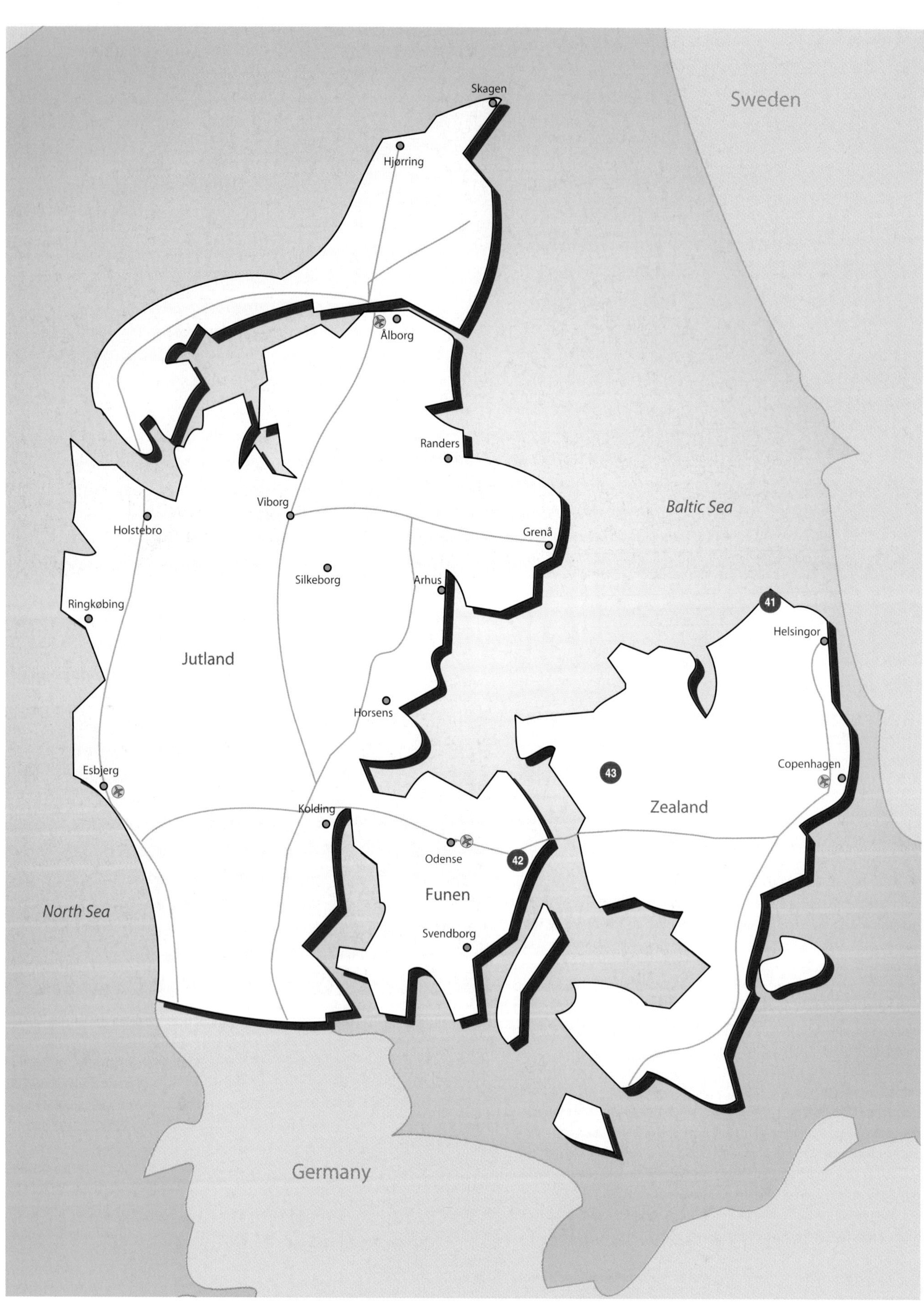

Havreholm Slot

KLOSTERRISVEJ 4, HAVREHOLM, 3100 HORNBÆK, DENMARK

Surrounded by 40 acres of immaculately preserved forest and meadows, overlooking a beautiful lake, this elegant hotel exudes romance and splendour. Breathtaking paintings of the Garden of Eden create a magnificent background to the restaurant, which serves a wonderful selection of food and fine wines. Guest rooms are stylish and the ultimate in comfort; sports facilities include horse riding, indoor and outdoor swimming pools, 5 tennis courts, squash, rowing and a 9-hole golf course.

Entouré par 16 ha de forêt et prés impeccablement préservés et donnant sur un beau lac, cet hôtel élégant exude romance et splendeur. Des tableaux du Jardin d'Eden à couper le souffle créent un fond magnifique au restaurant, qui sert une sélection excellent de mets et de bons vins. Les chambres sont élégantes et offre le plus grand confort. Les facilités de sport comprennent l'équitation, piscine couverte et piscine en plein air, courts de tennis, squash, canotage et un parcours de golf à 9 trous.

Umgeben von 16ha makelloser Wald- und Wiesenlandschaft mit Blick auf einen schönen See, bietet dieses elegante, prachtvolle Hotel eine romantische Atmosphäre. Herrliche Gemälde des Garten Eden schaffen einen wundervollen Hintergrund für das Restaurant, in dem eine hervorragende Auswahl an Speisen und edlen Weinen serviert wird. Die Zimmer sind elegant und bieten höchsten Komfort. Sportliche Einrichtungen sind Hallen- und Freibad, 5 Tennisplätze, Squash-Courts und ein 9-Loch-Golfplatz, außerdem kann man reiten und rudern.

Our inspector loved: *Taking a ride on the rowing boat on the peaceful lake.*

Directions: The nearest airport is Copenhagen. E47 towards Helsingor > exit 4 (Hornbæk).

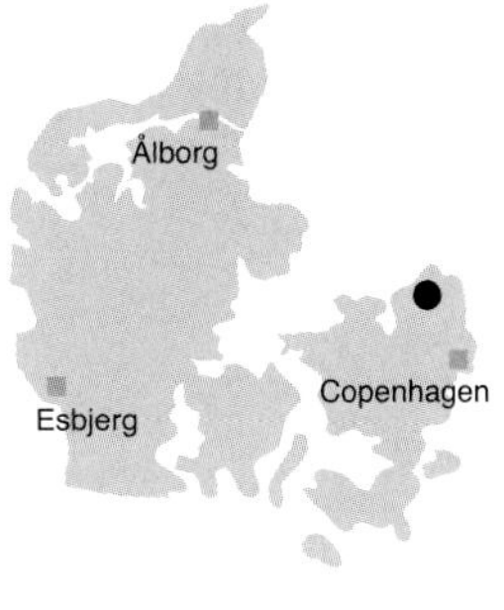

Ålborg
Esbjerg
Copenhagen

Web: www.johansens.com/havreholm
E-mail: havrehom@havreholm.dk
Tel: +45 49 75 86 00
Fax: +45 49 75 80 23

Price Guide: (room only)
single DKK1,140
double DKK1,790
suite DKK1,930

Hotel Hesselet

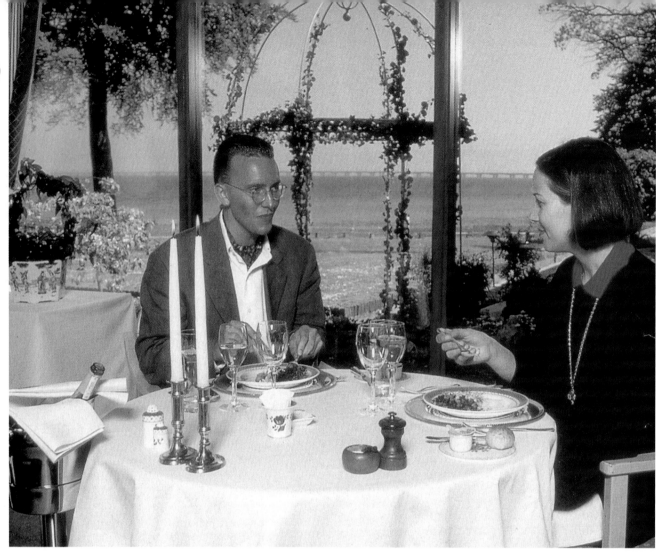

CHRISTIANSLUNDSVEJ 119, 5800 NYBORG, DENMARK

Situated on the island of Funen and surrounded by woodland, the renowned Hesselet offers simply awe-inspiring views over the sea. The Japanese influenced architecture is one of the hotel's most outstanding features, and visitors are not disappointed by the tasteful interior and spacious airy rooms. More active guests will enjoy the indoor pool with fitness equipment or may prefer to swim from the hotel jetty or play tennis.

Situé sur l'île de Funen et entouré de bois, le fameux Hesselet offre des vues extraordinaires sur la mer. L'architecture d'influence japonaise est un des traits de caractères principaux de l'hôtel et les visiteurs ne seront pas déçus de l'intérieur superbe et des chambres aériennes et luxueuses. Les visiteurs les plus actifs pourront profiter de la piscine couverte avec ses équipements sportifs ou pourront préférer une nage depuis la jetée ou jouer au tennis.

Das renommierte Hotel Hesselet auf der Insel Funen ist von Waldlandschaft umgeben und bietet atemberaubende Aussichten über das Meer. Die japanisch beeinflusste Architektur ist eine seiner Besonderheiten, und die geschmackvolle Inneneinrichtung und die geräumigen, luftigen Zimmern sind nicht weniger beeindruckend. Sportliche Gäste können Hallenbad und Fitnessgeräte nutzen, Tennis spielen oder vom hoteleigenen Steg aus schwimmen.

Our inspector loved: *The restaurant and excellent cuisine.*

Directions: E20 > exit 45 > Nyborg.

Web: www.johansens.com/hesselet
E-mail: hotel@hesselet.dk
Tel: +45 65 31 30 29
Fax: +45 65 31 29 58

Price Guide:
single DKK1,180–1,280
double/twin DKK1,680–1,780
suite DKK2,400–2,800

KRAGERUP GODS

KRAGERUPGÅRDSVEJ 33, 4291 RUDS-VEDBY, DENMARK

Built in 1801, surrounded by a moat and extensive private grounds, this historic fairytale mansion exudes charm and elegance. The 12 spacious en-suite bedrooms, with their high ceilings and unique antique furnishings, offer a welcoming atmosphere. The beautiful vaulted cellar, dating back to 1600, and the wonderful old manor kitchens have been refurbished and are an ideal setting for parties and meetings. Relax in the heated indoor pool and sauna, or enjoy a bicycle ride in the magnificent surrounding countryside.

Construite en 1801, de cette demeure historique de conte de fées entourée de douves, émane charme et élégance. Les 12 chambres spacieuses et leur salles de bain offrent une atmosphère accueillante avec leurs hauts plafonds et leur mobilier ancien unique. Le beau cellier en voûte datant de 1600 et les fantastiques cuisines du vieux manoir ont été rénovées, en faisant l'endroit idéal pour fêtes et réunions. Les hôtes peuvent se détendre dans la piscine intérieure chauffée et le sauna ou faire des promenades à vélo dans la magnifique campagne environnante.

Dieses 1801 erbaute historische Anwesen ist umgeben von einem Burggraben und ausgedehnten Ländereien und verströmt eine märchenhafte, elegante Atmosphäre. Die 12 geräumigen, einladenden Zimmer haben eigene Bäder, hohe Decken und sind mit einzigartigen antiken Möbeln gefüllt. Das Kellergewölbe aus dem Jahr 1600 und die zauberhaften alten Gutsküchen wurden renoviert und sind der ideale Ort für Festlichkeiten und Konferenzen. Das beheizte Hallenbad und die Sauna laden zur Entspannung ein, und man kann die herrliche Umgebung mit dem Fahrrad erkunden.

Our inspector loved: *Taking a tranquil morning stroll in the private grounds alongside the moat.*

Directions: The nearest airport is Copenhagen. Situated on Vest Sjealand, 10km north of Slagelse, 85km west of Copenhagen.

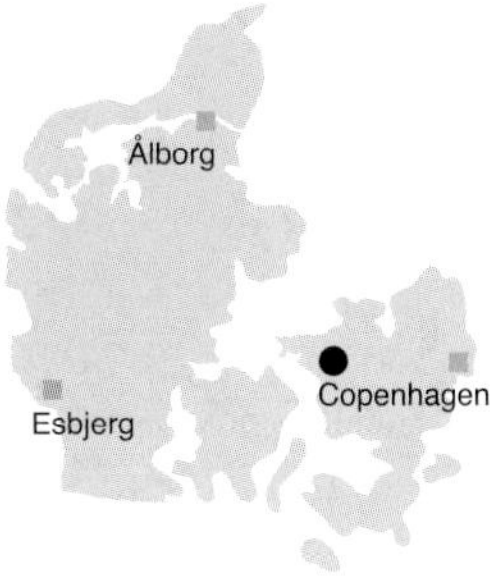

Web: www.johansens.com/kragerupgods
E-mail: bd@kragerup.dk
Tel: +45 58 26 12 50
Fax: +45 58 26 12 64

Ålborg
Esbjerg
Copenhagen

Price Guide:
(room only)
single DKK600
double DKK700

Estonia

Hotel location shown in red (hotel) or purple (spa hotel) with page number

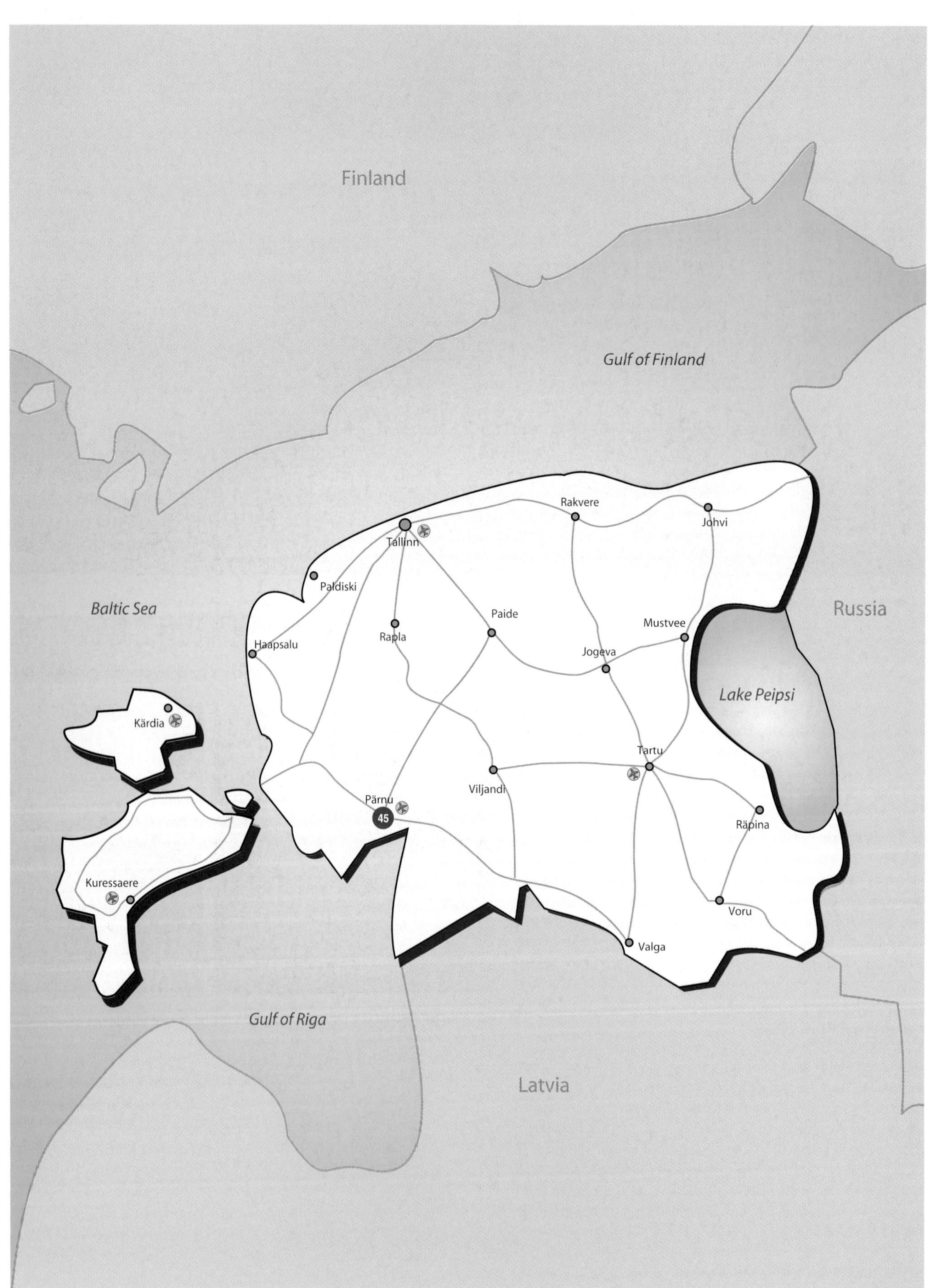

Villa Ammende

MERE PST. 7, 80010 PÄRNU, ESTONIA

Set in a romantic park close to the sea, this art nouveau hotel, built at the beginning of the 20th century, is Estonia's most fascinating building of its kind. All bedrooms are en suite, whilst the suites are decorated with restored original furniture and period details. The Suite Ammende boasts a sauna and whirlpool bath. Guests can enjoy French and Mediterranean cuisine accompanied by fine Old World wines in the elegant blue dining room, the green "wine room" or the crimson "hunting room". The famous Spa is only minutes away.

Dans un parepràs de la mer, cet hôtel art nouveau construit au début du XXe siècle, est l'un des bâtiments d'Estonie les plus fascinants de son genre. Toutes les chambres ont leur salle de bain; les suites sont décorées avec des meubles restaurés d'époque. La Suite Ammende contient un sauna et un bain à remous. Les invités peuvent apprécier, dans l'élégante salle à manger bleue, dans la "salle de vin" verte ou la "salle de chasse" rouge foncée, une cuisine française et méditerranéenne accompagnée de vins fins. Les célèbres Bains ne sont qu'à quelques minutes.

In einem romantischen Park am Strand liegt dieses Anfang des 20. Jahrhunderts erbaute Jugendstil-Hotel, Estlands faszinierendstes Gebäude seiner Art. Die Zimmer haben ihr eigenes Bad, und die Suiten sind mit restaurierten Originalmöbeln und dazugehörigen Details eingerichtet. Die Suite Ammende bietet Sauna und Bad mit Whirlpool. Französische und mediterrane Gerichte sowie feine Weine der Alten Welt werden im historischen blauen Speisesaal, grünen "Weinsaal" oder purpurfarbenen "Jadgsaal" serviert. Das berühmte Spa ist nur ein paar Minuten entfernt.

Our inspector loved: *The restoration of art nouveau architecture.*

Directions: On main road between Tallin and Riga. 2 hours from Tallin, 3 hours from Riga.

Web: www.johansens.com/villaammende
E-mail: ammende@ammende.ee
Tel: +372 44 73888
Fax: +372 44 73887

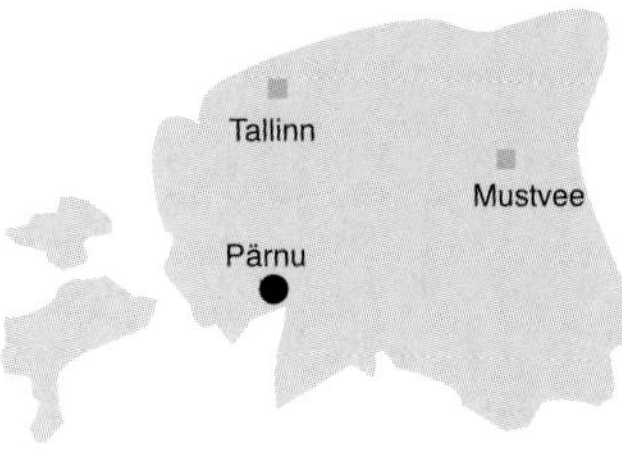

Tallinn
Mustvee
Pärnu

Price Guide:
deluxe €115–189
suite €190–390

France

Hotel location shown in red (hotel) or purple (spa hotel) with page number

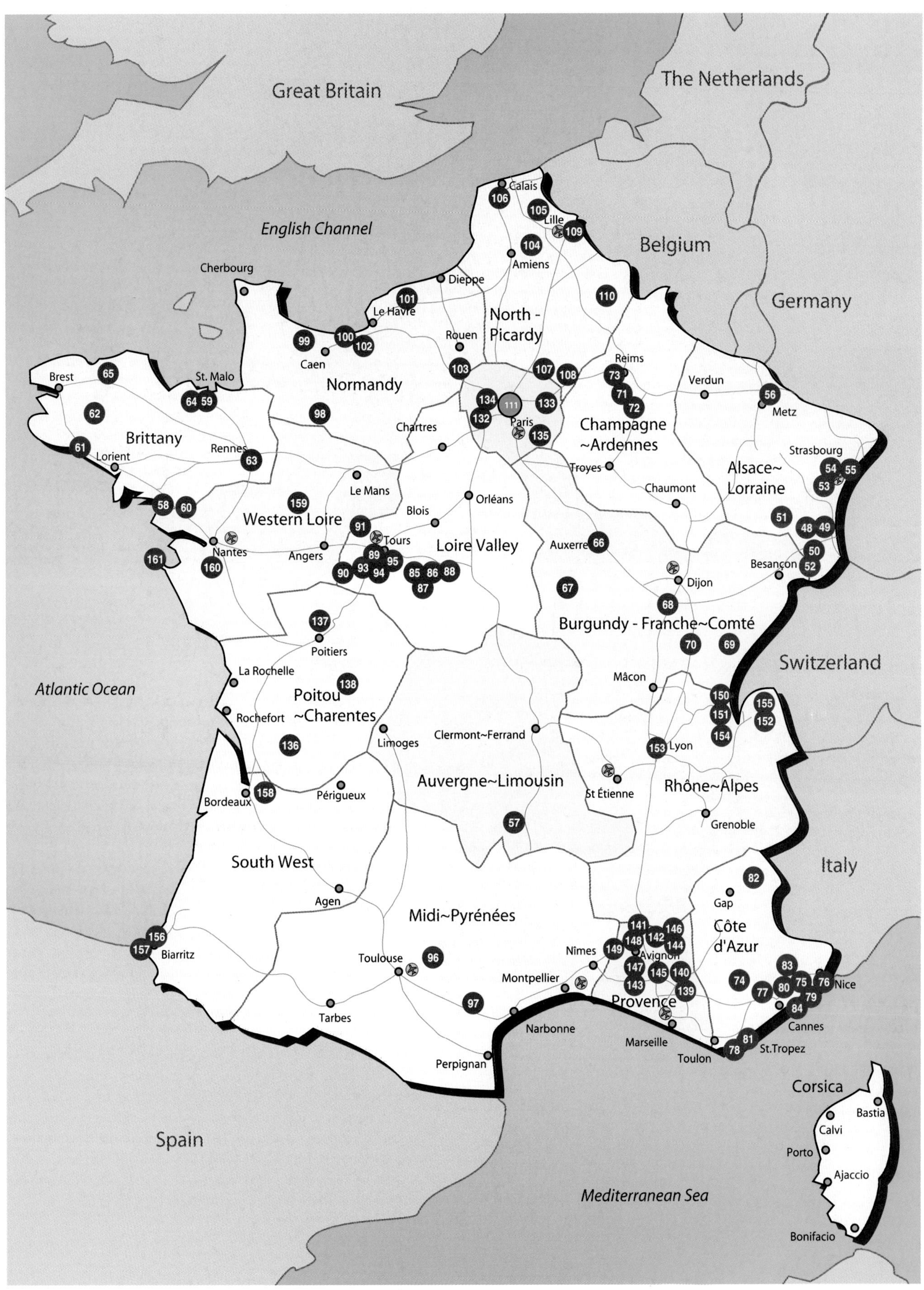

HOSTELLERIE LE MARÉCHAL

4 PLACE SIX MONTAGNES NOIRES, PETITE VENISE, 68000 COLMAR, FRANCE

Directions: From Strasbourg turn off the highway for Colmar Sud. Then follow the directions to Petite Venise.

Web: www.johansens.com/marechal
E-mail: marechal@calixo.net
Tel: +33 3 89 41 60 32
Fax: +33 3 89 24 59 40

Price Guide:
(breakfast excluded)
single €80–90
double €95–215
suites €245

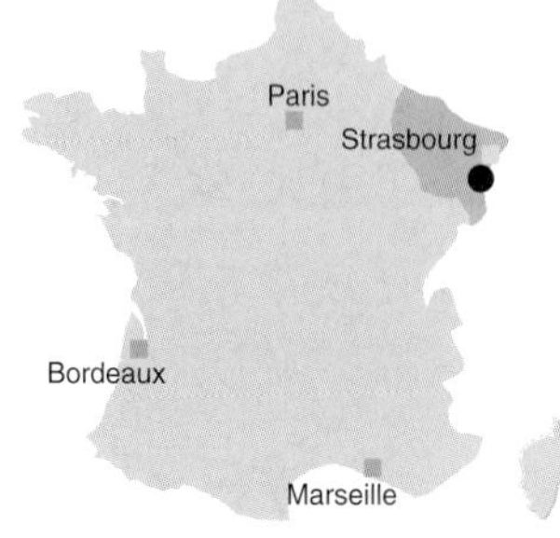

Set beside a canal in Colmar's most beautiful quarter, "Little Venice", this charming house is renowned for its exquisite cuisine, superb Alsatian wines and warm hospitality. After 2 years of renovation, the 4-star hotel now provides 30 delightful bedrooms, all named after famous musicians and equipped with air conditioning, satellite television and comfortable bathrooms. L'Echevin serves Alsatian delicacies by candlelight and classical music. This is the perfect place for a romantic weekend!

Située en bordure d'un canal dans le plus beau quartier de Colmar, "La Petite Venise", cette maison charmante est réputée pour sa cuisine, ses vins alsaciens et sa chaleureuse hospitalité. Après deux ans de rénovation, cet hôtel 4 étoiles a 30 chambres superbes, qui portent toutes le nom d'un musicien célèbre. Elles possèdent la climatisation, la télévision et par satellite ainsi que des salles de bain confortables. L'Echevin sert les plats fins alsaciens à la lueur des chandelles et au son de la musique classique. L'endroit idéal pour un week-end romantique!

An einem Kanal in "Petite Venise", dem schönsten Viertel Colmars liegt dieses 4-Sterne Hotel, das für seine exquisite Küche, köstlichen elsässischen Weine und herzliche Gastfreundschaft bekannt ist. Nach zweijähriger Renovierung stehen nun 30 zauberhafte Zimmer bereit, alle nach berühmten Musikern benannt und mit Klimaanlage, Satellitenfernsehen und komfortablen Bädern ausgestattet. Im L'Echevin werden bei Kerzenschein und klassischer Musik elsässische Köstlichkeiten serviert. Der perfekte Ort für ein romantisches Wochenende!

Our inspector loved: *Dinner overlooking the canal; a really romantic experience.*

Hôtel Les Têtes

19 RUE DE TÊTES, 68000 COLMAR, FRANCE

Situated at the heart of this labyrinthine cathedral town, this beautiful Renaissance hotel is truly unique. Covered by 105 grotesque masks, the Baroque theme extends into the interior, where an intimate courtyard allows guests to relax over coffee and cool drinks in summer. The bedrooms, complete with ancient beamed ceilings and attractive stonework, are highly atmospheric. The hotel's welcoming owner, Marc Rohfritsch, prepares sumptuous dishes served under glittering chandeliers in the restaurant La Maison des Têtes.

Situé au coeur de cette ville tentaculaire avec sa cathédrale, ce magnifique hôtel Renaissance est vraiment exceptionnel. Décoré de 105 masques de style grotesque, le thème baroque s'étend à l'intérieur, où une cour intime permet aux clients de se détendre autour d'un café ou de boissons rafraîchissantes en été. Les chambres, avec leurs poutres anciennes et leurs beaux murs en pierre, dégagent une ambiance extraordinaire. L'accueillant maître des lieux, Marc Rohfritsch, prépare de somptueux repas dans son restaurant La Maison des Têtes.

Inmitten dieser labyrinthischen Domstadt liegt dieses einzigartige Renaissancehotel. Das Barockthema wird mit 105 grotesken Masken im Interieur fortgesetzt, wo ein intimer Innenhof die Gäste zu Kaffee oder einem kühlen Drink im Sommer einlädt. Die Zimmer, mit alten Balkendecken und attraktiven Steinarbeiten verziert, sind besonders stimmungsvoll. Marc Rohfritsch, der Besitzer des Hotels, bereitet köstliche Speisen, die im Restaurant La Maison des Têtes unter glänzenden Lüstern serviert werden.

Our inspector loved: *The heavenly bedrooms.*

Directions: Colmar city centre.

Web: www.johansens.com/lestetes
Tel: +33 3 89 24 43 43
Fax: +33 3 89 24 58 34

Price Guide:
(breakfast excluded)
single €95-168
double/twin €95-168
suite €230

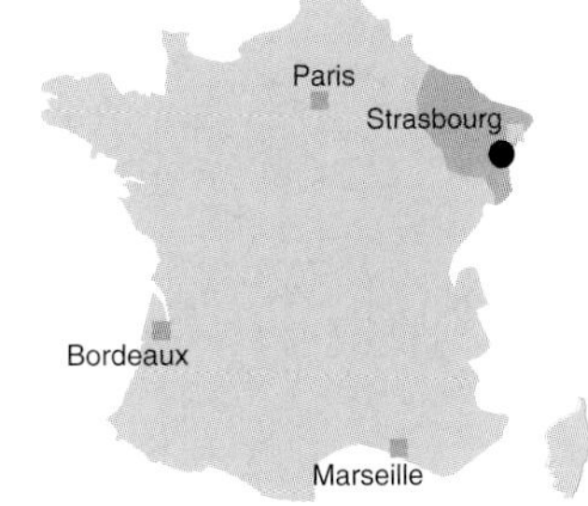

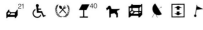

CHÂTEAU D'ISENBOURG

68250 ROUFFACH, FRANCE

Peace, comfort, luxury, discreet charm and attentive service are the hallmarks of this imposing, hillside château hotel which overlooks colourful gardens and vineyards towards the Vosges forest. Built on 12th and 14th-century cellars d'Isenbourg is a superb historical and gourmet retreat on the Alsace wine route. Its restaurants are famed, its bedrooms elegantly spacious and leisure facilities are excellent.

Paix, confort, charme discret et service attentif sont les marques de cet imposant hôtel-château, posé sur les coteaux et surplombant des jardins colorés et des vignobles en direction de la forêt de Visges. Construit sur les celliers d'Isenbourg datant du XIIe et XIVe siecle, c'est une superbe retraite historique gastronomique sur la route des vins d'Alsace. Ses restaurants sont célèbres, ses chambres élégantes sont spacieuses et ses équipements de loisirs sont excellents.

Ruhe, Komfort, Luxus, unaufdringlicher Charme und aufmerksamer Service sind die Maximen dieses eindrucksvollen, auf einem Hügel gelegenen Schlosshotels, das auf farbenfrohe Gärten und Weinberge in Richtung Vogesen blickt. Das auf Weinkellern aus dem 12. und 14. Jahrhundert erbaute Château d'Isenbourg ist ein einmaliges historisches und gastronomisches Erlebnis auf der Elsässer Weinroute. Seine Restaurants genießen einen exzellenten Ruf, die eleganten Zimmer sind geräumig und das Freizeitangebot ist hervorragend.

Our inspector loved: *The view from the Jacuzzi over the vineyards.*

Directions: A35 > exit Colmar.

Web: www.johansens.com/isenbourg
E-mail: isenbourg@grandesetapes.fr
Tel: +33 3 89 78 58 50
Fax: +33 3 89 78 53 70

Price Guide:
single €108–290
double €108–290
suite €276–475

Hostellerie Les Bas Rupts

88400 GÉRARDMER, VOSGES, FRANCE

Close to Lake Gérardmer, in the heart of Les Vosges Mountain region, the Hostellerie and its adjoining Chalet Fleuri is a magical retreat all year round. A homely and welcoming ambience is accompanied by warm hospitality – the bedrooms are comfortable and uniquely attractive, with hand-painted flowers adorning the walls and doors. The succulent dishes, an inspired interpretation of local specialities are complemented by fine wines and served in the panoramic restaurant.

Tout près du lac de Gérardmer, au coeur des Vosges, l'Hostellerie Les Bas Rupts et son annexe, le Chalet Fleuri, offrent une retraite idyllique tout au long de l'année. L'accueil cordial est complété par une atmosphère intime et chaleureuse - les chambres sont confortables et très jolies, avec des portes et des murs ornés de fleurs peintes à la main. Des plats succulents, une brillante interprétation des spécialités locales, accompagnés de vins exceptionnels sont servis dans le restaurant panoramique.

Nahe am Géradmer See und inmitten der Vogesen liegt die Hostellerie Les Bas Rupts und das dazugehörende Chalet Fleuri. Eine heimelige und warme Atmosphäre verbindet sich hier mit herzlicher Gastfreundschaft – die zauberhaften Zimmer sind gemütlich eingerichtet und die Wände und Türen mit Blumen handbemalt. Köstliche Speisen, eine gelungene Interpretation einheimischer Spezialitäten, und erlesene Weine werden im Panoramarestaurant serviert.

Our inspector loved: *The smell of wood burning in the fireplace in this lovely mountain chalet.*

Directions: Paris > Nancy > Remiremont > Gérardmer.

Web: www.johansens.com/lesbasrupts
E-mail: bas-rupts@wanadoo.fr
Tel: +33 3 29 63 09 25
Fax: +33 3 29 63 00 40

Price Guide: (room only)
single €140-180
double/twin €119-198
suite €240-280

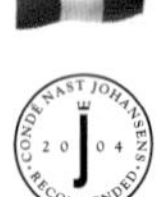

HOSTELLERIE ST BARNABÉ

68530 MURBACH – BUHL, FRANCE

The warmest of welcomes and the chance to really get away from it all are offered by this marvellous hostellerie in the heart of the Alsace. Set amidst spectacular forest scenery and beside a meandering mountain stream, each of the charming beamed bedrooms is named after one of the Alsatian grand cru wines. One of the cosy chalets has its own wood-burning stove. The hosts are true professionals and will ensure guests of impeccable service and breathtaking views.

Un accueil des plus chaleureux vous attend dans cette merveilleuse hostellerie alsacienne où vous pourrez vous reposer loin de tout. Construite au milieu d'une magnifique forêt et au bord d'un ruisseau de montagne, elle offre de ravissantes chambres aux poutres apparentes, qui portent toutes des noms de grands crus d'Alsace. Un poêle à bois chauffe l'un des chalets douillets. Les patrons sont de vrais professionnels, qui garantissent aux visiteurs un service impeccable, dont ils peuvent profiter en admirant des vues à couper le souffle.

Ein herzlicher Empfang erwartet Gäste in dieser wunderbaren Hostellerie im Herzen des Elsass. Inmitten atemberaubender Waldumgebung und neben einem Gebirgsbach gelegen, ist dies ein idealer Ort, um jeglichem Alltagsstress zu entkommen. Die bezaubernden Zimmer sind alle nach elsässischen Grand Cru Weinen benannt, und eines der gemütlichen Chalets hat einen eigenen Holzofen. Die Gastgeber sind wahre Experten und garantieren ihren Gästen makellosen Service und traumhafte Umgebung.

Our inspector loved: *The mountain chalet suite in the garden, for all honeymooners.*

Directions: D429 to Guebwiller, then direction Murbach D429II.

Web: www.johansens.com/stbarnabe
E-mail: hostellerie.st.barnabe@wanadoo.fr
Tel: +33 3 89 62 14 14
Fax: +33 3 89 62 14 15

Price Guide:
single€95-190
double €95–190

27 20

A L'Ami Fritz

8 RUE DES CHÂTEAUX, 67530 OTTROTT, FRANCE

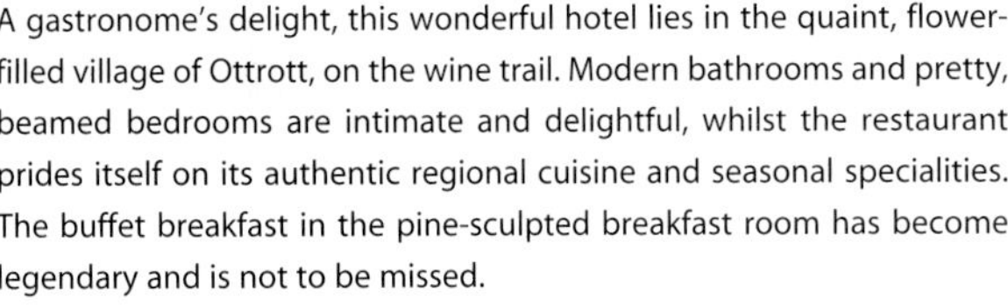

A gastronome's delight, this wonderful hotel lies in the quaint, flower-filled village of Ottrott, on the wine trail. Modern bathrooms and pretty, beamed bedrooms are intimate and delightful, whilst the restaurant prides itself on its authentic regional cuisine and seasonal specialities. The buffet breakfast in the pine-sculpted breakfast room has become legendary and is not to be missed.

Un plaisir de gastronome, cet adorable hôtel se situe sur la route des vins dans le pittoresque village fleuri d'Ottrott. Les salles de bain modernes et les chambres à poutres apparentes sont intimes et charmantes, alors que le restaurant s'enorgueillit de sa véritable cuisine régionale et de ses spécialités de saison. Le petit déjeuner buffet servi dans la salle à manger en pin sculpté est légendaire et ne doit être manqué sous aucun prétexte.

Dieses an der Weinroute gelegene wundervolle Hotel im kleinen, blumengeschmückten Dorf Ottrott ist ein wahres Paradies für Feinschmecker. Die modernen Bäder und hübschen Zimmer mit Holzbalkendecken sind gemütlich und einfach zauberhaft, und im Restaurant kann man authentische regionale Küche und Spezialitäten der Saison genießen. Das schon legendäre Frühstücksbuffet sollte man sich keinesfalls entgehen lassen.

Our inspector loved: *The cosy and romantic suite.*

Directions: A35, exit Obernai > then continue in the direction of Ottrott.

Web: www.johansens.com/amifritz
E-mail: hotel@amifritz.com
Tel: +33 3 88 95 80 81
Fax: +33 3 88 95 84 85

Price Guide:
double €62–90
suite €99–130

Romantik Hotel Beaucour Baumann

5 RUE DES BOUCHERS, 67000 STRASBOURG, FRANCE

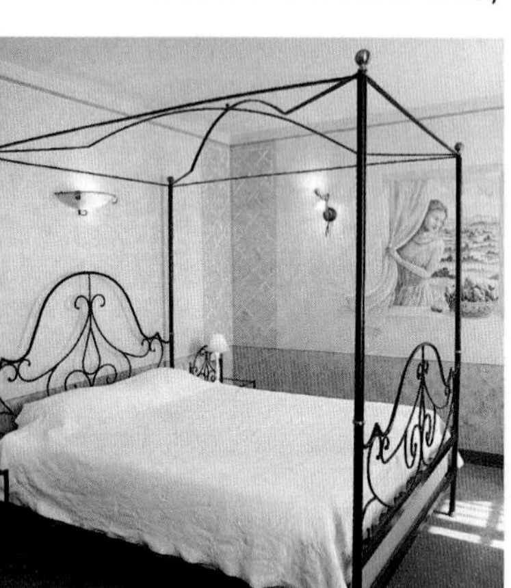

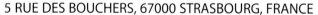

Just a stone's throw from the cathedral, this authentic timber-framed hotel is ideally situated for discovering Strasbourg. Built around a narrow courtyard, its exposed beams, warm colours and hand-painted frescoes create a homely and comfortable Alsatian ambience. Bedrooms are individually decorated and have Jacuzzi baths. A sumptuous breakfast is served daily, and guests can relax in the cosy lounge with its log fire. All visitors are given a hearty welcome from the staff and also the resident talking parrot!

A deux pas de la cathédrale, cet hôtel en style typique de la région est parfaitement situé pour découvrir Strasbourg. Construit autour d'une cour intérieure étroite, ses poutres apparentes, des couleurs chaudes et des fresques peintes à la main créent une ambiance confortable et alsacienne. Les chambres sont décorées de façon individuelle et disposent d'un Jacuzzi. Un petit déjeuner somptueux est servi tous les jours et les hôtes peuvent se détendre dans le salon intime autour du feu de bois. Le personnel, ainsi que le perroquet parlant, attend tous les visiteurs avec un accueil chaleureux !

Dieses mit echtem Fachwerk geschmückte Hotel liegt nur einen Katzensprung von der Kathedrale entfernt, ideal um Straßburg zu erkunden. Das Haus ist um einen schmalen Innenhof herum gebaut, und Holzbalken, warme Farben und handbemalte Fresken schaffen eine heimelige, typisch elsässische Atmosphäre. Die unterschiedlich gestalteten Zimmer haben Jacuzzibäder. Täglich wird ein üppiges Frühstück serviert, und Gäste entspannen sich in der gemütlichen Lounge mit offenem Kamin. Das Personal sorgt für einen herzlichen Empfang – und ebenso der sprechende Papagei!

Our inspector loved: *The talking parrot in the reception area who welcomes you.*

Directions: The hotel is in the town centre, near the old customs house. The nearest airport is Strasbourg.

Web: www.johansens.com/beaucour
E-mail: beaucour@hotel-beaucour.com
Tel: +33 3 88 76 72 00
Fax: +33 3 88 76 72 60

Price Guide:
(room only)
single €63-89
double €126-151
suite €153-169

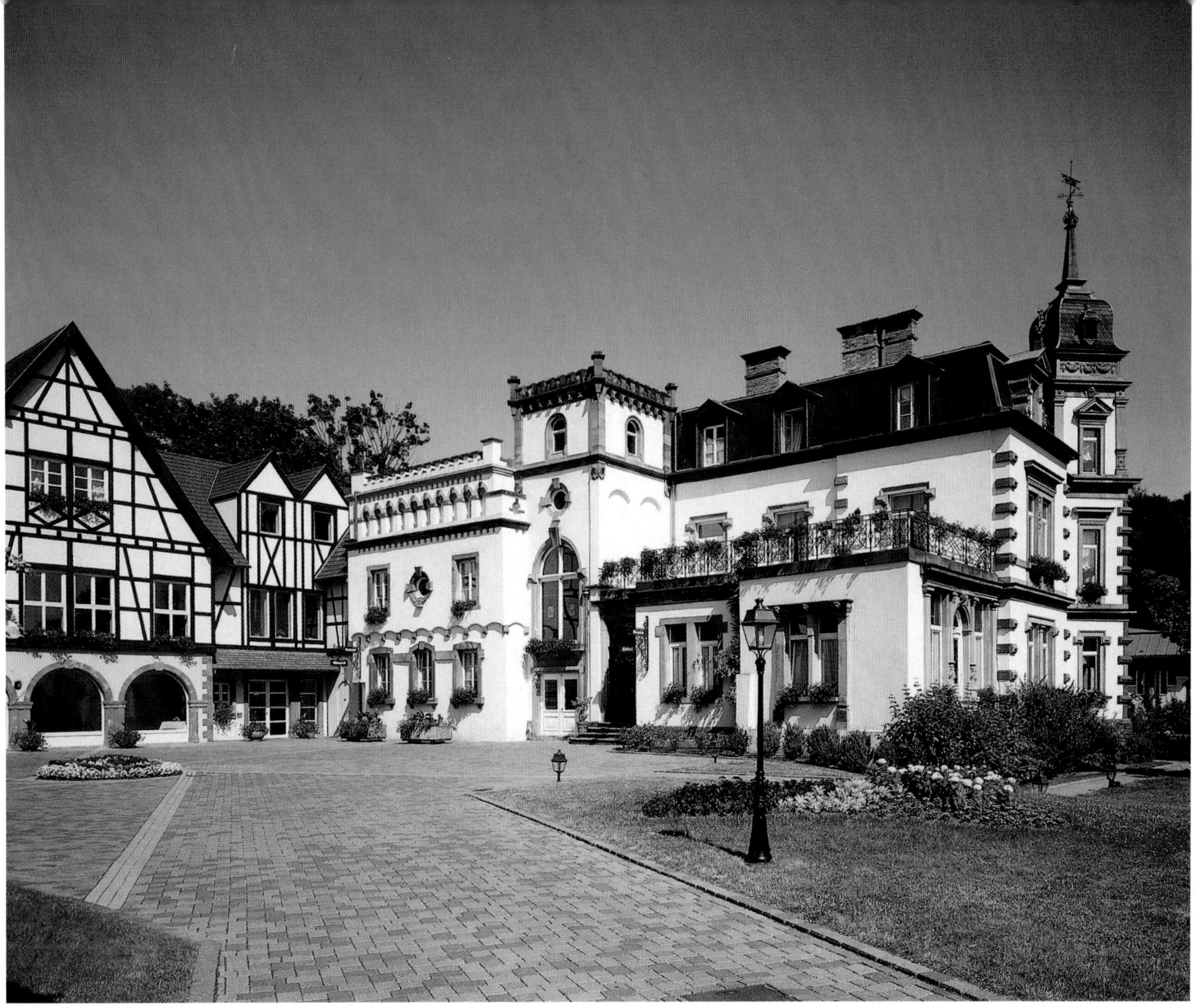

Château de L'Ile

4 QUAI HEYDT, 67540 OSTWALD, FRANCE

Here is total luxury and absolute quality. Nestling in 10 acres of parkland in a loop of the river Ill, this gorgeous château is elegant and spacious while at the same time being intimate and cosy. Individually decorated guest rooms with their refined bathrooms, air conditioning and balconies are simply a dream. Diners enjoy views over river and woods. Spa with pool and fitness centre.

Tout ici est synonyme de luxe et de complète qualité. Niché au cœur de 4 hectares de parc dans un méandre de l'Ill, ce superbe château est élégant et spacieux tout en bénéficiant d'une atmosphère intime et douillette. Les chambres à la décoration unique avec balcon, salles de bain raffinées et disposant de l'air conditionné sont de vraies merveilles. Les dîneurs peuvent profiter de la vue sur la rivière et les bois. L'hôtel dispose d'un spa et d'un centre de remise en forme.

Hier findet man Luxus und Qualität der höchsten Güte. Dieses wundervolle, inmitten von 4ha Parklandschaft an einer Schleife des Flusses Ill gelegene Château ist elegant und geräumig, hat jedoch eine gemütliche und intime Atmosphäre. Die unterschiedlich gestalteten Zimmer haben elegante Bäder, Klimaanlage und Balkone. Beim Abendessen kann man die herrliche Sicht auf den Fluss und die Wälder genießen. Ein Spa mit Pool und Fitnesszentrum steht zur Verfügung.

Our inspector loved: *The Asszimmer - the new red dining room.*

Directions: A35, exit Ostwald.

Web: www.johansens.com/chateaudelile
E-mail: ile@grandesetapes.fr
Tel: +33 3 88 66 85 00
Fax: +33 3 88 66 85 49

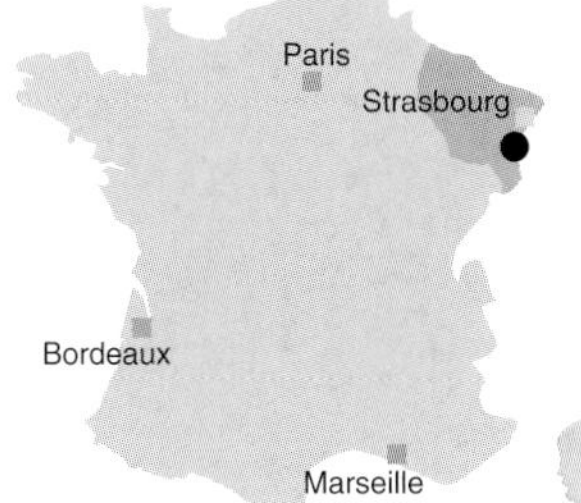

Price Guide:
single €122–355
double €122–355
suite €323–615

62 250 SPA

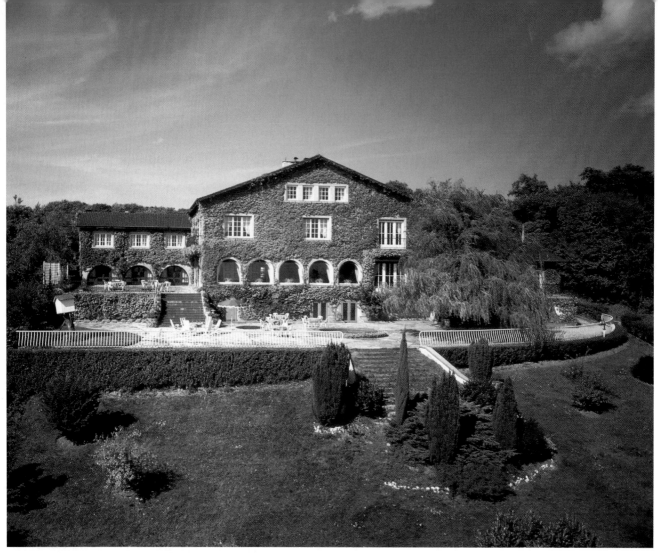

Romantik Hotel L'Horizon

50 ROUTE DU CRÈVE~CŒUR, 57100 THIONVILLE, FRANCE

Directions: A31> exit 40 > follow signs for Crève~Cœur.

Web: www.johansens.com/lhorizonfrance
E-mail: hotel@lhorizon.fr
Tel: +33 3 82 88 53 65
Fax: +33 3 82 34 55 84

Price Guide:
single €75–95
double €95–135
suite €180

Set on the Crève-Cœur hill overlooking Thionville and the surrounding countryside, this 3-star hotel is the perfect base from which to explore the beautiful Lorraine region. The individually decorated bedrooms are furnished with antiques and offer all modern comforts. Panoramic views can be enjoyed from the terrace and the popular restaurant where guests can sample delicious, simple dishes complemented by excellent wines. Luxembourg is within easy reach and guests can visit several Maginot Line forts nearby.

Situé sur la colline de Crève-Cœur surplombant Thionville et la campagne environnante, cet hôtel trois étoiles est la base idéale à partir de laquelle explorer la belle région de Lorraine. Les chambres décorées individuellement sont meublées avec des antiquités et offrent tout le confort moderne. Les vues panoramiques peuvent être appréciées de la terrasse et le restaurant reputé ou les hôtes peuvent déguster des plats délicieux quoique simples, accompagnés d'excellents vins. Le Luxembourg est facile d'accès et les hôtes peuvent visiter la ligne Maginot toute proche.

Dieses auf dem Crève-Cœur-Hügel gelegene 3-Sterne-Hotel mit Blick auf Thionville und die Umgebung ist der ideale Ausgangspunkt, um Lothringen zu erkunden. Die mit Antiquitäten gefüllten, individuell gestalteten Zimmer sind mit jeglichem modernen Komfort ausgestattet. Panoramablicke bieten sich von der Terrasse und dem beliebten Restaurant, wo köstliche Gerichte und erlesene Weine serviert werden. Luxemburg ist nicht weit, und mehrere Festungen der Maginot-Linie können in der Nähe besichtigt werden.

Our inspector loved: *Room 1 for its lovely decoration and view.*

Hostellerie Château de Varillettes

15100 SAINT~GEORGES PAR SAINT~FLOUR, FRANCE

This stunning 15th-century castle is ideally located in a green and quiet valley overlooking the Margeride hills, yet within a mile of Saint-Flour. Great care has been taken to preserve the ancient features and character of the building whilst ensuring guests' total comfort and relaxation. The medieval and herb gardens give a fascinating glimpse into the castle's former spirit, and the outdoor dining terrace is a charming setting from which to savour the delicious cuisine.

Cet incroyable château du XVe siècle a une location idéale dans une vallée tranquille, avec vue sur les Monts de La Margeride, à moins de 2 km de Saint-Flour. Les caractéristiques anciennes du bâtiment ont été préservées avec soin tout en assurant à ses hôtes tout le confort et une détente complète. Les jardins médiévaux et d'herbes aromatiques donnent un aperçu fascinant de l'esprit passé du château, et la salle à manger en terrasse est un endroit charmant pour savourer une cuisine délicieuse.

Diese prachtvolle Burg aus dem 15. Jahrhundert liegt inmitten eines ruhigen, üppig grünen Tales mit Blick auf die Margeride-Hügel, nur 1½km von Saint-Four entfernt. Gäste finden hier jeglichen modernen Komfort, wobei jedoch beim Umbau der ursprüngliche Charakter der Burg sorgfältig erhalten blieb. Der mittelalterliche und Kräutergarten bieten Einblicke in die einstige Geschichte der Burg, und die Terrasse ist ein hervorragender Ort, um die köstliche Küche zu genießen.

Our inspector loved: *The magical atmosphere of the château by night.*

Directions: A75 > exit 29.

Web: www.johansens.com/chateaudevarillettes
E-mail: varillettes@leshotelsparticuliers.com
Tel: +33 4 71 60 45 05
Fax: +33 4 71 60 34 27

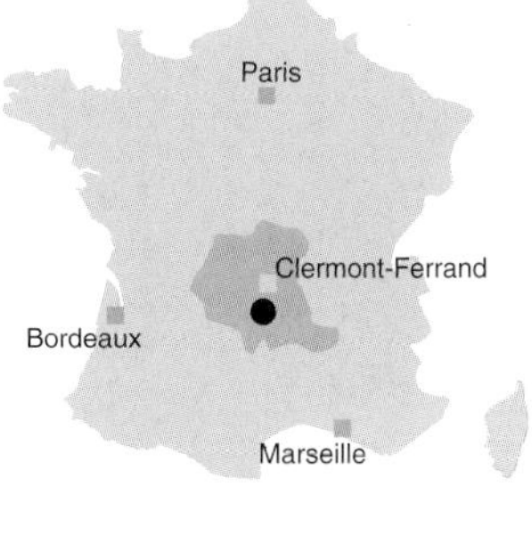

Price Guide:
double €107–123
suite €123–242

Domaine de Rochevilaine

POINTE DE PEN LAN, 56190 BILLIERS, FRANCE

Perched on the edge of the rocky Pointe de Pen Lan, this historic manor house affords a panoramic vista across the waterfront. The bedrooms are all designed in a stylish manner, whilst Aubusson tapestries adorn the walls of the comfortable lounge, where visitors enjoy pre-prandial drinks. Afterwards they can revel in the delicious French cuisine that chef Patrice Caillaut crafts from the freshest of local produce.

Perché sur la pointe rocheuse de Pen Lan, ce manoir historique bénéficie d'une vue panoramique sur le bord de mer. Les chambres sont toutes décorées avec soin. Les tapisseries d'Aubusson décorent les murs du confortable salon et le visiteur se délectera d'apéritifs délicieux. Ensuite, il pourra évoluer vers la divine table française que le chef Patrice Caillaut concocte à partir des meilleurs produits locaux.

Dieses historische Herrenhaus liegt auf der Felspitze von Pen Lan und bietet eine traumhafte Sicht auf die Küste. Die Zimmer sind höchst elegant, Aubusson-Gobelins zieren die Wände des gemütlichen Aufenthaltsraums, in dem sich die Gäste auf einen Apéritif treffen. Für die herrlichen französischen Speisen verwendet Chefkoch Patrice Caillaut die frischesten und besten Zutaten der Region.

Our inspector loved: *The Nomads massage in the Moorish massage parlour.*

Directions: From Nantes > E60 > Vannes > Billiers > Pen Lan.

Web: www.johansens.com/domainederochevilaine
Tel: +33 2 97 41 61 61
Fax: +33 2 97 41 44 85

Price Guide:
(room only)
single €110–336
double/twin €110–336
suites €310–462

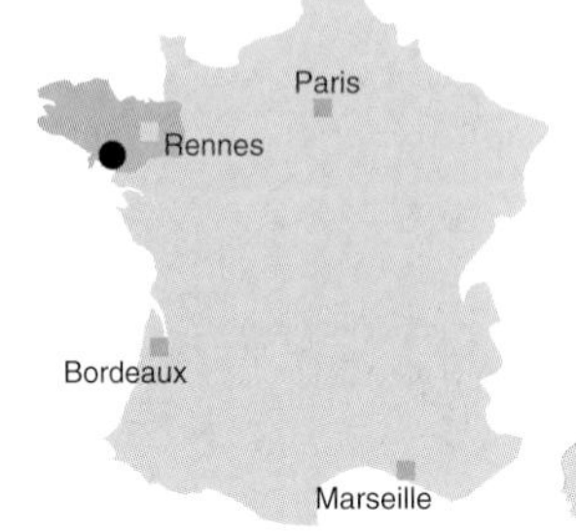

Château de Bonaban

35350 La Gouesnière, France

Situated on a wooded estate in the midst of the Pays Malouin, this 17th-century château offers best service in a friendly ambience. Boasting an opulently decorated chapel and a vast marble staircase, this idyllic country hideaway gives the impression of time standing still. The rooms are adorned with historical paintings, whilst the dining room invites guests to indulge in sumptuous traditional French fare. 5 high-quality golf courses are in close proximity.

Situé au coeur de la région boisée du Pays Malouin, ce château du XVIIe siècle offre le meilleur service dans une ambiance amicale. Exhibant une chapelle superbement décorée et une cage d'escalier en marbre, cette retraite idyllique campagnarde évoque une ambiance où le temps s'arrête. Les chambres sont ornées de peintures historiques et la salle à manger invite les clients aux plaisirs somptueux d'un menu français traditionnel. 5 superbes parcours de golf sont situés à proximité.

Auf einem bewaldeten Gut inmitten des Pays Malouin bietet dieses Schloss aus dem 17. Jahrhundert anspruchsvollen Service in einem freundlichen Ambiente. Mit einer opulent gestalteten Kapelle und einer riesigen Marmortreppe erweckt dieses idyllische ländliche Versteck den Eindruck, als ob hier die Zeit stehengeblieben wäre. Die Zimmer sind mit historischen Gemälden geschmückt, und im Speisesaal werden köstliche traditionelle französische Gerichte serviert. 5 hervorragende Golfplätze liegen in der Nähe.

Our inspector loved: *The candle-lit dinner in the small dining room.*

Directions: N137 > St Malo > La Gouesnière > signposts.

Web: www.johansens.com/chateaudebonaban
E-mail: chateau.bonaban@wanadoo.fr
Tel: +33 2 99 58 24 50
Fax: +33 2 99 58 28 41

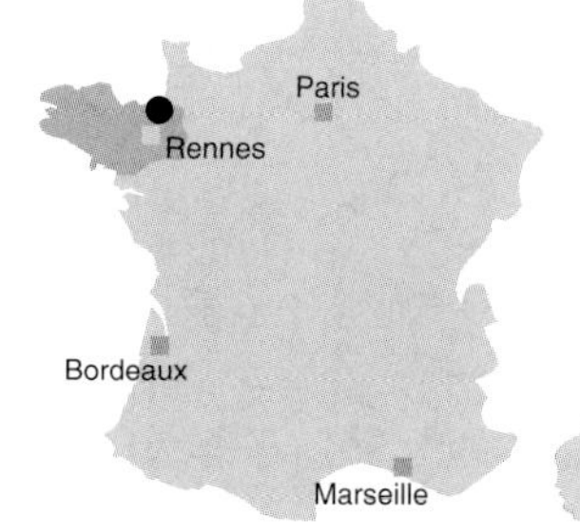

Price Guide:
single €75–235
double/twin €81–235
suites €206–275

Domaine de La Bretesche

44780 MISSILLAC, FRANCE

Directions: N165 Nantes-Brest, exit Missillac/La Bretesche.

Web: www.johansens.com/domainedelabretesche
E-mail: hotel@bretesche.com
Tel: +33 2 51 76 86 96
Fax: +33 2 40 66 99 47

Price Guide:
(room only)
single €130–250
double/twin €130–250
suite €250–320

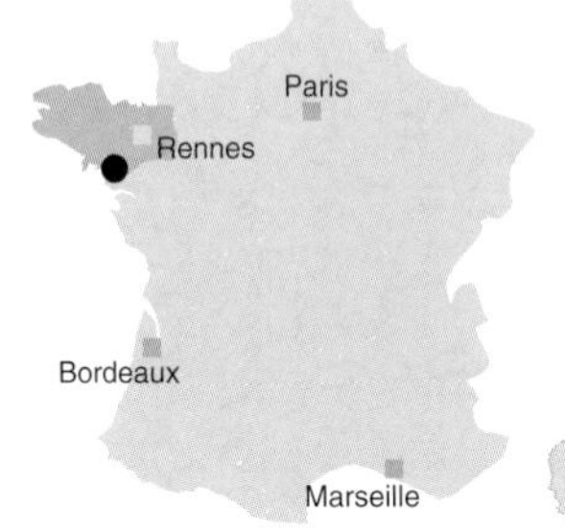

Guests staying in the airy, well-appointed rooms at Hôtel de la Bretesche could be forgiven for thinking they had walked into a fairy tale. Its lush green gardens border a lake and its restaurant looks onto beautiful Château de la Bretesche. Immaculate buildings surround a central courtyard where guests dine under pristine white umbrellas close to colourful banks of flowers. The restaurant offers stunning views whilst serving exquisite cuisine. The magnificent grounds also include an 18-hole golf course.

Les hôtes séjournant dans les belles chambres spacieuses de l'Hôtel de la Bretesche se croient en plein conte de fée. Son parc luxuriant borde un lac et le restaurant a une vue sur le magnifique Château de la Bretesche. Les bâtiments, immaculés et splendides, cernent une cour où les visiteurs dînent à l'ombre de parasols blancs, à côté de massifs de fleurs multicolores. Le restaurant, d'où l'on jouit de vues spectaculaires, propose une cuisine exquise. Le ravissant parc comprend un golf 18 trous.

Wer in den nonchalanten, gut ausgestatteten Zimmern des Hotels übernachtet, wird glauben, in einem Märchen gelandet zu sein. Üppig grüne Gärten grenzen an einen See und vom Restaurant blickt man auf das Château. Herrliche Gebäude umgeben einen zentralen Hof, wo die Gäste unter weißen Sonnenschirmen in der Nähe der bunten Blumenbeete dinieren. Bei exquisiter Cuisine kann man atemberaubende Aussichten genießen. Die großartigen Anlagen schließen auch einen 18-Loch Golfplatz mit ein.

Our inspector loved: *The view from the dining room and the bar in the old stables. Guests can sip champagne in the old stalls.*

Manoir de Kertalg

ROUTE DE RIEC-SUR-BELON, 29350 MOËLAN~SUR~MER, FRANCE

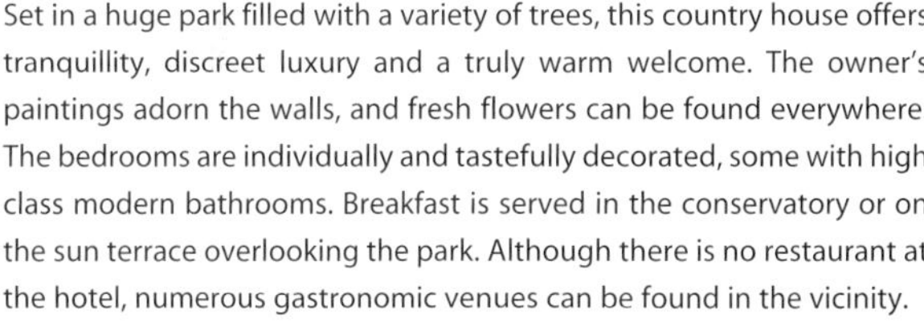

Set in a huge park filled with a variety of trees, this country house offers tranquillity, discreet luxury and a truly warm welcome. The owner's paintings adorn the walls, and fresh flowers can be found everywhere. The bedrooms are individually and tastefully decorated, some with high class modern bathrooms. Breakfast is served in the conservatory or on the sun terrace overlooking the park. Although there is no restaurant at the hotel, numerous gastronomic venues can be found in the vicinity.

Blotti au milieu d'un parc peuplé de différentes espèces d'arbres, ce manoir vous accueille cordialement dans un cadre au luxe discret baigné d'une douce tranquillité. Les tableaux du propriétaire ornent les murs, et des fleurs fraîches égayent toute la demeure. Les chambres sont décorées individuellement et avec goût, certaines s'accompagnent de salles de bains modernes. Le petit déjeuner est servi dans le jardin d'hiver ou sur la terrasse avec vue sur le parc. L'hôtel n'a pas de restaurant, mais les environs regorgent d'établissements gastronomiques.

Dieses Landhaus liegt inmitten eines riesigen, mit verschiedensten Bäumen gefüllten Parks und bietet Ruhe, unaufdringlichen Luxus und warme Gastfreundschaft. Eigene Bilder des Besitzers zieren die Wände und frische Blumen sind im ganzen Haus zu finden. Die Zimmer sind individuell und geschmackvoll eingerichtet, einige haben hochmoderne Bäder. Das Frühstück genießt man im Wintergarten oder auf der Terrasse mit Blick auf den Park. Zwar wird kein Abendessen serviert, aber zahlreiche Gourmetrestaurants liegen in nächster Nähe.

***Our inspector loved:** Room 4 - spacious and overlooking the park.*

Directions: Take the N165 and exit at Quimperlé centre.

Web: www.johansens.com/manoirdekertalg
E-mail: kertalg@free.fr
Tel: +33 2 98 39 77 77
Fax: +33 2 98 39 72 07

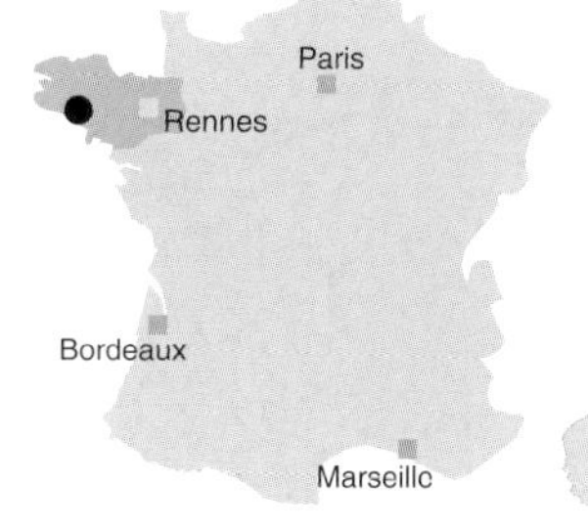

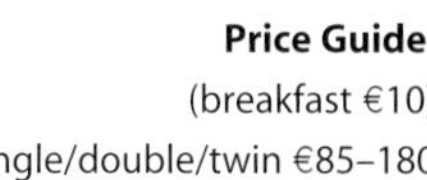

Price Guide:
(breakfast €10)
single/double/twin €85–180
suite €205

Château du Launay

56160 PLOERDÜT, FRANCE

Directions: Pontivy > Gourin, turn right after Toubahado on the D1.

Web: www.johansens.com/chateaudelaunay
E-mail: info@chateaudulaunay.com
Tel: +33 2 97 39 46 32
Fax: +33 2 97 39 46 31

Price Guide:
(room only)
single €115
double/twin €125-150

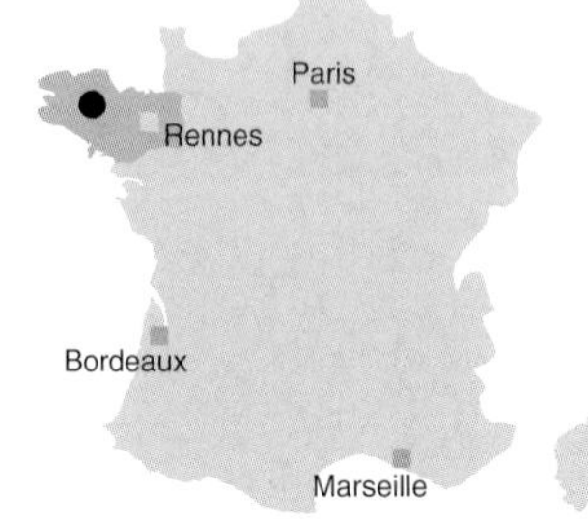

Serene and sophisticated, Château du Launay offers a step back into a timeless and peaceful era. Its charming hosts have designed their hotel entirely with this purpose, and the tasteful, stylish décor and tranquil ambience testify to their success. There is a well-stocked, cosy library, and musical evenings are held in the drawing room. Although there is no restaurant, table d'hôte is served on request. The hotel offers numerous outdoor pursuits such as tennis and riding; fishing is possible from a shady river bank within the grounds.

Paisible et élégant, le Château du Launay nous replonge dans le passé, vers une époque sereine. Les charmants propriétaires ont aménagé leur hôtel dans cet esprit, et le décor raffiné ainsi que la tranquillité des lieux témoignent de leurs efforts. Le château abrite une bibliothèque confortable et un salon accueillant des soirées musicales. L'hôtel n'a pas de restaurant, mais une table d'hôte est disponible sur demande. De nombreuses activités de plein air sont possibles telles que le tennis, l'équitation et la pêche sur la berge ombragée d'une rivière, dans le parc.

Das ruhige und elegante Château du Launay bietet eine Reise zurück in eine zeitlose und friedvolle Ära. Die Besitzer haben ihr Hotel in diesem Sinne gestaltet, und das geschmackvolle Décor und die ruhige Atmosphäre zeugen von ihrem Erfolg. Eine gutbestückte, gemütliche Bibliothek steht zur Verfügung, und im Aufenthaltsraum finden musikalische Abende statt. Zwar gibt es kein Restaurant, aber auf Wunsch wird für die Gäste gekocht und zusammen gegessen. Das Freizeitangebot umfasst Tennis, Reiten und Angeln am Fluss innerhalb des Grundstücks.

***Our inspector loved:** Sipping coffee in the library after dinner when listening to music.*

LeCoq~Gadby

156 RUE D'ANTRAIN, 35700 RENNES, FRANCE

This delightful family-run hotel boasts a stylish and newly-opened health spa. The ambience is one of elegance combined with intimacy with cosy treatment rooms, attentive staff and stunning views over the gardens. The Moroccan/Hammam sauna and oriental massages are deeply relaxing, and even the most discerning palate will be tempted by the delightful cuisine served in the restaurant overlooking the pretty gardens.

Ce délicieux hôtel familial s'enorgueillit d'un spa chic et tout nouveau. L'ambiance qui émane est celle de l'élégance associée à des chambres intimes et cabines de soins, un personnel attentif et des vues incroyables sur le jardin. Le hammam marocain et les massages orientaux sont la promesse d'une détente complète; le plus fin gourmet sera tente par la délicieuse cuisine servie dans le restaurant qui ouvre sur les jolis jardins.

Dieses freundliche, familiengeführte Hotel ist vor allem für sein chices neues Kurzentrum bekannt. Gemütliche Behandlungsräume, aufmerksames Personal und herrliche Blicke auf die Gärten schaffen ein einladendes, elegantes Ambiente, und die marokkanische Sauna und orientalische Massagen sorgen für totale Entspannung. Die köstlichen Speisen, die im Restaurant mit Blick auf die hübschen Gärten serviert werden, begeistern selbst den anspruchsvollsten Gast.

Our inspector loved: *The health spa and Turkish bath.*

Directions: North of the centre of Rennes > direction of Mont St Michel/Caen.

Web: www.johansens.com/lecoqgadby
E-mail: lecoq-gadby@wanadoo.fr
Tel: +33 2 99 38 05 55
Fax: +33 2 99 38 53 40

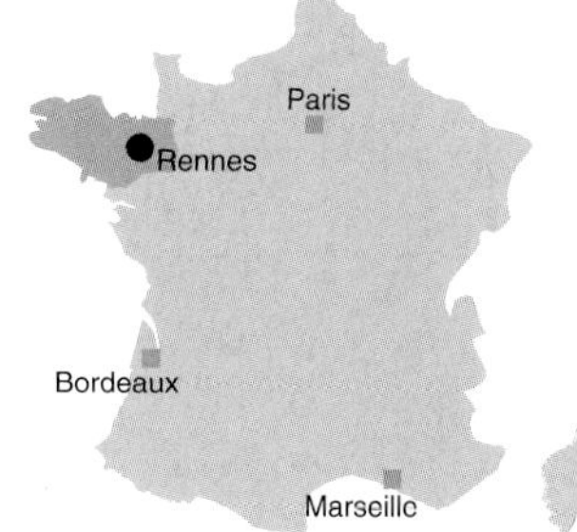

Price Guide:
(room only)
single €125–150
double €145–165
suite €265–305

SPA

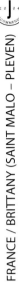

Manoir du Vaumadeuc

22130 PLEVEN, FRANCE

The magnificent Hunaudaye forest encompasses this luxurious former 15th-century manor house, which fuses modern comfort and medieval grandeur. Sculpted beams, ornate fireplaces and wooden floors set the tone in the public rooms, whilst an imposing granite staircase leads to the individually decorated rooms. Exclusive use of the château is available; this is an ideal venue for a special family function.

La somptueuse forêt de Hunaudaye abrite ce luxueux et ancien manoir du XVe siècle, qui allie un cadre médiéval authentique avec le confort moderne. Des poutres sculptées, des cheminées ornées et des parquets en bois plantent le décor des salons, alors qu'un magnifique escalier en granit vous amène aux chambres décorées de manière individuelle. L'utilisation exclusive du château est disponible; c'est l'endroit idéal pour des fêtes en famille.

Der herrliche Hunaudaye Forst umgibt dieses luxuriöse Herrenhaus aus dem 15. Jahrhundert, eine Mischung aus modernem Komfort und mittelalterlicher Opulenz. Zierbalken, prunkvolle Kamine und Holzböden verleihen den Empfangsräumen einen besonderen Charakter, und die Zimmer können über eine imposante Granittreppe erreicht werden. Das Château kann exklusiv gemietet werden und ist der ideale Ort für eine ganz besondere Familienfeier.

Our inspector loved: *Curling up with a book in the baronial salon in front of a roaring log fire.*

Directions: N168 > Planceot > Lamballe > Pleven.

Web: www.johansens.com/manoirduvaumadeuc
E-mail: manoir@vaumadeuc.com
Tel: +33 2 96 84 46 17
Fax: +33 2 96 84 40 16

Price Guide:
(room only)
single €90-195
double/twin €90–195
suites €205

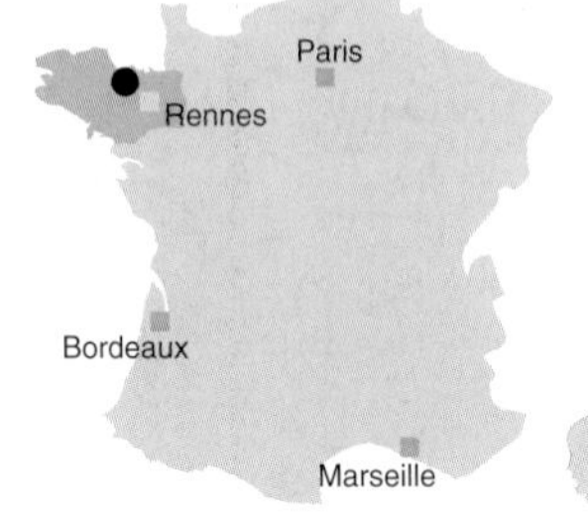

Ti Al Lannec

14 ALLÉE DE MÉZO~GUEN, BP 3, 22560 TREBEURDEN, FRANCE

This Breton manor house commands imposing views, perched high on a cliff top overlooking the rose granite coast - one of the most spectacular reaches of Brittany. Professionalism is key here with a warm welcome from the attentive staff and a keen eye for detail. The public rooms are well-appointed and inviting, whilst the bedrooms are luxurious, with many having private balconies and sea views.

Ce manoir breton, à la vue incroyable, est solidement posé sur la colline surplombant la côte de granite rose — l'une des plus spectaculaires de Bretagne. Ici le professionnalisme est de mise, accompagné d'un accueil chaleureux de la part d'un personnel attentif et d'une attention particulière pour le détail. Les salles communes sont bien placées et accueillantes, alors que les chambres sont luxueuses, beaucoup d'entre elles ayant un balcon privé et vue sur la mer.

Dieses bretonische Herrenhaus befindet sich an einem der spektakulärsten Orte der Bretagne und bietet von seiner Lage hoch auf einer Klippe atemberaubende Blicke auf die Küste. Professionalität und ein Auge fürs Detail sind das Erfolgsrezept des Hotels, und das Personal bereitet jedem Gast einen herzlichen Empfang. Die attraktiven Aufenthaltsräume sind sehr einladend und viele der luxuriösen Gästezimmer haben einen eigenen Balkon und Blick auf das Meer.

Our inspector loved: *Room 35 and the view over the bay.*

Directions: From North> towards Lannion> then towards Trebeurden.

Web: www.johansens.com/tiallannec
E-mail: resa@tiallannec.com
Tel: +33 296 15 01 01
Fax: +33 2 96 23 62 14

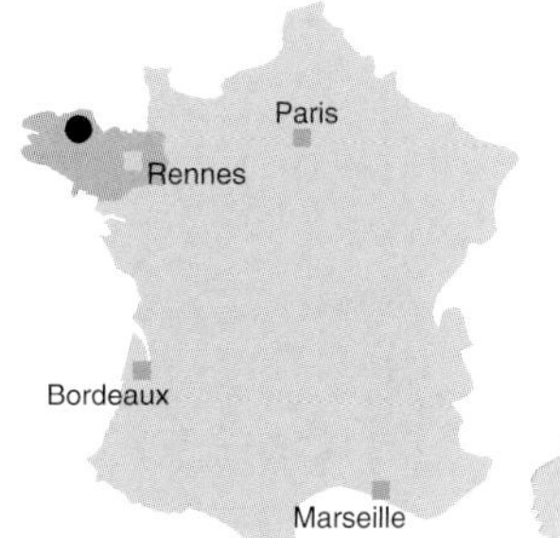

Price Guide:
(room only)
single €78-97
double €144-253
suite €288-317

33 SPA

LE PETIT MANOIR DES BRUYÈRES

5 ALLÉE DE CHARBUY, LES~BRUYÈRES, 89240 AUXERRE - VILLEFARGEAU, FRANCE

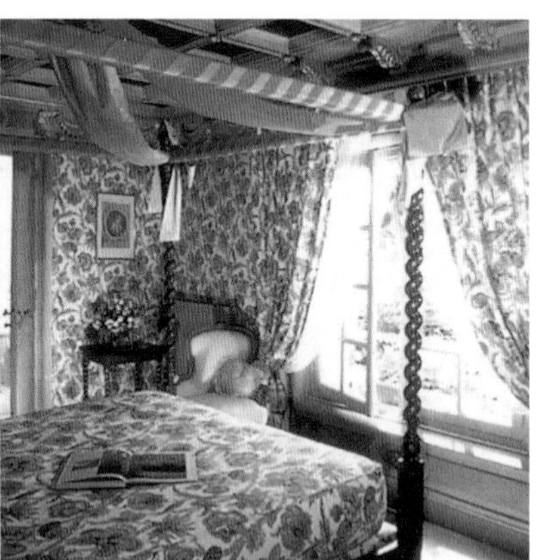

In the heart of a 250-acre forest and amidst a fragrant garden lies this charming, welcoming and old-fashioned guest house with its glazed-tile roof typical of the Burgundy region. The individually decorated bedrooms and suites are equipped with period furniture and luxurious bathrooms and overlook the park. Madame Joullié lovingly prepares delicious meals in her splendid kitchen, and after an apéritif comprising a glass of the famous Chablis wine, guests can feast on local specialities.

Perdue au milieu de 100 hectares de forêt et entourée d'un jardin parfumé, cette demeure accueillante vous invite à découvrir le charme désuet qui se cache sous son toit en tuiles vernissées typique de la Bourgogne. Les chambres et les suites sont dotées de meubles d'époque et de salles de bains luxueuses et jouissent d'une vue sur le parc. Madame Joullié prépare des repas délicieux dans sa superbe cuisine et, après leur avoir offert un verre de Chablis, elle propose à ses hôtes de goûter d'excellentes spécialités locales.

Dieses charmante, freundliche und altmodische Haus mit seinem regionstypischen Ziegeldach liegt inmitten eines 100ha großen Waldes in einem duftenden Garten. Die individuell gestalteten Zimmer und Suiten sind mit Stilmöbeln und luxuriösen Badezimmern ausgestattet und haben Blick auf den Park. Madame Joullié bereitet köstliche Speisen in ihrer eindrucksvollen Küche zu, und nach einem Apéritif – meist ein Glas des berühmten Chablis – erfreuen sich die Gäste an einheimischen Spezialitäten.

Our inspector loved: *Monsieur and Madame Joullié's delicious cuisine and superb selection of wines.*

Directions: A6 exit Auxerre-Sud or Auxerre-Nord.

Web: www.johansens.com/lepetitmanoirdesbruyeres
E-mail: jchambord@aol.com
Tel: +33 3 86 41 32 82
Fax: +33 3 86 41 28 57

Price Guide:
double €107–137
suite €152–195

Château de Vault de Lugny

11 RUE DU CHÂTEAU, 89200 AVALLON, FRANCE

Dating from the 16th century, this magical rural hideaway is surrounded by an authentic 13th-century moat weaving its way through the verdant estate. The interior is no less dramatic, with its marvellous panelling, elaborate fireplaces and ornate ceilings. Some of the splendid bedrooms have four-poster beds and fireplaces. The château is renowned for the variety of its food, which is taken around a large table exclusively for hotel residents (closed on Wednesdays), and its magnificent 100-acre garden and vegetable garden. There is also a terrace overlooking the river.

Ce ravissant château du XVIe siècle est encerclé de ses douves authentiques du XIIIe siècle. L'intérieur est tout aussi impressionnant, avec ses lambris magnifiques, ses cheminées élaborées et ses plafonds à la Française. Certaines chambres splendides ont des lits à baldaquins et des cheminées. Le château est renommé pour sa table d'hôte (restauration exclusivement pour résidents de l'hôtel, fermé le mecredi) et son magnifique jardin de 40 ha et potager. Terrasse sur la rivière.

Dieses zauberhafte Landversteck aus dem 16. Jahrhundert liegt inmitten eines üppigen Parks und ist von einem Burggraben aus dem 13. Jahrhundert umgeben. Im Inneren sorgen herrliche Holzvertäfelung, opulente Kamine und reichverzierte Decken für ein dramatisches Ambiente. Einige der prachtvollen Schlafzimmer besitzen Himmelbett und offenen Kamin. Das Château ist bekannt für seine große kulinarische Auswahl, die am "Table d'hôte" serviert wird (exklusiv für Hotelgäste, mittwochs geschlossen) und für seinen 40ha großen Garten und Gemüsegarten sowie eine Terrasse mit Blick auf den Fluss.

Our inspector loved: *The beautiful lawn and park where ducks, peacocks and hens roam freely.*

Directions: A6 > Avallon > Vezelay > Pontaubert.

Web: www.johansens.com/vaultdelugny
E-mail: hotel@lugny.com
Tel: +33 3 86 34 07 86
Fax: +33 3 86 34 16 36

Price Guide:
double/twin €160–460
suite €440

Ermitage de Corton

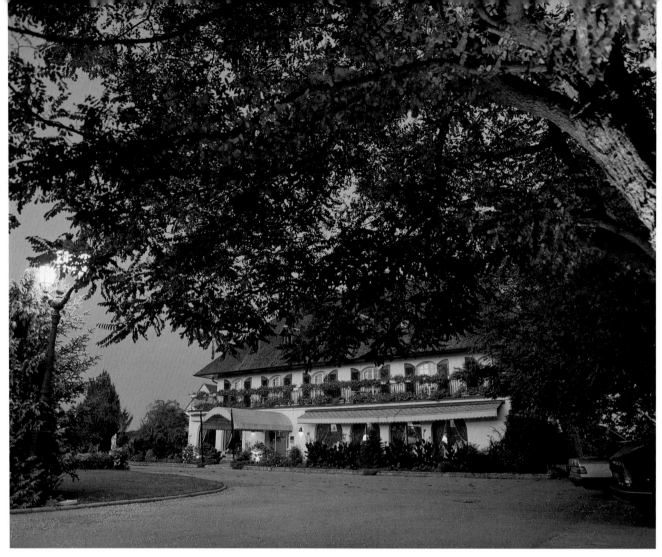

R.N. 74, 21200 CHOREY~LES~BEAUNE, FRANCE

Set in acres of glorious vineyards, this old burgundy-style mansion offers comfortable accommodation and warm hospitality in fine surroundings. The individually decorated rooms range from the grandiose to the simple yet elegant. The restaurant is undoubtedly the centre-point; the traditional French fare is prepared by a maître cuisinier de France, and is complemented by a fine selection of wines.

Entouré d'hectares de merveilleux vignobles, ce vieux manoir de style bourguignon offre des séjours confortables et une chaleureuse hospitalité dans un beau cadre. Les chambres décorées de manière individuelle varient d'un style grandiose au simple et élégant. Le restaurant est sans nul doute l'attraction centrale; la cuisine traditionnel le française est préparé par un Maître Cuisinier de France, et est complété par une fine sélection de vins.

Inmitten herrlicher Weinberge liegt dieses alte Haus im Burgunder Stil, das seinen Gästen ein herzliches Willkommen bietet. Die gemütlichen Zimmer sind in unterschiedlichen Stilen gestaltet, von prunkvoll bis einfach aber elegant. Das Restaurant, zweifellos Mittelpunkt des Hotels, serviert unvergleichliche französische Küche, kreiert von einem „Maître Cuisinier de France", und durch eine erlesene Auswahl an Weinen ergänzt.

Our inspector loved: *Madame Parra's warm welcome and Monsieur Parra's delicious cuisine.*

Directions: A6 > Beaune > exit 24 > Dijon.

Web: www.johansens.com/ermitagedecorton
E-mail: ermitage.corton@wanadoo.fr
Tel: +33 3 80 22 05 28
Fax: +33 3 80 24 64 51

Price Guide:
(Continental breakfast €25, lunch €40, dinner €40, à la carte menu €65-100)
double/twin €210-285
suite €250-350

Hostellerie des Monts de Vaux

LES MONTS DE VAUX, 39800 POLIGNY, FRANCE

This wonderful family-run coaching inn perched high on a mountain top is of beautifully old-fashioned charm. With its traditional décor and furnishings, it takes you back into a bygone era. It is a true home from home, with warming logfires in the lounges creating a cosy and welcoming atmosphere. After a day spent exploring the breathtaking surroundings by bicycle or on foot, guests can enjoy the extensive menu featuring delicious regional cuisine, complemented by an extraordinary wine list.

Perchée au sommet d'une montagne, cette superbe auberge familiale dégage un charme merveilleusement ancien. Son décor et son mobilier traditionnels vous transportent dans l'ancien temps. On se sent vraiment chez soi à la lueur des feux de bois qui réchauffent les salons en créant une atmosphère douillètte et accueillante. Après une journée passée à explorer les alentours pittoresques à vélo ou à pied, les clients pourront apprécier le menu complet qui propose une délicieuse cuisine régionale, accompagné d'une carte des vins extraordinaire.

Diese zauberhafte, familiengeführte alte Poststation liegt hoch auf einem Berg im Jura, und versprüht einen herrlich altmodischen Charme. Die traditionelle Einrichtung erinnert an längst vergangene Zeiten. Hier fühlt man sich wie zu Hause, und wärmende offene Kamine schaffen eine gemütliche und freundliche Atmosphäre. Die Gäste können die traumhaft schöne Umgebung zu Fuß oder mit dem Fahrrad erkunden, bevor sie sich von den regionalen Köstlichkeiten auf der umfangreichen Speisekarte und der phantastischen Weinkarte verwöhnen lassen..

Our inspector loved: *The truly personal welcome from the Carrion family.*

Directions: N5 from Poligny towards Switzerland.

Web: www.johansens.com/montdevaux
E-mail: mtsvaux@hostellerie.com
Tel: +33 3 84 37 12 50
Fax: +33 3 84 37 09 07

Price Guide:
(breakfast €13.50)
rooms and apartments from €145-220

CHÂTEAU DE GILLY

GILLY~LES~CÎTEAUX, 21640 VOUGEOT, FRANCE

With its moats, parkland gardens and magnificent 14th-century vaulted dining room this former residence of the Priors of the Cistercian Abbey in the heart of Burgundy is a superb hotel of history. Restoration, refurbishment, modernisation in no way diminished its authenticity and charm. The architecture is superb, the interior décor and furnishings stunning and guest rooms are of the highest standard.

Avec ses douves, son parc et sa magnifique salle à manger sous voûtes, cette ancienne résidence des moines de l'abbaye cistercienne du cœur de la Bourgogne est un splendide monument historique. Restauration, redécoration et modernisation n'ont en rien diminué son authenticité et son charme. L'architecture est superbe, les intérieurs et le mobilier magnifiques et les chambres d'un niveau exceptionnel.

Diese ehemalige Residenz der Priore der Zisterzienserabtei im Herzen des Burgund mit ihren Gräben, parkartigen Gärten und herrlichem Speisesaal mit gewölbter Decke aus dem 14. Jahrhundert ist ein einzigartiges und geschichtsträchtiges Hotel. Restaurierungs- und Modernisierungsarbeiten konnten der Authentizität und dem Charakter keinen Abbruch tun. Die Architektur ist atemberaubend, das Décor und die Einrichtung der Innenräume einmalig, und die Zimmer bieten höchsten Komfort.

Our inspector loved: *The very impressive vaulted dining room and the many activities organised for children.*

Directions: A6 > A31 exit Nuits-Saint-Georges > follow signs to Gilly-Les-Cîteaux.

Web: www.johansens.com/gilly
E-mail: gilly@grandesetapes.fr
Tel: +33 3 80 62 89 98
Fax: +33 3 80 62 82 34

Price Guide:
single €108–290
double €108–290
suite €276–510

Hostellerie La Briqueterie

4 Route de Sézanne, 51530 Vinay – Épernay, France

Standing at the foot of the Côte des Blancs and surrounded by beautiful flower-filled gardens, this friendly family-owned hotel is ideal for the champagne lover. Elegant salons reflect the beauty of the surroundings whilst the newly refurbished bedrooms are simply stunning. Vintages from the Trouillard family's own Champagne House are among the prestigious champagnes enjoyed in the conservatory bar, before diners choose from an enticing range of succulent dishes in the handsome, beamed 1-Michelin-star restaurant.

Cet hôtel familial accueillant se dresse dans un beau jardin fleuri, au pied de la Côte des Blancs, un paradis pour les amateurs de champagne. Les salons élégants et les superbes chambres récemment rénovées reflètent la beauté du paysage environnant. La famille Trouillard produit son propre champagne, et ses millésimes figurent parmi les prestigieuses bouteilles que les visiteurs peuvent déguster dans le bar aménagé dans le jardin d'hiver avant de succomber au grand choix de plats savoureux proposé dans le beau restaurant aux poutres apparentes et 1 étoile Michelin.

Dieses freundliche Hotel liegt Am Fuße der Côte des Blancs und ist von blumengefüllten Gärten umgeben. Elegante Salons und herrliche neue Zimmer spiegeln die Schönheit der Umgebung wider. Das Hotel ist ein Paradies für den Champagnerfreund – die Familie besitzt eine eigene Champagnerkellerei, und die Gäste können die erlesenen Jahrgänge in der Wintergarten-Bar genießen, bevor sie sich im zauberhaften Restaurant (1 Michelin-Stern) von einer großen Auswahl an köstlichen Speisen verlocken lassen.

Our inspector loved: *Swimming in the pool with a view over the champagne vineyards.*

Directions: Épernay > Route de Sézanne > signposted.

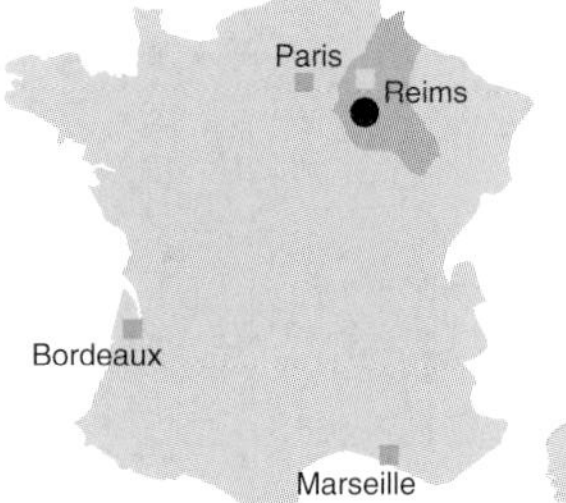

Web: www.johansens.com/labriqueterie
E-mail: info@labriqueterie.com
Tel: +33 3 26 59 99 99
Fax: +33 3 26 59 92 10

Price Guide:
single €160–170
double/twin €180–190
suite €240–250

CHÂTEAU D'ETOGES

51270 ETOGES EN CHAMPAGNE, FRANCE

Nestling in the Champagne Region on the Paris-Strasbourg road, this magnificent château is surrounded by a moat and 45 acres of parkland and gardens sprinkled with fountains and water features. Formerly a medieval fortress, the château was rebuilt in the 17th century by the counts of Anglure and prior to the revolution was a favourite stopping point for French royalty. Bright and spacious public rooms create a comfortable ambience, whilst the bedrooms are individually decorated and furnished, some in period style, others more cosy and intimate.

Niché au coeur de la Champagne, sur la route de Paris á Strasbourg, ce magnifique château est entouré de larges douves et d'un parc de 18ha. Ancien château-fort, il fut reconstruit au XVIIe siècle par les Comtes d'Anglure et fut, avant la Révolution, la halte privilégiée des Rois de France. Les chambres, intimes et confortables, sont aménagées et décorées avec raffinement. Mobilier authentique et vastes salons sont les témoins précieux des fastes du passé d'Etoges.

Dieses herrliche Château bei Etoges an der Straße von Paris nach Straßburg ist umgeben von einem Burggraben und 18ha Park mit zahlreichen Springbrunnen und Wasseranlagen. Diese einstige mittelalterliche Festung wurde im 17. Jahrhundert von den Grafen zu Anglure wieder erbaut und war vor der Revolution ein beliebter Rastort für Mitglieder der französischen Königsfamilie. Helle, geräumige Aufenthaltsräume schaffen ein freundliches Ambiente, und die Zimmer sind unterschiedlich eingerichtet und gestaltet, einige im Originalstil, andere eher klein und gemütlich.

Our inspector loved: *The Alizé bedroom with its exotic décor.*

Directions: The hotel is situated beside the D933 Montmirail, Chalons en Champagne road. The nearest airport is Paris Roissy.

Web: www.johansens.com/www.johansens.com/etoges
E-mail: contact@etoges.com
Tel: +33 3 26 59 30 08
Fax: +33 3 26 59 35 57

Price Guide: (room only)
single €80-110
double €110-190

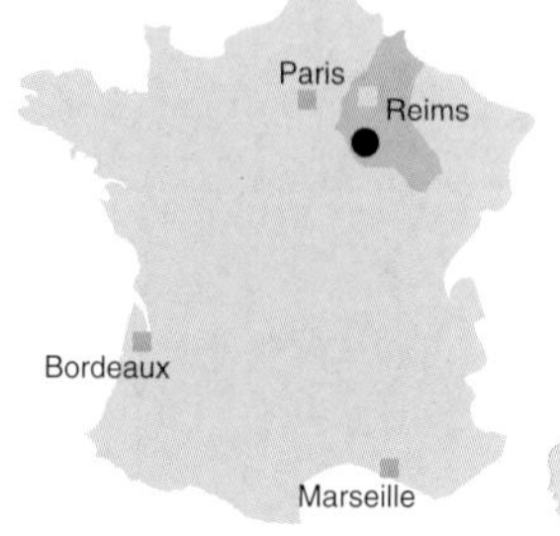

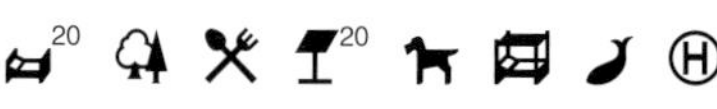

L'Assiette Champenoise

40 AVENUE PAUL VAILLANT COUTURIER, 51430 TINQUEUX, FRANCE

A truly warm welcome awaits visitors to this family-orientated hotel, highly reputed for its delicious modern and traditional cuisine. Complemented by a cosy and welcoming bar, a superb dining room opens out onto an amazing terrace. Guests may relax in the lawned gardens filled with trees and flowers, take advantage of the indoor swimming pool and sauna or visit Reims and some of the numerous champagne cellars in the vicinity, some of which house the finest bottles in the world.

Un accueil très chaleureux vous attend dans cet hôtel hautement réputé pour sa délicieuse cuisine moderne et traditionnelle. Complétée par un bar intime, l'élégante salle de restaurant s'ouvre sur une magnifique terrasse. Les visiteurs se reposent sur les pelouses du jardin rempli de fleurs et d'arbres, profitent de la piscine et du sauna ou visitent Reims et les innombrables caves à champagne des environs, dont certaines renferment les meilleures bouteilles du monde.

Ein herzlicher Empfang erwartet Besucher dieses familienorientierten Hotels, das für seine köstliche moderne und traditionelle Küche weithin bekannt ist. Es gibt eine gemütliche Bar, und ein eleganter Speisesaal führt auf eine fantastische Terrasse hinaus. Die Gäste entspannen sich im gepflegten, mit Bäumen und Blumen gefüllten Garten, Hallenbad oder in der Sauna oder erkunden Reims und die zahllosen Champagnerkeller in der Umgebung, von denen einige die besten Champagnersorten der Welt beherbergen.

Our inspector loved: *The amazing choice of crockery on which dinner is served, modern and innovative!*

Directions: A4 > exit Tinqueux.

Web: www.johansens.com/lassiettechampenoise
E-mail: info@assiettechampenoise.com
Tel: +33 3 26 84 64 64
Fax: +33 3 26 04 15 69

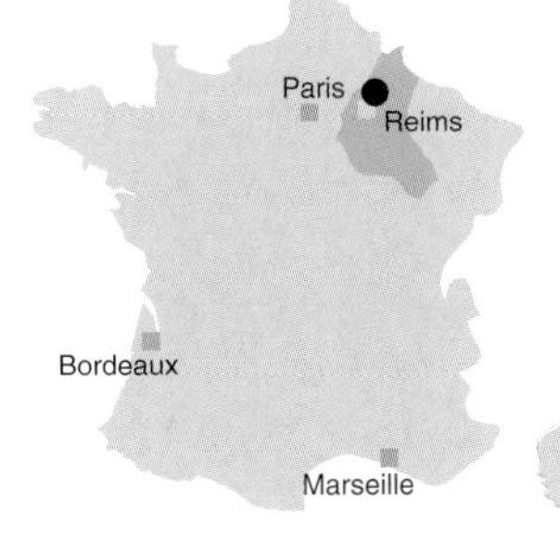

Price Guide:
double/twin €125–165
suite €245

BASTIDE DU CALALOU

MOISSAC-BELLEVUE, 83630 AUPS, FRANCE

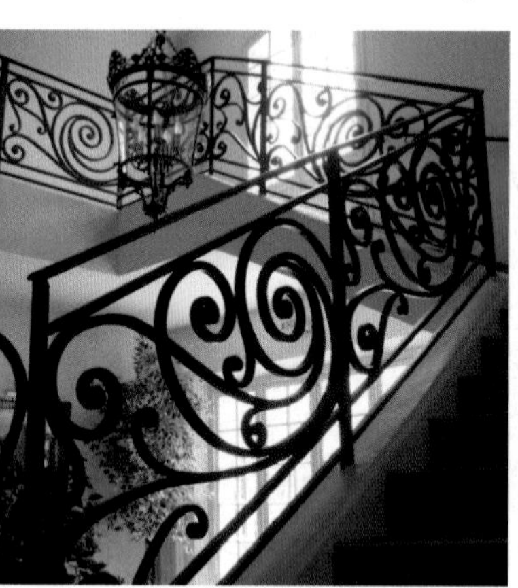

Directions: From the A8 > exit either St Maximin or Le Muy.

Web: www.johansens.com/calalou
E-mail: bastide.du.calalou@wanadoo.fr
Tel: +33 4 94 70 17 91
Fax: +33 4 94 70 50 11

Price Guide:
(room only)
double €93-191
apartment €180-230

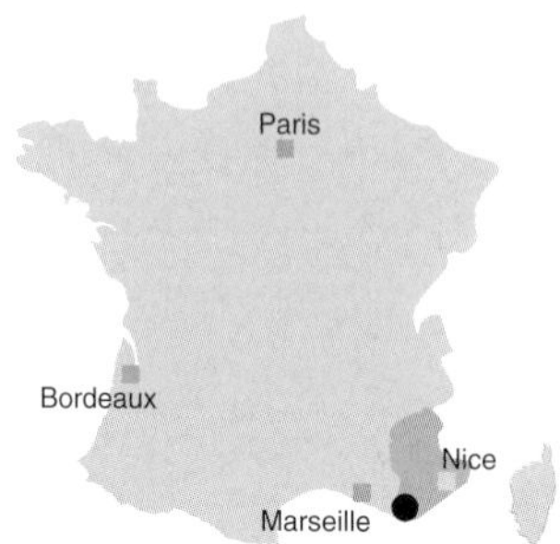

Perched high on a hill overlooking the Var countryside and surrounded by olive trees, Bastide du Calalou is a delightful retreat from hectic city life. Provençal tones and fine antique furnishings create a feeling of tranquillity, and each of the individually designed bedrooms overlooks the swimming pool, gardens or surrounding valley. Breakfast and apéritifs are served on the sunlit terrace, whilst high-quality dining can be enjoyed in the restaurant. The region offers plenty of attractions including the Var vineyards, where delicious rosé and red wines are produced.

Perché en haut sur une colline donnant sur la campagne de Var et entouré d'oliveraies, Bastide de Calalou est un retrait charmant de la vie trépidante. Des tons provençaux et ameublements anciens créent une ambiance tranquille, et chacune des chambres ornées de façon individuelle donne sur la piscine, les jardins ou la vallée environnante. Le petit-déjeuner et l'apéritif sont servis sur la terrasse ensoleillée, alors que la cuisine haute-qualité est servie au restaurant. Il y a de nombreuses attractions comprenant les vignobles de la Var, où des vins rouges et rosés délicieux sont produits.

Hoch auf einem Hügel mit Blick auf die Var-Region gelegen und von Olivenbäumen umgeben ist dieses Hotel ein wunderbares Versteck vor der Hektik der Stadt. Provenzalisches Décor und edle antike Einrichtungen sorgen für ein Gefühl der Ruhe, und die individuell gestalteten Zimmer blicken auf den Pool, Garten oder das Tal. Frühstück und Apéritif werden auf der sonnigen Terrasse serviert, und im Restaurant genießt man köstliche Küche. Die Region bietet zahlreiche Sehenswürdigkeiten, z.B. die Var-Weinberge, wo köstliche Rosé - und Rotweine hergestellt werden.

Our inspector loved: *The breathtaking views over the war region and warm welcome from the entire staff and owners.*

Domaine Cocagne

COLLINE DE LA ROUTE DE VENCE, 30, CHEMIN DU PAIN DE SUCRE, 08600 CAGNES~SUR~MER, FRANCE

A perfect French Riviera hideaway, Domaine Cocagne is tucked into a small hill with views of the old village of Cagnes-sur-Mer and the sea. Recently refurbished by a famous Dutch designer, its style is beautifully modern yet restrained. The pure white main building houses a bar and restaurant, airy seating area and large terrace, all overlooking the pool. Spacious, light bedrooms are decorated in subtle tones and a number of suites and a separate villa are also available.

Une cachette parfaite sur la Côte d'Azur, le Domaine Cocagne est blotti dans une petite colline avec vue sur le vieux village de Cagnes-sur-Mer et sur la mer. Il a été récemment admirablement redécoré par un designer hollandais célèbre, dans un style moderne quoique sobre. Le bâtiment principal, d'un blanc immaculé, abrite un bar et restaurant, un endroit clair pour s'asseoir et une grande terrasse, le tout surplombant la piscine. Les chambres, décorées dans des tons subtils, sont spacieuses et lumineuses et un certain nombre de suites ainsi qu'une villa indépendante sont disponibles.

Dieses perfekte "Versteck" an der Französischen Riviera liegt an einem kleinen Hügel mit Sicht auf das Meer und den alten Teil von Cagnes-sur-Mer. Kürzlich von einem bekannten holländischen Designer renoviert, bietet es einen unaufdringlich modernen Stil. Im strahlend weißen Hauptgebäude befinden sich Bar und Restaurant, eine Sitzecke und eine große Terrasse mit Blick auf den Pool. Die geräumigen, hellen Zimmer sind in subtilen Farben gehalten. Suiten und eine Einzelvilla stehen ebenfalls zur Verfügung.

Our inspector loved: *The terrace overlooking the pool where you can enjoy the chef's delicious cuisine.*

Directions: A8 > Cagnes-sur-Mer > centre ville > hotel signposted.

Web: www.johansens.com/domainecocagne
E-mail: hotel@domainecocagne.com
Tel: +33 4 92 13 57 77
Fax: +33 4 92 13 57 89

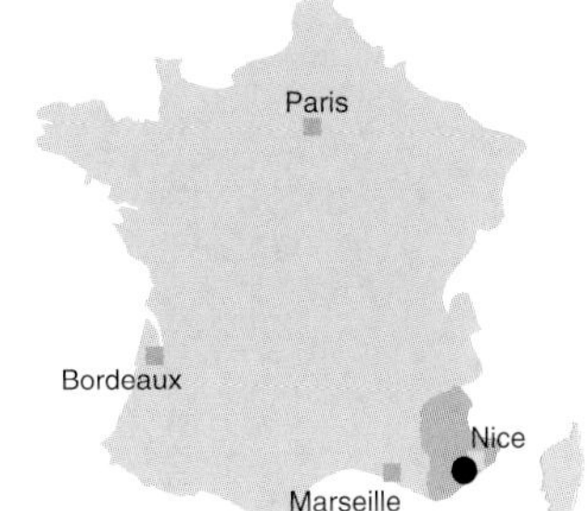

Price Guide:
single €115–154
double €125–192
suite €200–292

CHÂTEAU EZA

RUE DE LA PISE, 06360 ÈZE VILLAGE, FRANCE

From its vantage point, 1300 feet above the Mediterranean Sea, Château Eza enchants its guests as its location and history suggest. The original stone walls, oak beams, alcoves and fireplaces of several 13th-century houses are preserved in 10 sumptuous suites, 7 with their own balcony, and faultless modern facilities. Breathtaking views are guaranteed as an accompaniment to the award-winning meals served on the outdoor terrace or panoramic restaurant.

Perché à plus de 400 mètres au-dessus de la Méditerranée, Château Eza émerveille les visiteurs par sa situation et son histoire privilégiées. Les murs de pierre, les poutres en chêne, les alcôves et les cheminées de plusieurs maisons du XIIIe siècle subsistent dans les 10 suites somptueuses, 7 d'entre elles avec leur propre balcon, toutes dotées de commodités modernes de premier ordre. Des vues spectaculaires accompagnent la dégustation des plats primés servis sur la terrasse ou dans le restaurant panoramique.

Das etwa 450m über dem Mittelmeer gelegene Châtau Eza verzaubert seine Gäste durch seine Aussicht und seine Geschichte. In 10 luxuriösen, modern eingerichteten Suiten – 7 mit eigenem Balkon – sind die Steinwände, Eichenbalken, Alkoven und Kamine mehrerer Häuser aus dem 13. Jahrhundert erhalten. Eine atemberaubende Aussicht begleitet preisgekrönte Gaumenfreuden, die auf der Außenterrasse oder im Panorama-Restaurant serviert werden.

Our inspector loved: *The restaurant's private little balconies - amazing views and perfect for a romantic dinner.*

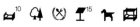

Directions: On Moyenne Corniche between Nice and Monaco.

Web: www.johansens.com/eza
E-mail: chateza@wanadoo.fr
Tel: +33 4 93 41 12 24
Fax: +33 4 93 41 16 64

Price Guide:
single €280–630
double/twin €280–630
suite €530–730

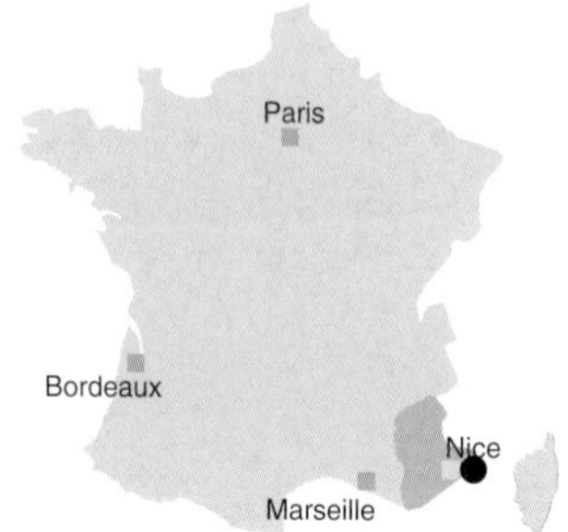

Bastide Saint Mathieu

35 CHEMIN DE BLUMENTHAL, 06130 ST. MATHIEU, GRASSE, FRANCE

This 18th-century Provençal Bastide is situated in the heart of the "Golden Triangle," just south east of the perfume town of Grasse. Owners, Mr and Mrs van Osch, personally welcome guests into this exclusive yet homely country residence. Each of the individually designed and spacious suites feature exquisite antiques and luxurious cashmere blankets. Breakfast may be taken on the terrace overlooking the sloping hills of Mougins and Cannes or in the intimate stone breakfast room. Within the beautiful, extensive gardens the secluded pool offers a relaxing haven.

Cette bastide provençale, datant du XVIIIe siècle est située au coeur du "triangle d'or" au sud-est de la ville de Grasse, célèbre pour le parfum. Les propriétaires, M et Mme van Osch, accueillent leurs hôtes personnellement dans cette résidence de campagne, qui est également exclusive et confortable. Toutes les suites, spacieuses et décorées de manière individuelle, sont parées d'antiquités et de couvertures luxueuses de cachemire. Le petit déjeuner est servi sur la terrasse donnant sur les collines de Mougins et de Cannes, ou dans la petite salle à manger construite en pierre. Dans les beaux jardins vastes, la piscine isolée offre un havre relaxant.

Diese provenzalische Bastide befindet sich im Herzen des "Goldenen Dreiecks", südöstlich der Parfümstadt Grasse. Die Eigentümer, Herr und Frau van Osch heißen ihre Gäste persönlich in ihrem exklusiven und familiären Landsitz willkommen. Jede der individuell gestalteten geräumigen Suiten bietet exquisite Antiquitäten und Kaschmirdecken. Das Frühstück wird auf der Terrasse mit Blick auf die Hügel von Mougins und Cannes oder im gemütlichen Frühstücksraum serviert. Innerhalb der herrlichen weitläufigen Gärten sorgt ein abgeschiedener Pool für Entspannung.

Our inspector loved: *The superb and original toiletries.*

Directions: From the A8 exit at 42 Cannes / Mougins / Grasse > Grasse > exit Grasse Sud. The nearest airport is Nice, Côte d'Azur.

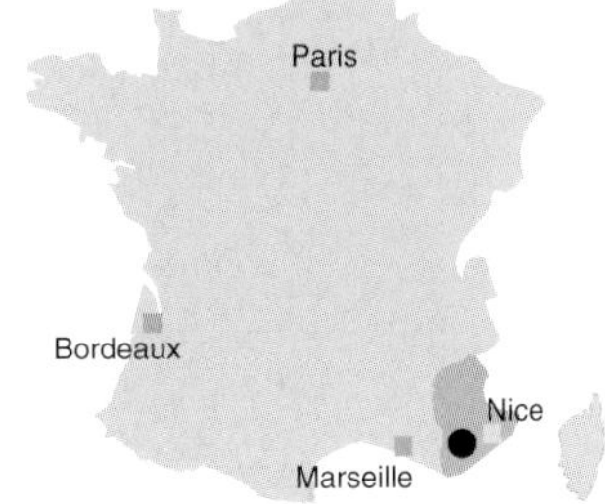

Web: www.johansens.com/saintmathieu
E-mail: info@bastidestmathieu.com
Tel: +33 4 97 01 10 00
Fax: +33 4 97 0110 09

Price Guide:
single €230-340
double €230-340

FRANCE / CÔTE D'AZUR (LE RAYOL – CANADEL)

Le Bailli de Suffren

AVENUE DES AMÉRICAINS, GOLFE DE SAINT~TROPEZ, 83820 LE RAYOL – CANADEL, FRANCE

This superb hotel facing the islands of Port-Cros and Levant is located in one of the most beautiful coves of the Saint-Tropez Gulf. Spacious and cosy lounges overlook the sea and the 53 junior suites are tastefully decorated in a Provençal style with balconies and terraces which boast views of the islands. Guests may dine at the gastronomic restaurant La Praya or the beach restaurant L'Escale, which is ideal for lunch by the sea. There is a heated swimming pool overlooking the sea, fitness room, sauna, private beach and yacht; all the ingredients for a fantastic break.

Ce superbe hôtel est situé face aux îles de Port-Cros et du Levant, au bord d'une des criques les plus séduisantes du Golfe de Saint-Tropez, dans un site totalement préservé. Vastes salons ouverts sur la mer, 53 suites junior décorées avec goût dans le style provençal avec balcons et terrasses orientés vers les îles, piscine d'eau douce chauffée surplombant la mer, salle de fitness, sauna, plage privée de sable fin, splendide voilier; tous les ingrédients de la Dolce Vita s'y trouvent réunis. Restaurant gastronomique La Praya et restaurant de plage 'L'Escale' pour déjeuner les pieds dans l'eau.

Dieses einmalige Hotel mit Blick auf die Inseln Port-Cros und Levant befindet sich in einer der schönsten Buchten am Golf von Saint-Tropez. Die geräumigen, gemütlichen Aufenthaltsräume blicken auf das Meer und die 53 Junior-Suiten sind geschmackvoll im provenzalischen Stil eingerichtet. Von den Balkonen und Terrassen sieht man die Inseln. Man kann im Gourmetrestaurant La Praya oder im Strandrestaurant L'Escale essen - der ideale Ort für ein Mittagessen direkt am Meer. Es gibt einen beheizten Swimmingpool mit Meerblick, Fitnessraum, Sauna, Privatstrand und eine herrliche Jacht: alles Zutaten für einen wunderbaren Aufenthalt.

Our inspector loved: *Its superb seaside location with breathtaking views.*

Directions: A8 > exit Le Muy > St Tropez> Cavalaire > Le Rayol - Canadel.

Web: www.johansens.com/lebaillidesuffren
E-mail: info@lebaillidesuffren.com
Tel: +33 4 98 04 47 00
Fax: +33 4 98 04 47 99

Price Guide:
double €145–519
junior suite €145–519

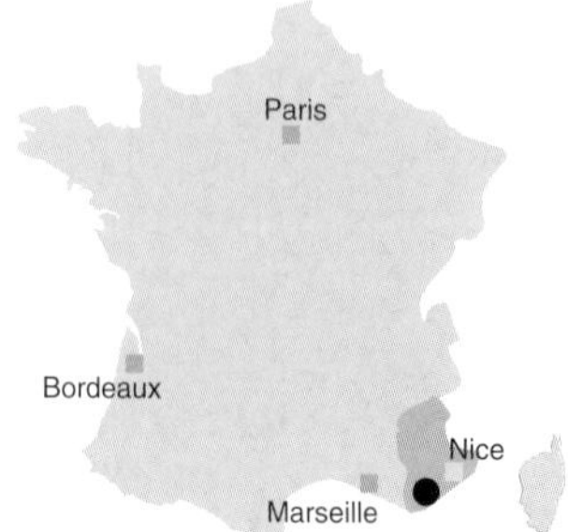

HÔTEL LA PÉROUSE

11, QUAI RAUBA~CAPEU, 06300 NICE, FRANCE

Perched high on a hill overlooking the Baie des Anges, the Hôtel la Perouse enjoys a unique and peaceful setting in the heart of the city. Completely renovated in 2000, the hotel offers a comfortable stay in charming surroundings, enhanced by elegant bedrooms decorated in Provençal style and flower-filled terraces and gardens. There is an outdoor swimming pool, gymnasium, sauna and Jacuzzi as well as a sun terrace with panoramic view of the surroundings. From May to September, simple Provençal dishes are served on the terrace in the shade of the lemon trees.

Dominant la Baie des Anges, l'Hôtel la Perouse bénéficie d'une situation privilégiée, véritable havre de paix en plein centre ville. Entièrement renové en 2000, l'hôtel offre un grand confort dans une atmosphère de charme et de convivialité avec ses chambres élégantes de style provençal, ses terrasses fleuries et ses jardins ombragés. L'hôtel dispose d'une piscine extérieure d'un solarium panoramique avec salle de gymnastique, sauna et jacuzzi au dernier étage avec vue imprenable sur la mer. Une cuisine provençale simple et fraîche est servie en terrasse à l'ombre des citronniers de mai à septembre.

Mit seiner herrlichen Lage am Schlossberg mit Blick auf die Baie des Anges ist dieses Hotel eine Oase der Ruhe mitten in der Stadt. Nach umfassender Renovierung im Jahr 2000 bietet das Hotel mit seinen eleganten Zimmern im provenzalischen Stil, blumengeschmückten Terrassen und schattenspendenden Gärten großen Komfort in charmanter Atmosphäre. Es gibt einen Außenpool, Fitnessraum, Sauna und Jacuzzi sowie eine Sonnenterrasse mit Panoramablick auf die Umgebung. Von Mai bis September wird auf der Terrasse im Schatten der Zitronenbäume einfache provenzalische Küche serviert.

Our inspector loved: *The superb top floor terrace with panoramic views.*

 62

 25

Directions: At the end of the Promenade des Anglais, before the harbour.

Web: www.johansens.com/hotellaperouse
E-mail: lp@hroy.com
Tel: +33 4 93 62 34 63
Fax: +33 4 93 62 59 41

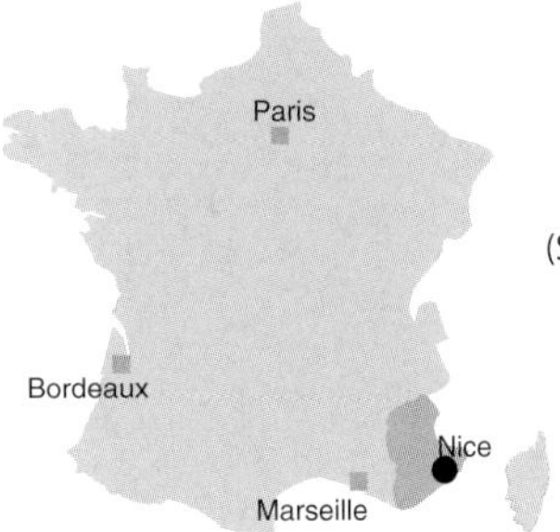

Paris
Bordeaux
Nice
Marseille

Price Guide:
(Special conditions for Johansens readers, breakfast €17)
single €150-405
double €150-405
suite €580-800

LE MAS D'ARTIGNY

ROUTE DE LA COLLE, 06570 SAINT~PAUL~DE~VENCE, FRANCE

Le Mas d'Artigny stands in 20 acres of hillside pine forest overlooking the Mediterranean and the medieval city of Saint-Paul-de-Vence between Nice and Cannes. Guests have the choice of bedroom, apartment or 2 to 8-bedroom villa with garden. All are spacious and individually decorated. Award-winning cuisine is served in an elegant restaurant with panoramic views. Extensive leisure and sport facilities.

Le Mas d'Artigny se tient au sein de 8ha de forêt de pins sur les côteaux de collines surplombant la Méditerranée et la cité médiévale de Saint-Paul-de-Vence entre Nice et Cannes. Les hôtes ont le choix entre chambres, appartements ou villas de 2 à 8 chambres avec jardin. Tous ces logements sont spacieux et décorés individuellement. Une cuisine primée est servie dans un restaurant élégant avec vue panoramique. De nombreux loisirs et sports sont disponibles.

Le Mas d'Artigny liegt zwischen Nizza und Cannes inmitten von 8ha hügeligem Pinienwald mit Blick auf das Mittelmeer und die mittelalterliche Stadt Saint-Paul-de-Vence. Man hat die Wahl zwischen einem Zimmer, Appartement oder einer Villa mit 2 bis 8 Zimmern und Garten. Alle Räumlichkeiten sind großzügig und individuell gestaltet. In einem eleganten Restaurant mit Panoramablick wird preisgekrönte Küche serviert. Das Sport- und Freizeitangebot ist sehr umfangreich.

Our inspector loved: *The giant chess board by the swimming pool.*

Directions: A8 from Nice, exit Cagnes-sur-Mer > follow signs to Vence > Saint Paul.

Web: www.johansens.com/masdartigny
E-mail: mas@grandesetapes.fr
Tel: +33 4 93 32 84 54
Fax: +33 4 93 32 95 36

Price Guide:
single €111–440
double €111–440
suite €416–990

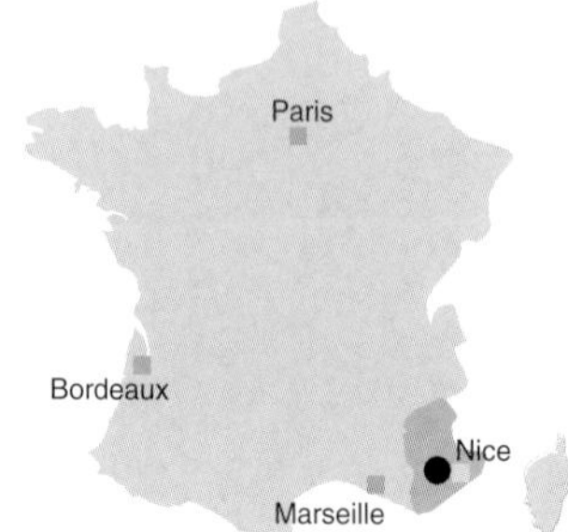

LA FERME D'AUGUSTIN

PLAGE DE TAHITI, 83350 RAMATUELLE, NR SAINT-TROPEZ, FRANCE

This delightful family-run hotel combines traditional French charm with modern hospitality to create an idyllic retreat from the buzzing pace of the Côte d'Azur. The pretty bedrooms and suites are furnished with antiques and have whirlpool baths – some even have private gardens. A hydrotherapy pool in the charming gardens and wonderful homemade cooking create a sense of luxury and complement the impeccable standards set by the owners, the Vallet family.

La famille Vallet a complété le charme français traditionnel de cet hôtel séduisant par un accueil moderne pour créer un havre de paix idyllique, à l'écart de la vie trépidante de la Côte d'Azur. Les jolies chambres et suites sont pourvues de meubles anciens et d'un bain bouillonnant, parfois même d'un jardin privatif. La piscine hydrothérapique aménagée dans le ravissant jardin et la cuisine maison succulente soulignent le caractère luxueux et la qualité exceptionnelle de cet établissement.

Dieses freundliche, familiengeführte Hotel, das traditionelles französisches Flair mit moderner Gastfreundschaft verbindet, liegt idyllisch fernab vom geschäftigen Treiben Côte d'Azur. Die hübschen Zimmer und Suiten sind mit Antiquitäten ausgestattet und haben Jacuzzibäder. Einige bieten auch einen privaten Garten. Ein Hydrotherapie-Pool im Garten und köstliche Hausmannskost schaffen ein Gefühl von Luxus und spiegeln perfekt das hohe Niveau wider, das sich die Eigentümer, die Familie Vallet, zum Ziel gesetzt haben.

Our inspector loved: *The friendliness of the staff and the relaxed atmosphere.*

Directions: A8 > exit Le Muy > Saint-Tropez > Plage de Tahiti.

Web: www.johansens.com/fermedaugustin
E-mail: vallet.ferme.augustin@wanadoo.fr
Tel: +33 4 94 55 97 00
Fax: +33 4 94 97 40 30

Price Guide:
(breakfast €12)
double/twin €150–182
suite €250-514

L'AUBERGE DU CHOUCAS

05220 MONETIER~LES~BAINS, SERRE~CHEVALIER, HAUTES~ALPES, FRANCE

This 17th-century mountain farmhouse is situated in an old Alpine village, on the edge of the Écrins National Park, in the Serre-Chevalier skiing area and offers many activities both in winter and summer. It is a warm and charming family-run hotel just a few minutes' walk from the foot of the ski slopes. The friendly ambience is enhanced by big log fires in the winter and the aroma of high living – herbs, flowers, wines and cooking. Many of the light and airy bedrooms, with their Alpine-style décor, have balconies. The Auberge restaurant serves inventive and delicious cuisine.

Cette ferme de montagne du XVIIe siècle est située dans un vieux village alpin, sur les bords du Parc National des Ecrins, au cœur du domaine skiable de Serre Chevalier. De nombreuses activités y sont proposées été comme hiver. Ce charmant et accueillant hôtel de famille n'est qu'à quelques minutes à pieds des pistes de ski. L'ambiance amicale est accrue par les grands feux de cheminée en hiver et par les arômes d'herbes, de fleurs, de vins et de cuisine. Les chambres claires et douillettes sont décorées dans un style montagnard et possèdent pour la plupart des balcons. Une cuisine délicieuse et inventive est servie à l'auberge.

Dieses Bergbauernhaus aus dem 17. Jahrhundert liegt in einem alten Alpendorf am Rande des Écrins Nationalparks. Das im Skigebiet von Serre-Chevalier gelegene herzliche familiengeführte Haus bietet sommers wie winters zahlreiche Aktivitäten und ist nur ein paar Minuten von den Skipisten entfernt. Die freundliche Atmosphäre wird durch offene Kaminfeuer im Winter und den herrlichen Duft von Kräutern, Blumen, Wein und Kochen noch verstärkt. Viele der hellen und luftigen im Alpenstil eingerichteten Zimmer bieten einen eigenen Balkon. Im Auberge werden einfallsreiche Köstlichkeiten serviert.

Our inspector loved: *The family atmosphere and the very warm welcome.*

Directions: Between Grenoble and Briançon. Follow signs for Monterier-les-Bains and the farmhouse is behind the church opposite the town hall.

Web: www.johansens.com/laubergeduchoucas
E-mail: auberge.du.choucas@wanadoo.fr
Tel: +33 4 92 24 42 73
Fax: +33 4 92 24 51 60

Price Guide:
single €115–165
double/twin €130–215
suite €215–300

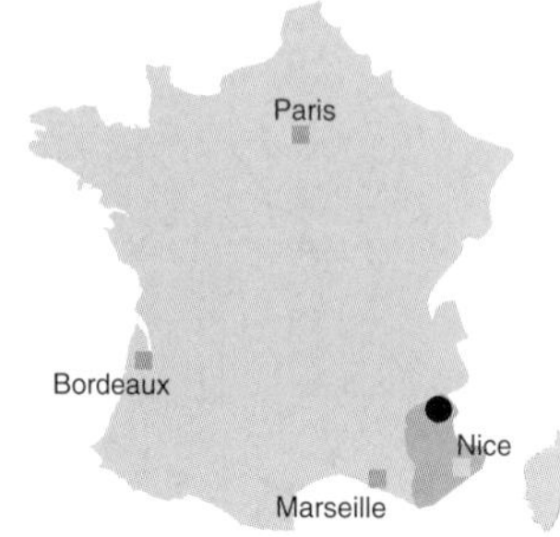

Hôtel Cantemerle

258 CHEMIN CANTEMERLE, 06140 VENCE, FRANCE

Nestling on a wooded hillside, this hotel is a haven of peace. Everything seems far away, yet Cannes, Nice and the airport, the sea and a few museums are within easy reach, and the towns of Vence and Saint-Paul, whose Provençal charm has inspired great artists such as Matisse and Chagall, are nearby. The comfortable rooms and suites have private terraces and each has its own individual style. Large lawns border the pool and the solarium, overlooking the Mediterranean. The indoor pool and Turkish bath, the lounges, the bar and the restaurant open onto large terraces.

Cet hôtel se niche sur une colline boisée et est un vrai havre de calme. Tout semble très loin, quand tout n'est qu'à quelques minutes: Cannes, Nice et son aéroport, la mer, les musées, et, à deux pas, Vence et Saint-Paul, petites cités dont le charme provençal a inspiré les plus grands artistes, comme Matisse ou Chagall. Les chambres et les duplex confortables avec terrasse privée offrent une grande diversité de décors raffinés. Une grande pelouse borde la piscine et le solarium, face à la Méditerranée. La piscine couverte et son hammam, les salons, le bar et le restaurant s'ouvrent sur de vastes terrasses.

Dieses auf einem Hügel gelegene Hotel ist eine Oase der Ruhe, scheinbar abgeschieden, doch unweit von Cannes, Nizza, dem Flughafen, dem Meer, ein paar Museen, und den Städtchen Vence und Saint-Paul, die bereits große Meister wie Matisse und Chagall mit ihrem provenzalischen Charme bezauberten. Die individuell gestalteten, komfortablen Zimmer und Suiten haben eigene Terrassen. Ein Swimmingpool ist von Rasen umgeben und das Solarium blickt auf das Meer. Das Hallenbad, Türkische Bad, die Aufenthaltsräume, Bar und Restaurant öffnen sich auf große Terrassen.

Our inspector loved: *The bedrooms in the new building where the exceptional steam bath is located.*

Directions: A8 exit Cagnes-sur-Mer > follow signs to Vence. The hotel is signposted.

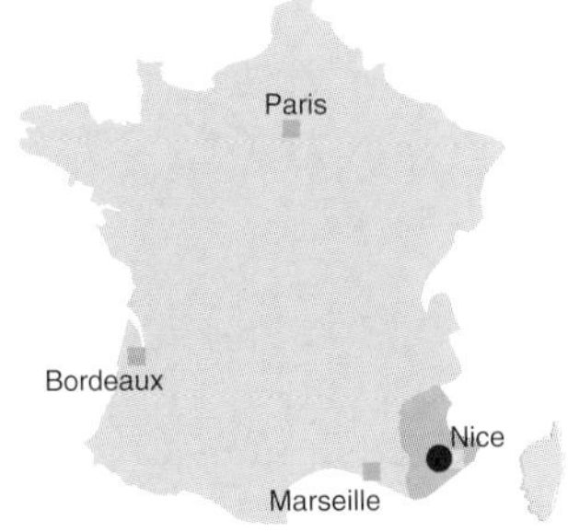

Web: www.johansens.com/hotelcantemerle
E-mail: info@hotelcantemerle.com
Tel: +33 4 93 58 08 18
Fax: +33 4 93 58 32 89

Price Guide:
double €170-198
duplex €195-223

Hôtel Juana

LA PINÈDE, AVENUE G. GALLICE, 06160 JUAN~LES~PINS, FRANCE

Built in 1931 and recently extensively restored, this art deco hotel is a real gem. Its heritage has been carefully preserved with bespoke furniture and fabrics, and the tastefully decorated bedrooms have elegant marble bathrooms featuring handmade tiles. At La Terrasse, awarded 2 Michelin stars and 5 diamonds, guests can enjoy traditional Provençal cuisine and fine wines in a romantic setting. There is a small white marble swimming pool, whilst the hotel's sandy beach is a 3-minute walk away, offering another 3 restaurants.

Construit en 1931 et récemment rénové, cet hôtel art déco est un vrai joyau. Son héritage a été soigneusement préservé par un ameublement sur mesures, et les chambres sont décorées avec goût avec des salles de bains en marbre et carrelages fait-main. A La Terrasse, 2 étoiles au Michelin et 5 diamants, les hôtes peuvent déguster une cuisine provençale typique et des vins délicats dans un cadre romantique. Pour les nageurs, il y a une petite piscine en marbre blanc, et la plage de sable de l'hôtel est à 3 minutes à pied, proposant 3 restaurants.

Dieses 1932 erbaute und ausgiebig restaurierte Art-Deco-Hotel ist ein wahres Juwel, dessen Erbe mit eigens angefertigten Möbeln und Stoffen bewahrt wurde. Die geschmackvoll eingerichteten Zimmer haben elegante Bäder mit handgefertigten Kacheln. Im mit 2 Michelinsternen und 5 Diamanten ausgezeichneten La Terrasse werden traditionelle provenzalische Küche und feine Weine in romantischem Ambiente serviert. Ein kleiner Marmorswimmingpool steht zur Verfügung und der Sandstrand ist nur 3 Minuten zu Fuß entfernt. Hier findet man 3 weitere Restaurants.

***Our inspector loved:** The panoramic views from the top floor bedrooms.*

Directions: A8 > exit Antibes/Juan-les-Pins > hotel is signposted.

Web: www.johansens.com/juana
E-mail: info@hotel-juana.com
Tel: +33 4 93 61 08 70
Fax: +33 4 93 61 76 60

Price Guide:
double €230-620
suite upon request

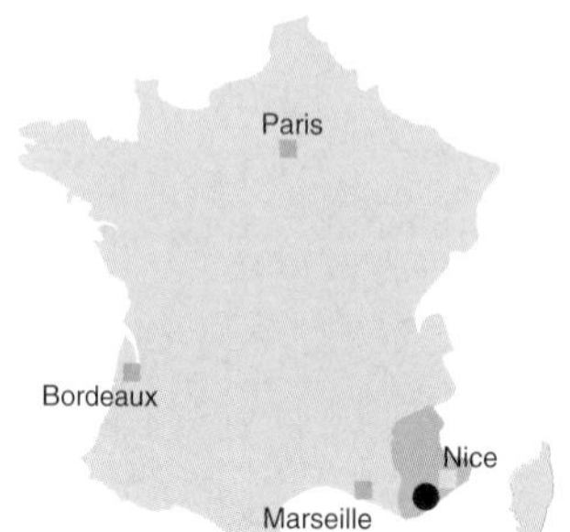

Château de Pray

ROUTE DE CHARGÉ, 37400 AMBOISE, FRANCE

Nestled on the sunny terraced slopes overlooking the tranquil Loire river, Château de Pray is simply steeped in history. Surrounded by peaceful gardens, the imposing round towers bear witness to its Renaissance origins. The traditional ambience extends to the interior, where wood panelling, heavy beams and rich fabrics abound. The en-suite bedrooms, many of which have stunning views, are tastefully furnished. Award-winning gourmet cuisine is served in the restaurant.

Niché sur les côteaux ensoleillés des collines des eaux tranquilles de la Loire, Le Château de Pray est imprégné d'histoire. Entouré de jardins paisibles, ses tours rondes sont témoins de son origine Renaissance. L'ambiance traditionnelle s'étend à l'intérieur où les boiseries, les lourdes poutres et riches étoffes abondent. Les chambres dont la plupart ont de superbes vues, sont meublées avec goût. La cuisine y est gourmande et soignée.

In die sonnigen, terrassenförmigen Hänge oberhalb der Loire schmiegt sich das geschichtsträchtige Château de Pray. Umgeben von ruhigen Gärten zeugen die imposanten runden Türme von seinen Ursprüngen aus der Renaissance. Das traditionsreiche Ambiente wird durch reichlich vorhandene Holzvertäfelung sowie schwere Balken und üppige Stoffe betont. Ausblick. Im Restaurant wird feinste Gourmetküche serviert.

Our inspector loved: *The hotel's vegetable garden.*

Directions: D31 > Blois.

Web: www.johansens.com/chateaudepray
E-mail: chateau.depray@wanadoo.fr
Tel: +33 2 47 57 23 67
Fax: +33 2 47 57 32 50

Price Guide:
single €95
double/twin €165
suite €185-230

Le Choiseul

SYMBOLES de FRANCE

36 QUAI CHARLES GUINOT, 37400 AMBOISE, FRANCE

Situated in a quiet and charming area around Amboise, Le Choiseul lies tucked between the hillside and the Loire river. The surrounding grounds of this ensemble of 3 delightful 18th-century houses feature a labyrinth of superb Italian-style terraced gardens. 32 tastefully decorated guest rooms with elegant bathrooms offer every comfort and there is excellent dining in a refined restaurant with panoramic views.

Situé dans un coin charmant et calme près d'Amboise, Le Choiseul est blotti entre les flancs de coteaux et la Loire. Sur les terrains environnants de ce complexe de 3 demeures charmantes du XVIIIe siècle, existe un labyrinthe de jardins en terrasses, dessiné dans un style italien superbe. Les 32 chambres décorées avec goût et disposant d'élégantes salles de bain offrent tout le confort et les dîners servis dans un restaurant raffiné avec vue panoramique sont délicieux.

In der ruhigen, zauberhaften Gegend um Amboise befindet sich Le Choiseul, ganz versteckt zwischen einem Hügel und der Loire. Die Umgebung dieser 3 herrlichen Häuser aus dem 18. Jahrhundert besteht aus einem Labyrinth aus wundervollen terrassenförmigen Gärten in 32 geschmackvoll eingerichteten Zimmer mit ihren eleganten Bädern bieten jeglichen Komfort, und im stilvollen Restaurant genießt man hervorragende Küche mit Panoramablick.

Our inspector loved: *The pool area - a haven of peace and tranquillity.*

Directions: D751 east of town centre.

Web: www.johansens.com/lechoiseul
E-mail: choiseul@grandesetapes.fr
Tel: +33 2 47 30 45 45
Fax: +33 2 47 30 46 10

Price Guide:
(room only)
single €92–267
double €92–267
suite €210–335

Le Manoir Les Minimes

34 QUAI CHARLES GUINOT, 37400 AMBOISE, FRANCE

This authentic 18th-century manor house was built on the foundations of the ancient medieval Monastère des Minimes and is situated in proximity of the old town. It is the ideal place from which to explore the châteaux and vineyards of the Loire Valley. This selected stopping place offers its visitors comfort "à la française," a harmonious blend of sophistication and intimacy, whilst affording glorious views of the Château Royale d'Amboise and the River Loire. Air-conditioned rooms; private enclosed parking; no restaurant.

Authentique demeure du XVIIIe siècle, érigée sur les fondations de l'ancien monastère médiéval des Minimes, située à proximité immédiate de la vieille ville. Le Manoir les Minimes est un lieu de villégiature rêvé pour découvrir les châteaux et les vignobles de la Loire. Cette halte de choix offre à ses visiteurs ce confort "à la française", harmonieux dosage de délicatesse et d'intimité, avec une vue exceptionnelle sur le Château Royale d'Amboise et la Loire. Chambres climatisées et parking privé clos. Sans restaurant.

Dieses authentische Herrenhaus aus dem 18. Jahrhundert wurde auf dem Fundament des mittelalterlichen Klosters Monastère des Minimes erbaut und befindet sich in unmittelbarer Nähe zur Altstadt. Es liegt ideal, um die Schlösser und Weinberge des Loire-Tals zu erkunden und bietet typischen Komfort "à la française", eine harmonische Mischung aus Intimität und Raffinesse, mit atemberaubenden Blicken auf das Château Royale d'Amboise und die Loire. Klimatisierte Zimmer; private, abgeschlossene Parkplätze; kein Restaurant.

Our inspector loved: *The total attention to detail.*

Directions: A10 > exit Amboise > D751 on the south bank of the river.

Web: www.johansens.com/lemanoirlesminimes
E-mail: manoir-les-minimes@wanadoo.fr
Tel: +33 2 47 30 40 40
Fax: +33 2 47 30 40 77

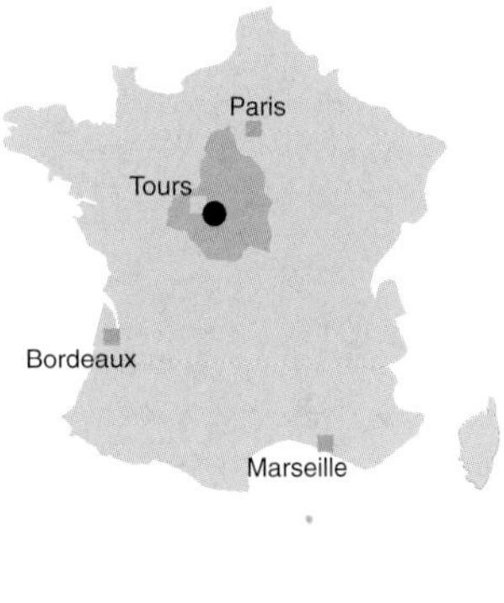

Paris
Tours
Bordeaux
Marseille

Price Guide:
(room only)
single €85–160
double €85–160
suites €195–230

Hostellerie Château de Chissay

41400 CHISSAY~EN~TOURAINE, FRANCE

With towers, turrets, inner courtyard and stunning views of the countryside, this historic, fairytale château was home to 2 French kings as well as the government during the 1940 retreat. All the comfortable rooms are elegantly decorated and guests can take a step back in time with interesting period details, exposed stonework and a serene private chapel. Delicious local French cuisine and wines are offered in the superb restaurant. Walking and cycling in the beautiful Loire Valley is a delight.

Avec donjon et tourelles, une cour intérieure et une vue sur la campagne, ce château historique, qui rappelle les contes de fée, fut la demeure de deux rois français et le gouvernement y séjourna pendant la retraite de 1940. Toutes les chambres sont confortables et élégamment décorées et grâce aux détails d'époque, une maçonnerie apparente et une paisible chapelle privée, les hôtes peuvent remonter le temps. Une cuisine et des vins régionaux sont servis dans un beau restaurant. La vallée de la Loire est le lieu idéal pour des excursions à pied ou à bicyclette.

Dieses historische Märchenschloss mit seinen Türmen, Zinnen, dem Innenhof und herrlichen Ausblicken auf die Umgebung war bereits Sitz zweier französischer Könige und der Regierung während der Beratungszeit 1945. Die komfortablen Zimmer sind elegant gestaltet, und interessante Stildetails, freiliegendes Mauerwerk und eine freundliche Privatkapelle bringen einen zurück in die Vergangenheit. Köstliche französische Küche und Weine werden in einem hervorragenden Restaurant serviert. Das herrliche Loire-Tal lädt zum Wandern und Fahrradfahren ein.

Our inspector loved: *The extremely romantic, troglodyte bedroom.*

Directions: D176 Chenonceaux–Montrichard.

Web: www.johansens.com/chateaudechissay
E-mail: chissay@leshotelsparticuliers.com
Tel: +33 2 54 32 32 01
Fax: +33 2 54 32 43 80

Price Guide:
(room only)
double €121–185
suite €210–265

Château de Rochecotte

SAINT~PATRICE, 37130 LANGEAIS, FRANCE

Formerly the home of Prince Talleyrand, this exquisite château is surrounded by acres of immaculate parkland. The salons are spacious and inviting, and the exceptional Italianate terrace overlooks the French gardens. The bedrooms are ethereal, furnished with delicately patterned chintz and antiques. The delightful dining room has terracotta columns, palm trees and splendid views over the park.

Autrefois la demeure du Prince de Talleyrand, cet exquis château est entouré d'un immense parc magnifique. Les salons sont accueillants et la terrace d'inspiration italienne surplombe les jardins français. Les chambres sont divines, avec des chintz délicats et des antiquités. La superbe salle à manger a des colonnes en terracotta, des palmiers et une vue splendide sur le parc.

Dieses exquisite Château, einst Heim des Prinzen Talleyrand, ist von einem herrlichen, weitläufigen Park umgeben. Die großzügigen Aufenthaltsräume laden zum Verweilen ein, und eine italienisch geprägte Terrasse gibt den Blick auf die französischen Gärten frei. Die traumhaften Schlafzimmer sind mit delikat gemustertem Chintz und feinen Antiquitäten ausgestattet. Vom Speisesaal mit seinen Terrakotta-Säulen und Palmen hat man eine fantastische Sicht auf den Park.

Our inspector loved: *Room 14, ideal for a romantic break.*

Directions: A10 towards Tours > Exit 23 > A85 > Langeais > N152 > Saint Patrice > D35. The nearest airport is Tours.

Web: www.johansens.com/rochecotte
E-mail: chateau.rochecotte@wanadoo.fr
Tel: +33 2 47 96 16 16
Fax: +33 2 47 96 90 59

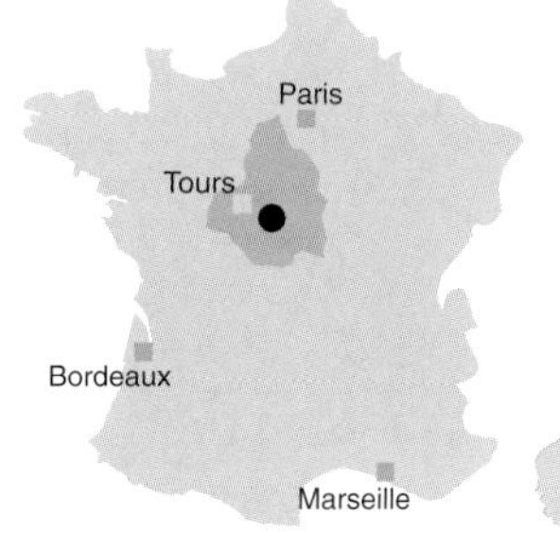

Price Guide:
(room only)
double/twin €125–206
suites €275

35 50

Le Prieuré

49350 CHÊNEHUTTE~LES~TUFFEAUX, FRANCE

Directions: On the D751 between Saumur and Gennes.

Web: www.johansens.com/leprieure
E-mail: prieure@grandesetapes.fr
Tel: +33 2 41 67 90 14
Fax: +33 2 41 67 92 24

Price Guide:
single €92–255
double €92–255
suite €221–295

This historic, local stone built former priory stands majestically in 17 acres of magnificent parkland featuring centuries-old trees just 7km from Saumur, the Loire Valley's capital city of horse riding. Guests are accommodated in the elegant château or small, modern chalets in the grounds. All are extremely comfortable and offer stunning views. There is an excellent restaurant with equally good, friendly service. Heated pool.

Cet ancien prieuré historique construit en pierre locale, se tient majestueusement dans les 7 hectares d'un parc magnifique aux arbres centenaires et à seulement 7 kilomètres de Saumur, la capitale de l'équitation de la vallée de la Loire. Les hôtes sont logés dans l'élégant château ou dans des petits pavillons modernes. Tous sont extrêmement confortables et offrent une vue imprenable. Le restaurant est excellent avec un service amical. Piscine chauffée.

Diese historische, aus einheimischem Stein erbaute ehemalige Abtei steht majestätisch inmitten von 7ha Parklandschaft mit jahrhundertealten Bäumen, nur 7km von Saumur, der Reiterhauptstadt des Loiretales entfernt. Man wohnt entweder im eleganten Château oder in kleinen, modernen Chalets auf dem Grundstück. Alle Zimmer sind extrem komfortabel und bieten herrliche Ausblicke. Im Restaurant genießt man hervorragende Küche, der Service ist sehr freundlich. Ein beheizter Swimmingpool ist vorhanden.

Our inspector loved: *The views from the restaurant.*

LA HUNAUDERIE

72500 THOIRÉ~SUR~DINAN, LOIRE VALLEY, FRANCE

Within a valley, at the bottom of a winding country road, stands this pretty farmhouse. Set amidst 17 acres of rolling hills, La Hunauderie is a true home from home where guests are instantly made to feel welcome. Following a careful restoration the hotel now offers 3 en-suite bedrooms and a large, comfortable lounge. Picturesque views of the surrounding fields can be enjoyed whilst sampling delicious home-cooked meals, prepared by owner, Carolyn Hayward. The Loire Valley and Le Mans are within easy reach.

Cette jolie maison de ferme est nichée dans une vallée au bout d,une petite route de campagne sinueuse. Au milieu de 7 hectares de collines onduleuses, on se sent vraiment chez soi grâce à l'accueil chaleureux. Suite à une restauration soigneuse, la Hunauderie a 3 chambres attenantes et un grand salon confortable. Les hôtes peuvent jouir des vues pittoresques des alentours, pendant qu'ils mangent la délicieuse cuisine de la propriétaire, Carolyn Hayward. La vallée de la Loire et Le Mans ne sont pas loin.

Dieses zauberhafte Bauernhaus befindet sich am Fuße einer sich durch ein Tal schlängelnden Landstraße, inmitten von 7ha sanfter Hügellandschaft. La Hunauderie ist ein wahres zweites Zuhause, wo man sich sofort willkommen fühlt. Nach sorgfältigen Restaurierungsarbeiten bietet das Hotel nun 3 Gästezimmer mit eigenem Bad und einen großen, gemütlichen Aufenthaltsraum. Die malerische Sicht auf die umliegenden Felder genießt man am besten bei der köstlichen, von der Hotelbesitzerin Carolyn Hayward zubereiteten Küche. Das Loiretal und Le Mans befinden sich ganz in der Nähe.

Our inspector loved: *The fabulous homely welcome.*

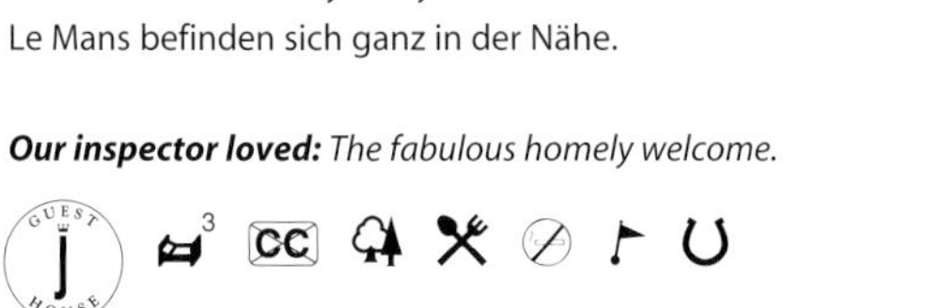

Directions: La Hunauderie is off the D216 west of Thoiré-sur-Dinan, the nearest town is Château-du-Loir on the N138. Full directions are available upon request. The nearest airport is Tours.

Web: www.johansens.com/lahunauderie
Tel: +33 2 43 79 32 20

Price Guide:
single €75
double €115

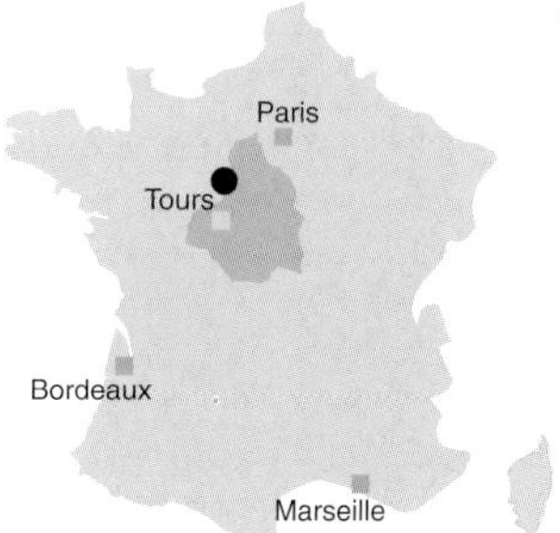

Celebration Gourmet Dinners or Prestigious 2 Night Breaks. (Flowers, a bottle of Champagne and bathrobes)

A VIP welcome, candlelit dinner, a lakeside walk, breakfast in bed overlooking the gardens full of flowers.

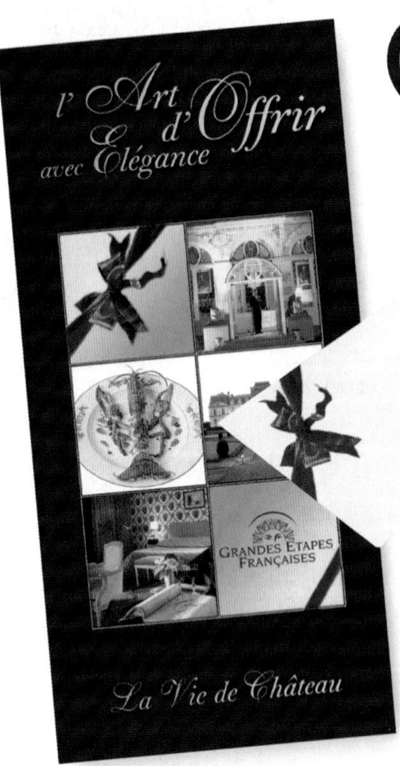

Offer the Unforgettable

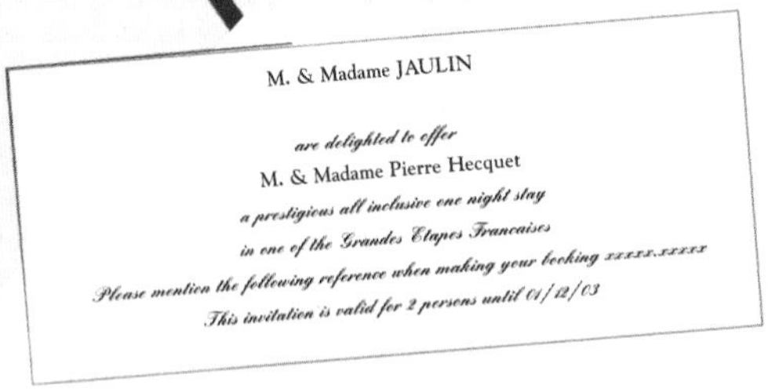

M. & Madame JAULIN

are delighted to offer

M. & Madame Pierre Hecquet

a prestigious all inclusive one night stay

in one of the Grandes Etapes Françaises

Please mention the following reference when making your booking xxxxx.xxxxx

This invitation is valid for 2 persons until 01/12/03

There are certain moments which merit a truly exceptional gift

THE ELEGANCE AND THE DISTINCTION OF AN INVITATION

A personalised invitation which clearly explains, without indication of price, the gift that is being offered, (dinner or a break in the selected category) is sent to your guest.

THE PRIVILEGE OF HAVING FREEDOM OF CHOICE

He or she can choose from amongst any the 10, 4 star " GRANDES ETAP FRANÇAISES " hotels, the location, the d of stay - the gift voucher is valid for 1 ye

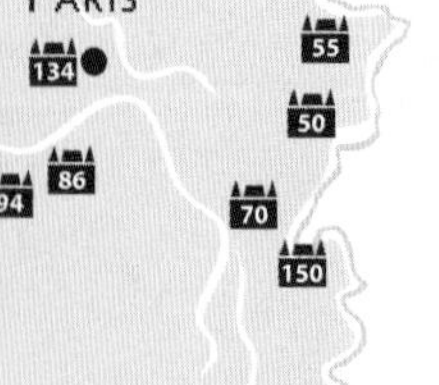

Discover 10 different ways to offer the truly unforgettable in any one of our 10, 4 star châteaux hotels.

For further information and bookings contact +33 1 40 02 99 99 or E-mail : cadeaux@grandesetapes.fr

GRANDES ETAP
FRANÇAISES

FRANCE / LOIRE VALLEY (TOURS - LUYNES)

Domaine de Beauvois

LE PONT CLOUET, ROUTE DE CLÉRÉ~LES~PINS, 37230 LUYNES, FRANCE

Situated on the banks of Lake Briffaut, in the heart of peaceful Tourain countryside, this gracious former manor house offers stunning views over beautiful gardens and 350 acres of glorious woodland. It is a true and historically attractive getaway hotel providing visitors with every comfort and excellent cuisine and service. Lounges are intimate, dining rooms elegant, bedrooms superb – and silence almost absolute.

Situé sur les rives du Lac Briffaut, au cœur de la paisible Touraine, cet élégant ancien manoir offre une vue imprenable sur des beaux jardins et plus de 140 hectares de bois magnifiques. Cet hôtel procure un véritable échappatoire à ses visiteurs dans un confort total, une cuisine et un service excellents, avec des salons à l'atmosphère feutrée, des salles à manger élégantes et des chambres superbes – le tout dans un silence presque absolu.

Mit seiner Lage am Ufer des Briffaut Sees im Herzen der friedlichen Landschaft westlich von Tours bietet dieses anmutige ehemalige Herrenhaus eine atemberaubende Sicht auf wundervolle Gärten und 140ha Waldlandschaft. Das historisch faszinierende Hotel ist ein wahres Versteck und gewährt seinen Gästen jeden Komfort bei exquisiter Küche und hervorragendem Service. Die Aufenthaltsräume sind gemütlich und intim, die Speisesäle elegant und die Gästezimmer einfach herrlich – und Ruhe ist garantiert.

Our inspector loved: *Room 22 for a romantic stay.*

Directions: N152 Tours - Langeais > exit at Luynes > direction Cléré.

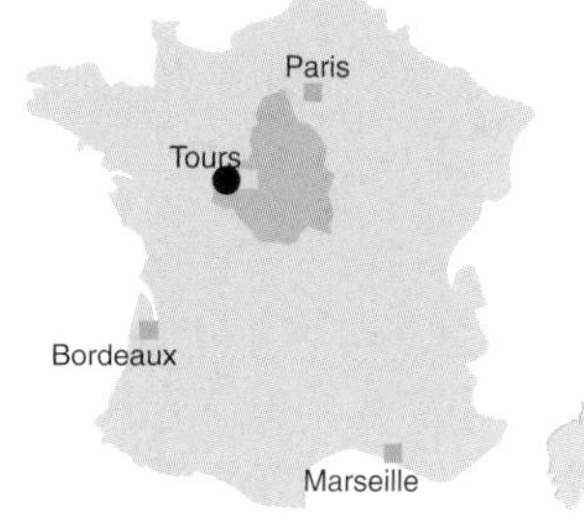

Web: www.johansens.com/domianedebeauvois
E-mail: beauvois@grandesetapes.fr
Tel: +33 2 47 55 50 11
Fax: +33 2 47 55 59 62

Price Guide:
(room only)
single €130–267
double €130–267
suite €210–280

Château d'Artigny

37250 MONTBAZON, FRANCE

Built by the perfumer Coty in 18th-century style, this palatial hotel creates an immediate impression. Its startling white exterior with soaring entrance pillars is in striking contrast to the lush greens of the surrounding 25 acres of parkland and formal gardens. The interior is equally majestic with imposing stone staircase, stunning public rooms, superb spacious bedrooms and 2 elegant gourmet restaurants.

Construit par le parfumeur Coty dans un style du XVIIIe siècle, cet hôtel magnifique fait une impression immédiate. Ses saisissants extérieurs blancs et l'entrée aux piliers élancés créent un contraste frappant avec les verts luxuriants des 10 hectares de parc et jardins alentours. L'intérieur est tout aussi majestueux avec d'impressionnants escaliers de pierre, d'incroyables salles communes, des superbes chambres spacieuses et 2 élégants restaurants gastronomiques.

Dieses vom Parfumeur Coty im Stil des 18. Jahrhunderts erbaute palastartige Hotel beeindruckt schon auf den ersten Blick. Das strahlend weiße Exterieur mit seinen eleganten Eingangssäulen steht in starkem Gegensatz zu der üppig grünen Umgebung der 10ha Parklandschaft und Gärten. Das Interieur ist ebenso majestätisch, hier findet man ein eindrucksvolles steinernes Treppenhaus, herrliche Aufenthaltsräume, wundervolle Gästezimmer und 2 elegante Feinschmeckerrestaurants.

Our inspector loved: *The circular dining room and the views.*

Directions: A10 exit 23 > direction Montbazon > in the centre of the village turn right.

Web: www.johansens.com/dartigny
E-mail: artigny@grandesetapes.fr
Tel: +33 2 47 34 30 30
Fax: +33 2 47 34 30 39

Price Guide:
(room only)
single €113–300
double €113–300
suite €289–530

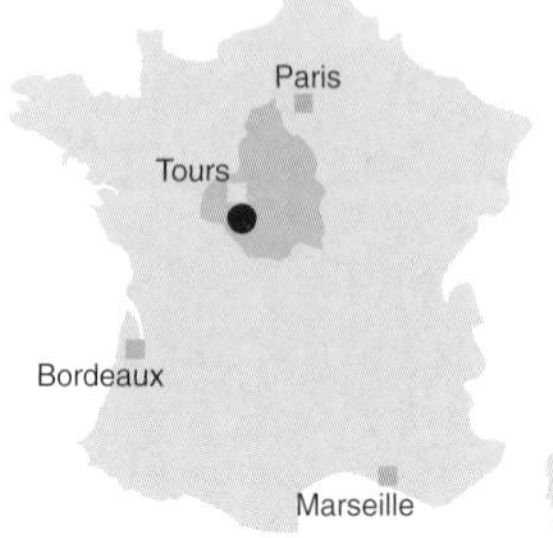

Domaine de La Tortinière

ROUTE DE BALLAN~MIRÉ, 37250 MONTBAZON, FRANCE

This fairytale château lies in the very heart of the Loire Valley and has breathtaking views over the Indre River. The welcome is warm and genuine and indicative of a winning formula that creates a sense of intimacy amongst classically elegant high ceilings, moulded doors and grand mirrors. Each of the bedrooms is individually decorated, whilst the "cottage rooms" in the park outbuildings are enchanting and even older than the château itself.

Ce château de conte de fées se situe au cœur de la Vallée de la Loire et a une vue à couper le souffle sur l'Indre. L'accueil est chaleureux, sincère et indicatif de la recette gagnante qui crée une sensation d'intimité au sein de hauts plafonds classiques et élégants, de portes à moulures et de grands miroirs. Chaque chambre est décorée individuellement, alors que les pavillons dans le parc, plus anciens que le château lui-même, sont absolument enchanteurs.

Dieses mitten im Herzen des Loiretales gelegene Märchenschloss bietet eine traumhafte Sicht über den Fluss Indre. Gäste erwartet ein warmer und herzlicher Empfang und ein Gefühl von Vertrautheit inmitten des mit klassisch hohen Decken, verzierten Türen und edlen Spiegeln geschmückten Interieurs. Die Zimmer sind individuell gestaltet, und die zauberhaften Cottagezimmer in den Außengebäuden im Park sind sogar noch älter als das Schloss selbst.

Our inspector loved: *Suite 6, with its comfortable lounge and bedroom in the tower.*

Directions: A10 > exit 23 direction Montbazon > turn right in the direction of Ballan-Miré.

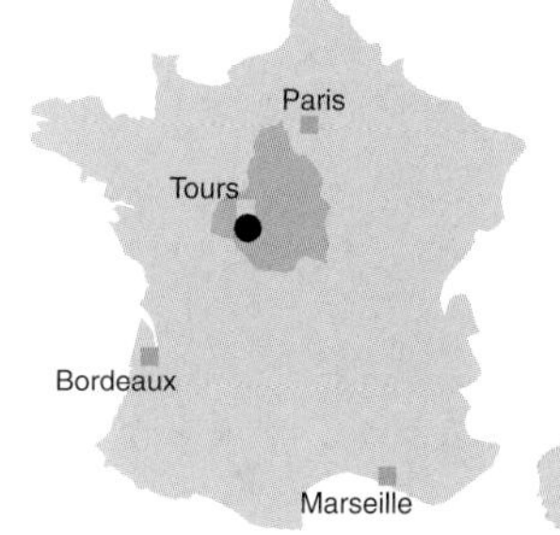

Web: www.johansens.com/domainetortiniere
E-mail: domaine.tortiniere@wanadoo.fr
Tel: +33 2 47 34 35 00
Fax: +33 2 47 65 95 70

Price Guide:
(room only)
single €98–170
double €98–170
suite €275

LE GRAND ECUYER

HAUT DE LA CITÉ, 81170 CORDES~SUR~CIEL, FRANCE

The beautiful medieval village of Cordes sits atop a hill, and Le Grand Ecuyer is located within its cobbled streets. Once home to the Comte de Toulouse, it is furnished in a medieval style with wonderfully rich furniture and fabrics. Most bedrooms have four-poster beds and views across the surrounding countryside. Renowned chef Yves Thuriès creates delicious cuisine, and dinner is served in one of 3 impressive dining rooms. Nearby places of interest include Toulouse and Gaillac, a wine-producing region.

Le beau village médiéval de Cordes se situe au sommet d'une colline et le Grand Ecuyer dans le dédale de ses rues pavées. Autrefois le foyer du Comte de Toulouse, il est meublé dans le style médiéval avec un superbe mobilier et des tissus riches. La plupart des chambres ont des lits à baldaquin et vue sur la campagne environnante. Le célèbre chef Yves Thuriès créé une cuisine délicieuse et le dîner est servi dans l'une des 3 impressionnantes salles à manger. A visiter tout près, Toulouse et la région viticole de Gaillac.

Mitten in dem auf einem Hügel gelegenen mittelalterlichen Dorf Cordes mit seinen Kopfsteingässchen liegt das zauberhafte Le Grand Ecuyer. Das einstige Zuhause des Comte de Toulouse ist in mittelalterlichem Stil mit üppigen Stoffen und Möbeln eingerichtet. Die meisten Zimmer bieten Himmelbetten und eine herrliche Sicht auf die Umgebung. Der bekannte Chefkoch Yves Thuriès kreiert köstliche Speisen, die in 3 eindrucksvollen Speisesälen serviert werden. Ausflugsziele in der Nähe sind Toulouse und die Weingegend Gaillac.

Our inspector loved: *The feeling of being in another era.*

Directions: A68 > exit between Toulouse and Albi > follow signs to Cordes.

Web: www.johansens.com/grandecuyer
E-mail: grand.ecuyer@thuries.fr
Tel: +33 5 63 53 79 50
Fax: +33 5 63 53 79 51

Price Guide:
double €90–155
suite €230

Château de Floure

1, Allée Gaston Bonheur, 11800 Floure, France

Only 10 minutes from Carcassonne, facing the majestic Mount Alaric, this beautiful château, which was formerly the residence of French writer Gaston Bonheur, lies peacefully within a lush park, surrounded by vineyards and exquisite traditional French gardens. Charming bedrooms are the ultimate in comfort whilst irresistible French cuisine and superb wines are served in the 17th-century restaurant, featuring impressive original woodwork. Guests can stroll through the grounds, play tennis or swim in the pool.

A seulement 10 minutes de Carcassonne, face au mont Alaric, le beau Château de Floure, ancienne résidence de Gaston Bonheur l'écrivain, se niche au cœur d'un parc luxuriant entouré de vignobles et d'adorables jardins typiques de la région. Les chambres charmantes sont ultra confortables et une cuisine succulente accompagnée de vins délicieux est servie au restaurant dans un cadre du XVIIe siècle à l'ébénisterie impressionnante. Les hôtes peuvent se promener dans le parc, jouer au tennis ou profiter de la piscine.

Nur 10 Minuten von Carcassonne entfernt und mit Blick auf den majestätischen Mont Alaric liegt dieses Château, die einstige Residenz des französischen Schriftstellers Gaston Bonheur, umgeben von üppiger Parklandschaft, Weinbergen und herrlichen traditionellen Gärten. Die bezaubernden Zimmer bieten höchsten Komfort, und im Restaurant aus dem 17. Jahrhundert mit seinen eindrucksvollen ursprünglichen Holzarbeiten werden unwiderstehliche französische Küche und edle Weine serviert. Man kann herrliche Spaziergänge machen, Tennis spielen oder im Pool schwimmen.

Our inspector loved: *The extremely warm welcome from the owners and lovely views over The French gardens towards the mountains.*

Directions: A61 > exit Carcassonne Est, no. 24 > RN113 towards Narbonne.

Web: www.johansens.com/floure
E-mail: contact@chateau-de-floure.com
Tel: +33 4 68 79 11 29
Fax: +33 4 68 79 04 61

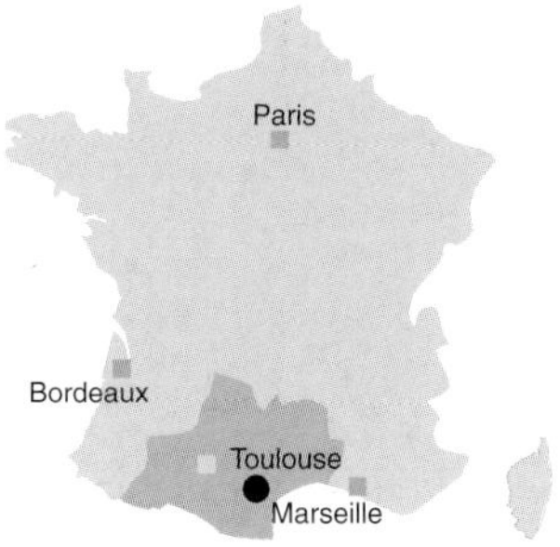

Price Guide:
(room only)
double €100-170
suite €230

LE BOIS JOLI

12, AVENUE PHILIPPE DU ROZIER, 61140 BAGNOLES DE L'ORNE, FRANCE

Just a stone's throw from the centre of the historic spa town of Bagnoles de L'Orne lies this charming 19th-century house, described as being "free as air." Lovingly restored by its owners and offering the warmest of welcomes, the hotel has a light and intimate atmosphere and boasts the most wonderful surroundings. Many of the bedrooms look out over the centuries-old sequoia trees that lie in the glorious parkland on the edge of the Forêt d'Andaine.

Situé à deux pas du centre de la station thermale historique de Bagnoles de l'Orne, Bois Joli est une charmante demeure du XIXe siècle d'où émane un sentiment de liberté. Parfaitement restauré par ses propriétaires qui offrent un accueil très chaleureux, l'hôtel bénéficie non seulement d'une atmosphère légère et intime mais aussi d'environs superbes. La plupart des chambres ont vue sur le superbe parc aux vénérables séquoïas à la lisière de la forêt d'Andaine.

Nur einen Steinwurf vom Zentrum der historischen Kurstadt Bagnoles de L'Orne entfernt liegt dieses charmante Hotel aus dem 19. Jahrhundert. Gäste erwartet ein herzlicher Empfang in diesem liebevoll von den Eigentümern restaurierten Haus. Die Atmosphäre ist freundlich und familiär, die Umgebung einfach atemberaubend. Viele der Zimmer blicken auf die jahrhundertealten Mammutbäume in herrlicher Parklandschaft am Rande des Forêt d'Andaine.

Our inspector loved: *The "Magnolia" room which overlooks the gardens.*

Directions: In the centre of Bagnoles de L'Orne.

Web: www.johansens.com/boisjoli
E-mail: boisjoli@wanadoo.fr
Tel: +33 2 33 37 92 77
Fax: +33 2 33 37 07 56

Price Guide:
(room only)
single €60–98
double €82–126

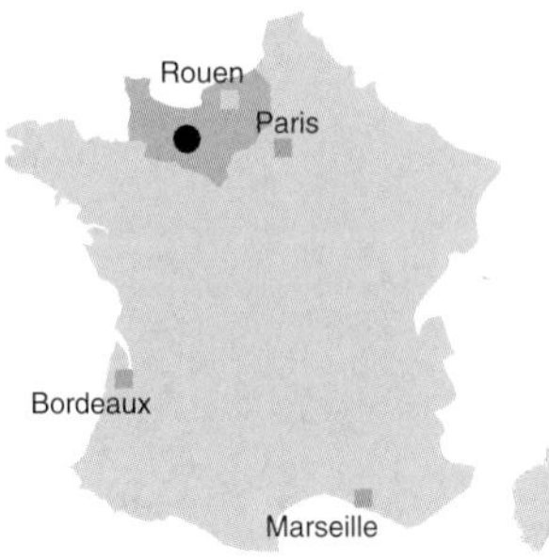

SYMBOLES de FRANCE

Château de Goville

14330 BREUIL~EN~BESSIN, FRANCE

Visitors to this charming château enjoy the warm welcome that has awaited famous guests in the past, such as The Duke of Orléans. Owner Jean-Jacques Vallée has honoured the château's fascinating history by restoring its 18th-century grandeur, with antique furniture and elegant yet comfortable bedrooms providing unique character. An amazing dolls house collection can be marvelled at, and Le Baromètre restaurant serves fine food in a graceful setting.

L'accueil chaleureux dont bénéficiaient autrefois les invités célèbres, comme le duc d'Orléans, est réservé aujourd'hui à tous les visiteurs de ce beau château. Le propriétaire, Jean-Jacques Vallée, a honoré l'histoire fascinante de cette demeure ancestrale en lui rendant sa splendeur du XVIIIe siècle. Le mobilier d'époque et les chambres élégantes et confortables donnent au lieu un charme incomparable. Une impressionante collection de maisons de poupée peut être admirée, et Le Baromètre, un restaurant au décor raffiné, propose une excellente cuisine.

Besucher dieses bezaubernden Schlosses werden so herzlich willkommen geheissen wie einst berühmte Gäste wie z. B. der Herzog von Orleans. Eigentümer Jean-Jacques Vallée hält die faszinierende Geschichte des Schlosses in Ehren und hat es in seiner ursprünglichen Pracht des 18. Jahrhunderts mit antiken Möbeln und eleganten, komfortablen Schlafzimmern restauriert. Eine einzigartige Puppenhaussammlung kann bestaunt werden, und das Restaurant Le Baromètre serviert erlesene Speisen in eleganter Atmosphäre.

Our inspector loved: *The charming lounge where you can soak up the country house atmosphere.*

Directions: D5 Bayeux-Le Molay Littry > 2km before Le Molay Littry.

Web: www.johansens.com/chateaudegoville
E-mail: chateaugoville@wanadoo.fr
Tel: +33 2 31 22 19 28
Fax: +33 2 31 22 68 74

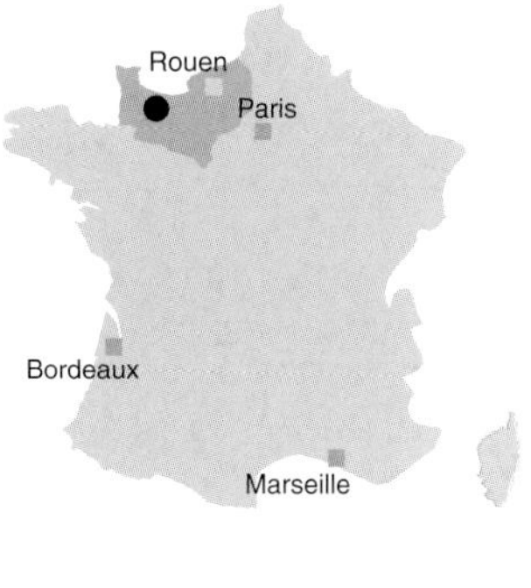

Rouen
Paris
Bordeaux
Marseille

Price Guide:
(room only)
single from €105
double/twin €145

Hostellerie de Tourgéville

CHEMIN DE L'ORGUEIL, TOURGÉVILLE, 14800 DEAUVILLE, FRANCE

Directions: Exit Deauville on the A13. Take the D27 after Canapville and turn left at the roundabout, then the first left turning. The hotel is 300 metres on the right . The nearest airport is Caen.

Web: www.johansens.com/tourgeville
E-mail: hostellerie@hotel-de-tourgeville.com
Tel: +33 231 14 48 68
Fax: +33 2 31 14 48 69

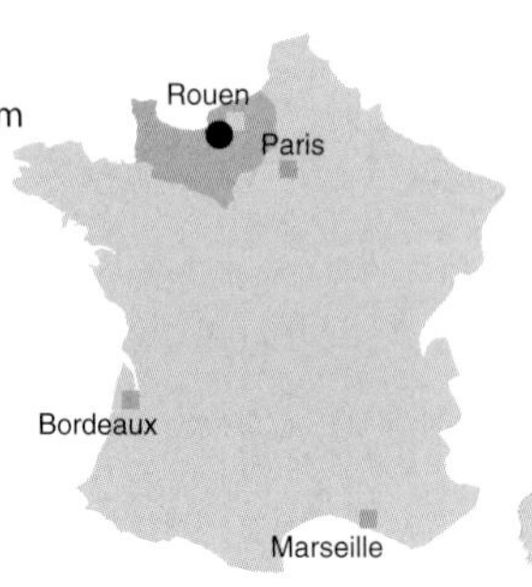

Price Guide:
single €110-160
double €110-225
suite €270-340

Hostellerie de Tourgéville is situated in extensive parklands, just a few minutes from Deauville. The individually and tastefully decorated guest rooms are named after film stars and boast picturesque views. Each suite features log fires in the lounge area and compact, well-equipped bathrooms with fluffy towels and bathrobes. The Claude Lelouch Pavillion, which is situated within the grounds, is ideal for honeymooners. With an indoor pool and 3 tennis courts as well as a private cinema available for group bookings, the hotel offers a variety of facilities with attentive, welcoming staff on hand.

Au sein d'un parc vaste, Hostellerie de Tourgéville est aussi à deux pas de Deauville. Les chambres décorées de manière individuelle possèdent un nom de star et se ventent d'une vue magnifique. Les suites ont un feu de bois dans le salon et une salle de bains bien équipée avec des serviettes et des peignoirs de bain luxueux. Le pavillon Claude Lalouch, situé dans le parc, est idéal pour des couples en voyage de noces. Avec une piscine à l'intérieur et 3 courts de tennis ainsi qu'un cinéma privé, l'hôtel vous propose une variété d'activités et un personnel attentif et accueillant.

Diese inmitten weitläufiger Parklandschaft gelegene Hostellerie ist nur ein paar Minuten von Deauville entfernt. Die individuell und geschmackvoll gestalteten Zimmer sind nach Filmstars benannt und haben malerische Ausblicke. Jede Suite bietet Kaminfeuer im Wohnbereich und kompakte, vollausgestattete Bäder mit flauschigen Handtüchern und Bademänteln. Der Claude Lelouch Pavillion auf dem Gelände ist ideal für Hochzeitsreisende. Vom Hallenbad und den 3 Tennisplätzen bis hin zum Privatkino für Gruppenvorstellungen bietet das Hotel eine Vielfalt von Einrichtungen sowie aufmerksames, herzliches Personal.

Our inspector loved: The different decorative themes for each room.

Domaine Saint Clair, Le Donjon

CHEMIN DE SAINT CLAIR, 76790 ETRETAT, FRANCE

The colour and character of this ivy-clad château are as inspiring as its breathtaking coastal views. Rooms are cosy and intimate with antique furnishings, and each of the superb newly decorated bedrooms in the adjoining villa are themed after a person who lived as a house guest between 1890 and 1920. After a delicious dinner in one of 3 unique dining rooms guests can retire to the cigar lounge, relax in the pretty courtyard or enjoy a drink on the poolside terrace.

La couleur et le caractère de ce château couvert de vigne vierge sont tout aussi inspirants par leur beauté qu'est la vue à couper le souffle sur la côte. Les pièces sont douillettes et intimes avec des antiquités pour mobilier, et chaque chambre de la villa adjacente, a été superbement décorée récemment selon quelqu'un qui a séjourné dans la maison entre 1890 et 1920. Après un délicieux dîner dans l'une des 3 salles à manger, les hôtes peuvent se retirer dans le salon, se détendre dans la petite cour intérieure ou déguster un verre sur la terrasse près de la piscine.

Farben und Charakter dieses efeubewachsenen Schlosses sind ebenso atemberaubend wie die Sicht auf die Küste. Die Zimmer sind herrlich gemütlich und mit Antiquitäten eingerichtet, und jedes der eindrucksvollen Zimmer in der anliegenden Villa wurde nach einer bestimmten Person gestaltet, die hier zwischen 1890 und 1920 zu Gast war. Nach einem köstlichen Abendessen in einem der 3 einzigartigen Speisesäle kann man sich ins Zigarrenzimmer zurückziehen, im Innenhof entspannen oder auf der Terrasse am Pool einen Drink genießen.

Our inspector loved: *The "Docteur François" bedroom, for its decoration and balcony.*

Directions: Town centre, follow signs.

Web: www.johansens.com/donjon
E-mail: info@hoteletretat.com
Tel: +33 2 35 27 08 23
Fax: +33 2 35 29 92 24

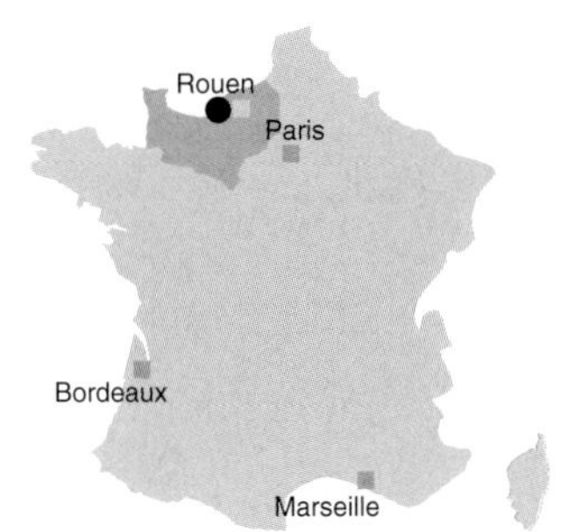

Price Guide:
(room only)
single €90-250
double/twin €90–250
suites €255-300

Manoir de la Poterie

CHEMIN PAUL RUEL, 14113 CRICQUEBOEUF, FRANCE

Situated between Honfleur and Trouville, the Manoir de la Poterie combines the atmosphere of a grand country manor with the hospitality and elegance of a small château. Fine cuisine is served in the dining room, whilst guests can also enjoy a drink in the American Bar or relax in the salon with its fireplace. The bedrooms are luxuriously appointed, featuring marble bathrooms and stunning views of the sea or the surrounding countryside, which beckons to be explored on a leisurely walk along the coast.

Entre Honfleur et Trouville, le Manoir de la Poterie offre l'espace d'une grande propriété de campagne ajouté à la chaleur et l'élégance d'un petit château. La salle à manger où est servie une cuisine raffinée est complétée par un Bar Américain et salon avec cheminée. Les chambres luxueuses avec salle de bain en marbre ont vue sur la mer ou sur la campagne. De nombreux endroits vous attendent pour d'agréables promenades le long de la côte.

Das zwischen Honfleur und Trouville gelegene Manoir de la Poterie bietet die Geräumigkeit eines vornehmen Landhauses und die Eleganz und Freundlichkeit eines kleinen Schlosses. Im Speisesaal werden erlesene Gerichte serviert, daneben gibt es eine Amerikanische Bar und einen Aufenthaltsraum mit Kamin. Die luxuriösen Zimmer haben Marmorbäder und Blick auf das Meer oder die Umgebung, und die schöne Landschaft lädt zu Spaziergängen entlang der Küste ein.

***Our inspector loved:** The elegant lounge with its log fire.*

Directions: Detailed directions available from the hotel.

Web: www.johansens.com/manoirdelapoterie
E-mail: info@honfleur-hotel.com
Tel: +33 2 31 88 10 40
Fax: +33 2 31 88 10 90

Price Guide:
(room only)
single €113–160
double €113–160
suites €134–198

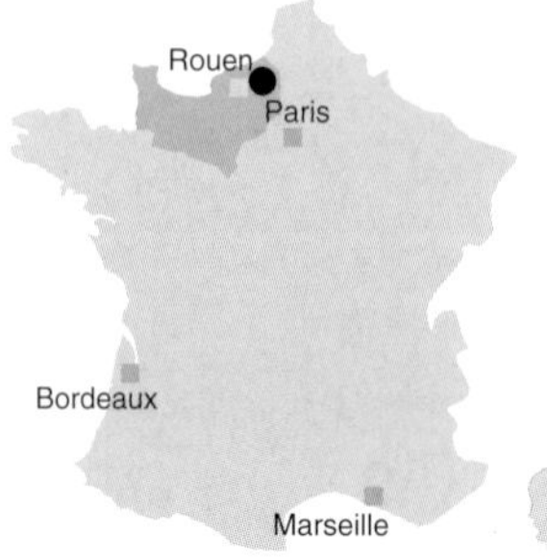

Hostellerie Château de Brécourt

DOUAINS, 27120 PACY~SUR~EURE, FRANCE

Only 1 hour from Paris and surrounded by woodlands and moats, Château de Brécourt exudes charm with a friendly welcome from attentive staff. Huge rooms, stone floors, high ceilings and blazing log fires create a wonderful, warm atmosphere. The spacious bedrooms are decorated in traditional château style with beautiful antique furniture and impressive draperies. Gastronomic delights are enjoyed in the elegant dining room overlooking the park. Guests can relax in the swimming pool or play tennis.

Situé à seulement 1 heure de Paris, entouré de bois et de douves, du Château de Brécourt émane un charme certain. L'accueil par un personnel attentif est amical. Des pièces immenses, sols en pierre, plafonds hauts et feux de bois chatoyants créent une merveilleuse et chaleureuse atmosphère. Les chambres spacieuses sont décorées dans le style traditionnel du château avec un très beau mobilier ancien et de superbes draperies. Une cuisine gastronomique est servie dans l'élégante salle à manger qui donne sur le parc. Pour la détente, il y a une piscine et un court de tennis.

Nur 1 Stunde von Paris enfernt und von Wald und Burggräben umgeben, bietet dieses Schloss einen herzlichen Empfang. Riesige Räume, Steinböden, hohe Decken und knisternde Kaminfeuer schaffen eine behagliche Atmosphäre. Die geräumigen Gästezimmer sind im traditionell Schlossstil mit herrlichen antiken Möbeln und traumhaften Stoffdrapierungen eingerichtet. Gastronomische Köstlichkeiten werden im eleganten Speisesaal mit Blick auf den Park geboten. Zur Entspannung gibt es einen Swimmingpool und einen Tennisplatz.

Our inspector loved: *The lounge and bar area, old beams, and the log fire.*

Directions: A13 > exit 16.

Web: www.johansens.com/chateaudebrecourt
E-mail: brecourt@leshotelsparticulier.com
Tel: +33 2 32 52 40 50
Fax: +33 2 32 52 69 65

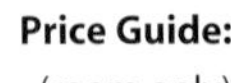

Price Guide:
(room only)
double €75–172
suite €180–261

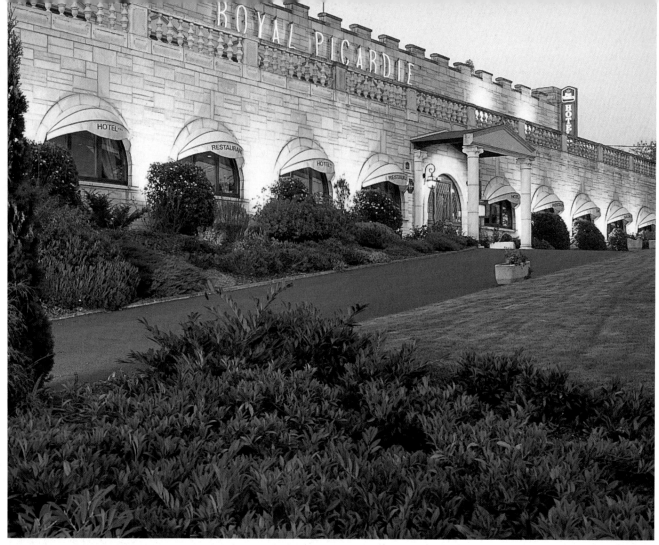

Hotel Royal Picardie

AVENUE DU GÉNÉRAL LECLERC, 80300 ALBERT, FRANCE

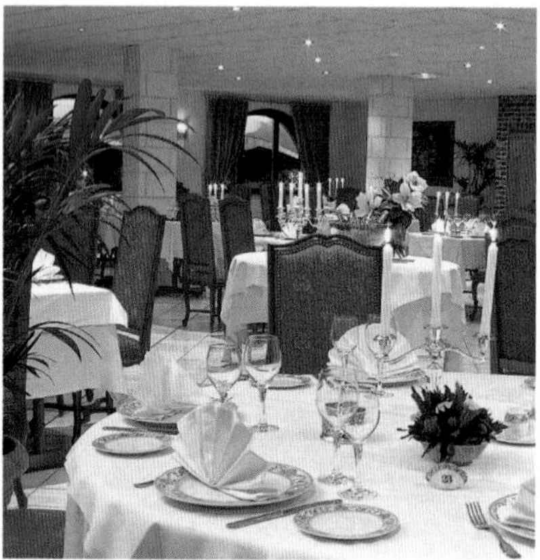

Directions: A1 > Paris > Lille exit 14 > D929 Amiens/Albert. The hotel is immediately south west of Albert. The nearest airport is Lille or Charles de Gaulle.

Web: www.johansens.com/royalpicardie
E-mail: royalpicardie@wanadoo.fr
Tel: +33 3 22 75 37 00
Fax: +33 3 22 75 60 19

Price Guide:
(Breakfast €10)
single €97-153
double €97-153

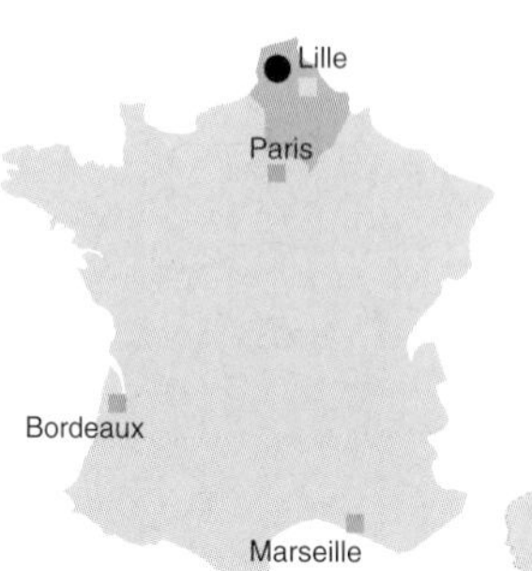

With its location close to Lille and Arras, in the heart of Picardy and its First World War battlefields, this splendid white stone building offers plenty to discover nearby. Its architecture was inspired by ancient fortresses, and guests are treated like royalty. Particular care has been taken in the comfortable en suite bedrooms, which feature marble bathrooms. Before sampling seasonal regional cuisine in the light and elegant Louis-XIV-style dining room, guests may relax in the bar by the inviting fireplace. The restaurant, conference rooms, bar and reception area are air-conditioned.

Tout proche de Lille et Arras, au coeur de la Picardie et de ses champs de batailles de la 1ère guerre mondiale, cette splendide construction de pierres blanches offre beaucoup de choses à découvrir à proximité. Son architecture s'inspire des châteaux forts d'autrefois et les hôtes sont traités royalement. Un soin tout particulier a été apporté à chaque chambre confortable avec salle de bain en marbre. Avant de savourer la cuisine régionale dans la salle à manger lumineuse et élégamment décorée en style Louis XIV, les hôtes peuvent se détendre dans le bar autour de la cheminée. Restaurant, salle de séminaires, bar et réception climatisés.

Mit seiner Lage nahe bei Lille und Arras im Herzen der Picardie mit ihren Schlachtfeldern aus dem 1. Weltkrieg bietet dieses strahlend weiße Steingebäude einiges an Attraktionen in der Umgebung. Die Architektur ist von alten Festungen inspiriert, und jeder Gast wird hier wie ein König behandelt. Jedes komfortable, liebevoll gestaltete Zimmer hat ein eigenes Marmorbad. Bevor man im hellen, eleganten Speisesaal im Stil Ludwigs des XIV. regionale Köstlichkeiten genießt, entspannt man sich am Kamin in der Bar. Restaurant, Konferenzräume, Bar und Rezeption sind klimatisiert.

***Our inspector loved:** The inglenook fireplace in the bar.*

La Chartreuse du Val St Esprit

62199 GOSNAY, FRANCE

Situated in the heart of the Pas-de-Calais region, this superb former distillery is steeped in history and legend. Particular care has been taken to personalise each of the elegant bedrooms and everything is done to ensure the utmost comfort. Local gastronomic dishes can be savoured in any of the 3 restaurants. As well as several historic and cultural attractions, there is a dry-ski slope nearby.

Situé dans le cœur du Pas de Calais, cette superbe ancienne chartreuse est ancrée dans l'histoire et la légende. Un soin particulier a été apporte pour que chacune des élégantes chambres soit personnalisée, et tout est fait pour assurer le plus grand confort. Une gastronomie locale peut être appréciée dans chacun des 3 restaurants. Ajoutant à l'attraction historique de l'hôtel, une piste de ski artificielle est à proximité.

Um diese geschichtsreiche, im Herzen der Region Pas-de-Calais gelegene ehemalige Schnapsbrennerei ranken sich zahlreiche Legenden. Jedes der eleganten Zimmer wurde mit viel Liebe eingerichtet, und höchster Komfort ist geboten. In 3 Restaurants kann man köstliche Feinschmeckerküche der Region genießen. Außer zahlreichen historischen und kulturellen Attraktionen gibt es ganz in der Nähe eine Trockenskipiste.

Our inspector loved: *The gastronomic dinner in the elegant restaurant.*

Directions: A26 > exit 6 for Bethune.

Web: www.johansens.com/lachartreuse
E-mail: lachartreuse@gofornet.com
Tel: +33 3 21 62 80 00
Fax: +33 3 21 62 42 50

Price Guide:
single €80–116
double €91–297
suite €297

Château de Cocove

62890 RECQUES~SUR~HEM, FRANCE

This classically proportioned château nestles within 11 hectares of its own pretty parkland and is an idyllic setting in which to enjoy fine regional cuisine. The elegant and panoramic dining room is the backdrop for romantic candle-lit dinners, whilst afternoon tea and apéritifs served by attentive staff can be savoured from the terrace. A carefully planned menu and fine wine selection ensure a gastronomic delight.

Ce château de style XVIIe niché au sein des 11 ha de son joli parc, est l'endroit idéal où apprécier une cuisine régionale raffinée. La salle à manger panoramique élégante est la toile de fond pour des dîners romantiques aux chandelles, alors que le thé de l'après-midi et les apéritifs servis par un personnel attentif peuvent être dégustés sur la terrasse. Un menu soigneusement planifié et une sélection de vins fins sont la garantie d'un régal gastronomique.

Dieses klassische Schloss befindet sich inmitten von 11 ha Parklandschaft und ist ein idyllischer Ort, um feinste regionale Küche zu genießen. Der elegante Speisesaal mit Panoramablick bietet den idealen Hintergrund für ein romantisches Abendessen bei Kerzenschein, und auf der Terrasse serviert das aufmerksame Personal Nachmittagstee und Apéritifs. Die sorgfältig zusammengestellte Speisekarte und eindrucksvolle Weinkarte versprechen gastronomischen Hochgenuss.

Our inspector loved: *The exposed stone bar for a pre-dinner drink.*

Directions: A26 > Calais > Paris exit No. 2 > Cocove.

Web: www.johansens.com/chateaudecocove
E-mail: chateaudecocove@hotmail.com
Tel: +33 3 21 82 68 29
Fax: +33 3 21 82 72 59

Price Guide:
(breakfast €10)
single €78–155
double €84–155

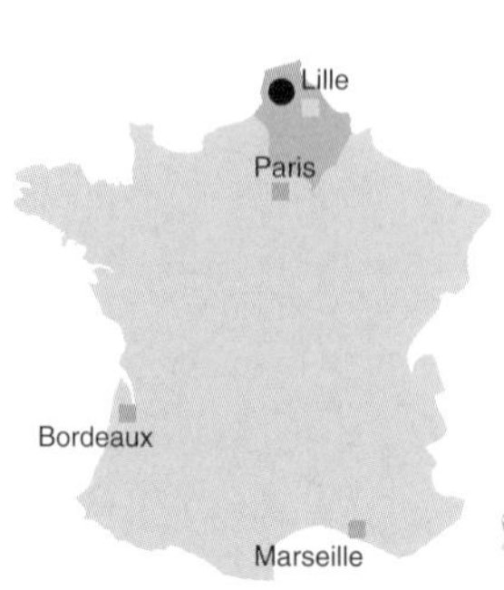

Hostellerie Château d'Ermenonville

60950 ERMENONVILLE, FRANCE

A flower-decked bridge and moat lead you towards this beautifully proportioned and elegant château, which lies just half an hour from the centre of Paris, yet seemingly in another world. The bedrooms overlook the park and lake or the enchanting central courtyard, and a grand sweeping staircase is reminiscent of fairy tales. After a day in the city there could be no finer place to savour an after-dinner cognac and enjoy the delicious cuisine in the Table de Poète restaurant.

Un pont de bois fleuri et des douves conduisent à cet élégant château, à l'architecture joliment proportionnée, qui se trouve à seulement une demie heure du cœur de Paris et qui pourtant semble situé dans un autre monde. Les chambres ont toutes vue sur le parc et le lac ou sur l'enchanteresse cour intérieure centrale et son escalier majestueux, évocateur des contes de fées. Après une journée en ville, il n'y a pas de meilleur endroit pour savourer un cognac ou déguster une délicieuse cuisine que le restaurant de la Table des Poètes.

Eine mit Blumen geschmückte Brücke über einen Burggraben führt zu diesem herrlichen, eleganten Schloss, das nur eine halbe Stunde vom Zentrum von Paris enfernt ist und doch in einer völlig anderen Welt zu liegen scheint. Die Zimmer haben Blick auf den Park und See oder den bezaubernden Innenhof, und ein eindrucksvolles gewundenes Treppenhaus erinnert an Märchen. Nach einem Tag in der Stadt ist dies der ideale Ort, um ein köstliches Diner im Table de Poète mit einem Cognac abzuschließen.

Our inspector loved: *The suites in the tower overlooking the lake.*

Directions: A1 > exit Ermenonville > N2 towards Paris/Soissons.

Web: www.johansens.com/chateaudermenonville
E-mail: ermenonville@leshotelsparticuliers.com
Tel: +33 3 44 54 00 26
Fax: +33 3 44 54 01 00

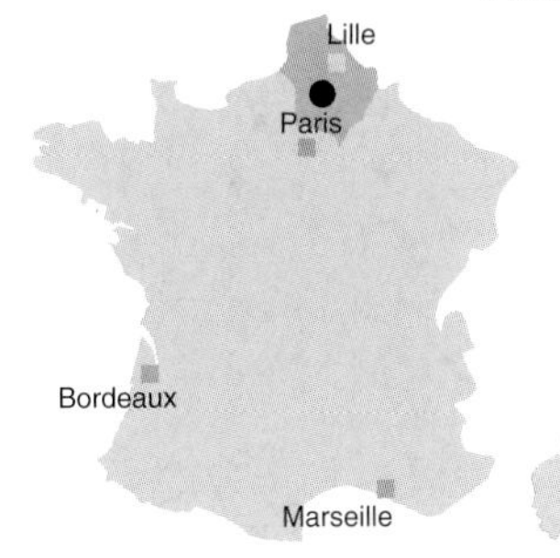

Price Guide:
double €75–155
suite €165–270

49 60

CHÂTEAU DE FÈRE

02130 FÈRE~EN~TARDENOIS, FRANCE

Directions: From Paris on the A4, exit at Château-Thierry. From Calais on the A26, exit at Reims.

Web: www.johansens.com/chateaudefere
E-mail: chateau.fere@wanadoo.fr
Tel: + 33 3 23 82 21 13
Fax: +33 3 23 82 37 81

Price Guide:
(room only)
single/double/twin €140–320
suites €220–380

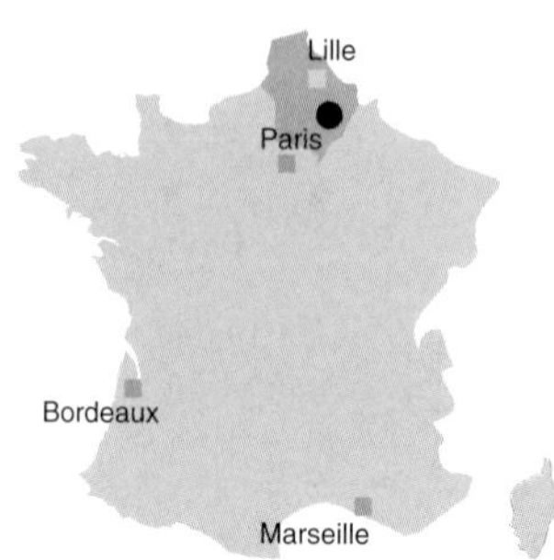

Side by side with the impressive ruins of a medieval castle, this grand and exclusive 18th-century château is situated in beautiful, wooded countryside just 1 hour's drive from Paris. The guest rooms are tastefully furnished, maintained to the highest standard and offer spectacular views. Excellent gourmet meals are served in 3 individual and stylishly designed dining rooms where the service is impeccable. The treasures of the Champagne region can be enjoyed on a tour of the Château's cellars.

Dominé par les ruines impressionnantes d'un château fort, cet hôtel de luxe occupe un magnifique château du XVIIIe siècle, au milieu d'un beau parc boisé, à une heure seulement de Paris. Des chambres de premier ordre, meublées avec goût, offrent des vues spectaculaires sur les environs. 3 salles à manger différentes proposent des menus gourmands dans un cadre élégant. Le service est d'une qualité irréprochable. Un tour des caves du château permet aux œnophiles de savourer les délices de la région champenoise.

Inmitten der imposanten Ruinen einer mittelalterlichen Burg und umgeben von herrlicher Waldlandschaft liegt dieses elegante und exklusive Schloss aus dem 18. Jahrhundert, nur eine Stunde Fahrt von Paris entfernt. Die Zimmer sind geschmackvoll eingerichtet und bieten höchstes Niveau und eindrucksvolle Aussichten. In 3 unterschiedlichen, eleganten Speisesälen werden exzellente Gerichte serviert; der Service ist tadellos. Champagnerfreunde werden sich über die Champagnerkeller des Schlosses freuen

Our inspector loved: *The tables in the dining room, which overlook the Château.*

Carlton Hotel

RUE DE PARIS, 59000 LILLE, FRANCE

A new health and fitness facility and solarium as well as stunning new double floor luxury suite are the latest additions to this historic city centre hotel. Situated in the Cupole, the suite has its own lounge, bar and bathroom, and is the ideal place in which to relax after a day enjoying Lille's shopping, museums and opera. The hotel is furnished in Louis XV and XVI styles and is easily accessible by plane or rail.

Un centre de remise en forme et un solarium ainsi qu'une superbe suite luxueuse sur deux niveaux sont les dernières nouveautés de cet hôtel historique du centre ville. Située dans la coupole la suite a son propre salon, bar et salle de bain et est l'endroit idéal pour se détendre après avoir profiter d'une journée de shopping, de musées et d'opéra à Lille. L'hôtel est meublé en style Louis XV et Louis XVI et est d'accès facile par avion ou train.

Ein neues Gesundheits- und Fitnesszentrum mit Solarium sowie eine atemberaubende, zweistöckige Luxussuite sind die neuesten Ergänzungen dieses historischen Hotels im Zentrum von Lille. Die in der Kuppel untergebrachte Suite mit Lounge, Bar und Bad ist der ideale Ort, um sich nach einem mit Einkaufen, Museumsbesuchen und Oper gefüllten Tag zu entspannen. Das im Stil Ludwigs des XV. und XVI. eingerichtete Hotel ist vom Flughafen oder Bahnhof gut zu erreichen.

Our inspector loved: *The new suite - uninhibited luxury.*

Directions: In the centre of Lille, near the railway station and opera.

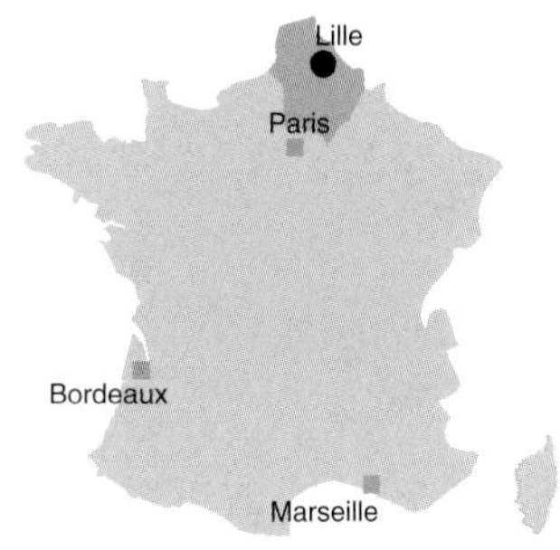

Web: www.johansens.com/carltonlille
E-mail: carlton@carltonlille.com
Tel: +33 3 20 13 33 13
Fax: +33 3 20 51 48 17

Price Guide:
(breakfast €17)
single/double €208
suite €250-1,150

LA TOUR DU ROY

02140 VERVINS, FRANCE

This charming hotel is set in the 11th -entury ramparts of the town and is steeped in history. A warm welcome is assured from the host, who has lovingly restored this building over the past 33 years. Now fully refurbished, bedrooms boast spectacular views of the valley and 4 of the antique-style bathrooms have Jacuzzi baths, whilst the suite found high in the tower is a true gem. The dining room is home to stunning antiques and is clad in wood and marble, making this an inviting setting in which to sample some of Madame Annie's renowned cuisine.

Imprégné d'histoire, ce charmant hôtel se dresse sur les remparts du XIe siècle de la ville. Le propriétaire, qui a restauré le bâtiment au fil des 33 dernières années, vous y réserve un accueil chaleureux. Entièrement remises à neuf, les chambres jouissent de vues spectaculaires sur la vallée de 4 salles de bains avec jacuzzi. La suite, qui occupe le haut de la tour, est une véritable merveille avec baignoires à deux habillée de bois et de marbre. La salle à manger abrite de belles antiquités et offre un cadre attrayant et panoramique, où il fait bon savourer la cuisine renommée de la patronne Annie. Cordon bleu aux doigts de fée (Ducasse) fait la cuisine comme loiseau chante (Courtine).

Dieses bezaubernde, geschichtsträchtige Hotel liegt in einem Stadtteil aus dem 11. Jahrhundert. Der Besitzer, der das Gebäude über die letzten 33 Jahren liebevoll restauriert hat, heißt seine Gäste hier herzlich willkommen. Die Zimmer, perfekt renoviert, haben herrliche Sicht auf das Tal und 4 der im antiken Stil gehaltenen Badezimmer haben Jacuzzibäder. Die Suite im oberen Teil des Turmes ist ein wahres Juwel, und der mit Holz und Marmor gestaltete Speisesaal bietet die ideale Umgebung, um Madame Annies köstliche Speisen zu probieren.

Our inspector loved: *The room in the tower, and exposed stone and wood-work.*

Directions: Between Paris and Brussels on the N2. Take the A26 from Calais to Reims, exit 13, then the N2 towards Vervins.

Web: www.johansens.com/tourduroy
E-mail: latourduroy@wanadoo.fr
Tel: +33 3 23 98 00 11
Fax: +33 3 23 98 00 72

Price Guide:
(breakfast €13)
single €60
double €92–183
suite €230

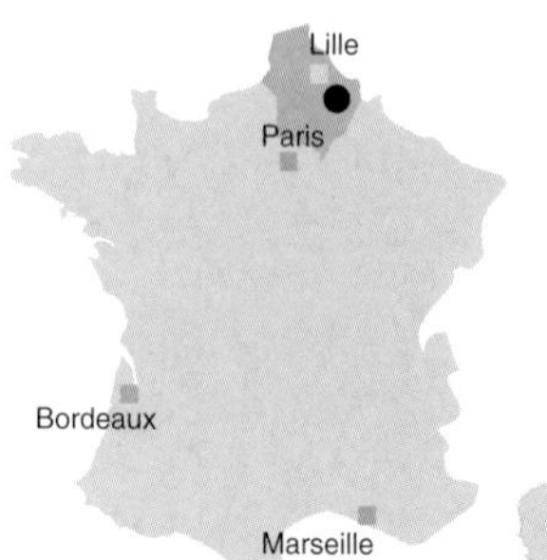

Paris

Hotel location shown in red (hotel) or purple (spa hotel) with page number

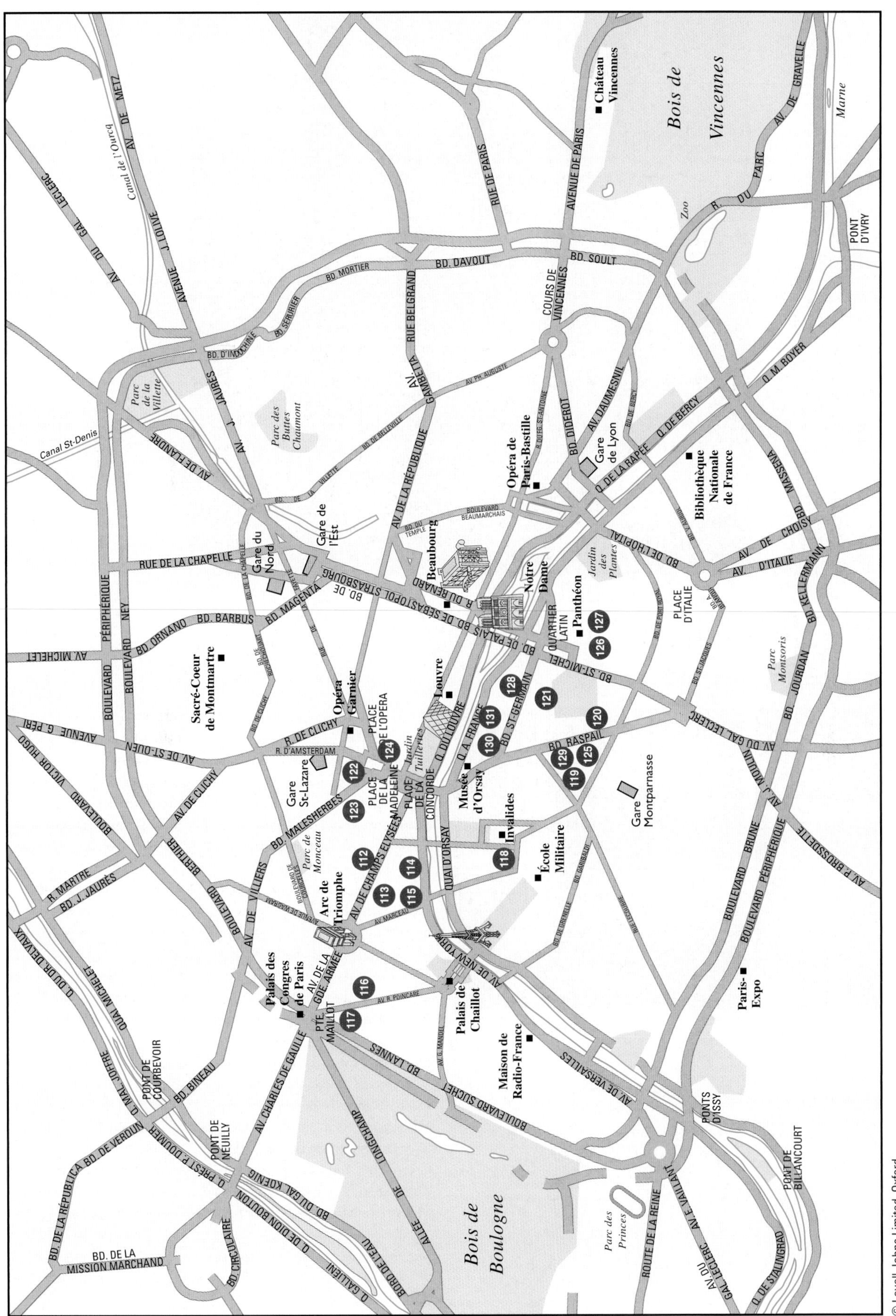

Hôtel Monna Lisa

DES IGN HOT ELS

97 RUE DE LA BOÉTIE, 75008 PARIS, FRANCE

Directions: Rue de la Boétie is located between the Faubourg St Honóré and the Champs-Elysées.

Web: www.johansens.com/monnalisa
E-mail: contact@hotelmonnalisa.com
Tel: +33 1 56 43 38 38
Fax: +33 1 45 62 39 90

Price Guide:
(room only)
double €235-265
suite €230-380

Conveniently located, within close proximity to the Arc de Triomphe, Hôtel Monna Lisa is an impressive mid 19th century hotel tastefully furnished with all modern conveniences. Guests are welcomed into this warm and contemporary style hotel by inviting, helpful staff where all 22 bedrooms have modern décor and feature wooden floors, quality fabrics and walnut furniture. The elegant and intimate restaurant, Caffe Ristretto, serves innovative Italian cuisine created from local produce.

Superbement situé, à deux pas de l'Arc de Triomphe, Hôtel Monna Lisa est un hôtel impressionnant du XIXe siècle orné avec goût et offrant tout le confort moderne. Un personnel chaleureux et obligeant accueille les hôtes dans cet établissement contemporain, où toutes les 22 chambres ont des planchers en bois, des tissus de qualité et des meubles en noyer. Caffè Ristretto, le restaurant élégant et intime, sert une cuisine italienne innovatrice, créée avec des ingrédients locaux.

Das Hotel Monna Lisa mit seiner günstigen Lage nahe des Arc de Triomphe ist ein eindrucksvolles Haus aus dem 19. Jahrhundert, das seinen Gästen jeglichen modernen Komfort bietet. Das herzliche, hilfsbereite Personal sorgt für einen angenehmen Empfang in diesem freundlichen, zeitgenössisch gestalteten Hotel. Alle 22 Zimmer sind modern mit Holzböden, hochqualitativen Stoffen und Möbeln aus Walnussholz eingerichtet. Im eleganten, gemütlichen Caffe Ristretto wird innovative italienische Küche aus einheimischen Zutaten serviert.

Our inspector loved: *The paintings; especially those in the de luxe bedrooms and suites, which each feature a segment of the famous "Mona Lisa" painting.*

HÔTEL PLAZA ATHÉNÉE

25 AVENUE MONTAIGNE, 75008 PARIS, FRANCE

Since opening in 1911 this elegant hotel has become synonymous with luxury and charm. Situated on the exclusive Avenue Montaigne in the heart of Paris, the Hôtel Plaza Athénée has undergone a complete redecoration, preserving and combining classical French and art deco styling on the top 2 floors with 21st-century facilities in all rooms. Alain Ducasse opened his gastronomic restaurant at the Plaza Athénée, and also oversees the other restaurants, the Relais Plaza and the summer courtyard restaurant. A member of the Dorchester group.

Depuis son ouverture en 1911, cet élégant hôtel est devenu un symbole de luxe et de charme. Il se dresse au coeur de Paris, sur l'avenue Montaigne, une des rues les plus chics de la capitale. Entièrement re-décoré, le Plaza Athénée a su garder son style français classique et innover avec le style art déco aux 2 derniers étages, tout en intégrant les commodités du XXIe siècle. Alain Ducasse a ouvert son restaurant gastronomique au Plaza Athénée; il supervise également les autres restaurants, le Relais Plaza, et l'été la Cour Jardin. Un membre du groupe Dorchester.

Seit seiner Eröffnung 1911 ist dieses elegante Hotel zu einem Symbol von Luxus und Charme geworden. An der exklusiven Avenue Montaigne im Herzen von Paris gelegen, wurde das Hôtel Plaza Athénée vollständig renoviert und vereint seinen klassisch Französischen Stil mit dem Art-Deco-Décor auf den 2 obersten Etagen perfekt mit dem Komfort des 21. Jahrhunderts. Alain Ducasse eröffnete hier sein Gourmetrestaurant und leitet daneben auch die anderen Restaurants: Le Relais Plaza und La Cour Jardin, das Sommerrestaurant. Mitglied der Dorchestergruppe.

Our inspector loved: *The innovative and stylish bar - the place to be in Paris!*

Directions: Centre of Paris, 5-minute walk from Champs-Elysées.

Web: www.johansens.com/plazaathenee
E-mail: reservation@plaza-athenee-paris.com
Tel: +33 1 53 67 66 65
Fax: +33 1 53 67 66 66

Price Guide:
(breakfast €33-45)
single €498-550
double/twin €620-740
suite €795-6,300

Hôtel San Régis

12 RUE JEAN GOUJON, 75008 PARIS, FRANCE

Deep in the heart of Paris's fashion district lies this small, intimate and beautifully appointed hotel. Built in 1857, the interior charmingly combines modern comforts with 19th-century furniture and antiques. Each of the 44 bedrooms has been individually decorated and boasts a marble bathroom as well as all modern conveniences. The restaurant, set in an old library, is a haven of tranquillity and serves simply impeccable fare.

Ce luxueux petit hôtel parisien à l'atmosphère intime jouit d'une situation privilégiée au coeur du quartier de la mode. Construit en 1857, le San Régis marie à merveille des meubles et des objets d'art du XIXe siècle avec un confort des plus modernes. Chacune des 44 chambres a son propre charme et dispose d'une salle de bains en marbre et des dernières commodités. Le restaurant, aménagé dans une ancienne bibliothèque, est un havre de paix propice à la dégustation de mets exquis.

Dieses persönliche und attraktive Hotel wurde im Jahr 1857 errichtet und liegt mitten im Pariser Modeviertel. Moderner Komfort verbindet sich perfekt mit Möbeln und Antiquitäten aus dem 19. Jahrhundert. Die 44 Zimmer sind individuell gestaltet und besitzen Marmorbäder und jegliche modernen Annehmlichkeiten. Das herrlich ruhige Restaurant liegt in einer alten Bibliothek und serviert hervorragende Gerichte.

Our inspector loved: *The intimate restaurant in the old library.*

Directions: Rue Jean Goujon is off the Champs-Elysées and Avenue Montaigne.

Web: www.johansens.com/sanregis
E-mail: message@hotel-sanregis.fr
Tel: +33 1 44 95 16 16
Fax: +33 1 45 61 05 48

Price Guide:
(room only)
single €300–395
double/twin €395–540
suite €590–1,025

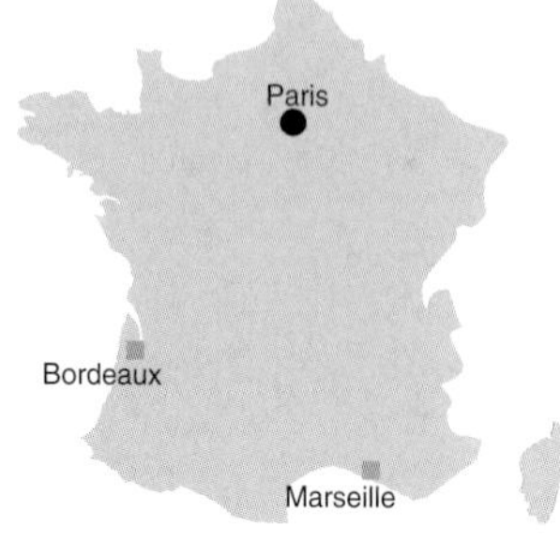

LA TRÉMOILLE

14 RUE DE LA TRÉMOILLE, 75008 PARIS, FRANCE

Recently reopened after extensive refurbishment this boutique-style hotel is now the epitome of 21st-century elegance. The bedrooms are beautifully designed in muted tones with inspiring use of fabric and equipped to a high standard (Internet access, CD and DVD players). The public rooms house a superb collection of Parisian photographic artwork. The restaurant and bar Senso offers superb French cuisine in an original setting designed by Sir Terence Conran. There is a new health and beauty centre with sauna, fitness facilities and superb treatment and massage rooms.

Récemment ré-ouvert après un programme de rénovations ce boutique hôtel est l'exemple même de l'élégance du XXIe siècle. Les chambres sont décorées dans des tons doux avec une utilisation inhabituelle des tissus et offrent un équipement très haut de gamme (accès internet, lecteur CD & DVD). Les pièces communes abritent une collection d'ouvres photographiques sur Paris. Le restaurant and bar Senso offre le meilleur de la cuisine française dans un décor original imaginé par le célèbre decorateur Sir Terence Conran. Nouveau centre de remise en forme avec sauna et des salons de beauté et de massage.

Dieses nach umfangreicher Renovierung wieder eröffnete Boutiquehotel ist nun der Inbegriff innovativer Eleganz des 21. Jahrhunderts. Die Zimmer sind mit gedämpften Tönen und interessanten Stoffen gestaltet und bieten Internetzugang, CD- und DVD-Player. Die Aufenthaltsräume beherbergen eine Sammlung Pariser Kunstfotografien. Das Restaurant und die Bar Senso bietet beste französische Küche in originellem, von Sir Terence Conran gestalteten Ambiente. Ein neues Health- und Beautyzentrum mit Sauna, Fitness und Schönheits- und Massagesalons steht zur Verfügung.

Our inspector loved: *The "Hatch" for room service without disturbance.*

Directions: Metro stations: Alma-Marceau or Franklin Roosevelt.

Web: www.johansens.com/tremoille
E mail: reservation@hotel-tremoille.com
Tel: +33 1 56 52 14 00
Fax: +33 1 40 70 01 08

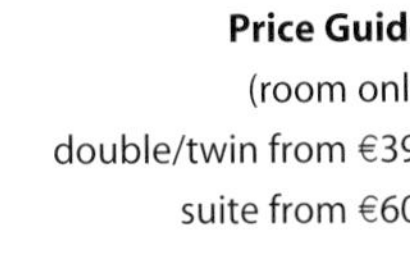

Price Guide:
(room only)
double/twin from €399
suite from €600

L'Hôtel Pergolèse

DES IGN HOT ELS

3 RUE PERGOLÈSE, 75116 PARIS, FRANCE

Directions: Close to Porte Maillot.

Web: www.johansens.com/pergolese
E-mail: hotel@pergolese.com
Tel: +33 1 53 64 04 04
Fax: +33 1 53 64 04 40

Price Guide:
single €218–273
double/twin €266–331
suite €416

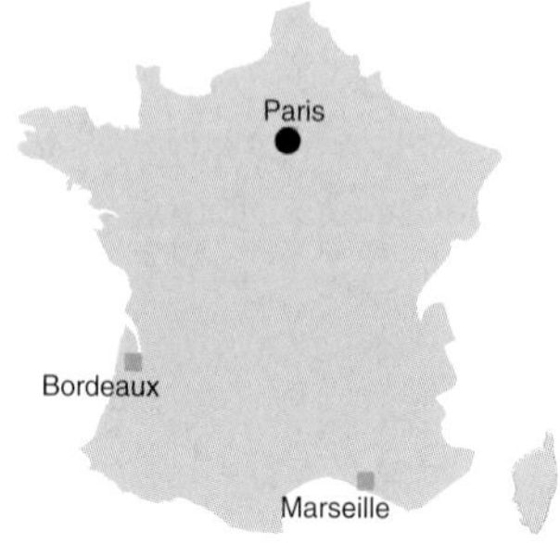

Originally a 19th-century bourgeois town house, this vibrant hotel, designed by Rena Dumas-Hermès, is the height of sophistication. The light, warmth and colour of the elegant interior leave an immediate impression on visitors, whilst the parquet floors and stylish leather chairs create a charismatic ambience. The colourful bedrooms combine serene comfort with cutting edge furnishings. Breakfast and drinks are served in the foyer, with glass walls opening onto the courtyard.

Cet hôtel particulier du XIXe siècle est aujourd'hui le comble de l'élégance. Dans cet établissement éblouissant, décoré par Rena Dumas-Hermès, les visiteurs sont d'emblée frappés par la chaleur, la clarté et les couleurs qui règnent dans les pièces distinguées et par la note charismatique apportée par le parquet et les beaux fauteuils en cuir. Confort et sérénité caractérisent les chambres aux couleurs gaies et au mobilier dernier cri. Le petit déjeuner et des rafraîchissements sont servis dans le hall dont les murs en verre s'ouvrent sur une cour intérieure.

Dieses charmante, von Rena Dumas-Hermès gestaltete Hotel war ursprünglich ein Stadthaus im 19. Jahrhundert, und ist heute der Inbegriff von Eleganz. Licht, Wärme und Farbe durchfluten das Interieur und fallen sofort ins Auge, während die Parkettböden und herrlichen Ledersessel ein gemütliches Ambiente schaffen. Die farbenfrohen Schlafzimmer verbinden Komfort und modernste Ausstattung. Frühstück und Drinks werden im Foyer serviert, dessen Glaswände den Blick auf den Innenhof freigeben.

Our inspector loved: *The superb and original "Pergolèse" suite.*

LA VILLA MAILLOT

143 AVENUE DE MALAKOFF, 75116 PARIS, FRANCE

A short walk from the Champs-Elysées, the Villa Maillot is a charming, elegant and discreet haven in the centre of Paris. Behind the façade of this unique historic residence lies a friendly, modern interior, with pastel colours, fireplace and wooden floors creating creating an atmosphere of warmth and hospitality. The bedrooms are all well appointed and have rose-coloured marble bathrooms. Breakfast, selected from the enticing buffet, may be enjoyed in the newly redesigned garden conservatory.

A deux pas des Champs-Elysées, la Villa Maillot est un havre de charme, élégant et discret au coeur de la capitale. La façade de cet ancien hôtel particulier cache un hôtel moderne et amical, avec de subtiles nuances de pastels, une cheminée et des sols de bois créant une atmosphère chaleureuse et conviviale. Les chambres sont toutes bien équipées et offrent des salles de bains en marbre rose. Un superbe buffet petit déjeuner dressé dans les salons est servi dans la verrière complètement reconçue, nichée dans un jardin.

Nur einen kurzen Spaziergang von den Champs-Élysées entfernt liegt die charmante Villa Maillot, die Eleganz und Diskretion mitten im Stadtzentrum bietet. Hinter der Fassade dieses außergewöhnlichen alten Hotels versteckt sich ein freundliches, modernes Interieur, das mit Pastellfarben, Kamin und Holzböden ein behagliches und einladendes Ambiente schafft. Die Zimmer sind alle bestens ausgestattet und verfügen über Marmorbäder in Rosétönen. Ein herrliches Frühstücksbuffet steht im Salon bereit und wird im neugestalteten Wintergarten serviert.

Our inspector loved: *The top-floor duplex suites overlooking Paris's rooftops.*

  42   12     SPA

Directions: Close to Porte Maillot.

Web: www.johansens.com/lavillamaillot
E-mail: resa@lavillamaillot.fr
Tel: +33 1 53 64 52 52
Fax: +33 1 45 00 60 61

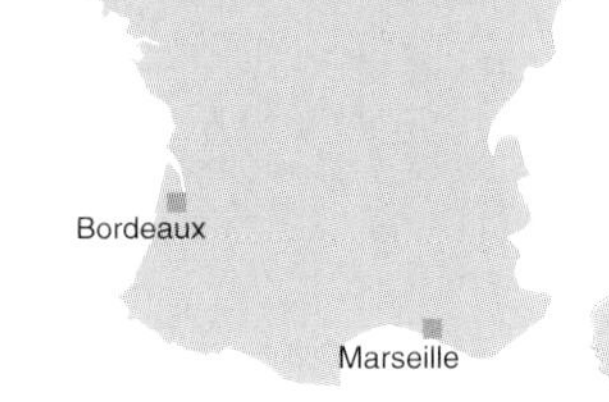

Price Guide:
(room only)
double/twin €310–360
suite €450–490

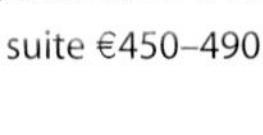

HÔTEL LE TOURVILLE

16 AVENUE DE TOURVILLE, 75007 PARIS, FRANCE

Though located in the heart of Paris, close to the Eiffel Tower, this neo-classical hotel enjoys a unique atmosphere of refined tranquillity. Soft pastel colours form a warm ambience and ideal background for the wealth of antique furniture and paintings that grace its salons and bedrooms. Guests are cosseted by the fine breakfasts served in the vaulted cellar room and the large range of toiletries that are thoughtfully provided in the marble bathrooms.

Bien qu'il se situe au coeur de Paris, à deux pas de la Tour Eiffel, cet hôtel néoclassique jouit d'une tranquillité raffinée. Les couleurs pastel créent une ambiance chaleureuse et soulignent à merveille la beauté des nombreux meubles et objets d'art anciens qui ornent les salons et les chambres. Les visiteurs choyés dégustent d'excellents petits déjeuners dans la cave voûtée et profitent du vaste choix d'articles de toilette gracieusement mis à leur disposition dans les salles de bains en marbre.

Trotz seiner Lage im Herzen von Paris und in der Nähe des Eiffelturms genießt dieses neoklassizistische Hotel eine Atmosphäre herrlicher Ruhe. Sanfte Pastellfarben schaffen ein warmes Ambiente und einen idealen Hintergrund für die Vielfalt antiker Möbel und Gemälde, welche die Salons und Schlafzimmer schmücken. Die Gäste werden durch das erlesene Frühstück im Gewölbekeller verwöhnt, des Weiteren durch das große Angebot an Toilettenartikeln, die sorgfältig ausgewählt in den Marmorbadezimmern bereitstehen.

Our inspector loved: *The superb top-floor suite.*

Directions: Between the Eiffel Tower and Les Invalides.

Web: www.johansens.com/tourville
E-mail: hotel@tourville.com
Tel: +33 1 47 05 62 62
Fax: +33 1 47 05 43 90

Price Guide:
(breakfast €12)
double/twin €150–240
junior suite €310

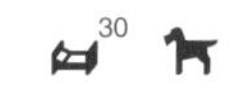

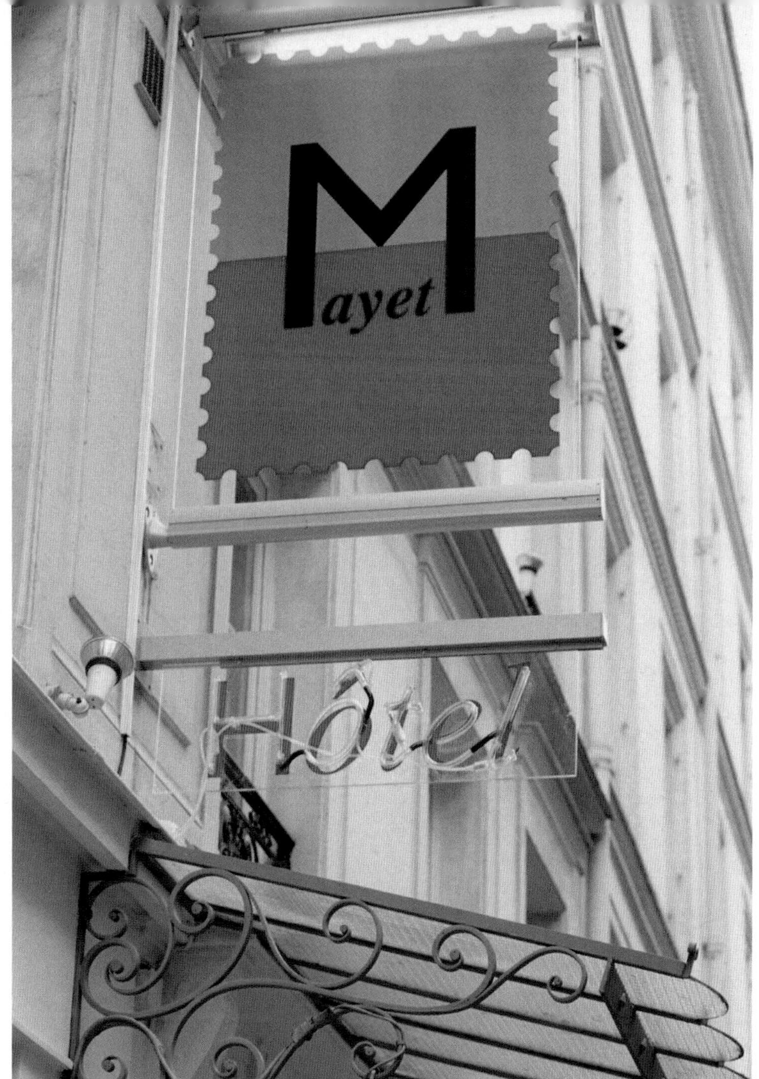

Hôtel Mayet

3 RUE MAYET, 75006 PARIS, FRANCE

Set in the heart of the vibrant Rive Gauche quarter, this beautiful small hotel is the ideal place for a young and energetic clientele, who wish to experience a relaxed yet sophisticated atmosphere. Laurence Raymond, owner of the ArtusHôtel, has decorated the entire hotel, and every detail has been thought of. The bright and comfortable bedrooms offer a modern design, including grey-and-raspberry coloured walls. Complimentary breakfast can be enjoyed in a beautiful room with vaulted ceiling and exposed stone walls, and is served on a long table d'hôte.

Situé au cœur de la rive gauche, ce petit bel hôtel est l'endroit l'idéal pour une clientèle jeune et pleine d'énergie, désirant ressentir une atmosphère détendue et sophistiquée. Laurence Raymond, propriétaire de l'ArtusHôtel a décoré tout l'hôtel et il ne manque aucun détail. Les chambres claires et confortables ont un design moderne avec des murs en gris et framboise. Le petit déjeuner est gratuit et servi sur un long table d'hôte, dans une belle salle avec plafond voûté et les murs en pierre exposés.

Dieses hübsche kleine Hotel im Herzen des lebhaften Rive Gauche ist der ideale Ort für ein junges, dynamisches Publikum, das eine gediegene und doch entspannte Atmosphäre schätzt. Laurence Raymond, Eigentümerin des ArtusHôtels, war für das Décor verantwortlich und hat dabei jedes Detail bedacht. Die hellen, komfortablen Zimmer sind modern gestaltet und haben grau und himbeerfarbene Wände. Frühstück ist inklusive und wird am Table d'hôte in einem herrlichen Raum mit hohen Decken und freiliegendem Mauerwerk serviert.

Our inspector loved: *The brilliant concept of this hotel and its lively atmosphere as well as its excellent value for money.*

 23

Directions: In the centre of Paris, close to Duroc métro station.

Web: www.johansens.com/mayet
E-mail: hotel@mayet.com
Tel: +33 1 47 83 21 35
Fax: +33 1 40 65 95 78

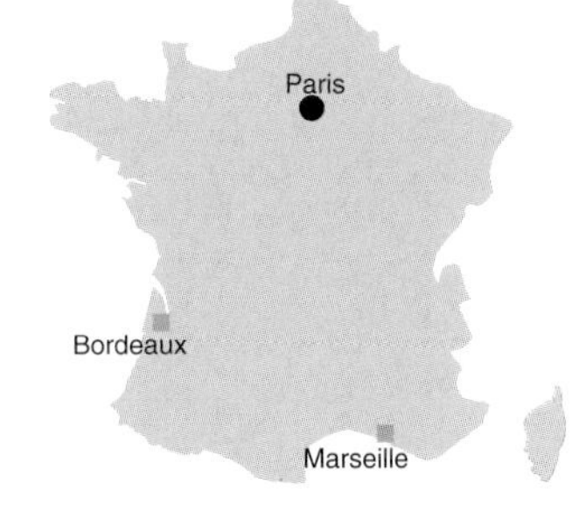

Price Guide:
room €100-140

Le Sainte~Beuve

9 RUE SAINTE~BEUVE, 75006 PARIS, FRANCE

Situated on a quiet street, this superbly renovated hotel is excellently positioned near to Saint-Germain-des-Près, Saint-Sulpice and the Jardin du Luxembourg. The charming Le Sainte-Beuve has the atmosphere of a chic Parisian home, complemented by friendly and welcoming service. The bedrooms are attractively decorated with pastel colours and antique furnishings, whilst the suite is simply beautiful. The fashionable shops and cultural attractions of central Paris are all within easy reach.

Dans une rue calme et idéalement situé près de Saint-Germain-des-Prés, Saint-Sulpice et les Jardins du Luxembourg, l'hôtel Sainte-Beuve a l'atmosphère d'une maison chic parisienne, complétée par un service amical et accueillant. Toutes les chambres sont agréablement décorées avec des couleurs pastel et un mobilier ancien, alors que la suite est tout simplement superbe. Les magasins en vogue et attractions culturelles du centre de Paris sont tous d'accès facile.

Dieses charmante, perfekt renovierte Hotel liegt in einer ruhigen Straße in der Nähe von Saint-Germain-des-Près, Saint-Sulpice und dem Jardin du Luxembourg. Die Atmosphäre ist die eines eleganten Pariser Privathauses, und wird durch den freundlichen, herzlichen Service noch verstärkt. Die Zimmer sind wunderschön mit Antiquitäten eingerichtet und in Pastellfarben gehalten, und die Suite ist einfach traumhaft. Die zahlreichen Einkaufsmöglichkeiten und kulturellen Attraktionen von Paris liegen alle in nächster Nähe.

Our inspector loved: *The warm welcome from the owner and the very friendly staff.*

Directions: Between Saint~Germain~des~Prés and Jardin du Luxembourg.

Web: www.johansens.com/saintbeuve
E-mail: saintebeuve@wanadoo.fr
Tel: +33 1 45 48 20 07
Fax: +33 1 45 48 67 52

Price Guide: (breakfast €13.50)
Rooms €126–315

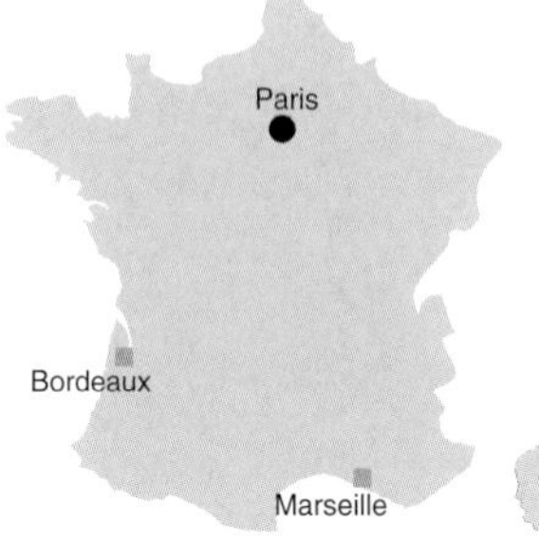

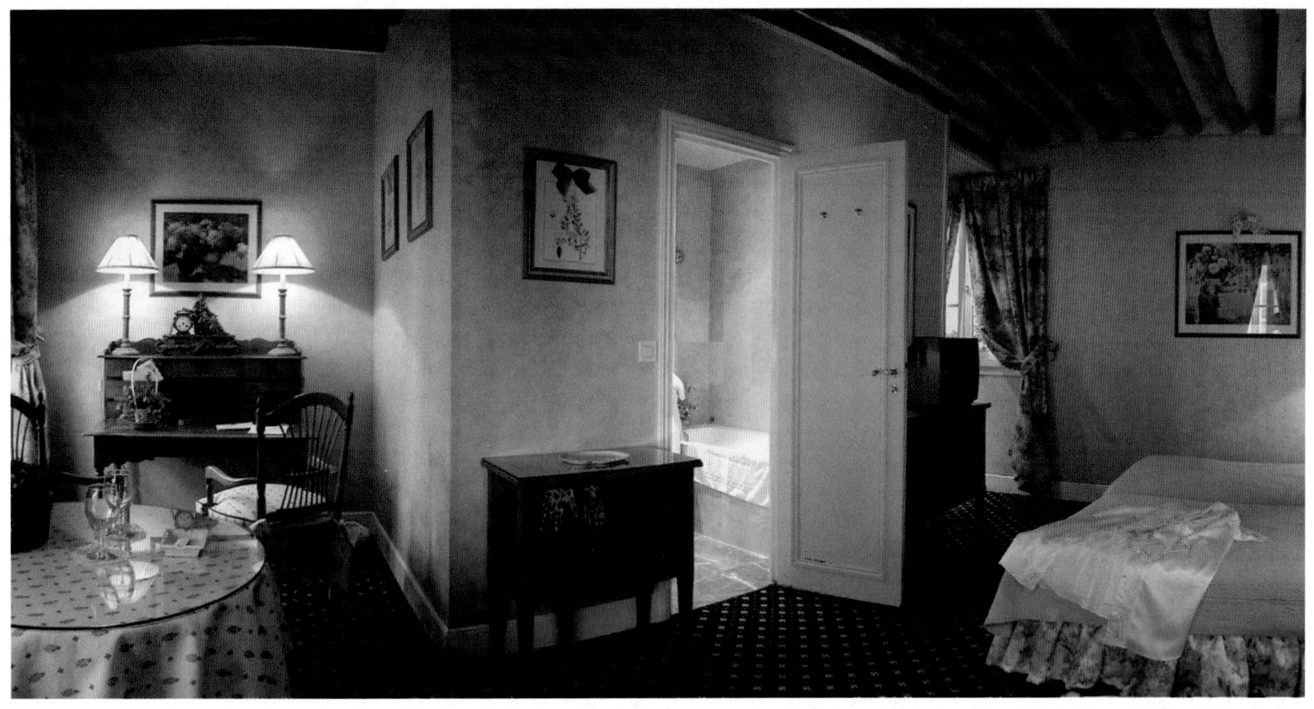

Relais Médicis***Luxe

23 RUE RACINE, 75006 PARIS, FRANCE

Tucked away just a few minutes from l'Odéon, the Jardin du Luxembourg and the Boulevard St Germain, this delightful hotel is arranged around a charming patio that is lavishly planted between April and September. Antique pieces, painted woodwork, Impressionist-style printed curtains and vintage photographs create a warm atmosphere. The 16 cosy bedrooms are surprisingly spacious and decorated with cheerful colours reminiscent of Provence and Italy; all have marble bathrooms and air conditioning. Numerous sights and attractions are within easy reach.

Situé à quelques minutes du Jardin du Luxembourg et du Boulevard St. Germain, cet hôtel de charme est construit autour d'une fontaine et d'un joli patio très fleuri des mois d'Avril à Septembre. Des meubles antiques, des boiseries peintes, des rideaux "impressionnistes" et des photos très anciennes créent une ambiance chaleureuse. Les 16 chambres sont à la fois intimes et spacieuses et sont décorées de couleurs qui rappellent celles de Provence et de l'Italie. Elles disposent toutes de salles de bain en marbre et sont climatisées. De nombreuses attractions sont d'accès facile.

Dieses zauberhafte, nur ein paar Minuten dem Jardin du Luxembourg und dem Boulevard St Germain entfernte Hotel ist um eine hübsche Terrasse herum gebaut, die von April bis September üppig bepflanzt ist. Antiquitäten, bemaltes Holz, impressionistisch bedruckte Vorhänge und alte Fotografien sorgen für ein warmes Ambiente. Die 16 gemütlichen Zimmer sind überraschend geräumig und mit bunten, an die Provence und Italien erinnernden Farben dekoriert. Alle haben Marmorbäder und Klimaanlange. Zahlreiche Sehenswürdigkeiten liegen in nächster Nähe.

Our inspector loved: *The lounge that gives the feeling of being in a private home.*

Directions: The hotel is a few yards from Place de l'Odéon and a few minutes from Boulevard Saint-Germain.

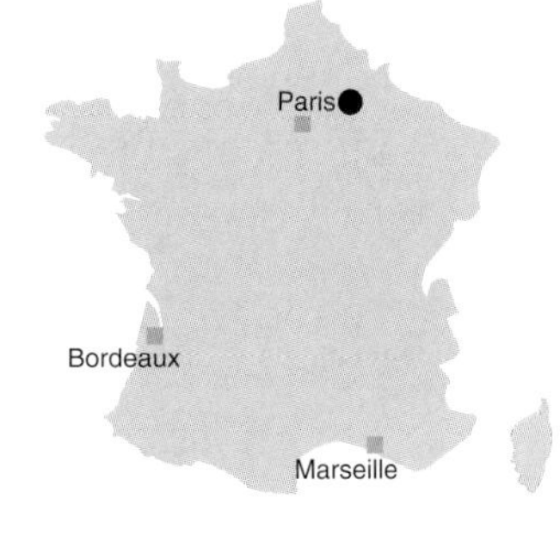

Web: www.johansens.com/medicis
Tel: +33 1 43 26 00 60
Fax: +33 1 40 46 83 39

Price Guide:
single €135-188
double €155-239
double de luxe €212-258

Hôtel de L'Arcade

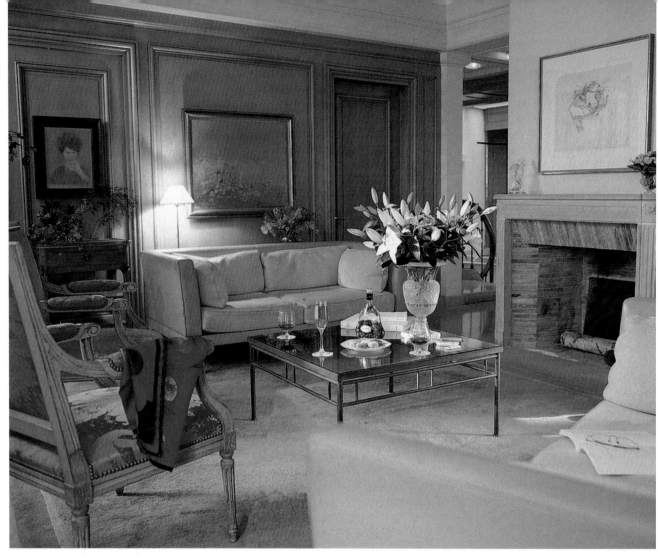

9 RUE DE L'ARCADE, 75008 PARIS, FRANCE

This 19th-century town house is ideally located just a few steps from the Opéra Gamier, the Place de la Concorde and the "grands magasins" on boulevard Haussman. This private home has been designed for those looking for discreet elegance. The subtly coloured lounges create a tranquil atmosphere, whilst the bedrooms are decorated in soft tones and have a functional design. Bathrooms boast marble and ceramic from Sardinia. Only breakfast is served here, but numerous cafés and restaurants can be found within easy reach.

L'Hôtel de l'Arcade, maison de ville du XIXe siècle, est idéalement situé à quelques minutes de l'Opéra Gamier, de la place de la Concorde et des grands magasins du boulevard Haussman. Cette maison privée a été conçue pour les amoureux à la recherche d'une élégance discrète. Décorés en couleurs subtiles, les salons créent une atmosphère de tranquillité. Les chambres en teintes douces sont lumineuses et fonctionnelles. Marbre et céramique de Sardaigne dans les salles de bains. Seul le petit-déjeuner y est servi mais de nombreux cafés et restaurants se situent dans les environs.

Dieses Stadthaus aus dem 19. Jahrhundert liegt ideal nur ein paar Minuten von der Opéra Gamier, der Place de la Concorde und den "grands magasins" des Boulevard Haussman entfernt. Dieses Privathaus ist ein Traum für diejenigen, die diskrete Eleganz lieben. Die Aufenthaltsräume sind mit subtilen, eine ruhige Atmosphäre schaffenden Farben gestaltet, und die Zimmer sind funktionell und in sanften Tönen gehalten. In den Bädern findet man Marmor und Keramik aus Sardinien. Das Hotel serviert nur Frühstück, doch zahlreiche Restaurants und Cafés liegen in nächster Nähe.

Our inspector loved: *The superb and welcoming lounge with its fireplace and bouquets of fresh flowers.*

Directions: Off Place de la Madeleine.

Web: www.johansens.com/larcade
E mail: contact@hotel-arcade.com
Tel: +33 1 53 30 60 00
Fax: +33 1 40 07 03 07

Price Guide:
single €140-163
double/twin €180
duplex apartment €215

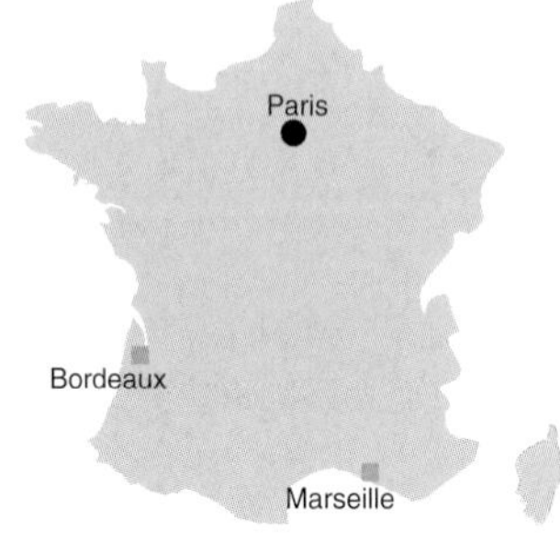

Hôtel Le Lavoisier

21 RUE LAVOISIER, 75008 PARIS, FRANCE

One of the most chic hotels in Paris, Hôtel le Lavoisier is mere minutes away from Place de la Concorde and the famous shops of the Boulevard Haussman. Well-chosen antique furniture and warm, elegant colour schemes compose a refinement that makes this hotel an ideal retreat from the busy streets of Paris. The intimacy of communal areas such as the cellar breakfast room, and the attentive service of the staff are suggestive of comforts from outside the city.

L'Hôtel Le Lavoisier, l'un des plus chics de Paris, n'est qu'à quelques minutes de la place de la Concorde et des célèbres magasins du boulevard Haussmann. Les meubles anciens choisis avec soin et les couleurs élégantes et chaleureuses du décor créent une ambiance raffinée qui fait de cet hôtel un refuge idéal pour échapper à la fébrilité des rues parisiennes. L'intimité des salles communes, telles que la petite salle à manger occupant la cave, et la prévenance du personnel évoquent le charme des hôtels provinciaux.

Dieses nur wenige Minuten vom Place de la Concorde und den Geschäften des Boulevard Haussman entfernt gelegene Hotel ist eines der elegantesten von Paris. Geschmackvolles, antikes Mobiliar und warme, elegante Farben schaffen eine erlesene Atmosphäre, die dieses Hotel zu einer Oase inmitten der geschäftigen Straßen von Paris macht. Die Abgeschiedenheit der Aufenthaltsräume, z. B. des Frühstücksraums im Kellergewölbe, sowie aufmerksamster Service bieten einen Komfort, wie man ihn sonst nur außerhalb der Stadt erwarten würde.

Our inspector loved: *The superb decoration of the lounge including the 19th-century paintings of children.*

Directions: Near Place Saint-Augustin.

Web: www.johansens.com/lelavoisier
E-mail: info@hotellavoisier.com
Tel: +33 1 53 30 06 06
Fax: +33 1 53 30 23 00

Price Guide:
double/twin €215–230
suite €285–415

30

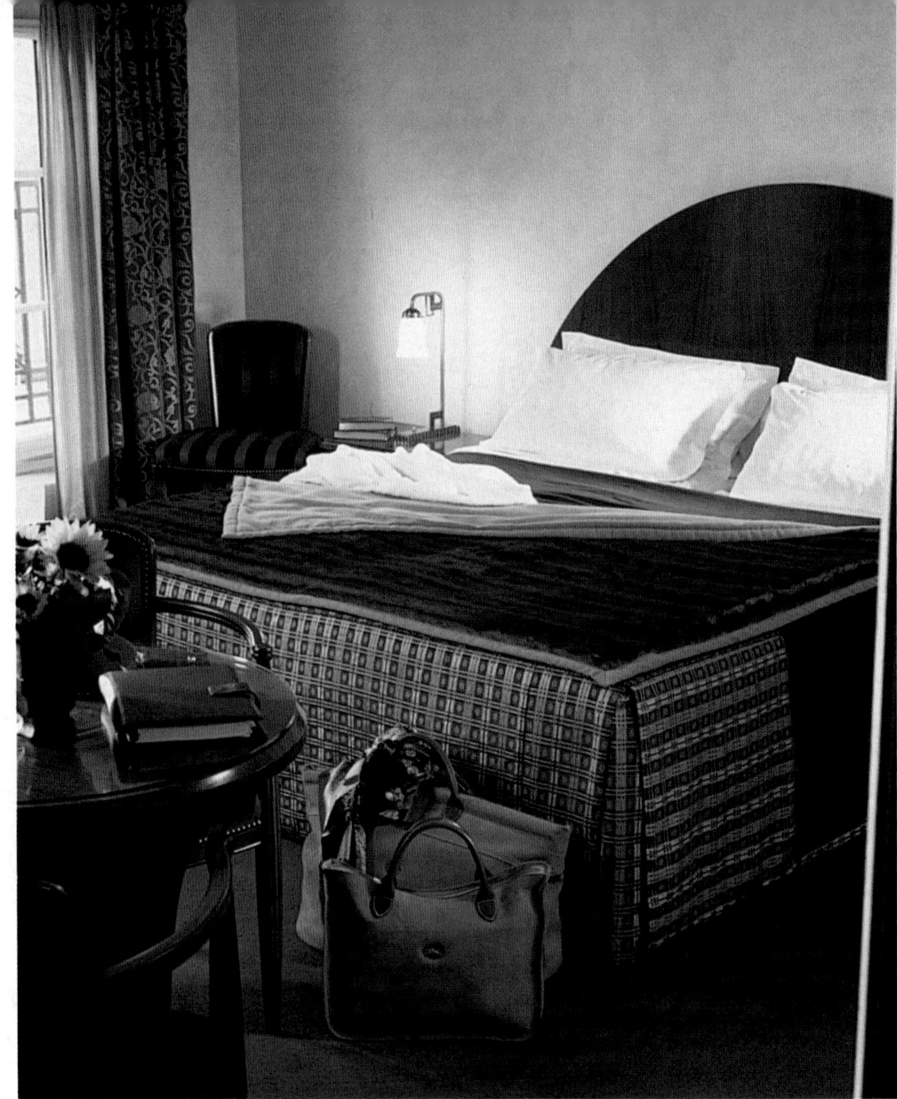

Hôtel Opéra Richepanse

14 RUE DU CHEVALIER DE SAINT-GEORGE, 75001 PARIS, FRANCE

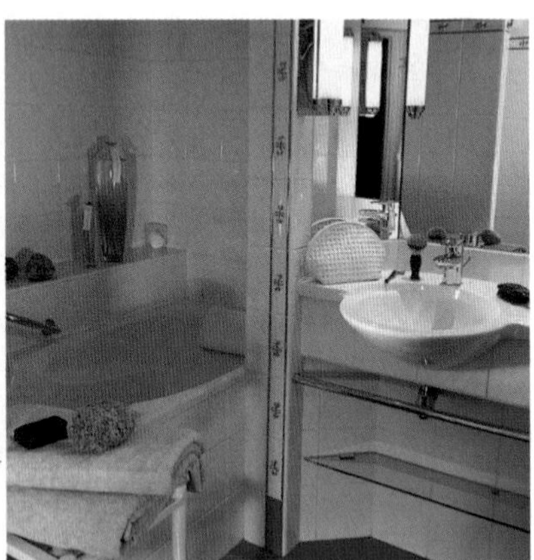

Directions: Centrally located, near to la Madeleine and Place de la Concorde.

Web: www.johansens.com/richepanse
E-mail: richepanseotel@wanadoo.fr
Tel: +33 (0) 1 42 60 36 00
Fax: +33 (0) 1 42 60 13 03

Price Guide:
(room only)
double €230-420
suite €450-708

In the heart of old Paris, this refined and private hotel is within close proximity to rue du Faubourg St Honoré, Place de la Concorde, Place de la Madeleine, Louvre Museum and Place Vendôme. Rooms and suites have been furnished in art deco style with warm, relaxing colours. Guests are entitled to complimentary use of the sauna and staff will organise all business and leisure schedules such as theatre tickets, restaurant bookings and sightseeing trips. This is an ideal base from which to explore Parisian delights.

Au cœur du vieux Paris, ce petit hôtel raffiné est proche rue du Faubourg St Honoré, Place de la Concorde, Place de la Madeleine, Musée du Louvre and Place Vendôme. Les chambres et les suites sont meublées d'un style art déco dans des couleurs chaudes et relaxantes. Les hôtes ont accès au sauna et le personnel organisera vos programmes affaires et loisirs tels que billets de théâtre, réservations restaurant et visites. C'est la base idéale d'où explorer les plaisirs parisiens.

Dieses elegante, private Hotel im Herzen des alten Paris liegt nahe der Rue Faubourg St Honoré, Place de la Concorde, Place de la Madeleine, dem Louvre und Place Vendôme. Die Zimmer und Suiten sind im Art-Deco-Stil mit warmen, entspannenden Farben gestaltet. Eine Sauna steht zur Verfügung, und das Personal hilft bei der Organisierung von Geschäfts- und Freizeitaktivitäten, wie z.B. Buchungen von Theaterkarten, Restaurants und Stadtrundfahrten. Der ideale Ausgangspunkt für Erkundungsgänge.

Our inspector loved: *The breakfast room with its superb vaulted ceiling.*

Victoria Palace Hôtel

6, RUE BLAISE DESGOFFE, 75006 PARIS, FRANCE

Conveniently situated on the left bank, within walking distance of most tourist sights in the city, this charming hotel has friendly, attentive staff and an atmosphere of luxury and elegance. Beautiful public rooms are decorated in a traditional Victorian style with eye-catching colour schemes, comfortable furniture and stunning works of art. A delicious buffet breakfast is served and there is also a 24-hour concierge service. The hotel is ideally situated for exploring the city's numerous attractions.

Bien situé sur la rive gauche, avec les attractions touristiques d'accès facile à pied, cet hôtel charmant a un personnel accueillant qui répond au moindre désir des clients et une ambiance de luxe et d'élégance. Les belles salles publiques sont décorées en style traditionnel victorien avec une combinaison de couleurs qui tire l'œil, des meubles confortables et des œuvres d'art magnifiques. Le petit déjeuner-buffet est servi et il y a un service concierge disponible 24h/24. L'hôtel est parfaitement situé pour explorer les nombreuses attractions de la ville.

Dieses charmante Hotel mit seiner günstigen Lage am linken Seineufer und nicht weit von zahlreichen Attraktionen der Stadt entfernt bietet freundliches, aufmerksames Personal und eine Atmosphäre von Luxus und Eleganz. Die herrlichen Aufenthaltsräume sind traditionell viktorianisch mit auffallenden Farben gestaltet und mit bequemen Möbeln und eindrucksvollen Kunstwerken gefüllt. Das Frühstück ist ein verlockendes Buffet, und ein Concierge steht rund um die Uhr zur Verfügung. Das Hotel liegt ideal, um die vielen Sehenswürdigkeiten von Paris zu erkunden.

Our inspector loved: *The beautifully decorated bedrooms each with superb paintings.*

Directions: The hotel is situated between rue de Renner and rue de Vaugirard, close to Saint Placide tube station.

Web: www.johansens.com/victoriapalace
E-mail: info@victoriapalace.com
Tel: +33 1 45 49 70 00
Fax: +33 1 45 49 23 75

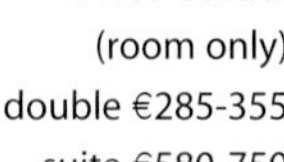

Price Guide:
(room only)
double €285-355
suite €580-750

Hôtel des Grands Hommes

17 PLACE DU PANTHÉON, 75005 PARIS, FRANCE

Situated next door to the Panthéon in the heart of Paris, this enchanting hotel is elegant and welcoming. Delightful public rooms are filled with antiques, precious woodwork and fine fabrics to create a serene ambience and stylish bedrooms are decorated in the Empire style. Terraces and balconies on the top floor bedrooms have beautiful views of the Panthéon and the Sacré Coeur.

Au cœur de Paris, à côté du Panthéon, ce charmant hôtel est élégant et accueillant. Les plaisantes salles publics sont décorées avec des antiquités, de précieuses oeuvres d'ébénisterie, et de belles draperies créant une ambiance sereine, et les chambres raffinées sont du style Empire. Les terrasses et balcons des chambres du dernier étage ont vue sur le Panthéon et le Sacré Coeur.

Dieses bezaubernde Hotel im Herzen von Paris besitzt eine elegante, herzliche Atmosphäre. Die Aufenthaltsräume sind mit Antiquitäten, kostbarer Holzverzierung und edlen Stoffen geschmückt, die Zimmer sind im Empirestil gestaltet. Von den Terrassen und Balkonen im obersten Stockwerk hat man eine herrliche Sicht auf das Panthéon und Sacré Coeur.

Our inspector loved: *The top floor bedrooms with little balconies that overlook the Panthéon; ideal for a romantic breakfast.*

Directions: Close to Jardin du Luxembourg.

Web: www.johansens.com/hoteldesgrandshommes
E-mail: reservation@hoteldesgrandshommes.com
Tel: +33 1 46 34 19 60
Fax: +33 1 43 26 67 32

Price Guide:
single €168–213
double €183–213
triple €244
suite €275–382

Hôtel du Panthéon

19 Place du Panthéon, 75005 Paris, France

Overlooking the Panthéon, this recently refurbished hotel has the comfortable and refined ambience of an 18th-century French town house. Great attention to detail has been paid to the tastefully decorated bedrooms, each of which offering a completely different colour scheme, style and atmosphere. The Jardin du Luxembourg is just 200 metres away, and, due to its central location, this exquisite hotel is the ideal base from which to explore Paris with its numerous sights and attractions.

Cet hôtel récemment réaménagé connaît le confort et le raffinement des hôtels particuliers français du XVIIIe siècle. Les chambres, qui se distinguent les unes des autres par des coloris, un style et une ambiance très différents, sont décorées avec goût et témoignent d'un grand souci du détail. Faisant face au Panthéon, à 200 mètres seulement du Jardin du Luxembourg, ce charmant établissement jouit d'une situation centrale idéale pour explorer Paris et ses nombreuses attractions,

Dieses erst kürzlich renovierte Hotel mit Blick auf das Panthéon besitzt die gemütliche und elegante Atmosphäre eines französischen Stadthauses aus dem 18. Jahrhundert. Die geschmackvoll eingerichteten Zimmer zeigen viel Liebe zum Detail, und jedes hat seinen eigenen Stil, Farben und Atmosphäre. Der Jardin du Luxembourg ist nur 200 Meter entfernt, und die zentrale Lage dieses exquisiten Hotels macht es zu einem idealen Ausgangspunkt für die vielen Sehenswürdigkeiten und Attraktionen von Paris.

Our inspector loved: *The beautifully designed and intimate bedrooms.*

Directions: Close to Jardin du Luxembourg.

Web: www.johansens.com/hoteldupantheon
E-mail: reservation@hoteldupantheon.com
Tel: +33 1 43 54 32 95
Fax: +33 1 43 26 64 65

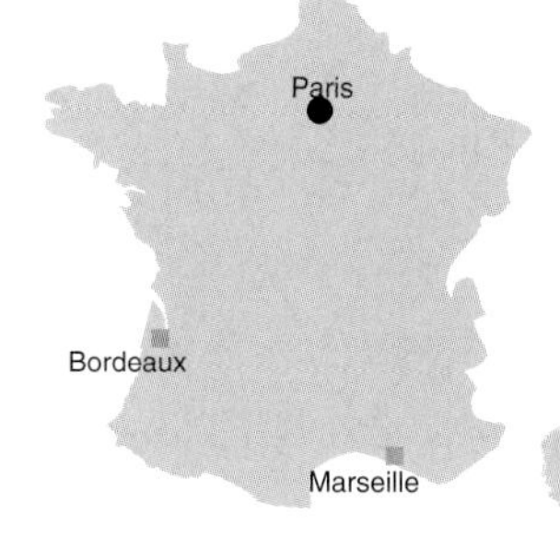

Price Guide:
single €168–213
double/twin €168–213
triple €198–229

FRANCE / PARIS (SAINT~GERMAIN)

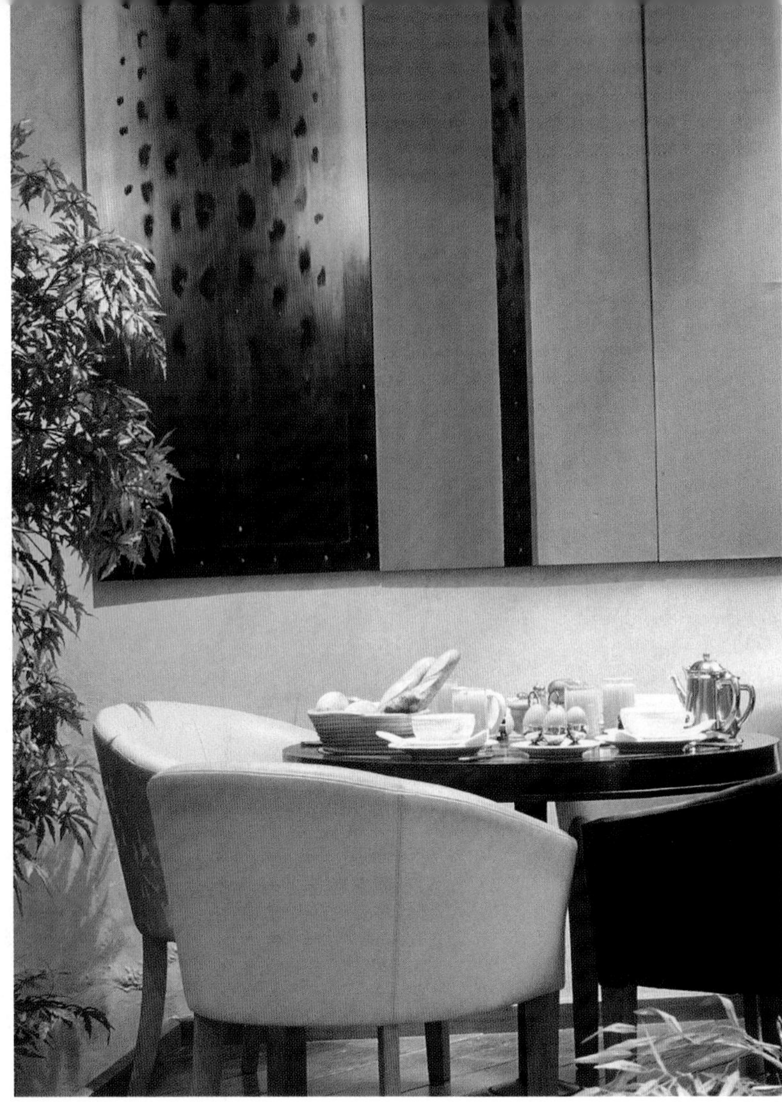

ArtusHôtel

DES IGN HOT ELS

34 RUE DE BUCI, 75006 PARIS, FRANCE

Regular Francophiles visiting the ArtusHôtel will be reassured to learn that only the name has changed from its former Buci Latin. The same attentive team are still on hand to attend to guests' every whim, whilst the intriguing and stylish décor remains undisturbed. Situated in the heart of the Latin quarter, the atmosphere is truly vibrant and exhilarating.

Les francophiles habitués de l'ArtusHôtel seront rassurés d'apprendre que seulement le nom de l'ancien Buci Latin a changé. La même équipe attentive est toujours là pour satisfaire les caprices des hôtes dans un décor toujours aussi chic et fascinant. Situé au cœur du Quartier Latin, l'atmosphère est réellement stimulante et vibrante.

Treue Gäste dieses Hotels können beruhigt aufatmen: es handelt sich um das altvertraute Buci Latin, lediglich der Name hat sich geändert. Das gleiche aufmerksame Personal steht zur Verfügung, und auch das faszinierende, stilvolle Décor hat sich nicht verändert. Mit seiner Lage im Herzen des Quartier Latin bietet dieses Hotel eine wundervoll lebhafte und mitreissende Atmosphäre.

Our inspector loved: *The bedroom doors, which have each been designed and decorated by a modern artist.*

Directions: Saint-Germain-des-Prés is the nearest metro.

Web: www.johansens.com/artushotel
E-mail: info@artushotel.com
Tel: +33 1 43 29 07 20
Fax: +33 1 43 29 67 44

Price Guide:
double/twin €190–235
suites €300–320

FRANCE / PARIS (SAINT~GERMAIN)

Hôtel Le Saint~Grégoire

43 RUE DE L'ABBÉ GRÉGOIRE, 75006 PARIS, FRANCE

Set at the heart of the Rive Gauche, this small 18th-century hotel offers guests refined elegance in a tranquil environment. Overlooking the interior garden, the charming lobby with an open fire becomes a cosy retreat during winter. 20 unique bedrooms are adorned with period paintings and antiques and offer every modern amenity. Guests enjoy an imaginative breakfast in the stonewall cellar before exploring the Saint Germain quarter.

Situé en plein coeur de la Rive Gauche, cet hôtel du XVIIIe siècle offre à ses visiteurs une élégance raffinée dans un environnement tranquille. Surplombant le jardin intérieur, le charmant hall de réception est encore plus attrayant en hiver avec son feu de cheminée. Les 20 chambres, toutes uniques, sont décorées de peintures d'époques et d'antiquités et offrent tout le confort moderne. Les hôtes peuvent déguster un petit déjeuner imaginatif dans la salle voutée aux murs de pierre, avant d'explorer le quartier Saint-Germain.

Mitten im Herzen des rechten Seine-Ufers gelegen bietet dieses kleine Hotel aus dem 18. Jahrhundert subtile Eleganz in einer ruhigen Umgebung. Der auf den Garten blickende Empfangsraum sorgt mit seinem offenen Kaminfeuer im Winter für Behaglichkeit. 20 einzigartige Zimmer sind mit Bildern und Antiquitäten des 18. Jahrhunderts geschmückt und bieten modernsten Komfort. Im Kellergeschoss mit seinen Steinwänden genießt man ein einfallsreiches Frühstück, bevor Saint Germain mit seinen vielen Attraktionen lockt.

Our inspector loved: *The manager's warm welcome and the feeling of entering a private home.*

Directions: Near Rue du Bac.

Web: www.johansens.com/saintgregoire
E-mail: hotel@saintgregoire.com
Tel: 33 1 45 48 23 23
Fax: +33 1 45 48 33 95

Price Guide:
single €175
double/twin €215
suite €248

Hôtel Pont Royal

7 RUE DE MONTALEMBERT, 75007 PARIS, FRANCE

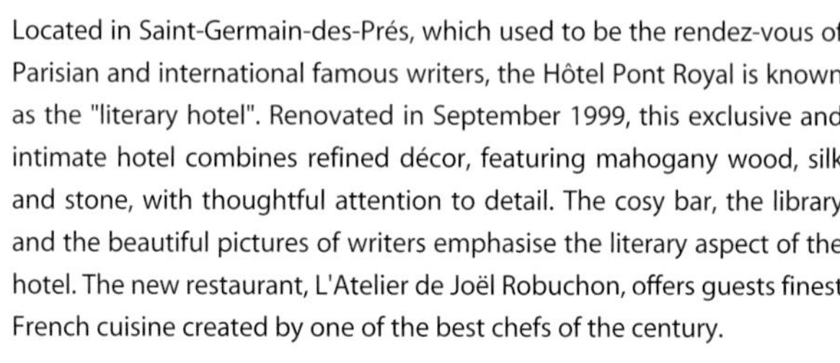

Located in Saint-Germain-des-Prés, which used to be the rendez-vous of Parisian and international famous writers, the Hôtel Pont Royal is known as the "literary hotel". Renovated in September 1999, this exclusive and intimate hotel combines refined décor, featuring mahogany wood, silk and stone, with thoughtful attention to detail. The cosy bar, the library and the beautiful pictures of writers emphasise the literary aspect of the hotel. The new restaurant, L'Atelier de Joël Robuchon, offers guests finest French cuisine created by one of the best chefs of the century.

Situé à Saint-Germain-des-Prés, longtemps renommé pour être le rendez-vous des Arts et des Lettres où se sont succédés les Prix Nobels, l'Hôtel Pont Royal se distingue par son raffinement intérieur et son savoir accueillir. Complètement renové en 1999, le mariage des soies, de l'acajou et du travertin est en harmonie avec son passé littéraire dont témoignent les portraits d'écrivains célèbres et le splendide salon bibliothèque. Son nouveau restaurant, L'Atelier de Joël Robuchon, offre la possibilité de goûter à l'exquise cuisine gastronomique de l'un des plus grands chef de ce siècle.

Dieses 1999 komplett renovierte "Literaturhotel" liegt mitten in Saint-Germain, dem einstigen Treffpunkt der Pariser und internationalen Literaturszene. Das exklusive, familiäre Hotel bietet eine harmonische und elegante Verbindung von Seide, Mahagoni und Stein mit viel Liebe zum Detail. Die gemütliche Bar, die Bibliothek und viele Portraits berühmter Schriftsteller betonen das literarische Ambiente. Im neuen Restaurant L'Atelier kreiert Chefkoch Joël Robuchon, einer der besten Köche des Jahrhunderts, feinste französische Küche.

Our inspector loved: *The top floor suite overlooking the Paris rooftops.*

Directions: Metro Rue du Bac.

Web: www.johansens.com/pontroyal
E-mail: hpr@hotel-pont-royal.com
Tel: +33 1 42 84 70 00
Fax: +33 1 42 84 71 00

Price Guide:
(breakfast €26)
classic room €370
de luxe room €420
suite €570–1,000
Special conditions for Johansens website users.

Paris
Bordeaux
Marseille

 75   15    

L' HÔTEL

13, RUE DES BEAUX ARTS, 75006 PARIS, FRANCE

Brimming with history, L'Hôtel was once visited by artists and other distinguished guests. Today a magnificent refurbishment keeps its spirit alive with stunning effect. Enchanting bedrooms, each with their own theme and style, descend from the magnificent skylight which looks out into the Paris sky. The sophisticated public rooms are superbly decorated; especially in the intimate bar and gourmet restaurant, Le Bélier, with its patio and fountain. Downstairs, a swimming pool reminiscent of old Roman hot baths awaits guests.

Lieu historique, l'hôtel était autrefois privilégié par les artistes et autres hôtes de marque. Récemment rénové, il a préservé son esprit de manière remarquable. Des chambres enchanteresses, chacune avec son propre thème et style, sont disposées sous la magnifique coupole qui s'ouvre sur le ciel de Paris. Les pièces communes sont décorées avec sophistication; surtout un bar intime et le restaurant gastronomique, Le Bélier, son patio et fontaine. Au sous-sol, une piscine qui évoque les vieux Bains chauds romains est à la disposition des hôtes.

Das geschichtsträchtige L'Hôtel wurde einst von Künstlern und anderen distinguierten Gästen besucht. Durch gekonnte Renovierung blieb der alte Geist des Hauses erhalten. Zauberhafte, nach unterschiedlichen Motiven gestaltete Zimmer reihen sich um ein fantastisches Deckenfenster mit Blick auf den Pariser Himmel. Die eleganten Aufenthaltsräume sind wundervoll eingerichtet, vor allem die gemütliche Bar und das Gourmetrestaurant Le Bélier mit Terrasse und Springbrunnen. Ein Swimmingpool, der an römische Thermen erinnert, steht zur Verfügung.

Our inspector loved: *The little swimming pool designed and decorated like a Roman bath.*

Directions: Saint-Germain-des-Prés is the nearest Métro.

Web: www.johansens.com/lhotel
E-mail: reservation@l-hotel.com
Tel: +33 1 44 41 99 00
Fax: +33 1 43 25 64 81

Price Guide:
double €248–625
suite €529–625
apartment €625–721

Hostellerie Abbaye des Vaux de Cernay

78720 CERNAY~LA~VILLE, FRANCE

Situated within the stunning Rambouillet Forest, this breathtaking former Cistercian abbey is a haven of peace and tranquillity, lovingly restored with original period features and glorious architecture. Galleried landings lead to spacious bedrooms with superb décor and views over well-kept grounds. The stone vaulted bar, lounge and restaurant make dining a romantic experience. Tennis, hunting and fishing are available, and guests can relax in the hotel's sauna, Jacuzzi or the outdoor swimming pool.

Situé au sein de la belle forêt domaniale de Rambouillet, cette ancienne abbaye cistercienne est un havre de paix et de tranquillité, restaurée avec passion avec les caractéristiques d'époque et son architecture sensationnelle. Des paliers en galerie conduisent à des chambres spacieuses, superbement décorées et avec vue sur le parc parfaitement entretenu. Le bar, salon et restaurant situés sous les voûtes de pierre, rendent le dîner en une expérience romantique. Les hôtes peuvent profiter du tennis, de la chasse et pêche ou se détendre dans le sauna, le jacuzzi ou la piscine extérieure.

Diese inmitten des herrlichen Rambouillet-Forsts gelegene Zisterzienserabtei ist eine Oase der Ruhe und Beschaulichkeit, liebevoll mit Stildetails und atemberaubender Architektur restauriert. Galerien führen in geräumige, zauberhaft gestaltete Gästezimmer mit Blick auf die gepflegten Ländereien. Die Bar mit ihren Steingewölben, der Aufenthaltsraum und das Restaurant schaffen ein romantisches Ambiente. Tennis, Jagd und Angeln stehen auf dem Programm, und zur Entspannung gibt es Sauna, Jacuzzi und Freibad.

Our inspector loved: *Wandering around the ruins of the former abbey.*

Directions: A10 > exit Les Ulis > N10 > exit Le Perray.

Web: www.johansens.com/abbayedesvauxdecernay
E-mail: cernay@leshotelsparticuliers.com
Tel: +33 1 34 85 23 00
Fax: +33 1 34 85 11 60

Price Guide:
(room only)
double €96–260
suite €330–590

LE MANOIR DE GRESSY

77410 GRESSY~EN~FRANCE, ROISSY CDG, NR PARIS, FRANCE

Built on the site of a 17th-century fortified farmhouse, Le Manoir de Gressy is a restful country retreat that recreates the cosy atmosphere of an old-fashioned inn. Whether you choose to relax by the pool or cycle through the countryside, the Manoir's tranquil surroundings offer respite from the bustle of everyday life. On the terrace, a selection of the very best fresh produce form the market is served. The luxuriously appointed bedrooms are charmingly decorated and look out over the pool and landscaped courtyard garden.

Sur le site d'une ferme fortifiée du XVIIe siècle, le Manoir vous offre un cadre reposant à la campagne. Redécouvrez l'atmosphère feutrée d'une étape d'autrefois. A bicyclette le long des chemins de halage ou bien autour de la piscine, le Manoir de Gressy offre un cadre privilégié à tous ceux qui désirent oublier leur vie trépidante. Dans une ambiance chaleureuse, dégustez une sélection des meilleurs produits du marché sur la terrasse. Les chambres raffinées, d'un charme et d'un luxe discret, s'ouvrent toutes sur la piscine et le jardin intérieur paysager.

An der Stelle eines befestigten Landgutes aus dem 17. Jahrhundert befindet sich das idyllische Manoir de Gressy. Hier fühlt man sich wahrlich in eine vergangene Zeit zurückversetzt. Ob man mit dem Fahrrad die Gegend erkundet oder sich am Pool erholt, hier findet man Ruhe vom hektischen Alltagsleben. In herzlicher Atmosphäre wird auf der Terrasse eine verlockende Auswahl an frischen Produkten vom Markt serviert. Die zauberhaften, eleganten Zimmer bieten diskreten Luxus und alle haben Blick auf den Pool und den gepflegten Garten.

Our inspector loved: *The courtyard garden and the pool.*

Directions: Paris > A1 or A3 > A104, N2 > D212 > Gressy.

Web: www.johansens.com/manoirdegressy
Tel: +33 1 60 26 68 00
Fax: +33 1 60 26 45 46

Price Guide:
(room only)
single/double €210–265
suite €265

CHÂTEAU D'ESCLIMONT

28700 ST. SYMPHORIEN~LE~CHÂTEAU, FRANCE

Directions: A11 exit 1 > Ablis > direction of Chartres.

Web: www.johansens.com/esclimont
E-mail: esclimont@grandesetapes.fr
Tel: +33 2 37 31 15 15
Fax: +33 2 37 31 57 91

Price Guide:
rooms €170–412
double €170–412
suite €620–1,090

A French château as it should be - tranquil moat, colourful gardens, picturesque towers, acres of parkland, large lake. And inside, high ceiling rooms, period elegance and delicate décor reminiscent of d'Esclimont's original 15th to 16th-century era. Spacious en-suite guest rooms have every comfort, whilst excellent cuisine is prepared by leading chef Olivier Dupart with inventive pre-dinner cocktails served by master barman Jean Jacques Venneugges.

Un château français comme il se doit. Des douves tranquilles, des jardins colorés, des tours pittoresques, des hectares de parc, un grand lac. Et à l'intérieur, des hauts plafonds, une élégance d'époque et un décor délicat évocateurs de l'original Esclimont du XVe et XVIe siècles. Les chambres spacieuses ont tout le confort. Une cuisine excellente est préparée par le chef Olivier Dupart avec des cocktails d'apéritifs inventifs servis par le barman Jean Jacques Venneugges.

Genau so sollte ein französisches Château aussehen: ein ruhiger Burggraben, farbenprächtige Gärten, malerische Türmchen, weite Parklandschaft und ein großer See, und im Inneren hohe Decken, Eleganz vergangener Zeiten und erlesenes Décor, das an Esclimonts Zeit im 15. und 16. Jahrhundert erinnert. Die geräumigen Zimmer mit eigenen Bädern bieten jeglichen Komfort. Chefkoch Olivier Dupart kreiert exzellente Speisen, und vor dem Abendessen serviert Bartender Jean Jacques Venneugges einfallsreiche Cocktails.

Our inspector loved: *Room 12 with its round bed.*

Hostellerie Château du Maréchal de Saxe

DOMAINE DE LA GRANGE, 91330 YERRES, FRANCE

This historic château sits at the end of an imposing drive, and within 65 hectares of glorious parkland. Perfectly proportioned, it has recently undergone a total refurbishment. Now its restaurant and rooms have been re-opened so guests can enjoy the stunning high-ceilinged lounge, intimate dining salons and large, elegant bedrooms. Attentive staff are on hand to attend to every need, and golf and horse riding are available nearby. The city of Paris with its numerous attractions lies just 20km north west of the château.

Ce château se situe au bout d'une allée imposante, et au sein d'un superbe parc privé de 65 ha. Avec une architecture parfaitement proportionnée, il a récemment été complètement restauré. Son restaurant et ses chambres ont maintenant réouvert et ses hôtes peuvent apprécier son salon à plafond haut, ses salles à manger intimes et ses grandes chambres élégantes. Un personnel attentif est à disposition pour satisfaire les moindres désirs des invités, et golf et équitation sont disponibles tout près. Paris et ses nombreuses attractions ne se trouvent qu'à 20 km au nord-ouest de château.

Dieses historische, kürzlich komplett renovierte Schloss liegt am Ende einer imposanten Auffahrt, inmitten von 65ha herrlicher Parklandschaft. Restaurant und Zimmer sind nun für Gäste geöffnet, und man kann den beeindruckenden Aufenthaltsraum mit seiner hohen Decke, die gemütlichen Speisesäle und die großzügigen, eleganten Gästezimmer bewundern. Aufmerksames Personal erfüllt jeden Wunsch. Golf und Reiten sind in der Nähe möglich, und Paris mit seinen zahlreichen Attraktionen liegt nur 20km nordwestlich vom Schloss.

Our inspector loved: *The ground-floor suite; graceful and elegant.*

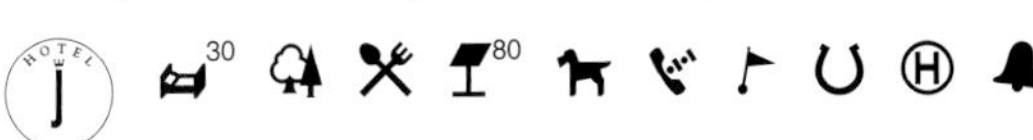

Directions: N19 > D941 > the entrance is to the left of roundabout.

Web: www.johansens.com/marechaldesaxe
E-mail: saxe@leshotelsparticuliers.com
Tel: +33 1 69 48 78 53
Fax: +33 1 69 83 84 91

Price Guide:
double/twin €122–244
suite €275–382

Château de L'Yeuse

65 RUE DE BELLEVUE, QUARTIER DE ECHASSIER, 16100 CHÂTEAUBERNARD, FRANCE

Directions: N141 from Angoulème > turn right in the direction of L'Echassier.

Web: www.johansens.com/chateaudelyeuse
E-mail: reservations.yeuse@wanadoo.fr
Tel: +33 5 45 36 82 60
Fax: +33 5 45 35 06 32

Price Guide:
(room only)
single €89–153
double €89–153
suite €199–305

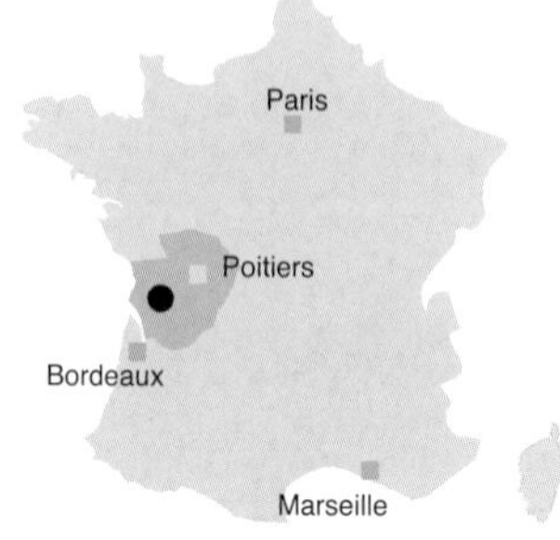

Perfectly enlarged and restored with tasteful interiors, the château's superb décor includes wonderful furnishings and fabrics. Beautiful suites have stunning views across the park, the river Charente and surrounding countryside and are adjoined by spacious, well-equipped bathrooms. In the elegant high-ceilinged dining room attentive staff serve inventive local cuisine. There is an outdoor pool and indoor Jacuzzi and sauna, and guests can choose to relax on the large sun terrace or beneath the shade of the ancient oak trees, or "Yeuses".

Agrandie et restaurée parfaitement avec goût, le superbe décor du Château inclut un fantastique ameublement et tissus. Les suites superbes, avec salle de bain contiguë spacieuse et parfaitement équipée, ont une vue imprenable sur le parc, la Charente et la campagne environnante. Dans l'élégante salle à manger à hauts plafonds, un personnel attentif sert une cuisine locale inventive. Les hôtes peuvent choisir d'utiliser la piscine extérieure ou le jacuzzi en salle, ou encore de se détendre sur la grande terrasse ensoleillée ou à l'ombre des vieux chênes appelés Yeuses.

Dieses restaurierte, erweiterte Schloss besitzt ein geschmackvolles Interieur mit einem Décor aus wundervollen Einrichtungen und Stoffen. Die Suiten bieten herrliche Ausblicke auf den Park, den Fluss Charente und die Umgebung und haben geräumige Bäder. Im eleganten Speisesaal serviert aufmerksames Personal kreative regionale Küche. Ein Außenswimmingpool sowie ein Jacuzzi und eine Sauna stehen zur Verfügung, und man kann sich auf der großen Sonnenterrasse oder im Schatten der alten Eichenbäume („Yeuses") entspannen.

Our inspector loved: *The extensive and adventurous wine list.*

FRANCE / POITOU~CHARENTES (POITIERS – SAINT~MAIXENT~L'ECOLE)

LOGIS ST. MARTIN

CHEMIN DE PISSOT, 79400 SAINT~MAIXENT~L'ECOLE, FRANCE

Renowned for its excellent gastronomic restaurant, this charmingly restored 17th-century manor is nestled in the peaceful surroundings of the beautiful Poitou valley. Delicious and inventive cuisine is served in the elegant dining room, complemented by fine wines and great vintages, rare liquors and a choice of cigars. Friendly and attentive staff cater for every need. Guests may relax on the terrace or explore the beautiful countryside and enjoy golf, horse riding and fishing.

Réputé pour son excellent restaurant gastronomique, ce charmant pavillon restauré du XVIIe siècle est niché au calme dans la superbe vallée du Poitou. La cuisine délicieuse et inventive est servie dans l'élégante salle à manger et est agrémentée de vins fins, de grands crus, de digestifs uniques et d'un large choix de cigares. Le personnel, prévenant et accueillant, répond au moindre besoin. Les hôtes peuvent se relaxer sur la terrasse, explorer les superbes environs ou pratiquer le golf, l'équitation ou la pêche.

Dieses herrlich renovierte Haus aus dem 17. Jahrhundert liegt im friedvollen und traumhaft schönen Tal von Poitou und ist berühmt für sein exzellentes Gourmetrestaurant. Im eleganten Speisesaal wird köstliche und einfallsreiche Küche serviert, begleitet von erlesenen Spitzenweinen, seltenen Likören und einer großen Auswahl an Zigarren. Das freundliche und aufmerksame Personal erfüllt jeden Wunsch. Die Gäste können auf der Terrasse entspannen, die herrliche Landschaft erkunden und Golf spielen, reiten oder angeln.

Our inspector loved: *The constant quality year in, year out.*

Directions: A10 > exit 32.

Web: www.johansens.com/logisstmartin
E-mail: courrier@logis-saint-martin.com
Tel: +33 549 0558 68
Fax: +33 549 7619 93

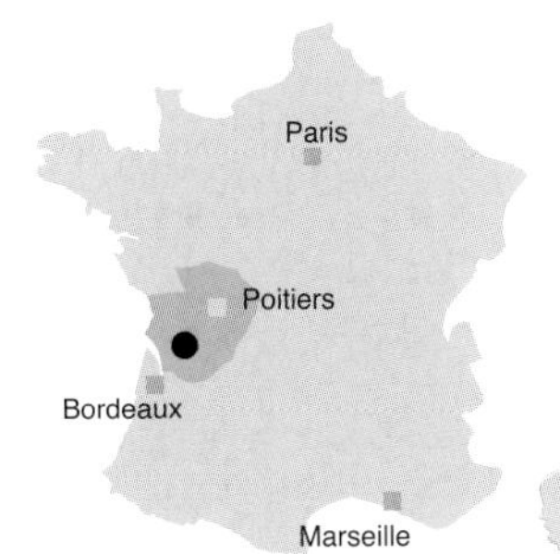

Price Guide:
(room only)
single €90–115
double/twin €90–120
suite €130

11 15

DOMAINE DES ETANGS

16310 MASSIGNAC, FRANCE

Directions: Nearest airport: Limoges; nearest station: Angoulême (45 minutes). Angoulême > Limoges road N141; at La Rochefoucauld, go towards Montemboeuf (D13).

Web: www.johansens.com/etangs
E-mail: info@domainedesetangs.fr
Tel: +33 5 45 61 85 00
Fax: +33 5 45 61 85 01

Price Guide:
single €137-242
double €137-242
suite €222-242

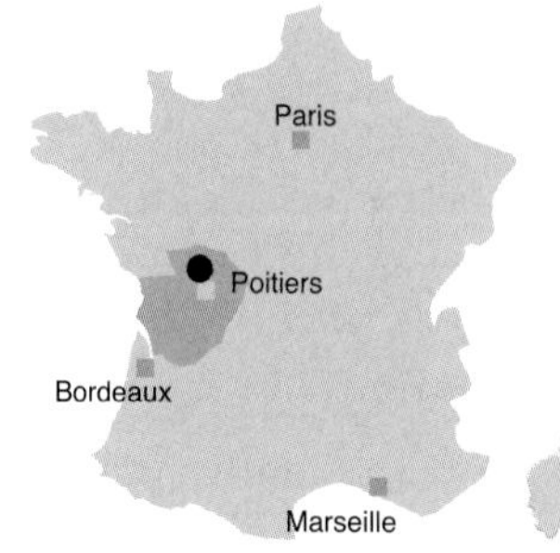

The Domaine is a vast, partially wooded property of over 2,000 acres including 76 acres of ponds and over 25km of private roads. Dotted around this immaculately kept piece of nature are an elegant château and 7 hamlets, housing 17 4-star guest rooms and suites. Most of the rooms, which are charmingly decorated with stone, glass, wood and copper, have impressive fireplaces, which can also be found in the salons and the Les Tournelles restaurant, where guests can enjoy delicious seasonal cuisine. Activities include tennis, swimming in the pool, boating on the lake and much more.

Le Domaine est une vaste propriété partiellement boisée de 850 ha, ponctués par 31 ha d'étangs et 25 km de routes privées. Dans une nature soigneusement préservée, se dressent un élégant château et 7 hameaux principaux dans lesquels sont aménagés 17 chambres ou suites 4 étoiles. La plupart des pièces, chaleureusement décorées en pierre, verre, bois et cuivre, possède une imposante cheminée a l'instar des salons d'accueil et du restaurant Les Tournelles, qui sert une délicieuse cuisine de saison. Pour la détente, le domaine propose le court de tennis, la piscine chauffée, le canotage et toutes sortes de loisirs.

Dieses weitläufige, teilweise bewaldete Anwesen umfasst 850ha Land mit 31ha Teichen und 25km Privatstraßen. In sorgfältig gepflegter Natur befinden sich ein elegantes Schloss und 7 kleine Dörfchen mit 17 4-Sterne-Zimmern und Suiten. Die meisten der mit Stein, Glas, Holz und Kupfer gestalteten, einladenden Zimmer bieten eindrucksvolle Kamine, wie man sie auch in den Aufenthaltsräumen und im Les Tournelles findet, das erlesene, saisonbedingte Küche serviert. Aktivitäten sind Tennis, Schwimmen im Pool, Bootfahren und vieles mehr.

***Our inspector loved:** The total freedom to do whatever you want.*

Le Pigonnet

5 AVENUE DU PIGONNET, 13090 AIX~EN~PROVENCE, FRANCE

This beautiful Bastide Provençale lies in the heart of Aix-en-Provence, less than 5 minutes' walk from the town centre. The décor is typically Provençal in its use of fabric and colour, and is both elegant and extremely welcoming. Many of the bedrooms overlook the beautiful manicured grounds with wide varieties of plants, flowers and trees and stunning fountains, whilst the typical regional cuisine will have guests returning again and again.

Cette belle bastide provençale se situe au cœur d'Aix-en-Provence, à moins de 5 minutes à pied du centre ville. Le décor est typiquement provençal dans son utilisation de tissus et couleurs, et est à la fois élégant et accueillant. La plupart de ses chambres surplombent les jardins superbement entretenus avec toute une variété de plantes, fleurs, arbres et fantastiques fontaines, alors que la cuisine typiquement régionale verra ses hôtes revenir encore et encore.

Diese wundervolle Bastide Provençale liegt inmitten eines Parks in Aix-en-Provence, knapp 5 Minuten zu Fuß vom Stadtzentrum entfernt. Das Décor aus typisch provenzalischen Stoffen und Farben schafft eine elegante und freundliche Atmosphäre. Viele Zimmer haben Blick auf die herrlich mit den verschiedensten Blumen, Bäumen und faszinierenden Springbrunnen gestalteten Gärten, und die köstliche regionale Küche sorgt dafür, dass Gäste immer wieder hierher kommen.

Our inspector loved: *The beautifully quiet park surrounding this town centre hotel.*

Directions: From A8 exit Pont de l'Arc > follow signs to town centre > after roundabout the hotel is located at the third red light on left.

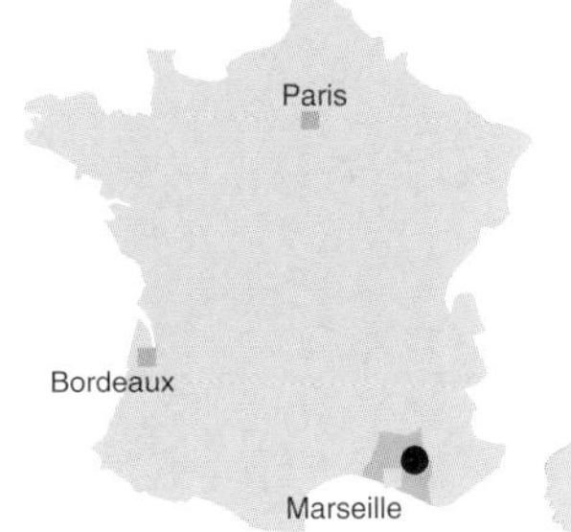

Web: www.johansens.com/lepigonnet
E-mail: reservation@hotelpigonnet.com
Tel: +33 4 42 59 02 90
Fax: +33 4 42 59 47 77

Price Guide:
single €160-250
double €180-400
suite from €500

La Bastide de Capelongue

84480 BONNIEUX, FRANCE

Directions: A7 > exit Avignon Sud > Apt. Bonnieux is then signposted.

Web: www.johansens.com/capelongue
E-mail: bastide@francemarket.com
Tel: +33 4 90 75 89 78
Fax: +33 4 90 75 93 03

Price Guide:
(room only)
double €220-320
junior suite €380

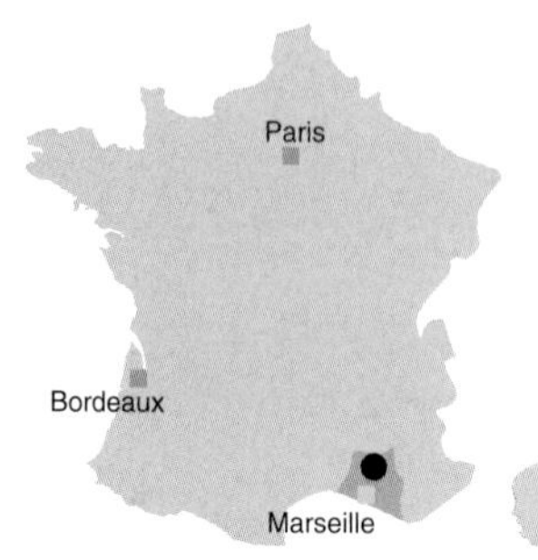

This beautiful property, set in the heart of the Lubéron region, overlooks the delightful old village of Bonnieux and is surrounded by lavender fields and rolling plains. The attention to detail throughout the hotel is immaculate; the spacious bedrooms are decorated with elegant soft furnishings and neutral pastel tones and offer terrace or balcony. Stunning panoramic views can be enjoyed from the superb restaurant, which overlooks the beautiful garden and its hidden swimming pool.

Cette belle propriété, située au cœur du Lubéron, donne sur le vieux village charmant de Bonnieux et est entourée par des champs de lavande et des pleines onduleuses. L'attention apportée au détail dans tout l'hôtel est impeccable; les chambres spacieuses sont ornées avec des ameublements doux et des tons pastel neutres, et offrent une terrasse ou balcon. On peut jouir de vues panoramiques à couper le souffle depuis le restaurant superbe, qui donne sur le beau jardin et sa piscine cachée.

Dieses wundervolle Hotel befindet sich im Herzen des Lubéron mit Blick auf das hübsche alte Dorf Bonnieux und ist umgeben von Lavendelfeldern und weiten Ebenen. Liebe zum Detail ist überall sichtbar, und die geräumigen Zimmer sind elegant in neutralen Pastelltönen eingerichtet und bieten Terrasse oder Balkon. Vom exquisiten Restaurant hat man einen herrlichen Panoramablick auf den traumhaften Garten und den versteckten Swimmingpool.

Our inspector loved: *The beautiful garden full of lavender and the breathtaking views.*

Le Clair de la Plume

PLACE DU MAIL, 26230 GRIGNAN, FRANCE

Situated at the foot of an imposing castle in the picturesque village of Grignan, in the heart of the Drôme Provençale, this delightful guesthouse is a true gem and was originally constructed in the 17th century. Breakfast is prepared in a vaulted-ceiling kitchen, the legacy of the monks who founded the site. The charming bedrooms are individually designed with typical Provençal bedcovers and curtains. Grignan with its numerous restaurants and attractions offers plenty of entertainment.

Situé au pied de l'imposant château dans le village médiéval de Grignan, au cœur de la Drôme provençale, cette adorable maison d'hôtes est un véritable joyau construit au XVIIe siècle. Le petit déjeuner est préparé dans la cuisiné voûtée héritage des moines à l'origine des lieux. Les chambres charmantes ont toutes une décoration unique, avec dessus de lits et rideaux typiquement provençaux. De nombreux loisirs sont disponibles a Grignan, avec entre autres de nombreux restaurants.

Am Fuße einer eindrucksvollen Burg im malerischen Dorf Grignan mitten im Drôme Provençale liegt dieses einladende Gästehaus, ein wahres Juwel, das ursprünglich im 17. Jahrhundert erbaut wurde. Das Frühstück wird in einer Küche mit gewölbter Decke zubereitet, ein Andenken an die Mönche, die diese Stätte gründeten. Die zauberhaften Zimmer sind individuell mit typisch provenzalischen Bettdecken und Vorhängen gestaltet. Grignan mit seinen Restaurants und Attraktionen bietet zahlreiche Unterhaltungsmöglichkeiten.

Our inspector loved: *The hotel's intimate atmosphere and the owner's warm welcome.*

Directions: From North > A7 > exit 18 Montelimar Sud > D541 to Nyons > hotel in the heart of Grignan. From South > A7 > exit 19 Bollene > D26 to St Paul 3 châteaux > D59 then D71 to Grignan > hotel in the heart of Grignon.

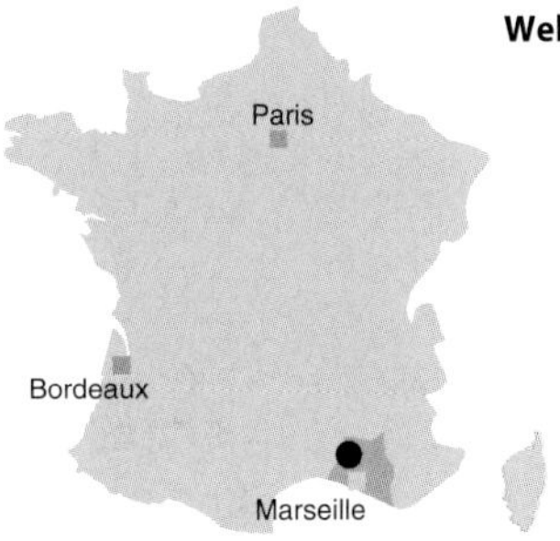

Paris

Bordeaux

Marseille

Web: www.johansens.com/leclairdelaplume
E-mail: plume2@wanadoo.fr
Tel: +33 4 75 91 81 30
Fax: +33 4 75 91 81 31

Price Guide:
double €90–165

Manoir de la Roseraie

ROUTE DE VALRÉAS, 26230 GRIGNAN, FRANCE

Directions: A7 > Montelimar Sud > Nyons Sud.

Web: www.johansens.com/manoirdelaroseraie
E-mail: roseraie.hotel@wanadoo.fr
Tel: +33 4 75 46 58 15
Fax: +33 4 75 46 91 55

Price Guide:
double/twin €155–205
suite €300–330

Situated in the Drôme Provençale and surrounded by 5 acres of lush lawns and gardens that seem to explode into a riot of colours, this is a luxurious and welcoming 19th-century manor. Fusing past and contemporary décor, the interior has been appointed in stylish fabrics and comfortable furnishings. The fresh taste of home-grown vegetables and fruit entices visitors towards the restaurant, where the inspired dishes are complemented by a selection of fine wines.

Situé en Drôme Provençale et entouré de 2 hectares de parc, de pelouses et de jardins qui semblent exploser dans une fête colorée, il s'agît ici d'un accueillant et luxueux manoir du XIXe siècle. Mariant le passé et le présent, la décoration a été arrangée avec de beaux tissus et des meubles confortables. Les légumes et les fruits cultivés sur place ajoutent à l'authenticité du restaurant, où les plats inspirés sont complétés par une sélection de vins fins.

Dieses luxuriöse und einladende Haus aus dem 19. Jahrhundert liegt im Drôme Provençale, inmitten von 2ha grünem Rasen und farbenfrohen Gärten. Vergangenheit vermischt sich mit zeitgenössischem Décor, die Innenräume sind mit stilvollen Stoffen und bequemem Mobiliar eingerichtet. Der köstliche Geschmack von Gemüse und Obst aus eigenem Anbau lockt die Gäste ins Restaurant, wo einfallsreiche Gerichte von einer Auswahl erlesener Weine ergänzt werden.

Our inspector loved: *The magnificent garden with hundreds of different varieties of roses.*

Mas de l'Oulivie

13520 LES~BAUX~DE~PROVENCE, FRANCE

Surrounded by olive trees, this beautiful and very welcoming "mas provençal" nestles at the bottom of one of the most amazing villages in Provence. All bedrooms are decorated with rustic wood furniture and Provençal fabrics. 2 beautiful suites, one of which has it's own terrace and garden are also available. The stunning pool and Jacuzzi are an oasis of peace, and here, a variety of snacks and salads are served at lunchtime. After a day of sightseeing, this is the perfect place to enjoy the colours and overwhelming scents that are so typical of the region.

Niché au pied de l'un des plus prestigieux villages de Provence, ce beau mas provençal entouré d'oliviers cache une hospitalité cordiale. Toutes les chambres sont agrémentées de meubles en bois rustiques et de tissus provençaux. Deux belles suites, dont l'une s'ouvre sur une terrasse et un jardin privatifs, sont également disponibles. La magnifique piscine et le jacuzzi forment une oasis de paix où sont servies diverses collations légères et salades à midi. Après une journée d'exploration, le mas est l'endroit rêvé pour se laisser griser par les couleurs et les parfums enivrants de la région.

Umgeben von Olivenbäumen liegt dieses zauberhafte "Mas provençal" am Fuße eines der außergewöhnlichsten Dörfer der Provence. Alle Zimmer sind mit rustikalem Mobiliar und provenzalischen Stoffen ausgestattet, und eine der beiden schönen Suiten mit Terrasse besitzt einen eigenen Garten. Der herrliche Pool und Jacuzzi verbreiten eine Atmosphäre der Ruhe, und mittags wird hier eine Vielzahl von Snacks und Salaten serviert. Nach einem langen Erkundungstag ist dies der ideale Ort, um die typischen Farben und Gerüche der Region zu genießen.

Our inspector loved: *The superb swimming pool with its unusual stone features and the Jacuzzi.*

Directions: 2 km from the village towards Fontvieille/Arles on the D78f secondary road.

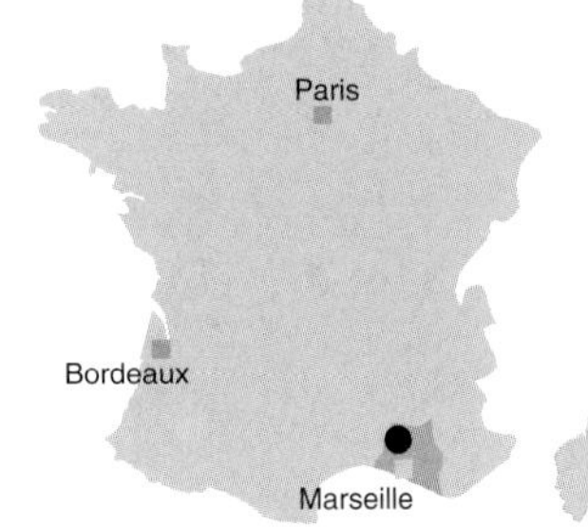

Web: www.johansens.com/masdeloulivie
E-mail: contact@masdeloulivie.com
Tel: +33 4 90 54 35 78
Fax: +33 4 90 54 44 31

Price Guide:
double/twin €115–230
suite €360–390

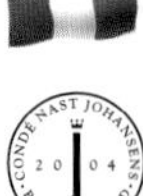

Château Talaud

84870 LORIOL~DU~COMTAT, FRANCE

Directions: A7 > exit no. 22 Carpentras > D950 towards Carpentras, after Sarrians > Monteux on D107 > turn right after 500m.

Web: www.johansens.com/talaud
E-mail: chateautalaud@infonie.fr
Tel: +33 4 90 65 71 00
Fax: +33 4 90 65 77 93

Price Guide:
double €155-195

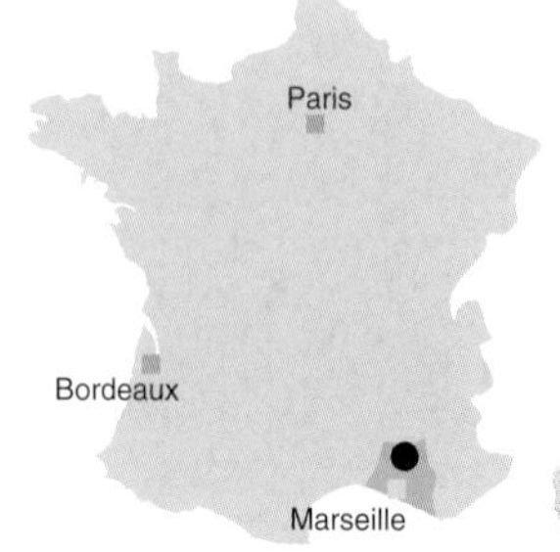

This charming 18th-century castle is situated in a stunning expanse of park estate, surrounded by beautiful Provençal vineyards. The spacious bedrooms are tastefully decorated with wonderful antiques and boast every modern amenity. Each room has been carefully designed to offer a relaxing and tranquil ambience, and affords glorious views over the estate. The hospitable owners will ensure their guests have a memorable stay and are on hand to offer suggestions on places to explore in this wonderful region.

Ce charmant château du XVIIIe siècle est situé dans une étendue fantastique du domaine entourée de vignobles, au sein de la superbe Provence. Les chambres spacieuses sont décorées avec goût avec de magnifiques antiquités et s'enorgueillissent des facilités les plus modernes. Chaque chambre a été soigneusement dessinée pour la tranquillité et la détente. Toutes les chambres ont de très belles vues sur le domaine. L'accueil des propriétaires, qui sont à disposition pour des conseils sur les endroits à voir dans la région, assure les hôtes d'un séjour mémorable.

Dieses zauberhafte Schloss aus dem 18. Jahrhundert liegt inmitten eines weitläufigen Parks umgeben von provenzalischen Weinbergen. Die geräumigen Zimmer sind geschmackvoll mit herrlichen Antiquitäten und jeglichem modernen Komfort eingerichtet. Jedes Zimmer spiegelt perfekt die entspannte und friedliche Atmosphäre wider und bietet traumhafte Ausblicke auf die Ländereien. Die gastfreundlichen Besitzer des Hotels sorgen für einen unvergeßlichen Aufenthalt und machen gerne Vorschläge zu Exkursionen in diese herrliche Region.

Our inspector loved: *The superb and amazing setting of this beautiful château.*

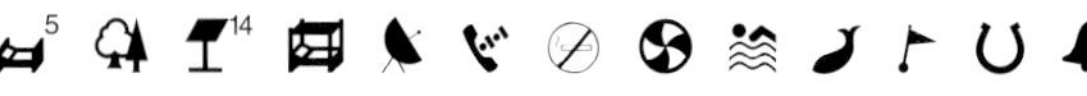

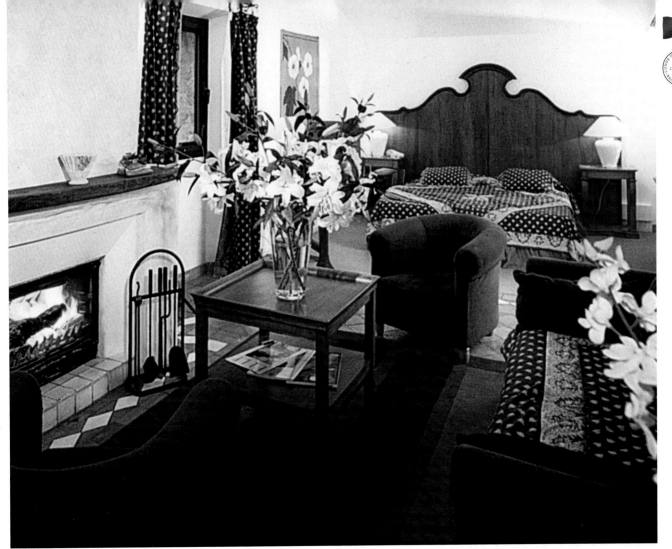

LE MOULIN DE LOURMARIN

84160 LOURMARIN, PROVENCE, FRANCE

This 18th-century former mill is located in the delightful village of Lourmarin in the heart of the Lubéron, and boasts a winning combination of contemporary style within a traditional stone building. Wrought iron blends effortlessly with dark wooden furniture, and the impressive vaulted dining room opens onto a stunning terrace with ancient olive trees. The exquisite cuisine is prepared by Edouard Loubet, the youngest chef in France to be awarded 2 Michelin stars.

Cet ancien moulin datant du XVIIIe siècle est situé dans l'adorable village de Lourmarin au cœur du Lubéron, et s'enorgueillit d'un mélange réussi de style contemporain dans un bâtiment traditionnel en pierre. Les fers forgés se fondent parfaitement avec les bois foncés, et l'impressionnante salle à manger sous voûte ouvre sur une superbe terrasse aux vieux oliviers. La délicieuse cuisine est préparée par Edouard Loubet, le plus jeune chef en France à s'être vu décerner 2 étoiles Michelin.

Diese einstige Mühle aus dem 18. Jahrhundert befindet sich in dem hübschen Dorf Lourmarin im Herzen des Lubéron und bietet eine wundervolle Mischung aus zeitgenössischem Stil in einem traditionellen Steingebäude. Schmiedeeiserne Gegenstände schmiegen sich an Möbel aus dunklem Holz und der eindrucksvolle Speisesaal mit seiner gewölbten Decke öffnet sich auf eine herrliche, von alten Olivenbäumen umgebene Terrasse. Die exquisiten Speisen werden von Edouard Loubet zubereitet, dem jüngsten Koch Frankreichs mit 2 Michelinsternen.

Our inspector loved: *The beautiful public areas on 2 levels and the wheat on the ceiling.*

  19      

Directions: A7 > exit Sénas > D973 towards Pertuis > follow the signs to Lourmarin.

Web: www.johansens.com/moulindelourmarin
E-mail: info@moulindelourmarin.com
Tel: +33 4 90 68 06 69
Fax: +33 4 90 68 31 76

Paris
Bordeaux
Marseille

Price Guide:
(room only)
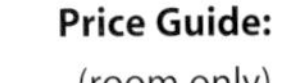
double €190-310

suite €430-655

CHÂTEAU DE MAZAN

PLACE NAPOLÉON, 84380 MAZAN, FRANCE

Built in 1720, the hotel is the former residence of the Marquis de Sade. Its setting in the heart of Mazan, a typical Provençal village, is a magnificent park filled with mulberry trees, paths of lavender and centuries old olive trees. Inside, the 25 bedrooms are all individually decorated in a traditional style. Attention to detail is evident everywhere from the high ceilings to the impressive ancient tiled floors dating back to the 19th century. Food is innovative and highlights fresh local ingredients.

Construit en 1720, cet hôtel était la résidence du Marquis de Sade. Sa situation au cœur de Mazan, village provençal typique, est un parc magnifique de mûriers, de chemins de lavande et d'oliviers centenaires. A l'intérieur, les 25 chambres sont toutes individuellement décorées dans le style traditionnel. L'attention au détail est partout évidente, des hauts plafonds aux impressionnants carrelages anciens datant du XIXe siècle. La cuisine est originale et met en valeur les ingrédients frais locaux.

Dieses 1720 erbaute Hotel ist der einstige Wohnsitz des Marquis de Sade. Es liegt inmitten eines herrlichen, mit Maulbeerbäumen, Lavendel und jahrhundertealten Olivenbäumen gefüllten Parks im Herzen von Mazan, einem typisch provenzalischen Dorf. Die 12 Gästezimmer sind unterschiedlich im traditionellen Stil gestaltet, und Liebe zum Detail ist überall sichtbar, von den hohen Decken bis hin zu eindrucksvollen alten Fliesenböden aus dem 19. Jahrhundert. Das Essen ist innovativ und basiert hauptsächlich auf frischen einheimischen Zutaten.

Our inspector loved: *The superb and original bathrooms in the superior garden rooms and suites.*

Directions: From the A7 > exit Avignon Nord > Carpentras on D942 > from Carpentras follow Mont Ventoux then Mazan > in Mazan the hotel is in first road on the right.

Web: www.johansens.com/mazan
E-mail: contact@chateaudemazan.fr
Tel: +33 4 90 69 62 61
Fax: +33 4 90 69 76 62

Price Guide:
(room only)
double €120-270
suite €240-400

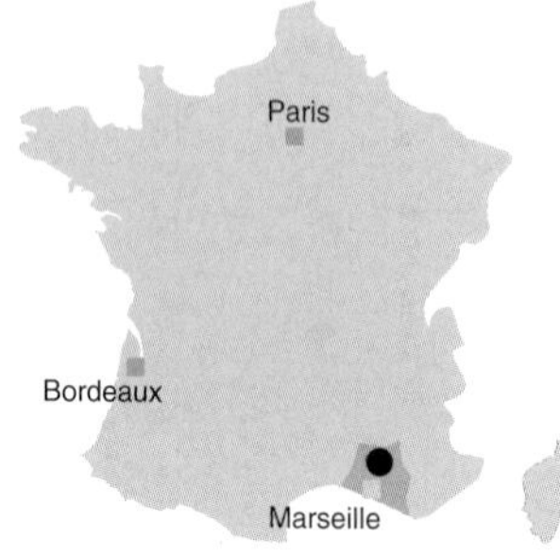

Château des Alpilles

ROUTE DÉPARTEMENTALE 31, ANCIENNE ROUTE DU GRÈS, 13210 SAINT~RÉMY~DE~PROVENCE, FRANCE

Surrounded by verdant grounds in which rare old trees offer a touch of the exotic, this elegant 19th-century château offers wonderful seclusion. The salons reflect its age-old grandeur, with moulded ceilings, mosaic floors, tapestries and enormous gilt mirrors. Many bedrooms reflect this ancient splendour, whilst some are more contemporary. Adjoining the cosy bar is the dining room, where visitors can enjoy simple regional dishes.

Entouré de terrains verdoyants où de vieux arbres offrent une touche exotique, cet élégant château du XIXe siècle offre une merveilleuse occasion de retraite. La salon reflète la grandeur d'époque, avec moulures, sols en mosaïque, tâpisseries et d'énormes miroirs dorés. La plupart des chambres reflète cette grandeur ancienne, alors que certaines sont plus contemporaines. A côté du bar chaleureux se trouve le restaurant, où les visiteurs peuvent déguster des plats régionaux simples.

Umgeben von einer Parkanlage mit seltenen alten Bäumen bietet dieses elegante Château aus dem 19. Jahrhundert herrliche Abgeschiedenheit. Die Salons spiegeln mit ihren Stuckverzierungen, Mosaikböden, Gobelins und riesigen vergoldeten Spiegeln eine Erhabenheit aus vergangenen Zeiten wider. Einige Zimmer zeigen die gleiche ehrwürdige Pracht, andere sind modern gestaltet. Neben der behaglichen Bar können die Gäste einfache, regionale Gerichte im Speisesaal genießen.

Our inspector loved: *The superb park surrounding the château, with its swimming pool and tennis courts.*

Directions: D31 > Tarascon.

Web: www.johansens.com/chateaudesalpilles
E-mail: chateau.alpilles@wanadoo.fr
Tel: +33 4 90 92 03 33
Fax: +33 4 90 92 45 17

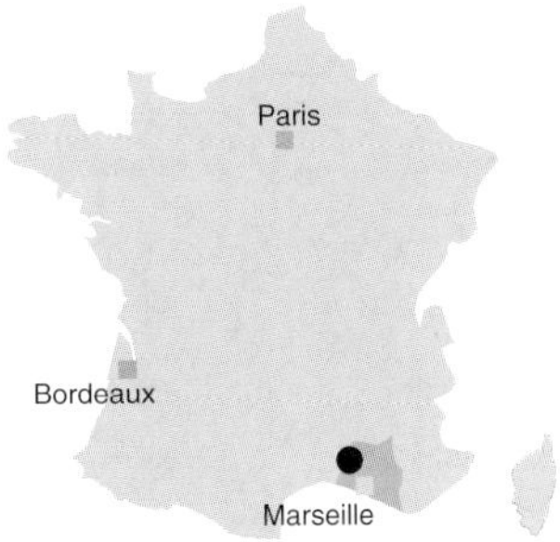

Price Guide:
single €180
double/twin €180–230
suite €258–360

FRANCE / PROVENCE (SAUVETERRE)

CHÂTEAU DE VARENNE

30150 SAUVETERRE, FRANCE

Directions: A7 > exit Orange > N480 towards Avignon. Alternatively: A7 > Avignon Nord > Villeneuve les Avignon > Roguemaure.

Web: www.johansens.com/varenne
E-mail: info@chateaudevarenne.com
Tel: +33 4 66 82 59 45
Fax: +33 4 66 82 84 83

Price Guide:
(room only)
double €90-159
suite €150-210

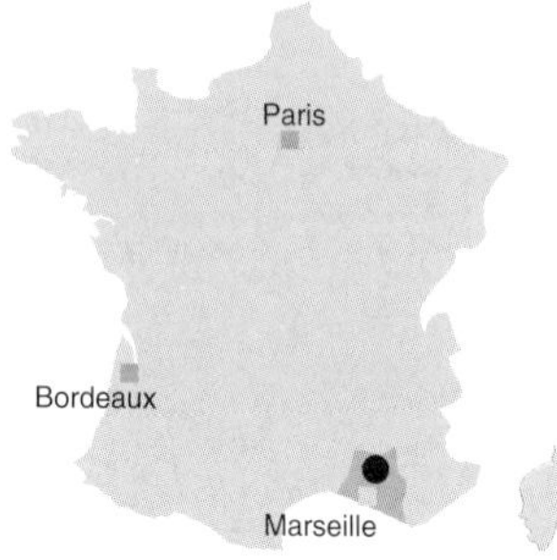

This "Hôtel de Charme" is a hidden gem nestled in 3 acres of magnificent parkland. Originally built in 1738, recent renovations unearthed original stone and wooden floors, a stone vault, marble fireplace and main staircase, which have been restored to their former splendour. The 14 bedrooms are attractively decorated; one has a staircase leading to a private terrace. Although there is no restaurant, the superb kitchen accommodates guests who wish to enjoy an apéritif before venturing out for dinner. For relaxation there is a pool, a terrace and 2 lounges.

Cet "Hôtel de Charme" est un joyau dissimulé au sein d'un parc magnifique de plus d'1 ha. Construit en 1738, des rénovations récentes ont découvert la pierre et les parquets d'origine, une voûte de pierre, des cheminées en marbre et l'escalier principal, restauré dans sa splendeur d'antan. Les 14 chambres sont joliment décorées, l'une ayant un escalier privé conduisant à une terrasse privée. Bien qu'il n'y ait pas de restaurant, la superbe cuisine accommode les hôtes souhaitant prendre un apéritif dînatoire. La piscine, la terrasse et deux salons sont les lieux où se détendre.

Dieses 1738 erbaute wundervolle "Hôtel de Charme" liegt versteckt inmitten von 1,2ha herrlicher Parklandschaft. Kürzliche Renovierungsarbeiten brachten die ursprünglichen Stein- und Holzfußböden, einen Marmorkamin und das Haupttreppenhaus zum Vorschein, und stellten die einstige Pracht wieder her. Die 14 Zimmer sind attraktiv gestaltet, eines bietet eine über eine Treppe erreichbare Privatterrasse. Es gibt kein Restaurant, doch man kann in der Küche einen Apéritif zu sich nehmen. Zur Entspannung gibt es einen Swimmingpool, eine Terrasse und 2 Aufenthaltsräume.

***Our inspector loved:** The magnificent 400-year-old cedar of Lebanon watching over this superb and relaxing hotel.*

FRANCE / PROVENCE (UZÈS)

Château d'Arpaillargues

HÔTEL MARIE D'AGOULT, 30700 UZÈS, FRANCE

Protected by thick stone walls, this château offers a warm welcome and all the charm and authenticity of a Provençal stately home. The bedrooms and apartments are elegantly furnished, and the superb dining rooms with their vaulted ceilings are warmed by crackling fires in autumn. In fine weather, delicious meals are served in the lovely courtyard. Guests may relax on the huge terrace, play tennis or swim in the fantastic swimming pool surrounded by a beautiful park. Golf can be arranged nearby.

Protégé par d'épais murs en pierre, ce château accueillant cache le charme et l'authenticité d'un logis seigneurial de Provence. Les chambres et les appartements sont aménagés dans un style élégant. En automne, des feux de cheminée crépitent dans les belles salles à manger aux plafonds voûtés. Par beau temps, des repas savoureux sont servis dans la jolie cour. Les visiteurs lézardent sur la terrasse, jouent au tennis ou se baignent dans la fabuleuse piscine entourée d'un beau parc. Golf possible à proximité.

Von dicken Steinmauern umgeben verkörpert dieses freundliche Château den Charme und die Authentizität der Provence. Die Zimmer und Appartements sind elegant ausgestattet, und die herrlichen Speisesäle mit ihren gewölbten Decken werden im Herbst von offenem Kaminfeuer gewärmt. Bei gutem Wetter werden im zauberhaften Innenhof köstliche Gerichte serviert. Die Gäste können sich auf der großen Terrasse entspannen, Tennis spielen oder im eindrucksvollen Pool schwimmen. Auch Golf ist in der Nähe möglich.

Our inspector loved: *The amazing terrace where one can relax under the shade of beautiful trees.*

Directions: A9 exit Remoulins > follow signs to Uzès.

Web: www.johansens.com/arpaillagues

E-mail: savrychateau30@aol.com

Tel: +33 4 66 22 14 48

Fax: +33 4 66 22 56 10

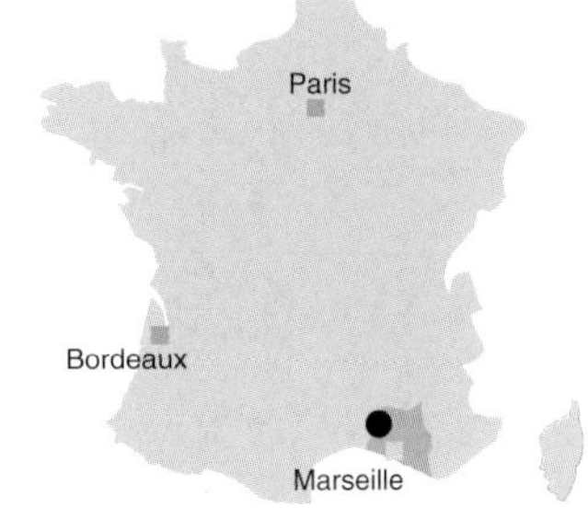

Price Guide:

single €77-115

double/twin €92-115

suite €130-182

Château de Divonne

01220 DIVONNE~LES~BAINS, FRANCE

Standing proudly on a small hill and surrounded by 22 hectares of lush parkland, this is a luxurious and welcoming 19th-century gourmet hotel that offers peace, tranquillity and spectacular lake and mountain views. Delightfully fusing the traditional and the modern, the interior is appointed in stylish décor, fabrics and furniture, with each bright and spacious guest room individually and elegantly furnished to the highest standard.

Ce luxueux et accueillant hôtel gastronomique du XIXe siècle qui se tient fièrement sur une petite colline et est entouré de 22 hectares de parc luxuriant, offre paix, tranquillité et des vues spectaculaires sur le lac et la montagne. Mélangeant de manière délicieuse le traditionnel et le moderne, la décoration intérieure, les tissus et meubles sont élégants et les chambres lumineuses et spacieuses sont individuellement décorées selon les plus hauts standards.

In stolzer Lage auf einer Anhöhe und umgeben von 22ha üppiger Parklandschaft, bietet dieses einladende und luxuriöse Gourmethotel aus dem 19. Jahrhundert absolute Ruhe und atemberaubende Blicke auf See und Berge. Das Interieur, eine attraktive Mischung aus traditionell und modern, ist mit stilvollen Stoffen und Möbeln gestaltet, und jedes der hellen und geräumigen Zimmer ist individuell und elegant eingerichtet und bietet höchsten Komfort.

Our inspector loved: *The large terrace with amazing views over the French Alps and Mont Blanc.*

Directions: A6 > A40 exit Bellegarde > Gex / Divonne.

Web: www.johansens.com/chateaudedivonne
E-mail: divonne@grandesetapes.fr
Tel: +33 4 50 20 00 32
Fax: +33 4 50 20 03 73

Price Guide:
single €104–290
double €104–290
suite €293–360

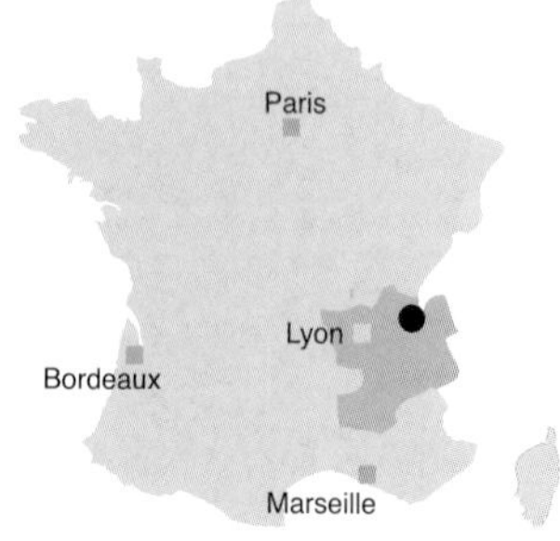

Le Domaine de Divonne Casino, Golf & Spa Resort

AVENUE DES THERMES, 01220 DIVONNE~LES~BAINS, FRANCE

The Domaine de Divonne is one of the most exclusive French resorts, the nearest to Geneva and the Swiss border. The magnificent estate consists of a 1930 art deco residence, the Grand Hotel, an 18-hole golf course, a casino and a night club. The elegant guest rooms offer balconies overlooking the Alps or Jura mountains and state-of-the-art technology. 5 restaurants, including the 1 Michelin star La Terrasse, offer a diversity of cuisine. A new spa provides the most innovative water treatments and an indoor pool with aqua gym. The Atelier de Beauté Anne Sémonin offers a wide range of treatments.

Le Domaine de Divonne est un resort unique en France. C'est également le plus proche de Genève et de la frontière suisse. Cet éstablissement de grand luxe, dans un style art déco des anées 30, réunit Le Grand Hôtel, un golf 18 trous, un casino et une discothèque. Les chambres luxueuses disposent de balcons avec vue sur les Alpes et le Jura et un équipement technique trés complet. Il y a 5 restaurants, dont La Terrasse a l'étoile Michelin. Un nouveau Spa offre les traitements d'eau les plus innovatifs et une aqua gym. L'Ateleir de Beaute Anne Sémonin offre des sains personnalisés et relaxants.

Domaine de Divonne, eines der exklusivsten Resorts in Frankreich, nahe bei Genf und der Schweizer Grenze. Das luxuriöse Anwesen im 30er Jahre Art-Déco-Stil besteht aus dem Grand Hotel, einem 18-Loch Golfplatz, Casino und einem Nightclub. Die eleganten Zimmer bieten Balkon mit Blick auf die Alpen und modernste Technologie. 5 Restaurants stehen zur Auswahl, darunter das mit 1 Michelin-Stern ausgezeichnete La Terrasse. Ein neues Kurzentrum bietet innovative Wasserbehandlungen und ein Hallenbad mit Aqua-Gym. Zahlreiche Behandlungen sind im Atelier de Beauté Anne Sémonin geboten.

Our inspector loved: *The wide range of activities available especially the spa.*

Directions: N1 from Geneva > Coppet/Divonne exit.

Web: www.johansens.com/domainededivonne
E-mail: info@domaine-de-divonne.com
Tel: +33 4 50 40 34 34
Fax: +33 4 50 40 34 24

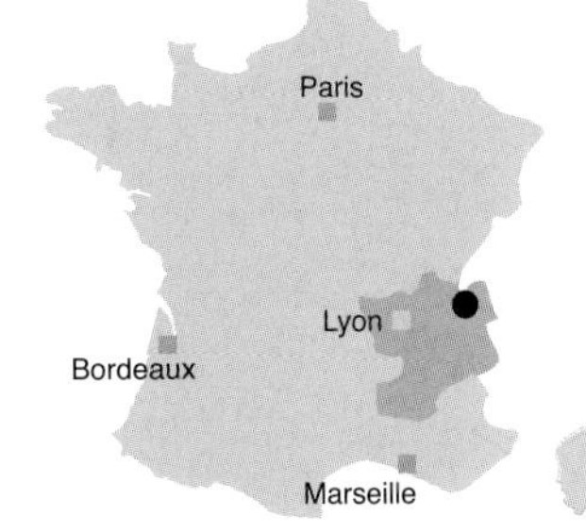

Price Guide:
single €190–270
double/twin €260–350
suite €465–2760

Chalet Hôtel La Marmotte

61 RUE DU CHÉNE, 74260 LES GETS, FRANCE

Situated amidst the beautiful alpine trails and ski slopes of the French Alps, the very family-orientated La Marmotte is friendly and cosy and the perfect base from which to explore this exciting region. Guests of all ages will appreciate the range of activities, including on-site gym, indoor swimming pool, spa and beauty facilities. Exhilarating ski slopes, golf courses and Lac de Baignade are nearby, and lively Les Gets with its shops and restaurants is within easy reach of other "Portes du Soleil" ski resorts.

Au pied des pistes de ski et des sentiers pédestres des Alpes, vous attend un grand chalet convivial et confortable, la base parfaite pour explorer une région fascinante. Idéal pour les familles, cet hôtel offre des activités aux visiteurs de tout âge, qui peuvent profiter notamment du gymnase, de la piscine couverte, du spa et du centre de beauté. Pistes grisantes, golfs et lac de baignade ne sont qu'à deux pas. Et si l'animation des Gets, avec ses restaurants et ses magasins, ne vous suffit pas, vous pouvez facilement accéder aux autres stations des "Portes du Soleil".

Umgeben von herrlichen Wanderwegen und Skipisten der französischen Alpen bietet das freundliche, familienorientierte Hotel La Marmotte den perfekten Ausgangspunkt, um diese faszinierende Gegend zu erforschen. Gäste aller Altersstufen nutzen das umfassende Freizeitangebot, wie Fitnessraum, Hallenbad, Spa und Schönheitsfarm. Traumhafte Abfahrten, Golfplätze und der Lac de Baignade sind in der Nähe, und vom lebhaften Les Gets mit seinen Restaurants und Geschäften sind auch andere "Portes du Soleil" Skigebiete leicht erreichbar.

Our inspector loved: *The indoor swimming pool overlooking the ski slopes.*

Directions: Leave the A40 and exit at Cluses.

Web: www.johansens.com/chaletlamarmotte
E-mail: info@hotel-marmotte.com
Tel: + 33 4 50 75 80 33
Fax: +33 4 50 75 83 26

Price Guide:
(half-board)
double/twin €99–185

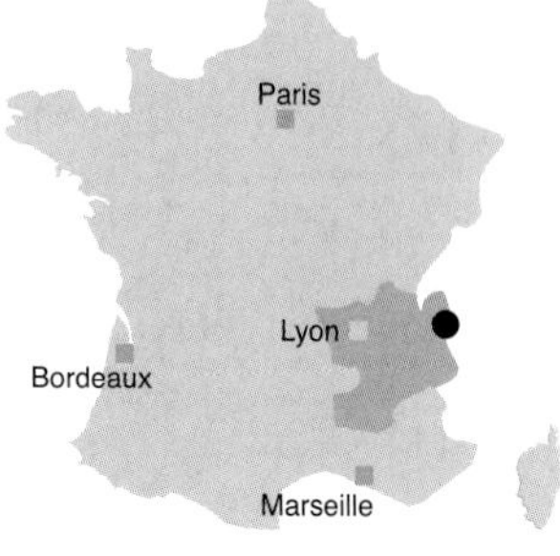

FRANCE / RHÔNE~ALPES (LYON)

La Tour Rose

22 RUE DU BOEUF, 69005 LYON, FRANCE

Boasting a Tuscan garden with terraces, waterfalls and ornamental pools, this striking collection of 3 Renaissance buildings is perhaps Lyon's most luxurious hotel. Each of the suites has been designed by one of Lyon's most famous silk manufacturers. A former chapel, leading onto a terrace, the restaurant serves classically-inspired nouvelle cuisine. Afterwards, visitors can relax in the stylish bar or one of the sunlit gardens.

La Tour Rose a pour cadre un jardin toscan avec terrasses, cascades et bassins d'agrément. Ses 3 bâtiments Renaissance composent probablement l'un des hôtels les plus luxueux de Lyon. Chaque suite a été décorée par de célèbres fabricants de soie. Le restaurant, jadis une chapelle, mène à la terrasse et sert une cuisine nouvelle teintée de classicisme. Les visiteurs pourront également se relaxer dans le bar stylé ou dans un des jardins ensoleillés.

Mit seinem toskanischen Garten, herrlichen Terrassen, Wasserfällen und farbenfrohen Teichen ist dieser eindrucksvolle Komplex aus 3 Renaissancebauten das wohl luxuriöseste Hotel in Lyon. Jede der Suiten wurde von einem bekannten Lyoner Seidenfabrikanten entworfen. Das Restaurant, eine ehemalige Kapelle, führt auf eine Terrasse und serviert moderne und doch klassisch inspirierte Gerichte, und die Gäste können sich in der eleganten Bar oder in einem der sonnigen Gärten vergnügen.

Our inspector loved: *Its ideal location in the heart of the old town, perfect to explore Lyon's historic treasures.*

Directions: Vieux-Lyon.

Web: www.johansens.com/tourrose
E-mail: latourose@free.fr
Tel: +33 4 78 92 69 10
Fax: +33 4 78 42 26 02

Price Guide:
(breakfast €18)
double/twin €230–290
suite €335–540

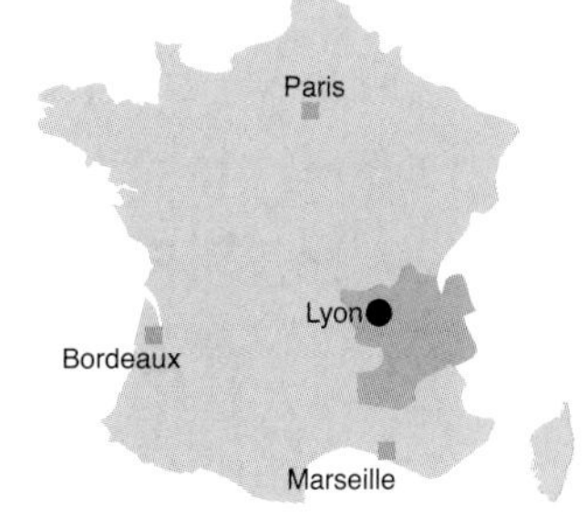

Chalet Hôtel de la Croix-Fry

74230 MANIGOD, FRANCE

Directions: A41 > exit Annecy Nord > follow signs to Thônes > Manigod > Col de la Croix Fry.

Web: www.johansens.com/croixfry
E-mail: hotelcroixfry@wanadoo.fr
Tel: +33 4 50 44 90 16
Fax: +33 4 50 44 94 87

Price Guide:
(per person, including dinner)
double €120-130
suite €175-195
chalet (per week) €800-3,300

Set at an altitude of 1,400m with stunning views, this welcoming property, run by Marie-Ange Guelpa-Veyrat and her children, offers traditional hospitality with an emphasis on friendly service and exquisite Savoyard cuisine. Accommodation comprises a range of chalets for 2 to 8/10 persons and 10 bedrooms and suites in the main hotel, which have either a balcony or terrace; some boast whirlpool baths. Guests can enjoy walks, mountain biking and picnics, and in winter, there is a complimentary shuttle service to the skiing slopes of La Clusaz (1.5km).

A 1400 m d'altitude, cette charmante propriété aux vues fantastiques, gérée par Marie-Ange Guelpa-Veyrat et ses enfants, offre un accueil chaleureux. L'accent est mis sur un service amical et une délicieuse cuisine savoyarde. L'hébergement se fait dans l'un des chalets individuels pouvant accueillir de 2 à 8/10 personnes ou dans les 10 chambres et suites de l'hôtel, certaines équipées de bains balnéo et qui ont toutes balcon ou terrasse. Les hôtes peuvent faire des randonnées, du VTT et des pique-niques et en hiver une navette avec chauffeur les emmène jusqu'aux pistes de La Clusaz (1,5 km).

In 1400m Höhe mit herrlichem Panorama liegt dieses einladende, von Marie-Ange Guelpa-Veyrat und ihren Kindern geführte Hotel, das traditionelle Gastfreundschaft mit Betonung auf freundlichem Service und köstlicher Küche der Haute-Savoie bietet. Die Unterkunft umfasst Chalets für 2 bis 8/10 Personen und 10 Zimmer und Suiten mit Balkon oder Terrasse im Hotel, einige davon mit Whirlpoolbädern. Spaziergänge, Mountainbiken und Picknicks sind an der Tagesordnung, und im Winter wird gratis Shuttleservice zu den 1,5km entfernten Pisten von La Clusaz geboten.

Our inspector loved: *The very warm welcome from the owners and the most breathtaking view of mountains ever experienced.*

CHÂTEAU DE COUDRÉE

DOMAINE DE COUDRÉE, BONNATRAIT, 74140 SCIEZ~SUR~LÉMAN, FRANCE

Perched on the edge of Lake Geneva, this 12th-century château with its turrets and pinnacles offers a truly fairy tale experience. With a mere 19 guest rooms, all furnished with antiques, this is an elite hotel. Exquisite salons, and a big terrace overlooking the pool and gardens down to the water's edge all contribute to the visitors' overall pleasure. A memorable gastronomic experience is also guaranteed.

Niché sur les bords du Lac de Genève, ce château du XIIe siècle avec ses 19 chambres meublées d'antiquités, offre une vision de conte de fée, avec ses tourelles et ses donjons. Des salons raffinés, un bar accueillant, une grande terrasse avec vue sur la piscine et le jardin descendant jusqu'au bord du lac rendent les séjours encore plus agréables. Une mémorable expérience gastronomique est également garantie.

Am Ufer des Genfer Sees gelegen bietet dieses Château aus dem 12. Jahrhundert mit seinen Türmen und Zinnen einen märchenhaften Aufenthalt. Mit nur 19 Zimmern, alle mit erlesenen Antiquitäten möbliert, ist Exklusivität garantiert. Herrliche Salons, eine große Terrasse mit Blick über den Pool und ein Garten bis zum Seeufer schaffen ein Gefühl der totalen Entspannung. Die Küche verspricht gastronomischen Hochgenuss.

Our inspector loved: *Its fantastic location on the shore of Lake Geneva, with its private boating stage and amazing views.*

Directions: A40 > Annemasse/Thonon/Evian > Sciez Bonnatrait.

Web: www.johansens.com/decoudree
E-mail: chcoudree@coudree.com
Tel: +33 4 50 72 62 33
Fax: +33 4 50 72 57 28

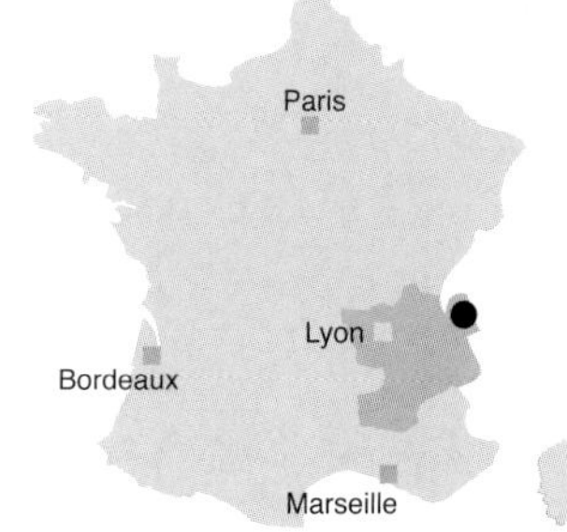

Price Guide:
single/double/twin €120.45–327.80
apartments €280.55–344.55

Hôtel du Palais

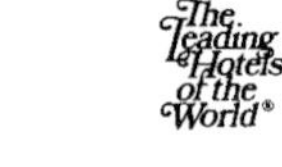

1 AVENUE DE L'IMPÉRATRICE, 64200 BIARRITZ, FRANCE

Directions: The hotel is situated in the centre of Biarritz.

Web: www.johansens.com/palais
E-mail: reception@hotel-du-palais.com
Tel: +33 5 59 41 64 00
Fax: +33 5 59 41 67 99

Price Guide:
(room only)
single €250–425
double/twin €350–500
suite €500–1,350
royal suite upon application

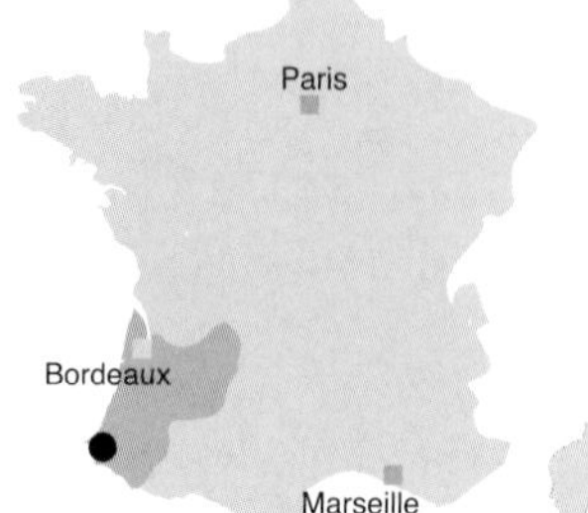

The auspicious history of this exceptional waterfront residence echoes proudly today. Marble pillars and glistening chandeliers adorn its palatial foyer and exquisite antique furniture is set throughout the sophisticated bars and luxurious bedrooms. One of the 2 new opulent Royal Suites also boasts an ocean view. Built by request of Napoleon III for his wife Eugénie in 1855, the hotel offers a dazzling range of entertainment. The elegance of its 1 Michelin Star restaurant is worthy of the many notable guests who have chosen this magnificent hotel as their summer retreat.

Cadeau impérial de Napoléon III à son épouse Eugénie, cette somptueuse demeure, construite sur le front de mer en 1855, témoigne d'un riche passé. Des colonnes de marbre et des lustres scintillants ornent le hall grandiose, et des meubles anciens raffinés agrémentent les bars élégants et les chambres luxueuses. Une des nouvelles suites royales luxueuses s'enorgueillit d'une vue sur la mer. L'hôtel offre en outre un choix impressionnant de loisirs. Quant à l'élégant restaurant une étoile Michelin, il est digne des nombreux hôtes prestigieux qui ont fait de ce palais leur résidence d'été.

Dieses prächtige, direkt am Wasser gelegene Anwesen ist reich an Geschichte – Napoleon III. baute es 1855 für seine Gemahlin Eugénie. Marmorsäulen und glänzende Lüster zieren das palastartige Foyer, und die eleganten Bars und luxuriösen Schlafzimmer sind mit erlesenen antiken Möbeln gefüllt. Eine der neuen Royal Luxussuiten bietet Blick auf das Meer. Umfassende Freizeitmöglichkeiten stehen zur Verfügung, und das elegante 1 Michelin Stern Restaurant begeistert die zahlreichen Gäste, die sich dieses superbe Hotel als "Sommerresidenz" ausgewählt haben.

***Our inspector loved:** The grandeur of this palatial hotel.*

HOTEL LEHEN TOKIA

CHEMIN ACHOTARRETA, 64500 CIBOURE, SAINT~JEAN~DE~LUZ, FRANCE

This beautiful little hotel is situated in the hills of Saint-Jean-de-Luz and has a glorious panoramic view of the bay. The building is classified as a historic monument because of a massive stained-glass window, and its new-Basque-style architecture is perfectly complemented by the predominantly art-deco interior. Most of the individually designed en-suite bedrooms and suites have views of the ocean. Guests can enjoy water sports, explore the town and the Basque country and visit nearby Biarritz.

Ce petit hôtel charmant se dresse dans les collines de Saint-Jean-de-Luz, d'où elle jouit d'une splendide vue panoramique de la baie. Classé monument historique pour son énorme vitrail, le Tokia se caractérise par une architecture néo-basque en parfaite harmonie avec le style art déco qui domine à l'intérieur. La plupart des chambres et des suites, toutes décorées de façon individuelle, ont vue sur l'océan. Les visiteurs pratiquent des sports nautiques, explorent le Pays basque et visitent Biarritz tout près.

Dieses zauberhafte kleine Hotel liegt in den Hügeln von Saint-Jean-de-Luz und bietet einen atemberaubenden Panoramablick auf die Bucht. Das Gebäude ist dank eines riesigen Buntglasfensters ein historisches Monument, und seine neo-baskische Architektur wird durch das vorwiegend im Art-Deco-Stil gehaltene Interieur perfekt ergänzt. Die unterschiedlich eingerichteten Zimmer und Suiten haben alle ein eigenes Bad, die meisten haben Meerblick. Die Gäste können Wassersport betreiben, die Stadt und das Baskenland erkunden oder Biarritz besuchen.

Our inspector loved: *The warm welcome from the owner and the feeling of privacy.*

Directions: A63 > exit Saint-Jean-de-Luz Sud > Ciboure.

Web: www.johansens.com/lehentokia
E-mail: info@lehen-tokia.com
Tel: +33 5 59 47 18 16
Fax: +33 5 59 47 38 04

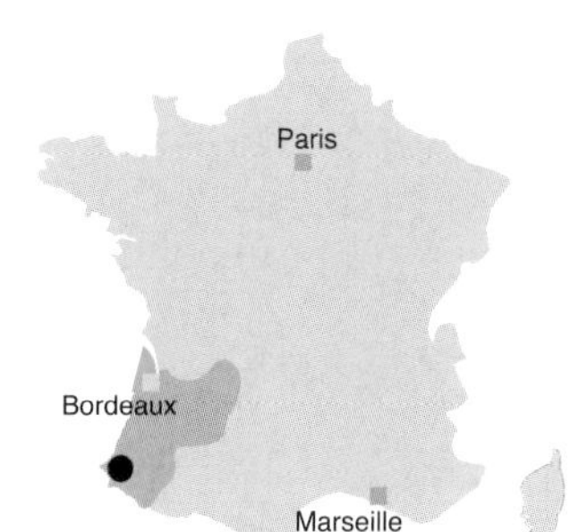

Price Guide:
(breakfast €10)
double/twin €80–145
suite €185–215

Château de Sanse

33350 SAINTE~RADEGONDE, FRANCE

Situated in the Bordeaux region, only 20 minutes from the famous vineyards of Saint-Emilion, this charming château is surrounded by a 5-ha estate. Bright and airy living rooms create a wonderfully comfortable ambience. The extremely spacious bedrooms are decorated with simple, light colours and many have direct access to a private balcony or terrace with views over Gensac or the Dordogne valley. In the cosy dining room guests can enjoy local specialities featuring fresh produce, much of which is grown in the private garden.

Situé dans le Bordelais, à seulement 20 minutes des célèbres vignobles de Saint-Emilion, cet établissement de charme est entouré d'un parc de 5ha. Ses pièces lumineuses et aérées créent une ambiance merveilleusement confortable. Les chambres spacieuses à la décoration raffinée et personnalisée ont pour la plupart un accès direct à un balcon privé ou une terrasse avec vue sur Gensac et la vallée de la Dordogne. Dans la salle intime du restaurant, les hôtes pourront apprécier les spécialités locales cuisinées avec les produits frais, la plupart provenant du jardin potager.

Dieses charmante, von 5ha Land umgebene Château befindet sich in Bordeaux, nur 20 Minuten von den berühmten Saint-Emilion Weinbergen entfernt. Helle, luftige Aufenthaltsräume schaffen eine entspannende Atmosphäre, und die geräumigen Zimmer sind in einfachen, sanften Farben gehalten; einige haben direkten Zugang auf einen eigenen Balkon oder Terrasse mit Blick auf Gensac oder das Dordognetal. Im Speisesaal werden einheimische Spezialitäten serviert, für die frische, meist im eigenen Garten angebaute Zutaten verwendet werden.

Our inspector loved: *The beautiful suites with their open-plan bathrooms.*

Directions: Bordeaux > N89 > Libourne > D936 > Castillon La Bataille > D17 > Pujols > D18 > Gensac.

Web: www.johansens.com/chateaudesanse
E-mail: contact@chateaudesanse.com
Tel: +33 5 57 56 41 10
Fax: +33 5 57 56 41 29

Price Guide:
double/twin €90-125
suite €150-185

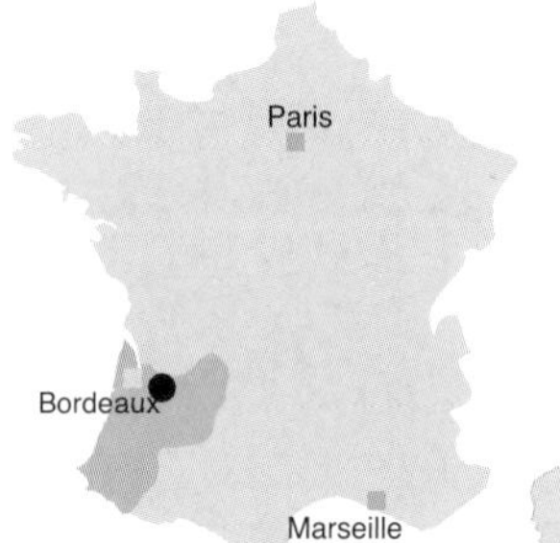

Château des Briottières

49330 CHAMPIGNÉ, FRANCE

Surrounded by 360 acres of parkland "à l'anglaise", this magnificent family-owned stately home is set in the heart of peaceful Anjou. The luxurious interior, with its pervading air of serenity, features Louis XV antiques and quirky memorabilia. The immaculately presented bedrooms have windows overlooking the estate, inviting the rich perfumes of herbs and flowers. Traditional Anjou meals are served in the impressive period dining room.

Entouré d'un jardin anglais de 150ha, cette magnifique maison familiale est en plein coeur de la paisible région d'Anjou. L'intérieur luxueux dégage une ambiance sereine et présente des pièces Louis XV et des objets de collection. Les chambres immaculées donnent sur le domaine et laissent entrer le doux parfum des herbes aromatiques et des fleurs. Les repas traditionnels d'Anjou sont servis dans l'ancienne salle à manger impressionnante.

Umgeben von 150 ha Parklandschaft „à l'anglaise" liegt dieses prächtige, im Familienbesitz befindliche Herrenhaus im Herzen des friedlichen Anjou. Die luxuriöse Inneneinrichtung mit Antiquitäten aus der Zeit Louis XV. schafft eine ruhige Atmosphäre. Die perfekt gestalteten Zimmer bieten einen Blick über das Gut und durch die Fenster strömt der Duft von Kräutern und Blumen. Die traditionsreiche Küche des Anjou wird im eindrucksvollen Speisezimmer serviert.

Our inspector loved: *"La Chambre Rose", an elegant suite with stunning views over the park.*

Directions: A11 > exit 11 > D859 > Champigné > 4km.

Web: www.johansens.com/chateaudesbriottieres
E-mail: briottieres@wanadoo.fr
Tel: +33 2 41 42 00 02
Fax: +33 2 41 42 01 55

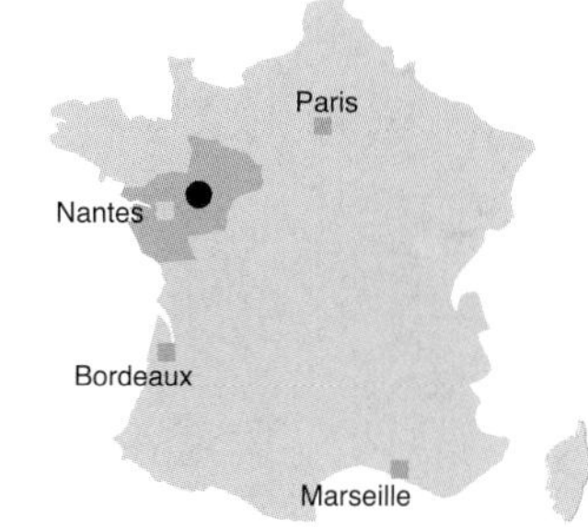

Price Guide:
(room only)
single €140–230
double/twin €120–240
suites €275–320

HOSTELLERIE ABBAYE DE VILLENEUVE

44480 NANTES – LES SORINIÈRES, FRANCE

This beautifully restored abbey was founded before the 15th century. Now part of the house is made up of the old Cistercian guest quarters and it still boasts an impressive stone staircase. The cloister entrance leads into the elegant L'Epicurien restaurant, whilst the public rooms have high ceilings and open fireplaces and the bedrooms display beautiful timbering and elegant décor. Outside, a pretty, centrally positioned pool completes the air of calm and tasteful luxury.

Cette abbaye admirablement bien restaurée a été fondée avant le XVe siècle. De nos jours, une partie des logements est constituée des anciens quartiers d'hôtes cisterciens, et s'enorgueillit d'un impressionnant escalier de pierre. L'entrée du cloître conduit à l'élégant restaurant L'Epicurien, alors que les salles communes ont des plafonds hauts et cheminées ouvertes et les chambres affichent de beaux bois d'œuvre et un décor élégant. Dehors, une petite piscine centrale ajoute au sentiment de calme et de luxe raffiné.

Diese schöne Abtei wurde bereits vor dem 15. Jahrhundert gegründet. Heute besteht ein Teil des Hauses aus den ehemaligen Zisterzienser-Gästezimmern, und ein eindrucksvolles steinernes Treppenhaus ist auch noch vorhanden. Der Klostereingang führt in das elegante Restaurant L'Epicurien. Hohe Decken und offene Kamine zieren die Aufenthaltsräume, und die Gästezimmer haben herrliche Vertäfelungen und sind elegant gestaltet. Draußen sorgt ein attraktiver, zentral gelegener Pool für eine Atmosphäre von bescheidenem Luxus.

Our inspector loved: *The cloistered entrance hall.*

Directions: Nantes circular south > exit Les Sorinières.

Web: www.johansens.com/abbayedevilleneuve
E-mail: villeneuve@leshotelsparticuliers.com
Tel: +33 2 40 04 40 25
Fax: +33 2 40 31 28 45

Price Guide:
(room only)
double €80–155
suite €190

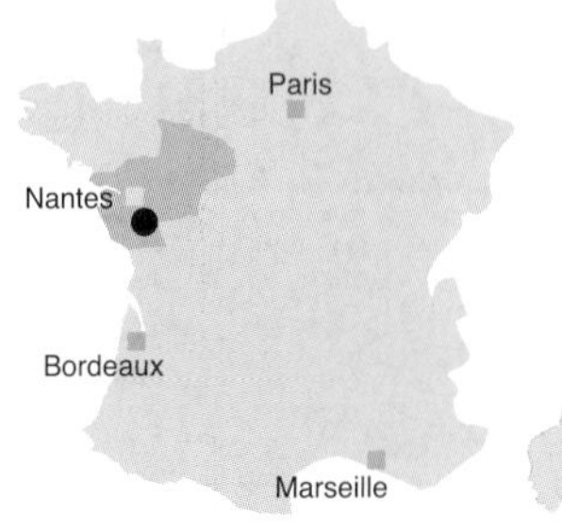

Hostellerie du Général d'Elbée

PLACE DU CHÂTEAU, 85330 NOIRMOUTIER~EN~L'ISLE, FRANCE

Accessed by bridge or causeway to the Isle of Noirmoutier, this idyllic portside mansion affords wonderful views of the port and the medieval castle, and is a real oasis of tranquillity. Cosy lounges, pretty bedrooms, some of which have oak-beams, delightful interior courtyard and charming pool settings all add to the sense of simplistic charm that characterise the area, and make this the ideal place to relax and unwind, or to enjoy the many fine sandy beaches of the Vendée.

Sur l'île de Noirmoutier, où l'on accède par le pont ou par la route à marée basse, cet hôtel idyllique particulier offre une vue imprenable sur le port et le château médieval et est un havre de paix et de tranquillité. Des salons confortables, de jolies chambres, certaines avec poutres apparentes, une ravissante cour intérieure et un charmant arrangement autour de la piscine, tout ajoute au charme simple des environs, et en fait l'endroit idéal pour se détendre ou jouir des nombreuses plages de sable fin de la Vendée.

Erreichbar über eine Brücke oder einen Damm zur Insel Noirmoutier, bietet dieses idyllische Hotel herrliche Blicke auf den Hafen und die mittelalterliche Burg – eine wahre Oase der Ruhe. Gemütliche Aufenthaltsräume, attraktive Zimmer (einige mit Eichenholzdecke), ein zauberhafter Innenhof und hübscher Swimmingpool unterstreichen das Gefühl von Einfachheit, das so typisch für diese Gegend ist und diesen Ort ideal zum Entspannen machen. Die zahlreichen Sandstrände der Vendée liegen in nächster Nähe.

Our inspector loved: *The super swimming pool and courtyard area.*

Directions: A11 > exit Nantes > direction of Noirmoutier.

Web: www.johansens.com/generaldelbee
E-mail: elbee@leshotelsparticuliers.com
Tel: +33 2 51 39 10 29
Fax: +33 2 51 33 08 23

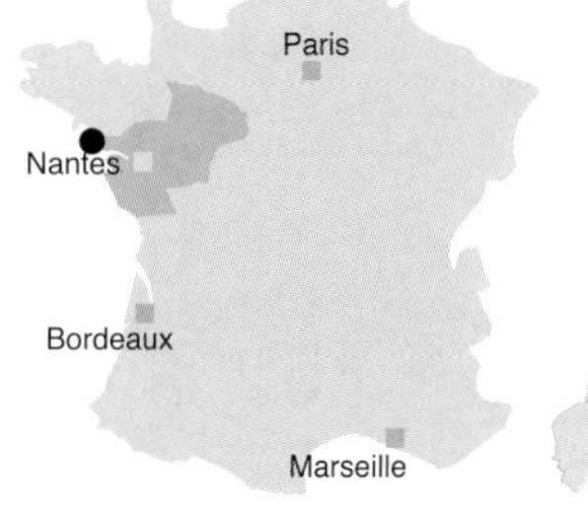

Price Guide:
(room only)
double €75–€210
suite €178–277

Germany

Hotel location shown in red (hotel) or purple (spa hotel) with page number

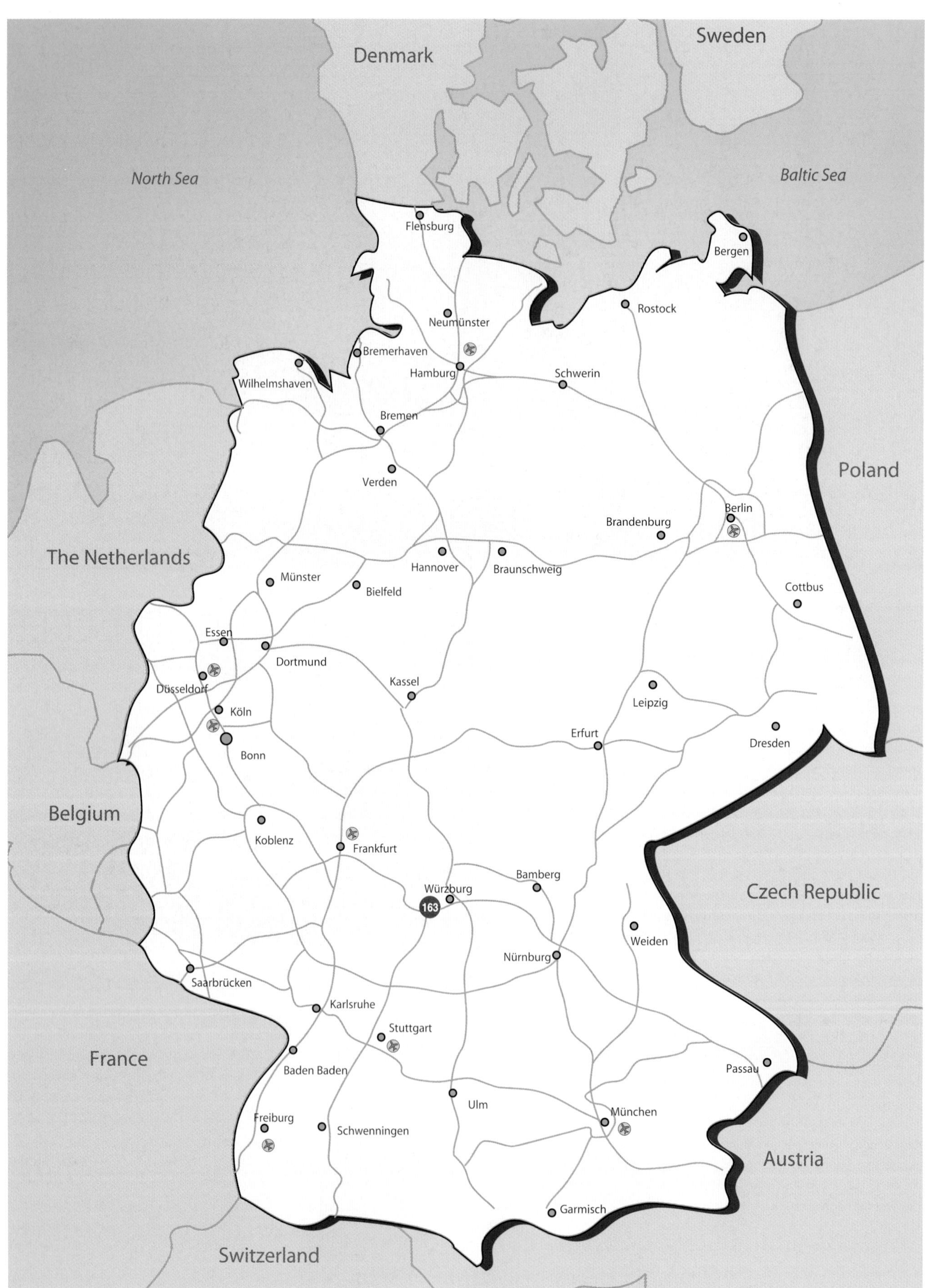

Hotel Eisenhut

HERRNGASSE 3-7, 91541 ROTHENBURG OB DER TAUBER, GERMANY

Situated in the middle of the unspoilt medieval town of Rothenburg, the Eisenhut is an attractive hotel created from 4 14th-century town houses. Its historic origins are reflected in the interior, which is adorned with gleaming suits of armour, marvellous antiques and relics of imperial armies. The bedrooms are luxurious and spacious, with gorgeous flowered bedcovers and big gilt mirrors adding to their charm. Sophisticated international menus also include local specialities, and are complemented by fine wines from the cellar.

Composé de 4 demeures du XIVe siècle, le Eisenhut est un bel hôtel situé au coeur de la ville médiévale préservée de Rothenburg. Ses origines historiques sont reflétées à l'intérieur, qui est agrémenté par de superbes armures, de belles antiquités et des reliques des armées impériales. Le charme des chambres, luxueuses et spacieuses, est accentué par de magnifiques dessus-de-lit fleuris et de grands miroirs dorés. Les menus sophistiqués de cuisine internationale proposent également des spécialités régionales agrémentées de bons vins.

Dieses attraktive Hotel im Zentrum der mittelalterlichen Stadt Rothenburg besteht aus 4 Patrizierhäusern aus dem 14. Jahrhundert. Die historischen Ursprünge zeigen sich in der Einrichtung: schimmernde Rüstungen, eine Hinterlassenschaft der kaiserlichen Armee, und herrlichste Antiquitäten zieren die Räume. Die großen Zimmer sind luxuriös, und vergoldete Spiegel und zauberhafte geblümte Bettdecken sorgen für Persönlichkeit. Auf der Speisekarte stehen exquisite internationale Gerichte sowie regionale Spezialitäten und erlesene Weine.

***Our inspector loved:** The professional staff and the elegant décor throughout.*

Directions: A7 > Rothenburg > Marktplatz.

Web: www.johansens.com/eisenhut
E-mail: hotel@eisenhut.com
Tel: +49 9861 7050
Fax: +49 9861 70545

Price Guide:
single €111–121
double/twin €155–205
suites €280–340

Great Britain & Ireland

Hotel location shown in red (hotel) or purple (spa hotel) with page number

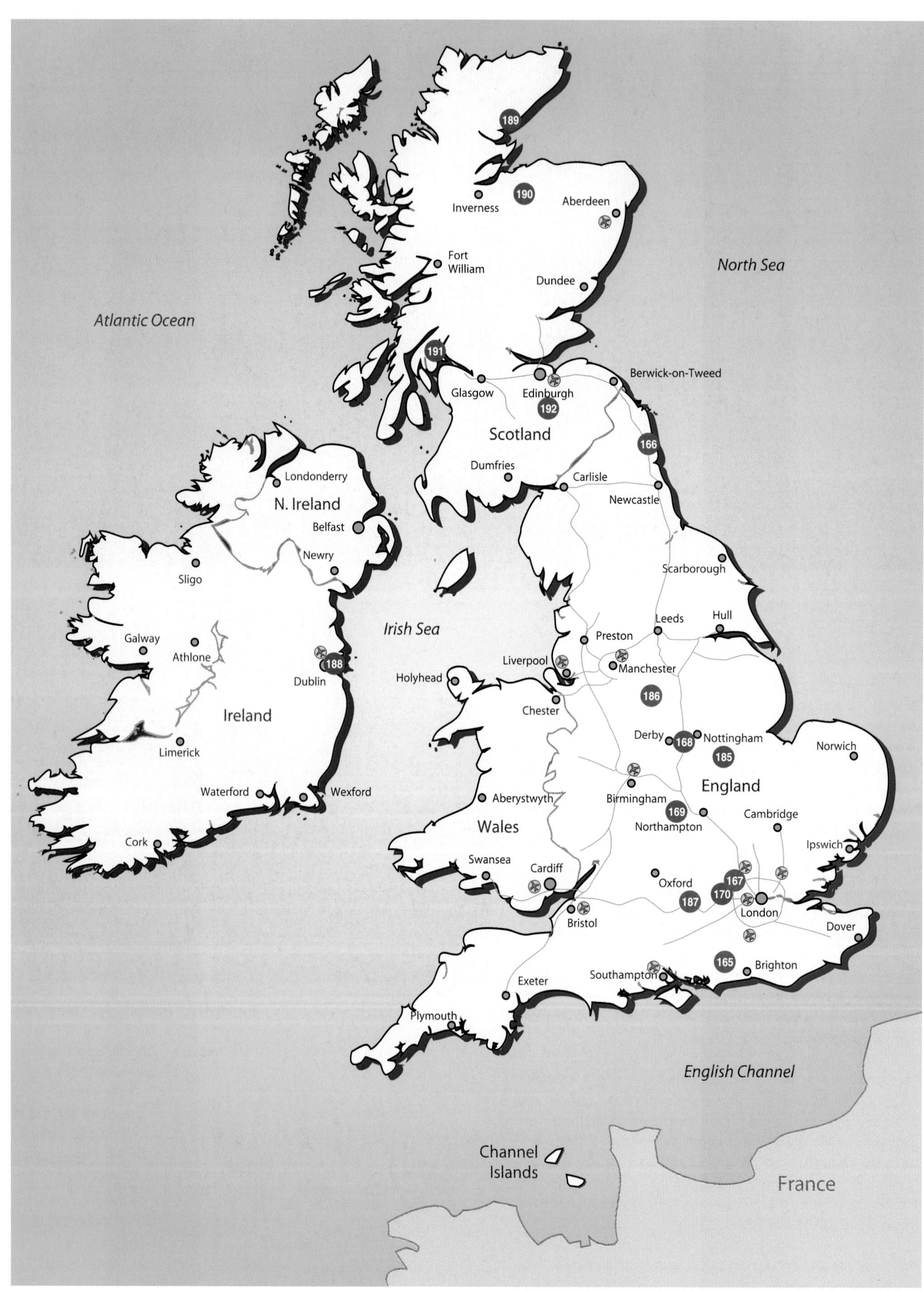

Amberley Castle

AMBERLEY, NEAR ARUNDEL, WEST SUSSEX BN18 9ND, ENGLAND

Winner of the Johansens Award for Outstanding Excellence and Innovation 2003, this medieval fortress is over 900 years old and boasts a fascinating history. Today it offers a warm welcome and the ultimate in contemporary yet timeless luxury. Distinctive new suites have been added, and each room is individually designed with its own Jacuzzi bath. The exquisite 12th-century Queen's Room makes the perfect setting for the hotel's creative cuisine, whilst nearby, Roman ruins, antiques, horse-racing and stately homes are found in abundance.

Le gagnant du prix Johansens Award for Outstanding Excellence and Innovation en 2003 a plus de 900 ans et un passé fascinant. Aujourd'hui, il réserve un accueil chaleureux à ses visiteurs qui y découvrent un luxe à la fois moderne et hors du temps. L'hôtel comprend de nouvelles suites et des chambres avec jacuzzi décorées de manière individuelle. Datant du XIIe siècle, la ravissante chambre de la reine forme un cadre parfait pour la cuisine de l'hôtel, situé dans une région où abondent les ruines romaines, les antiquaires, les champs de courses et les demeures ancestrales.

Diese mittelalterliche Festung wurde 2003 mit dem Johansens Award for Outstanding Excellence and Innovation ausgezeichnet. Das über 900 Jahr alte Anwesen ist heute ein einladendes Hotel, das das Beste an zeitgemäßem und doch zeitlosen Luxus bietet. Hervorragende neue Suiten wurden eingerichtet, und jedes Zimmer ist individuell gestaltet und hat ein Jacuzzi-Bad. Der Queen's Room aus dem 12. Jahrhundert ist das ideale Umfeld, um die Küche des Hotels zu genießen, und in der Nähe kann man zahlreiche Ruinen und Landsitze erkunden, Antiquitäten kaufen oder zum Pferderennen gehen.

Directions: A29 - B2139 between Bury and Storrington.

Web: www.johansens.com/amberleycastleeuro
E-mail: info@amberleycastle.co.uk
Tel: +44 1798 831 992
Fax: +44 1798 831 998

Price Guide:
(room only)
double/twin £145–340
suite £275–340

Our inspector loved: *The castle walls, black swans and white peacocks.*

Waren House Hotel

WAREN MILL, BAMBURGH, NORTHUMBERLAND NE70 7EE, ENGLAND

Situated in 6 acres of gardens and woodland on the edge of the Budle Bay Bird Sanctuary, the Waren House Hotel offers discerning visitors peace and quiet even during the busy summer months. Throughout the hotel, the antique furnishings and the immaculate and well-chosen décor evoke a warm and friendly ambience. In the intimate candle-lit dining room, guests can choose from an eclectic menu and extensive wine list.

Situé dans un parc et une forêt de 2½ hectares sur le bord de la Baie de Budle Bird Sanctuary, le Waren House Hotel offre à ses visiteurs une paix et une tranquillité inégalables même durant les mois estivaux. Dans l'hôtel, les meubles anciens et la décoration extrêment soignés évoquent une ambiance chaleureuse et amicale. Dans la salle à manger intime éclairée aux bougies, les visiteurs pourront se régaler d'un menu éclectique et d'une superbe liste de vins.

Das Waren House Hotel liegt in 2½ ha Park- und Waldlandschaft am Rande des Budle Bay Vogelschutzgebietes und bietet anspruchsvollen Gästen selbst während der geschäftigen Sommermonate völlige Ruhe. Im ganzen Hotel befinden sich Antiquitäten und geschmackvolle Einrichtungen, die ein behagliches und freundliches Ambiente schaffen. Im intimen und mit Kerzenlicht beleuchteten Speisesaal erfreuen sich die Gäste an abwechslungsreichen Speisen und einer ausführlichen Weinkarte.

Our inspector loved: *This delightful small hotel on the heritage coast overlooking Budle Bay.*

Directions: B1342 > Waren Mill > south-west of Budle Bay.

Web: www.johansens.com/warenhouseeuro
E-mail: enquiries@warenhousehotel.co.uk
Tel: +44 1668 214581
Fax: +44 1668 214484

Price Guide:
single £90–£110
double £120–£140
suite £165–£195

The Greyhound Inn

HIGH STREET, CHALFONT ST PETER SL9 9RA, ENGLAND

This 14th-century coaching inn, set in the historic village of Chalfont St Peter, is easily accessed from central London and Heathrow Airport and moments away from glorious English countryside. The 12 en-suite bedrooms feature marble bathrooms and solid oak furniture and some guest rooms boast original 14th-century oak beams and Georgian period furnishings. The restaurant's daily changing menu offers classic British cuisine with a modern twist and is created from fresh local produce, accompanied by a fine selection of wines.

Ce relais de poste du XIVe siècle, situé dans le village historique de Chalfont St Peter, d'accès facile du centre de Londres et de l'aéroport d'Heathrow ainsi que de la célèbre campagne anglaise. Ses 12 chambres présentent des salles de bain en marbre et meubles en chêne, certaines d'entre elles ont des poutres apparentes datant du XIVe siècle et mobilier de style anglais classique. Au restaurant, le menu change tous les jours et offre une cuisine britannique classique avec une touche de modernité, créée à partir de produits locaux frais et accompagnée d'une sélection de vins fins.

Diese Kutschstation aus dem 14. Jahrhundert liegt im historischen Dorf Chalfont St Peter, ist leicht von der Londoner Innenstadt und dem Flughafen Heathrow erreichbar und befindet sich doch inmitten herrlicher englischer Landschaft. Die 12 Zimmer haben eigene Marmorbäder und solide Eichenmöbel, einige sogar die Originaleichenbalken aus dem 14. Jahrhundert und Stilmöbel der Zeit König Georges. Im Restaurant kann man täglich neue, mit frischen einheimischen Zutaten zubereitete britische Klassiker mit moderner Note sowie feine Weine genießen.

Our inspector loved: *The contemporary style and traditional comfort.*

Directions: M25 > junction 16 > M40 > junction 1 > A40 > A413 > village centre.

Web: www.johansens.com/greyhoundeuro
E-mail: reception@thegreyhound.net
Tel: +44 1753 883404
Fax: +44 1753 891627

Price Guide:
single £105
double £140
suite £170

Risley Hall

DERBY ROAD, RISLEY, DERBYSHIRE DE72 3SS, ENGLAND

Dating from Elizabethan times, Risley Hall has been splendidly restored to its former glory. Its peaceful atmosphere is enhanced by spectacular, colourful gardens. The décor inside features oak beams, ornate fireplaces and individually decorated bedrooms. The cosy Drawing Room is a convivial place to enjoy afternoon tea, whilst the Cocktail Lounge serves lunchtime drinks or apéritifs. The hotel is ideal for corporate meetings or special occasions, and guests are free to explore the wealth of historic buildings in the vicinity.

Datant de l'époque élisabéthaine, Risley Hall a retrouvé sa splendeur d'origine grâce à une restauration soignée. Un beau parc fleuri accentue l'atmosphère paisible des lieux. L'hôtel ouvre sur des pièces dotées de poutres en chêne et de cheminées richement ornées et des chambres au style individuel. Le salon convivial est l'endroit indiqué pour prendre le thé, et le bar vous attend pour l'apéritif. Risley Hall est idéal pour organiser des réunions d'affaires ou des réceptions et découvrir les nombreux monuments historiques de la région.

Risley Hall stammt aus der Zeit Elizabeths I. und erlangte durch ausführliche Renovierung seine ursprüngliche Pracht wieder. Die friedliche Atmosphäre verstärkt sich noch durch prachtvolle, bunte Gärten. Eichenbalken und verzierte Kamine schmücken die Innenräume und die Zimmer sind individuell gestaltet. Der Aufenthaltsraum lädt zum Nachmittagstee ein, und in der Cocktail Lounge werden Drinks und Apéritifs serviert. Das Hotel ist ideal für Geschäftstreffen, und zahlreiche historische Bauten können in der Nähe erkundet werden.

***Our inspector loved:** The quiet enviroment and attention to detail offered. "A little oasis." So near to excellent air, rail and road links.*

Directions: M1 > exit junction 25 towards Sandiacre.

Web: www.johansens.com/risleyhalleuro
E-mail: johansens@risleyhallhotel.co.uk
Tel: +44 115 939 9000
Fax: +44 115 939 7766

Price Guide:
single £105–£125
double/twin £125–£145
suite £150–£195

FAWSLEY HALL

FAWSLEY, NEAR DAVENTRY, NORTHAMPTONSHIRE NN11 3BA, ENGLAND

Set amidst beautiful countryside and surrounded by parkland, Fawsley Hall combines the charm and character of a manor house with the comforts of a modern hotel. 43 wonderfully decorated rooms offer a range of styles; many have four-poster beds. Guests dine at the excellent Knightley Restaurant, whilst the Old Laundry Bar provides delicious lunches. The hotel's new spa in the Georgian cellar includes a beauty salon, fitness studio, steam room, sauna and spa bath as well as conference facilities for up to 140.

Au sein de belle campagne et entouré par un parc, Fawsley Hall marie à merveille le charme et le caractère d'un manoir avec le confort d'un hôtel moderne. Les 43 chambres magnifiques sont décorées dans une variété de styles divers; plusieurs d'entre elles ont un lit à colonnes. Les hôtes dînent au restaurant superbe Knightley, alors que Old Laundry Bar propose des déjeuners délicieux. Le nouveau spa dans la cave géorgienne comprend un salon de beauté, studio de remise en forme, hammam, sauna et bain spa, ainsi que des facilités de conférences pour jusqu'à 140 personnes.

Inmitten herrlicher Landschaft und umgeben von Park bietet Fawsley Hall den Charme und Charakter eines Landsitzes mit allen Annehmlichkeiten eines modernen Hotels. Die 43 Zimmer sind in unterschiedlichen Stilen gehalten, viele haben Himmelbetten. Im hervorragenden Knightley Restaurant wird feine Küche serviert, und die Old Laundry Bar ist hervorragend für ein leichtes Mittagessen. Im neuen Spa des Hotels im georgianischen Keller befinden sich Schönheitssalon, Dampfbad, Sauna und Kurbad sowie Konferenzeinrichtungen für bis zu 140 Personen.

Our inspector loved: *The views of the rolling countryside from the bedroom windows.*

Directions: Fawsley Hall can be reached by the M40, junction 11 or the M1, junction16. Both are 10 miles from the hotel.

Web: www.johansens.com/fawsleyhalleuro
E-mail: reservations@fawsleyhall.com
Tel: +44 1327 892000
Fax: +44 1327 892001

Price Guide:
single from £135
double from £160
suite from £275

STOKE PARK CLUB

PARK ROAD, STOKE POGES, BUCKINGHAMSHIRE SL2 4PG, ENGLAND

Directions: M4, junction 6 or M40 junction 2 > A344 > at double roundabout at Farnham Royal take B416. Entrance is approximately 1 mile on the right.

Web: www.johansens.com/stokeparkeuro
E-mail: info@stokeparkclub.com
Tel: +44 1753 717171
Fax: +44 1753 717181

Price Guide:
single £270
suite £390

Set amidst 350 acres of parkland, this elegant hotel has played host to numerous noblemen, kings and queens. Great attention to detail is evident in the décor, with antiques, exquisite fabrics and original paintings and prints creating a lavish setting. The individually designed bedrooms and suites, some with their own terrace, are complemented by marble bathrooms. The hotel is home to one of the finest 27-hole championship golf courses in the world – Stoke Poges. Spa facilities include 11 treatment rooms, indoor swimming pool, state-of-the-art gym and 13 tennis courts.

Au milieu de 140 ha de parc, cet élégant hôtel fut une halte royale pour de nombreux rois, reines et aristocrates. L'attention apportée aux détails est évidente dans le décor; des objets d'art, tissus exquis, et tableaux originaux créent un cadre somptueux. Les chambres et suites décorées de façon individuelle, quelques-unes avec leur propre terrasse, sont complétées par des salles de bains en marbre. L'hôtel a un parcours de golf championnat de 27 trous – Stoke Poges, un des meilleurs parcours au monde. Le spa comprend 11 salles de traitement, piscine couverte, centre de remis en forme du dernier cri et 13 courts de tennis.

Dieses inmitten von 140ha Park gelegene elegante Hotel beherbergte bereits zahlreiche Adelige, Könige und Königinnen. Liebe zum Detail ist überall sichtbar, und Antiquitäten, exquisite Stoffe und Originalgemälde und -drucke schaffen ein edles Ambiente. Die unterschiedlich gestalteten Zimmer und Suiten (einige mit Terrasse) haben Marmorbäder. Gäste können auf dem Stoke Poges, einem der besten 27-Loch-Golfplätze der Welt spielen. Wellnesseinrichtungen umfassen 11 Behandlungsräume, Hallenbad, hochmodernen Fitnessraum und 13 Tennisplätze.

Our inspector loved: *The wonderful setting, comfy rooms and stunning spa.*

LONDON

Hotel location shown in red (hotel) or purple (spa hotel) with page number

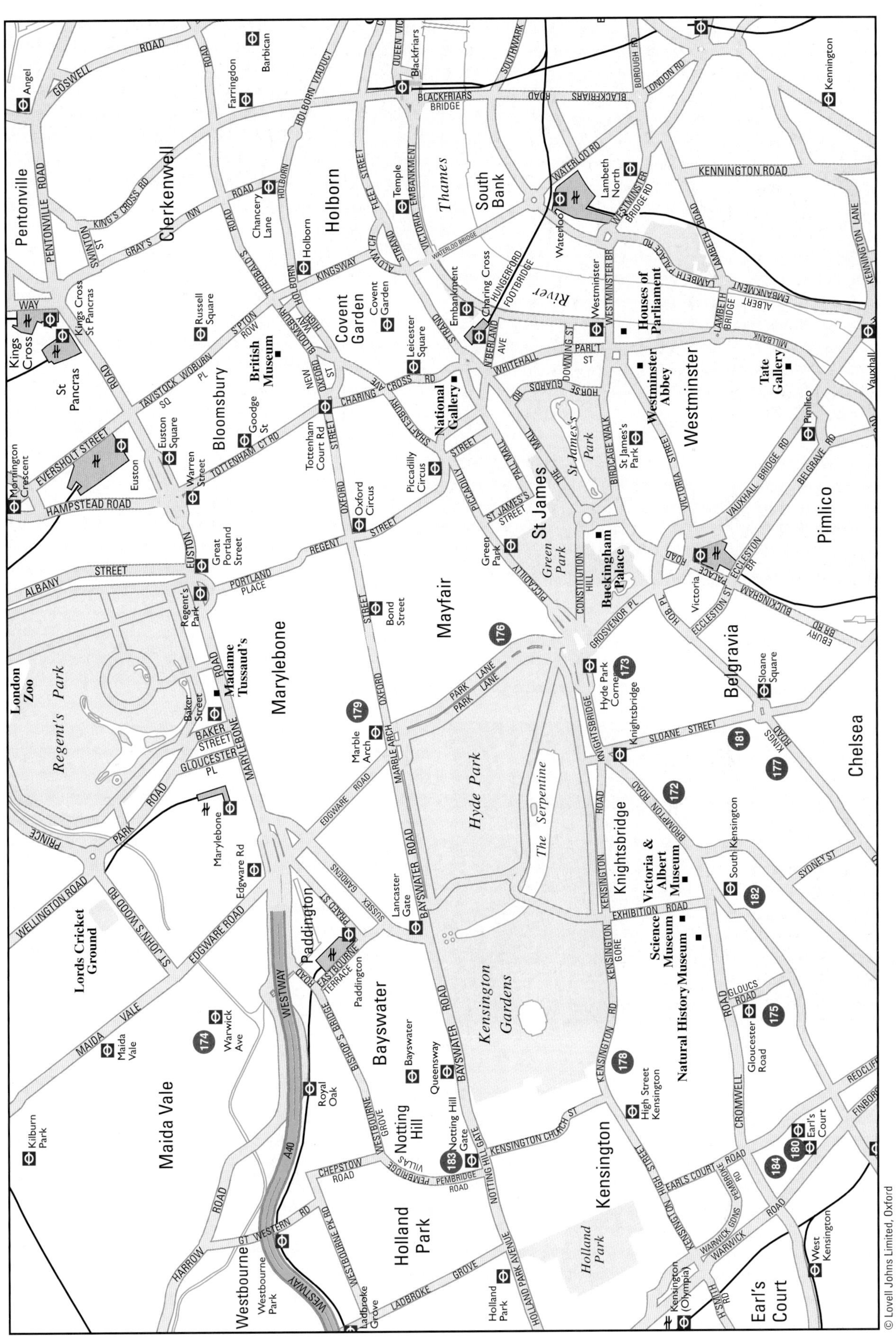

Beaufort House Apartments

45 BEAUFORT GARDENS, KNIGHTSBRIDGE, LONDON SW3 1PN, ENGLAND

Situated in a quiet tree-lined Regency cul-de-sac in the heart of Knightsbridge, Beaufort House comprises 21 self-contained apartments of 5-star standard. Each has been individually and traditionally decorated, with direct dial telephones and high-speed Internet. Every apartment has a fully-fitted kitchen. A concierge is on duty 24 hours a day. Complimentary membership to Aquilla's health club is also offered to all guests during their stay.

Situé dans une impasse calme et longée d'arbres dans Knightsbridge, Beaufort House comprend 21 appartements indépendants de catégorie 5 étoiles. Chacun est décoré de manière individuelle et traditionnelle et possède téléphone direct et ADSL. Tous sont équipés de cuisine. Un concierge est à votre disposition 24h/24. Une adhésion complémentaire au club de remise en forme Aquilla est également offerte à tous les visiteurs durant leur séjour.

In einer ruhigen, von Bäumen eingefassten Straße im Herzen von Knightsbridge liegt Beaufort House, das aus 21 abgeschlossenen 5-Sterne Appartements besteht. Jedes ist individuell und traditionell eingerichtet und bietet neben Telefon mit Direktdurchwahl auch ADSL-Internetzugang sowie eine voll ausgestattete Küche. Ein Pförtner ist rund um die Uhr im Dienst. Während des Aufenthalts haben die Gäste freie Mitgliedschaft in Aquilla's Fitnessclub.

Our inspector loved: *This well-equipped and comfortable establishment, as ideal for weekend breaks as it is for longer stays.*

Directions: Off Brompton Road in Knightsbridge.

Web: www.johansens.com/beauforthouseapartmentseuro
E-mail: info@beauforthouse.co.uk
Tel: +44 20 7584 2600
Fax: +4 20 7584 6532

Price Guide:
(excluding VAT)
apartment £230–650

THE BERKELEY

WILTON PLACE, LONDON SW1 7RL, ENGLAND

Perfectly located in the heart of fashionable Knightsbridge, the luxurious Berkeley is a stunning mix of traditional and contemporary design. Beautiful bedrooms are decorated with antiques and exquisite fabrics in striking colours. Very calm and friendly staff attend to guests' every need. Gordon Ramsay's Boxwood Café and Michelin-star chef Marcus Wareing's new Pétrus restaurant make the hotel one of the city's top gastronomic destinations.

Parfaitement situé, au cœur du quartier de Knightsbridge, cet hôtel de luxe est un mélange fascinant de design traditionnel et contemporain. Les belles chambres sont décorées avec des antiquités et des tissus exquis en couleurs vivantes. Le personnel calme et sympathique répond au moindre désir des hôtes. Le Boxwood Café de chef Gordon Ramsay et Pétrus, le restaurant nouveau de Marcus Wareing, attribué une étoile Michelin, rendent l'hôtel une des meilleures destinations gastronomiques de Londres.

Mitten im Herzen des beliebten Viertels Knightsbridge gelegen, bietet das luxuriöse Berkeley eine eindrucksvolle Mischung aus traditionellem und zeitgenössischem Design. Die hübschen Zimmer sind mit Antiquitäten gefüllt und mit exquisiten Stoffen in kräftigen Farben dekoriert. Das ruhige und sehr freundliche Personal kommt allen Wünschen nach. Gordon Ramsays Boxwood Café und das Pétrus Restaurant des Michelin-Sterne-Kochs Marcus Wareing machen dieses Hotel zu einem der besten Gourmettreffs der Stadt.

Our inspector loved: *The rooftop heated swimming pool and spa with retractable roof and stunning panoramic views over central London.*

Directions: Heathrow Airport is 45 minutes by car. Knightsbridge tube station is a 5-minute walk. The hotel is situated on the corner of Wilton Place and Knightsbridge overlooking Hyde Park.

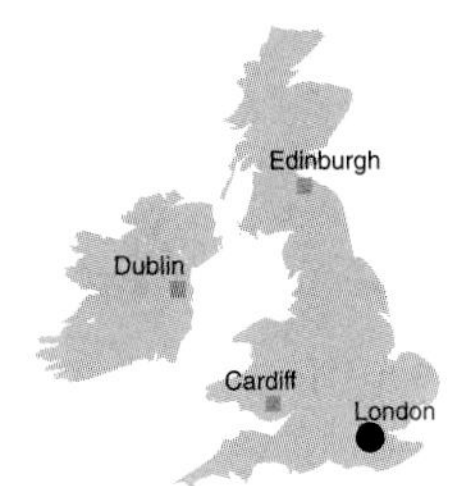

Web: www.johansens.com/berkeleyeuro
E-mail: reservations@the-berkeley.co.uk
Tel: +44 (0) 20 7235 6000
Fax: +44 (0) 20 7235 4330

Price Guide:
double £295-420
suite £490-3,300
four poster £855-940

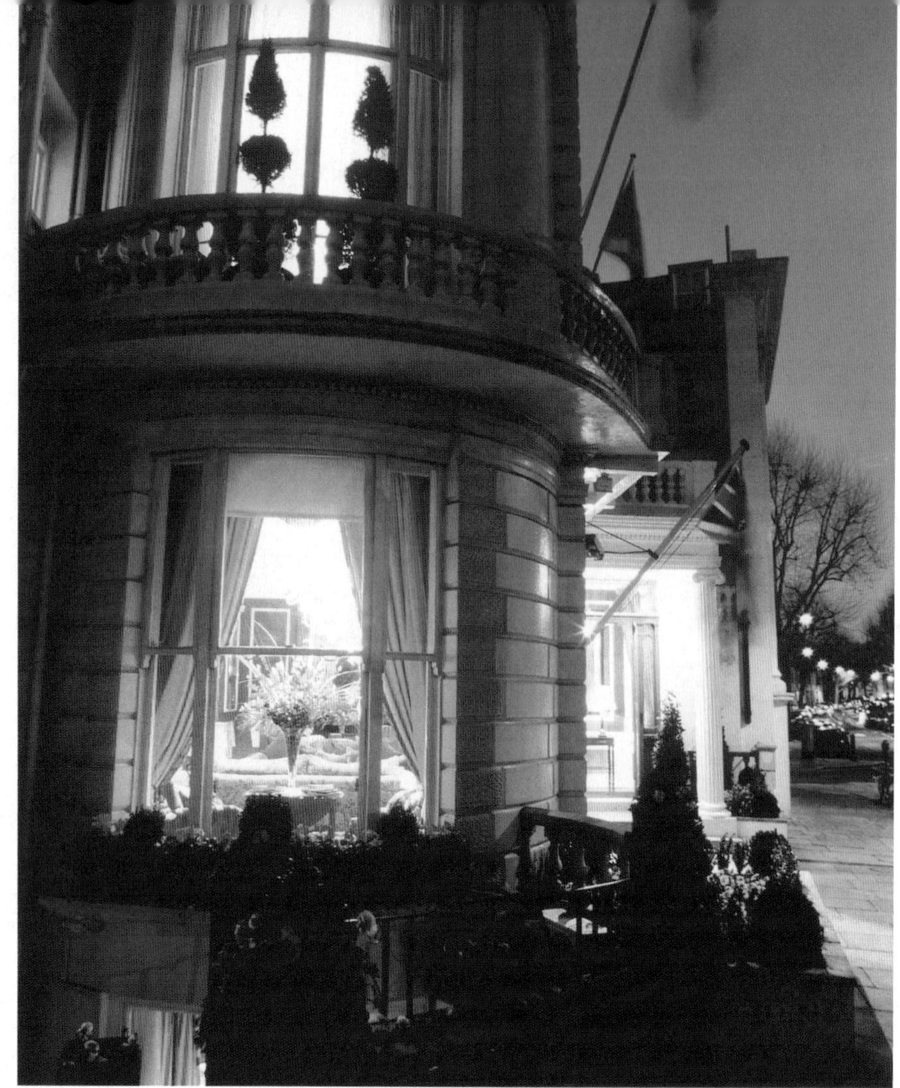

THE COLONNADE, THE LITTLE VENICE TOWN HOUSE

2 WARRINGTON CRESCENT, LONDON W9 1ER, ENGLAND

Situated at the heart of London's Little Venice, The Colonnade is a tall, elegant Victorian house that simply exudes charm and sophistication. Dating from the middle of the 19th century it has been refurbished to the very highest of standards. Each of the 43 bedrooms has been individually designed with sumptuous fabrics and antiques, and the intimate drawing room completes the feeling of a true "home away from home". The Enigma restaurant serves an unforgettable Town House breakfast, Mediterranian cuisine for lunch and dinner.

Situé en plein coeur de la Petite Venise à Londres, Le Colonnade est une grande et élégante maison victorienne qui dégage une ambiance de charme et de sophistication. Dâtant du milieu du XIXe siècle, l'hôtel a été superbement rénové. Chacune des 43 chambres a été décorée de manière individuelle et est agrémentée de somptueux tissus et d'antiquités. L'intimité du salon complète le sentiment d'être "comme à la maison". Le restaurant "Enigma sert un petit déjeuner "Town House" inoubliable et un cuisine méditerranéen pour le déjeuner et le dîner.

Das Colonnade, im Herzen von Londons Little Venice gelegen, ist ein hohes, elegantes viktorianisches Haus mit Charme und Raffinesse. Es wurde Mitte des 19. Jahrhunderts erbaut und in exklusivem Stil renoviert. Jedes der 43 Zimmer ist individuell gestaltet und mit herrlichsten Stoffen und erlesenen Antiquitäten eingerichtet, und der heimelige Aufenthaltsraum sorgt dafür, dass man sich wie zu Hause fühlt. Das Restaurant Enigma serviert ein unvergeßliches "Town House" Frühstück und mittags und abends genießt man Mittelmeerküche.

Our inspector loved: *Its elegance, sophistication and warmth - all rolled into one. Please discover it for yourself.*

Directions: Near Warwick Avenue underground station.

Web: www.johansens.com/colonnadetownhouseeuro
E-mail: res_colonnade@eton.com
Tel: +44 20 7286 1052
Fax: +44 20 7286 7286

Price Guide:
(excluding VAT)
single £126
suites from £230

THE CRANLEY

10–12 BINA GARDENS, SOUTH KENSINGTON, LONDON SW5 0LA, ENGLAND

Standing in the heart of Kensington, this charming and sophisticated town house blends traditional style and service with 21st-century technology. Beautiful antiques, hand-embroidered fabrics, striking colour combinations and stone are used throughout. Some of the delightful bedrooms feature four-poster beds and all benefit from luxurious bathrooms. Copious continental breakfasts, English afternoon tea and evening apéritifs are served. Many of London's restaurants and attractions are within walking distance.

Charmant et raffiné, cet hôtel particulier au coeur de Kensington allie un style et un service traditionnels à un confort moderne. L'intérieur est rehaussé par de belles antiquités, des tissus brodés à la main, des combinaisons de couleurs remarquables et l'usage de la pierre. Des lits à baldaquin trônent dans certaines des chambres, toutes équipées de salles de bains luxueuses. L'hôtel sert de copieux petits déjeuners continentaux, le thé de cinq heures et l'apéritif avant le dîner. Nombre des restaurants et des attractions de la capitale ne sont qu'à deux pas.

Dieses charmante und elegante mitten in Kensington gelegene Stadthaus verbindet traditionellen Stil und Service mit der Technologie des 21. Jahrhunderts. Herrliche Antiquitäten, handbestickte Stoffe, auffällige Farbkombinationen und Stein zieren das Interieur. Einige der hübschen Zimmer haben Himmelbetten und alle besitzen luxuriöse Bäder. Gäste genießen ein üppiges Frühstück, englischen Nachmittagstee und Apéritifs am Abend. Zahlreiche Restaurants und Attraktionen befinden sich in nächster Nähe.

Our inspector loved: *This charming hotel with its abundance of four-poster beds.*

Directions: Underground stations: Gloucester Road or South Kensington.

Web: www.johansens.com/cranleyeuro
E-mail: info@thecranley.com
Tel: +44 20 7373 0123
Fax: +44 20 7373 9497

Price Guide:
single £182.12
double/twin £211.50
suite from £300

THE DORCHESTER

PARK LANE, MAYFAIR, LONDON W1A 2HJ, ENGLAND

Recently restored to its original splendour, The Dorchester is quite plainly one of the finest hotels in the world . Each of the bedrooms and suites has been luxuriously designed, and benefits from marble bathrooms. Apart from the renowned Grill Room, there is an exquisite Chinese restaurant. Specialised health and beauty treatments are available in The Dorchester Spa, impressive with its statues and glass and water fountain.

Récemment restauré, Le Dorchester est tout simplement un des hôtels les plus raffinés du monde. Chaque chambre et suite a été luxueusement conçue avec des salles de bain en marbre. Outre la fameuse rotisserie, l'hôtel dispose d'un exquis restaurant chinois. Le Spa du Dorchester propose des traitements spéciaux de beauté et de santé. Il se distingue par ses impressionnantes statues, ses fontaines et ses miroirs

Vor kurzem zu seiner ursprünglichen Pracht renoviert, ist das Dorchester eines der besten Hotels der Welt. Jedes Zimmer sowie jede Suite ist luxuriös gestaltet und verfügt über ein Marmorbad. Außer dem renommierten Grill Room gibt es auch ein herrliches kantonesisches Restaurant. Besondere Schönheits- und Gesundheitsanwendungen werden im Dorchester Spa angeboten, das die Gäste mit Statuen und Glas- und Wasser-Springbrunnen beeindruckt.

***Our inspector loved:** The superb example of English elegance, charm and superb service.*

Directions: Hyde Park Corner end of Park Lane.

Web: www.johansens.com/thedorchestereuro
E-mail: reservations@dorchesterhotel.com
Tel: +44 (0)20 7629 8888
Fax: + 44 (0)20 7409 0114

Price Guide:
(excluding VAT)
single £275–330
double/twin £345–380
suite £525–2,125

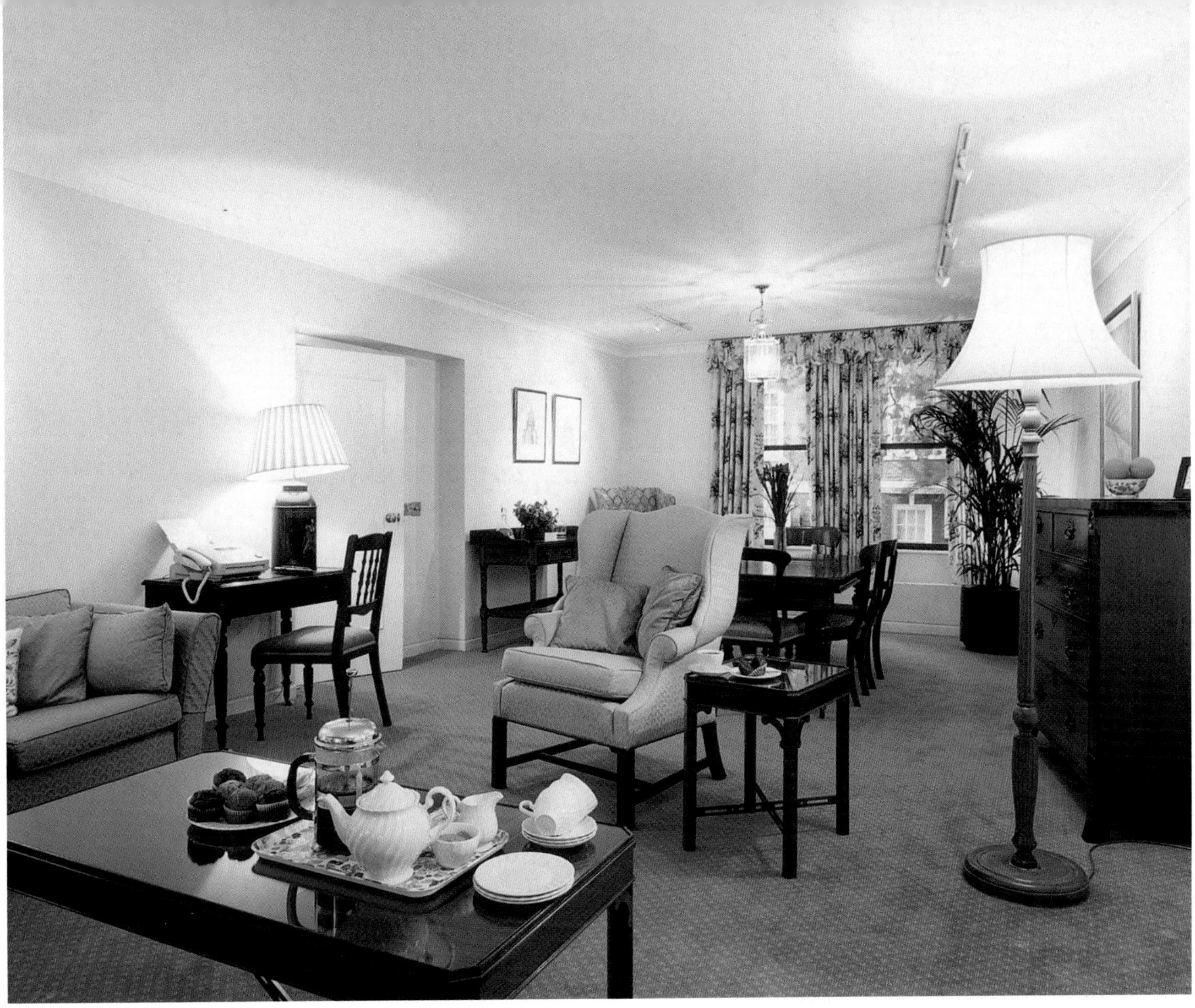

Draycott House Apartments

10 DRAYCOTT AVENUE, CHELSEA, LONDON SW3 3AA, ENGLAND

Draycott House stands in a quiet tree-lined avenue in the heart of Chelsea and offers luxury accommodation in 1, 2 or 3-bedroomed apartments. Combining comfort, privacy and security, the apartments are spacious, luxurious and well-equipped. Draycott House will organise cars, airport transfers, catering and theatre arrangements etc., as well as an introduction to an exclusive health club. There is 5-day maid service, in-house laundry facilities and garage parking.

Draycott House s'élève dans une rue paisible bordée d'arbres en plein coeur de Chelsea et offre un logement luxueux. Les appartements avec 1, 2 ou 3 lits allient confort, intimité et sécurité. Ils sont spacieux, luxueux et bien équipés. Draycott House organise sur demande des taxis, des transferts aéroport, des services de restauration, des places de théâtre, etc. Il offre également son club de remise en forme prestigieux. Le service de femmes de chambre est tous les cinq jours, et des services de blanchisserie ainsi qu'un garage sont disponibles.

Die großzügigen Zimmer 1-, 2- und 3-Appartements des Draycott House liegen in einer ruhigen Allee im Herzen von Chelsea. Geräumig, luxuriös und bestens ausgestattet bieten sie eine Mischung aus Komfort, Abgeschiedenheit und Sicherheit. Taxis, Flughafentransfer, Verpflegung, Theaterkarten etc. können organisiert werden, ebenso wie die Einführung in einen exklusiven Fitnessclub. Ausserdem stehen 5-Tages-Zimmerservice, Waschmaschine und Trockner wie auch überdachte Parkplätze zur Verfügung.

Our inspector loved: *The light and comfortable spacious apartments decorated in a traditional English style, in a fabulous location.*

Directions: Close to Sloane Square.

Web: www.johansens.com/draycotthouseapartmentseuro
E-mail: sales@draycotthouse.co.uk
Tel: +44 20 7584 4659
Fax: +44 20 7225 3694

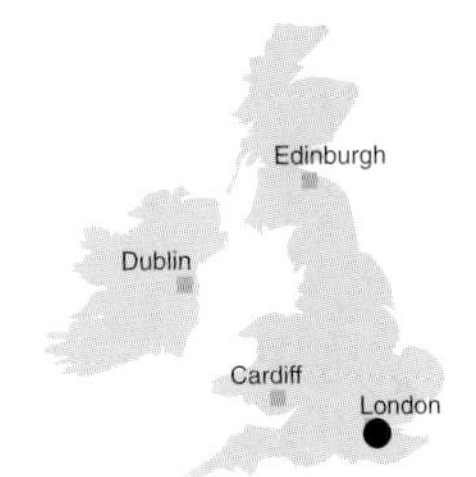

Price Guide: (excluding VAT)
£195–490 per night
£1215–3095 per week

GREAT BRITAIN & IRELAND / ENGLAND (LONDON)

Kensington House Hotel

15-16 PRINCE OF WALES TERRACE, KENSINGTON, LONDON W8 5PQ, ENGLAND

This attractive hotel with pillared entrance and ornate windows stands grandly on a 19th-century site, long associated with style and elegance. Its intimate bedrooms are bright and airy with contemporary yet classic furniture and fittings. The stylish Tiger Bar is a popular venue for cocktails and dining on traditional and modern dishes. A gentle stroll down leafy streets leads to the serenity of Kensington Gardens and many of London's most fashionable shops, restaurants and attractions are also within walking distance.

Ce bel hôtel avec entrée à colonnades et fenêtres fleuries se tient majestueusement dans un quartier du XIXe siècle, synonyme depuis toujours de classe et élégance. Ses chambres intimes sont claires et aérées avec un mobilier contemporain quoique classique. L'élégant Tiger Bar est un endroit populaire pour un cocktail et pour dîner une cuisine traditionnelle ou moderne. Une petite marche le long des rues arborées conduit aux Jardins de Kensington et de nombreux magasins, restaurants et attractions en vogue sont également accessibles à pied.

Dieses attraktive Hotel aus dem 19. Jahrhundert mit seinem von Säulen umfassten Eingang ist seit langem der Inbegriff von Stil und Eleganz. Die gemütlichen Zimmer sind hell und luftig und zeitgenössisch und doch klassisch eingerichtet. In der eleganten Tiger Bar trifft man sich zum Cocktail oder genießt die traditionelle und moderne Küche. Ein kurzer Spaziergang führt zu den Kensington Gardens und viele der besten Geschäfte, Restaurants und Attraktionen Londons liegen in nächster Nähe.

Our inspector loved: *The fresh contemporary feel of this hidden away town house hotel.*

Directions: The nearest underground station is High Street Kensington.

Web: www.johansens.com/kensingtonhouseeuro
E-mail: reservations@kenhouse.com
Tel: +44 20 7937 2345
Fax: +44 20 7368 6700

Price Guide:
single £150
double/twin £175–£195
junior suites £215

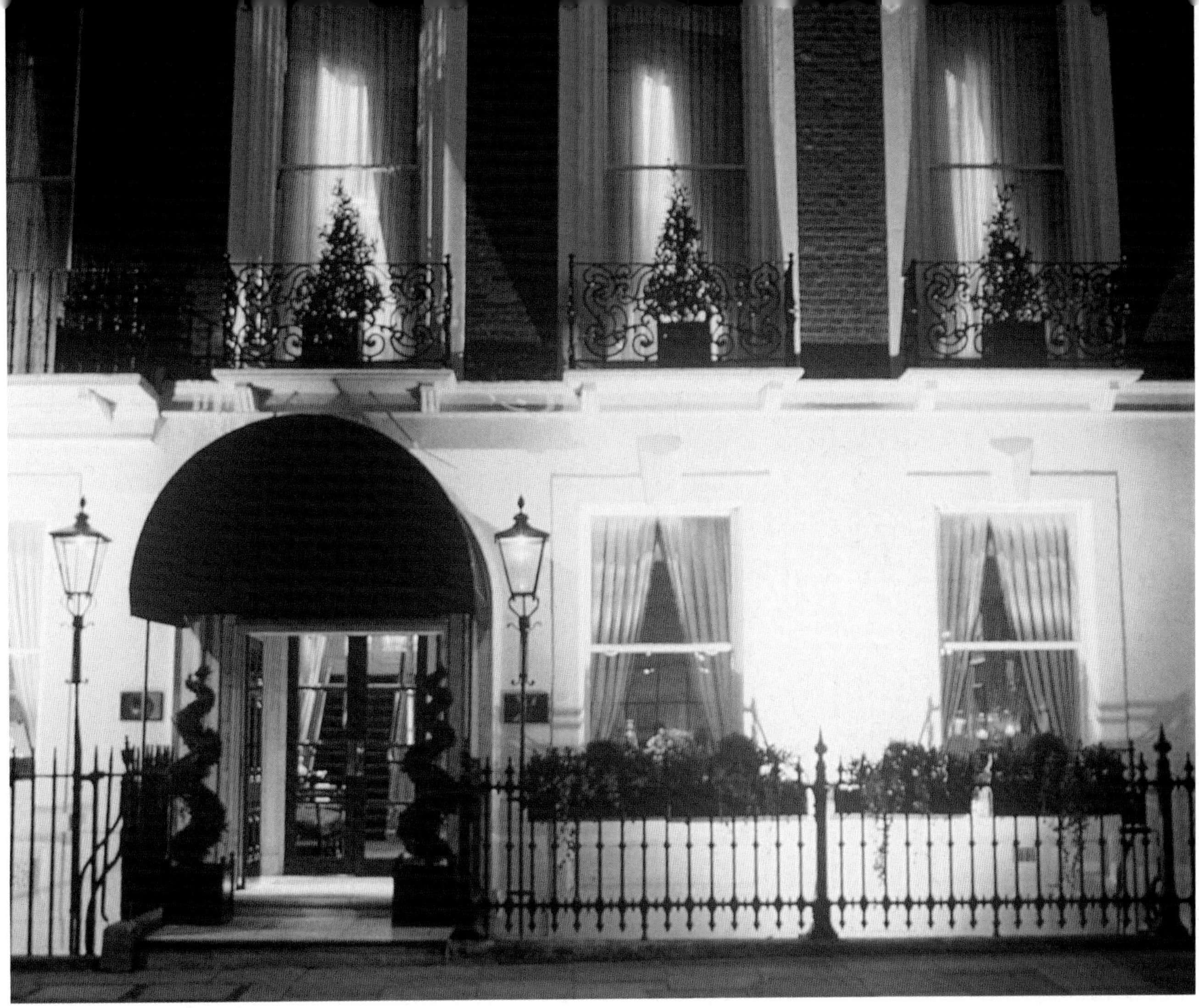

The Leonard

15 SEYMOUR STREET, LONDON W1H 7JW, ENGLAND

4 late Georgian town houses are the basis of this discreet central hotel, which has been imaginatively reconstructed and decorated to a very high standard. Colourful wall coverings and exquisite French furnishings create a warm, luxurious atmosphere. The air-conditioned bedrooms benefit from spacious marble-finished bathrooms, and guests can enjoy eating at the hotel's café bar. Complimentary Internet access is available in reception. 5 serviced apartments are available for longer stays, in a property across the road.

4 hôtels particuliers georgiens composent cet hôtel de charme dans le centre de Londres qui a été reconverti avec goût et décoré selon les meilleurs standards. Les tentures murales colorées complétées par d'exquis tissus français créent une atmosphère chaleureuse et luxueuse. Les chambres sont climatisées et ont de spacieuses salles de bain en marbre. Le déjeuner est servi dans le café de l'hôtel. Un service gratuit Internet est disponible à la réception. Il ya 5 appartements pour un plus long séjour dans une propriété d'en face.

4 georgianische Stadthäuser sind die Basis dieses diskreten Hotels im Zentrum von London, das einfallsreich umgebaut und eingerichtet wurde. Bunte Tapeten und exquisite französische Einrichtungsstoffe schaffen eine luxuriöse und gediegene Atmosphäre. Die vollklimatisierten Zimmer verfügen über geräumige Marmorbäder. Mittagessen wird in der Café-Bar des Hotels serviert. Gratis-Internetzugang in der Rezeption. 5 Appartements mit Service sind in einem Gebäude gegenüber für längere Aufenthalte verfügbar.

Our inspector loved: *The pretty patio roof terrace and the warm, relaxed atmosphere of the reception.*

Directions: North of Marble Arch, off Portman Square.

Web: www.johansens.com/leonardeuro
E-mail: the.leonard@dial.pipex.com
Tel: +44 20 7935 2010
Fax: +44 20 7935 6700

Price Guide:
(excluding VAT)
double/twin from £220
suites £280–550

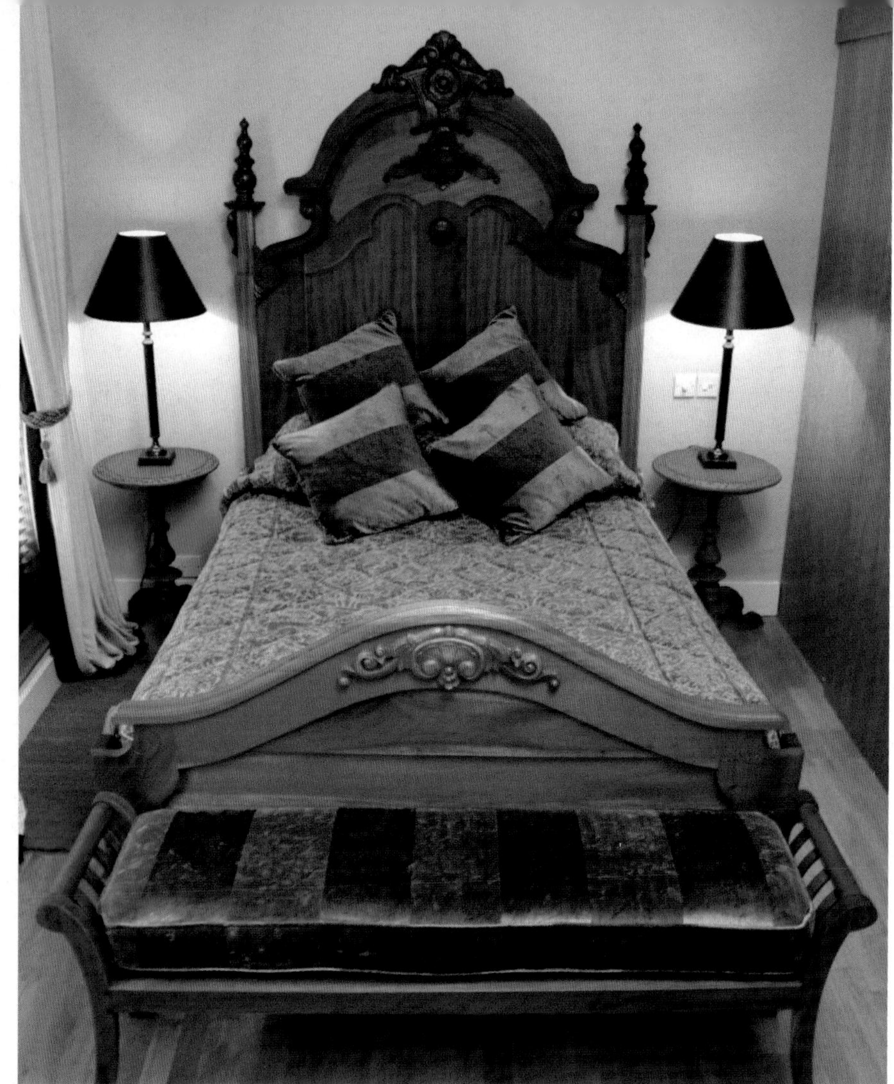

Mayflower Hotel

24-28 TREBOVIR ROAD, LONDON SW5 9NJ, ENGLAND

This recently renovated hotel offers an intriguing blend of eastern influences and modern luxury. Vibrant fabrics and Indian and oriental antiques abound in the individually decorated bedrooms, 4 of which have balconies. High ceilings and hand-carved wardrobes and bedside tables are complemented by stylish bathrooms and state-of-the-art technology with Internet access and wide-screen televisions. Knightsbridge and Chelsea, the V&A and the Natural History and Science Museum are on the doorstep, whilst Earls Court Exhibition Centre is close by.

Cet hôtel récemment remis à neuf offre un mélange fascinant d'influences de l'Est et de luxe moderne. Des tissus vifs et objets d'art de l'Orient et de l'Inde ornent les chambres décorées de façon individuelle, dont 4 ont des balcons. Des plafonds hauts, armoires et tables de chevet sculptées à la main sont complétés par des salles de bains élégantes et équipements du dernier cri, comprenant accès Internet et des grands télévisions. Knightsbridge et Chelsea, les musées V&A et Natural History and Science sont tout proches, alors que le centre d'expositions Earls Court n'est pas loin.

Dieses kürzlich renovierte Hotel bietet eine interessante Mischung aus östlichen Einflüssen und modernem Luxus. Farbenfrohe Stoffe und indische und asiatische Antiquitäten füllen die unterschiedlichen Zimmer (4 mit Balkon), und hohe Decken, handgeschnitzte Schränke und Nachttische, edle Bäder und modernste Technologie mit Internetzugang und Widescreen-Fernsehen sorgen für das gewisse Extra. Knightsbridge und Chelsea, das V&A, das Natural History and Science Museum sowie das Ausstellungszentrum Earls Court liegen in nächster Nähe.

Our inspector loved: *The Eastern influence in all the bedrooms.*

Directions: Situated between Earls Court Road and Warwick Road. The nearest underground station is Earls Court.

Web: www.johansens.com/mayflowereuro
E-mail: mayflower@aol.com
Tel: +44 20 7370 0991
Fax: +44 20 7370 0994

Price Guide:
single £79
double £109
family room £130

Number Eleven Cadogan Gardens

11 CADOGAN GARDENS, SLOANE SQUARE, KNIGHTSBRIDGE, LONDON SW3 2RJ, ENGLAND

In a quiet tree-lined street between Harrods and King's Road, Number Eleven is an elegant town house hotel with a reputation for first-class service. The well-appointed bedrooms are covered with antiques and Oriental rugs, while the Garden Suite has a spacious drawing room overlooking attractive gardens. Pre-dinner drinks and canapés are served in the Drawing Room or the Library, which can also be reserved for private parties. Sauna and massage facilities are available, and a personal trainer is on call in the in-house gymnasium.

Situé dans une paisible rue bordée d'arbres entre Harrods et King's Road, le Number Eleven est un élégant établissement citadin avec une réputation hors pair. Les merveilleuses chambres sont meublées d'antiquités et de tapis orientaux, et la suite Garden a un salon avec vue sur de superbes jardins. Les apéritifs et canapés sont servis dans le salon ou dans la bibliothèque, également disponibles pour des réunions privées. L'hôtel dispose de facilités de sauna et massage et un entraîneur personnel est disponible au centre de remise en forme.

In einer ruhigen, von Bäumen umsäumten Straße zwischen Harrods und der King's Road steht Number Eleven, ein elegantes Stadthaus, das für seinen erstklassigen Service bekannt ist. Die schön eingerichteten Zimmer sind mit Antiquitäten und Perserteppichen ausgestattet, und die Garden Suite verfügt über ein geräumiges Wohnzimmer mit Ausblick auf herrliche Gärten. Apéritifs und Canapés werden im Drawing Room oder der Bibliothek serviert, die auch für private Anlässe reserviert werden kann. Sauna und Massageeinrichtungen sind vorhanden, und ein Personal Trainer steht im hauseigenen Fitnessstudio zur Verfügung.

Our inspector loved: *This very traditional town house and its lovely staff.*

  60     12    

Directions: Off Sloane Street.

Web: www.johansens.com/numbereleveneuro
E-mail: reservations@number-eleven.co.uk
Tel: +44 20 7730 7000
Fax: +44 20 7730 5217

Edinburgh
Dublin
Cardiff
London

Price Guide:
(excluding VAT)
single from £145
double/twin from £185
suites from £275

NUMBER SIXTEEN

16 SUMNER PLACE, SOUTH KENSINGTON, LONDON SW7 3EG, ENGLAND

Freshly refurbished behind its beautifully pillared façade, this elegant hotel is a haven of calm, seclusion and friendly service amidst its bustling surroundings. There is a light and airy drawing room and a conservatory that opens out onto an award-winning private garden, perfect for al fresco dining. Each of the 41 spacious bedrooms is individually decorated in a modern English style with hand-embroidered bedspreads and crisp linen. Some of London's best restaurants, shops and museums are virtually on the doorstep.

Derrière la façade avec de belles colonnes, cet élégant hôtel récemment remis à neuf est un havre de tranquillité, solitude et service chaleureux au milieu d'environs bruyants. Il y a un salon de réception clair alors que le jardin d'hiver donne sur un jardin privé primé, l'endroit parfait pour diner al fresco. Chacune des 41 chambres est décorée en style anglais moderne avec des dessus-de-lit brodés à la main et linge apprêté. Certains des meilleurs restaurants, magasins et musées de Londres sont tout près.

Hinter der schönen Säulenfassade verbirgt sich ein elegantes, komplett neu hergerichtetes Hotel, eine Oase der Ruhe mit freundlichem Service inmitten lebhafter Umgebung. Der Aufenthaltsraum ist hell und luftig, und der Wintergarten öffnet sich auf einen preisgekrönten Garten, perfekt zum Essen unter freiem Himmel. Jedes der 41 Zimmer ist individuell in modernem englischen Stil gestaltet und bietet handbestickte Bettüberwürfe und frischgestärkte Wäsche. Einige der besten Restaurants, Geschäfte und Museen Londons befinden sich direkt vor der Tür.

Our inspector loved: *The calming, elegant interior and pretty secret back garden.*

Directions: Sumner Place is off the old Brompton Road near Onslow Square. South Kensington underground station is a 2-minute walk away.

Web: www.johansens.com/numbersixteeneuro
E-mail: reservations@numbersixteenhotel.co.uk
Tel: +44 20 7589 5232
US Toll Free: 1 800 553 6674
Fax: +44 20 7584 8615

Price Guide:
(excluding VAT)
single from £130
double/twin from £165

Pembridge Court Hotel

34 PEMBRIDGE GARDENS, LONDON W2 4DX, ENGLAND

Beautifully restored to its 19-century origins, this gracious Victorian town house offers the high level of service demanded by today's discerning traveller. The well-appointed bedrooms are individually decorated with pretty fabrics and the walls are adorned with a collection of framed Victorian fans. It is situated in the heart of Notting Hill, renowned for its vibrant nightlife and one of the largest antiques markets in the world.

Superbement restauré en fonction de ses origines du XIXe siècle, cette jolie maison de ville victorienne offre un grand standing de service. Les jolies chambres sont toutes individuellement décorées avec des superbes tissus et les murs sont ornés d'une collection d'évantails victoriens. Il est situé au coeur de Notting Hill, renommé pour sa vie nocturne animée et pour être un des plus grands marchés aux puces du monde.

Dieses elegante viktorianische Herrenhaus aus dem 19. Jahrhundert wurde perfekt restauriert und bietet dem anspruchsvollen Gast von heute höchsten Standard an Service. Die gutausgestatteten Zimmer sind individuell mit hübschen Stoffen gestaltet, und eine Sammlung von viktorianischen Fächern ziert die Wände. Das Pembridge Court liegt im Herzen von Notting Hill, das für sein reges Nachtleben und einen der weltgrößten Antiquitätenmärkte bekannt ist.

Our inspector loved: *The welcome from the staff and the cats, as well as the excellent atmosphere.*

Directions: The hotel is 2 minutes from Portobello Road.

Web: www.johansens.com/pembridgecourteuro
E-mail: reservations@pemct.co.uk
Tel: +44 20 7229 9977
Fax: +44 20 7727 4982

Price Guide:
single £130–170
double/twin £190–200

Twenty Nevern Square

20 NEVERN SQUARE, LONDON SW5 9PD, ENGLAND

This elegant town house has been sumptuously restored with an emphasis on natural materials – linen, cotton and silks – and beautiful hand-carved beds and furniture. Each of the 20 intimate bedrooms is individually designed echoing both Asian and European influences. The hotel overlooks a tranquil garden square and has its own delightful restaurant, Café Twenty, serving modern European food. Guests are a mere 10 minutes from London's most fashionable shopping areas, restaurants, theatres and cultural attractions.

Restauré avec faste, cet élégant hôtel particulier privilégie aujourd'hui les matières naturelles – lin, coton et soie – et les beaux lits et autres meubles artisanaux. Chacune des 20 chambres intimes est décorée dans un style individuel aux influences asiatiques et européennes. L'hôtel donne sur un square paisible et dispose d'un restaurant raffiné, le Café Twenty, qui sert une cuisine européenne moderne. Les restaurants, les théâtres, les attractions culturelles et les rues commerçantes les plus chics de Londres ne sont qu'à 10 minutes.

Dieses elegante Stadthaus wurde im großen Stil renoviert, wobei man vornehmlich natürliche Materialien wir Leinen, Baumwolle und Seide sowie herrliche handgeschnitzte Betten und Möbel verwendete. Jedes der 20 gemütlichen Zimmer ist individuell gestaltet und von asiatischen und europäischen Einflüssen geprägt. Das Hotel blickt auf einen ruhigen Garten, und das eigene Restaurant Café Twenty serviert moderne europäische Küche. Londons beliebteste Einkaufsstraßen, Restaurants, Theater und kulturelle Attraktionen sind nur 10 Minuten entfernt.

Our inspector loved: *The fusion of Eastern and European influences in all the rooms.*

Directions: 2 minutes from Earls Court underground station.

Web: www.johansens.com/twentynevernsquareeuro
E-mail: hotel@twentynevernsquare.co.uk
Tel: +44 20 7565 9555
Fax: +44 20 7565 9444

Price Guide:
single £130
double £165–195
suite £275

STAPLEFORD PARK HOTEL, SPA, GOLF & SPORTING ESTATE

NR MELTON MOWBRAY, LEICESTERSHIRE LE14 2EF, ENGLAND

Situated within 500 acres of wooded parkland, this award-winning 16th-century stately home and sporting estate is the essence of luxury in beautiful surroundings. Sumptuous bedrooms are individually decorated with designer names such as Mulberry, Wedgwood, Liberty and Crabtree & Evelyn. Delicious English cuisine and superb wines are served in the elegant dining rooms. Guests can take advantage of the indoor pool, Jacuzzi, sauna, fitness room and health therapies. Shooting, riding, tennis and golf are available.

Demeure ancestrale et domaine sportif du XVIe siècle, cet hôtel primé entouré de 200 ha de parc boisé est le comble du luxe dans un cadre magnifique. Mulberry, Wedgwood, Liberty, Crabtree & Evelyn et d'autres signatures renommées se reconnaissent dans le décor des chambres somptueuses. Les visiteurs savourent la cuisine anglaise et des vins remarquables servis dans les élégantes salles à manger et profitent de la piscine, du jacuzzi, du sauna, de la salle de culture physique et des thérapies de remise en forme. Tir, équitation, tennis et golf sont aussi possibles.

Dieses in 200ha bewaldeter Parklandschaft gelegene preisgekrönte Anwesen aus dem 16. Jahrhundert ist der Inbegriff von Luxus in herrlichster Umgebung. Die prunkvollen Zimmer sind unterschiedlich mit Designs von Mulberry, Wedgwood, Liberty und Crabtree & Evelyn gestaltet. Köstliche englische Küche und erlesene Weine werden in den eleganten Speisesälen serviert. Hallenbad, Jacuzzi, Sauna, Fitnessraum und therapeutische Anwendungen werden angeboten, Schießen, Reiten, Tennis und Golf sind ebenfalls möglich.

Our inspector loved: *The stunning views from the new clubhouse overlooking the golf course.*

Directions: By train from London Kings Cross/Grantham in 1 hour. Take the A1 to Colsterworth then the B676 via Saxby.

Web: www.johansens.com/staplefordparkeuro
E-mail: reservations@stapleford.co.uk
Tel: +44 1572 787 522
Fax: +44 1572 787 651

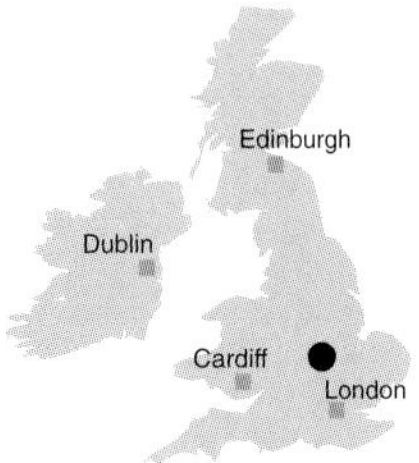

Edinburgh
Dublin
Cardiff
London

Price Guide:
double/twin £205–345
suites from £425.

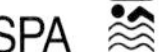

THE PEACOCK AT ROWSLEY

ROWSLEY, NEAR MATLOCK, DERBYSHIRE DE4 2EB, ENGLAND

This superb 17th-century country house has been refurbished to reflect its wonderful ambience. Numerous antiques have been exquisitely restored, and the comfortable en-suite bedrooms, 1 of which has a four-poster, are equipped with all modern amenities. Guests enjoy contemporary English cuisine based on local produce and game from the estate. Conference and banqueting facilities for up to 30 are available. The hotel is a paradise for fishing enthusiasts, whilst the Peak District National Park, Haddon Hall and Chatsworth are all within easy reach.

Cette maison de campagne datant du XVIIe siècle a été remis à neuf pour refléter son ambiance superbe. De nombreux objets d'art ont été finement restaurés et les chambres attenantes confortables, dont 1 a un lit à baldaquin, offrent toutes les facilités modernes. Les hôtes peuvent savourer la cuisine anglaise contemporaine créée avec des ingrédients locaux et du gibier de la propriété. Les facilités de conférence et banquet sont disponibles pour jusqu'à 30 personnes. L'hôtel est un paradis pour les passionnés de la pêche, alors que le Peak District National Park, Haddon Hall et Chatsworth sont tous d'accès facile.

Dieses herrliche Landhaus aus dem 17. Jahrhundert wurde im Einklang mit dem Ambiente des Hauses komplett neu hergerichtet. Wundervolle Antiquitäten wurden hervorragend restauriert, und die komfortablen Zimmer (1 mit Himmelbett) bieten jeglichen modernen Komfort. Serviert wird moderne englische Küche mit einheimischen Zutaten und eigenem Wild. Konferenz- und Bankettseinrichtungen für bis zu 30 Personen sind vorhanden. Das Hotel ist ein Anglerparadies, und der Peak District Nationalpark, Haddon Hall und Chatsworth liegen in nächster Nähe.

Our inspector loved: *The history and welcome of this ancient dower house.*

Directions: M1 > exit 28 > towards A6 > midway between Matlock and Bakewell.

Web: www.johansens.com/peacockeuro
E-mail: office@thepeacockatrowsley.com
Tel: +44 1629 733518
Fax: +44 1629 732671

Price Guide:
single £55
double £125

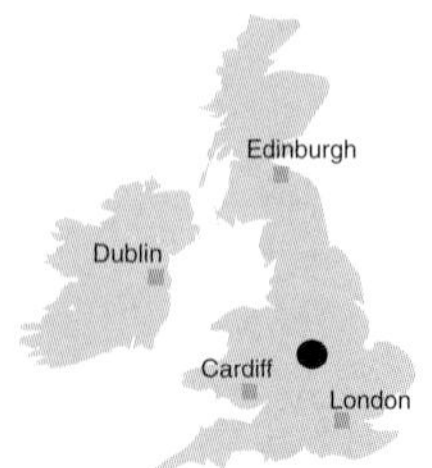

The French Horn

SONNING ON THAMES, BERKSHIRE RG4 6TN, ENGLAND

This luxurious, charming hotel and gourmet restaurant is the epitome of the quaint, quintessential English riverside village retreat. Set near Windsor and the historic village of Sonning, there are 4 riverside cottages, each with its own patio, and 12 suites and en-suite double rooms to choose from. The family-run restaurant looks out onto the Thames and serves classic French cuisine alongside traditional English dishes, and the wine list is reputed to be amongst the finest in Europe. Meeting facilities for up to 16 delegates are available.

Ce charmant hôtel luxueux avec son restaurant gastronome est la quintessence d'un village retrait au charme vieillot au bord de la rivière. Situé près de Windsor et le village historique de Sonning, l'hôtel propose 4 petites maisons, chacune avec sa propre terrasse ainsi que 12 suites et chambres attenantes. Le restaurant familial donne sur le Thames et sert une cuisine française classique ainsi que des plats traditionnels anglais et les vins sont réputés être parmi les meilleurs en Europe. Des facilités de conférence pour jusqu'à 16 personnes sont disponibles.

Dieses zauberhafte, luxuriöse Hotel und Gourmetrestaurant ist der Inbegriff eines typischen englischen, an einem Fluss gelegenen Dorfhotels. Das Hotel befindet sich in der Nähe von Windsor und dem historischen Ort Sonning und umfasst 4 Cottages direkt an der Themse und 12 Suiten und Doppelzimmer mit eigenem Bad. Das familiengeführte Restaurant blickt ebenfalls auf den Fluss und serviert klassische französische Küche und traditionelle englische Gerichte, und die Weinkarte ist eine der besten in ganz Europa. Konferenzeinrichtungen für bis zu 16 Personen vorhanden.

Our inspector loved: *The glorious riverside setting and the Old World charm.*

Directions: M4 > exit junction 8/9 > follow A404 > at Thickets roundabout turn left > A4 towards Reading for 8 miles > Sonning > cross Thames on B478 > hotel is on the right.

Web: www.johansens.com/frenchhorneuro
E-mail: thefrenchhorn@compuserve.com
Tel: +44 1189 692204
Fax: +44 1189 442210

Price Guide:
single £105–£160
double/twin £130–£195

Aberdeen Lodge

53-55 PARK AVENUE, BALLSBRIDGE, DUBLIN 4, IRELAND

Located in the south city centre, set within formal gardens on a serene tree-lined avenue, this classic example of Edwardian architecture prides itself on ensuring that the needs of its guests are met wholeheartedly. Elegant bedrooms are furnished in complete harmony with the house, spacious suites feature Jacuzzis and period furniture, whilst the award-winning intimate dining room serves a special menu and good selection of fine wines. The hotel provides an ideal base from which to enjoy Dublin's sights and shopping in the famous Grafton Street. Private car park.

Situé au centre sud de la ville, ce bel exemple d'architecture édouardienne se dresse au milieu d'un jardin à la française, dans une paisible avenue bordée d'arbres, et met un point d'honneur à satisfaire tous les besoins des visiteurs. Les chambres élégantes sont en harmonie avec le reste de l'hôtel et les suites spacieuses comportent des jacuzzis et des meubles d'époque. La petite salle à manger primée propose un menu exceptionnel et un excellent choix de vins fins. L'hôtel est idéal pour visiter Dublin et faire du shopping dans la célèbre Grafton Street. Parking privé.

Dieses inmitten formeller Gärten an einer Allee gelegene Hotel im sudlichen Zentrum der Stadt ist ein klassisches Beispiel Edwardischer Architektur. Kein Wunsch bleibt hier unerfüllt. Die eleganten Zimmer sind im Einklang mit der Umgebung gestaltet, und die geräumigen Suiten bieten Jacuzzis und Stilmöbel. Im preisgekrönten Speisesaal wird ein Sondermenü und eine gute Auswahl an erlesenen Weinen serviert. Das Hotel liegt ideal, um Dublin zu erkunden und in der berühmten Grafton Street einkaufen zu gehen. Privatparkplatz vorhanden.

Our inspector loved: *The quiet seclusion so close to the city centre.*

Directions: Off Ailesbury Road, 7 minutes from the city centre by D.A.R.T. bus.

Web: www.johansens.com/aberdeenlodge
E-mail: aberdeen@iol.ie
Tel: +353 1 283 8155
Fax: +353 1 283 7877

Price Guide:
single €99–129
double/twin €124–189
suite €159–239

Royal Marine Hotel

GOLF ROAD, BRORA, SUTHERLAND KW9 6QS, SCOTLAND

Standing midway between Inverness and John O'Groats, this former private home has been refurbished to provide all modern amenities, whilst still retaining original features such as the wooden arches of the entrance hall, carved wood fireplaces and the grand staircase. Particular emphasis is placed on quality and service, complementing the pleasing décor and comfort throughout. Many of the attractive guest rooms offer splendid scenic views. Guests can use the facilities of the leisure club, play golf, go fishing on Loch Brora, or explore the numerous attractions nearby.

Situé entre Inverness et John O'Groats, cette ancienne résidence privée a été rénovée pour offrir tout le confort moderne, alors qu'elle garde ses détails originaux comme les voûtes en bois de l'entrée, les cheminées en bois et le splendide escalier. Une importance particulière est accordée à la qualité, le service, le confort et le décor agréable. Plusieurs chambres offrent des vues scéniques spectaculaires. Les hôtes peuvent profiter du club de remise en forme, jouer au golf, aller à la pêche sur Loch Brora ou découvrir les nombreuses attractions dans les alentours.

Dieses einstige Privathaus auf halber Strecke zwischen Inverness und John O'Groats wurde renoviert und mit modernsten Einrichtungen versehen, wobei einige ursprüngliche Details wie z.B. die Holzbögen in der Eingangshalle, geschnitzte offene Kamine und das herrliche Treppenhaus erhalten blieben. Die Betonung liegt hier auf Qualität, Service, Komfort und angenehmem Décor. Einige Zimmer bieten eine traumhafte Sicht auf das Umland. Ein Freizeitkomplex steht zur Verfügung, man kann Golf spielen, auf dem Loch Brora angeln oder die Umgebung erkunden.

Our inspector loved: *The excellent facilities; great golf on the doorstep, and proximity to Inverness.*

Directions: Inverness > A9 north > follow signs for Wick > at Brora cross bridge turn right.

Web: www.johansens.com/royalmarineeuro
E-mail: info@highlandescape.com
Tel: +44 1408 621252
Fax: +44 1408 621181

Price Guide:
single £75
double £120-150

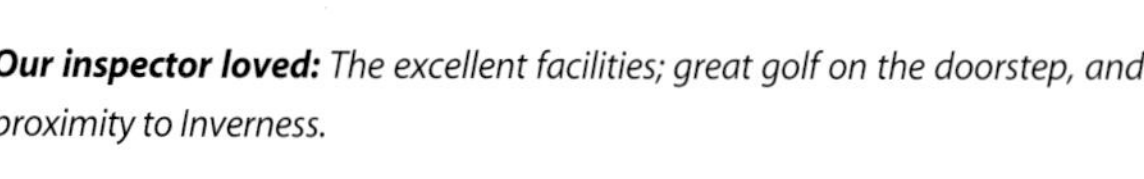

Muckrach Lodge Hotel & Restaurant

DULNAIN BRIDGE, BY GRANTOWN-ON-SPEY, INVERNESS-SHIRE PH26 3LY, SCOTLAND

With its welcoming log fires, fresh flowers, comfortable sofas and country house charm this former sporting lodge has a relaxed, informal ambience. Surrounded by 10 acres of landscaped grounds, amazing scenery featuring the Cairngorm Mountains, River Spey, lochs and moors, Muckrach boasts a rare natural beauty. Bedrooms are spacious and imaginative cuisine is served in the AA Rosette awarded restaurant complemented by fine wines and rare malts. Guests can explore nearby ancient ruined castles, forts and the Culloden battlefield.

Avec ses feux de bois, ses fleurs coupées, ses canapés confortables et son charme de maison de campagne, cet ancien pavillon de chasse a une ambiance détendue et sans façons. Entouré de 4 ha de terres aménagées, de paysages tels que les monts Cairngorm, la rivière Spey, des lochs et des landes, Muchrach peut s'enorgueillir d'une beauté naturelle rare. Les chambres sont spacieuses et une cuisine inventive est servie au restaurant à 1 Rosette AA, complétée par des vins fins et des malts rares. Les hôtes peuvent explorer des ruines de châteaux et forts ainsi que le champ de bataille de Culloden.

Mit seinen Kaminfeuern, frischen Blumen, bequemen Sofas und Landhauscharme bietet dieses einstige Jagdhaus eine entspannte, informelle Atmosphäre. Muckrach besitzt eine seltene natürliche Schönheit, umgeben von 4ha gepflegtem Garten, den Cairngormbergen, dem Fluss Spey, mehreren Lochs und Mooren. Die Zimmer sind geräumig und im mit einer AA Rosette ausgezeichneten Restaurant werden einfallsreiche Speisen, edle Weine und seltene Whiskys serviert. Gäste können nahegelegene Burgruinen, Festungen und das Schlachtfeld von Culloden besichtigen.

Our inspector loved: *The relaxed style and the abscence of pretentiousness.*

Directions: Muckrach Lodge is 3 miles South West of Grantown-on-Spey on the B9102 and A95, through Dulnain Bridge Village on the A938.

Web: www.johansens.com/muckrachlodgeeuro
E-mail: stay@muckrach.co.uk
Tel: +44 1479 851257
Fax: +44 1479 851325

Price Guide:
single £60–£85
double/twin £120–£140

Enmore Hotel

MARINE PARADE, KIRN, DUNOON, ARGYLL PA23 8HH, SCOTLAND

Attractive, small and personal, this undiscovered gem overlooks the Firth of Clyde and is surrounded by beauty and tranquillity. Pretty gardens set the scene, echoed by uplifting colourful décor inside and luxurious four-poster beds - one room even has a double whirlpool bath. Fresh local produce is used to create superb traditional Scottish dishes. For leisure there is walking, pony trekking, fishing as well as many historic sites. A championship golf course is nearby.

Charmante, petite et intime, cette merveille inconnue donnant sur l'estuaire de la Clyde est entourée par la beauté et la tranquillité. De beaux jardins vous préparent pour le décor coloré et réjouissant à l'intérieur et les chambres avec lits à colonnes; une chambre est même équipée avec un double bain à remous. Des produits locaux frais créent des plats écossais traditionnels superbes. Les hôtes peuvent jouir de randonnées à pied ou à poney, aller à la pêche ou visiter les nombreuses attractions historiques. Un parcours de golf utilisé pour des championnats est tout près.

Dieses attraktive, kleine familiäre Juwel blickt auf den Firth of Clyde und ist umgeben von Schönheit und Ruhe. Hübsche Gärten bilden den Rahmen für ein erfrischendes, farbenfrohes Décor und luxuriöse Himmelbetten - ein Zimmer bietet sogar ein Doppel-Whirlpoolbad. Hervorragende schottische Speisen werden mit den frischesten einheimischen Zutaten zubereitet. Das Freizeitangebot umfasst Wandern, Pony-Trekking, Angeln sowie die Besichtigung zahlreicher historischer Stätten. Ein Championship-Golfplatz ist in der Nähe.

Our inspector loved: *The total escape and the magical scenery yet only 1 hour from Glasgow.*

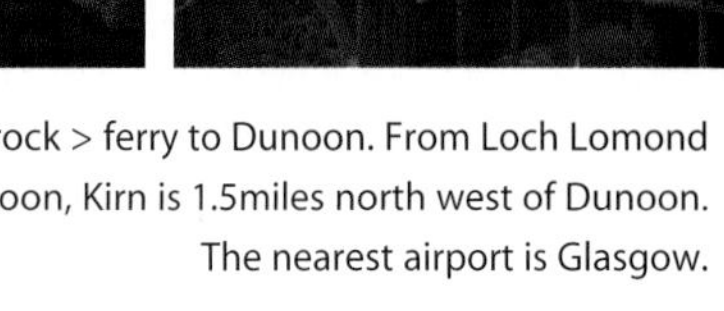

Directions: From Glasgow > Gourock > ferry to Dunoon. From Loch Lomond > A82/A83 > A815 towards Dunoon, Kirn is 1.5miles north west of Dunoon. The nearest airport is Glasgow.

Web: www.johansens.com/enmoreeuro
E-mail: enmorehotel@btinternet.com
Tel: +44 1369 702230
Fax: +44 1369 702148

Price Guide:
single £65-95
double £90-158

Castle Venlaw Hotel

EDINBURGH ROAD, PEEBLES, SCOTLAND EH45 8QG

Directions: Edinburgh > A703 to Peebles > the hotel is then signposted on the left just after the 30mph sign.

Web: www.johansens.com/venlaweuro
E-mail: enquiries@venlaw.co.uk
Tel: +44 1721 720384
Fax: +44 1721 724066

Price Guide:
single £60-85
double/twin £120-180

Overlooking the ancient town of Peebles in the peaceful Borders countryside, yet only 40 minutes from Edinburgh, this majestic hotel has an air of elegance and relaxed informality. Great care has been taken to preserve the charm and character of the castle and the restaurant, with its 2 AA-Rosettes provides fresh, locally produced meals of superb quality with an international flavour. Acres of beautiful woodlands can be explored or there is golf, fishing and many historic buildings in the area.

Donnant sur l'ancienne ville de Peebles dans la campagne paisible de Borders, mais seulement à 40 minutes d,Edimbourgcet, cet hôtel majestueux a une ambiance également élégante et détendue. Le charme et le caractère du château ont été soigneusement préservés. Le restaurant, attribué 2 rosettes AA, sert des plats frais avec une influence internationale, utilisant des produits locaux de très bonne qualité. Les hôtes peuvent explorer les bois, jouer au golf, aller à la pêche ou visiter les nombreux bâtiments historiques dans les alentours.

Dieses majestätische Hotel mit Blick auf die alte Stadt Peebles inmitten der Borders-Region, doch nur 40 Minuten von Edinburgh entfernt, besitzt eine Aura der Eleganz kombiniert mit entspannter Atmosphäre. Der Charme und Charakter des Hotels wurde sehr sorgfältig beibehalten, und im mit einer AA-Rosetten ausgezeichneten Restaurant werden hervorragende, aus frischen, einheimischen Zutaten zubereitete Gerichte mit internationaler Note serviert. Die Gäste können die herrliche umliegende Waldlandschaft erkunden, Golf spielen, angeln oder die zahlreichen historischen Stätten der Region besichtigen.

Our inspector loved: *The exceptionally large rooms, the peace and quiet and the proximity to Edinburgh.*

GREECE

Hotel location shown in red (hotel) or purple (spa hotel) with page number

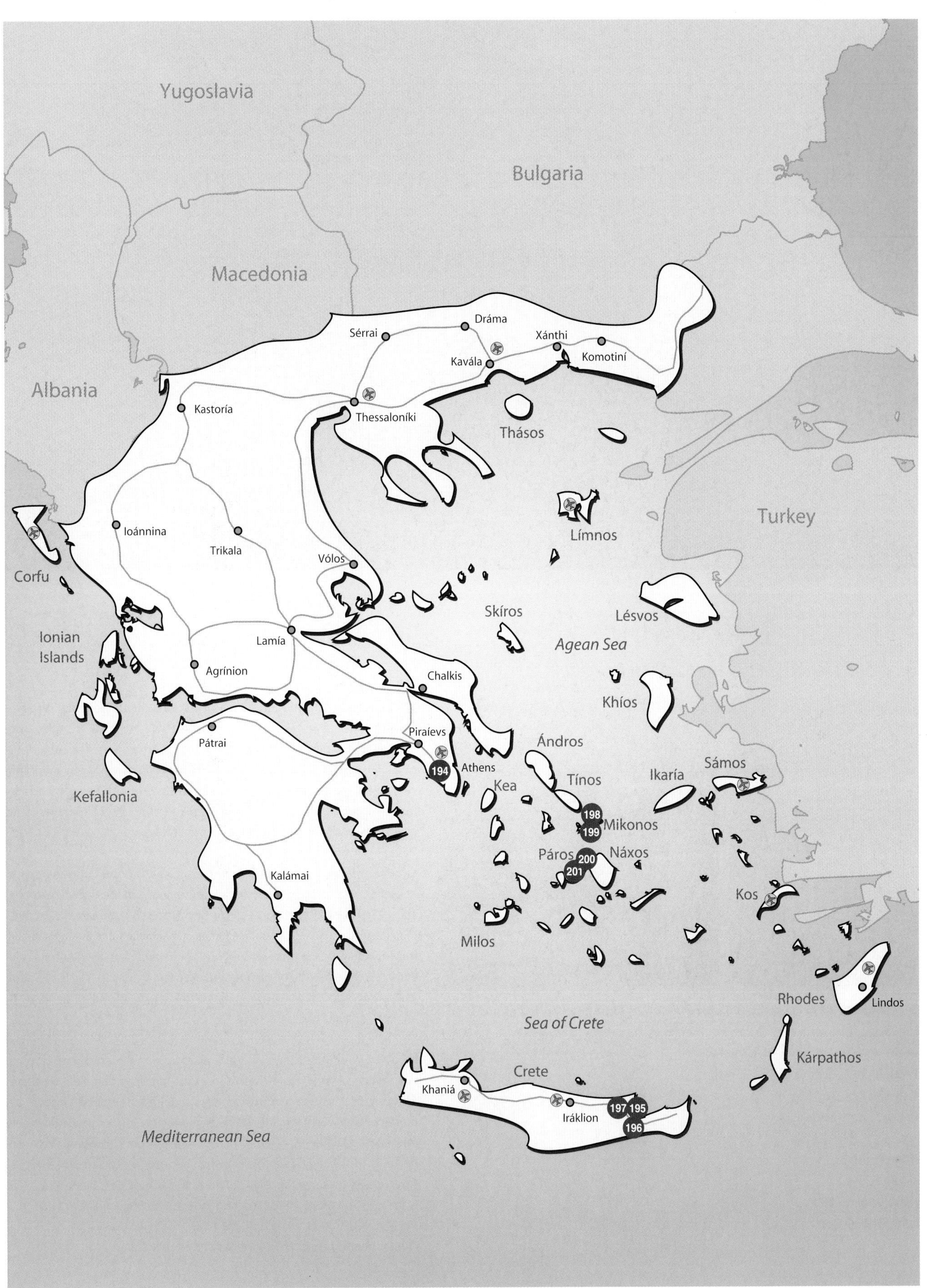

Hotel Pentelikon

66 DILIGIANNI STREET, 14562 ATHENS, GREECE

Directions: Set in the suburb of Kifissia. Venizelos Airport is 30 minutes away.

Web: www.johansens.com/pentelikon
E-mail: pentelik@otenet.gr
Tel: +30 2 10 62 30 650-6
Fax: +30 2 10 80 19 223

Price Guide:
single €750
double/twin €890
suite €1,100-2,060

Set in a peaceful residential area of Athens, this impressive, discreet small hotel is the essence of style. Fine antiques, silk curtains and immaculate staff contribute to its select ambience. The luxurious bedrooms are individually decorated in French fabrics with harmonising wall coverings. Cuisine is a delight with the informal La Terrasse and the gourmet Vardis restaurant, the only restaurant in Greece that has been awarded a Michelin Star for 4 consecutive years.

Situé dans un quartier calme d'Athènes, ce petit hôtel impressionnant et discret est une figure de style. Des antiquités raffinées, des rideaux de soie et un personnel impeccable contribuent à son ambiance sélective. Les chambres luxueuses sont décorées individuellement avec des tissus français coordonnés aux papiers muraux. La table est divine tant sur la Terrace détendue qu'au restaurant gastronomique le Vardis, le seul restaurant en Grèce à avoir gagnée une étoile Michelin pendant 4 années consécutives.

In einer ruhigen Wohngegend von Athen gelegen bietet dieses vortreffliche kleine Hotel Diskretion und einzigartigen Stil. Kostbare Antiquitäten, seidene Vorhänge und tadelloses Personal tragen zu diesem exklusiven Ambiente bei. Die luxuriösen Zimmer sind individuell mit französischen Stoffen und damit harmonisierenden Tapeten gestaltet. Köstliche Gerichte werden im informellen La Terrasse oder im Gourmetrestaurant Vardis serviert, das einzige Restaurant in Griechenland, das 4 Jahre hintereinander einen Michelinstern bekam.

Our inspector loved: *The courteous and friendly staff.*

The Peninsula at Porto Elounda De Luxe Resort

72053 ELOUNDA, CRETE, GREECE

Located on a peninsula, within the famous Porto Elounda De Luxe Resort, this hotel boasts spectacular views over the bay. Large, airy suites are decorated with Greek marble and teak floors and have access to either a shared or private heated seawater pool. There is a private beach, tennis, 9-hole golf course with academy, water sports, wellness, indoor pool, gym and a children's club. A wine cellar and several restaurants complete the resort. Inspired by a Greek village square, the "Playiada" with its boutiques, jewellers, an art gallery and an orthodox chapel is the venue for evening festivities.

Situé sur une péninsule, au sein du célèbre Porto Elounda De Luxe Resort, cet hôtel s'enorgueillit de vues spectaculaires sur la baie. Les grandes suites sont décorées de marbre grec et de planchers en teck et ont accès à des piscines privées ou publiques ou privées d'eau de mer chauffée. Le resort dispose de sa plage privée, tennis, golf à 9 trous avec école, centre de bien-être et de remise en forme, piscine couverte, club des enfants, une cave et plusieurs restaurants. La place "Playiada" avec des boutiques, des bijouteries, une galérie d'art et une chapelle orthodoxe, est l'endroit pour des festivités du soir.

Dieses Hotel auf einer Halbinsel innerhalb des berühmten Porto Elounda De Luxe Resorts bietet eine herrliche Sicht auf die Bucht. Die großen Suiten sind mit griechischem Marmor und Teakböden gestaltet und haben Zugang zu einem Gemeinschafts- oder eigenem beheizten Salzwasserpool. Es gibt einen Strand, Tennis, 9-Loch-Golfplatz mit Golfakademie, Wellness- und Fitness-Centre, Hallenbad, Kinderclub, einen Weinkeller und mehrere Restaurants. Am Dorfplatz "Playiada" mit seinen Boutiquen, Juwelieren, einer Kunstgalerie und einer orthodoxen Kappelle finden Abendfestivitäten statt.

Our inspector loved: *The views over the water and the poolside bar.*

Directions: Available on request. The nearest airport is Heraklion.

Web: www.johansens.com/peninsulacrete
E-mail: peninsula@elounda-sa.com
Tel: +30 28410 68000
Fax: +30 28410 41889

Price Guide:
suites €340–8,100

Athens
Rhodes
Iráklion - *Crete*

32

SPA

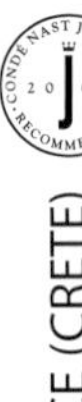

Pleiades Luxurious Villas

PLAKES-72, 100 AGHIOS NIKOLAOS, CRETE, GREECE

Directions: From Heraklion airport head towards Elounda. Hotel is located before Aghios Nikolaos on the left.

Web: www.johansens.com/pleiades
E-mail: pleia@otenet.gr
Tel: +30 28410 90450
Fax: +30 28410 90473

Price Guide:
(self-catering)
2-bedroom villa €240-680
3-bedroom villa €350-950

Set in a quiet location with beautiful views over the Mirabello gulf, just 2km from Aghios Nikolaos, this new complex consists of 7 individually designed villas sleeping 4-6 persons. Each villa has a spacious living area, fireplace, fully equipped kitchen and dining room as well as its own swimming pool and offers all modern amenities including Internet access. Upon arrival, guests receive a complimentary bottle of champagne and a fruit basket. A daily maid service and cook are available upon request. Activities include water skiing, windsurfing, diving, horse riding and tennis.

Situé dans une position tranquille avec de belles vues sur le golfe de Mirabello et à 2 km de Aghios Nikolaos, ce nouveau complexe comprend 7 villas décorées de façon individuelle pour 4-6 personnes. Chaque villa a un espace vital spacieux, une cheminée, une cuisine et salle à manger bien équipées, ainsi que sa propre piscine. Elles offrent toute facilité moderne, comprenant accès Internet. En arrivant, les hôtes sont offerts une bouteille de champagne et une corbeille de fruits. Femme de ménage et chef de cuisine disponibles sur demande. Loisirs: ski nautique, planche à voile, plongée, équitation et tennis.

In ruhiger Lage mit herrlicher Sicht auf den Golf von Mirabello, nur 2km von Aghios Nikolaos entfernt, liegt dieser neue Komplex, der aus 7 unterschiedlich gestalteten Villen für 4-6 Personen besteht. Jede Villa ist geräumig, hat einen Kamin, vollausgestattete Küche und Esszimmer sowie einen eigenen Pool und moderne Einrichtungen wie z.B. Internetzugang. Bei der Ankunft wartet eine Flasche Champagner und ein Obstkorb auf die Gäste. Täglicher Reinigungsdienst und Koch auf Anfrage. Aktivitäten: Wasserski, Windsurfen, Tauchen, Reiten und Tennis.

***Our inspector loved:** The spacious villas with their individual character.*

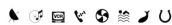

St Nicolas Bay Hotel

PO BOX 47, 72100 AGHIOS NIKOLAOS, CRETE, GREECE

Flower-filled gardens with olive, lemon and orange trees surround this bungalow hotel. With its own quiet sandy beach, it offers excellent accommodation, mouth-watering cuisine and superb service. All rooms and suites enjoy stunning views from their balconies or terraces, whilst the suites have marble bathrooms with Jacuzzi; some boast a private heated pool. Facilities include water sports, scuba diving, boats for sea excursions, gym, sauna, steam bath, Jacuzzi, massage, hydromassage, aromatherapy and beauty treatments. Member of the Charming Hotels Consortium.

Des jardins remplis de fleurs et d'oliviers, de citronniers et d'orangers entourent cet hôtel formé de pavillons. Outre sa plage privée tranquille, l'hôtel offre un excellent logement, une table savoureuse et un service impeccable. Les chambres et suites possèdent des balcons ou des terrasses avec une vue imprenable. Les suites, certaines avec piscine privée chauffée, ont des salles de bain en marbre avec jacuzzi. Loisirs: sports nautiques, plongée, excursions en bateau, gymnase, sauna, hammam, jacuzzi, massage, hydro-massage, aromathérapie et traitements de beauté. Membre de Charming Hotels.

Mit Blumen und Oliven-, Zitronen- und Orangenbäumen gefüllte Gärten umgeben dieses Bungalow-Hotel mit eigenem ruhigen Sandstrand. Küche, Service und Unterkunft sind hervorragend; die Zimmer und Suiten bieten vom Balkon oder der Terrasse traumhafte Ausblicke. Die Suiten, einige mit beheiztem Pool, haben Marmorbad mit Jacuzzi. Aktivitäten: Wassersport, Tauchen, Bootsexkursionen aufs Meer, Fitness, Sauna, Dampfbad, Whirlpool, Massage, Hydromassage, Aromatherapie und Schönheitsbehandlungen. Mitglied der Charming Hotels.

Our inspector loved: *The luxury suites with their private little pools and gardens.*

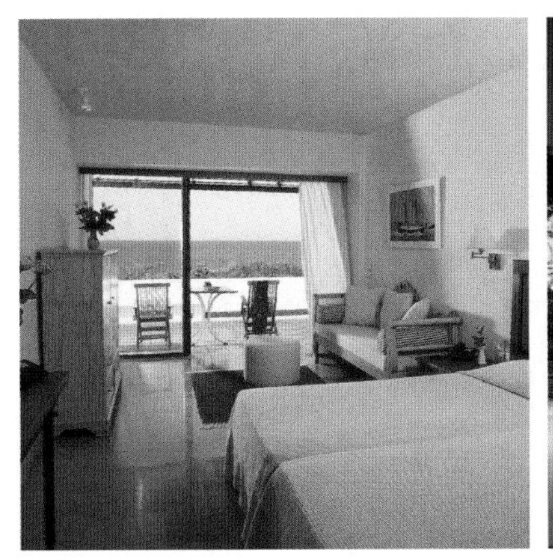

Directions: Heraklion > Aghios Nikolas.

Web: www.johansens.com/stnicolasbay
E-mail: stnicolas@otenet.gr
Tel: +30 2841 025041
Fax: +30 2841 024556

Price Guide:
single €180-330
double/twin €240–440
suite €290–700
suite with private pool €550–1,800

Apanema

TAGOO, MYKONOS, GREECE

This elegant boutique hotel is set on the waterfront, just a 10-minute walk from Mykonos town. Built in 2000 and partially refurbished every year, the hotel has only 17 large rooms with balcony or terrace, thus providing a cosy and relaxed retreat from the island's vibrant lifestyle. Offering all the amenities of a large hotel, it is particularly suited for those who wish to relax and enjoy a private environment, with a choice between a soft or hard mattress, Hermès or Trussardi bath products and breakfast until 1pm. Johansens guests receive a fruit salad and a bottle of wine upon arrival.

Cet élégant boutique hôtel est situé au bord de la mer, à 10 minutes à pied de la ville de Mykonos. Construit en 2000 et partiellement remis à neuf chaque année, l'hôtel ne dispose que de 17 grandes chambres avec balcon ou terrasse et donc offre un refuge intime pour échapper la vie trépidante de l'île. Offrant toutes les facilités d'un grand hôtel, il est idéal pour ceux qui veulent se dérouler dans un environnement privé. Il offre un choix de matelas forts et doux et des produits de bains Hermès ou Trussardi. Le petit déjeuner est servi jusqu'à 13 h. En arrivant, les clients de Johansens reçoivent une salade de fruits et une bouteille de vin.

Dieses elegante Boutique-Hotel liegt direkt am Meer, nur 10 Minuten zu Fuß von Mykonos-Stadt entfernt. Das 2000 erbaute und jährlich weiter erneuerte Hotel hat nur 17 große Zimmer mit Balkon oder Terrasse und bietet so ein gemütliches Versteck vor dem regen Inseltreiben. Alle Annehmlichkeiten eines großen Hotels sind geboten, ideal um in familiärer Atmosphäre zu entspannen. Man hat die Wahl zwischen harter oder weicher Matratze und Hermès oder Trussardi-Badeartikeln, Frühstück bis 13 Uhr. Johansens-Gäste bekommen frischen Obstsalat und eine Flasche Wein.

***Our inspector loved:** Watching the magnificent sunset from the poolside.*

Directions: Mykonos Airport > across the main sea port > 800m towards Tagoo on the right.

Web: www.johansens.com/apanema
E-mail: mail@apanemaresort.com
Tel: +30 22890 28590
Fax: +30 22890 79250

Price Guide:
single €135-240
double €170-330
suite €260-385

THARROE OF MYKONOS

ANGELIKA, 84600 MYKONOS, GREECE

This hilltop location enjoys breathtaking sunsets and glorious views over the Aegean Sea. Mykonos town centre is just 15 minutes away and Ornos beach is within walking distance. Décor is modern and minimalist, and the en-suite bedrooms have a balcony or terrace. Traditional Greek and Mediterranean cuisine, organic and vegetarian menus are served in the Barbarossa restaurant, fine wines, organic beers and cocktails, in the Colors of the Sunset Bar. The Princess Shanhaz Ayurvedic natural herbal centre offers hair and body spa treatments.

Sa location au sommet d'une colline offre des couchers de soleil à couper le souffle et des vues splendides sur la mer Egée. Le centre de la ville de Mykonos n'est qu'à 15 minutes et la plage Ornos est accessible à pied. Le décor est moderne et minimaliste, et les chambres avec salle de bain ont un balcon ou une terrasse. Une cuisine grecque et méditerranéenne et des menus biologiques et végétariens sont servis au restaurant Barbarossa; des vins fins, des bières biologiques et des cocktails sont servis au Colors of the Sunset Bar. Le Princess Shanhaz centre ayurvédique offre des traitements bains et soins de beauté.

Von seiner Hügellage bietet dieses Hotel herrliche Sonnenuntergänge und Ausblicke auf die Ägäis. Mykonos Stadtzentrum ist nur 15 Minuten entfernt, und der Ornos-Strand ist zu Fuß erreichbar. Das Décor ist modern und minimalistisch, die Zimmer haben eigenes Bad und Terrasse oder Balkon. Das Barbarossa serviert traditionelle griechische und Mittelmeerküche und vegetarische und Bio-Menüs, in der Colors of the Sunset Bar gibt es edle Weine, Bier aus biologischem Anbau und Cocktails. Das Princess Shanhaz Ayurveda-Zentrum bietet Kur- und Schönheitsbehandlungen.

Our inspector loved: *The view of Mykonos Bay and town from the poolside.*

Directions: The hotel is 800m from Mykonos town centre.

Web: www.johansens.com/tharroe
E-mail: tharroe@myk.forthnet.gr
Tel: +30 22890 27370
Fax: +30 22890 27375

Price Guide:
single €100-460
double €120-600
suite €180-2,000

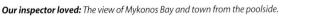

GREECE (PAROS)

Acquamarina Resort

NEW GOLDEN BEACH, 84400 PAROS, GREECE

Directions: Paros Airport > Paros Port > towards New Golden Beach Road (Neachrisiakti) > at the beach the hotel is signposted.

Web: www.johansens.com/acquamarina
E-mail: acquamarina@cybex.gr
Tel: +30 228404 3281
Fax: +30 228404 3236

Price Guide:
single €98-140
double €140-200
suite €180-300

This intimate, family-run resort is situated directly on the seafront and offers every guest individual care and attention in a relaxed atmosphere. The whitewashed bungalow villas are built in traditional Cycladian design, with spacious marble floored rooms and either a balcony or veranda. The outdoor pool is one of the largest in the Cycladic islands and is complemented by a poolside bar, whilst the alluring gardens reflect the tranquillity of the resort. Guests can enjoy mouth-watering cuisine in the taverna or the à la carte restaurant.

Cet ensemble balnéaire familial intime est situé directement en bordure de mer et offre à ses hôtes une attention individualisée dans une atmosphère détendue. Les bungalows aux murs blanchis sont construits dans le style traditionnel des Cyclades, avec de grandes pièces aux sols en marbre et soit un balcon soit une véranda. La piscine extérieure est la plus grande des Cyclades avec bar au bord, alors que des jardins émane la tranquillité de la station. Les hôtes peuvent déguster une cuisine savoureuse à la taverne ou au restaurant à la carte.

Dieses kleine, familiengeführte Resort befindet sich direkt am Meer und bietet jedem Gast höchst individuelle Aufmerksamkeit in entspannter Atmosphäre. Die weißgetünchten Bungalow-Villen sind in traditionellem kykladischen Design gestaltet und haben geräumige Zimmer mit Marmorböden und entweder Balkon oder Veranda. Der Swimmingpool – komplett mit Bar – ist einer der größten der Kykladischen Inseln und die hübschen Gärten spiegeln die Beschaulichkeit des Resorts wider. In der Taverne oder im à la carte Restaurant wird köstliche Küche serviert.

Our inspector loved: *The charming restaurant by the seaside.*

ASTIR OF PAROS

KOLYMBITHRES, NAOUSSA, 84401 PAROS, GREECE

Set amid endless gardens overlooking the Aegean Sea, this model "Cycladic village" is the ideal place for a relaxing, traditional Greek break. The rooms are light and spacious, and flowers are everywhere. The Poseidon restaurant serves Greek and international delights in a candle-lit setting, whilst the Aeolos Thai Restaurant offers Thai cuisine and live music; the Amfitriti bar and the Nereus bar serve exotic cocktails. On site is the Venus Art Gallery, where Greek and international artists exhibit contemporary paintings and sculptures.

Entouré de jardins qui donnent sur la mer Egée, ce village "cycladique" est l'endroit idéal pour un séjour grec reposant et traditionnel. Les chambres sont claires et spacieuses, les fleurs y sont partout présentes. Au restaurant Poseidon, les clients pourront goûter des plats grecs et internationaux, ou des délices thaïs et musique en direct dans le Aeolos Thai Restaurant. Le bar Amfitriti et le bar Nereus servent des cocktails. Vous trouverez sur place la Galerie d'art Venus, où les artistes grecs et internationaux exposent leurs tableaux contemporains et leurs sculptures.

Inmitten endloser Gärten mit Blick auf das Ägäische Meer liegt dieses Modell eines Cycladischen Dorfes, ideal für einen erholsamen und traditionellen griechischen Urlaub. Die Zimmer sind hell und geräumig, und überall sind Blumen. Im Poseidon kann man griechische und internationale Köstlichkeiten bei Kerzenschein genießen, das Aeolos Thai Restaurant bietet Thai-Küche und die Amfitriti und die Nereus Bar servieren exotische Cocktails. In der Venus-Kunstgallerie stellen griechische und internationale Künstler zeitgenössische Malereien und Skulpturen aus.

Our inspector loved: *The extensive garden.*

Directions: 20 minutes from airport, 15 minutes from port.

Web: www.johansens.com/astirofparos
E-mail: astir@hol.gr
Tel: +30 22840 51976
Fax: +30 22840 51842

Price Guide:
double €160-230
suite €186-670

Hungary

Hotel location shown in red (hotel) or purple (spa hotel) with page number

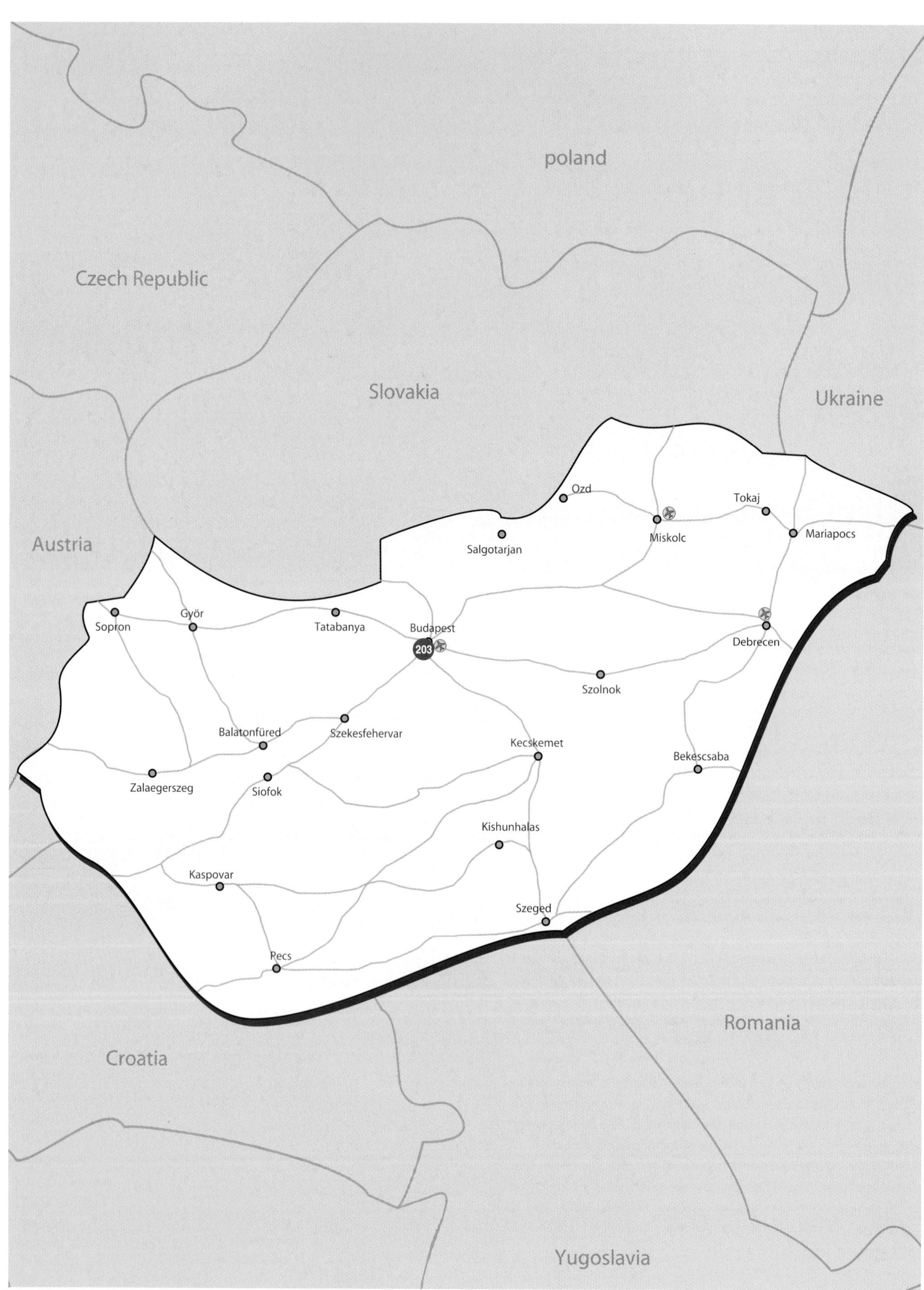

Uhu Villa

1025 BUDAPEST, KESELYÜ U. 1/A, HUNGARY

Uhu Villa is situated just 20 minutes from the River Danube, the Castle area and the centre of Budapest. Built in the late 1800s the Villa stands in a hidden valley among the hills of Buda. The 10 modern bedrooms are elegantly furnished; beamed ceilings and old prints feature throughout the hotel. The restaurant serves Italian cuisine, offering a lighter and healthier variation to the spicy, opulent native cuisine. The Uhu Villa Fitness & Relax Centre features a warm water swimming pool, massage treatments and sauna.

Uhu Villa est située à 20 minutes de la Danube, du quartier du château et du centre de Budapest. Construit à la fin du XIXe siècle, la Villa se trouve au cœur d'une vallée cachée parmi les collines de Buda. Les 10 chambres sont meublées de manière élégante et il y a des poutres au plafond et des vielles gravures dans tout l'hôtel. La cuisine italienne est servie dans le restaurant, offrant un choix plus légère au plats épissés et riches de la cuisine locale. Les hôtes peuvent se détendre dans le centre de fitness et relax, offrant un sauna, une piscine chauffée et des traitements de massage.

Die Ende des 19. Jahrhunderts erbaute Uhu Villa liegt in einem Tal in den Hügeln von Buda, nur 20 Minuten von der Donau, dem Burgviertel und dem Zentrum Budapests entfernt. Die 10 modernen Gästezimmer sind elegant eingerichtet, Balkendecken und alte Drucke zieren das gesamte Hotel. Im Restaurant wird italienische Küche serviert, eine etwas leichtere und gesündere Alternative zur scharfen, üppigen einheimischen Küche. Das Uhu Villa Fitness & Relax Centre bietet Warmwasserbecken, Massagen und Sauna.

Our inspector loved: *The location; in the middle of a forest yet within easy reach of busy city life.*

Directions: The hotel is located north west of the city. Moskva Place > along the tram line 56 > Pasareti Street > turn right uphill. The nearest airport is Budapest.

Györ
Budapest
Szeged

Web: www.johansens.com/www.uhuvilla.hu
E-mail: uhuvilla@uhuvilla.hu
Tel: +36 1 275 1002
Fax: +36 1 398 0571

Price Guide:
single €85
double €100
suite €150-200

Italy

Hotel location shown in red (hotel) or purple (spa hotel) with page number

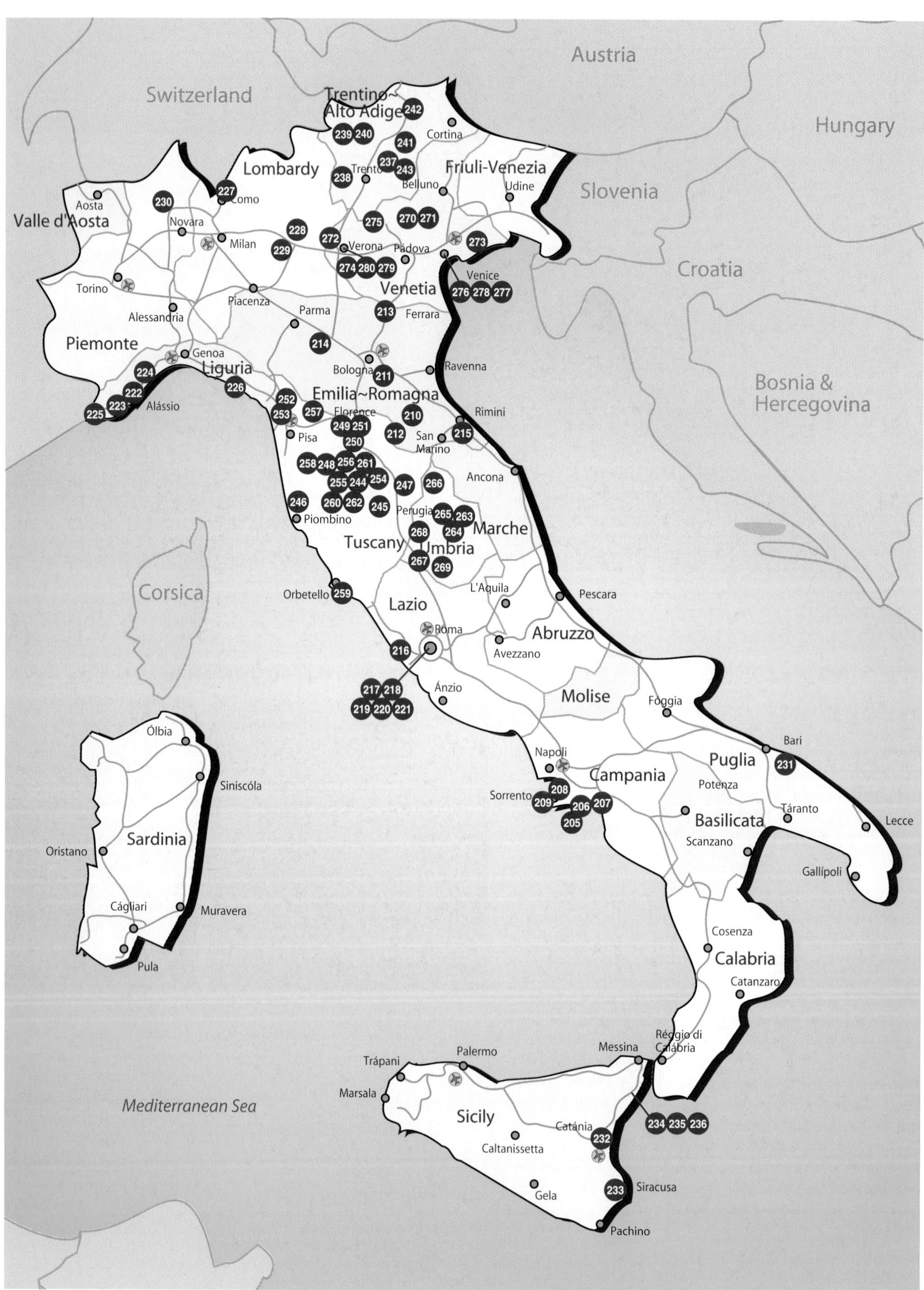

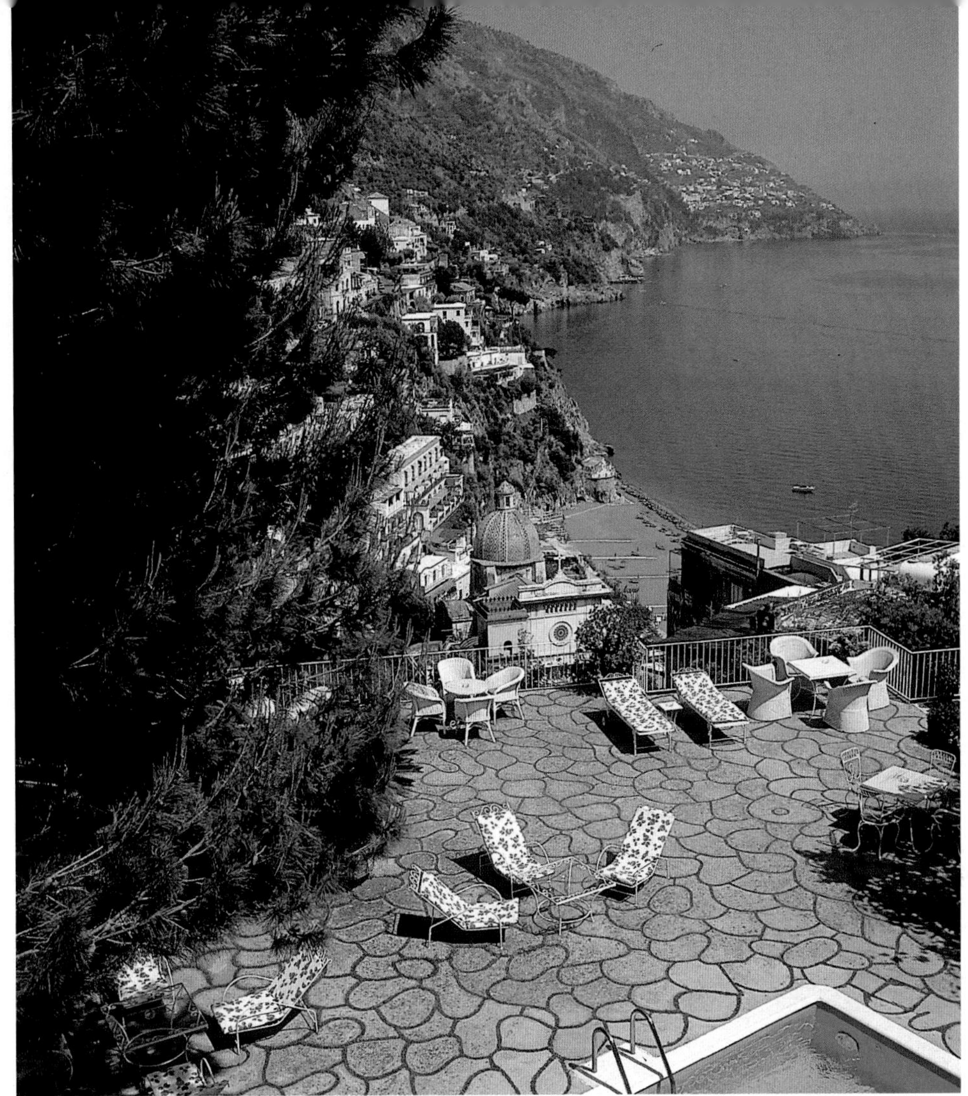

Hotel Poseidon

VIA PASITEA 148, 84017 POSITANO (SALERNO), ITALY

This 4-star hotel is located in the heart of the town. The charming, pristine bedrooms, decorated with rustic furniture, have balconies overlooking the village. The spacious, comfortable living room and bar are nearby to the sunbathing terrace and swimming pool, which is heated during the winter months. In summer, the restaurant service is on a vast terrace covered with vines. There is a well equipped gym and massages are available on request.

Cet hôtel 4 étoiles est situé en plein coeur de la ville. Les chambres, charmantes et immaculées, sont décorées avec des meubles rustiques et ont des balcons surplombant le village. La salle de séjour et le bar, spacieux et confortables, donnent sur une terrasse ensoleillée avec une piscine chauffée pendant l'hiver. En été, le service de restauration est assuré sur une grande terrasse ombragée de vignes. Il ya un gymnase bien équipé et des massages sont disponibles sur demande.

Dieses 4-Sterne-Hotel liegt mitten im Zentrum von Positano. Die zauberhaften traditionellen Zimmer sind mit rustikalen Möbeln ausgestattet und haben Balkone mit Blick auf das Dorf. Der große, gemütliche Aufenthaltsraum und die Bar liegen neben einer Sonnenterrasse mit Swimmingpool, der im Winter beheizt wird. Im Sommer diniert man auf einer von Weinlaub überdachten Terrasse. Ein gutausgestatteter Fitnessraum steht zur Verfügung und Massagen werden auf Anfrage angeboten.

Our inspector loved: *The spa, great treatment, outstanding professionality and lovely music in the background.*

Directions: A3 > Castellammare di Stabia > Meta di Sorrento > Positano.

Web: www.johansens.com/hotelposeidon
E-mail: info@hotelposeidonpositano.it
Tel: +39 089 811111
Fax: +39 089 875833

Price Guide:
single €245–274
double/twin €255–284
suite €441–483

50 50 SPA

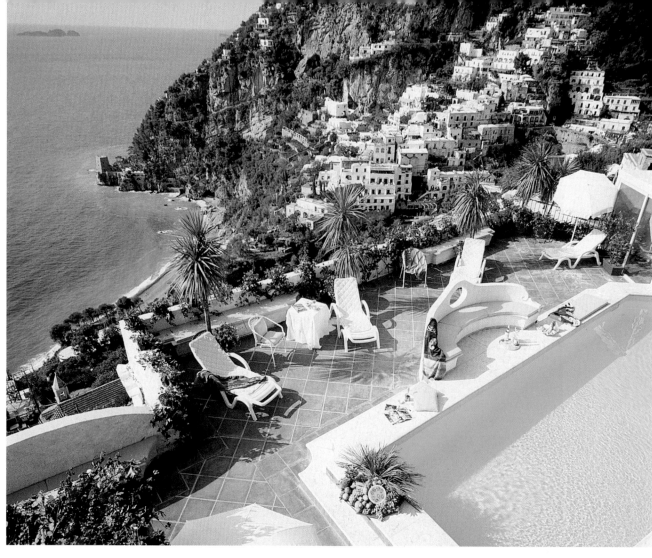

HOTEL VILLA FRANCA

VIALE PASITEA 318, 84017 POSITANO (SA), ITALY

Perched high on the cliffs and facing the sea and the village, this hotel has a truly spectacular outlook. The roof garden also holds the swimming pool, and there can be few more beautiful places in which to enjoy a chilled glass of wine and admire the view. The owner has a distinct gourmet flair and the Li Galli restaurant offers haute cuisine with a local flavour, as well as various surprise dishes that never fail to delight!

Perché en haut des falaises et face à la mer et du village, cet hôtel a une vue spectaculaire. Le jardin perché sur le toit dispose également d'une piscine, et est l'endroit parfait où déguster un verre de vin frais ou simplement apprécier la vue. Le propriétaire est un fin gourmet et le restaurant Li Galli offre de la grande cuisine à la saveur locale, ainsi qu'une myriade de plats surprenants qui sont toujours un régal !

Dieses hoch auf den Klippen über dem Meer gelegene Hotel bietet ein wahrhaft spektakuläres Panorama. Auf der Dachterrasse befindet sich ein Swimmingpool, und man kann sich kaum einen besseren Ort vorstellen, um ein Glas Wein und die herrliche Sicht zu genießen. Der Besitzer hat einen ausgeprägten Sinn für Feinschmeckerküche, und im Restaurant Li Galli wird Haute Cuisine mit einheimischer Note serviert, außerdem stehen stets verlockende Überraschungen auf der Speisekarte.

Our inspector loved: *The dining experience: the view is enchanting and the food is simply delicious.*

Directions: A3 > Sorrento > Positano.

Web: www.johansens.com/villafranca
E-mail: info@villafrancahotel.it
Tel: +39 089 875655
Fax: +39 089 875735

Price Guide:
single €170–220
double €190–340

Hotel Villa Maria

VIA S.CHIARA 2, 84010 RAVELLO (SA), ITALY

Situated with a unique and breathtaking view of the Amalfi coast and the hills that gently slope down to it lies this family-owned hotel, which has a romantic and intimate ambience, as if staying in a private villa. The rooms are large and spacious overlooking the orchard that provides ingredients for the elegant dinner table. Guests also have use of the swimming pool at the nearby sister hotel, Hotel Giordano.

Cet hôtel familial à l'ambiance romantique et intime comme celle d'une villa privée, a des vues uniques et à couper le souffle sur la côte d'Amalfi et sur les collines qui descendent doucement vers celle-ci. Les chambres sont grandes et spacieuses et s'ouvrent sur les vergers d'où viennent certains ingrédients utilisés pour l'élégante table du dîner. Les hôtes peuvent également utiliser la piscine de l'hôtel partenaire tout proche, l'hôtel Giordano.

In einzigartiger Lage mit atemberaubender Sicht auf die Amalfiküste und die sanft bis zur Küste hinunterführenden Hügel liegt dieses familiengeführte Hotel, das ein romantisches und familiäres Ambiente besitzt, so dass man sich wie in einer privaten Villa fühlt. Die Zimmer sind groß und geräumig und blicken auf den Garten, der stets für frische Zutaten für ein elegantes Abendessen sorgt. Gäste können den Swimmingpool des nahegelegenen Schwesterhotels Giordano benutzen.

Our inspector loved: *The stunning view.*

Directions: A3 (Naples – Salerno) exit Angri > Costa Amalfitana > Ravello.

Web: www.johansens.com/villamaria
Email: villamaria@villamaria.it
Tel: +39 089 857255
Fax: +39 089 857071

Price Guide:
single €145–175
double €175–270
suite €385–425

Grand Hotel Cocumella

VIA COCUMELLA 7, 80065 SANT'AGNELLO, SORRENTO, ITALY

This former Jesuit monastery was transformed into a hotel in 1822. Traces of the past remain; the elegant hall was once the cloisters and the chapel is still used for weddings and concerts. Many of the guest rooms have magnificent antique furnishings and the bridal suite has an exquisite painted ceiling. Guests feast on aromatic Mediterranean dishes, and in summer, light buffet lunches are enjoyed by the pool.

Cet ancien monastère jésuite a été transformé en hôtel en 1822. Les traces du passé sont encore présentes, le hall élégant occupe l'ancien cloître et la chapelle continue d'être utilisée pour des mariages ou des concerts. De magnifiques meubles anciens agrémentent les chambres et une peinture raffinée orne le plafond de la suite nuptiale. Les visiteurs dégustent des plats méditerranéens aux saveurs aromatiques l'été et des buffets légers sont proposés au bord de la piscine.

Dieses ehemalige Jesuitenkloster wurde 1822 zu einem Hotel umgebaut, und Spuren der Vergangenheit sind immer noch vorhanden. Die elegante Halle war einst der Kreuzgang und die Kapelle wird noch heute für Hochzeiten und Konzerte genutzt. Viele der Zimmer sind mit prächtigen Antikmöbeln eingerichtet und die Hochzeitssuite ziert eine beeindruckend bemalte Decke. Die Gäste erfreuen sich an köstlichen mediterranen Gerichten, und in den Sommermonaten sind leichte Buffetlunches am Pool zu genießen.

Our inspector loved: *The scent of the garden: a revitalising experience.*

Directions: Naples > Castellammare di Stabia > Sorrento.

Web: www.johansens.com/grandcocumella
E-mail: hcocum@tin.it
Tel: +39 081 878 2933
Fax: +39 081 878 3712

Price Guide:
single €200–237
double/twin €300–420
suite €435–692

GRAND HOTEL EXCELSIOR VITTORIA

PIAZZA TASSO 34, 80067 SORRENTO (NAPLES), ITALY

Built at the turn of the century and set on the Sorrento waterfront with its own moorings, the architecture of this fine hotel is graceful fin de siècle. The grounds are beautiful, filled with exotic subtropical plants and scented from the orange groves and olive trees. Guests can dine al fresco in the panoramic Bosquet Restaurant or enjoy the ambience in the grand Vittoria Restaurant, with its impressive marble pillars. The hotel boasts new prestigious and evocative suites, such as the Pompei Suite, created in original Pompeian style and the Imperial Suite in Liberty style.

Construit au début du siècle, l'Excelsior Vittoria se dresse sur le front de mer de Sorrente et dispose de ses propres mouillages. Cet hôtel raffiné se distingue par son élégante architecture de fin de siècle. Le parc est magnifique, rempli de plantes subtropicales et parfumé par des orangers et des oliviers. Les clients peuvent dîner à l'extérieur au restaurant panoramique Le Bosquet ou préférer l'ambiance du grand restaurant Vittoria avec ses impressionnants piliers en marbre. L'hôtel peut se vanter de ses nouvelles suites évocatrices telles que la Suite Pompéi, décorée dans un style pompéien, et la Suite Impériale dans un style Liberté.

Dieses herrliche Hotel im eleganten Fin-de-siècle-Stil wurde um die Jahrhundertwende erbaut und hat seinen eigenen Anlegeplatz direkt am Meer von Sorrento. Die herrlichen Gärten sind voll von exotischen subtropischen Pflanzen und dem zarten Duft von Orangen- und Olivenbäumen. Man kann entweder in Freien im Panoramarestaurant Bosquet oder im stimmungsvollen Vittoria mit seinen eindrucksvollen Marmorsäulen dinieren. Das Hotel bietet neue, luxuriöse Suiten wie z.B. die im ursprünglichen Pompei-Stil eingerichtete Pompei Suite oder die Imperial Suite im Liberty-Stil.

Our inspector loved: *The apéritif on the terrace, accompanied by live jazz and the best sunset ever!*

Directions: A3 > Castellammare di Stabia > Sorrento.

Web: www.johansens.com/excelsiorvittoria
E-mail: exvitt@exvitt.it
Tel: +39 081 807 1044
Fax: +39 081 877 1206

Price Guide:
single €305
double/twin €350–500
suite €630–2,010

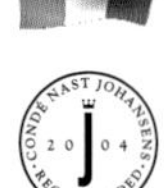

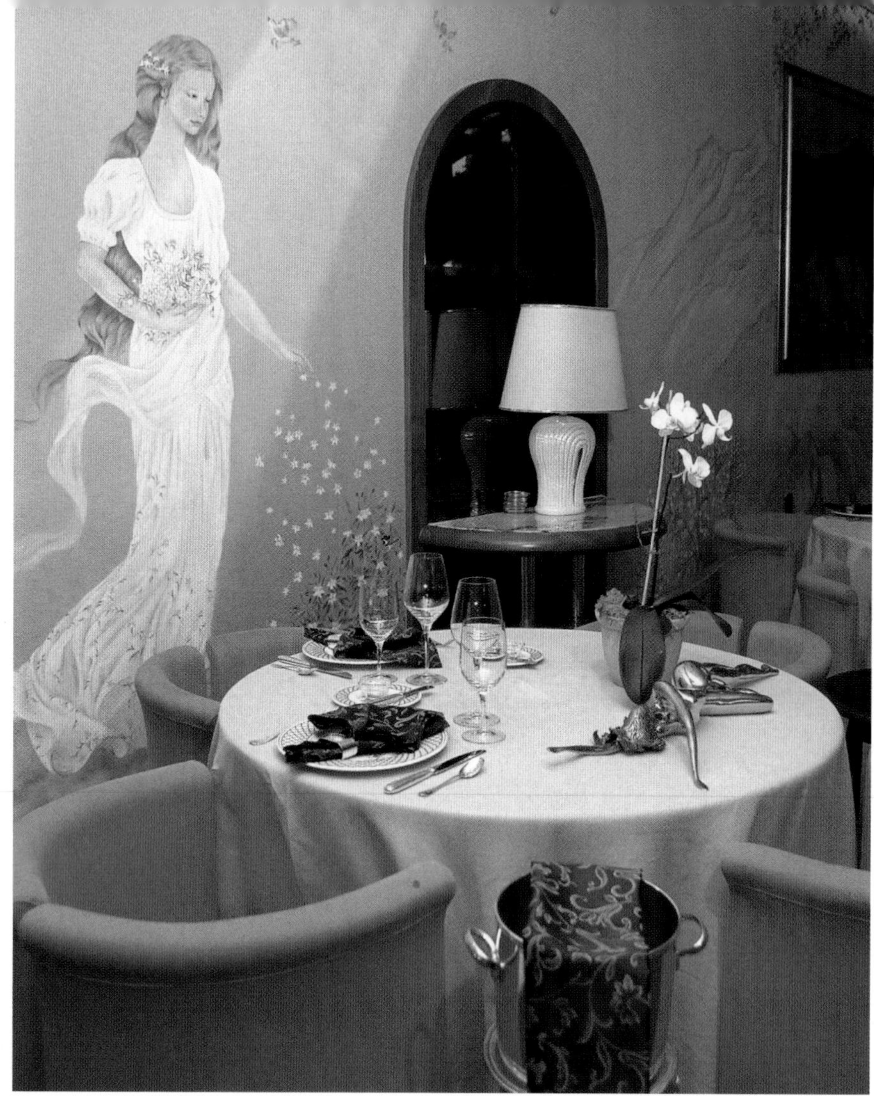

Hotel Tosco Romagnolo

PIAZZA DANTE ALIGHIERI 2, 47021 BAGNO DI ROMAGNA TERME, ITALY

Situated in an ancient village and surrounded by fascinating landscape only a few miles from the Adriatic Sea, this friendly, family-run hotel offers pure relaxation, refined cuisine, modern accommodation and a sense of elegance. Guests can choose between 2 restaurants, the Tosco Romagnolo and the Paolo Teverini, which has received many awards for its exquisite cuisine and wide selection of fine wines. For those wishing to be pampered, there is a beauty farm and health centre. Beautiful Tuscany and Umbria are within easy driving distance.

Situé dans un vieux village, au milieu d'une contrée fascinante, à quelques kilomètres de l'Adriatique, cet hôtel familial est une invitation à la douceur de vivre. Dans un cadre accueillant et élégant, les visiteurs découvrent des chambres modernes confortables et une cuisine raffinée, proposée par 2 restaurants différents, le Tosco Romagnolo et le Paolo Teverini. Ce dernier a obtenu maintes distinctions pour ses plats exquis et son grand choix d'excellents vins. Des soins attentifs sont dispensés par un centre de beauté et de remise en forme. La Toscane et l'Ombrie ne sont pas loin.

In einem alten Dorf nur ein paar Kilometer von der Adria entfernt gelegen und von faszinierender Landschaft umgeben bietet dieses elegante, freundliche, familiengeführte Hotel reinste Erholung, komfortable Zimmer und hervorragende Küche. Man hat die Wahl zwischen 2 Restaurants, dem Tosco Romagnolo und dem Paolo Teverini, das mehrfach für seine exquisiten Gerichte und erlesenen Weine ausgezeichnet wurde. Ein Schönheits- und Gesundheitszentrum steht ebenfalls zur Verfügung. Die Toskana und Umbrien sind leicht mit dem Auto zu erreichen.

Our inspector loved: *Chef Paolo Teverini's exquisite cuisine.*

Directions: E45 from Cesena towards Perugia > exit Bagno di Romagna.

Web: www.johansens.com/toscoromagnolo
E-mail: lacasa@paoloteverini.it
Tel: +39 0543 911260
Fax: +39 0543 911014

Price Guide:
single €150
junior suite €160–300
suite €300–420

Relais Torre Pratesi

VIA CAVINA 11, 48013 BRISIGHELLA (RA), ITALY

This 16th-century tower has only recently been converted into a peaceful and elegant hotel, which has lost nothing of its historic charm. Each bedroom is lovingly furnished with pieces of antique and hand-crafted furniture. The Fireplace room is the candle-lit setting for dinners of delicate local cuisine. Guests can enjoy a Jacuzzi and swimming pool in the garden. Close to Tuscany, this is an area of immense culture, which guests are encouraged and helped to explore by their welcoming hosts.

Récemment transformée en un hôtel reposant et raffiné, cette tour du XVIe siècle ne manquera pas de séduire les visiteurs par son charme historique. Dans les chambres aménagées avec soin trônent des meubles anciens et artisanaux. Le restaurant et sa cheminée forment un cadre idéal pour goûter les délicates saveurs de la cuisine locale à la lueur des chandelles. L'hôtel dispose d'un jacuzzi et une piscine situés dans le jardin. Proche de la Toscane, cette région est d'une grande richesse culturelle, que des hôtes vous encourageront et aideront à découvrir.

Dieser Turm aus dem 16. Jahrhundert wurde erst kürzlich in ein elegantes und friedliches Hotel umgewandelt, das nichts von seinem ursprünglichen Charme verloren hat. Die Zimmer sind liebevoll mit Antiquitäten und handgefertigten Möbeln eingerichtet. Im Kaminsaal werden bei Kerzenschein köstliche regionale Gerichte serviert. Diese sehr nahe an der Toskana gelegene Region ist unglaublich reich an Kultur, und lädt zur Erforschung ein, wobei die Gastgeber gerne behilflich sind.

Our inspector loved: *Savouring the rich culture in peaceful harmony with nature.*

Directions: A14 exit at Faenza > SS302 Brisighella–Florence road > Fognano > direction Zattaglia.

Web: www.johansens.com/torrepratesi
E-mail: torrep@tin.it
Tel: +39 0546 84545
Fax: +39 0546 84558

Price Guide:
double €150–180
suite €180–210

Monte del Re

40050 DOZZA (BOLOGNA), ITALY

This ancient convent, which enjoys a prestigious location within a park overlooking the hills, offers the perfect combination of tranquillity and comfort needed in today's hectic world. Guests at Monte del Re are immediately surrounded by its magical, romantic atmosphere, enhanced by the charming surroundings. Superb culinary delights are served in the restaurant, and guests will appreciate the richly elegant furnishings, the panoramic swimming pool and the beautiful garden. The ancient church is now used as a conference centre or for banquets.

Ce couvent très ancien, qui jouit d'une position prestigieuse au sein d'un parc donnant sur les collines, offre la combinaison parfaite de tranquillité et confort, dont nous avons tellement besoin dans la vie trépidante de nos jours. Les hôtes sont immédiatement entourés par une ambiance romantique, mise en valeur par les environs charmants. Des délices culinaires superbes sont servies dans le restaurant, et les hôtes apprécieront les mobiliers élégants, la piscine panoramique et le beau jardin. L'église ancienne a été transformée en centre de conférences et banquets.

Dieses einstige Kloster in seiner herrlichen Lage inmitten eines Parks mit Blick auf die Hügellandschaft bietet die perfekte Verbindung von Ruhe und Komfort, so dringend nötig in unserer hektischen Welt. Man ist hier sofort von einer magischen, romantischen Atmosphäre umgeben, die durch die zauberhafte Umgebung noch verstärkt wird. Im Restaurant wird hervorragende Küche serviert, und die üppig-elegante Einrichtung, der Panorama-Swimmingpool und der hübsche Garten runden das Ganze wunderbar ab. Die alte Kirche dient nun als Konferenz- oder Bankettsaal.

Our inspector loved: *The magical atmosphere and the superb restaurant.*

Directions: From the A1 > A14 towards Ancona > exit Castel San Pietro Terme > follow directions to Imola - Dozza SS9 (Via Emilia).

Web: www.johansens.com/montedelre
E-mail: montedelre@tiscali.it
Tel: +39 0542 678400
Fax: +39 0542 678444

Price Guide:
single €97-170
double €125-230
junior suite €175-260

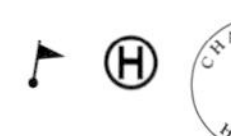

RIPAGRANDE HOTEL

VIA RIPAGRANDE 21, 44100 FERRARA, ITALY

This superbly restored 15th-century palace features a Renaissance interior, appropriate to the history of the hotel. The entrance hall is spectacular with its marble staircase and pillars, wrought-iron banisters and beamed ceiling. The attractive Ripa restaurant serves many traditional Ferrarese specialities. 2 enchanting courtyards make wonderful settings for banquets. Guests relax in the cool salons or upon terraces, some of which are privately adjoined to the spacious bedrooms, which have been recently refurbished.

Ce palais du XVe siècle superbement restauré est agrémenté d'un intérieur Renaissance. Le hall d'entrée est spectaculaire en raison de sa cage d'escalier orné d'une rampe en fer forgé, de ses colonnes en marbre et de son plafond orné de poutres. Le charmant restaurant Ripa sert nombre de spécialités traditionnelles de Ferrare. Enfin, 2 délicieuses cours forment un cadre idéal pour les banquets. Les hôtes peuvent se relaxer dans les salons ou sur les terrasses, dont certaines privées rejoignent les chambres spacieuses et récemment renovées.

Das Interieur dieses perfekt restaurierten Palais aus dem 15. Jahrhundert ist im Renaissance-Stil gehalten und passt somit zur Geschichte des Hotels. Die Eingangshalle beeindruckt mit Marmortreppe und -säulen, schmiedeeisernen Geländern und Balkendecke. Das Restaurant Ripa serviert traditionelle Spezialitäten aus Ferrara, und 2 zauberhafte Innenhöfe sind perfekt für Bankette. Entspannen kann man in den kühlen Salons oder auf den Terrassen, von denen einige zum Privatgebrauch direkt an die geräumigen, kürzlich renovierten Zimmer angrenzen.

Our inspector loved: *The 2 magnificent Renaissance courtyards and the exquisite cuisine.*

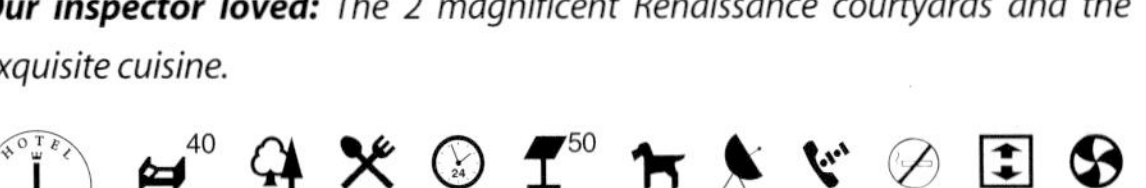

Directions: The hotel is halfway between Venice and Florence. A13 > Ferrara.

Web: www.johansens.com/ripagrande
E-mail: ripahotel@mbox.4net.it
Tel: +39 0532 765250
Fax: +39 0532 764377

Price Guide:
single €125
double/twin €195
suite €175–190

Hotel Posta

PIAZZA DEL MONTE, 2, 42100 REGGIO EMILIA, ITALY

Located in the town's historic centre, this imposing medieval building was built in 1280 as Palazzo del Capitano (Magistrate's House) and has a long tradition of hospitality. The influence of the different centuries can be appreciated in the charming blend of styles throughout the hotel. The bar with its refined and unusual atmosphere is particularly delightful, whilst the splendid Salone del Capitano is available for meetings and banquets. Excursions in and out of town can be organised, including a visit to a cheese factory, where the legendary Parmigiano Reggiano (parmesan cheese) is produced.

Situé au cœur de la ville historique, cette maison médiévale imposante fut construite en 1280 comme Palazzo del Capitano (la maison du magistrat) et possède une longue tradition d'hospitalité. L'influence des siècles passés se montre dans le mélange de styles dans tout l'hôtel. Le bar avec son atmosphère élégante et exceptionnelle est splendide, alors que le Salone del Capitano est l'endroit idéal pour des conférences ou des banquets. Des excursions peuvent être organisées, comprenant une visite à une fromagerie produisant le Parmigiano Reggiano légendaire.

Dieses eindrucksvolle mittelalterliche Haus befindet sich im Zentrum der Altstadt und erfreut sich einer langen Tradition der Gastfreundschaft. 1280 als Palazzo del Capitano (Haus des Stadtverwalters) erbaut, zeigen sich auch heute noch die Einflüsse der Jahrhunderte in einer zauberhaften Stilmischung. Besonders die Bar mit ihrer einmaligen Atmosphäre ist ein Genuss. Der Salone del Capitano bietet sich sowohl für Konferenzen als auch Bankette an. Exkursionen werden organisiert, darunter der Besuch einer Käserei, in der der berühmt Parmigiano Reggiano hergestellt wird.

Our inspector loved: *The magnificent medieval style façade.*

Directions: From the A1 (Milano/Roma) exit at Reggio Emilia, then follow signs to the town centre.

Web: www.johansens.com/posta
E-mail: info@hotelposta.re.it
Tel: +39 05 22 43 29 44
Fax: +39 05 22 45 26 02

Price Guide:
single €135
double €175
suite €205-250

HOTEL DES NATIONS

LUNGOMARE COSTITUZIONE 2, 47838 RICCIONE (RN), ITALY

Situated on the beach, this quiet, charming hotel was conceived according to the wellness philosophy. Stunning sea views and beautiful antique furniture enhance the elegant bedrooms. Natural organic food and local delicacies are served in the harmoniously decorated breakfast room, and guests can make reservations at the excellent adjacent restaurant. Health treatments such as massage, reflexology and mud therapy are available, whilst outdoor pursuits include tennis, excursions and fishing.

Situé sur la plage, ce charmant hôtel a été conçu suivant les principes du bien-être. Une vue imprenable sur la mer et de beaux meubles anciens mettent en valeur les chambres élégantes. Une nourriture naturelle et biologique et des spécialités locales sont servies dans la salle du petit-déjeuner. Les repas peuvent être pris dans le délicieux restaurant adjacent à l'hôtel, mais uniquement sur réservation. Les hôtes peuvent profiter de traitements de santé tels que massage, réflexologie et bains de boue, alors que les activités incluent tennis, voile, excursions et pêche.

Dieses ruhige, am Strand gelegene Hotel wurde gemäß der Wellness-Philosophie erbaut. Traumhafte Meeresblicke und schöne antike Möbel verstärken das elegante Ambiente der Zimmer. Im harmonisch gestalteten Frühstücksraum werden biologische Kost und einheimische Köstlichkeiten serviert, und die Gäste können das hervorragende Restaurant im Haus besuchen (Reservierung erforderlich). Gesundheitsanwendungen wie Massage, Reflexologie und Schlammtherapie werden angeboten; Tennis, Exkursionen und Angeln sind ebenfalls möglich.

Our inspector loved: *The emphasis on well-being, from the natural delicacies at breakfast to the therapies for body and mind.*

Directions: A14 > exit Riccione > follow directions to Riccione Mare.

Web: www.johansens.com/hoteldesnations
E-mail: info@desnations.it
Tel: +39 0541 647878
Fax: +39 0541 645154

Price Guide:
single €140–175
double €210–270
suite €306–545

LA POSTA VECCHIA

PALO LAZIALE, 00055 LADISPOLI, ROME, ITALY

Overlooking the sea and surrounded by natural parkland, the sumptuous Posta Vecchia, built on ancient Roman foundations, has a quiet luxuriousness. Many of the original structures such as stone doorways and fireplaces are preserved whilst stunning mosaics and antiques have been carefully restored and displayed in the hotel's museum. Exquisite décor and warm colour schemes create a welcoming atmosphere and the Italian cooking is simply delicious. There is a private beach and excellent leisure facilities inlcuding a beauty salon.

Surplombant la mer et entouré d'un parc naturel, le somptueux Posta Vecchia, construit sur d'anciennes fondations romaines, bénéficie d'un luxe tranquille. La plupart des installations originelles telles qu'encadrements de porte en pierre et cheminées a été préservée alors que d'étonnantes mosaïques et antiquités ont été restaurées avec soin et sont présentées dans le musée de l'hôtel. Le décor raffiné et les couleurs chaudes créent une atmosphère accueillante; la cuisine italienne est tout simplement délicieuse. L'hôtel dispose d'une plage privée et d'excellentes installations de loisirs, incluant un salon de beauté.

Dieses auf römischen Fundamenten erbaute, von Parklandschaft umgebene Hotel mit Meerblick bietet Eleganz und unaufdringlichen Luxus. Viele ursprüngliche Strukturen wie steinerne Torbögen und Kamine blieben erhalten, zauberhafte Mosaiken und Antiquitäten wurden sorgfältig restauriert und im Hotelmuseum ausgestellt. Exquisites Décor und warme Farben schaffen eine einladende Atmosphäre, und die italienische Küche ist einfach unübertroffen. Ein Privatstrand sowie Freizeiteinrichtungen sind vorhanden, darunter ein Beautysalon.

Directions: A12 > Cerveteri - Ladispoli > follow SSI south > exit Palo Laziale.

Web: www.johansens.com/postavecchia
E-mail: info@lapostavecchia.com
Tel: +39 0699 49501
Fax: +39 0699 49507

Price Guide:
(including visit to Roman Museum)
superior room €570
junior suite €920
master suite €1,400

Our inspector loved: *The many Roman antiques displayed around the hotel.*

 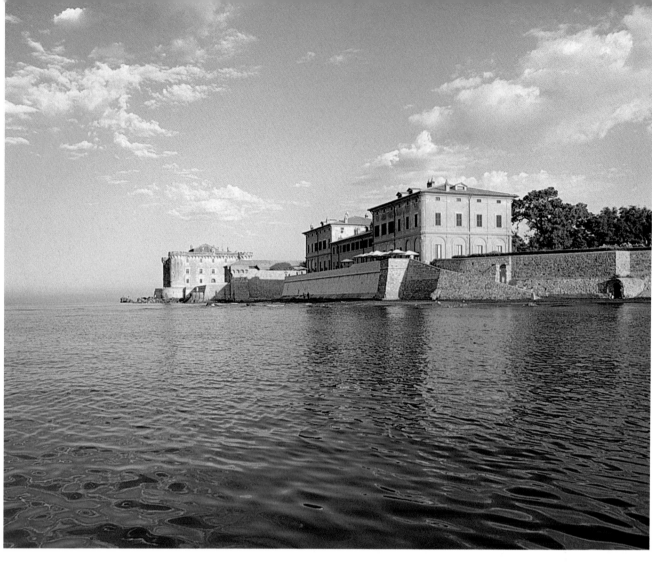

The Duke Hotel

VIA ARCHIMEDE 69, 00197 ROME, ITALY

Located in the prestigious and elegant residential district of Parioli, the Duke is a peaceful and stylish 4-star hotel that offers attentive and personal service for the most exacting guest. The style is a winning combination of classic Italian bourgeois design and the ambience of an English Gentleman's Club, creating a warmth of atmosphere that is mirrored by the attitude of its staff. The hotel is set between the parks of Villa Borghese and Villa Glori, and numerous sights are within easy reach.

Situé dans le prestigieux et élégant quartier résidentiel de Parioli, le Duke est un hôtel 4 étoiles chic et paisible qui offre un service personnel et attentif pour les hôtels les plus exigeants. Le style est une combinaison gagnante de style italien bourgeois classique et d'ambiance de Club de gentleman anglais, créant ainsi une atmosphère chaleureuse reflétée dans l'attitude du personnel. Cet hôtel est situé entre les parcs de la Villa Borghèse et de la Villa Glori, et proche de nombreuses curiosités touristiques.

Das inmitten des vornehmen, edlen Wohnviertels Parioli gelegene Duke Hotel ist ein friedliches und elegantes 4-Sterne-Hotel, dessen aufmerksamer, persönlicher Service selbst den anspruchsvollsten Gast zufrieden stellt. Der Stil ist eine attraktive Mischung aus klassischem italienischen bürgerlichem Design und dem Ambiente eines englischen Gentlemen Clubs, dessen herzliche Atmosphäre sich in der Freundlichkeit des Personals widerspiegelt. Das Hotel befindet sich zwischen den Parks der Villa Borghese und der Villa Glori, und zahlreiche Sehenswürdigkeiten liegen in nächster Nähe.

Our inspector loved: *The perfect blend between Italian Rationalist style and the warmth of an English Gentlemen's Club.*

Directions: 45 minutes from Ciampino and Fiumicino Airports.

Web: www.johansens.com/dukehotel
E-mail: theduke@thedukehotel.com
Tel: +39 06 367221
Fax: +39 06 36004104

Milan
Venice
Rome

Price Guide:
single €198-280
double €285-380
suite €470-895

Hotel Aventino

VIA SAN. DOMENICO 10, 00153 ROME, ITALY

Newly restored with care and respect for the district's historic past this charming city centre hotel enjoys an atmosphere of refined and innovative tranquillity. Décor and furnishings evoke a world of genteel and traditional relaxation, which radiates out from elegant public rooms and spacious guest rooms with all modern facilities to the attractive shady garden. The lounge boasts an antique fireplace, which during the colder months creates a very romantic and charming atmosphere. An ideal base for exploring Rome's treasures.

Récemment restauré avec soin et respect de l'histoire du quartier, cet hôtel charmant du centre ville bénéficie d'une atmosphère tranquille et raffinée. Le décor et le mobilier évoquent un monde de distinction associé à une détente traditionnelle, qui irradient des élégantes salles communes et des chambres spacieuses disposant de tout le confort moderne, jusqu'au beau jardin ombragé. Le salon a une cheminée antique, qui pendant des moins plus froids, crée une atmosphére romantique et charmante. Une base idéale pour explorer les trésors de Rome.

Dieses zauberhafte, erst kürzlich mit viel Liebe und Respekt für die historische Vergangenheit dieses Bezirks restaurierte Hotel im Stadtzentrum besitzt eine Atmosphäre der Eleganz und Ruhe. Décor und Einrichtung sorgen für ein Gefühl der Entspannung, das in den eleganten Aufenthaltsräumen, großen Gästezimmern mit jeglichem modernem Komfort und dem attraktiven, schattenspendenden Garten zu spüren ist. Der Aufenthaltsraum hat einen antiken Kamin, der während der kälteren Monate eine romantische und bezaubernde Atmosphäre erstellt. Der ideale Ausgangspunkt, um Roms Schätze zu erkunden.

Our inspector loved: *The refined elegance of the bedrooms and the relaxing gardens.*

Directions: Located in the heart of the city.

Web: www.johansens.com/aventino
E-mail: info@aventinohotels.com
Tel: +39 06 5745 174 / 5783 214
Fax: +39 06 5783 604

Price Guide:
single €109
double (single occupancy) €155
double €166
triple €192

Hotel dei Borgognoni

VIA DEL BUFALO 126 (PIAZZA DI SPAGNA), 00187 ROME, ITALY

Within the heart of Rome, this distinguished hotel boasts modern convenience whilst maintaining traditional elegance. In an ideal location, the hotel is a short walk from the Trevi Fountain and the Spanish Steps as well as many cultural delights. All 50 en-suite bedrooms overlook the hotel's enclosed garden, featuring an abundance of flowers. Each guest is made to feel welcome by the personal service, and the refined lounge offers a relaxing place to take a drink. Conference rooms are also available.

Au cœur de Rome, cet hôtel a gardé son élégance originale alors qu'il a tout confort moderne. Situé dans un endroit idéal, l'hôtel est tout près de la fontaine de Trévi, la Piazza di Spagna ainsi que d'autres délices culturelles. Toutes les 50 chambres avec salle de bains attenante, donnent sur le jardin fleuri. Le service du personnel fait le bon accueil aux hôtes et le salon raffiné offre un environnement relaxant pour prendre un verre. Des salles de conférence sont aussi disponibles.

Dieses ganz besondere Hotel im Herzen von Rom bietet modernsten Komfort vereint mit traditioneller Eleganz. Das Hotel liegt ideal nur einen kurzen Spaziergang vom Trevibrunnen, der Spanischen Treppe und vielen anderen kulturellen Attraktionen entfernt. Alle 50 Zimmer haben ein eigenes Bad und blicken auf das Blumenmeer im Hotelgarten. Durch den persönlichen Service fühlt man sich ganz besonders willkommen, und in der eleganten Lounge kann man bei einem Drink wunderbar entspannen. Konferenzräume sind vorhanden.

Our inspector loved: *The private patios facing the internal garden.*

Directions: The hotel is a short walk from Piazza di Spagna metro station.

Web: www.johansens.com/borgognoni
E-mail: info@hotelborgognoni.it
Tel: +39 06 6994 1505
Fax: +39 06 6994 1501

Price Guide:
single €210-230
double €295-305
suite Upon Request

  50   80   

Hotel dei Consoli

VIA VARRONE 2/D, 00193 ROME, ITALY.

In the heart of town, near the Tiber river and close to the Vatican, this charming hotel welcomes guests into a peaceful retreat. Its history dates back to the 19th century and ornate public rooms feature soaring stucco decorations, Murano chandeliers, antique furniture, fresh flowers and excellent paintings. Guest rooms and suites, many of which overlook St Peter's dome, are beautifully appointed with period style furniture, rich fabrics, objets d'art and spacious bathrooms. The hotel boasts a superb location for the business and leisure traveller alike and takes great pride in its impeccable level of service.

Situé en plein centre ville, près du fleuve de Tibre et du Vatican, cet hôtel charmant offre à ses hôtes un refuge de paix. L'hôtel date du XIXe siècle et les salles publiques fleuries sont ornées de grandes décorations de stuc, lustres de Murano, des meubles antiques, des belles peintures et des fleurs. Les chambres et les suites, dont plusieurs donnent sur le Dôme Saint Pierre, sont meublées dans le style de l'époque et décorées avec des tissus de luxe et des objets d'art. Les salles de bains sont toutes spacieuses. L'hôtel revendique un endroit superbe pour le voyageur d'affaires ainsi que pour le voyageur de loisirs et le personnel est fier de son niveau impeccable de service.

Dieses zauberhafte, nahe am Tiber und am Vatikan gelegene Hotel bietet seinen Gästen ein ruhiges Versteck mitten im Herzen der Stadt. Seine Geschichte geht bis ins 19. Jahrhundert zurück, und in den Aufenthaltsräumen kann man Stuckverzierungen, Muranolüster, antikes Mobiliar, frische Blumen und herrliche Gemälde bewundern. Die Zimmer und Suiten - zahlreiche mit Blick auf den Petersdom - sind wundervoll mit Stilmöbeln, üppigen Stoffen, Kunstgegenständen und geräumigen Badezimmern eingerichtet. Das Hotel liegt ideal sowohl für Geschäftsreisende als auch Touristen und ist zurecht stolz auf seinen tadellosen Service.

***Our inspector loved:** The utmost privacy.*

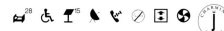

Directions: The hotel is a 2-minute walk from the Vatican and 15 minutes from the Spanish Steps.

Web: www.johansens.com/deiconsoli
E-mail: info@hoteldeiconsoli.com
Tel: +39 0668 892972
Fax: +39 0668 212274

Price Guide:
single €100-200
double €150-290
junior suites €200-440

Hotel Giulio Cesare

VIA DEGLI SCIPIONI 287, 00192 ROME, ITALY

The Giulio Cesare, situated close to some of the most glorious streets in Rome, is the essence of comfort. Offering its guests a unique blend of hospitality, relaxation and excellent service, this 18th-century neo-classical hotel is ideal for either business or pleasure. The intimate bar is delightful with a fine collection of wines. Whilst there is no restaurant, sumptuous dishes are served at all times of the day in the bar and garden.

Le Giulio Cesare, proche des rues les plus prestigieuses de Rome, est la quintessence du confort. Offrant un degré exceptionnel d'hospitalité, de détente et de qualité de service, cet hôtel néo-classique est idéal pour les voyageurs d'affaires comme pour les touristes. Le bar intime est charmant et offre une palette de grands vins exceptionnelle. Bien qu'il n'y ait pas de restaurant, de succulents plats sont servis à toute heure de la journée dans le bar ou dans le jardin.

Das Giulio Cesare liegt in der Nähe einiger der prachtvollsten Straßen Roms und ist der Inbegriff von Komfort. Mit seiner einzigartigen Mischung aus Gastfreundschaft, Entspannung und exzellentem Service ist dieses neoklassizistische Hotel aus dem 18. Jahrhundert ideal sowohl für Urlauber als auch Geschäftsreisende. Die intime Bar wartet mit einer erlesenen Auswahl an Weinen auf. Zwar besitzt das Hotel kein Restaurant, doch in der Bar oder im Garten werden rund um die Uhr verlockende Speisen serviert.

***Our inspector loved:** The buffet breakfast: simply delicious, as is its friendly and attentive service.*

Directions: Lepanto tube.

Web: www.johansens.com/giuliocesare
E-mail: giulioce@uni.net
Tel: +39 06 321 0751
Fax: +39 06 321 1736

Price Guide:
single €250
double/twin €300

Diana Grand Hotel

VIA GARIBALDI 110, 17021 ALASSIO (SV), RIVIERA DEI FIORI, ITALY

Set in a sunny position at the gulf of the prestigious Riviera del Ponente, this hotel has its own private sandy beach and is conveniently close to the historical centre of Alassio, with its pretty streets full of shops, boutiques and coffee bars. There are 2 restaurants offering creative international cuisine, the Sun Terrace and the beach-facing A Marina, which has a more relaxed atmosphere and offers a great selection of seafood. There is also a lively American bar.

Situé dans une position ensoleillée au golfe de la prestigieuse Riviera del Ponente, cet hôtel dispose de sa propre plage de sable privée. Il se trouve près du centre historique d'Alassio avec ses rues jolies remplies de magasins, boutiques et cafés. 2 restaurants servent une cuisine créative internationale: le Sun Terrace et l'A Marina près de la mer, qui a une atmosphère plus détendue et offre un grand choix de fruits de mer. Un autre endroit populaire est le bar américain très vivant.

Dieses Hotel liegt in sonnenbeschienener Lage am Golf der vornehmen Riviera del Ponente und hat seinen eigenen Sandstrand. Es befindet sich günstig nahe am historischen Zentrum von Alassio mit seinen hübschen Sträßchen, Geschäften, Boutiquen und Cafés. In 2 Restaurants wird kreative internationale Küche serviert, dem Sun Terrace und dem am Strand gelegenen A Marina, das für seine entspannte Atmosphäre und große Auswahl an Meeresfrüchten bekannt ist. Außerdem gibt es eine lebhafte amerikanische Bar.

Our inspector loved: *The hotel's fantastic position, set directly on the sea.*

Directions: A10 > exit Albenga > then follow directions to Alassio. The nearest international airport is Genoa/Nice, the local airport, Villanova, is 15km away.

Web: www.johansens.com/diana
E-mail: hotel@dianagh.it
Tel: +39 0182 642 701
Fax: +39 0182 640 304

Price Guide:
single from €100-140
double from €140-210
suite from €245-272

54 200 SPA

Grand Hotel Diana Majestic

VIA OLEANDRI 15, 18013 DIANO MARINA (IM), ITALY

This small resort hotel has a great position just by the sea with its own private sandy beach, and is set in delightful ancient olive groves. The comfortable bedrooms all have a balcony and sea view, whilst the new suites have the added temptation of a large terrace with outdoor Jacuzzi. Excellent Mediterranean cuisine is served nightly, whilst the terrace by the sea provides a stunning backdrop for candle-lit dining or sampling one of the hotel's 50 brands of whisky.

Cette petite station de vacances se trouve tout près de la mer avec sa propre plage de sable et parmi des anciennes oliveraies merveilleuses. Toutes les chambres confortables ont un balcon avec vue sur la mer, et les nouvelles suites offrent une grande terrasse avec Jacuzzi en plein air. Une cuisine excellente méditerranéenne est servie chaque soir, alors que la terrasse près de la mer est l'endroit parfait pour des dîners aux chandelles ou pour savourer une des 50 marques de whisky de la maison.

Dieses kleine Resort-Hotel befindet sich in bevorzugter Lage inmitten alter Olivenhaine direkt am Meer und hat einen eigenen Sandstrand. Die komfortablen Zimmer haben alle Balkon und Meerblick, und die neuen Suiten bieten zudem noch eine große Terrasse mit Jacuzzi im Freien. Jeden Abend wird exzellente Mittelmeerküche serviert, die man bei Kerzenschein auf der Terrasse direkt am Meer genießen kann. So mancher Gast wird sich auch über die 50 Sorten Whisky des Hotels freuen.

Our inspector loved: *The terrace overlooking the sea and the new suites.*

Directions: Exit A10 at San Bartolomeo Al Mare, then follow signs for Diano Marina. Easy access from Genoa and Nice airports.

Web: www.johansens.com/dianamajestic
E-mail: grandhotel@dianamajestic.com
Tel: +39 0183 402 727
Fax: +39 0183 403 040

Price Guide:
single €110-200
double €160-220
suite €260-750

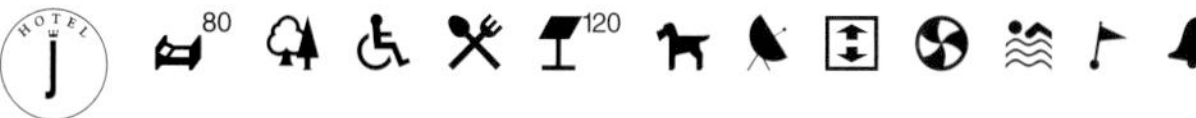

Hotel Punta Est

VIA AURELIA 1, 17024 FINALE LIGURE (SV) ITALY

This elegant 18th-century villa was once a private summer residence. Today, it is a unique hotel, nestled in its own park with shaded pathways and olive groves, and fabulous panoramic views over the Ligurian Sea. Relaxation is guaranteed both by the swimming pool and the private beach, and the Aladdin's Cave with its stalagmites and stalactites provides a unique setting for musical events, weddings and parties.

Cette élégante villa du XVIIIe siècle fût une résidence priveé. Aujourd'hui, c'est un hôtel unique, niché dans son propre parc aux allées ombragées et oliveraies, et aux vues panoramiques fabuleuses sur la Mer Ligurienne. La détente est garantie tout aussi bien grâce à la piscine et aux plages privées, mais aussi aux caves d'Aladin avec ses stalagmites et stalactites qui procure un décor unique pour des évènements musicaux, mariages et fêtes diverses.

Diese elegante Villa aus dem 18. Jahrhundert war einst eine private Sommerresidenz. Heute ist sie ein einzigartiges Hotel inmitten eines eigenen Parks mit schattigen Wegen, Olivenhainen und herrlichem Panoramablick auf das Ligurische Meer. Swimmingpool und Privatstrand sorgen für Entspannung, und die Aladdinhöhle mit ihren Stalagmiten und Stalaktiten bietet eine einmalige Bühne für Musikveranstaltungen, Hochzeiten und andere Feste.

Our inspector loved: *The amazing view and the magnificent "Aladdin's Cave".*

Directions: Genoa > Autostrada A10 > San Remo > Finale Ligure.

Web: www.johansens.com/puntaest
E-mail: info@puntaest.com
Tel: +39 019 600611
Fax: +39 019 600611

Price Guide:
single €140
double/twin €250
suite €260–450

HOTEL SAN GIORGIO - PORTOFINO HOUSE

VIA DEL FONDACO, 11, 16034 PORTOFINO (GENOVA), ITALY

This charming hotel is situated in a quiet location just a few steps from the main square and harbour of Portofino and offers guests an elegant alternative to the usual type of accommodation in this area. The hotel's greatest treasure is its wonderful garden, where guests can enjoy spectacular views while walking along its paths. Local traditional décor abounds throughout; local "Ardesia" slate has been used for the floors and bathrooms. A meeting room can accommodate up to 15 people, and a small wellness centre and gym will open in 2004.

Ce charmant hôtel est situé dans un endroit calme à quelques pas de la place principale et du port de Portofino, et offre une alternative élégante au logement typique de cette région. Le plus grand trésor de cet hôtel est son jardin magnifique, où les hôtes peuvent jouir de vues à couper le souffle pendant qu'ils se promènent le long de ses sentiers. Un décor traditionnel est présent dans tout l'hôtel; les sols et salles de bains sont carrelés en ardoise locale "Ardesia". Il y a une salle de conférences pour jusqu'à 15 personnes et un petit centre de beauté et de remise en forme s'ouvre en 2004.

Dieses zauberhafte Hotel befindet sich in ruhiger Lage nur ein paar Schritte vom Hafen und Hauptplatz von Portofino entfernt und bietet eine elegante Alternative zur sonstigen ortsüblichen Ferienunterkunft. Besonders herrlich ist der Hotelgarten, von dessen hübschen Wanderpfaden man wundervolle Ausblicke hat. Das Hotel ist in traditionellem Décor der Region gestaltet und für die Fliesen und die Bäder wurde ortstypischer "Ardesia"-Schiefer verwendet. Das Konferenzzimmer fasst 15 Personen, und 2004 eröffnet ein Wellness-Centre mit Fitnessraum.

Our inspector loved: *The wonderful combination of tradition and design, especially in the bathrooms.*

Directions: From A12, exit Rapallo > follow signs to Santa Margherita - Portofino.

Web: www.johansens.com/portofinohouse
E-mail: info@portofinohsg.it
Tel: +39 0185 26991
Fax: +39 0185 267139

Price Guide:
double €250-400
suite €400-700

Hotel Vis à Vis & Ristorante Olimpo

VIA DELLA CHIUSA 28, 16039 SESTRI LEVANTE (GE), ITALY

Set on an idyllic hillside overlooking Sestri Levante and 2 spectacular bays, this family-run hotel is surrounded by olive trees and is an enchanting place to stay. Guests will be mesmerised by the breathtaking view from the hotel's elegant restaurant Olimpo, which serves delicious food complemented by the finest regional wines. There is an open-air barbecue on the terrace and a magnificent roof garden, Ponte Zeus. An outside lift links the hotel to the centre of town.

Situé sur les flancs idylliques d'une colline avec vue sur le Sestri Levante et 2 baies superbes, cet hôtel familial entouré d'oliviers est un endroit enchanteur où séjourner. Les hôtes seront ébahis par la vue à couper le souffle qu'ils auront à partir de l'élégant restaurant Olimpo, qui sert une cuisine délicieuse accompagnée des meilleurs vins régionaux. Il y a un barbecue en plein air sur la terrasse et un jardin sur le toit magnifique, Ponte Zeus. Un ascenseur extérieur relie l'hôtel au centre-ville.

Dieses auf einem idyllischen Hügel mit Blick auf Sestri Levante und 2 herrliche Buchten gelegene und von Olivenbäumen umgebene familiengeführte Hotel ist ein zauberhafter Aufenthaltsort. Eine atemberaubende Sicht genießt man auch aus dem eleganten Restaurant Olimpo, in dem köstliche Speisen und erlesene Weine der Region serviert werden. Es gibt einen offenen Grill auf der Terrasse und einen herrlichen Dachgarten, Ponte Zeus. Ein Lift verbindet das Hotel mit dem Stadtzentrum.

Our inspector loved: *The spectacular view of the 2 bays from the restaurant and terrace.*

Directions: A12 > Genoa > Livorno > Sestri Levante > follow the signs to Centro > the hotel is signposted.

Web: www.johansens.com/visavis
E-mail: visavis@hotelvisavis.com
Tel: +39 0185 42661/480801
Fax: +39 0185 480853

Price Guide:
single €115–150
double €155–220
suite €220–330

Grand Hotel Villa Serbelloni

VIA ROMA 1, 22021 BELLAGIO, LAKE COMO, ITALY

Built in the early 19th century, this majestic villa stands in a beautiful and sunny position on a promontory between the two halves of Lake Como, and has an air of grandeur and luxury that few can rival. Elegantly frescoed ceilings, stunning crystal chandeliers and lush carpeting are complemented by stylish antique pieces, whilst 2 restaurants serve the very best in international cuisine. 2 swimming pools, a private beach and a luxury health spa complete the feeling of total relaxation.

Cette villa majestueuse fut construite au début du XIXe siècle et se trouve dans un endroit ensoleillé sur un promontoire entre les deux parties du lac Como. Son air de grandeur et de luxe est incomparable. L'hôtel est pourvu de plafonds ornés de fresques élégantes, de lustres magnifiques de cristal, de tapis somptueux et de pièces antiques raffinées. Les 2 restaurants servent des plats délicieux internationaux, alors que les 2 piscines, une plage privée et un centre de remise en forme luxueux créent une ambiance de détente absolue.

Diese Anfang des 19. Jahrhunderts erbaute majestätische Villa befindet sich in herrlicher, sonnenbeschienener Lage auf einer Landzunge zwischen den beiden Hälften des Comer Sees und besitzt eine unvergleichliche Aura von Eleganz und Luxus. Mit wundervollen Fresken verzierte Decken, traumhafte Kristalllüster und üppige Teppiche wechseln sich mit edlen antiken Stücken ab, und in 2 Restaurants wird hervorragende internationale Küche serviert. 2 Swimmingpools, ein Privatstrand und ein luxuriöses Wellnesszentrum sorgen für Entspannung pur.

Our inspector loved: *The gorgeous location and the most precious ceilings ever seen.*

Directions: A9, exit Como Sud > follow directions to Bellagio.

Web: www.johansens.com/serbelloni
E-mail: inforequest@villaserbelloni.it
Tel: +39 031 950 216
Fax: +39 031 951 529

Price Guide:
single €165-245
double €250-475
suite €495-805

Grand Hotel Gardone Riviera

VIA ZANARDELLI 84, 25083 GARDONE RIVIERA (BS), LAGO DI GARDA, ITALY

Directions: A4 > exit Desenzano > towards Salò-Gardone.

Web: www.johansens.com/gardoneriviera
E-mail: ghg@grangardone.it
Tel: +39 0365 20261
Fax: +39 0365 22695

Price Guide:
single €98-121
double €160-220
junior suite €200-260

This magnificent hotel, built in 1888, exudes a refined atmosphere of a bygone era. Beyond the ivy-clad, rose-covered façade the elegantly decorated guest rooms and suites boast beautiful lakeside views. During summer a lunch buffet is served on the garden terrace and a romantic dinner, complete with stunning backdrop, can be enjoyed at the Veranda Restaurant. Winnies Piano Bar offers a relaxed environment with live music and dancing. Guests receive a 10-20% discount when using 2 local golf courses and have exclusive use of the hotel's private beach.

De cet hôtel magnifique construit en 1888, émane l'atmosphère raffinée des temps passés. Derrière la façade rose couverte de lierre, les chambres et suites élégamment décorées s'enorgueillissent de vues splendides sur le lac. L'été, un buffet est servi pour le déjeuner dans le jardin en terrasse et un dîner romantique, sur une toile de fond superbe, peut être dégusté au restaurant Veranda. Le piano-bar Winnies offre un environnement détendu, avec musique live et danse. Les hôtes ont l'accès exclusif à la plage privée de l'hôtel alors que 2 cours de golf locaux offrent une réduction de 10-20%.

Dieses wundervolle, 1888 erbaute Hotel verströmt die Atmosphäre einer längst vergangenen Zeit. Hinter der mit Efeu bewachsenen und von Rosen bedeckten Fassade verstecken sich elegante Zimmer und Suiten mit herrlicher Sicht auf den See. Im Sommer wird auf der Gartenterrasse ein Mittagsbuffet serviert und abends genießt man das romantische Ambiente des Veranda Restaurants. Winnies Piano Bar bietet das perfekte Umfeld für Live-Musik und Tanz. Die Gäste können den Privatstrand exklusiv nutzen, und 2 örtliche Golfplätze bieten einen Rabatt von 10-20%.

Our inspector loved: *The enchanting position and landscape.*

DES IGN HOT ELS

DELLEARTI DESIGN HOTEL

VIA BONOMELLI 8, 26100 CREMONA, ITALY

Set in the heart of Cremona, this intriguing hotel is the perfect place for those looking for a truly different experience. Furnished in vibrant warm colours, the interior is a creative blend of comfort, clean architectural lines and modern art, displaying an incredible attention to detail. All bedrooms are decorated with simple, pure elegance and equipped with ultramodern amenities. Cold, light meals may be enjoyed in the bedrooms. A conference room, Turkish bath, sauna, Jacuzzi and gym are available. The wellness centre offers face and body massages on request from Monday-Friday.

Au coeur de Crémone, cet hôtel original est l'endroit parfait pour ceux qui sont à la recherche d'une expérience différente. Décoré dans des couleurs vives et chaleureuses, l'intérieur est un mélange créatif de confort, de lignes architecturales nettes et d'art moderne, démontrant une attention au détail impressionnante. Toutes les chambres sont meublées dans la plus pure et simple élégance, complétée par des équipements ultramodernes. Des repas legeres peuvent y être servis. Une salle de conférence, des bains turcs, sauna, jacuzzi et gym sont également disponibles. Sur demande, le centre de beauté offre des massages (lundi-vendredi).

Dieses faszinierende Hotel im Herzen von Cremona ist ideal für einen ganz besonderen Aufenthalt. Das Interieur, eine Mischung aus Komfort, klaren architektonischen Linien und moderner Kunst, ist in warmen, kräftigen Farben gehalten. Liebe zum Detail ist überall deutlich. Die Zimmer sind mit einfacher, reiner Eleganz gestaltet und bieten ultramoderne Einrichtungen. Man kann hier auch leichte Mahlzeiten zu sich nehmen. Konferenzraum, Dampfbad, Sauna, Jacuzzi und Fitnessraum sind vorhanden, und das Wellness-Centre bietet auf Anfrage montags-freitags Massagen.

Our inspector loved: *The feeling of being carried away from the ordinary.*

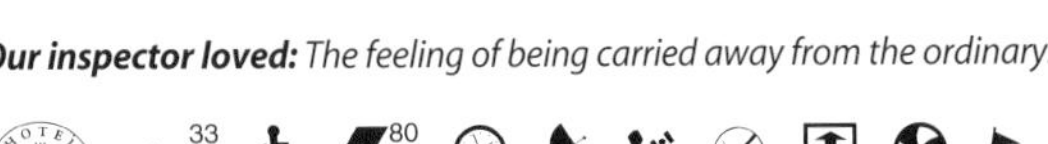

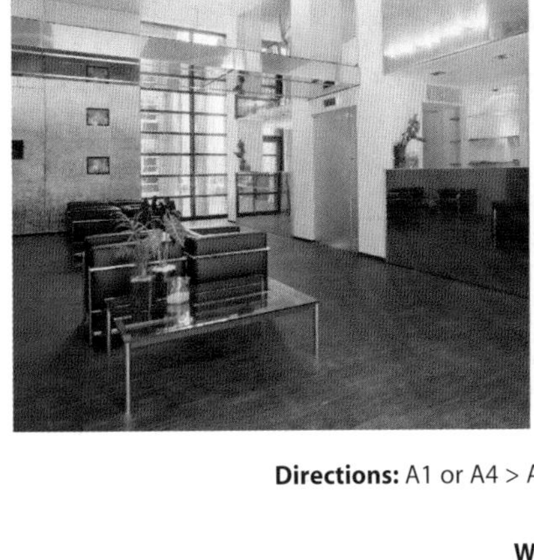

Directions: A1 or A4 > A21, exit Cremona (near Piacenza).

Web: www.johansens.com/dellearti
E-mail: info@dellearti.com
Tel: +39 0372 23131
Fax: +39 0372 21654

Milan
Venice
Rome

Price Guide:
single €114
double €165
suite €196

Hotel Villa Aminta

VIA SEMPIONE NORD 123, 28838 STRESA (VB), ITALY

Directions: A8 Motorway from Milan > direction Lago Maggiore, exit Carpugnino > follow signs to Stresa.

Web: www.johansens.com/aminta
E-mail: h.villaminta@stresa.net
Tel: +39 0323 933 818
Fax: +39 0323 933 955

Price Guide:
double €252
junior suite €298
suite €596

This recently renovated 5-star de luxe hotel is a charming villa situated on the shores of Lake Maggiore, one of the most enchanting lakes in Italy. All bedrooms have a romantic décor, stucco works, precious furniture and look out over the gorgeous lake. Gastronomic delights are served in the Le Isole restaurant, and in summer, romantic dinners can be enjoyed on the terrace. Sightseeing tours, lake cruises and water-skiing are just some of the activities guests may enjoy, whilst nearby places of interest include Isola Bella, Villa Pallavicino and Locarno.

Ce charmant et luxueux hôtel à 5 étoiles récemment rénové est située sur les bords du Lac Maggiore, l'un des lacs les plus enchanteurs d'Italie. Les chambres ont un décor romantique, des ornements en stuc, un meublier de valeur et vue sur le lac. Les plaisirs gastronomiques sont servis au restaurant Le Isole, et la terrasse est l'endroit idéal l'été, pour un dîner romantique. De nombreuses activités sont disponibles, telles qu'excursions, croisières sur le lac et ski nautique; parmi les sites proches à visiter, on compte Isola Bella, Villa Pallavicino et Locarno.

Diese neu renovierte Villa ist ein luxuriöses 5-Sterne Hotel am Ufer des Lago Maggiore, eines der bezauberndsten Seen Italiens. Die Zimmer sind romantisch mit kostbaren Möbeln eingerichtet und haben Stuckdecken und herrliche Sicht auf den See. Kulinarische Köstlichkeiten werden im Le Isole serviert, und im Sommer kann man romantisch auf der Terrasse dinieren. Gäste können Besichtigungstouren und Fahrten auf dem See machen, Wasserski fahren oder Sehenswürdigkeiten in der Nähe, wie z.B. Isola Bella, Villa Pallavicino und Locarno besuchen.

Our inspector loved: *The enchanting views of the islands on Lake Maggiore.*

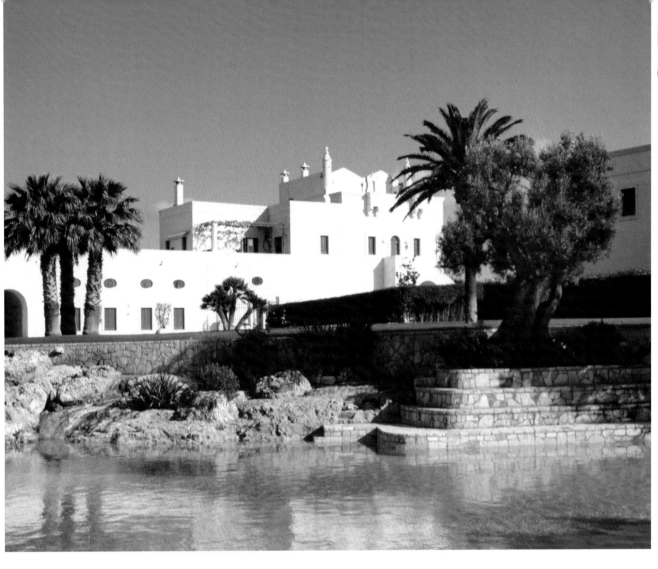

Masseria San Domenico

LITORANEA 379, 72010 SAVELLETRI DI FASANO (BRINDISI) ITALY

The Masseria is an ancient watchtower dating from the 15th century, built overlooking the Adriatic by the knights of Malta to ward off attacks by the Ottomans. Surrounded by more than 3,700 acres of olive groves and vineyards, its architectural glory has been restored and its facilities include a spectacular seawater pool, tennis courts, Thalassotherapy Spa, and a brand new 18-hole golf course. Places of historic interest nearby include Egnazia, Alberobello and Castellana.

La Masseria est une ancienne tour de garde du XVe siècle, surplombant l'Adriatique et construite par les Chevaliers de Malte pour prévenir les attaques des ottomans. Entourée de plus de 500ha d'oliveraies et vignobles, sa gloire architecturale a été restaurée et ses installations incluent une spectaculaire piscine d'eau de mer, des courts de tennis, un centre de thalassothérapie et un tout nouveau golf 18 trous. D'un point de vue historique, Egnazia, Alberobello et Castellana sont à visiter.

Dieser alte Wachturm aus dem 15. Jahrhundert mit Blick auf die Adria wurde von den maltesischen Rittern erbaut, um Angriffe der Ottomanen abzuwehren. Die architektonische Pracht der inmitten von über 1500ha Olivenhainen und Weinbergen gelegenen Masseria wurde komplett restauriert. Zu den Einrichtungen gehören ein spektakulärer Salzwasserpool, Tennisplätze, ein Thalassotherapie-Spa und ein brandneuer 18-Loch-Golfplatz. Ausflugsziele sind Egnazia, Alberobello und Castellana.

Our inspector loved: *The Spa - effective thalassotherapy treatments are given with great care and attention.*

Directions: Bari YSS16 > Brindisi > Litoranea 379 > Fasano Savelletri.

Web: www.johansens.com/masseriasandomenico
E-mail: info@masseriasandomenico.com
Tel: +39 080 482 7769
Fax: +39 080 482 7978

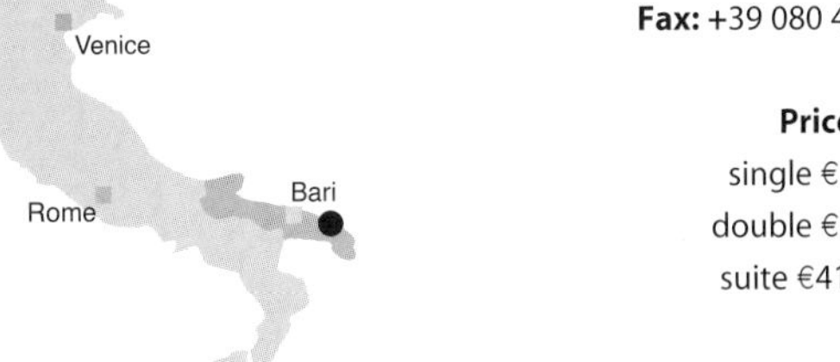

Price Guide:
single €190–245
double €264–484
suite €412–2,150

50 SPA

Katane Palace Hotel

VIA FINOCCHIARO APRILE 110, 95129 CATANIA, ITALY

Directions: The hotel is in the city centre. The nearest airport is Catania.

Web: www.johansens.com/katane
E-mail: info@katanepalace.it
Tel: +39 095 747 0702
Fax: +39 095 747 0172

Price Guide:
single €180
double €206-221
suite €353

This splendid, elegant hotel is set in the heart of Catania, close to its historical centre and the Ionian Sea. Well connected to public transport and motorways, this ancient building was renovated and turned into a prestigious hotel, offering spacious and gracefully decorated accommodation as well as a wonderfully cosy lounge. Sumptuous breakfasts and Sicilian delicacies are served in the attractive Il Cuciniere restaurant, which is located in the old cloister. The hotel has its own congress centre, where guests can enjoy regular musical events.

Ce splendide et élégant hôtel est situé au cœur de Catania, près du centre historique et la mer Ionienne. Avec les transports en commun et les autoroutes d'accès facile, ce bâtiment très ancien a été rénové et transformé en hôtel, offrant des chambres spacieuses et gracieusement décorées, ainsi qu'un salon douillet. Des petits déjeuners délicieux et des spécialités de Sicile sont servis dans le restaurant Il Cuciniere, situé dans le vieux cloître. L'hôtel dispose de son propre centre de congrès où les hôtes peuvent assister aux concerts.

Dieses prächtige, elegante Hotel liegt im Herzen von Catania, nahe der Altstadt und dem Ionischen Meer mit guter Verkerhsanbindung. Das alte Gebäude wurde renoviert und in ein edles Hotel umgewandelt, das heute geräumige und erlesen eingerichtete Zimmer sowie eine herrlich gemütliche Lounge bietet. Ein üppiges Frühstück sowie sizilianische Köstlichkeiten werden im Restaurant Il Cuciniere serviert, das im ehemaligen Kreuzgang untergebracht ist. Das Hotel hat sein eigenes Konferenzzentrum, in dem regelmäßig Musikabende stattfinden.

Our inspector loved: *To wine and dine in the ancient cloister, an oasis of peace and quiet.*

45 40

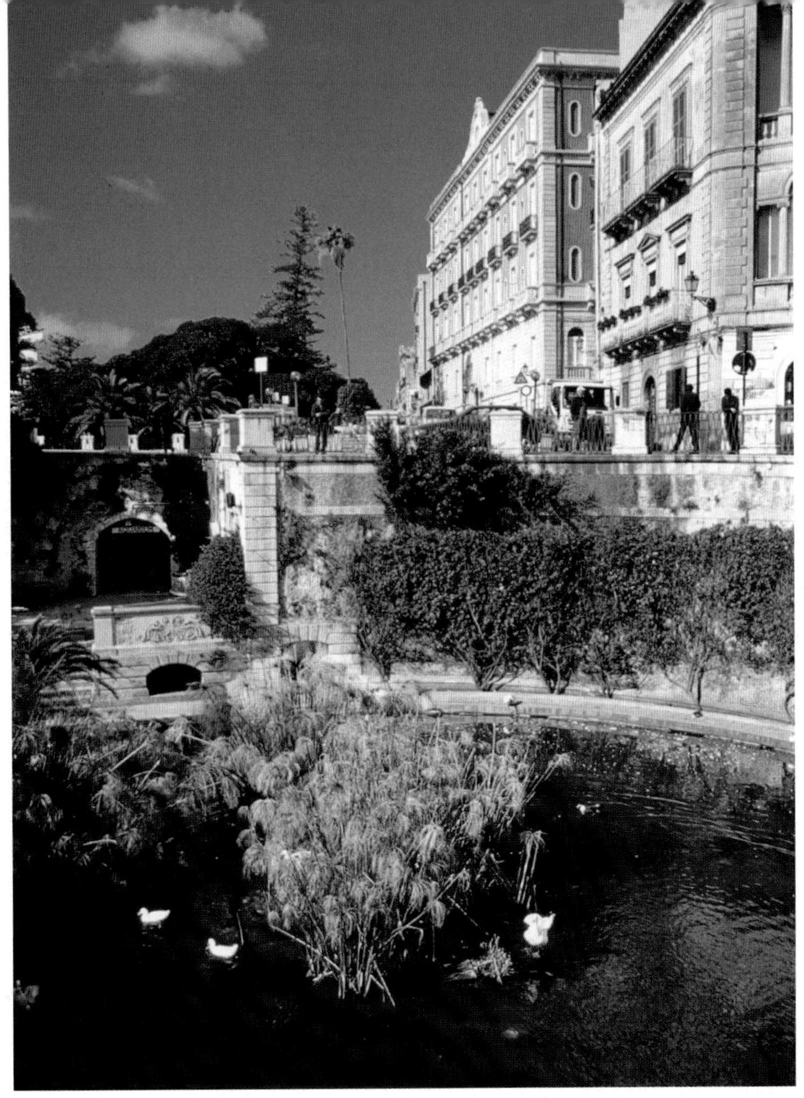

Hotel des Etrangers et Miramare

PASSEGGIO ADORNO 10/12, 96100 SIRACUSA, ITALY

Just reopened after 30 years, this prestigious hotel lies in the heart of the unique city of Ortigia. Facing directly onto the fine sandy beach, it is a haven of simple elegance and luxury, with just 80 rooms, many of which have sea views. There are 2 restaurants – the stunning Medusa boasts dramatic panoramic views over the coastline, whilst the Roof Garden has a wonderful terrace for outdoor dining – both of which offer some of the finest Italian dishes.

Réouvert après 30 ans de fermeture, cet hôtel renommé est situé au cœur de la ville unique d'Ortigia. L'hôtel donne sur la plage de sable et offre un havre d'élégance et de luxe avec 80 chambres, dont plusieurs ont une vue sur la mer. Il y a 2 restaurants – l'excellent Medusa qui offre des vues panoramiques dramatiques sur la côte et le jardin sur le toit avec sa terrasse parfaite pour manger au frais – ils offrent tous les deux des meilleurs plats italiens.

Dieses prestigereiche, nach 30 Jahren neueröffnete Hotel befindet sich im Herzen der einzigartigen Stadt Ortigia und blickt direkt auf einen herrlichen Sandstrand. Das Haus ist eine Oase der einfachen Eleganz und des Luxus, mit nur 80 Zimmern, viele davon mit Blick aufs Meer. Es gibt 2 Restaurants – das eindrucksvolle Medusa mit Panoramablick auf die Küste und den Dachgarten mit seiner traumhaften Terrasse – in denen feinste italienische Küche serviert wird.

Our inspector loved: *The breathtaking views of the coast.*

Directions: Catania Airport > highway to Siracusa > last exit, Siracusa Centro > direction Ortigia.

Web: www.johansens.com/etrangersetmiramare
E-mail: desetrangers@medeahotels.com
Tel: +39 0931 62671
Fax: +39 0931 65124

Price Guide: (half board rates available, €60 supplement charge for sea view)
single €101-174
double €90-174
junior suite €150-235
de luxe suite €180-295

Grand Hotel Atlantis Bay

VIA NAZIONALE 161, TAORMINA MARE, ITALY

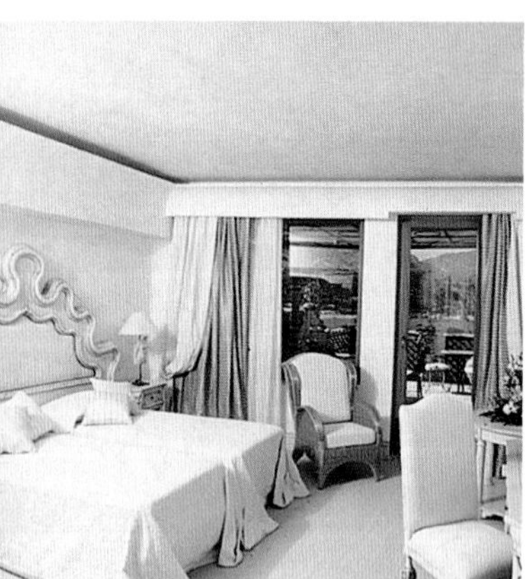

The toast of Taormina beach, this newly opened hotel has already become home to many celebrities and international guests. Entering the hotel is like walking into an enchanted cave and its lavishly decorated stone walls, carved out of the stone of the bay, hold a huge aquarium of colourful tropical fish. Guest rooms are decorated with cool white washed walls and simple, delicate fabrics. From the candle-lit restaurant to the terraces and panoramic views, it is impossible not to be swept away by the hotel's exotic ambience.

La coqueluche de la baie de Taormina, cet hôtel récemment ouvert est déjà devenu la nouvelle base de nombreuses célébrités et hôtes internationaux. Entrer dans cet hôtel est comme pénétrer dans une cave enchantée et sur ses murs de pierre somptueusement décorés, sculptés dans le roc de la baie, se tient un immense aquarium de poissons tropicaux. Les chambres sont décorées de murs lessivés blancs et d'étoffes simples et délicates. Du restaurant éclairé aux chandelles, aux terrasses et vues panoramiques, il est impossible de ne pas être ensorcelé par l'ambiance exotique de l'hôtel.

Dieses fantastische neueröffnete Hotel am Strand von Taormina ist bereits ein beliebter Zweitwohnsitz zahlreicher Prominenter und Gäste aus aller Welt. Man betritt das Hotel wie eine verzauberte Höhle, und die üppig dekorierten, in den Fels gehauenen Steinwände bergen ein riesiges Aquarium voller tropischer Fische. Die Gästezimmer haben kühle weiße Wände und mit einfachen, feinen Stoffen bezogene Betten. Vom mit Kerzen beleuchteten Restaurant bis hin zu den Terrassen und Panoramablicken – das exotische Ambiente des Hotels raubt einem den Atem.

Our inspector loved: *The trendy setting and decoration, with an oriental flavour.*

Directions: Located on Taormina's seafront. Catania is the nearest airport.

Web: www.johansens.com/atlantis
E-mail: info@atlantisbay.it
Tel: +39 0942 618011
Fax: +39 0942 23194

Price Guide:
single €193-350
double €147-210

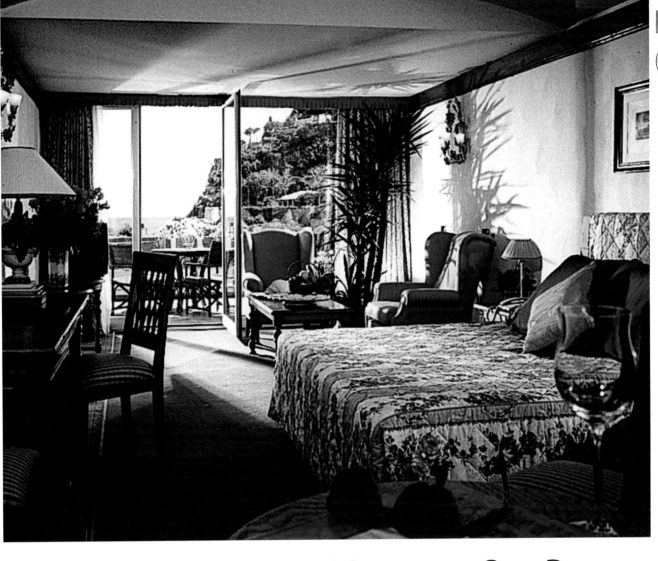

Grand Hotel Mazzarò Sea Palace

VIA NAZIONALE 147, 98030 TAORMINA (ME), ITALY

The Grand Hotel stands in one of Taormina's most enchanting spots right on the beach of a small bay and offers breathtaking views. The bedrooms are exquisitely furnished and have amazing terraces; some even boast private pools. Large windows look out onto the pool terrace and beyond to the sea. Guests can enjoy the private beach and the attention of exclusive and outstanding service provided by the extremely friendly staff. Taormina is easily reached by cable car.

L'hôtel se trouve dans un des endroits les plus enchanteurs de Taormina, sur la plage d'une petite baie, offrant des vues à couper le souffle. Les chambres meublées avec beaucoup de goût, ont des terrasses incroyables, et certaines ont des piscines privées. De grandes fenêtres ouvrent sur la terrasse autour de la piscine et le golfe. Les hôtes peuvent profiter de la plage privée et d'un service exclusif et impeccable d'un personal amical. Taormina est facilement accessible par téléphérique.

Dieses Hotel befindet sich an einem der schönsten Orte Taorminas, direkt am Strand einer kleinen Bucht mit atemberaubenden Ausblicken. Die Zimmer sind wundervoll gestaltet und bieten herrliche Terrassen, einige haben sogar einen eigenen Pool. Große Fenster geben den Blick frei auf die Poolterrasse und das Meer im Hintergrund. Die Gäste können den Privatstrand genießen und sich voll und ganz dem exklusiven, hervorragenden freundlichen Service hingeben. Taormina ist leicht mit der Gondelbahn zu erreichen.

Our inspector loved: *Having breakfast on the terrace overlooking the beach, watching the sunrise.*

Directions: Easily accessed from A18 ME - CT, exit Taormina towards Taormina mare-Mazzarò.

Web: www.johansens.com/mazzeroseapalace
E-mail: info@mazzaroseapalace.it
Tel: +39 0942 612111
Fax: +39 0942 626237

Price Guide:
single €193-350
double €147-210

Hotel Baia Taormina

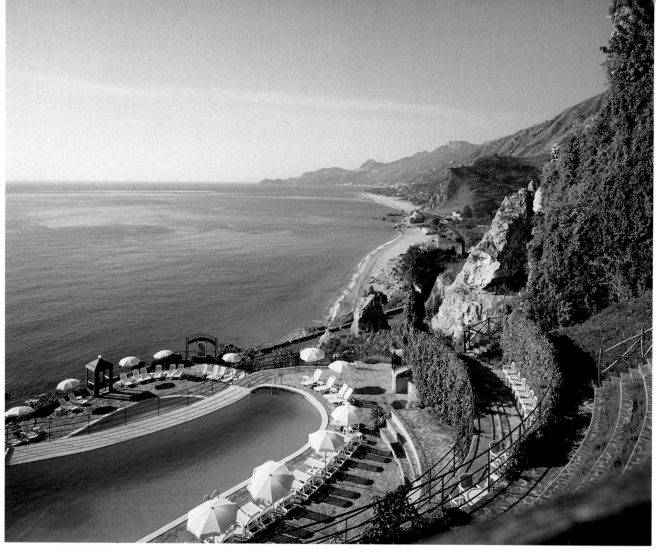

STATALE DELLO IONIO 39, 98030 MARINA D'AGRO (ME), ITALY

Overlooking the beautiful Baia di Taormina, this peaceful, brand new hotel is built on a cliff that gently slopes down to the sea. With its wide arches and terraces and the use of local materials, the hotel blends perfectly with its surroundings. All bedrooms have views over the sea and are furnished according to local tradition. Excellent cuisine is accompanied by live music on the terrace. For leisure, guests may enjoy the hotel's 2 swimming pools and a beauty centre.

Cet hôtel tout neuf se dresse sur une falaise qui descend doucement vers la mer, d'où il domine la superbe baie de Taormina. Grâce à ses grandes arches, à ses terrasses et à l'usage de matériaux de la région, l'hôtel se fond harmonieusement dans le décor paisible. Les chambres offrent une vue sur la mer et sont meublées dans le style traditionnel de la région. Des repas savoureux accompagnés de musique se prennent sur la terrasse. L'hôtel comprend 2 piscines et un centre de beauté.

Dieses brandneue Hotel mit Blick auf die herrliche Bucht von Taormina liegt auf einer sanft zum Meer hinunterführenden Klippe. Mit seinen großzügigen Torbögen und Terrassen und der Verwendung von einheimischen Materialien ist es perfekt an seine friedvolle Umgebung angepasst. Alle Zimmer bieten Meerblick und sind nach örtlicher Tradition eingerichtet. Köstliche Speisen werden zu Live-Musik auf der Terrasse serviert, und für Freizeitvergnügen sorgen 2 Swimmingpools und ein Beautyzentrum.

Our inspector loved: *The swimming pool: perched on the cliff that slopes down to the sea. The view is amazing!*

Directions: Catania > A18 towards Messina, exit Taormina > Messina > Letojanni > Forza d'Agrò.

Web: www.johansens.com/baiataormina
E-mail: hotel@baiataormina.com
Tel: +39 0942 756292
Fax: +39 0942 756603

Price Guide:
single €122–213
double/twin €174–296

Art Hotel Cappella

STR. PECEI 17, ALTA BADIA - DOLOMITES, 39030 COLFOSCO/CORVARA (BZ), ITALY

Dating back to 1894, this hotel has a long tradition of hospitality. The owner, an artist and photographer, has utilised her extensive cultural knowledge and travel experiences to create a warm and inviting atmosphere, carefully blending modern art, rare ethnic pieces and hand-crafted furnishings. 2 restaurants provide casual and gourmet dining. Many sports activities make for an action packed holiday, whilst there is a wellness centre for those in search of a more relaxed break. Starting right at the doorstep, guests are connected to the ski slopes of Sella Ronda and Alta Badia.

Datant de 1894, cet hôtel a une longue tradition d'hospitalité. La propriétaire, artiste et photographe, a utilisé ses connaissances artistiques et ses expériences de voyages pour créer une atmosphère chaleureuse, mélangeant art moderne, pièces ethniques et mobilier fait main. 2 restaurants offrent des dîners simples et gourmets. On peut choisir parmi de nombreuses activités sportives alors que ceux qui sont à la recherche d'un séjour plus reposant peuvent profiter du centre de bien-être. Depuis la porte les hôtes ont accès aux pistes de Sella Ronda et Alta Badia.

Seit 1894 bietet dieses Hotel seine Gastfreundschaft an. Die Eigentümerin, eine Künstlerin und Fotografin, nutzte ihr umfassendes kulturelles Wissen und ihre Reiseerfahrungen für die Mischung aus moderner Kunst, ethnischen Stücken und handgefertigten Einrichtungen, die eine einladende Atmosphäre schafft. 2 Restaurants bieten informelle und Gourmetküche. Zahlreiche sportliche Aktivitäten werden angeboten, es gibt aber auch ein Wellness-Centre für einen etwas entspannteren Urlaub. Man ist direkt ab der Haustür mit den Pisten der Sella Ronda und Alta Badia-Skigebiete verbunden.

Our inspector loved: *The entire experience; feeding the mind, body and soul.*

Directions: Enquire at hotel; ask for Renata Kostner.

Web: www.johansens.com/cappella
E-mail: info@hotelcappella.com
Tel: +39 0471 836183
Fax: +39 0471 836561

Price Guide:
single €93-195
double €136-370
suite €238-450

Hotel Lorenzetti

VIA DOLOMITI DI BRENTA 119, 38084 MADONNA DI CAMPIGLIO (TN) ITALY

This enchanting chalet-style hotel, with its flower-bedecked balconies, stands apart from the main ski lifts and village centre, offering tranquillity and spectacular views over the mountains. The interior is very elegant, and some of the superb suites have hydromassage facilities. Winter sports enthusiasts appreciate the fine skiing and the ice rink. In summer, residents stroll in the gardens, walk in the mountains and play golf. The hotel's new wellness centre boasts beauty facilities such as massage, sauna, steam bath and solarium.

Ce charmant hôtel de style chalet, avec ses balcons ornés de fleurs, se dresse à l'écart des remontée-mécaniques et du centre du village, offrant tranquillité et des vues spectaculaires sur les montagnes. L'intérieur est très élégant, et certaines des superbes suites ont des hydro-masseurs. Les mordus des sports d'hiver apprécieront les belles pistes et la patinoire. En été, les clients se prélassent dans les jardins, font des randonnées en montagne ou peuvent jouer au golf. Le nouveau centre de beauté comprend massage, sauna, bain turc et solarium.

Dieses hübsche Hotel im Chaletstil steht mit seinen blumengeschmückten Balkonen abseits der Skilifte und des Dorfzentrums und ermöglicht Ruhe, Entspannung und atemberaubende Aussichten. Das Interieur ist elegant und in einigen der einzigartigen Suiten gibt es Wassermassage. Anspruchsvolle Skipisten und eine Schlittschuhbahn begeistern die Wintersportler, und im Sommer kann man Spaziergänge in den Gärten und Wanderungen in den Bergen unternehmen oder Golf spielen. Das Wellness-Centre bietet Massage, Sauna, Türkisches Bad und Solarium.

Our inspector loved: *The hotel's excellent location and the cosy atmosphere.*

Directions: A4 > exit Brescia Est > SS. 45 bis SS. 237 > follow directions to Lago Idro > Madonna di Campiglio.

Web: www.johansens.com/lorenzetti
E-mail: hotellorenzetti@hotellorenzetti.com
Tel: +39 0465 44 14 04
Fax: +39 0465 44 06 88

Price Guide:
single €60–175
double/twin €95–325
suite €118–400

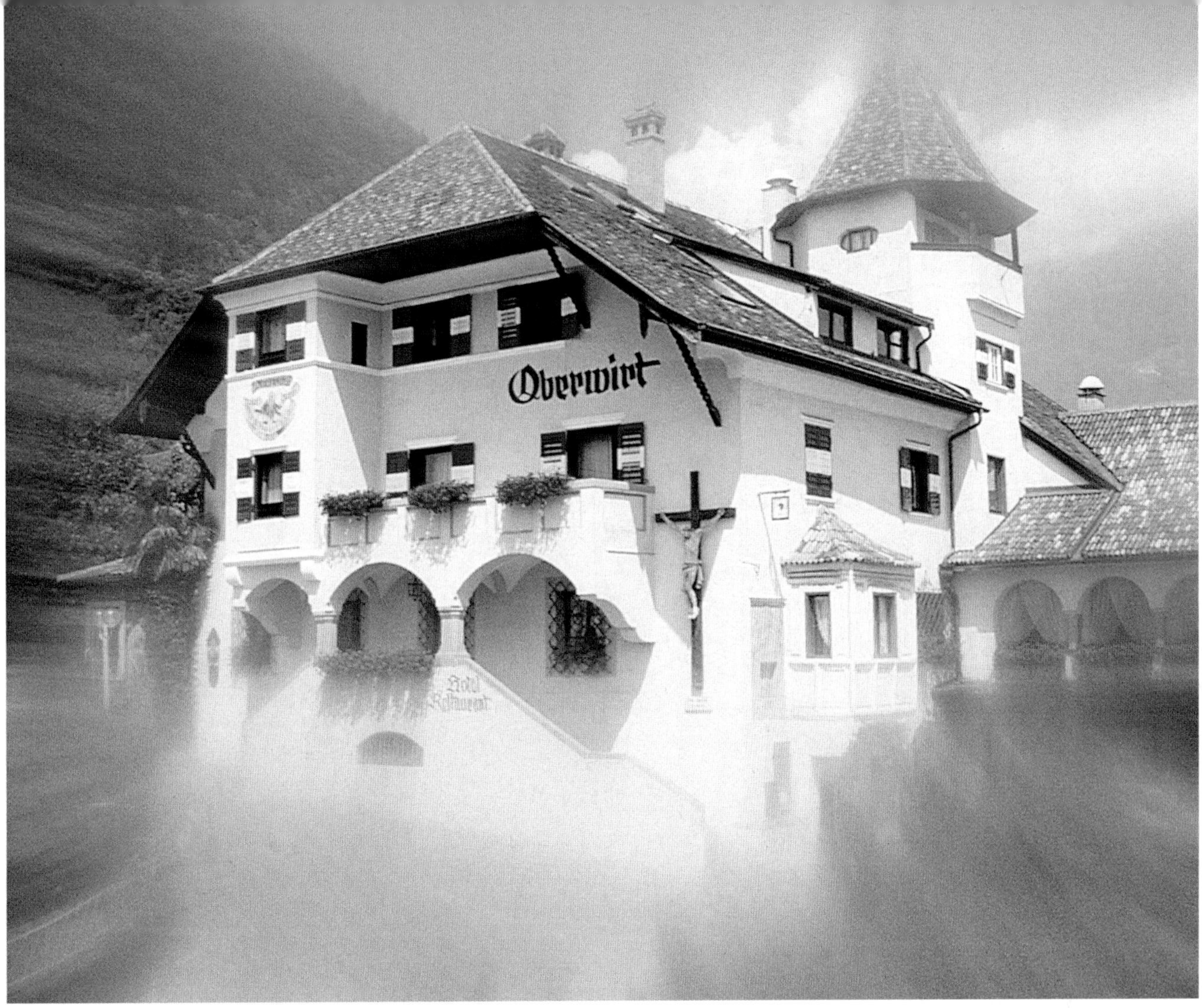

Romantik Hotel Oberwirt

ST FELIXWEG 2, 39020 MARLING – MERAN, ITALY

Owned by the Waldner family since 1749, this hotel has been offering hospitality since the 15th century. The extensive gardens, culinary delights and the cosy Tyrolean bar are reason enough to come and visit this historic house. A special highlight is the newly designed wellness and beauty residence Amadea. Sports enthusiasts will enjoy the fitness area, indoor and outdoor swimming pools and the hotel's own tennis school.

Propriété de la famille Waldner depuis 1749, cet hôtel offre de l'hospitalité depuis le XVe siècle. Les grands jardins, délices culinaires et le bar intime tyrolien sont parmi les attractions et une bonne raison de visiter cette maison historique. Une attraction particulière est le récemment dessiné centre de bien-être et beauté Amadea. Les personnes sportives apprécieront la zone fitness, la piscine couverte et la piscine en plein air ainsi que l'école de tennis de l'hôtel.

Dieses Hotel bietet seine Gastfreundschaft bereits seit dem 15. Jahrhundert an und befindet sich seit 1749 im Besitz der Familie Waldner. Der großzügige Gastgarten, die kulinarischen Genüsse sowie die gemütliche Tiroler Bar sind Grund genug, dieses historische Haus zu besuchen. Ein besonderes Highlight ist die neu gestaltete Wellness- und Beutyresidenz Amadea. Für alle Sportlichen gibt es einen Fitnessbereich, ein Hallenbad, ein Freischwimmbad und das hauseigene Tenniscamp.

Our inspector loved: *The romantic atmosphere and the impeccable service.*

Directions: Innsbruck Verona road > Bozen Sud > Meran > Marling.

Web: www.johansens.com/oberwirt
E-mail: info@oberwirt.com
Tel: +39 0473 22 20 20
Fax: +39 0473 44 71 30

Price Guide:
double €110–176
suite €144-235

Park Hotel Mignon

VIA GRABMAYR 5, 39012 MERANO, ITALY

Close to the famous promenades of Merano and surrounded by its own green park, lies the family-run Park Hotel Mignon. The hotel is bright and harmoniously decorated with a relaxing and regenerating atmosphere. For those whishing to be pampered, the health and beauty centre offers personalised programmes and treatments. The excellent cuisine includes South Tyrolean and Italian dishes. In the evenings, guests may enjoy live music at the piano bar or in the garden by the swimming pool.

A proximité des célèbres promenades de Merano, cet hôtel familial entouré d'un parc verdoyant invite à se détendre dans un cadre lumineux et harmonieux. Qui souhaite se faire dorloter sera comblé par les programmes et les traitements personnalisés offerts par le centre de beauté et de remise en forme. Le menu savoureux est composé de spécialités du Haut-Adige et de plats italiens. Le soir, les visiteurs se laissent bercer par la musique dans le piano-bar ou dans le jardin, au bord de la piscine.

In der Nähe der berühmten Meraner Promenaden und umgeben von seinem eigenen Park liegt das familiengeführte Park Hotel Mignon. Es ist hell und harmonisch eingerichtet und besitzt eine entspannende Atmosphäre. Wer sich verwöhnen lassen will, findet im wellness und Schönheitszentrum eine Reihe von individuellen Programmen und Behandlungen. Für kulinarischen Genuss sorgen köstliche Südtiroler und italienische Gerichte, und abends erfreuen sich die Gäste an Live-Musik in der Pianobar oder im Garten am Pool.

Our inspector loved: *The beautiful garden and the superb hospitality.*

Directions: Brennero > exit Bolzano Sud > Merano Sud > Maia Alta.

Web: www.johansens.com/parkhotelmignon
E-mail: info@hotelmignon.com
Tel: +39 0473 230353
Fax: +39 0473 230644

Price Guide:
single €75–104
double/twin €150–207
suite €196–259

Posthotel Cavallino Bianco

VIA CAREZZA 30, 39056 NOVA LEVANTE (BZ), DOLOMITES, ITALY

Situated in the Val d'Ega, at the heart of the Dolomites and close to Verona and Venice lies this former staging post, owned by the Wiedenhofer family since 1865. Today the hotel offers first-class comfort in an elegant setting; cuisine and cellar are a refined blend of Mediterranean and Alpine flavours. The new wellness centre offers indoor and outdoor swimming pool, Jacuzzi, saunas, relax areas, fitness room, beauty and spa treatments and massages. Activities: tennis, golf, skiing, cross-country skiing, golf, walking and climbing amidst the most stunning mountain scenery.

Situé au Val d'Ega au cœur des Dolomites et près de Vérone et de Venise, cet ancien relais est géré par la famille Wiedenhofer depuis 1865. L'hôtel offre aujourd'hui tout le confort moderne dans un cadre élégant. La cuisine et la cave proposent une combinaison de saveurs raffinées méditerranéennes et alpines. Le nouveau centre de bien-être offre piscine couverte, jacuzzi, saunas, zones de détente, piscine en plein air, salle de remise en forme, traitements de beauté, massages et bains. Acitivités: tennis, ski, ski de randonné, golf, randonnés et l'alpinisme en plein cœur d'une région magnifique.

Im Eggental in den Dolomiten, unweit von Verona und Venedig, liegt diese ehemalige Poststation, im Besitz der Familie Wiedenhofer seit 1865. Das Hotel bietet heue First-Class-Komfort in eleganter Atmosphäre, Küche und Keller sind eine edle Kombination aus mediterranem und alpendländischen Geschmack. Ein neuer Wellnessbereich bietet Hallenbad, Whirlpool, Saunen, Ruhezonen, Freibad und Fitnessraum, Schönheitsbehandlungen, Massagen und Bäderanwendungen, und man genießt Tennis, Ski- und Langlaufen, Golf, Wandern und Bergsteigen inmitten herrlichster Bergregion.

Our inspector loved: *The fabulous panoramic view and the warm hospitality.*

Directions: A22 > Bolzano North > Nova Levante > Val d'Ega-Lago di Carezza.

Web: www.johansens.com/weissesrossl
E-mail: posthotel@postcavallino.com
Tel: +39 0471 613113
Fax: +39 0471 613390

Price Guide:
single €80–120
double/twin €140–220
suite €190–260

          SPA 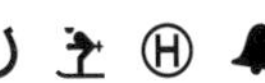 

Hotel & Spa Rosa Alpina

STRADA MICURA DE RUE 20, 39030 SAN CASSIANO, DOLOMITES (BZ) ITALY

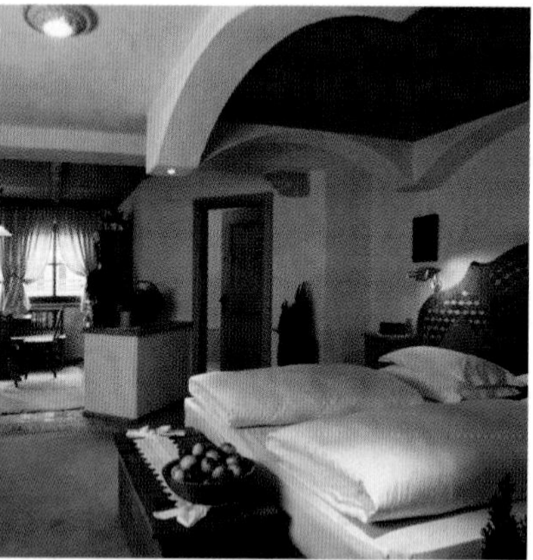

Directions: A22 to Brennero > Exit Varna-Bressanone > SS49 Valpusteria to Brunico >SS244 Val Badia > Follow signs to San Cassiano.

Web: www.johansens.com/rosaaplina
E-mail: info@rosalpina.it
Tel: +39 0471 849500
Fax: +39 0471 849377

Price Guide:
single €160–230
double €180–360
suite €370–495

A charming family-run hotel located in the Dolomites, the Rosa Alpina offers relaxation and an escape for lovers of skiing, golf, good food and fine wines. A combination of ancient Tyrolean style and modern elegance, bedrooms inspire peace and are furnished in linens, wood and marble. Guests can choose from 3 restaurants, and at the Michelin starred St. Hubertus cooking classes are organised. The hotel also arranges guided mountain excursions, personalised beauty programmes at the wonderful spa, and golfing tournaments.

Le Rosa Alpina est un charmant hôtel familial situé dans les Dolomites qui offre détente et une échappatoire idéale pour les amoureux du ski, golf, bonne nourriture et vins fins. Dans une combinaison de style ancien tyrolien et d'élégance moderne, les chambres sont paisibles et sont meublées de lins, bois et marbre. Les hôtes peuvent choisir entre 3 restaurants, et des cours de cuisine sont organisés au St Hubertus primé au Michelin. L'hôtel organise également des excursions guidées en montagne, des programmes-beauté personnalisés au superbe spa et des tournois de golf.

Dieses zauberhafte familiengeführte Hotel in den Dolomiten mit seiner entspannenden Atmosphäre ist der ideale Ort für Skifahrer, Golfer und Liebhaber von guter Küche und feinen Weinen. Die ruhigen Zimmer, eine Kombination aus altem Tiroler Stil und moderner Eleganz, sind mit Leinen, Holz und Marmor eingerichtet. Es gibt 3 Restaurants, und im mit einem Michelinstern gekrönten St. Hubertus findet Kochunterricht statt. Bergführungen, individuelle Schönheitsprogramme im Spa sowie Golfturniere können arrangiert werden.

Our inspector loved: *The exclusive ambience of the St. Hubertus restaurant.*

Romantik Hotel Turm

PIAZZA DELLA CHIESA 9, 39050 VÖLS AM SCHLERN, SÜD TIROL (BZ), ITALY

Located high up in the centre of a natural park, this stylish hotel is set in a tower dating back to the 13th century. The family are collectors of art, and many works, including paintings by Picasso and De Chirico, can be admired throughout the hotel. The charming bedrooms are decorated with local fabrics and old carved wood furniture. Exquisite dishes and excellent wines are served in the gourmet restaurant, whilst the hotel's breathtaking, newly opened wellness centre offers a wide range of hay, wine and herb treatments and baths.

Situé en haut au centre d'un parc naturel, cet hôtel élégant se trouve dans un tour datant du XIIIe siècle. La famille collectionne des tableaux, et de nombreux œuvres d'art, comprenant des tableaux de Picasso et De Chirico, peuvent être admirés dans tout l'hôtel. Les chambres charmantes sont ornées avec des tissus de la région et des meubles en bois sculpté. Des plats exquis et excellents vins sont servis dans le restaurant gourmet, alors que le nouveau centre de beauté sensationnel offre des traitements et bains de foin, de vin et d'herbes.

Hoch oben inmitten eines Naturparks befindet sich dieses elegante, in einem Turm aus dem 13. Jahrhundert untergebrachte Hotel. Die Familie sammelt Kunst, und zahlreiche Werke, darunter Malereien von Picasso und De Chirico, zieren das ganze Hotel. Die zauberhaften Zimmer sind mit Stoffen der Region und alten holzgeschnitzten Möbeln gestaltet. Exquisite Küche und hervorragende Weine werden im Gourmetrestaurant serviert, und das atemberaubende brandneue Wellness-Centre bietet eine große Auswahl an Heu-, Wein- und Kräuterbehandlungen.

Our inspector loved: *The salt grotto and the Emperor bath in the wellness centre.*

Directions: A22 > exit Bolzano Nord > follow signs to Brennero and Altopiano dello Schillar.

Web: www.johansens.com/turm
E-mail: info@hotelturm.it
Tel: +39 0471 725014
Fax: +39 0471 725474

Price Guide:
single €76–110
double/twin €172–250
suite €192–280

Castello di Leonina Relais

STRADA S. BARTOLOMEO, LOCALITÀ LEONINA, 53041 ASCIANO (SIENA), ITALY

Formerly the residence of Cardinal Fabio Chigi and later the home to Pope Alexander VII, this 13th-century fortress is set in the heart of Crete Senesi amidst beautiful rolling hills, considered by many to be the most enchanting countryside in the area. Bedrooms and public rooms are exquisitely furnished and the restaurant is an ideal venue for banquets. The conference room can accommodate up to 50 people. The piano bar and swimming pool, surrounded by magnificent gardens, are relaxing havens. Alternatively, a fitness centre features a Turkish bath, massage therapy, sauna and whirlpool.

Ancienne résidence du Cardinal Fabio Chigi puis du pape Alexandre VII, cette forteresse du XIIIe siècle est située au sein des collines arrondies de Crete Senesi, considéré par beaucoup comme la campagne la plus charmante de la région. Les chambres et pièces communes sont meublées avec goût, et le restaurant est l'endroit idéal pour un banquet. La salle de conférence peut contenir jusqu'à 50 personnes. Le piano bar et la piscine, entourés de jardins magnifiques, sont des havres de détente et le centre de remise en forme offre bain turc, massages thérapeutiques, sauna et bain à remous.

Diese Burg aus dem 13. Jahrhundert, einst die Residenz des Kardinal Fabio Chigi und später von Papst Alexander VII., liegt im Herzen von Crete Senesi inmitten herrlich sanfter Hügellandschaft, von vielen als schönstes Fleckchen der Region bezeichnet. Die Zimmer und Aufenthaltsräume sind exquisit eingerichtet, und das Restaurant ist der ideale Ort für Festlichkeiten. Der Konferenzraum fasst 50 Personen. Man kann in der Pianobar oder am Pool inmitten wundervoller Gärten entspannen, und das Fitness-Centre bietet türkisches Bad, Massage, Sauna und Whirlpool.

Our inspector loved: *The wonderful views of the "magical" landscape.*

Directions: A1 > exit Firenze-Certosa > highway to Siena > few km south east of Siena on the way to Asciano.

Web: www.johansens.com/leonina
E-mail: info@castellodileonina.com
Tel: +39 0577 716088
Fax: +39 0577 716054

Price Guide:
single €98-115
double (single occupancy) €109-160
double €135-200
senior suite €194-240
presidential suite €290-350

CasaBianca

LOC. CASABIANCA, 53041 ASCIANO (SI), ITALY

CasaBianca is an agricultural estate, made up of the elegant 17th-century main villa, ancient rural apartments, little streets, gardens and olive groves. Guests can get a real feel for its rich heritage from the incredibly detailed furnishings, the restoration of the original farm buildings and the excellent food, prepared with some of the estate's own fresh produce. The restaurant is situated in the cellars where old barrels are still visible. There is the chance to learn about Tuscan specialities during cookery classes or wine tastings.

Casa Bianca est un domaine agricole, constitué d'une élégante villa principale du XVIIe siècle, de petites rues, jardins, oliveraies et de vieilles maisons rurales. Les hôtes peuvent avoir une meilleure idée de son riche héritage via son ameublement incroyablement détaillé, la restauration des bâtiments d'origine de la ferme et sa nourriture excellente, préparée avec des produits frais de l'exploitation. Le restaurant est situé dans les celliers où les tonneaux sont toujours visibles. Il est également possible d'apprendre plus sur les spécialités toscanes au travers de cours de cuisine et de dégustation de vin.

Dieses Landgut besteht aus einer Hauptvilla aus dem 17. Jahrhundert, kleinen Sträßchen, Gärten, Olivenhainen und alten Landhäusern. Das reiche Erbe des Gutes wird besonders anhand der Einrichtungsdetails, der restaurierten ehemaligen Hofgebäude und der exquisiten Küche deutlich, für deren Zubereitung frische Zutaten aus eigenem Anbau verwendet werden. Das Restaurant befindet sich im Keller, wo zahlreiche alte Fässer aufbewahrt werden. Besonders gut lernt man die toskanischen Spezialitäten bei Kochstunden und Weinproben kennen.

Our inspector loved: *The breathtaking views of the amazing landscape and the restaurant.*

Directions: A1 exit Val di Chiana > follow directions to Sinalunga then Asciano.

Web: www.johansens.com/casabianca
E-mail: casabianca@casabianca.it
Tel: +39 0577 704362
Fax: +39 0577 704622

Price Guide:
double €163-190
suite €239-353

Castello di Magona

VIA DI VENTURINA 27, 57021 CAMPIGLIA MARITTIMA (LIVORNO), ITALY

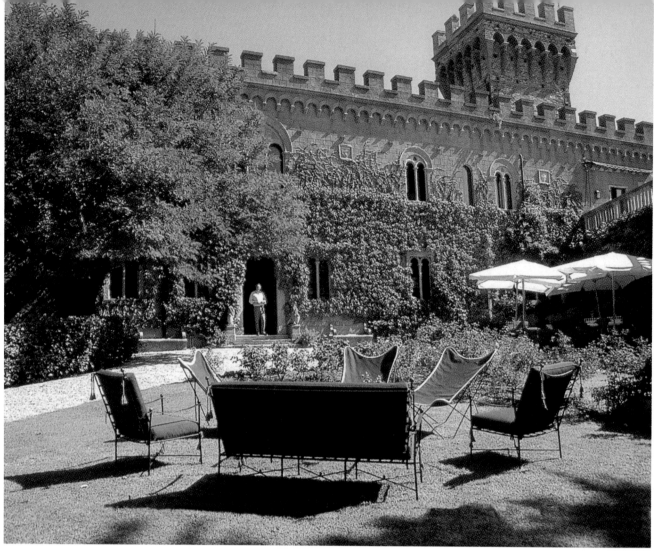

This magnificent villa on the Tuscan coast with breathtaking views across to the island of Elba can be rented on a weekly basis as an 11-bedroom holiday home and is ideally suited for a gathering with family or friends, exclusive meeting or unforgettable wedding. The 5 bedrooms and 6 suites are luxuriously appointed and equipped with all modern comforts. Guests can enjoy cookery classes, wine tastings, a swimming pool and fitness facilities. The Castello is the perfect base from which to explore the numerous artistic and natural riches in the vicinity.

Cette villa magnifique sur la côte toscane avec des vues à couper le souffle de l'île d'Elba, peut être loué pour une semaine en entière comme maison de vacances de 11 chambres, et offre l'endroit idéal pour des fêtes en famille, réunions exécutifs ou mariages inoubliables. Les 5 chambres et 6 suites sont luxueusement ornées et disposent de tout le confort moderne. Les hôtes peuvent participer aux cours de cuisine et aux dégustations de vins, et profiter d'une piscine et équipements de remis en forme. Le Castello est le base pour découvrir les nombreuses attractions artistiques et naturelles tout près.

Diese herrliche Villa an der toskanischen Küste mit atemberaubender Sicht auf die Insel Elba kann wöchentlich als 11-Zimmer-Ferienhaus gemietet werden und eignet sich hervorragend für Familientreffen, kleine Konferenzen, Hochzeiten oder Urlaub mit Freunden. Die 5 Zimmer und 6 Suiten sind luxuriös und bieten jeglichen modernen Komfort. Man kann an Kochkursen und Weinproben teilnehmen, im Pool schwimmen oder die Fitnesseinrichtungen nutzen. Das Castello liegt ideal, um die zahlreichen künstlerischen und natürlichen Schätze der Umgebung zu erkunden.

Our inspector loved: *Its splendid loction and rich, authentic furnishings.*

Directions: Available from hotel on request.

Web: www.johansens.com/magona
E-mail: relais@castellodimagona.it
Tel: +39 0565 851235
Fax: +39 0565 855127

Price Guide:
(minimum stay 3 nights)
7 nights €21,640–25,060

Relais San Pietro in Polvano

LOCALITÀ POLVANO, 52043 CASTIGLION FIORENTINO (AR), ITALY

This delightful hotel nestles in the green Tuscan hills and is a complete haven of peace and tranquillity. Guests will instantly feel relaxed in their romantic bedrooms, or by the swimming pool with its panoramic views of the surrounding countryside. Dining is a true experience with home-baked breads and pasta, and in the summer months the view from the outdoor dining terrace is unrivalled. This is a non-smoking establishment.

Cet adorable hôtel niché dans les vertes collines de Toscane est un havre de paix et de tranquillité. Les hôtes se sentent immédiatement détendus dans leurs chambres romantiques, ou au bord de la piscine aux vues panoramique sur la campagne environnante. Le dîner est une réelle expérience avec des pains et pâtes faits maisons, et l'été, la vue à partir de la terrasse extérieure est unique. C'est un établissement non-fumeur.

Dieses inmitten grüner toskanischer Hügellandschaft gelegene freundliche Hotel ist eine wahre Oase der Ruhe. In den romantischen Zimmern und am Swimmingpool mit Panoramablick auf die umliegende Landschaft fühlt man sich sofort entspannt. Das Essen hier ist ein wahrer Genuss - selbstgebackenes Brot und hausgemachte Pasta stehen auf der Speisekarte, und in den Sommermonaten hat man von der Außenterrasse eine unvergleichliche Sicht. Rauchen ist im gesamten Hotel nicht gestattet.

Our inspector loved: *The beautiful, peaceful location and the superb hospitality.*

Directions: A1 > exit Monte San Savino > follow directions to Castiglion Fiorentino.

Web: www.johansens.com/pietroinpolvano
E-mail: info@polvano.com
Tel: +39 0575 650100
Fax: +39 0575 650255

Price Guide:
single €130–150
double €170–200
suite €250–350

Relais della Rovere

VIA PIEMONTE 10, LOC. BADIA, 53034 COLLE VAL D'ELSA (SI), ITALY

Midway between Florence and Siena, this delightful Tuscan retreat epitomises the simple rustic elegance of the area. Formerly an abbey dating back to the 11th century, it cleverly combines old and modern styles, with elegant and spacious bedrooms and delightful cloistered dining. The restaurant serves a fantastic menu of local cuisine and wines, and the swimming pool is the ideal place from which to relax and enjoy the stunning Tuscan scenery.

A mi-chemin entre Florence et Sienne, cette ravissante retraite toscane incarne la simple élégance rustique de la région. Autrefois une abbaye construite au XIe siècle, elle combine des styles modernes et anciens, avec de belles chambres spacieuses et une délicieuse salle de restaurant cloîtrée. Le restaurant offre un menu superbe de cuisine et de vins locaux, et la piscine est l'endroit idéal où se détendre et apprécier la vue incroyable sur les paysages toscans.

Dieses wundervolle toskanische Hotel auf halber Strecke zwischen Florenz und Siena verkörpert perfekt die einfache, rustikale Eleganz der Region. Die einstige Abtei aus dem 11. Jahrhundert kombiniert geschickt alten und modernen Stil. Die Zimmer sind elegant und geräumig und man diniert in klösterlicher Atmosphäre. Im Restaurant wird eine verlockende Auswahl toskanischer Köstlichkeiten und Weine serviert, und der Swimmingpool ist der ideale Ort, um zu entspannen und die traumhafte Landschaft zu bewundern.

Our inspector loved: *The hotel's simple beauty.*

Directions: A1 exit Firenze Certosa > motorway to Siena, exit Colle Val D'Elsa Nord.

Web: www.johansens.com/dellarovere
E-mail: dellarovere@chiantiturismo.it
Tel: +39 0577 924696
Fax: +39 0577 924489

Price Guide:
rooms €176–290
suite €262–428

J AND J HISTORIC HOUSE HOTEL

VIA DI MEZZO 20, 50121 FLORENCE, ITALY

This is a veritable retreat for travellers, a charming transformation from a convent to a delightful small hotel, far from the bustle of the commercial world despite its central location. The individual bedrooms look out over the rooftops or down onto concealed courtyards and are furnished with antiques and hand-woven fabrics. The lounge is very elegant and a small bar leads into a courtyard which is a pleasant spot for drinks in fine weather.

Cet ancien couvent a été converti en un ravissant petit hôtel et constitue un vrai refuge pour le voyageur. Tout en étant situé de façon centrale, il reste protégé de l'agitation du monde extérieur. Les chambres individuelles donnent sur les toits de la ville ou sur des cours intérieures, et sont garnies de meubles anciens et d'étoffes tissées à la main. Le salon est très élégant et un petit bar mène à une cour intérieure, endroit fort agréable pour prendre un verre lorsque le temps le permet.

Dieses charmante kleine Hotel war ursprünglich ein Kloster und ist nun ein wahrer Erholungsort für Reisende, fernab von der Hektik der modernen Welt und doch zentral gelegen. Die individuell gestalteten Zimmer blicken über die Dächer der Stadt oder auf versteckte Innenhöfe und sind mit Antiquitäten und handgewebten Stoffen geschmückt. Der Aufenthaltsraum ist äußerst elegant, und eine kleine Bar führt in einen Hof – ein beliebter Ort, um einen Drink zu genießen.

Our inspector loved: *The view of the rooftops and the hidden courtyards, characteristic of the region.*

Directions: Borgo Pinti > city centre.

Web: www.johansens.com/jandj
E-mail: jandj@dada.it and reservations@jandj.it
Tel: +39 055 26312
Fax: +39 055 240282

Price Guide:
double/twin €210-315
suite €300-460

Hotel Lorenzo Il Magnifico

VIA LORENZO IL MAGNIFICO 25, 50129 FLORENCE, ITALY

This newly opened villa, located just a few steps from the heart of Florence, is the epitome of refined, simple elegance. The emphasis is on comfort and exceptional hospitality, provided by the wonderful staff. Each room is equipped with Jacuzzi bath or shower, whilst particular care has been taken in the selection of the superb bath and bed linens. A pretty garden, private garage and meeting room for up to 30 delegates complete the villa's amenities. Guests' cats and dogs are welcome.

Cette villa récemment ouverte et à deux pas du cœur de Florence est la quintessence d'élégance raffinée et simple. Une importance particulière est accordée au confort et à l'hospitalité exceptionnelle, offert par le personnel magnifique. Chaque chambre dispose d'un bain ou douche jacuzzi, alors qu'un soin particulier a été apporté à la sélection de linge, qui est superbe. La villa dispose aussi d'un beau jardin, garage privé et salle de conférences pour jusqu'à 30 délégués. Les chats et les chiens des hôtes sont accueillis.

Diese neu eröffnete Villa ist nur ein paar Schritte vom Stadtzentrum entfernt und der Inbegriff von edler, einfacher Eleganz. Die Betonung liegt hier auf Komfort und außergewöhnlichem Service. Jedes Zimmer bietet Jacuzzibad oder -dusche, und besondere Sorgfalt wurde auf die Auswahl der Bettwäsche und Handtücher gelegt. Ein hübscher Garten, eine Garage und ein Konferenzzimmer für bis zu 30 Personen vervollkommnen das Angebot. Auch die Hunde und Katzen der Gäste sind hier sehr willkommen.

Our inspector loved: *The simple elegance demonstrated by the fresh flowers and beautiful linens.*

Directions: A1 > any exit to Florence, then follow directions to Viali di Circonvallazione and Piazza della Libertà.

Web: www.johansens.com/lorenzomagnifico
E-mail: info@lorenzoilmagnifico.net
Tel: +39 055 4630878
Fax: +39 055 4630878

Price Guide:
double (single occupancy) €150-240
double €180-290
suite €350-500

Villa Montartino

Via Gherardo Silvani 151, 50125 Florence, Italy

Rising above the beautiful Ema Valley and surrounded by high stone walls, olive trees and vineyards, the excellent 11th-century Villa Montartino offers quality service within a peaceful setting. The luxurious, spacious rooms have panoramic views of the hills around Florence and contain original antiques, local handicrafts and modern conveniences. A buffet breakfast is served on the typical Loggia overlooking the whole valley. Lunches and dinners can be arranged upon prior notice.

S'élevant au dessus de la belle vallée de l'Ema et entourée de hauts murs de pierre, d'oliviers et de vignobles, l'excellente Villa Montartino, construite au XIe siècle, offre un service irréprochable dans un environnement paisible. Les chambres sont luxueuses et spacieuses, contenant des antiquités originales, de l'artisanat local et tout le confort moderne, et offrent toutes une vue panoramique sur les collines autour de Florence. Le buffet du petit déjeuner est servi dans la loggia surplombant la vallée. Déjeuners et dîners peuvent être organisés sur demande.

Diese eindrucksvolle Villa aus dem 11. Jahrhundert liegt hoch über dem Ema Tal und ist von hohen Steinmauern, Olivenbäumen und Weinbergen umgeben und bietet exzellenten Service in ruhiger Atmosphäre. Die luxuriösen, großen Zimmer haben Panoramablick auf die Hügel um Florenz und sind mit Antiquitäten, einheimischen Handwerksarbeiten und modernen Einrichtungen ausgestattet. Ein Frühstücksbuffet wird auf der typischen Loggia mit Blick auf das ganze Tal serviert. Mittag-und Abendessen können auf Anfrage zubereitet werden.

Our inspector loved: *The view of the hills and countryside surrounding Florence.*

Directions: A1 exit Firenze-Certosa > SS2 to Galluzzo > Via Gherardo Silvani.

Web: www.johansens.com/villamontartino
E-mail: info@montartino.com
Tel: +39 055 223520
Fax: +39 055 223495

Price Guide:
double/twin €284
suites €320
(weekly rate) apartments €930–1652

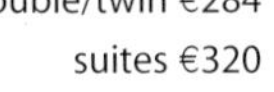

Hotel Villa Ariston

VIALE C. COLOMBO 355, 55043 LIDO DI CAMAIORE (LU), ITALY

Set in a quiet park only a few steps from the sea, this friendly early 20th-century villa offers guests various types of accommodation and the comfort of a 4-star hotel. The 20 charming bedrooms are located in the villa. Dinner is served in a romantic restaurant, whilst lunch can be taken by the pool. Guests can enjoy hydromassage and tennis, relax at the beach clubs opposite the hotel, play golf at a nearby golf course, or explore the beauty of Tuscany.

Située dans un parc à quelques pas seulement de la mer, cette amicale villa du début du XXe siècle offre à ses hôtes différents types de logement et le confort d'un hôtel 4 étoiles. Les 20 ravissantes chambres sont situées dans la Villa. Le dîner est servi dans un restaurant à l'atmosphère romantique, alors que le déjeuner peut être pris près de la piscine. Les hôtes peuvent profiter de l'hydromassage et du tennis, se détendre sur les plages privées en face de l'hôtel, jouer au golf sur le cours proche ou explorer les beautés de la Toscane.

Diese freundliche, in einem ruhigen Park nahe am Meer gelegene Villa aus dem frühen 20. Jahrhundert bietet Gästen mehrere Unterbringungsmöglichkeiten und den Komfort eines 4-Sterne Hotels. Die 20 zauberhaften Zimmer befinden sich in der Villa. Das Abendessen wird im romantischen Restaurant serviert, und mittags isst man am Pool. Hydromassage und Tenniplätze werden angeboten, die gegenüberliegenden Strände laden zur Entspannung ein, und Gäste können in der Nähe Golf spielen und die Toskana erkunden.

Our inspector loved: *Its joyful elegance and style.*

Directions: A12 exit at Versilia or Viareggio.

Web: www.johansens.com/villaariston
E-mail: info@villaariston.it
Tel: +39 0584 610633
Fax: +39 0584 610631

Price Guide:
single €130–220
double €180–300
suite €260–440

VILLA MICHAELA

VIA DI VALLE 6/8, 55060 VORNO - CAPANNORI (LU), ITALY

Set amidst its own 50 acres in the hills south of Lucca and surrounded by pine forests, this early 19th-century villa, with its consecrated chapel, is a popular venue for weddings and family reunions. Carefully restored to maintain its original character, the villa provides all modern comforts in 11 individually furnished en-suite double bedrooms and a separate coach house offering 3 en-suite double bedrooms. Guests can enjoy gastronomic delights or attend cookery classes in the impressive Tuscan kitchen, whilst for leisure there is a large swimming pool as well as a tennis court.

Au sein de ses propres 20 ha dans les collines au sud de Lucca et entourée de forêts de pin, cette villa datant du début du XIXe siècle a sa propre chapelle et elle est l'endroit idéal pour des noces et des fêtes en famille. Soigneusement restaurée pour maintenir son caractère original, la villa offre tout le confort moderne dans 11 chambres meublées de façon individuelle et avec salle de bain attenante et l'ancienne remise de carrosses separée offrant 3 chambres. Il y a une grande cuisine toscane, où les hôtes peuvent déguster des délices gastronomiques et participer aux cours de cuisine. La villa dispose d'une grande piscine et un court de tennis.

Diese Villa aus dem frühen 19. Jahrhundert liegt inmitten ihrer eigenen 20ha Land umgeben von Pinienwäldern in den Hügeln südlich von Lucca und ist mit ihrer eigenen Kapelle der ideale Ort für Hochzeiten und Familienfeiern. Die sorgfältig restaurierte Villa bietet jeglichen modernen Komfort in 11 unterschiedlich gestalteten Doppelzimmern mit Bad und der separaten ehemaligen Remise mit 3 Doppelzimmern und Bad. In der eindrucksvollen toskanischen Küche kann man köstlich speisen oder Kochkurse machen. Ein großer Swimmingpool und ein Tennisplatz stehen zur Verfügung.

Our inspector loved: *The huge kitchen, warm hospitality and friendliness.*

Directions: The villa is a 10-minute drive south of Lucca on the old road to Pisa. Take the A11 or A12.

Web: www.johansens.com/michaela
E-mail: info@villamichaela.com
Tel: +39 058 397 1371
Fax: +39 058 397 1292

Price Guide:
(minimum 2-night stay)
double/twin €280-600

Country House Casa Cornacchi

LOC. MONTEBENICHI, 52021 AREZZO, TUSCANY, ITALY

After an exhilarating drive through the breathtaking countryside between Siena and Arezzo, guests receive a warm welcome at this relaxing and tranquil country residence. Casa Cornacchi consists of fully restored stone buildings dating back to the 16th century and offers exquisitely furnished bedrooms, a panoramic swimming pool and Jacuzzi as well as some fine Tuscan wines. Guests can explore this enchanting region with its wonderful treasures of art, history and nature.

Après une promenade en voiture vivifiante à travers la belle campagne de Siena et Arezzo, les hôtes reçoivent le bon accueil à cette résidence de campagne tranquille et relaxante. Les bâtiments en pierre datant du XVIe siècle ont été restaurés et offrent des chambres exquisément ornées, une piscine panoramique et jacuzzi ainsi que de fins vins toscans. Cette région enchanteresse avec son art, son histoire et sa nature fascinants, est à découvrir.

Nach einer wundervollen Fahrt durch die atemberaubende Landschaft zwischen Siena und Arezzo wird man in diesem entspannten, ruhigen Landsitz mit offenen Armen empfangen. Casa Cornacchi besteht aus Steingebäuden aus dem 16. Jahrhundert und bietet exquisit eingerichtete Gästezimmer, einen Panorama-Swimmingpool und Jacuzzi sowie einige ausgezeichnete toskanische Weine. Diese zauberhafte Region mit ihren zahlreichen Kunstschätzen, geschichtsträchtigen Stätten und herrlicher Natur bietet etwas für jeden Geschmack.

Our inspector loved: *The feeling of joy and serenity of the hotel and surrounding area.*

Directions: From Florence take the A1 > exit Valdarno > Siena > Bucine > Ambra > Montebenichi.

Web: www.johansens.com/cornacchi
E-mail: info@cornacchi.com
Tel: +39 055 998229
Fax: +39 055 9983863

Price Guide:
single €120
double €160
suite €180

Hotel Monteriggioni

VIA 1 MAGGIO 4, 53035 MONTERIGGIONI (SI), ITALY

Set within the walls of the fortified village of Monteriggioni, with its 14 towers and parish church still preserved, this charming hotel has maintained its original character by sympathetic restoration and scrupulous interior design. The atmosphere is one of discreet luxury, with each of the bedrooms being individually dressed with elegant fabrics and antique furniture that are in perfect harmony with the Tuscan stone exterior. The beautiful gardens encourage relaxation, with an elegant swimming pool and shady olive groves.

À l'abri des remparts du village fortifié de Monteriggioni, dont les 14 tours et l'église paroissiale sont restées intactes, cet hôtel de charme a gardé son cachet d'origine tout en bénéficiant d'une restauration harmonieuse et d'une décoration soignée. Il y règne un luxe discret, distillé par les étoffes élégantes et le mobilier raffiné, en parfait accord avec la façade en pierre toscane, qui parent les chambres apprêtées de manière individuelle. Le superbe jardin, avec sa belle piscine et ses olivaies ombragées, est une invitation à la détente.

Dieses charmante, innerhalb der Festungsmauern des Dorfes Monteriggioni gelegene Hotel, dessen 14 Türme und die Kirche noch intakt sind, behielt während seiner Renovierung und Umgestaltung seinen ursprünglichen Charakter bei. Unaufdringlicher Luxus ist überall spürbar, und die individuell gestalteten Zimmer sind mit feinen Stoffen und antiken Möbeln eingerichtet, die perfekt mit dem toskanischen Steinmauern harmonieren. Der herrliche Garten mit seinem eleganten Swimmingpool und schattenspendenden Olivenbäumen ist ideal zum Entspannen.

Our inspector loved: *The fascinating fortified medieval village of Monteriggioni.*

Directions: A1 Florence–Siena road, exit at Monteriggioni > pass Colonna di Monteriggioni > SS2 Cassia for 1km > Siena > left.

Web: www.johansens.com/monteriggioni
E-mail: info@hotelmonteriggioni.net
Tel: +39 0577 305009
Fax: +39 0577 305011

Price Guide:
single €110
double/twin €220
suite €338

Castel Pietraio

STRADA DI STROVE 33, 53035 MONTERIGGIONI, ITALY

With even its later additions dating back to the 15th century, Castel Pietraio is steeped in local history and today is the centre of a strong wine-growing estate. Whilst marble bathrooms and Jacuzzi baths have been added to ensure every comfort, there is still a definite and enchanting medieval ambience. Considerately planned to accommodate guests' every requirement, there is an elegant swimming pool and playground on site, whilst the tower is lit by torches for grand banquets in the Capacci hall. There are 2 golf courses nearby.

Ce château imprégné d'histoire, dont même les agrandissements les plus récents remontent au XVe siècle, est aujourd'hui le noyau d'un important domaine viticole. L'installation de salles de bains en marbre et de jacuzzis pour le plus grand confort du visiteur n'a rien ôté au charme médiéval de l'endroit. Conçu de manière à satisfaire tous les besoins des visiteurs, cet hôtel dispose d'une élégante piscine et d'un terrain de jeu. La tour est illuminée par des torches lors des grands banquets organisés dans la salle Capacci. 2 parcours de golf se situent à proximité.

Diese geschichtsträchtige Burg, deren neueste Erweiterungen aus dem 15. Jahrhundert stammen, ist heute das Zentrum eines erfolgreichen Weinanbaugebietes. Zwar wurde mit Marmorbädern und Jacuzzis für modernen Komfort gesorgt, doch die herrliche mittelalterliche Atmosphäre ist noch deutlich spürbar. Alles wurde perfekt auf die Bedürfnisse heutiger Gäste abgestimmt. Es gibt einen eleganten Swimmingpool und einen Spielplatz, und der Turm wird für prunkvolle Bankette im Capacci-Saal mit Fackeln beleuchtet. 2 Golfplätze liegen in der Nähe.

Our inspector loved: *The Tuscan combination of nature, wine and modern comforts.*

Directions: A1Florence – Siena road, exit at Monteriggioni > SS541 towards Badia Isola.

Web: www.johansens.com/castelpietraio
E-mail: castelpietraio@tin.it
Tel: +39 0577 300020
Fax: +39 0577 300977

Price Guide:
single/double/twin €150–160
junior suite €180

ALBERGO PIETRASANTA - PALAZZO BARSANTI BONETTI

VIA GARIBALDI 35, 55045 PIETRASANTA (LUCCA), ITALY

An authentic 17th-century palace in true Renaissance style, the hotel has been restored and maintained in a unique fashion. Its main hall combines abstract paintings with antique furniture, marble chip floors and beautiful moulded stucco and fresco ceilings. The covered courtyard has been transformed into a bar, and the enchanting waterfall in one corner completes its evocative charm. Bedrooms feature attractive fabrics and antique décor, and many bistros and brasseries, including one of the most renowned restaurants of Versilia, are nearby.

Ce palais authentique du XVIe siècle en style de la Renaissance a été restauré et maintenu de manière unique. Sa salle principale marie à merveille des peintures abstraites avec des meubles antiques, un sol en marbre et des plafonds magnifiques de stuc et de fresques. La cour couverte a été transformée en bar et la fontaine au coin complète son charme évocateur. Les chambres sont décorées de manière antique avec des tissus attractifs. De nombreux bistrots et brasseries, comprenant une des plus célèbres de Versilia, sont à proximité.

Dieses echte Renaissance-Palais aus dem 17. Jahrhundert wurde auf einzigartige Weise restauriert und erhalten. In der Haupthalle mischen sich abstrakte Gemälde mit Antiquitäten, Marmorböden und wundervollen Stuck- und Freskodecken. Der überdachte Innenhof wurde in eine Bar umgewandelt, und der zauberhafte Wasserfall in der Ecke sorgt für ganz besonderen Charme. Die Zimmer sind mit hübschen Stoffen und antikem Décor ausgestattet, und zahlreiche Bistros und Brasserien, darunter eines der bekanntesten Restaurants von Versilia, liegen in nächster Nähe.

Our inspector loved: *The harmonious blend of abstract paintings (from their private collection) with the antique furniture.*

Directions: A12 (Genova-Livorno) > exit at Versilia > Pietrasanta > Viale Apua > historical centre > Vicolo Lavatoi.

Web: www.johansens.com/pietrasanta
E-mail: a.pietrasanta@versilia.toscana.it
Tel: +39 0584 793 727
Fax: +39 0584 793 728

Price Guide:
double €220-360
junior suite €320-480
suite €390-640

Hotel Relais La Suvera

53030 PIEVESCOLA – SIENA, ITALY

In 1989 the Marchess Ricci and his wife Principessa Eleonora Massimo created this elite and luxurious hotel composed of 4 beautifully restored houses surrounding a courtyard. The elegant reception has a welcoming ambience, enhanced by a display of wines from their own vineyard. The exquisite salons are bedecked with antiques and the family art collection. Guests feast on Tuscan dishes served in the hotel's restaurant.

C'est en 1989 que le marquis Ricci et son épouse la princesse Eleonora Massimo ont créé cet hôtel luxueux de grand standing formé de 4 maisons superbement restaurées autour d'une cour. L'élégante réception se caractérise par une ambiance chaleureuse, accentuée par une série de bouteilles de vins provenant du vignoble du Relais. Les salons ravissants sont agrémentés de belles pièces anciennes et d'une collection d'oeuvres d'art de la famille. Les hôtes se régalent de succulents plats toscans servis au restaurant de l'hôtel.

1989 schufen der Marquis Ricci und seine Gemahlin Principessa Eleonora Massimo dieses elitäre Luxushotel, das aus 4 wunderschön restaurierten Häusern besteht. Schon der elegante Empfangsraum, in dem einige der Weine aus dem eigenen Weinberg ausgestellt werden, strahlt warme Herzlichkeit aus. Die prachtvollen Aufenthaltsräume sind mit Antiquitäten und einer von der Familie zusammengestellten Kunstsammlung gefüllt. Für kulinarischen Genuss im Hotelrestaurant sorgen köstliche toskanische Speisen.

Our inspector loved: *The family's collection of antiques and the hotel's cultural heritage.*

Directions: Superstrada Siena-Florence > Colle Val d'Elsa > Grosseto.

Web: www.johansens.com/relaislasuvera
E-mail: lasuvera@lasuvera.it
Tel: +39 0577 960300
Fax: +39 0577 960220

Price Guide:
double/twin €360–560
suite €480–980

Il Pellicano Hotel & Spa

Loc. Sbarcatello, 58018 Porto Ercole (GR), Tuscany, Italy

This ivy-clad villa, surrounded by a cluster of cottages is set amongst old olive trees in spectacular gardens and situated on the breathtaking Argentario Peninsula; a real paradise. Each room and suite is uniquely decorated and guests can enjoy exquisite local and international cuisine and wine at The Pelican Point Restaurant or al fresco at La Terrazza. After a day of water skiing, tennis or swimming in the heated seawater pool guests can take advantage of the Paradise Spa and relax with a massage. The hotel boasts its very own private cove which can be reached by lift.

Cette villa recouverte de lierre et entourée de charmants cottages, est située parmi de vieux oliviers dans de spectaculaires jardins sur la péninsule Argentario: un vrai paradis. Chacune des chambres et suites est décorée de manière unique et les clients peuvent déguster une délicieuse cuisine locale et internationale au restaurant Pelican Point ou à l'extérieur à La Terrazza. Après une journée de ski nautique, de tennis ou au bord de la piscine d'eau de mer chauffée, les clients peuvent se rendre au Paradise Spa et apprécier un massage. L'hôtel possède sa propre anse que l'on rejoint en ascenseur.

Diese efeubewachsene, von Cottages umgebene Villa liegt inmitten von Olivenbäumen in einem Garten auf der paradiesischen Argentario-Halbinsel. Alle Zimmer und Suiten sind unterschiedlich eingerichtet, und im The Pelican Point Restaurant oder al fresco im La Terrazza werden exquisite einheimische und internationale Gerichte und Weine serviert. Man kann Wasserski fahren, Tennis spielen oder im beheizten Salzwasserpool schwimmen und danach bei einer Massage im Paradise Spa entspannen. Das Hotel bietet eine eigene kleine Bucht, die mit einem Lift zu erreichen ist.

Our inspector loved: *This magical place where life is a dream from which you never want to wake.*

Directions: Rome > A12 > Civitavecchia > Orbetello > Porto Ercole.

Web: www.johansens.com/ilpellicano
E-mail: info@pellicanohotel.com
Tel: +39 0564 858111
Fax: +39 0564 833418

Price Guide:
(room only)
double €390
suite €622
(half board)
double €818
suite €1,426

Palazzo Leopoldo

VIA ROMA 33, 53017 RADDA IN CHIANTI, ITALY

Directions: From Rome: A1 > exit Valdarno > follow signs to Radda in Chianti. From Florence: Superstrada to Siena > exit S. Donato > follow Castellina and Radda.

Web: www.johansens.com/palazzoleopoldo
E-mail: leopoldo@chiantinet.it
Tel: +39 0577 735605
Fax: +39 0577 738031

Price Guide:
double €150–220
junior suite €220–290
suite €290–490

Located in the charming medieval town of Radda, in the heart of the Chianti region, between Siena and Florence, this hotel offers a unique blend of ancient Tuscan nobility and modern comfort and has been restored with careful attention to detail. Breakfast can be enjoyed in the original 18th-century kitchen or on the terrace, whilst the La Perla restaurant serves excellent local and Italian cuisine. The well-stocked wine cellar hosts wine-tasting sessions. The health and beauty centre offers various treatments.

Situé dans la charmante ville médiévale de Radda, au cœur de la région de Chianti, entre Siena et Florence, cet hôtel offre un mélange unique de vieille noblesse toscane et de confort moderne et a été restauré avec une grande attention au détail. Le petit-déjeuner peut être dégusté dans la cuisine datant du XVIIIe siècle ou sur la terrasse, alors que le La Perla sert une excellente cuisine locale et italienne. Les hôtes peuvent participer aux dégustations de vins dans la cave bien approvisionnée, et le centre de remise en forme et de beauté offre des traitements divers.

Dieses in der mittelalterlichen Stadt Radda im Herzen der Chianti-Region zwischen Siena und Florenz gelegene Hotel bietet eine einzigartige Mischung aus alter toskanischer Eleganz und modernem Komfort und wurde mit viel Liebe zum Detail restauriert. Das Frühstück kann man in der Küche aus dem 18. Jahrhundert oder auf der Terrasse genießen, und im La Perla wird hervorragende einheimische und italienische Küche serviert. Im gutbestückten Weinkeller finden Weinproben statt. In der Schönheitsfarm kann man sich mit zahlreichen Behandlungen verwöhnen lassen.

Our inspector loved: *The beautiful view of Tuscany's rolling hills and vineyards.*

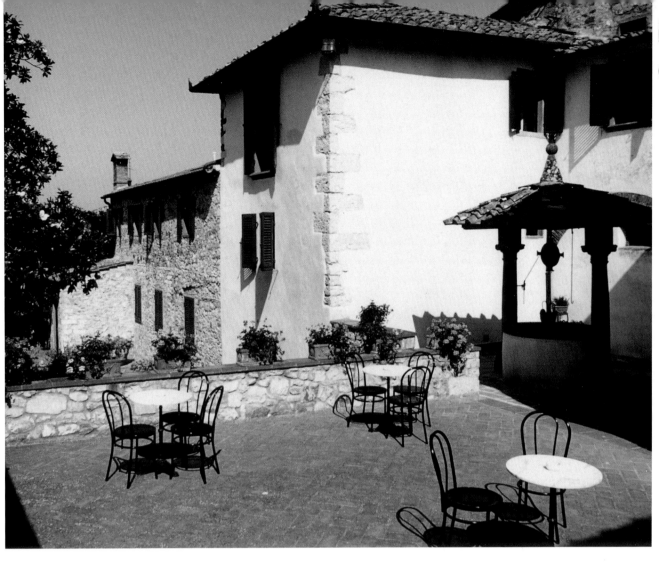

Relais Fattoria Vignale

VIA PIANIGIANI 8, 53017 RADDA IN CHIANTI (SIENA), ITALY

Located in the heart of the Chianti Classico region, just outside the medieval village of Radda, this 18th-century manor house was formerly a family-run wine estate. Bedrooms and public rooms feature antiques and some guest rooms have a Jacuzzi, terrace and panoramic view. Meals may be taken on the wisteria and jasmine-covered terrace. Alternatively, Vignale Restaurant, 300m away, serves seasonal cuisine complemented by Fattoria Vignale, national and Tuscan wines. The original wine cellars host wine tastings and the rustic-style Taverna.

Situé au cœur de la région de Chianti Classico, juste à l'extérieur du village médiéval de Radda, ce manoir du XVIIIe siècle était autrefois un domaine viticole familial. Des antiquités habillent ses pièces communes et chambres, certaines de ses dernières bénéficiant de jacuzzi et vues panoramiques. Les repas peuvent être pris sur la terrasse couverte de jasmin et glycine. Autrement, le restaurant Vignale, à 300 m, sert une cuisine de saison complétée par Fattoria Vignale, des vins nationaux et toscans. Les celliers originaux abritent un atelier de dégustation et une taverne de style rustique.

Im Herzen der Chianti Classico Region, außerhalb des mittelalterlichen Dorfes Radda befindet sich dieser Herrensitz aus dem 18. Jahrhundert, einst ein familiengeführtes Weingut. Die Zimmer sind mit Antiquitäten gefüllt, einige haben Jacuzzi, Terrasse und Panoramablick. Gegessen wird auf der mit Blauregen und Jasmin umrankten Terrasse, oder im 300m entfernten Vignale, wo man saisonbedingte Küche und italienische, toskanische oder Weine der Fattoria Vignale genießt. In den alten Weinkellern, wo sich auch die rustikale Taverne befindet, finden Weinproben statt.

Our inspector loved: *The sweet scented flower-covered terrace with splendid views.*

Directions: From north: A1 (north) > exit Florence Certosa 7 > main road to Siena for 22km > exit San Donato > Castellina > Rradda. From south: A1 (south) > exit Valdarno 7 (Montevarchi) > country road 408 towards Gaide Siena > Radda.

Web: www.johansens.com/vignale
E-mail: vignale@vignale.it
Tel: +39 0577 738300
Fax: +39 0577 738592

Price Guide:
single €135
double €165-300
suite €350

Hotel Certosa di Maggiano

STRADA DI CERTOSA 82, 53100 SIENA, ITALY

Directions: A1 > exit Firenze Certosa > Superstrada - Siena > exit Siena Sud > follow signs to Porta Romana.

Web: www.johansens.com/certosadimaggiano
E-mail: info@certosadimaggiano.it
Tel: +39 0577 288180
Fax: +39 0577 288189

Price Guide:
double €382–594
suite €647–982

A true escape from the world, this hotel is the oldest Carthusian monastery in Tuscany and dates from 1316. Its tranquillity is striking, and common rooms are splendid and rich in antique furniture, frescoes and paintings. The 17 bedrooms were once monastic cells, but are now elegantly furnished. Delicious cuisine is served either in the Il Canto restaurant or the beautiful colonnaded porch. Guests can relax by the pool and in the flower-filled garden, cycle, horse ride, or explore the stunning surrounding Chianti area.

Une réelle échappatoire au monde agité, cet hôtel datant de 1316, est le plus vieux monastère chartreux de Toscane. Sa tranquillité est saisissante, les salles communes sont splendides et riches en antiquités, fresques et peintures. Les 17 chambres qui furent des cellules de moines, sont maintenant élégamment meublées. Une cuisine délicieuse est servie soit dans le restaurant Il Canto ou dans la superbe véranda à colonnades. Les hôtes peuvent se détendre auprès de la piscine ou dans le jardin fleuri, ou faire de la bicyclette, de l'équitation, ou encore explorer la superbe la région de Chianti.

Dieses Hotel, das älteste Kartäuserkloster der Toskana, stammt aus dem Jahr 1316 und ist mit seiner unvergleichlichen Ruhe ein wahres Versteck vor der Hektik des Alltags. Die Aufenthaltsräume sind üppig mit Antiquitäten, Fresken und Malereien gefüllt, und die einstigen Mönchszellen wurden in 17 elegante Gästezimmer umgewandelt. Köstliche Speisen werden entweder im Il Canto oder auf der mit Säulen geschmückten Veranda serviert. Die Gäste können sich am Pool und im Garten entspannen oder die eindrucksvolle Chianti-Region erforschen.

Our inspector loved: *The colonnaded porchway and serene setting.*

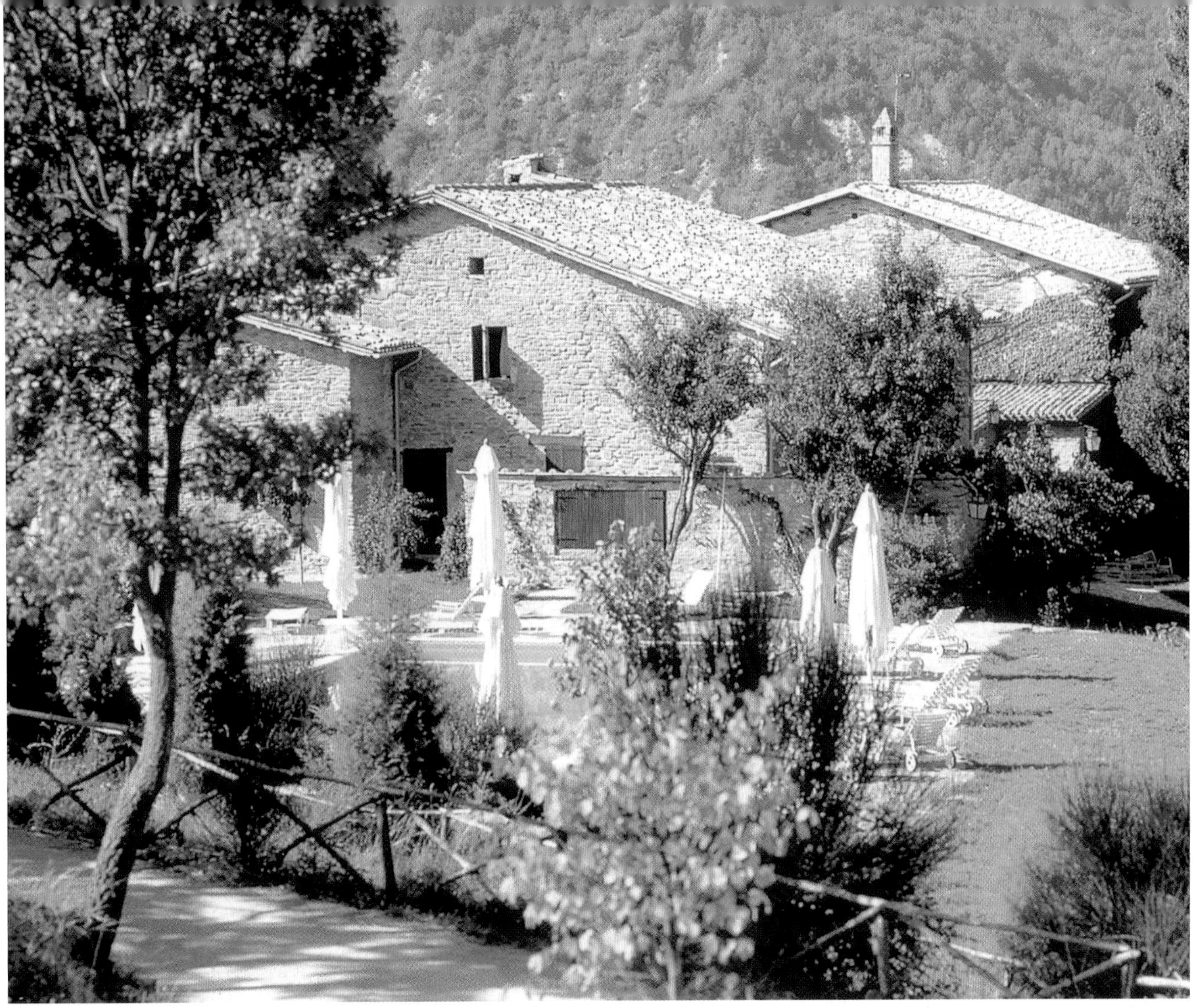

Romantik Hotel Le Silve di Armenzano

06081 LOC. ARMENZANO, ASSISI (PG), ITALY

This small hotel dates back to before the birth of St Francis of Assisi, the patron saint of animals. Le Silve is 700 metres above sea level, built on a plateau at the foot of the Subasio mountains. The air is scented by olive groves, and deer and horses ramble through the beautiful countryside. Umbrian cooking is delicious and here, the bread is baked traditionally in the fireplace. A charming sense of unspoilt rural simplicity is created by touches such as alfresco dining and country furniture.

Ce petit hôtel dâte d'avant la naissance de Saint François d'Assise, le saint patron des animaux. Le Silve se situe à 700 mètres au dessus du niveau de la mer. Il a été construit sur un plateau, au pied des montagnes du Subasio. L'air y est parfumé par les oliveraies et des biches et des chevaux gambadent dans le magnifique parc. La cuisine ombrienne est délicieuse et le pain proposé est cuit de façon traditionnelle dans la cheminée. Le diner servi à l'extérieur et le mobilier de style campagnard dégagent un agréable sentiment de simplicité rurale.

Dieses kleine Hotel existierte bereits vor der Geburt von Franz von Assisi, dem Schutzpatron der Tiere. Es liegt 700 Meter über dem Meeresspiegel auf einem Plateau am Fuße der Subasio-Berge und vom Duft der Olivenhaine umgeben. Wild und Pferde durchstreifen die herrliche Landschaft. Die Küche Umbriens ist einfach köstlich, und das Brot wird traditionell im Holzofen gebacken. Man spürt ein unbeschwertes Gefühl von ländlicher Schlichtheit, das durch rustikales Mobiliar und Essen unter freiem Himmel noch betont wird.

Our inspector loved: *The elegance of this charming retreat which offers you traditional dishes and homemade delicacies.*

 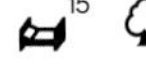     

Directions: Perugia > Assisi> S. 75 > Armenzano.

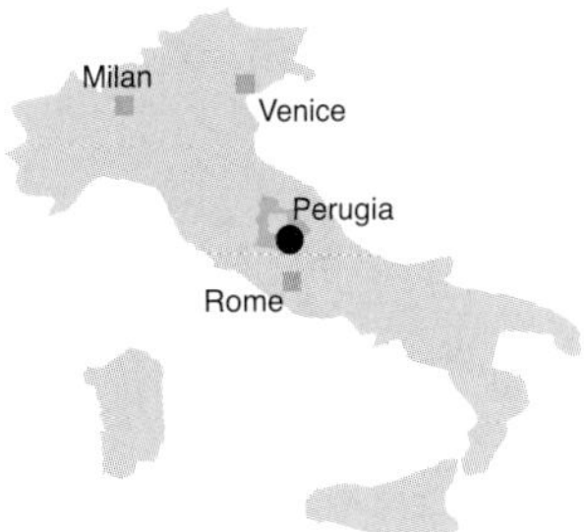

Web: www.johansens.com/silvediarmenzano
E-mail: hotellesilve@tin.it
Tel: +39 075 801 9000
Fax: +39 075 801 9005

Milan
Venice
Perugia
Rome

Price Guide:
single €83–91
double/twin €166–182

ITALY / UMBRIA (COLLE SAN PAOLO - PERUGIA)

Romantik Hotel Villa di Monte Solare

VIA MONTALI 7, 06070 COLLE SAN PAOLO - PANICALE (PG), ITALY

Directions: From A1 exit Chiusi towards Tavernelle - Colle San Paolo.

Web: www.johansens.com/montesolare
E-mail: info@villamontesolare.it
Tel: +39 075 832376
Fax: +39 075 8355818

Price Guide:
single €84–96
double €148–190
suite €182–216

The combination of its elegant Italian gardens, chapel and beautiful surroundings of woods and vineyards provide this elegant hotel with its sense of total tranquillity. The authenticity of the building has been painstakingly preserved in its restoration and today it offers individually designed bedrooms, some with their original frescoes and terracotta floors. Chef, Antonio Bondi, prepares high-quality Italian food (guests have the opportunity to join the cooking school) and more than 285 Umbrian wines are on offer.

La combinaison de ses beaux jardins italiens, de sa chapelle et des superbes bois et vignobles qui l'entourent, procure à cet élégant hôtel son sentiment de tranquillité absolue. L'authenticité du bâtiment a été préservée avec soin lors de sa restauration et il offre aujourd'hui des chambres individuellement décorées, certaines ayant gardé leurs fresques et sols en terre cuite d'origine. Le restaurant sert une cuisine italienne de grande qualité, préparée par Antonio Bondi (et aussi la chance de s'enrôler dans l'école de cuisine), et plus de 285 vins ombriens.

Die Kombination aus eleganten italienischen Gärten, einer Kapelle und der wunderschönen Umgebung aus Wäldern und Weinbergen gibt diesem eleganten Hotel eine Aura von Ruhe und Frieden. Die Authentizität des Gebäudes wurde bei der Restaurierung sorgfältig bewahrt, und heute findet man hier unterschiedlich gestaltete Zimmer, von denen einige noch die ursprünglichen Fresken und Terrakottaböden aufweisen. Chefkoch Antonio Bondi bereitet köstliche italienische Speisen zu (Gäste können hier auch einen Kochkurs machen), und über 285 umbrische Weine stehen zur Auswahl.

Our inspector loved: *The superb hospitality and the fabulous cuisine.*

Castello di Petroia

LOCALITÀ PETROIA, 06020 GUBBIO (PG), ITALY

Steeped in Italian history and the birthplace of Count Federico da Montefeltro, Duke of Urbino, Castello di Petroia is a beautiful collection of buildings housed within castle walls. The duke played a key part in the Italian Renaissance and the castle has been restored today in complete sympathy with its origins. Guests at the castle are assured of a quite unique experience. The common rooms are beautiful, and the swimming pool a truly relaxing haven overlooking the peaceful woods and grounds that surround the estate.

Imprégnée d'histoire italienne, et le lieu de naissance du Comte Federico da Montefeltro, Duc d'Urbino, Castello di Petroia est un ensemble de bâtiments situés au sein des murs du château. Le Duc joua un rôle important pendant la renaissance italienne et le château a maintenant été restauré en accord avec ses particularités d'origine; ses hôtes peuvent donc jouir d'une expérience unique. Les pièces communes sont superbes et la piscine, avec sa vue sur les bois et le parc entourant la propriété, est l'endroit idéal où se détendre.

Das geschichtsträchtige Castello di Petroia war Geburtsort des Grafen Federico da Montefeltro, Herzog von Urbino, der eine bedeutende Rolle in der italienischen Renaissance spielte. Es besteht aus mehreren herrlichen Gebäuden innerhalb der Burgmauern und wurde in völliger Harmonie mit seinen Ursprüngen restauriert. Gäste erwartet eine wahrhaft einzigartige Erfahrung. Die Aufenthaltsräume sind wunderschön gestaltet, und der Swimmingpool ist eine Oase der Ruhe mit Blick auf die friedliche Umgebung.

Our inspector loved: *The fascinating history behind this authentic castle.*

Directions: From E45 (Orte–Cesena) exit at Bosco > the castle is on the S.S.298.

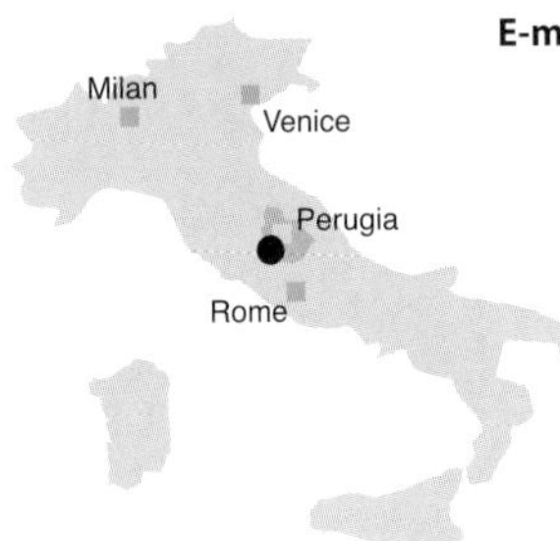

Web: www.johansens.com/castellodipetroia
E-mail: castellodipetroia@castellodipetroia.com
Tel: +39 075 92 02 87/92 01 09
Fax: +39 075 92 01 08

Price Guide:
double/twin €100–120
tower €100–120
suite €140–180

PALAZZO TERRANOVA

LOC. RONTI MORRA, 06010 MORRA (PG), ITALY

Directions: A1 towards Rome > exit Monte San Savino > Castiglion Fiorentino > over bridge > right at crossroads > right at traffic lights > left at third set of lights > Citta di Castello > Ronti > left before Cyprus trees > dirt track 2km.

Web: www.johansens.com/terranova
E-mail: bookings@palazzoterrannova.com
Tel: +39 075 857 0083
Fax: +39 075 857 0014

Price Guide:
(based on 2 persons, per night)
double €350-500
suite €620-775

Palazzo Terranova is quite simply a stunning hotel; both in its location at the top of a hill overlooking the rolling Umbrian landscape, and in terms of its style. Each of the 12 bedrooms has been immaculately designed featuring wrought-iron beds, antique pieces and creative use of colour. The new Bar and Enoteca serves delicious food including homemade salamis, cheese and olive oil as well as excellent wines, complementing the extremely warm welcome. There is a stunning pool, and for guests wishing to get away from it all, the hotel is available for exclusive use.

Palazzo Terranova est tout simplement un hôtel magnifique; sur le plan de sa position privilégiée donnant sur les collines onduleuses d'Ombrie et sur le plan de son style. Chacune des 12 chambres a un design impeccable avec des lits en fer forgé, des objets d'art et l'emploi créatif de couleur. Des salamis, fromages et huile d'olive faits à la maison ainsi que des vins excellents sont servis dans le nouveau bar et Enoteca, complétant l'accueil très chaleureux. Il y a une piscine superbe et pour les hôtes souhaitant laisser tous leurs ennuis derrière eux, l'hôtel est disponible pour l'utilisation exclusive.

Dieses Hotel ist einfach einmalig, sowohl was seine Lage auf einem Hügel mit Blick auf die umbrische Landschaft als auch seine Eleganz betrifft. Jedes der 12 Zimmer wurde mit schmiedeeisernen Betten, Antiquitäten und kreativen Farben gestaltet. In der neuen Bar und Enoteca gibt es köstliches Essen, darunter selbstgemachte Salami, Käse und Olivenöl und hervorragende Weine – die perfekte Ergänzung zum herzlichen Empfang. Ein herrlicher Swimmingpool steht zur Verfügung, und wer sich nach völliger Abgeschiedenheit sehnt, kann das Hotel exklusiv mieten.

Our inspector loved: *The stunning views and gardens ensuring a true haven away from chaotic daily life.*

Villa Ciconia

VIA DEI TIGLI 69, LOC. CICONIA, 05019 ORVIETO (TR), ITALY

This 16th-century villa located near the town of Orvieto is an elegant haven of tranquillity set amidst a beautiful park. Newly renovated, the villa has maintained its original character, apparent in its thick walls, large beams and terracotta flooring. 12 comfortable guest rooms look onto the park. Guests can enjoy traditional Umbrian delicacies complemented by fine wines from the well-stocked cellar. Villa Ciconia is the ideal base from which to explore the enchanting Umbrian countryside and picturesque villages.

Cette villa datant du XVIe siècle près de la ville d'Orvieto est un élégant havre de tranquillité au sein d'un beau parc. Récemment rénovée, la villa a gardé son caractère original, évident dans ses murs épais, ses grandes poutres apparentes et ses sols en terracotta. Les 12 chambres donnent sur le parc. Les hôtes peuvent savourer des spécialités ombriennes accompagnées de bons vins de la cave bien équipée. Villa Ciconia est la base idéale pour découvrir la campagne enchanteresse d'Ombrie et ses villages pittoresques.

Diese Villa aus dem 16. Jahrhundert nahe der Stadt Orvieto ist eine Oase der Ruhe und Eleganz inmitten eines herrlichen Parks. Die kürzlich renovierte Villa besitzt immer noch ihren ursprünglichen Charakter, sichtbar an den dicken Wänden, großen Holzbalken und Terrakottaböden. Die 12 komfortablen Zimmer blicken auf den Park. Die Gäste genießen traditionelle Köstlichkeiten Umbriens und erlesene Weine aus dem gutbestückten Weinkeller. Dies ist der ideale Ausgangspunkt für Ausflüge in die zauberhafte umbrische Landschaft mit ihren malerischen Dörfern.

Our inspector loved: *The simple elegance.*

Directions: Approximately 85km south of Perugia. From Orvieto Scalo follow directions towards Arezzo (SS71).

Web: www.johansens.com/villaciconia
E-mail: villaciconia@libero.it
Tel: +39 0763 305582/3
Fax: +39 0763 302077

Price Guide:
(lunch €18, dinner €18)
single €120-145
double €130-155

Alla Corte del Sole Relais

LOC. I GIORGI, 06061 PETRIGNANO DEL LAGO (PG), ITALY

This delightful, 15th-century monastic village with its renovated, rebuilt and refurbished accommodation stands near Lake Trasimeno, midway between Cortona and Montepulciano. It is the ideal retreat for anyone seeking to be pampered and enjoy the region's cultural centres. Each guest room is charmingly elegant, air-conditioned and has every home comfort. Superb cuisine, complemented by an extensive wine list, is served in the spacious and attractive restaurant. The beautifully maintained grounds feature a large swimming pool.

Ce charmant village monastique datant du XVe siècle avec des logements rénovés, reconstruit et remis à neuf, est situé près du lac Trasimeno, entre Cortona et Montepulciano. Il est l'endroit parfait pour des personnes cherchant à se dorloter et profiter des centres culturels de la région. Chaque chambre est élégante, climatisée et dispose de tout le confort moderne. Une cuisine superbe, arrosée par un grand choix de bons vins, est servie dans le restaurant spacieux et agréable. Il y a une grande piscine dans le parc superbement entretenu.

Dieses wundervolle klösterliche Dorf aus dem 15. Jahrhundert in der Nähe des Trasimener Sees auf halber Strecke zwischen Cortona und Montepulciano bietet komplett renovierte und neu gestaltete Unterkunft und ist der ideale Ort, um sich total zu entspannen und das kulturelle Angebot der Region zu nutzen. Jedes der eleganten, zauberhaften Zimmer bietet Klimaanlage und jeglichen Komfort. Im geräumigen, attraktiven Restaurant werden exquisite Gerichte und eine umfassende Auswahl edler Weine serviert. Ein großer Swimmingpool befindet sich ebenfalls auf dem herrlichen Gelände.

Our inspector loved: *The mouthwatering breakfast and the attention to detail.*

Directions: A1 > exit Valdichiana/Bettolle > take Superstrada to Perugia > exit Cortona > follow signs for Monte Pulciano.

Web: www.johansens.com/cortedelsole
E-mail: info@cortedelsole.com
Tel: +39 075 9689008/014
Fax: +39 075 9689070

Price Guide:
single €110-120
double €173-203
suite €203-303

Convento di Agghielli

FRAZIONE POMPAGNANO, LOCALITÀ AGGHIELLI, 06049 SPOLETO (PG), ITALY

Guests are guaranteed a truly unique experience at this 13th-century Country Resort for Wellness and Cooking, a remarkable retreat from the world. Everything here is designed in total harmony with nature, from the eco-friendly building materials to the ingredients used in the kitchen, which are all organically grown or raised on the property. Guests can attend cookery classes, explore the beautiful Umbrian countryside or simply relax and enjoy some well-deserved pampering sessions, including hydromassage, reflexology and ayurvedic treatments.

Les hôtes sont assurés d'une expérience unique dans ce lieu de vacances datant du XIIIe siècle et situé à la campagne, qui se spécialise dans le bien-être et l'art culinaire; une superbe retraite loin du monde. Tout a été créé en harmonie avec la nature, des matériaux de construction écologiques aux ingrédients utilisés dans la cuisine, issus de l'agriculture et de l'élevage biologiques de la propriété. Les hôtes peuvent assister à des cours de cuisine, explorer la belle campagne ombrienne ou simplement se détendre et se faire choyer lors de séances bien méritées d'hydrothérapie, réflexologie et traitements ayur-védiques.

Ein Aufenthalt in diesem Country Resort for Wellness and Cooking aus dem 13. Jahrhundert ist ein unvergleichliches Erlebnis. Alles in diesem wahrhaften Versteck vor der Welt ist in Harmonie mit der Natur gestaltet, von den Baumaterialien bis hin zu den Speisen, deren Zutaten ausschließlich aus eigenem biologischen Anbau oder eigener Aufzucht stammen. Man kann Kochkurse machen, die herrliche Landschaft Umbriens erkunden oder sich einfach mit Hydromassage, Reflexologie, Ayurweda-Behandlungen und vielem mehr verwöhnen lassen.

Our inspector loved: *The plunge into 100ha of pure nature.*

Directions: Approximately 66km south-east of Perugia and 2km south of Spoleto on the S3.

Web: www.johansens.com/agghielli
E-mail: info@agghielli.it
Tel: +39 0743 225 010
Fax: +39 0743 225 010

Price Guide:
double €124-155
suite €140-230

Hotel Ca' Sette

VIA CUNIZZA DA ROMANO 4, 36061 BASSANO DEL GRAPPA, ITALY

The Hotel Ca' Sette takes its name from a Venetian family who built the villa as a summer residence in the 18th century and is a truly stylish home from home. An atmosphere of quiet elegance is created by immaculate style and harmonious use of space whilst original local furniture and antiques create an authentic feel. Delicious food can be enjoyed in the award-winning restaurant. Bassano has a rich cultural life, stunning Venetian architecture, museums and a number of frescoed palazzi.

L' hôtel Ca' Sette tient son nom d'une famille vénitienne qui construit la villa comme résidence d'été au XVIIIe siècle. On se sent vraiment chez soi dans cet hôtel élégant. Une atmosphère d'élégance discrète est créée par le style immaculé et l'utilisation harmonieuse de l'espace, renforcée par un mobilier local original et des antiquités ajoutant au caractère authentique. Une cuisine délicieuse est servie dans le restaurant renommé. Bassano a une riche vie culturelle, une architecture vénitienne superbe, des musées et des palais ornés de fresques.

Dieses heimelige Hotel erhielt seinen Namen von einer venezianischen Familie, die die Villa im 18. Jahrhundert als Sommerresidenz erbaute. Makelloser Stil und harmonische Raumaufteilung schaffen eine ruhige Eleganz, während einheimisches Mobiliar und Antiquitäten für ein authentisches Flair sorgen. Im preisgekrönten Restaurant werden köstliche Speisen serviert. Bassano ist reich an Kultur, venezianischer Architektur, Museen und einer Anzahl von mit Fresken geschmückten Palazzi.

Directions: A4 > A31 towards Valdastico > exit at Dueville > take the main road to Bassano del Grappa.

Web: www.johansens.com/www.ca-sette.it
E-mail: info@ca-sette.it
Tel: +39 0424 383350
Fax: +39 0424 393287

Price Guide:
single €110–154
double €165–206
suite €240–362

Our inspector loved: *This stylish home away from home.*

CASTELBRANDO

VIA BRANDOLINI 29, 31030 CISON DI VALMARINO (TV), ITALY

A visit to Castelbrando is like a step back in time. Dating back to Roman times, this fortress at the foothills of the Alps of Treviso offers an unforgettable experience. Situated on 9 levels, this medieval "village" boasts 2 restaurants for casual or elegant dining, 8 bars, a spa and gym, 3 theatres, 4 museums, 4 conference halls and 47 tastefully furnished bedrooms. Guests may enjoy the magnificent views from the cable cars and take advantage of the extensive cultural entertainment, including guest performances by well-known musicians and theatre companies.

Un séjour à Castelbrando vous replonge dans le passé. Datant du temps des romains, ce château-fort dans les contreforts des alpes de Treviso offre une expérience inoubliable. Avec 9 niveaux, ce «village médiéval» s'enorgueillit de 2 restaurants pour des dîners élégants ou détendus, 8 bars, un spa et centre de remise en forme, 3 théâtres, 4 musées, 4 salles de conférences et 47 chambres ornées avec goût. Les hôtes peuvent apprécier les vues magnifiques depuis les téléphériques et profiter des divertissements culturels, comprenant des représentations et soirées musicales avec des artistes bien-connus.

Ein Aufenthalt hier ist wie eine Reise in die Vergangenheit. Diese am Fuße der Treviser Alpen gelegene Festung aus römischer Zeit ist ein ganz besonderer Ort. Das mittelalterliche „Dorf" liegt auf 9 Ebenen und besitzt 2 Restaurants (ein elegantes und ein eher legeres), 8 Bars, ein Kur- und Fitnesszentrum, 3 Theater, 4 Museen, 4 Konferenzsäle und 47 geschmackvoll eingerichtete Zimmer. Die Gondelbahnen bieten eine herrliche Sicht auf die Umgebung, und das umfassende kulturelle Angebot wird durch Gastspiele bekannter Musiker und Theatergruppen bereichert.

Our inspector loved: *The combination of a hotel with museums and theatres.*

Directions: From A27 > exit Vittorio Veneto Nord > follow directions to Follina Valdobbiadene > signposted.

Web: www.johansens.com/castelbrando
E-mail: hotel@castelbrando.it
Tel: +39 0438 976093
Fax: +39 0438 916020

Price Guide:
single €100
double €140
suite €260-350

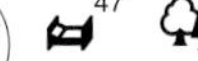

SPA

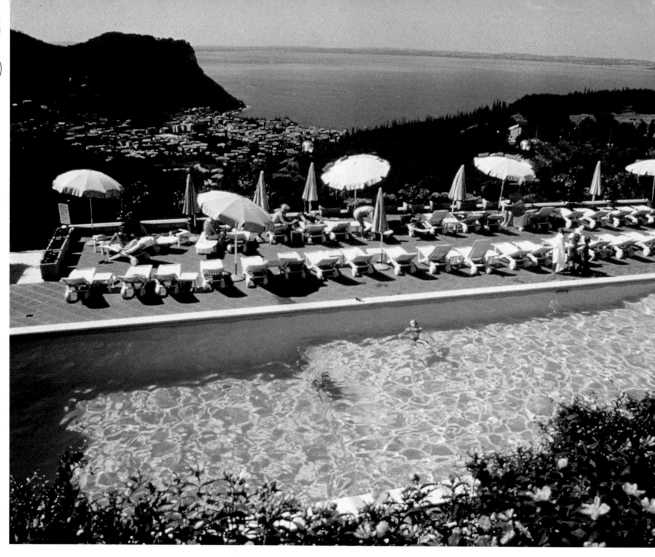

Hotel Madrigale

VIA GHIANDARE 1, 37016 MARCIAGA, BY GARDA (VR), ITALY

Set close to a golf course in the hills overlooking Lake Garda, this charming hotel is a haven of peace and tranquillity. All bedrooms have been recently renovated, offer great comfort and afford wonderful views of the lake from a pretty balcony. Excellent local and international cuisine is served in the panoramic restaurant, complemented by a great selection of wines. Guests can enjoy the 2 swimming pools in the grounds, whilst staff are happy to organise excursions to the lake and surrounding vineyards.

Situé près d'un parcours de golf parmi des collines surplombant le lac Garda, cet hôtel charmant est un havre de paix et de tranquillité. Les chambres récemment rénovées, offrent tout le confort et des balcons jolis avec vue sur le lac. Une excellente cuisine locale et internationale est servie au restaurant panoramique, accompagnée par une grande sélection de vins. L'hôtel dispose de 2 piscines, et des excursions au lac et aux vignobles des alentours peuvent être organisées.

Dieses zauberhafte Hotel nahe eines Golfplatzes in den Hügeln oberhalb des Gardasees ist eine wahre Oase der Ruhe. Alle Zimmer wurden kürzlich renoviert und bieten jeglichen Komfort, alle haben einen hübschen Balkon mit Blick auf den See. Im Panoramarestaurant werden hervorragende einheimische und internationale Gerichte sowie eine große Auswahl an Weinen serviert. Das Hotel besitzt 2 Swimmingpools, und Exkursionen zum See und den umliegenden Weinbergen können organisiert werden.

Our inspector loved: *The peacefulness and the panoramic views, especially from the swimming pool.*

Directions: From the A22 > direction Brenner > exit at Affi. Then follow signs to Garda.

Web: www.johansens.com/madrigale
E-mail: madrigale@madrigale.it
Tel: +39 045 627 9001
Fax: +39 045 627 9125

Price Guide:
single €75-100
double €117-170
suite €160-220

Park Hotel Brasilia

VIA LEVANTINA, 30017 LIDO DI JESOLO, ITALY

Located on the eastern side of the Lido di Jesolo across the lagoon from Venice, the hotel boasts a quiet position, a private sandy beach and 2 swimming pools. Recently refurbished in soft, elegant shades and fabrics, all bedrooms are comfortable and boast terraces and sea views. At the Ipanema Restaurant guests can enjoy candle-lit dinners of local and international cuisine and exquisite wines from the cellar. Lunch is served either on the veranda or alongside the pool.

Situé côté Est du Lido di Jesolo en face de Venise sur l'autre rive du lagon, l'hôtel bénéficie d'une position tranquille, d'une plage de sable privée et de 2 piscines. Récemment redécorées dans des tons et tissus doux et élégants, toutes les chambres sont confortables avec terrasses et vue sur la mer. Au restaurant Ipanema, les hôtes peuvent dîner aux chandelles une cuisine locale et internationale accompagnée de vins fins du cellier. Le déjeuner est servi soit sous la véranda soit au bord de la piscine.

Dieses Hotel am Ostende des Lido di Jesolo gegenüber der Lagune von Venedig bietet eine ruhige Lage mit privatem Sandstrand und 2 Swimmingpools. Alle Zimmer wurden kürzlich mit sanften, eleganten Farben und Stoffen neu gestaltet und haben Balkons oder Terrassen mit Meerblick. Im Ipanema Restaurant kann man bei Kerzenschein einheimische und internationale Gerichte sowie erlesene Weine genießen. Das Mittagessen wird entweder auf der Veranda oder am Pool serviert.

Our inspector loved: *The hotel's lovely position by the sea and its beautiful private sandy beach.*

Directions: A4 Motorway > Quarto D'Altino > Lido Di Jesolo > "Zona Est".

Web: www.johansens.com/parkhotelbrasilia
E-mail: info@parkhotelbrasilia.com
Tel: +39 0421 380851
Fax: +39 0421 92244

Price guide
double (single occupancy) €95–155
double €118–194
suite €192–230

Relais La Magioca

VIA MORON 3, 37024 NEGRAR (VERONA), ITALY

Directions: A4 > exit Verona Sud > Negrar–Valpolicella > A22 > exit Verona Nord > Valpolicella–Negrar.

Web: www.johansens.com/lamagioca
E-mail: info@magioca.it
Tel: +39 045 600 0167
Fax: +39 045 600 0840

Price Guide:
single €150–200
double/twin €170–240
suites €195–390

Set in an immaculate park, this charming relais offers breathtaking views, a romantic atmosphere and total peace and tranquillity. An ancient stone-built farmhouse, it has been furnished with refined taste and attention to detail. The 6 individually designed bedrooms are charming and comfortable, and together with the lounge and delightful breakfast room create a typical country house ambience. Nearby attractions include Verona, the vineyards of Valpolicella and Soave and Lake Garda. Venice is also within easy reach.

Situé dans un parc splendide, ce relais charmant, havre de paix, offre une vue à couper le souffle et une atmosphère romantique. Un ancien corps de ferme en pierre, il a été restauré et meublé avec raffinement jusque dans ses moindres détails. Les 6 chambres, décorées différemment, sont charmantes et confortables, et avec le salon et la ravissante salle du petit déjeuner, créent une ambiance typique de maison de campagne. Vérone, les vignobles de Valpolicella et de Soave et le Lac Garda sont des attractions touristiques très proches. Venise est également facile d'accès.

In einem herrlich gepflegten Park liegt dieses bezaubernde Relais, das sich durch seine atemberaubenden Ausblicke, romantische Atmosphäre und völlige Ruhe auszeichnet. Das alte, aus Stein gebaute Farmhaus wurde geschmackvoll und mit viel Liebe zum Detail eingerichtet. Die 6 individuell gestalteten Zimmer sind komfortabel und schaffen zusammen mit dem Aufenthalts- und dem Frühstücksraum ein typisches Landhausambiente. Verona, die Weinberge von Valpolicella und Soave und der Gardasee sind einen Besuch wert, und Venedig ist nicht weit.

Our inspector loved: *The romantic atmosphere and great attention to detail.*

Casa Belmonte Relais

VIA BELMONTE 2, 36030 SARCEDO (VI), ITALY

With breathtaking views over the Veneto's rolling plains from its position on top of a hill, and surrounded by olive groves and vineyards, this charming and elegant relais is a true haven of peace and relaxation. Each room is unique, and the tasteful furnishings and décor create a harmonious balance between tradition and refinement. Guests can enjoy breakfast in the Garden House, and relax on the veranda or in the lovely garden by the swimming pool. Finnish sauna, solarium and shiatsu massage are available.

Du sommet de sa colline, avec une vue sur les plaines onduleuses du Veneto et cerné par les oliveraies et les vignobles, ce relais charmant et élégant est un véritable havre de paix et de repos. Chaque chambre est unique et l'élégance du mobilier et du décor crée un équilibre harmonieux mêlant tradition et raffinement. Les clients peuvent prendre le petit-déjeuner dans la Maison du Jardin et se détendre sur la véranda ou dans le joli jardin situé à côté de la piscine. Un sauna finnois, un solarium et des massages shiatsu sont également à la disposition des clients.

Diese zauberhafte und elegante Herberge liegt auf einer Anhöhe mit herrlicher Aussicht auf das Veneto und umgeben von Olivenhainen und Weinbergen - eine Oase für Ruhe und Erholung. Jedes Zimmer ist individuell und geschmackvoll eingerichtet und bietet ein harmonisches Verhältnis zwischen Tradition und Raffinesse. Die Gäste können ihr Frühstück im Garden House genießen und sich auf der Veranda oder am Pool im Garten entspannen. Finnische Sauna, Solarium und Shiatsu-Massage werden ebenfalls angeboten.

Our inspector loved: *The excellent location - absolute peace and quiet.*

Directions: A4 motorway > Valdastico motorway (A31) > exit at Duevalle > follow signs to Bassano and Sarcedo.

Milan
Venice
Rome

Web: www.johansens.com/casabelmonte
E-mail: info@casabelmonte.com
Tel: +39 0445 884833
Fax: +39 0445884 134

Price Guide:
single €125–175
double €150–225
suite €200–275

HOTEL GIORGIONE

SS. APOSTOLI 4587, 30131 VENICE, ITALY

Directions: Airport > bus to Piazzale Roma > Vaporetto to Cà d'Oro. Railway station > Vaporetto to Cà d'Oro.

Web: www.johansens.com/giorgione
E-mail: giorgione@hotelgiorgione.com
Tel: +39 041 522 5810
Fax: +39 041 523 9092

Price Guide:
rooms from €200–700

A 15th-century building houses this charming hotel, which is set in a quiet location in the centre of the old town, close to the Rialto bridge and a few minutes from Piazza San Marco. The recently renovated hotel provides all modern comforts whilst retaining its original charm. All rooms are decorated in a romantic and refined style with antique Venetian pieces of furniture. Breakfast is served inside or outside in the beautiful garden. At the adjacent Osteria-Enoteca Giorgione guests can enjoy a great variety of wines and local dishes.

Un bâtiment du XVe siècle abrite ce charmant hôtel, situé dans un endroit calme au centre de la vieille ville, à proximité du pont Rialto et de la Piazza San Marco. Récemment rénové, l'hôtel est équipé de toutes les commodités modernes tout en conservant son charme d'origine. Les chambres sont décorées dans un style romantique et raffiné avec des meubles vénitiens antiques. Le petit-déjeuner est servi à l'intérieur ou à l'extérieur dans le jardin. Dans la Osteria-Enoteca Giorgione voisine, les clients peuvent goûter à une variété de vins et de plats locaux.

Ein Gebäude aus dem 15. Jahrhundert beherbergt dieses zauberhafte Hotel, das sich in ruhiger Lage im Zentrum der Altstadt nahe der Rialto-Brücke und dem Markusplatz befindet. Das kürzlich renovierte Hotel bietet jeglichen modernen Komfort, hat jedoch seinen ursprünglichen Charme beibehalten. Die Zimmer sind romantisch und elegant mit alten venezianischen Möbeln eingerichtet. Frühstück wird drinnen oder draußen im Garten serviert, und die Osteria-Enoteca Giorgione bietet eine große Auswahl an Weinen und hiesigen Gerichten.

Our inspector loved: *The warm welcome and the romantic Venetian courtyard with lovely fountain.*

Hotel Londra Palace

RIVA DEGLI SCHIAVONI, 4171, 30122 VENICE, ITALY

Just a few steps from the Piazza San Marco and the Grand Canal, this exclusive boutique hotel offers guests a feeling of unforgettable glamour and a romantic atmosphere. Each of the spacious, richly decorated bedrooms and suites, most of which afford stunning views of the lagoon, is a unique experience in itself, evoking a sense of discreet luxury. Guests can enjoy refined cuisine in a sophisticated setting at the hotel's restaurant, Do Leoni, and during the warmer months, lunch or drinks are served on the veranda.

A deux pas de la Place San Marco et le Grand Canal, cet hôtel exclusif propose aux visiteurs un sens de prestige inoubliable dans une atmosphère romantique. Chacune des chambres et suites spacieuses et somptueusement décorées, dont la plupart offrent une vue imprenable sur la lagune, est une expérience unique en soi, évoquant un sens de luxe discrète. Une cuisine raffinée est servie dans un cadre sophistiqué au restaurant Do Leoni, et pendant les mois plus chauds, les hôtes peuvent prendre un verre ou déjeuner sur la véranda.

Dieses exklusive Boutique-Hotel liegt nur ein paar Schritte vom Markusplatz und dem Canal Grande entfernt und bietet seinen Gästen unvergleichlichen Glamour und eine romantische Atmosphäre. Jedes der geräumigen, üppig dekorierten Zimmer und Suiten, von denen die meisten auf die Lagune blicken, ist ein Erlebnis für sich und weckt ein Gefühl von zurückhaltendem Luxus. Im edlen Hotelrestaurant Do Leoni werden raffinierte Gerichte serviert, und in den wärmeren Monaten kann man auf der Terrasse Mittag essen oder einen Drink zu sich nehmen.

Our inspector loved: *The superb location and the view of the lagoon.*

53

Directions: Located in the city centre, near Piazza S. Marco.

Milan
Venice
Rome

Web: www.johansens.com/londrapalace
E-mail: info@hotelondra.it
Tel: +39 041 5200533
Fax: +39 041 5225032

Price Guide:
double/twin (single occupancy) €265-475
double/twin €380-585
junior suite €485-790

Albergo Quattro Fontane - Residenza d'Epoca

30126 Lido di Venezia, Venice, Italy

A distinctive country house set in an idyllic garden on the Lido amongst orchards and productive vineyards, away from the hustle and bustle of Venice, the Albergo is only 10 minutes by water-bus from San Marco square. Signore Bevilacqua, whose family has owned the property for over 40 years, has collected some very unusual antique furniture, art and artefacts from all over the world. Venetian specialities complement wine from local vineyards.

Maison de campagne raffinée dans un jardin idyllique sur le Lido, l'Albergo, avec ses vergers et ses vignobles, est à seulement 10 minutes en navette-bateau de la place Saint Marc. Le Signore Bevilacqua, dont la famille est propriétaire depuis plus de 40 ans, a collectionné des meubles, de l'art et des objets façonnés originaux provenant du monde entier. Des spécialités vénitiennes complètent la carte de vins des producteurs locaux

Dieses herrliche Landhaus liegt in einem idyllischen Garten am Lido, umgeben von Obstplantagen und Weinbergen und fernab vom geschäftigen Treiben Venedigs, aber innerhalb von 10 Minuten per Boot vom Markusplatz zu erreichen. Signore Bevilacqua, dessen Familie das Hotel seit über 40 Jahren besitzt, hat eine Sammlung ungewöhnlicher Antiquitäten, Gemälde und Kunstgegenstände aus aller Welt. Für kulinarischen Genuss sorgen venezianische Spezialitäten und Weine aus einheimischen Weinbergen.

***Our inspector loved:** The hotel's originality and the precious collection of objets d'art from each corner of the world.*

Directions: Lido via San Marco > Albergo.

Web: www.johansens.com/albergoquattrofontane
E-mail: quafonve@tin.it
Tel: +39 041 526 0227
Fax: +39 041 526 0726

Price Guide:
single €130–270
double/twin €160–400
apartment €300-600

HOTEL GABBIA D'ORO

CORSO PORTA BORSARI 4A, 37121 VERONA, ITALY

Set in the historical centre of Verona, this very special small luxury hotel is housed in a 18th-century palazzo. Wooden ceilings, frescoes and precious paintings abound, whilst in the bedrooms antique furniture, oriental carpets, rich accessories, beautiful fabrics and lace create a romantic ambience. The Orangerie, a charming winter garden, is the perfect place to enjoy a cup of coffee or a light snack. The vineyards of Valpolicella and Lake Garda are all within easy reach, whilst Venice is a popular destination for a day trip.

Au cœur historique de Vérone, ce petit hôtel de luxe très spécial se situe au sein d'un palais du XVIIIe siècle. Les plafonds en bois, fresques et peintures précieuses, ainsi que le mobilier ancien des chambres, les tapis orientaux, les accessoires luxueux, les beaux tissus et dentelles créent une atmosphère particulièrement romantique. L'Orangerie, un charmant jardin d'hiver, est l'endroit idéal pour déguster une tasse de café ou un repas léger. Les vignobles de Valpolicella et le Lac Garda sont faciles d'accès et Venise est une destination populaire pour une journée de sortie.

Dieses kleine Luxushotel befindet sich im historischen Zentrum Veronas in einem Palazzo aus dem 18. Jahrhundert. Hölzerne Decken, Fresken und kostbare Malereien zieren das Interieur, und in den Schlafzimmern schaffen antike Möbel, orientalische Teppiche, schmuckvolle Accessoires, herrliche Stoffe und Spitze ein romantisches Ambiente. Die Orangerie, ein zauberhafter Wintergarten, ist der perfekte Ort für eine Tasse Kaffee oder einen Snack. Die Valpolicella-Weinberge und der Gardasee sind leicht erreichbar; Venedig ist eine beliebte Tagestour.

Our inspector loved: *The joyful Orangerie and the collection of fine silverware.*

Directions: In historical centre of Verona, near Piazza delle Erbe.

Web: www.johansens.com/gabbiadoro
E-mail: gabbiadoro@easyasp.it
Tel: +39 045 8003060
Fax: +39 045 590293

Price Guide:
single €160–284
double €232–351
suite €284–826

Palazzo San Fermo

STRADA SAN FERMO 8, 37121 VERONA, ITALY

Directions: From the A4 > exit Verona Sud. From the A22 > exit Verona Ovest. The hotel is in the centre of historic Verona.

Web: www.johansens.com/sanfermo
E-mail: info@palazzosanfermo.com
Tel: +39 045 800 3060
Fax: +39 045 590 293

Price Guide:
(apartment only, minimum stay 2 nights)
1-4 people €350-550
5-6 people €500-800

A unique alternative to a typical hotel experience, this wonderful 17th-century palazzo in the centre of Verona offers 5 stunning luxury apartments serviced by the Hotel Gabbia d'Oro. Guests may take advantage of all facilities offered by the hotel, which is just a few minutes' walk away. The beautifully decorated apartments range in size from 115 to 125m² and are fully equipped to provide all modern comforts. Guests also have a cellular phone at their disposal.

Une alternative unique à l'expérience typique d'hôtel, ce palais magnifique du XVIIe siècle au sein de Vérone consiste en 5 appartements de luxe fantastiques qui font partie de l'hôtel Gabbia d'Oro. Les hôtes peuvent profiter de toutes les facilités de l'hôtel, qui est à quelques minutes à pied. Les appartements, ornés à la perfection, sont de 115m² à 125m² en taille et offrent tout le confort moderne. Un téléphone portable est à la disposition des clients.

Dieses herrliche Palazzo aus dem 17. Jahrhundert im Herzen von Verona ist eine einzigartige Alternative zu einem typischen Hotelaufenthalt. Die 5 Luxusappartements gehören zum nur ein paar Minuten Fußmarsch entfernten Hotel Gabbia d'Oro, dessen Einrichtungen die Gäste selbstverständlich benutzen können. Die wunderschön eingerichteten Appartements sind 115m² bis 125m² groß und mit jeglichen modernen Annehmlichkeiten ausgestattet. Alle Gäste bekommen ein Mobiltelefon zur Verfügung gestellt.

Our inspector loved: *The opportunity to feel and live like a true noble citizen of Verona.*

HILDON
SPORT
STILL NATURAL MINERAL WATER
The ultimate refreshment for leisure & sport.
Hildon Ltd., Broughton, Hampshire SO20 8DQ,UK, ☏ +44 (0)1794 - 301 747, Fax +44 (0)1794 - 301 718
e-mail: hildon@hildon.com – www.hildon.com

LUXEMBOURG

Hotel location shown in red (hotel) or purple (spa hotel) with page number

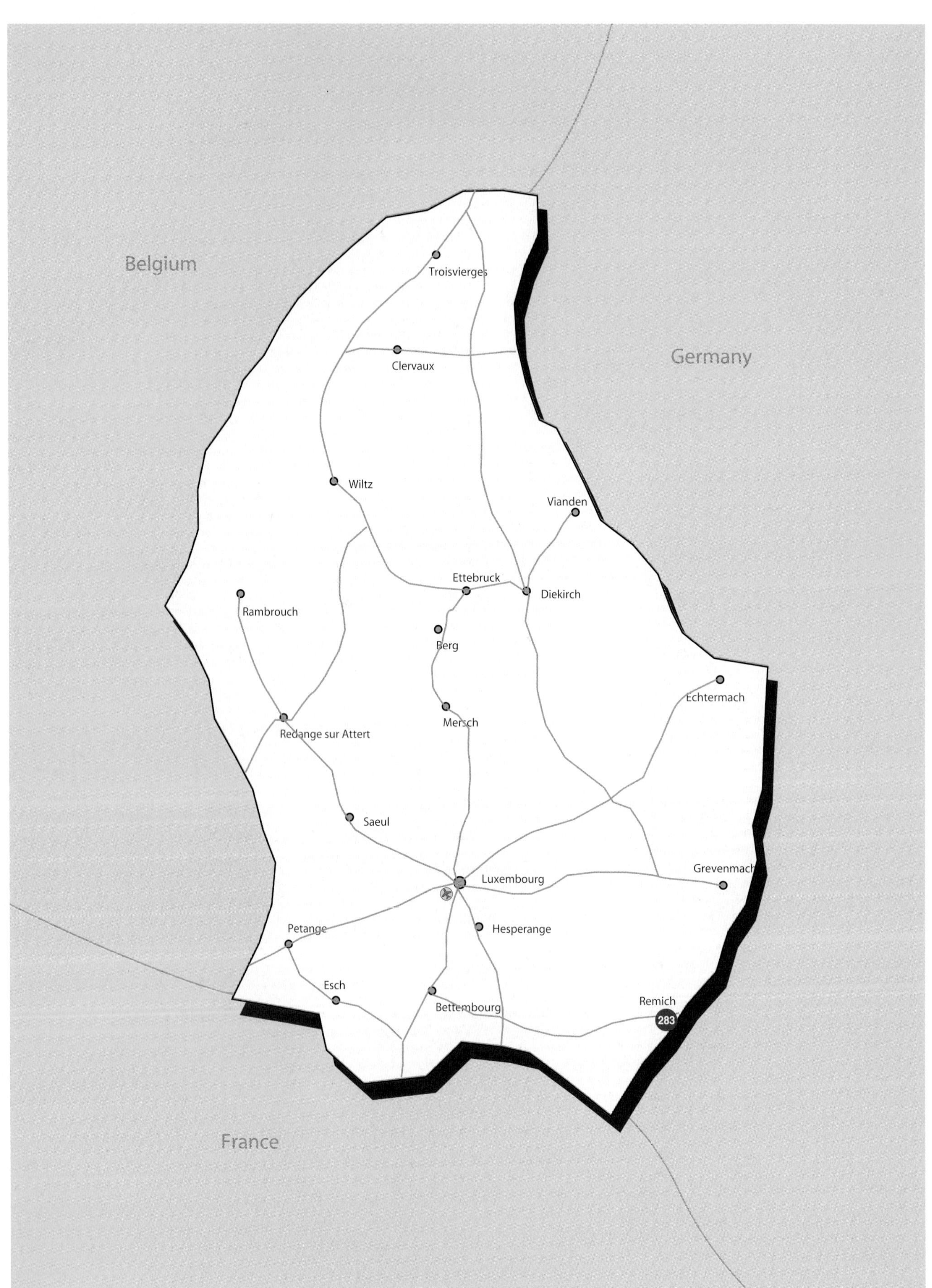

Hotel Saint~Nicolas

31 Esplanade, 5533 Remich, Luxembourg

Set in the picturesque town of Remich, this family-run hotel affords fantastic views across the esplanade and lush vineyards as it lies on the banks of the river Moselle. The eclectic hotel features unusual public rooms adorned with interesting paintings. The hotel's Lohengrin Restaurant serves traditional French cuisine; a true gastronomic delight. Complimentary broadband Internet access is available.

Situé dans la ville pittoresque de Remich, cet hôtel familial offre des vues fantastiques sur l'esplanande et les vignobles étant situé sur les berges de la rivière Moselle. Cet hôtel éclectique a des salles communes originales décorées de peintures uniques. Le restaurant de l'hôtel, le Lohengrin est un délice gastronomique proposant une cuisine traditionnelle française. Un service Internet ASDL gratuit est disponible.

Das familiengeführte Hotel Saint Nicolas, das an der Mosel mitten in der malerischen Stadt Remich gelegen ist, bietet spektakuläre Ausblicke auf die Uferpromenade und die üppigen Weinberge. Die Aufenthaltsräume sind originell und mit interessanten Bildern geschmückt. Das Restaurant Lohengrin mit seiner traditionellen französischen Küche bietet einen gastronomischen Hochgenuss. Gratis ADSL-Internetzugang ist vorhanden.

Our inspector loved: *Its promenade location and the wonderful service.*

Directions: Luxembourg > E29 > Remich or A13 > exit 13 Schengen.

Web: www.johansens.com/saintnicolas
E-mail: hotel@pt.lu
Tel: +352 2666 3
Fax: +352 2666 3666

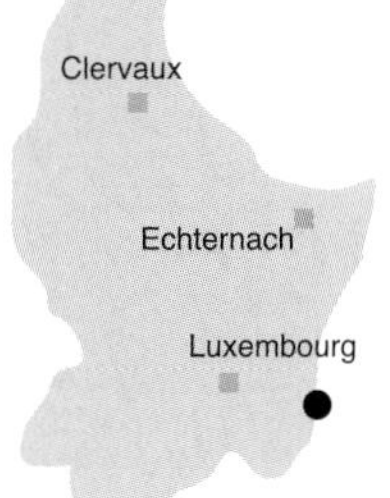

Price Guide:
single €79–104
double/twin €100–130
Gastronomic offer (incl. two nights) €170–195

Monaco

Hotel location shown in red (hotel) or purple (spa hotel) with page number

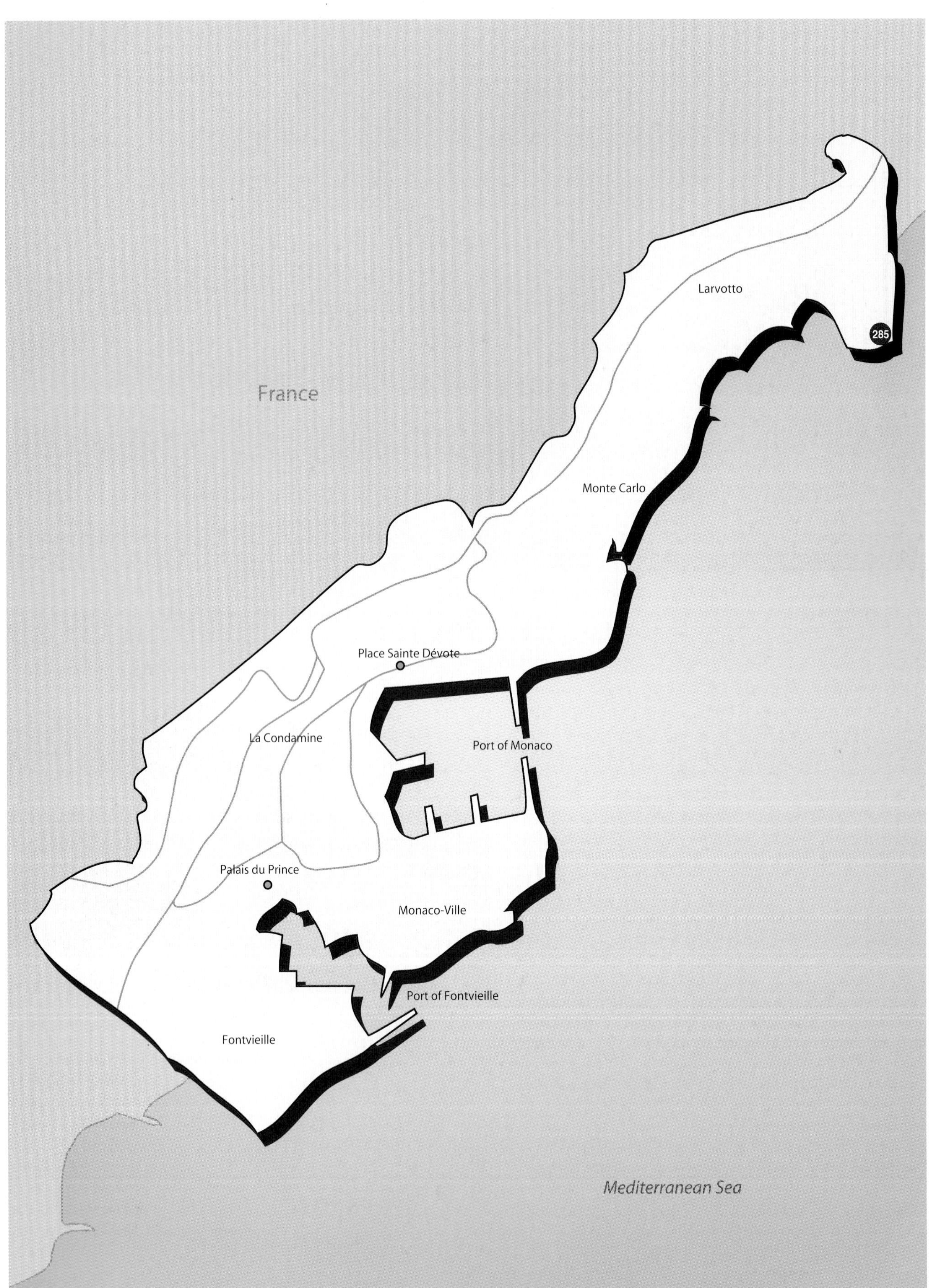

MONTE~CARLO BEACH HOTEL

AVENUE PRINCESSE GRACE, 06190 ROQUEBRUNE – CAP~MARTIN, FRANCE

Decorated throughout in Italian Riviera style, this charming yet lavish property has been a resting place for the glitterati since the 1930s, and its popularity remains to day. Bright colours adorn the bedrooms, and 4 excellent restaurants serve different flavours. The private beach and the olympic-sized swimming pool add to the appeal. Through the Société des Bains de Mer Resort, guests can enjoy tennis at the Country Club, golf at the 18-hole Golf Club, the famous Spa centre "Les Thermes Marins" as well as entertainment at the Sporting Monte-Carlo.

Ce petit palace de charme, empreint d'un air de Riviera italienne reçoit le beau monde depuis 1930, et sa popularité se perpétue aujourd'hui. Des couleurs vives égayent les chambres, et les 4 restaurants proposent des cuisines aux saveurs différentes. Sa plage privée et la piscine olympique rendent cet endroit magique encore plus irrésistible. Grâce au Resort de la Société des Bains de Mer, les hôtes profiteront également du Country Club et de ses 23 courts de tennis, du Golf Club (parcours à 18 trous), des Thermes Marins ainsi que du Sporting Monte-Carlo.

Dieses im Stil der italienischen Riviera eingerichtete Hotel beherbergt seit 1930 die Reichen und Schönen dieser Welt, und sein Charme ist bis heute ungebrochen. Einzigartige Farbkombinationen zieren die Zimmer und jedes der 4 vorzüglichen Restaurants bietet eine andere Geschmacksrichtung. Der Privatstrand und der olympische Pool machen diesen Ort unwiderstehlich. Dank des Resorts der Société des Bains de Mer können die Gäste im Country Club Tennis spielen und den Golf Club, die "Thermes Marins" und den Sportclub Monte-Carlo benutzen.

Our inspector loved: *The bedrooms, which all overlook the Mediterranean Sea with panoramic views.*

Directions: Nice Airport > 25km.

Web: www.johansens.com/montecarlo
E-mail: resort@sbm.mc
Tel: +377 92 16 25 25
Fax: +377 92 16 26 26

Price Guide:
(Continental breakfast €26)
single/double/twin €255–610
junior suite €390–765
suite €715–1,835

The Netherlands

Hotel location shown in red (hotel) or purple (spa hotel) with page number

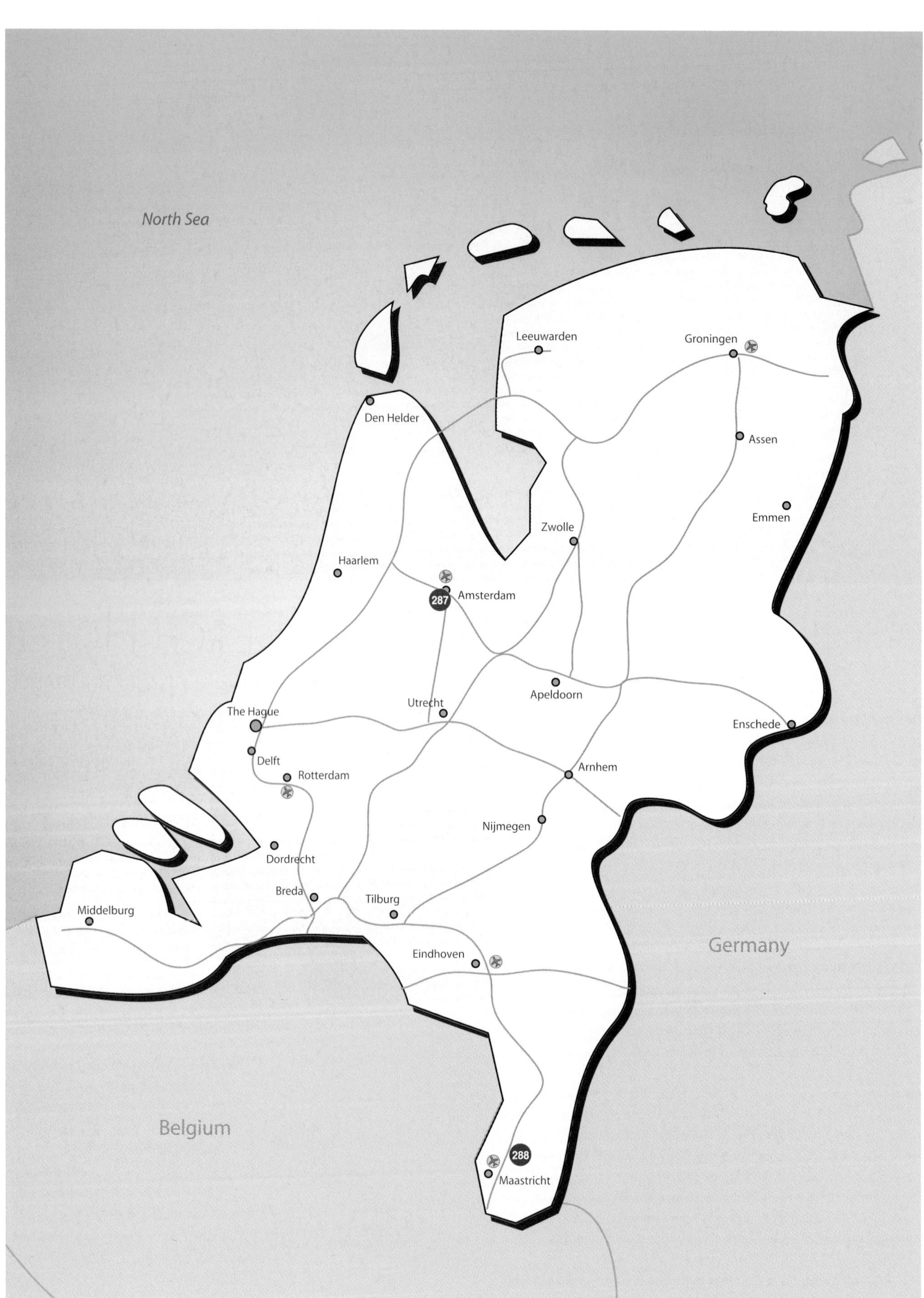

Ambassade Hotel

HERENGRACHT 341, 1016 AZ AMSTERDAM, THE NETHERLANDS

The Ambassade is a most attractive hotel in the heart of Amsterdam. Originally 10 separate houses, each the home of a wealthy merchant on the Herengracht ("the Gentlemen's Canal"), the hotel has been converted into one building which retains all the erstwhile interior architecture and the external façades. Over the years, numerous authors have stayed at this hotel; an extensive collection of signed books can be found in the library. A special Internet office is available free of charge. The hotel's luxurious float and massage centre Koan Float, is situated further along the street.

L'Ambassade est un hôtel très attrayant dans le coeur d'Amsterdam. Originellement 10 maisons séparées, chacune étant la maison d'un riche marchand de Herengracht (Le "Canal des Messieurs"), l'hôtel a été converti en un bâtiment qui comprend toute l'architecture intérieure ancienne et les façades extérieures d'époque. De nombreux auteurs ont visité cet hôtel, et on peut admirer une collection de livres signés dans la bibliothèque. Un bureau avec service Internet gratuit est disponible. Le centre de massage luxueux Koan Float, appartenant à l'hôtel, est situé à proximité.

Dieses attraktive Hotel im Herzen von Amsterdam bestand ursprünglich aus 10 separaten Häusern, jedes im Besitz eines reichen Kaufmanns auf der Herengracht ("Herrenkanal"). Das Hotel wurde zu einem einzigen Gebäude umgebaut, wobei das ehemalige Interieur sowie die Architektur und die Außenfassaden erhalten blieben. Viele Schriftsteller waren hier zu Gast, und in der Bibliothek findet man eine Sammlung signierter Bücher. Ein Büro mit gratis Internetzugang steht zur Verfügung. Das hoteleigene, luxuriöse Float- und Massagezentrum Koan Float befindet sich ein paar Häuser weiter.

Our inspector loved: *Breakfast in the elegant dining room overlooking the canal.*

Directions: Schiphol Airport > take a taxi, train or car to the centre of the city.

Web: www.johansens.com/ambassade
E-mail: info@ambassade-hotel.nl
Tel: +31 20 5550222
Fax: +31 20 5550277

Price Guide:
(breakfast €16)
single €158-165
double €188-195
suite €260-340

Château St Gerlach

JOSEPH CORNELI ALLÉE 1, 6301 KK VALKENBURG A/D GEUL, MAASTRICHT, THE NETHERLANDS

Directions: A2 > Exit 51, towards Valkenburg > A79 towards Valkenburg > Aachen > Exit 3 towards Valkenburg. The château is near to Maastricht Airport.

Web: www.johansens.com/stgerlach
E-mail: reservations@stgerlach.chateauhotels.nl
Tel: +31 43 608 88 88
Fax: +31 43 604 28 83

Price Guide:
(room only)
double €230
suite €270

This enchanting hotel lies between the hills of the picturesque Geul River Valley, and the owner has searched for furniture to decorate its wonderful rooms from all over Europe. A well-stocked cosy bar opens until late, and the restaurant and bistro are located within the original château, which has been restored to its past glory. The inner courtyard and fountain provide a quiet spot for relaxation, and walks within the grounds are thoroughly recommended as is a visit to the excellent indoor pool and beauty spa.

Cet hôtel enchanteur est niché entre les collines de la pittoresque vallée de la Geul, et pour les pièces, le propriétaire a cherché des meubles dans toute l'Europe. Le bar confortable bien fourni est ouvert tard, et le restaurant et bistro sont situés au sein du château d'origine qui a été restauré en accord avec sa gloire passée. La cour intérieure et la fontaine procurent un endroit tranquille où se détendre, et se promener dans le parc est hautement recommandé tout comme l'est une visite à l'excellente piscine couverte ou au centre de beauté.

Dieses zauberhafte Hotel liegt in den Hügeln des malerischen Geul-Tales. Der Besitzer sammelte die Einrichtung für die herrlichen Zimmer in ganz Europa. Eine gutbestückte, gemütliche Bar ist bis spät in die Nacht geöffnet, und Restaurant und Bistro befinden sich im ursprünglichen Château, dessen einstige Pracht durch Renovierung wiederhergestellt wurde. Der ruhige Innenhof mit Springbrunnen ist der ideale Ort zur Entspannung, und man kann auf dem Grundstück spazieren gehen oder das Hallenbad und die Schönheitsfarm besuchen.

Our inspector loved: *The stunning beamed restaurant and bistro located in the old château.*

NORWAY

Hotel location shown in red (hotel) or purple (spa hotel) with page number

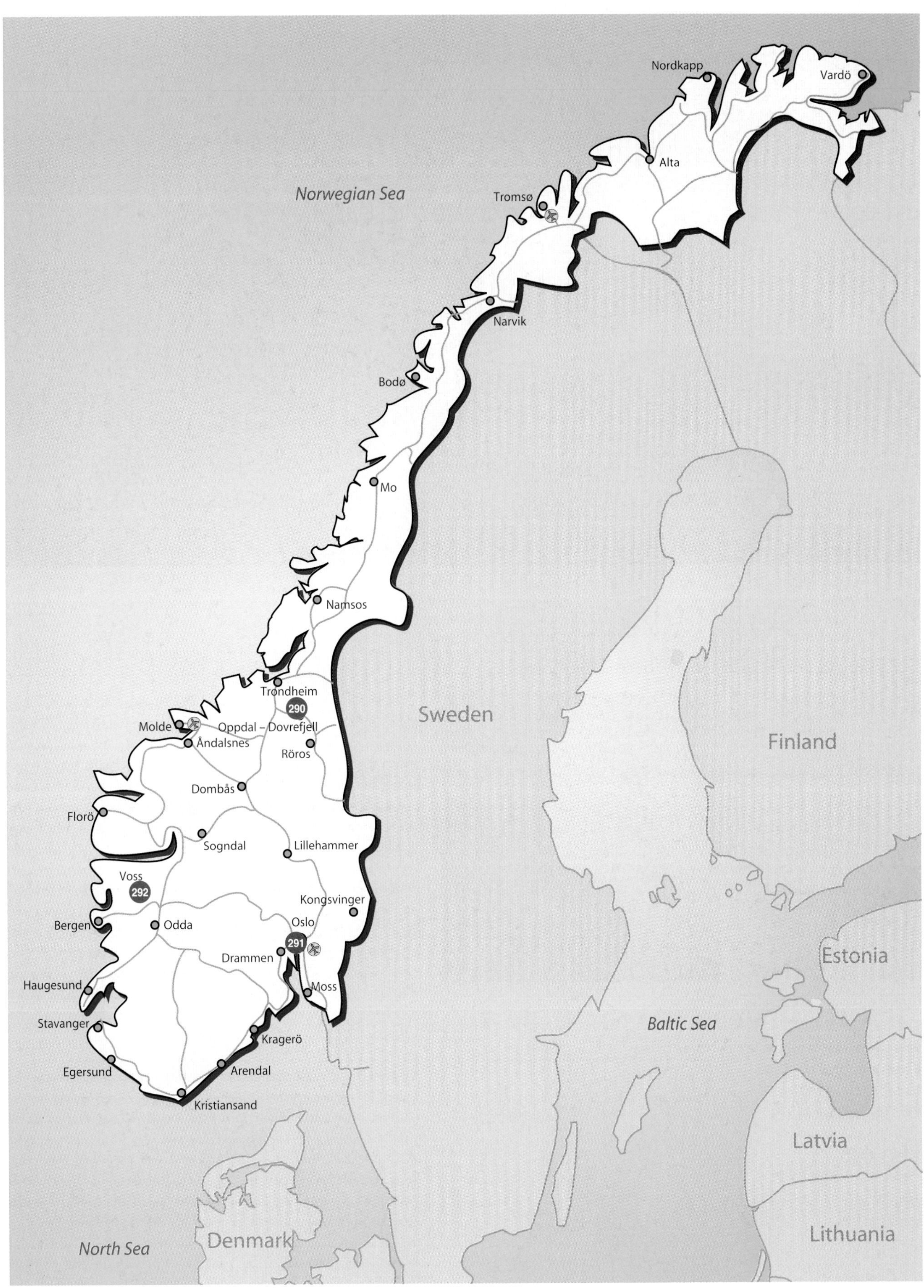

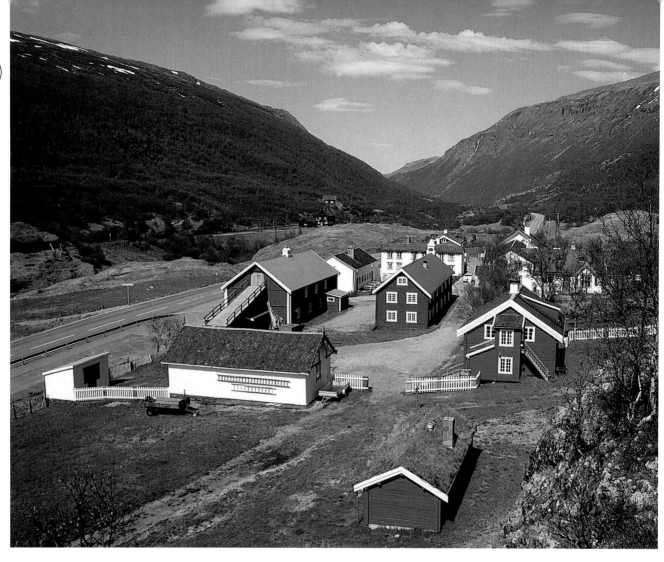

Kongsvold Fjeldstue

De Historiske Hotel

DOVREFJELL, 7340 OPPDAL, NORWAY

Situated amid outstanding scenery in the Dovrefjell National Park, this charming mountain lodge consists of 20 well-preserved historic buildings, furnished with an interesting collection of antique furniture. Numerous old photographs and paintings in the peaceful public rooms illustrate the history of the property. Gastronomic delights are served in the à la carte restaurant, which offers views of the beautiful surroundings. Guests can visit the Park and Alpine Garden, go on a Musk ox safari or enjoy activities such as hiking, cycling and riding.

Situé au sein du Parc National du Dovrefjell, ce charmant hôtel de montagne est constitué de 20 bâtiments historiques bien préservés, meublés avec une collection intéressante d'antiquités. De nombreuses vieilles photographies et peintures exposées dans les paisibles salles communes illustrent l'histoire de la propriété. Les plaisirs gastronomiques sont servis à la carte au restaurant, qui a vue sur les beaux environs. Les hôtes peuvent visiter le Parc et le Jardin Alpin, aller en safari au boeuf musqué ou apprécier des activités telles que randonnée pédestre, cycliste ou équestre.

Inmitten der atemberaubenden Landschaft des Dovrefjell Nationalparks liegt diese charmante historische Berg-Lodge, die aus 20 perfekt erhaltenen und mit einer interessanten Sammlung antiker Möbel ausgestatteten Gebäuden besteht. Alte Fotografien und Bilder in den ruhigen Aufenthaltsräumen erzählen die Geschichte der Lodge. Im à la carte Restaurant werden bei herrlicher Sicht auf die Umgebung gastronomische Köstlichkeiten serviert. Die Gäste können den "Alpengarten" erforschen, auf Moschusochsen-Safari gehen oder wandern, radfahren und reiten.

***Our inspector loved:** The fabulous scenery.*

Directions: E6 from Trondheim/Oslo.

Web: www.johansens.com/kongsvoldfjeldstue
E-mail: post@kongsvold.no
Tel: +47 72 40 43 40
Fax: +47 72 40 43 41

Price Guide:
rooms from NOK595

Hotel Bastion

SKIPPERGATEN 7, 0152 OSLO, NORWAY

Oslo's only privately owned boutique hotel, the Bastion is located in the old town, just a few minutes' walk from the heart of the city. With a unique style and atmosphere its many works of art are complemented by contemporary furniture and wooden floors. All suites have Jacuzzi baths, electronically adjustable beds and Internet access. Afternoon tea or an evening drink can be enjoyed in the intimate lounge with its fireplace. There is also a small fitness centre.

Le seul hôtel boutique privé d'Oslo, le Bastion est situé dans la vieille ville, à quelques minutes seulement du centre ville. Avec son style et son atmosphère uniques, ses nombreuses œuvres d'art sont complétées par un mobilier contemporain et des parquets. Toutes les suites disposent de jacuzzis, de lits positionnables électroniquement et d'accès à l'Internet. Thés l'après-midi ou un verre le soir peuvent être dégustés près des cheminées du salon intime. Il existe également un petit centre de remise en forme.

Oslos einziges privat geführtes Boutiquehotel befindet sich in der Altstadt, nur ein paar Schritte vom Herzen der Stadt entfernt. Stil und Atmosphäre sind einzigartig, und die zahlreichen Kunstwerke werden durch zeitgenössisches Mobiliar und Holzböden ergänzt. Alle Suiten bieten Whirlpoolbäder, elektronisch verstellbare Betten und Internetzugang. Nachmittagskaffee oder ein abendlicher Drink werden im gemütlichen Aufenthaltsraum mit seinem offenen Kamin serviert. Ein kleines Fitnesszentrum steht zur Verfügung.

Our inspector loved: *Afternoon tea by the fireplace in the intimate lounge.*

Directions: Old Oslo centre.

Web: www.johansens.com/bastion
E-mail: booking@hotelbastion.no
Tel: +47 22 47 77 00
Fax: +47 22 47 77 99

Price Guide:
single NOK690–1,245
double/twin NOK990–1,495

Fleischers Hotel

De Historiske Hotel

5700 VOSS, NORWAY

Directions: Bergen > E16 > Voss.

Web: www.johansens.com/fleischers
E-mail: hotel@fleischers.no
Tel: +47 56 52 05 00
Fax: +47 56 52 05 01

Price Guide:
single NOK1,125
double/twin NOK1,490–1,690

This grand hotel is set in a superb position, overlooking the lake. The façade, with its towers and pointed dormer windows, is reminiscent of Switzerland. Built in 1889 and still run by the same family, the hotel has been discreetly modernised without losing its original charm. There is a warm ambience in the foyer with its convivial and elegant salons. Delicious food including local fish and Norwegian specialities is served in the restaurant with its warm colour scheme.

Ce grand hôtel est situé idéalement au dessus du lac. La façade, avec ses tours et ses lucarnes pointues qui sont des reminiscences suisses. Construit en 1889 et toujours tenu par la même famille, l'hôtel a été modernisé intelligemment sans perdre son charme originel. Il y a une ambiance chaleureuse dans le salon avec ses salons amicaux et élégants. Le restaurant, qui se caractérise par des couleurs chaudes, propose une cuisine délicieuse, avec notamment du poisson de la région et des spécialités norvégiennes.

Dieses Grand Hotel hat eine herrliche Lage mit Aussicht über den See. Die Fassade mit ihren Türmen und spitzen Giebelfenstern erinnert an die Schweiz. 1889 erbaut und immer noch von der gleichen Familie geführt, wurde das Hotel umsichtig renoviert, ohne seinen ursprünglichen Charme zu verlieren. Das Foyer strahlt mit seinen freundlichen und eleganten Salons ein gemütliches Ambiente aus. Das Restaurant ist in warmen Farben gehalten und serviert köstliche norwegische Spezialitäten und Fisch der Region.

Our inspector loved: *Fleischers' fabulous breakfast buffet enjoyed at a window table with views of the fjord.*

PORTUGAL

Hotel location shown in red (hotel) or purple (spa hotel) with page number

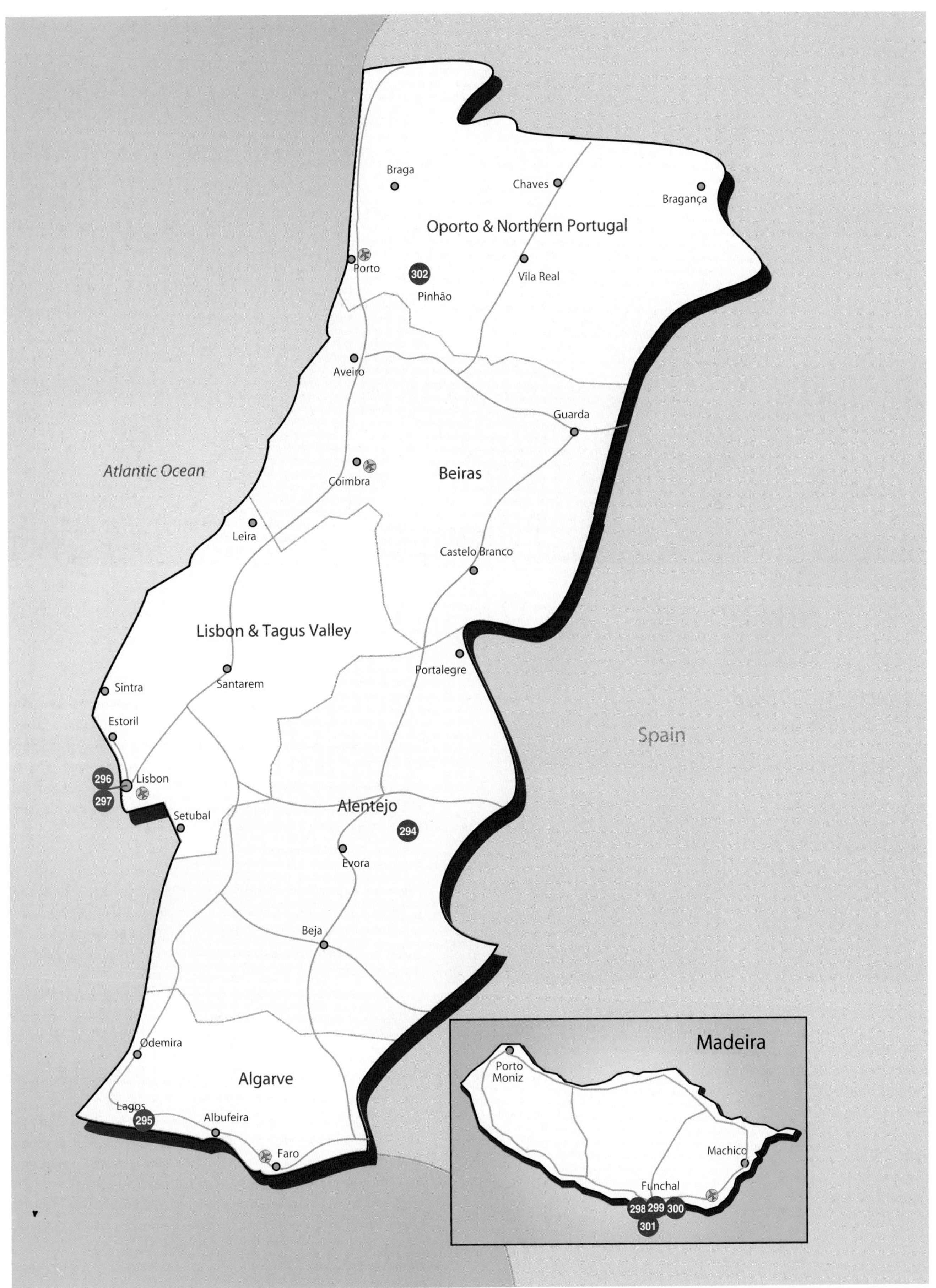

PORTUGAL / ALENTEJO (REDONDO)

Convento de São Paulo

ALDEIA DA SERRA, 7170 –120 REDONDO, PORTUGAL

Directions: Lisbon > A6 > Evora/Estremoz > Redondo.

Web: www.johansens.com/conventodesaopaulo
E-mail: hotelconvspaulo@mail.telepac.pt
Tel: +351 266 989160
Fax: +351 266 989167

Price Guide:
single €145–167
double/twin €180–195
suite €205–235

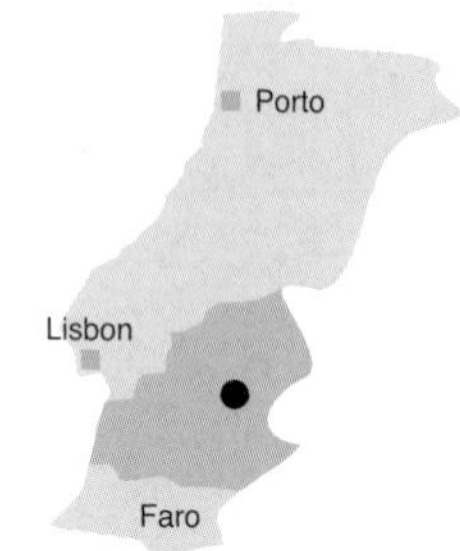

Situated between Estremoz and Redondo in the Alentejo, Convento de São Paulo, "the Monastery of Saint Paul", was constructed in 1182 by monks seeking a tranquil location to pray. Many vestiges of the 12th century have remained; the original chapel and church are popular venues for weddings and special events, whilst the bedrooms are the old chambers of the monks. Guests dine beneath the splendour of 18th-century fresco paintings in the stylish restaurant. The convent also has a collection of 50,000 tiles.

Situé dans l'Alentejo, entre Estremoz et Redondo, le Convento de São Paulo fût construit en 1182 par des moines en quête d'endroit tranquille pour prier. De nombreux vestiges du XIIe siècle ont été conservés; la chapelle et l'église originales sont des endroits populaires pour les mariages ou les occasions spéciales, et les anciennes cellules des moines servent aujourd'hui de chambres. Les hôtes dînent sous de somptueuses fresques du XVIIIe siècle, dans l'élégante salle à manger. Le couvent aussi dispose d'une collection de 50 000 carreaux.

Convento de São Paulo, "das Kloster des Heiligen Paulus", liegt zwischen Estremoz und Redondo und wurde 1182 von Mönchen erbaut – sie suchten einen ruhigen Platz, um zu beten. Viele Spuren aus dem 12. Jahrhundert sind hier erhalten geblieben: Die ursprüngliche Kapelle und die Kirche sind bei Hochzeiten und feierlichen Anlässen sehr begehrt, und die alten Kammern der Mönche sind die heutigen Gästezimmer. Im eleganten Restaurant diniert man unter herrlichen Fresken aus dem 18. Jahrhundert. Das Kloster besitzt auch eine Sammlung von 50.000 Kacheln.

Our inspector loved: *This peaceful haven - just the place to recharge your batteries.*

ROMANTIK HOTEL VIVENDA MIRANDA

PORTO DE MÓS, 8600 LAGOS, PORTUGAL

Vivenda Miranda is a delightful hotel, with Moorish influences evident in its architecture. It is nestled on a bluff above the sea, surrounded by a subtropical garden, and with captivating views from the terrace. Hearty breakfasts and light lunches anticipate the fantastic gourmet meal served in the evening, accompanied by fine wines. Tennis facilities are nearby, mountain bikes are available and water sports can be practised at the Marina. The hotel has its own PGA Golf Professional and the 8 golf courses in the vicinity offer superb green fee reductions.

Le Vivenda Miranda est un hôtel délicieux, avec, dans son architecture, une influence maure évidente. Il est niché sur une avancée au dessus de la mer, entouré d'un jardin subtropical, et bénéficie de vues captivantes de la terrasse. Des petits-déjeuners copieux et des déjeuners légers sont un préambule au fantastique repas gastronomique accompagné de vins fins servi le soir. Des courts de tennis sont tout proches, des VTT sont disponibles et les sports aquatiques peuvent être pratiqués à la marina. L'hôtel a sa propre PGA Golf Professional (Association des Professionnels du Golf) et les 8 parcours de golf du voisinage offrent de très bonnes réductions.

Dieses auf einer Klippe über dem Meer gelegene einladende Hotel ist von einem subtropischen Garten umgeben und bietet eine atemberaubende Sicht von der Terrasse. Maurische Einflüsse zeigen sich deutlich in der Architektur. Ein herzhaftes Frühstück und leichtes Mittagessen bereiten auf ein Feinschmeckermahl und erlesene Weine am Abend vor. Gäste können Tennis spielen, Mountainbiken und Wassersport betreiben. Das Hotel verfügt über seinen eigenen PGA Golf Professional, und 8 nahegelegene Golfplätze bieten reduzierte Green-Gebühren.

Our inspector loved: *Relaxing on the terrace, enjoying the view over the ocean.*

Directions: Faro Airport > IPI > Lagos > singposted.

Web: www.johansens.com/vivendamiranda
E-mail: reservations@vivendamiranda.pt
Tel: +351 282 763222
Fax: +351 282 760342

Price Guide:
single €95–130
double/twin €134–184
suite €174–290

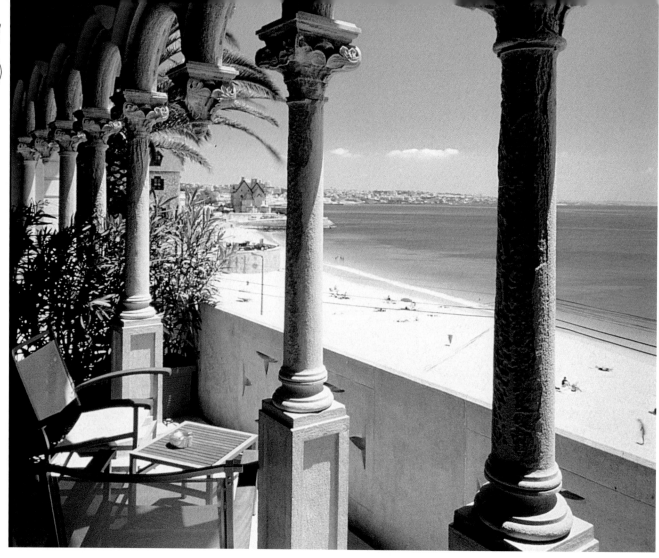

ALBATROZ PALACE, LUXURY SUITES

The Leading Small Hotels of the World

RUA FREDERICO AROUCA, 100, 27570-353 CASCAIS, LISBON, PORTUGAL

This carefully restored former royal summer retreat is situated on the cliffs above Conceição beach in the charming fishing village of Cascais. Sheer indulgence is reflected by the elegant décor featuring antique and modern furnishings. The 4 luxurious rooms and 2 suites boast sea views and with Albatroz Hotel a few metres away guests may dine in the locally renowned restaurant and swim in the hotel's pool with panoramic views of the bay below. Golf and sightseeing can be arranged. Guests can be picked up from the airport in a private taxi with English-speaking driver (€50).

Cet ancien retrait royal restauré est situé sur les falaises au-dessus de la plage de Conceição au village de Cascais. Une ambiance d'indulgence est reflétée dans le décor élégant avec des ameublements anciens et modernes exquis. Les 4 chambres et les 2 suites s'enorgueillissent d'une vue sur la mer, et Albatroz Hotel étant à quelques mètres, les hôtes peuvent passer des soirées dans son restaurant renommé et nager dans sa piscine avec des vues panoramiques. Golf et visites touristiques peuvent être organisés. Un service de taxi avec un chauffeur qui parle l'anglais, est disponible pour chercher les hotes de l'aéroport (€50).

Diese restaurierte ehemalige königliche Sommerresidenz liegt in den Klippen über dem Strand von Conceição im Fischerdorf Cascais. Das elegante Interieur ist mit herrlichen Antiquitäten und exquisitem modernen Mobiliar gestaltete. Die 4 luxuriösen Zimmer und 2 Suiten haben Meerblick, und das nur ein paar Meter entfernte Albatroz Hotel bietet ein beliebtes Restaurant und einen Swimmingpool mit Panoramablick auf die Bucht. Golf und Besichtigungstouren können arrangiert werden. Gäste können im Privattaxi mit englischsprachigem Fahrer vom Flughafen abgeholt werden (€50).

Our inspector loved: *The sheer luxury and ocean views.*

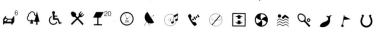

Directions: 24 km from the centre of Lisbon. 15 km from Sintra. 4 km from Estoril. 24km from Lissabon. From the airport take the A5 towards Cascais.

Web: www.johansens.com/albatroz
E-mail: albatroz@mail.telepac.pt
Tel: +351 21 484 73 80
Fax: +351 21 484 48 27

Price Guide:
single €315
double €362
suite €509

Solar do Castelo

RUA DAS COZINHAS 2, 1100–181 LISBON, PORTUGAL

Surrounded by the walls of Lisbon's St George's Castle, this historic building has been carefully transformed into a charming, contemporary hotel. Many of the original features have been brought back to life by architect Vasco Massapina, such as the elaborate design of the main façade and typical Portuguese Pombal tiling with its star and flower pattern. Guests can explore the castle grounds and visit numerous restaurants, shops and historical sites in the vicinity.

A Lisbonne, cerné par les murs du château de San Jorge, ce monument historique a été soigneusement transformé en un charmant hôtel contemporain. Pour la plupart, ses caractéristiques originelles, telles que la façade principale raffinée et ses céramiques Pombal si typiquement portugaises aux motifs floraux et d'étoiles, ont été "ranimées" par l'architecte Vasco Massapina. Les hôtes peuvent visiter les terres du château ainsi que les nombreux restaurants, magasins et sites historiques du voisinage.

Dieses von den Mauern der St.-Georgs-Burg umgebene historische Gebäude wurde sorgfältig in ein freundliches, zeitgenössisches Hotel umgewandelt, wobei der Architekt Vasco Massapina viele der Originalmerkmale zum Leben erweckte, so z.B. die kunstvoll verzierte Fassade und die typischen portugiesischen Fliesen im Pombal-Muster mit Sternen und Blumen. Die Gäste können das Schlossgelände erkunden und zahlreiche Restaurants, Geschäfte und historische Stätten in der Umgebung besuchen.

***Our inspector loved:** The calming décor and friendly service.*

Directions: Lisbon Airport > taxi to hotel.

Web: www.johansens.com/solardocastelo
E-mail: solar.castelo@heritage.pt
Tel: +351 218 870 909
Fax: +351 218 870 907

Price Guide:
(breakfast €12.50)
single €170–295
double €182–330

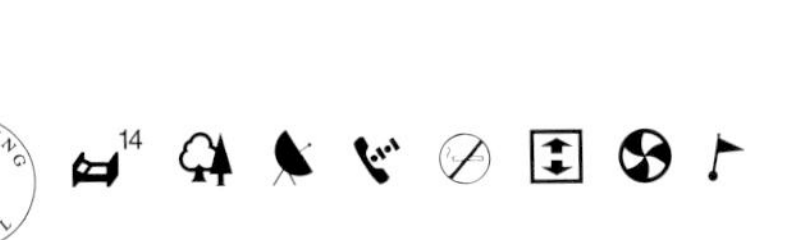

Quinta da Bela Vista

CAMINHO DO AVISTA NAVIOS 4, 9000 FUNCHAL, MADEIRA, PORTUGAL

It is a joy to stay in this traditional house, with its tall windows and green shutters, overlooking Funchal Bay and surrounded by exotic gardens. The interiors are a blend of sophistication and rich, classical furnishings. Guests enjoy their apéritifs in the cheerful bar or on the sunny terraces before choosing between the elegant restaurant serving fine food and the best wines or the more informal dining room.

Surplombant la baie de Funchal et entourée de jardins exotiques, c'est un vrai plaisir de séjourner dans cette maison traditionnelle, avec ses grandes fenêtres et ses volets verts. L'intérieur est un mélange de sophistication et de richesse, avec des meubles classiques. Les visiteurs dégusteront leur apéritif dans le bar animé ou sur les terraces ensoleillées avant de se décider entre le restaurant élégant servant des plats fins et les meilleurs vins ou la salle à manger plus informelle.

Ein Aufenthalt in diesem traditionellen Haus mit seinen großen Fenstern und grünen Fensterläden, das auf die Bucht von Funchal blickt und von exotischen Gärten umgeben ist, bleibt unvergessen. Die Räume sind höchst elegant, üppig und klassisch eingerichtet. Die Gäste können in der gemütlichen Bar oder auf der sonnigen Terrasse einen Apéritif nehmen, bevor sie sich im informellen Speisesaal oder dem eleganten Restaurant von feinen Speisen und edlen Weinen verwöhnen lassen.

Our inspector loved: *This elegant quinta with excellent service, set in lovely gardens.*

Directions: Main road > Rua do Dr Pita.

Web: www.johansens.com/quintadabelavista
E-mail: info@belavistamadeira.com
Tel: +351 291 706400
Fax: +351 291 706411

Price Guide:
single €118–209
double/twin €157–281
suite €299–339

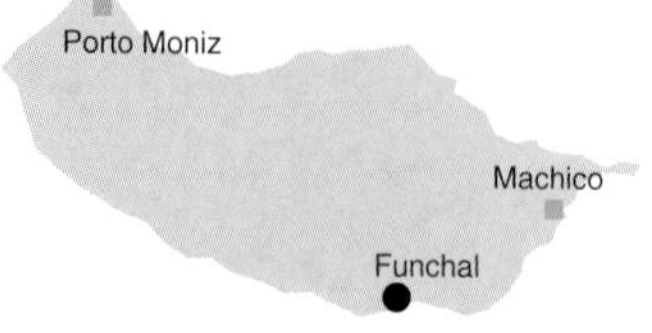

Quinta das Vistas Palace Gardens

CAMINHO DE SANTO ANTONIO 52, 9000-187 FUNCHAL, MADEIRA, PORTUGAL

Situated on the brow of a hill this 5-star hotel has magnificent views of Funchal, the Atlantic and the surrounding mountains. With an emphasis on personal detail guests check in within the relaxed atmosphere of the beautifully decorated bedrooms, where a traditional Madeiran gift awaits. The main restaurant serves creative dishes combining local produce and exotic herbs and spices. Visitors can enjoy Royal Tea on the veranda, swim in the indoor or outdoor pools and relax in the gardens or the health club.

Situé sur les bords d'une colline, cet hôtel cinq étoiles a une vue magnifique sur Funchal, l'Atlantique et les montagnes environnantes. Les hôtes sont accueillis dans des chambres superbement décorées bénéficiant d' une atmosphère relaxante où les attend un cadeau typiquement madeiran. Le restaurant principal sert des plats créatifs qui combinent produits locaux et herbes et épices exotiques. Les visiteurs peuvent déguster un Thé Royal sous la véranda, nager dans les piscines couverte et extérieure et se détendre dans les jardins ou le club de remise en forme.

Dieses auf einem Hügel gelegene 5-Sterne-Hotel bietet eine herrliche Sicht auf Funchal, den Atlantik und die umliegenden Berge. Die Atmosphäre ist entspannt und die Betonung liegt auf persönlichen Details – Gäste erwartet bei der Ankunft ein traditionelles Geschenk in den hübsch gestalteten Zimmern. Im Hauptrestaurant werden kreative Speisen aus einheimischen Zutaten und exotischen Kräutern und Gewürzen serviert, auf der Veranda kann man „Royal Tea" genießen, im Hallenbad oder Außenpool schwimmen oder im Health Club entspannen.

Our inspector loved: *The beautiful dining areas and impeccable service.*

Directions: A short taxi ride from the airport.

Web: www.johansens.com/quintadasvistas
E-mail: info@charminghotelsmadeira.com
Tel: +351 291 750 007
Fax: +351 291 750 017

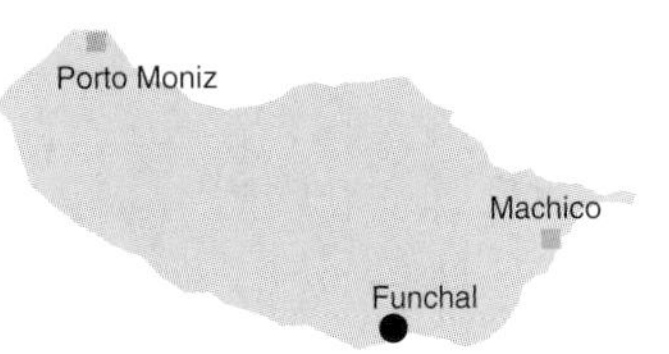

Price Guide:
single €130–240
double €170–375
suite €220–820

QUINTA DO ESTREITO

RUA JOSÉ JOAQUIM DA COSTA, ESTREITO DE CÂMARA DE LOBOS, FUNCHAL, 9325–034 MADEIRA, PORTUGAL

Tranquil luxury and exceptional beauty are manifest in this elegant hotel, which is beautifully decorated with great attention to detail. Friendly, discreet staff ensures superb personal service within a homely and intimate atmosphere. The subtly furnished bedrooms are a haven of peace with sweeping views of the ocean and surrounding countryside. Creative meals are served using fresh local produce, and guests can explore the lovingly landscaped gardens, olive groves and vineyards. Island tours are available.

Un luxe tranquille et une beauté exceptionnelle sont manifestes dans cet hôtel élégant, superbement décoré. Un personnel amical et discret assure un service personnel dans une atmosphère chaleureuse et intime. Les chambres subtilement meublées sont un havre de paix avec vue panoramique sur l'océan et la campagne environnante. Une cuisine novatrice, créée à partir de produits locaux, est servie et les hôtes peuvent explorer les charmants jardins aménagés, les oliveraies et les vignobles. Des tours de l'île sont disponibles.

Dieses elegante, mit viel Liebe zum Detail eingerichtete Hotel bietet Ruhe, Luxus und eine außergewöhnlich schöne Umgebung. Das freundliche, unaufdringliche Personal garantiert hervorragenden Service in heimeliger, familiärer Atmosphäre. Die hübschen Zimmer haben herrliche Sicht auf das Meer und die umliegende Landschaft, und die Gäste können kreative, mit frischesten Zutaten zubereitete Speisen genießen. Die gepflegten Gärten, Olivenhaine und Weinberge laden zum Spaziergang ein, und Inselexkursionen können organisiert werden.

Our inspector loved: *The exquisite lavender garden.*

Directions: Funchal Airport > taxi to hotel.

Web: www.johansens.com/quintadoestreito
E-mail: quintaestreito@charminghotelsmadeira.com
Tel: +351 291 910530
Fax: +351 291 910549

Price Guide:
single €150–190
double €190–240

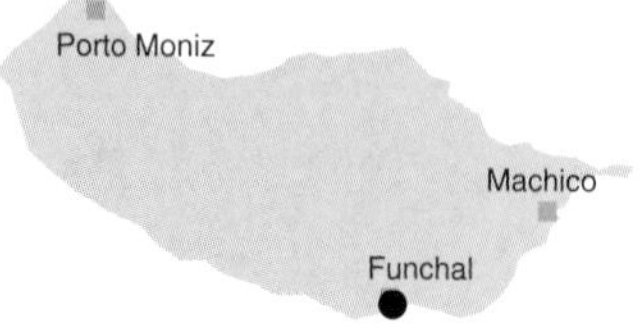

Quinta do Monte

CAMINHO DO MONTE 192, 9050-288 FUNCHAL, MADEIRA, PORTUGAL

Surrounded by lush gardens and fresh mountain air the hotel is in the heart of the historic leafy village of Monte. Tranquil and elegant, the manor house has been beautifully restored and features original wood floors, traditional Madeiran antique furniture and Persian carpets. A Turkish bath spa and Jacuzzi complement the indoor pool. Rooms have views across the sea, the hillside to Funchal, and the grounds, which feature the original chapel of the Quinta do Monte and many World Heritage plant species.

Entouré de jardins luxuriants et bénéficiant de l'air frais de la montagne, l'hôtel est au cœur du village historique entouré d'arbres de Monte. Elégant et tranquille, le manoir a été superbement restauré et garde ses particularités d'origine telles que planchers, mobilier madère traditionnels et tapis persans. Des bains turcs et un centre de remise en forme complètent la piscine couverte. Les chambres ont vue sur la mer, les collines de Funchal, et les terres où se situe l'originale chapelle de la Quinta do Monte ainsi que nombreuses espèces de plantes qui sont déclarées "héritage universel".

Umgeben von üppigen Gärten und frischer Bergluft liegt dieses Hotel im Herzen des historischen Dorfes Monte. Das ruhige und elegante Herrenhaus wurde wundervoll restauriert und ist mit ursprünglichen Holzböden, traditionellen Madeiramöbeln und persischen Teppichen geschmückt. Die Zimmer blicken auf das Meer, Funchal und das Grundstück, auf dem die ursprüngliche Kapelle Quinta do Monte und zahlreiche geschützte Pflanzenarten zu finden sind. Dampfbad, Hallenbad und Fitnesszentrum sind vorhanden.

Our inspector loved: *The abundance of fresh air in this green environment.*

Directions: A 30-minute drive from the airport.

Web: www.johansens.com/quintadomonte
E-mail: info@quintadomonte.com
Tel: +351 291 780 100
Fax: +351 291 780 110

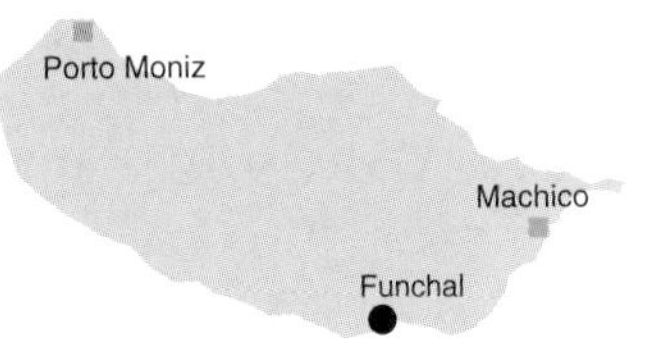

Price Guide:
single €135-175
double €170-250
suite €220-270

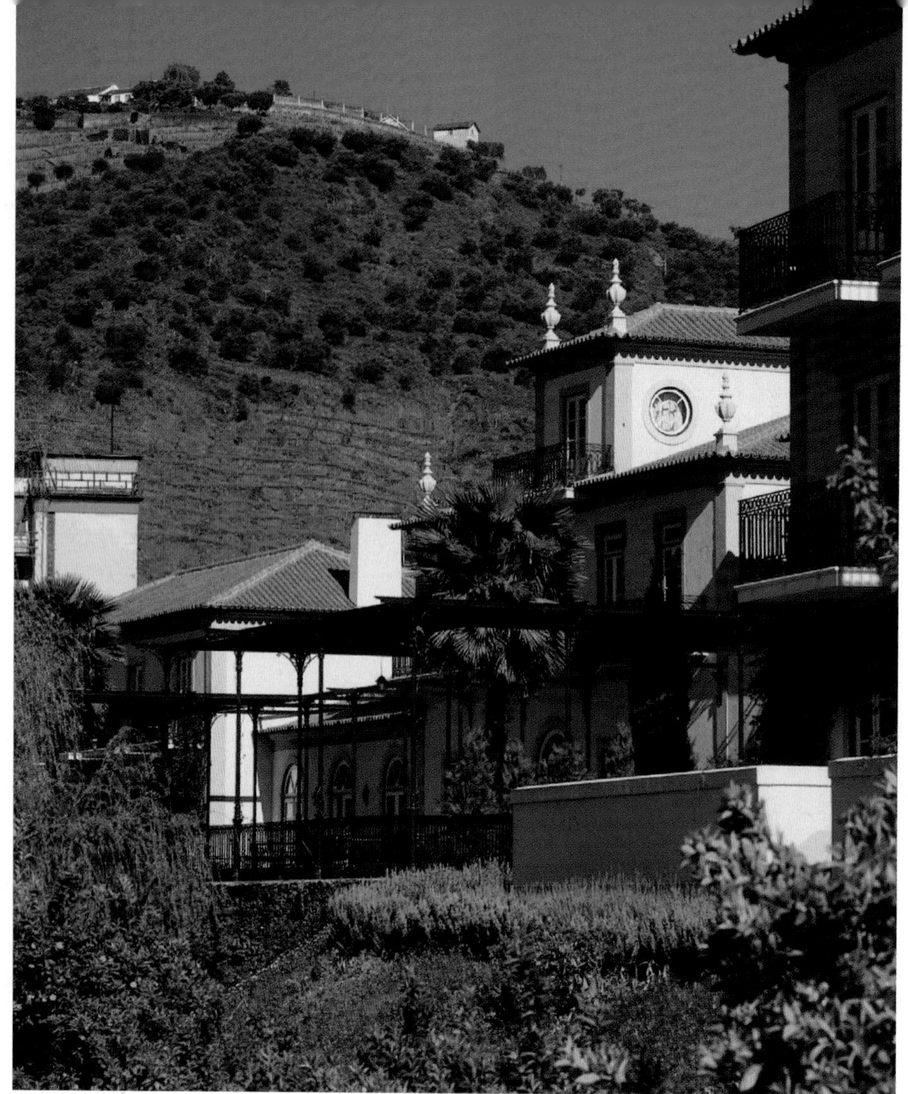

Vintage House Hotel

LUGAR DA PONTE, 5085-034 PINHÃO, PORTUGAL

Directions: From Porto > A4-IP4 > Vila Real > exit Mesão Frio/Régua > follow signs to Pinhão.

Web: www.johansens.com/vintagehouse
E-mail: vintagehouse@hotelvintagehouse.com
Tel: +351 254 730 230
Fax: +351 254 730 238

Price Guide:
single €103–149
double/twin €116–163
suite €198–298

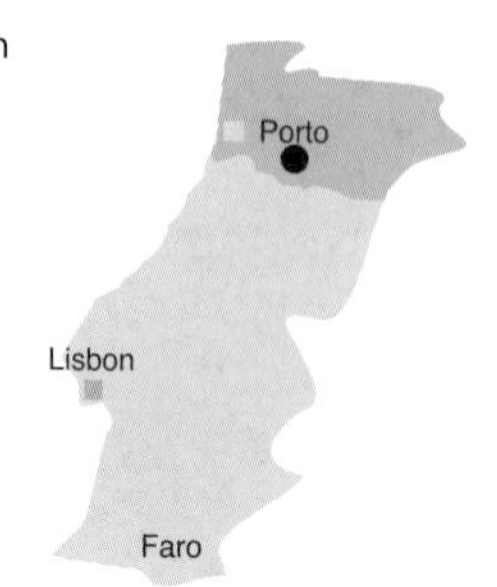

Steeped in history, this elegant hotel is situated on a former wine estate dating back to the 18th century, and takes its name from the surrounding Port vineyards. Today, the owners run specialist wine tasting courses for enthusiasts, and the bar is situated in the former Port wine lodge. The hotel has been refurbished to reflect the building's heritage and now manages to combine the character of a period property with modern comforts and facilities.

Ancré dans l'histoire, cet élégant hôtel est situé sur une ancienne exploitation viticole du XVIIIe siècle, et tient son nom des vignobles environnants de Porto. Aujourd'hui, les propriétaires organisent des cours de dégustation pour les passionnés, et le bar se trouve dans les anciennes "cuves". L'hôtel a été meublé pour refléter l'héritage du bâtiment et arrive maintenant à combiner le caractère de l'ancienne propriété avec le confort et facilités modernes.

Dieses elegante, geschichtsträchtige Hotel befindet sich auf einem ehemaligen Winzergut aus dem 18. Jahrhundert und bekam seinen Namen von den umliegenden Portweinbergen. Heute werden hier spezielle Weinkurse für Weinliebhaber abgehalten, und die Bar befindet sich im früheren Portweinhaus. Das Hotel wurde sorgfältig restauriert und spiegelt nun das Erbe und den einstigen Charakter des Hauses wider, wobei modernste Einrichtungen und Komfort geboten werden.

Our inspector loved: *The unique "wine academy".*

Spain

Hotel location shown in red (hotel) or purple (spa hotel) with page number

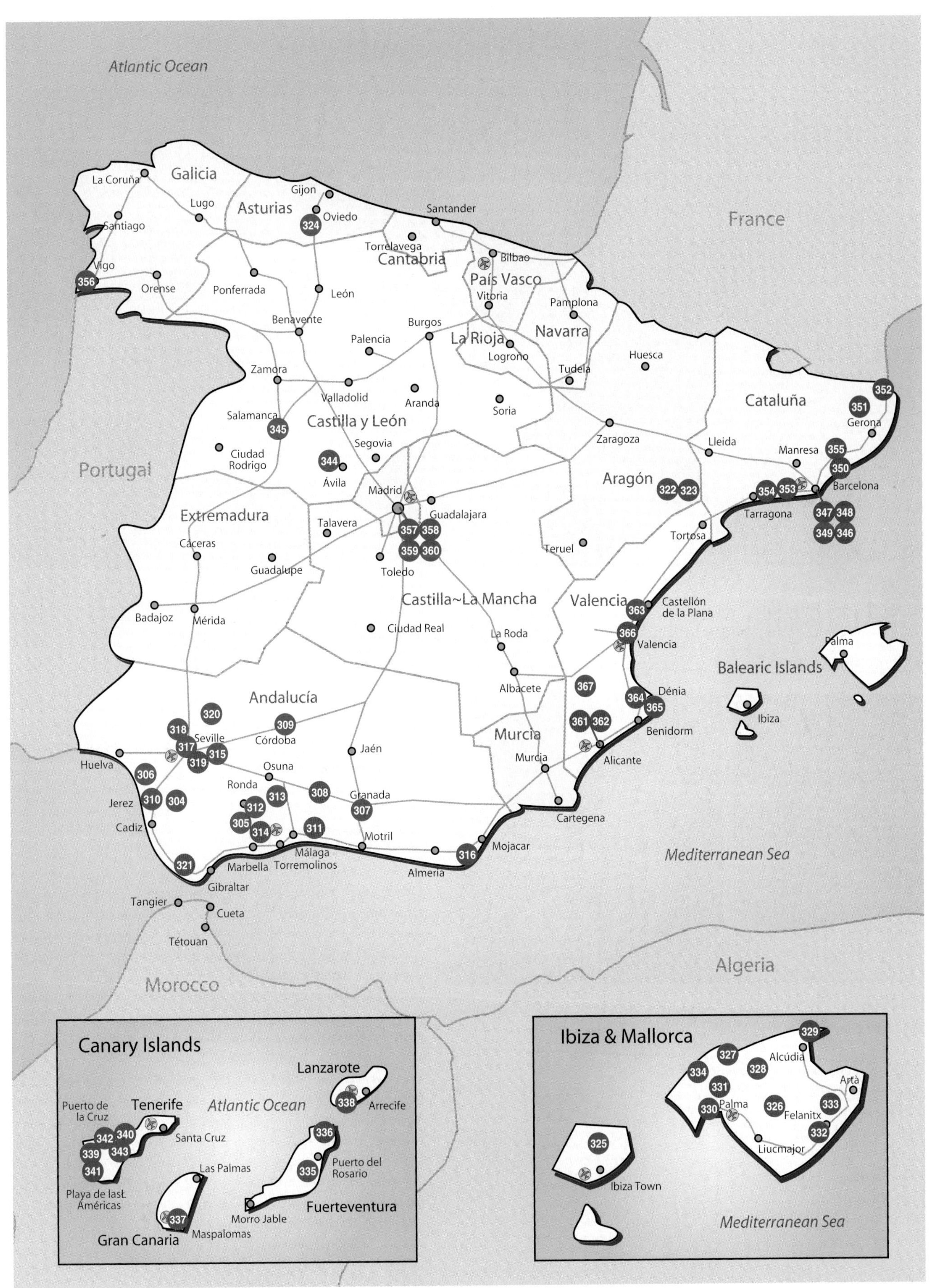

HACIENDA EL SANTISCAL

AVDA. EL SANTISCAL 129 (LAGO DE ARCOS), 11630 ARCOS DE LA FRONTERA, SPAIN

Directions: Sevilla > N1V to Jerez > N342 to Arcis de la Arcos de la Frontera > C372, take the first right to El Bosque > follow signs to the hotel.

Web: www.johansens.com/haciendaelsantiscal
E-mail: reservas@santiscal.com
Tel: +34 956 70 83 13
Fax: +34 956 70 82 68

Price Guide: (room only)
single €47.65-71.62
double/twin €64.68-99.39
suites €97.13-124.32

Surrounded by fields of sunflowers, this 15th-century manor house, exquisitely restored, offers glorious views of the lake and historic town of Arcos. A welcoming atmosphere envelopes the property as Señora Gallardo invites guests into her home to enjoy the ambience of a traditional Andalucían Hacienda. All rooms have been newly decorated. Traditional home-cooked dishes feature vegetables, olives and oranges grown in the Hacienda's own groves and gardens. A mobile phone is provided for the guests in each room.

Entouré de champs de tournesols, ce manoir du XVe siècle, restauré de façon exquise, offre des vues imprenables sur le lac et la ville historique d'Arcos. Une accueillante atmosphère caractérise la propriété, et Madame Gallardo invite les hôtes dans sa demeure afin de leur faire profiter de l'ambiance traditionnelle d'une Hacienda andalouse. Des plats traditionnels faits-maison sont composés des légumes, olives et oranges qui ont poussé dans le verger et le potager de la Hacienda. Un téléphone portable est mis à la disposition des clients dans chaque chambre.

Umgeben von Sonnenblumenfeldern bietet dieses perfekt restaurierte Herrenhaus aus dem 15. Jahrhundert herrliche Ausblicke auf den See und die historische Stadt Arcos. Eine herzliche Atmosphäre liegt über dem Anwesen und Señora Gallardo lädt ihre Gäste ein, das Ambiente einer typisch andalusischen Hazienda zu genießen. Für die traditionellen selbstgemachten Gerichte werden Gemüse, Oliven und Orangen aus den eigenen Hainen und Gärten verwendet. Die neu hergerichteten Zimmer sind mit Mobiltelefonen für die Gäste ausgestattet.

Our inspector loved: *The traditional Andalucían atmosphere and hospitality.*

Hotel Villa Padierna & Flamingos Golf Club

CTRA. DE CÁDIZ KM 166, 29679 MARBELLA, SPAIN

Reminiscent of an Italian villa, the hotel is surrounded by its own stunning golf course looking out across the Mediterranean and the mountains beyond. The impressive atrium complete with columns, statues, antique urns and a grand marble staircase, leads to a comfortable sitting room with doors opening onto a lovely sun-drenched terrace. Luxurious bedrooms are spacious with large bathrooms and windows and sumptuous furnishings. The manicured undulating lawns contain numerous trees, shrubs and flowers, providing colour and scent along with the breathtaking views.

Cet hôtel, qui rappelle une villa italienne, est entouré de son propre parcours de golf impressionnant, qui donne sur la Méditerranée et les montagnes lointaines. L'entrée avec des colonnes, statues, urnes anciennes et son grand escalier en marbre vous mène au salon confortable avec des portes donnant sur une terrasse ensoleillée. Les chambres luxueuses ont des meubles somptueux, grandes salles de bains et grandes fenêtres. Les jardins superbement entretenus avec toute une variété d'arbres, plantes et fleurs, fournissent des belles couleurs et du parfum ainsi que des vues imprenables.

Dieses an eine italienische Villa erinnernde Hotel liegt umgeben von seinem eigenen Golfplatz mit Blick auf das Mittelmeer und die Berge im Hintergrund. Vom Atrium mit seinen Säulen, Statuen, antiken Urnen und Marmortreppe gelangt man in einen bequemen Aufenthaltsraum, der auf eine sonnige Terrasse führt. Die luxuriösen, geräumigen Zimmer haben große Fenster und Bäder und sind stilvoll eingerichtet. Auf dem perfekt gepflegten, sanft hügeligen Rasen findet man zahlreiche Bäume, Sträucher und Blumen, die für Farbe und herrlichen Duft sorgen.

Our inspector loved: *Taking lunch on the terrace overlooking the green lawns, white birds dotting the lake and blue Mediterranean Sea.*

Directions: Málaga - Cádiz motorway > exit Marbella > N340 towards Cádiz > exit km166 > signs to Flamingos Golf Club and Hotel.

Web: www.johansens.com/villapadierna
E-mail: info@flamingos-golf.com
Tel: +34 952 88 91 50
Fax: +34 952 88 91 60

Price Guide:
(room only)
single €157-285
double €193-430
suite €277-1,200

  53  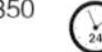 350     

El Cortijo de Los Mimbrales

CTRA DEL ROCIO - MATALASCAÑAS, KM 30, 21750 ALMONTE (HUELVA), SPAIN

Set on the border of the Doñana National Park, this former orange farm, which still retains 1300ha of orange groves, consists of rows of charmingly converted farmers' cottages. 6 self-contained cottages, held in rustic style with strong colours, have their own private gardens, whilst a further 21 bedrooms open onto the romantic and peaceful hotel garden with its enchanting fountains and courtyards and a Moor-style pool. The hotel has its own stables of 12 thoroughbreds; other activities include golf and ballooning over Doñana Park.

Construite en bordure du parc national de Doñana, cette ancienne ferme spécialisée dans la culture d'orangers, qui a gardé 1 300 ha d'orangeraies, est composée de cottages transformés. Les 6 charmants cottages indépendants au style rustique et peints en couleurs vives jouissent chacun d'un jardin privé. Les 21 chambres donnent sur le jardin paisible de l'hôtel agrémenté de ravissantes fontaines, de jolies cours et d'une piscine de style maure. L'hôtel a sa propre écurie avec 12 pur-sang et golf et des ascensions en ballon sont possibles.

Diese ehemalige Orangenplantage, die heute noch 1300ha Orangenhaine ihr eigen nennt, liegt am Rande des Doñana Nationalparks und besteht aus einer Reihe umgebauter Cottages ehemaliger Farmarbeiter. Gäste haben die Wahl zwischen 6 in sich geschlossenen Cottages mit eigenem Garten oder 21 Zimmern, die alle auf den romantischen Hotelgarten mit seinen Springbrunnen, Innenhöfen und den mauri-schen Pool blicken. Im hoteleigenen Stall stehen 12 Vollblüter, und Golf und Ballonfahrten über den Doñana Park werden angeboten.

Our inspector loved: *The fresh orange juice on arrival and the many delightful touches both decorative and practical.*

Directions: Seville E1/A49 > Huelva > Almonte - Matalascañas > hotel is signposted.

Web: www.johansens.com/cortijomimbrales
E-mail: info@cortijomimbrales.com
Tel: +34 959 44 22 37
Fax: +34 959 44 24 43

Price Guide:
(excluding VAT)
single €125-150
double €125-150
cottage €250-350

SPAIN / ANDALUCÍA (GRANADA)

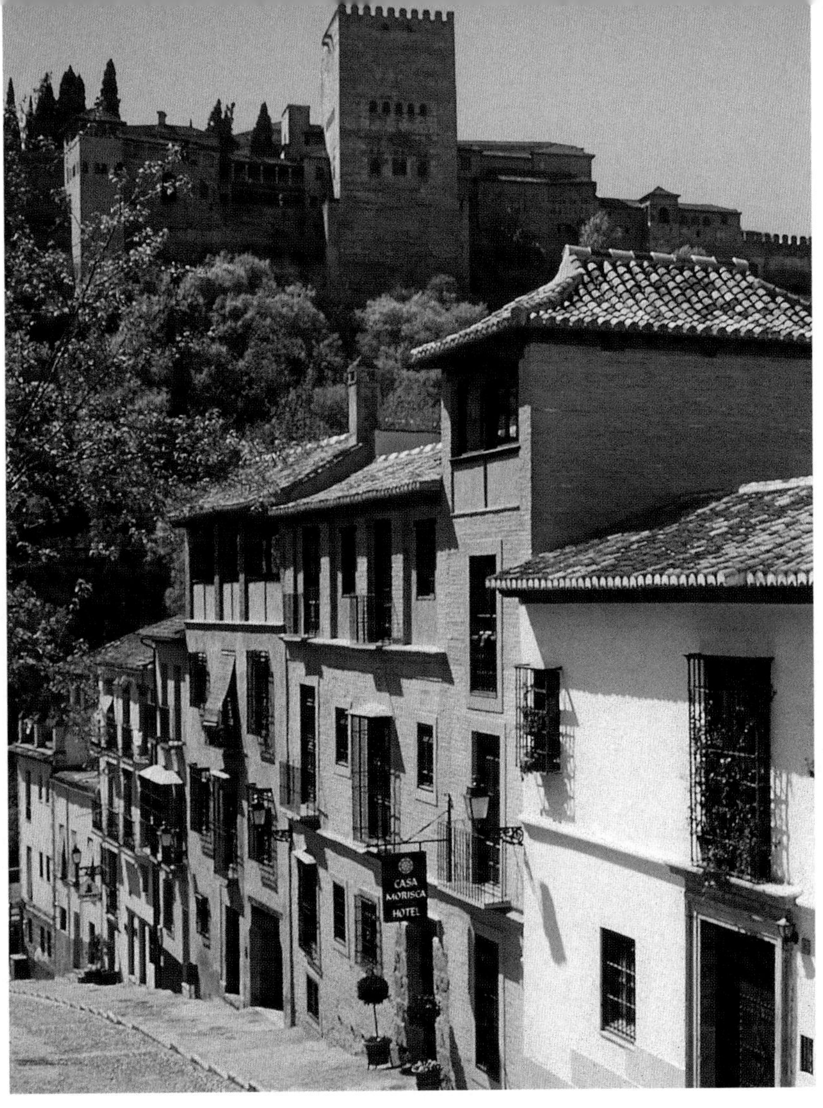

Hotel Casa Morisca

CUESTA DE LA VICTORIA 9, 18010 GRANADA, SPAIN

Situated in the historic "Albayzin" quarter with view of the Alhambra, this stunning, recently restored Moorish palace offers guests a true feel of this ancient city. The décor includes original features such as a beautiful Moorish brick façade, carved wooden ceilings dating from the 15th century, marble columns and old ceramic tiles. An interior courtyard with a skylight and fountains is surrounded by a 2-floor gallery, giving access to the 14 individually decorated bedrooms, some of which offer hydromassage baths.

Situé dans le quartier historique "Albayzin" avec vue de l'Alhambra, ce palais maure magnifique, récemment remis à neuf, offre une excellente impression de cette ville ancienne. Le décor comprend des caractéristiques originelles, telles que la façade en brique, des plafonds sculptés en bois datant du XVe siècle, des colonnes en marbre et des vieux carreaux en céramique. Une cour intérieure avec une lucarne et des fontaines est entourée par des galeries sur 2 niveaux, qui mènent aux 14 chambres décorées de façon individuelle, quelques-unes offrent des bains hydromassage.

Dieses wundervolle Hotel im historischen Albayzin-Viertel mit Blick auf die Alhambra wurde kürzlich restauriert und bietet seinen Gästen ein authentisches Stück Granada. Ursprüngliche Merkmale wie die maurische Fassade, geschnitzte Holzdecken aus dem 15. Jahrhundert, Marmorsäulen und alte Keramikfliesen sind erhalten. Ein Innenhof mit Deckenlicht und Springbrunnen ist von einer 2-stöckigen Gallerie umgeben, von der man zu den 14 unterschiedlichen Zimmern gelangt, einige mit Hydromassagebad.

Our inspector loved: *The breathtaking views of the Alhambra from room 15 and the magnificent carved wooden ceiling in room 8.*

Directions: Near the Alhambra in the town centre.

Web: www.johansens.com/morisca
E-mail: info@hotelcasamorisca.com
Tel: +34 958 221 100
Fax: +34 958 215 796

Price Guide:
(room only, excluding VAT)
single €112
double €140-190

Hotel La Bobadilla

FINCA LA BOBADILLA, APTO. 144, 18300 LOJA, GRANADA, SPAIN

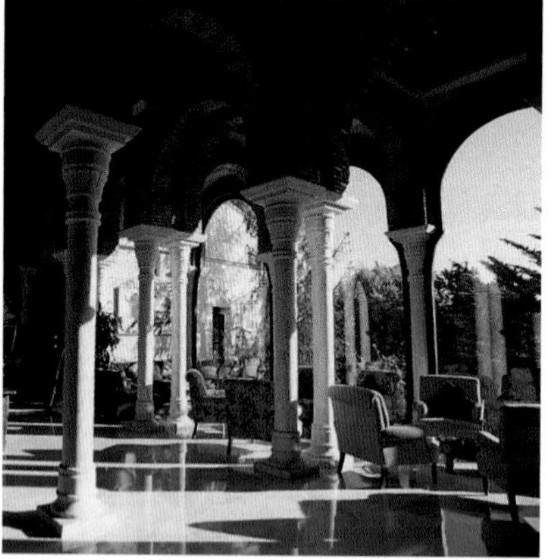

This hotel is a beautiful replica of an Andalusian village and a delight from the columned entrance hall to the enormous pool and the award-winning restaurant. The pretty bedrooms are spacious with sitting areas and decorated with typical local wood carved furniture; most have their own private terraces. The public areas have the atmosphere and décor of an Andalusian country manor. Guests can play tennis, go horse riding – the hotel has its own stables with 6 horses – or venture out in a beach buggy or bicycle.

Cet hôtel est une réplique d'un village andalou où tout est un régal pour les sens, du hall à colonnes au restaurant primé en passant par l'immense piscine. Les jolies chambres spacieuses sont dotées d'un coin séjour et décorées de meubles en bois sculpté typiques de la région. La plupart d'entre elles disposent d'une terrasse privée. Les salles communes se distinguent par une atmosphère et un décor dignes d'un manoir andalou. Les visiteurs pourront jouer au tennis, faire de l'équitation – l'hôtel a 6 chevaux – et découvrir les environs en buggy ou à vélo.

Diese Nachbildung eines andalusischen Dorfes ist zauberhaft, angefangen bei der Eingangshalle bis hin zum herrlich großen Swimmingpool und dem preisgekrönten Restaurant. Die hübschen Zimmer sind geräumig, haben Sitzecken und sind mit ortstypischen geschnitzten Holzmöbeln eingerichtet. Die meisten haben eine eigene Terrasse. Ambiente und Décor sind das eines andalusischen Landhauses. Zahlreiche Freizeitmöglichkeiten umfassen Tennis, Reiten – das Hotel besitzt 6 Pferde – und Ausflüge im Beach-Buggy oder mit dem Fahrrad.

Our inspector loved: *The breathtaking reception hall, reminiscent of Andalucia's rich Moorish heritage.*

Directions: A92 Granada–Seville road > exit 175 Salinas.

Web: www.johansens.com/bobadilla
E-mail: info@la-bobadilla.com
Tel: +34 958 32 18 61
Fax: +34 958 32 18 10

Price Guide:
(excluding VAT)
single €181–226
double/twin €264–391
suites €442–940

CORTIJO DE IZNÁJAR

VALDEARENAS, 14970 IZNÁJAR (CÓRDOBA), SPAIN

This relaxing retreat, located just outside the moorish town of Iznájar, is typically Andulcían in style with its large central courtyard, tiled fountain and welcoming ambience. Each individually decorated bedroom features a view of the lakes and surrounding mountains or courtyard. The colourful dining room opens onto the patio where alfresco meals from the interesting menu may be enjoyed complemented by fine wines. Granada, Córdoba, Málaga and Costa del Sol are all nearby and the hotel is an ideal base for fascinating nature walks.

Ce refuge relaxant est tout proche de la ville maure de Iznájar. Avec sa grande cour intérieure, sa fontaine carrelée et son ambiance chaleureuse, ce cortijo a un style typiquement andalou. Chaque chambre, décorée de manière individuelle, a une vue sur le lac, les montagnes, ou la cour intérieure. La salle à manger colorée donne sur la terrasse où les clients peuvent savourer la cuisine d,un menu intéressant et des bons vins au frais. Granada, Córdoba, Málaga et la Costa del Sol ne sont pas loin et l,hôtel est une base idéale pour des promenades fascinantes dans la nature.

Diese Oase der Entspannung liegt außerhalb der maurischen Stadt Iznájar und ist mit seinem großen, zentralen Innenhof, gekachelten Brunnen und einladenden Ambiente ein typisch andalusisches Cortijo. Die unterschiedlich gestalteten Zimmer bieten Sicht auf die Seen und umgebenden Berge oder den Innenhof. Der farbenfrohe Speisesaal geht in eine Terrasse über, wo man die Köstlichkeiten der interessanten Speisekarte und edle Weine „al fresco" genießen kann. Granada, Córdoba, Málaga und die Costa del Sol sind nicht weit, und das Hotel liegt ideal für Wanderungen in die Umgebung.

Our inspector loved: *The rural comfort in a peaceful setting close to nature.*

Directions: From Málaga take the N331 towards Granada > A92 towards Sevilla > exit 175 towards Villanueva de Tapia > Iznájar > the hotel is then signposted.

Web: www.johansens.com/iznajar
E-mail: info@cortijodeiznajar.com
Tel: +34 957 534 884
Fax: +34 957 534 885

Price Guide:
(breakfast excluded)
single €40-45
double €60-70
suite €75-85

Hotel Villa Jerez

AVDA. DE LA CRUZ ROJA 7, 11407 JEREZ DE LA FRONTERA, SPAIN

Small, classic, aristocratic. This adequately sums up Hotel Villa Jerez, a delightful, antique-filled retreat encompassed by beautiful mature gardens in the elegant residential area of Jerez. It has the atmosphere and ambience of a stately home. There is a superb marble staircase, a comfortable sitting room leading onto the gardens, and spacious, stylish bedrooms with French windows opening onto terraces or balconies.

En résumé petit, classique et aristocratique: l'Hôtel Villa Jerez est une délicieuse retraite remplie d'antiquités entourée de beaux jardins dans l'élégant quartier résidentiel de Jerez. Il a l'ambiance et l'atmosphère d'une maison imposante: un superbe escalier de marbre, un salon confortable qui conduit aux jardins, et de chics et spacieuses chambres avec des porte-fenêtres qui ouvrent sur des terrasses et balcons.

Klein, klassisch, aristokratisch – so könnte man das Hotel Villa Jerez in wenigen Worten beschreiben. Dieses herrliche, mit Antiquitäten gefüllte Haus liegt von traumhaften Gärten umgeben im eleganten Wohnviertel von Jerez. Atmosphäre und Ambiente sind vornehm und würdevoll, und innen beeindruckt ein herrliches marmornes Treppenhaus und ein gemütlicher Aufenthaltsraum mit Zugang zum Garten. Die Zimmer sind geräumig und elegant und haben große Glastüren, die auf eine Terrasse oder einen Balkon führen.

Our inspector loved: *An oasis of peace and elegance in the middle of the city.*

Directions: Located in the heart of Jerez. Only 7km from the airport.

Web: www.johansens.com/villajerez
E-mail: reservas@villajerez.com
Tel: +34 956 15 31 00
Fax: +34 956 30 43 00

Price Guide:
single €189–218
double €236–273
suite €294–660

El Molino de Santillán

CTRA. DE MACHARAVIAYA, KM 3, 29730 RINCÓN DE LA VICTORIA, MÁLAGA, SPAIN

Tucked away in its own large tract of hills, this Andalucían farmhouse is a rare gem. Each of the individually designed, rustic-styled bedrooms has its own terrace and views over the impeccably manicured grounds. The sea is just a 5km-walk away and can be glimpsed as one strolls down the delightful country paths. The fascinating towns of Granada, Seville and Córdoba as well as Málaga and its airport are all within easy driving distance, whilst a range of sporting activities including golf and horse riding can be arranged from the hotel.

Nichée au creux de ses propres collines, cette ferme andalouse est une vraie merveille. Chacune des chambres rustiques décorées de façon individuelle dispose d'une terrasse privée et jouit d'une belle vue sur le parc parfaitement entretenu. Une promenade de 5 km permet de rejoindre la mer, qui s'entrevoit tout au long de la descente par les ravissants chemins de campagne. Les villes fascinantes de Grenade, Séville et Cordoue ainsi que Málaga et son aéroport ne sont pas loin en voiture et des activités sportives comme le golf et l'équitation peuvent être organisées depuis l'hôtel.

Dieses andalusische Bauernhaus liegt versteckt inmitten von Hügellandschaft und ist ein wahres Juwel. Jedes der individuell im ländlichen Stil gestalteten Zimmer hat seine eigene Terrasse mit Blick auf den makellosen Rasen des Hotels. Das nur 5km entfernte Meer kann man auf einem Spaziergang erspähen, und die faszinierenden Städte Granada, Sevilla und Cordoba sowie Málaga und der Flughafen sind schnell zu erreichen. Diverse Sportarten wie Golf und Reiten können vom Hotel aus organisiert werden.

Our inspector loved: *The secluded environment amongst the hills.*

Directions: Málaga – Almería road > exit No 258 Macharaviaya > hotel is signposted.

Web: www.johansens.com/molinodesantillan
E-mail: msantillan@spa.es
Tel: +34 952 40 09 49
Fax: +34 952 40 09 50

Price Guide:
(room only)
single €77.50–98.90
double €99.90–119.90
suites €141.90–168.90

Hotel La Fuente de La Higuera

PARTIDO DE LOS FRONTONES, 29400 RONDA, MÁLAGA, SPAIN

Directions: From Málaga Airport > N340 towards Cádiz > San Pedro de Alcantara > A376 to Ronda > A376 towards Seville > turn right between km 117 and 116 > hotel is signposted.

Web: www.johansens.com/www.hotellafuente.com
E-mail: info@hotellafuente.com
Tel: +34 95 2 11 43 55
Fax: +34 95 2 11 43 56

Price Guide:
double €130
suites €160–250

Cool and tranquil with a colonial feel, this converted olive mill is surrounded by olive groves and has stunning views of the mountains and beautiful countryside. All rooms have private terraces and the suites feature fireplaces, which are perfect on cool winter evenings. Subtle décor and light colour schemes complement the spacious and airy hotel. Hiking, riding and ballooning is available or nearby Ronda and Seville make an interesting day out.

Calme et tranquille avec une atmosphère coloniale, ce pressoir à olives converti est entouré d'oliveraies et offre une vue imprenable sur les montagnes et le superbe paysage. Toutes les chambres disposent d'une terrasse privée, et les suites ont des cheminées, idéales pendant des soirées fraîches en hiver. Une décoration subtile et des tons clairs ajoutent au charme de cet hôtel aéré et spacieux. Randonnées pédestres et équestres et tours de montgolfières sont disponibles, et Ronda et Seville proches, sont idéales pour une journée de sortie.

Diese umgebaute Olivenmühle mit ihrer eleganten, beschaulichen Atmosphäre und kolonialem Flair liegt inmitten von Olivenhainen und bietet eine herrliche Sicht auf die Berge und die schöne Umgebung. Alle Zimmer haben eine eigene Terrasse, und die Suiten bieten Kamine, die besonders an kühlen Winterabenden für Wärme sorgen. Subtiles Décor und helle Farben schaffen ein Gefühl von Geräumigkeit und Frische. Man kann wandern, reiten, Ballon fahren oder Ausflüge nach Ronda und Sevilla unternehmen.

Our inspector loved: *The tranquil, spacious rooms full of light and wonderful views.*

La Posada del Torcal

29230 VILLANUEVA DE LA CONCEPCIÓN, MÁLAGA, SPAIN

This idyllic Andalucían cortijo is situated on a hilltop estate overlooking the magnificent El Torcal National Park. The 10 spacious and individually decorated rooms are filled with fine antiques and ceramics. There is an elegant salon, and innovative Spanish and international cuisine is served in the winter dining room or the spectacular terrace restaurant. For leisure, there is tennis, horse riding, a heated swimming pool and spa facilities. Córdoba, Ronda, Granada and Seville are all nearby. Helicopter transfers from Málaga Airport can be arranged.

Ce charmant cortijo andalou se dresse dans un domaine situé au sommet d'une colline dominant le magnifique parc national El Torcal. Les 10 chambres spacieuses et décorées de manière individuelle sont parées de meubles anciens et de céramiques. La Posada compte un élégant salon et une cuisine espagnole et internationale est servie dans la salle à manger ou sur la fabuleuse terrasse. Les activités incluent tennis, équitation et il y a une piscine chauffée et un spa. Cordoue, Ronda, Grenade et Séville ne sont pas loin. Héliportage de l'aéroport de Málaga est possible.

Dieses idyllische andalusische Cortijo liegt auf einer Anhöhe mit Blick aufden El Torcal Nationalpark. Die 10 geräumigen, individuell gestalteten Zimmer sind mit feinen Antiquitäten und Keramikarbeiten geschmückt. Innovative spanische und internationale Küche wird im Winterspeisesaal oder im sensationellen Terrassenrestaurant serviert. Das Freizeitangebot umfasst Tennis, Reiten, beheizten Swimmingpool und Spa. Córdoba, Ronda, Granada und Sevilla sind schnell zu erreichen. Hubschraubertransfer vom Flughafen Málaga kann organisiert werden.

Our inspector loved: *The relaxing atmosphere, excellent service and stunning views.*

Directions: From Málaga, N331 > Antequera > exit 148 > Casabermeja > Villanueva de la Concepción > La Jolla.

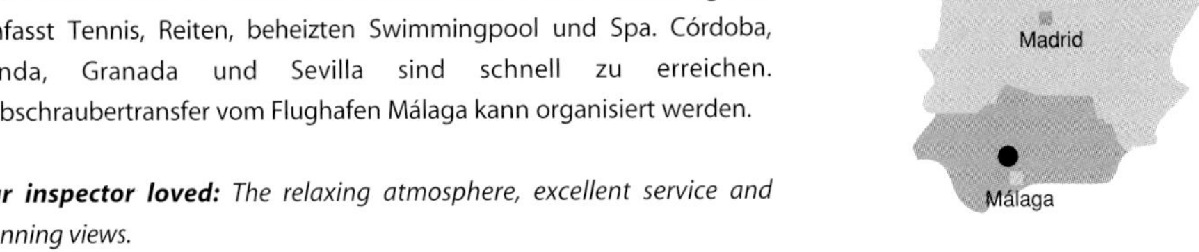

Web: www.johansens.com/posadadeltorcal
E-mail: hotel@eltorcal.com
Tel: +34 952 03 11 77
or +34 69 94 34 385
Fax: +34 952 03 10 06

Price Guide:
(room only)
double/twin €125-180
suite €260

HOTEL BYBLOS ANDALUZ

MIJAS GOLF, 29650 MIJAS~COSTA, MÁLAGA, SPAIN

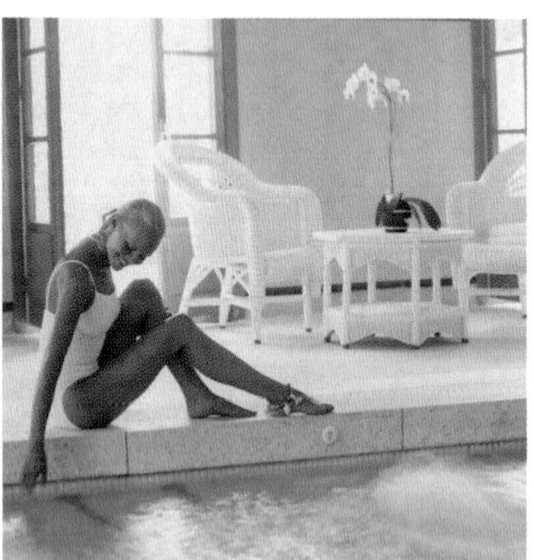

This luxurious property offers glorious views over the surrounding mountains, gardens and golf courses. The comfortable, sybaritic bedrooms have excellent en-suite facilities. There are 2 delightful restaurants, El Andaluz, with its Sevillian courtyard, and the sophisticated Le Nailhac. The Louison Bobet Institute of Thalassotherapy is the largest in Europe and offers many health facilities such as subaquatic massages, and includes the beauty centre "La Prairie".

Cette propriété luxueuse offre des vues imprenables sur les montagnes environnantes, les jardins et le terrain de golf. Les chambres confortables et sybarites ont de magnifiques salles de bains. L'hôtel a 2 délicieux restaurants, El Andaluz, avec sa cour sévillane et Le Nailhac plus sophistiqué. L'Institut Louison Bobet de thalassothérapie est le plus grand d'Europe et propose nombre de services de santé incluant des massages subaquatiques. Il y a un centre de beauté "La Prairie".

Dieses luxuriöse Anwesen trumpft mit traumhaften Blicken auf die umliegenden Berge, Parks und Golfplätze. Die gemütlichen Zimmer haben hervorragende En-suite-Annehmlichkeiten. Es gibt 2 exzellente Restaurants: El Andaluz mit seiner Sevillianer Innenhof, und das erlesene Le Nailhac. Das Louison Bobet Institut für Thalassotherapie ist das größte seiner Art in Europa und bietet zahlreiche Fitness- und Gesundheitsanwendungen, wie z.B. Unterwassermassagen, sowie ein "La Prairie" Beauty-Zentrum.

Our inspector loved: *The beautiful Andalucían patios and relaxing views over the golf course.*

Directions: Málaga–Cádiz motorway > exit Fuengirola-Coin > follow signs.

Web: www.johansens.com/byblosandaluz
E-mail: comerical@byblos-andaluz.com
Tel: +34 952 47 30 50
Fax: +34 952 58 63 27

Price Guide:
single €189.32–278.40
double/twin €242.09–354.21
suite €438.31–1265.91

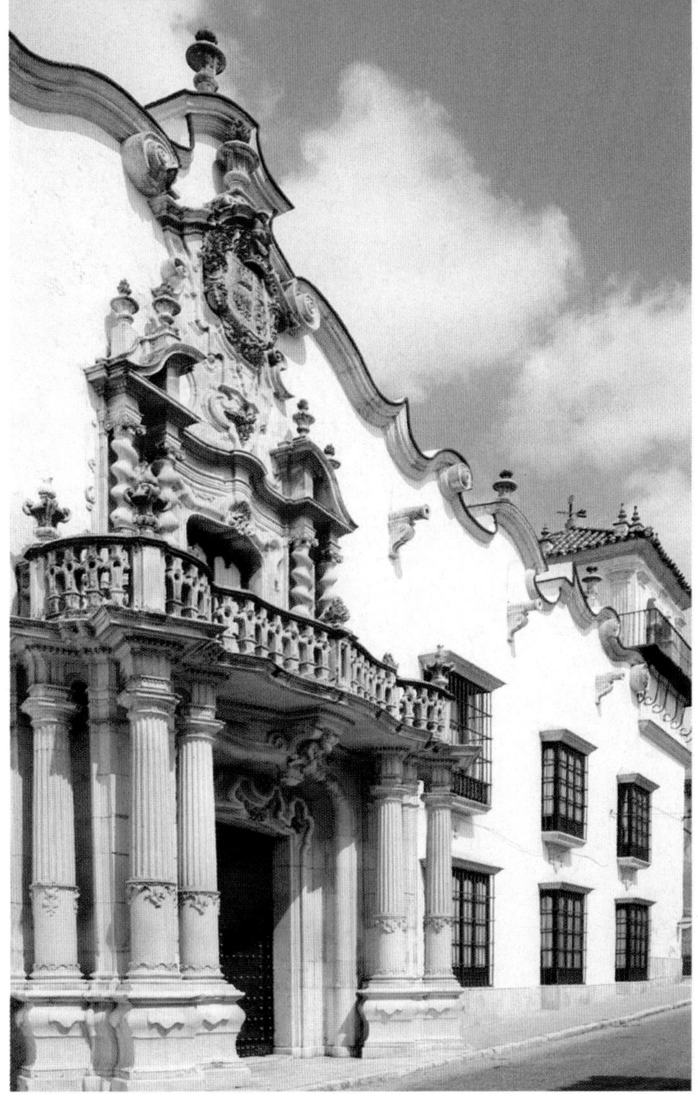

Palacio Marqués de la Gomera

C/ San Pedro 20, 41640 Osuna, Seville, Spain

Set in a street full of wonderful old aristocratic houses, the façade of the Palace is one of the best examples of 18th-century Baroque architecture. Walking into its typical Andalucían central courtyard is like stepping back in time. Behind graceful colonnade arches lie public rooms filled with antiques and paintings and bedrooms all with their own special atmosphere and features, from wooden beams to stone walls, French windows and the classic Suite 7 as used in Zeffirelli's film "Callas Forever".

Situé dans une rue pleine de vieilles maisons aristocratiques, la façade du Palace est l'un des meilleurs exemples du Baroque XVIIIe siècle et entrer dans sa cour intérieure typiquement andalouse est un saut dans le passé. Derrière de belles arches à colonnades, se tiennent des pièces communes emplies d'antiquités et de particularités, des poutres en bois aux murs de pierre, portes-fenêtres et au Suite 7 classique comme celui du film de Zefferelli "Callas Forever".

Dieses Palacio, dessen Fassade eines der besten Beispiele für weltlichen Barock des 18. Jahrhunderts ist, liegt in einer Straße mit herrlichen alten Adelshäusern, und wenn man den typisch andalusischen Innenhof betritt, fühlt man sich sofort in die Vergangenheit zurückversetzt. Hinter dem eleganten Säulengang liegen mit Antiquitäten und Malereien geschmückte Aufenthaltsräume und Zimmer mit ihrer ganz eigenen Atmosphäre und Einrichtung aus Holzbalken, Steinwänden, großen Glastüren und dem klassischen Suite 7, wie man ihn aus Zeffirellis Film „Callas Forever" kennt.

Our inspector loved: *The tower room with 180° views of the city and the surrounding countryside.*

Directions: From Seville > A92 to Osuna. From Málaga > Granada > Antequera > A92 to Osuna.

Web: www.johansens.com/palaciomarquesdelagomera
E-mail: palaciogomera@telefonica.net
Tel: +34 95 4 81 22 23
Fax: +34 95 4 81 02 00

Price Guide:
single €73.96
double €102.90-122.19
suite €180.07

19 360

SPAIN / ANDALUCÍA (SAN JOSÉ)

HOTEL CORTIJO EL SOTILLO

CARRETERA ENTRADA A SAN JOSÉ S/N, 04118 SAN JOSÉ-NÍJAR, SPAIN

Directions: Take the coastal motorway and exit at San José. Before entering the town, the hotel is on the left. Almeria Airport is 38 km away.

Web: www.johansens.com/sotillo
E-mail: sotillo@a2000.es
Tel: +34 950 61 11 00
Fax: +34 950 61 11 05

Price Guide:
(excluding VAT)
single €103
double €127.50
suite €161.50

Hotel Cortijo el Sotillo & Equestrian Centre is a charming, ranch-style hotel set in an idyllic location within 40 acres of the natural park of San José. Marble, wood and terracotta all work together to create a hacienda style, and open fireplaces in winter add a warm welcome and a feeling of total comfort. The restaurant serves a variety of traditional regional dishes and modern Mediterranean cuisine; and this combined with stables, archery centre, mini football pitch and small wildlife park make this an ideal venue for families.

L'Hotel Cortijo el Sotillo & Equestrian Centre est un charmant hôtel en style d'un ranch, situé dans une position idyllique parmi 16ha du parc naturel de San José. La mélange de marbre, de bois et de terracotta crée un style d'hacienda; en hiver des cheminées pourvoient un accueil chaleureux et un sens de confort absolu. Le restaurant sert des plats traditionnels de la région ainsi qu'une cuisine moderne méditerranéenne. Tout cela en combinaison avec un centre d'équitation, un centre de tir à l'arc, un mini terrain de football et une petite réserve naturelle rendent l'hôtel une destination parfaite pour toute la famille.

Das zauberhafte Hotel Cortijo el Sotillo & Equestrian Centre im Stil einer Ranch befindet sich idyllischer Lage inmitten des 16ha großen Naturparks von San José. Marmor, Holz und Terrakotta schaffen einen echten Haziendastil, und im Winter sorgt ein offenes Kaminfeuer für Wärme und Wohlbehagen. Im Restaurant wird eine Kombination aus traditionellen Gerichten und moderner Mittelmeerküche serviert, und zusammen mit Reitanlagen, Bogenschießeinrichtungen, Mini-Fußballplatz und kleinem Tierpark stellt dieses Hotel einen idealen Ferienort für die ganze Familie dar.

Our inspector loved: *The variety of outdoor activities for all the family.*

Hotel Casa Palacio Casa de Carmona

PLAZA DE LASSO 1, 41410 CARMONA, SEVILLE, SPAIN

Visitors to this enchanting 16th-century palace will enjoy service of the highest standard in a serene, relaxed atmosphere. The hotel is adorned throughout with stunning antique furniture and artwork which has been handed down through the family. The bedrooms are decorated with beautiful fabrics in colourful hues. Guests can relax in the outdoor pool, which blends discreetly with the palm trees and bougainvillea in the Arab-style garden. The restaurant, located in the old stables, serves succulent cuisine prepared from the finest local produce.

Les visiteurs de ce palace enchanteur du XVIe siècle bénéficient du meilleur service dans une atmosphère sereine et détendue. L'hôtel est meublé de splendides antiquités et d'œuvres d'art héritées des générations précédentes. Les chambres sont décorées de superbes draperies dans des nuances éclatantes. Les hôtes peuvent se détendre dans la piscine extérieure, qui se fond dans les palmiers et bougainvilliers des jardins de style arabe. Le restaurant, situé dans les anciennes écuries, sert une cuisine succulente préparée à partir de produits naturels de la meilleure qualité.

Gäste dieses bezaubernden Palastes aus dem 16. Jahrhundert erleben hier erstklassigen Service in heiterer, entspannter Atmosphäre. Das Hotel ist mit herrlichen Antiquitäten und Kunstwerken geschmückt, die von Generation zu Generation weitergereicht wurden, und die Zimmer sind mit hübschen, farbenfrohen Stoffen dekoriert. Der Swimmingpool schmiegt sich dezent an die mit Palmen und Bougainvillea gefüllten arabischen Gärten an, und das in den ehemaligen Stallungen untergebrachte Restaurant bietet köstliche, aus feinsten einheimischen Zutaten zubereitete Speisen.

Our inspector loved: *Feeling like a guest in the home of an old aristocratic family.*

Directions: From Seville > N IV towards Cordoba and Madrid > km25 > exit Carmona > follow signs to Centro Historico and Casa de Carmona.

Web: www.johansens.com/carmona
E-mail: reserve@casadecarmona.com
Tel: +34 954 191 000
Fax: +34 954 190 189

Price Guide:
single €115-235
double €120-240
junior suite €200-300
suite €500-900

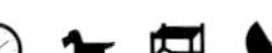

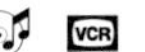

Hotel Cortijo Águila Real

CTRA. GUILLENA–BURGUILLOS KM 4, 41210 GUILLENA, SEVILLE, SPAIN

This charming Andalucían country house was perfectly restored as a hotel in 1991 and features well-appointed bedrooms and junior suites. Each room has been given its own individual décor and name. Hand-painted furniture and extravagant tapestries adorn the walls. The homemade dishes comprise fresh local produce as well as food grown on the hotel farm. The beautiful surrounding gardens create a peaceful, relaxing environment.

Cet élégant manoir andalou a été superbement restauré en hôtel en 1991 et propose des chambres et des junior suites impeccables. Chaque chambre se distingue par son propre nom et sa décoration spécifique. Des meubles peints à la main et de somptueuses tapisseries ornent les murs. Les plats faits-maison sont élaborés à partir de produits régionaux frais ou de la ferme de l'hôtel. Les superbes jardins environnants forment un cadre paisible et relaxant.

Dieses zauberhafte andalusische Landhaus wurde 1991 perfekt in ein Hotel umgewandelt und bietet nun gutausgestattete Zimmer und Suiten. Jeder Raum hat einen anderen Namen, ist individuell gestaltet und mit handbemalten Möbeln und extravaganten Wandbehängen geschmückt. Für die hauseigene Küche werden Produkte aus der Gegend oder aus eigenem Anbau verwendet. Die herrlichen umliegenden Gärten schaffen eine friedliche und erholsame Atmosphäre.

Our inspector loved: *The scent of roses and the singing of the birds in the attractive mature gardens.*

Directions: SE-30 > N630 > Merida > Guillena > signposted to hotel.

Web: www.johansens.com/cortijoaguilareal
E-mail: hotel@aguilareal.com
Tel: +34 955 78 50 06
Fax: +34 955 78 43 30

Price Guide:
double/twin €100–120
suite €140–190

HOTEL HACIENDA LA BOTICARIA

CTRA. ALCALÁ - UTRERA KM.2, 41500 ALCALÁ DE GUADAIRA (SEVILLE), SPAIN

This grand hacienda-style building is set around a large central courtyard, and its interior is decorated in an elegantly rustic style. Bedrooms are spacious and comfortable with lovely fabrics, and overlook pretty lawns, flowers and lemon trees. Excellent food is served with traditional Spanish cutlery and linens. The hotel's friendly welcome is faultless and guests can enjoy a visit to the private coach house featuring a collection of carriages, one of which belonged to the British royal family.

Ce grand bâtiment de type hacienda se trouve au centre d'une cour fermée, et son intérieur est meuble dans un style rustique élégant. Les chambres sont spacieuses et confortables avec de jolis tissus, et ont vue sur les belles pelouses, fleurs et sur les citronniers. Une cuisine excellente est servie avec des couverts et services de table traditionnels espagnols. L'accueil amical de l'hôtel est sans faute et les hôtes peuvent se promener jusqu'au "garage" privé qui présente une collection de diligences et carrosses, dont l'un a appartenu à la famille royale britannique.

Dieses anmutige Gebäude im Haziendastil ist um einen großen Innenhof herum gebaut und in elegant-rustikalem Stil eingerichtet. Die geräumigen, komfortablen Zimmer sind mit hübschen Stoffen dekoriert und blicken auf zauberhafte Gärten, Blumen und Zitronenbäume. Exquisite Speisen werden durch traditionelles spanisches Besteck und Tischtücher ergänzt, und Gäste werden aufs freundlichste willkommen geheissen. Man kann eine private Remise mit einer Sammlung von Kutschen bewundern, von denen eine der britischen Königsfamilie gehörte.

Our inspector loved: *The stylish décor and the impeccable service.*

Directions: Sevilla > A92 (Málaga-Granada) > exit Alcalá de Guadiara > Utrera (432) > km 2 > signposted.

Web: www.johansens.com/haciendalaboticaria
E-mail: info@laboticaria-hotel.com
Tel: +34 955 69 88 20
Fax: +34 955 69 87 55

Price Guide:
double €256–320
suite €428–642

SPAIN / ANDALUCÍA (SEVILLE)

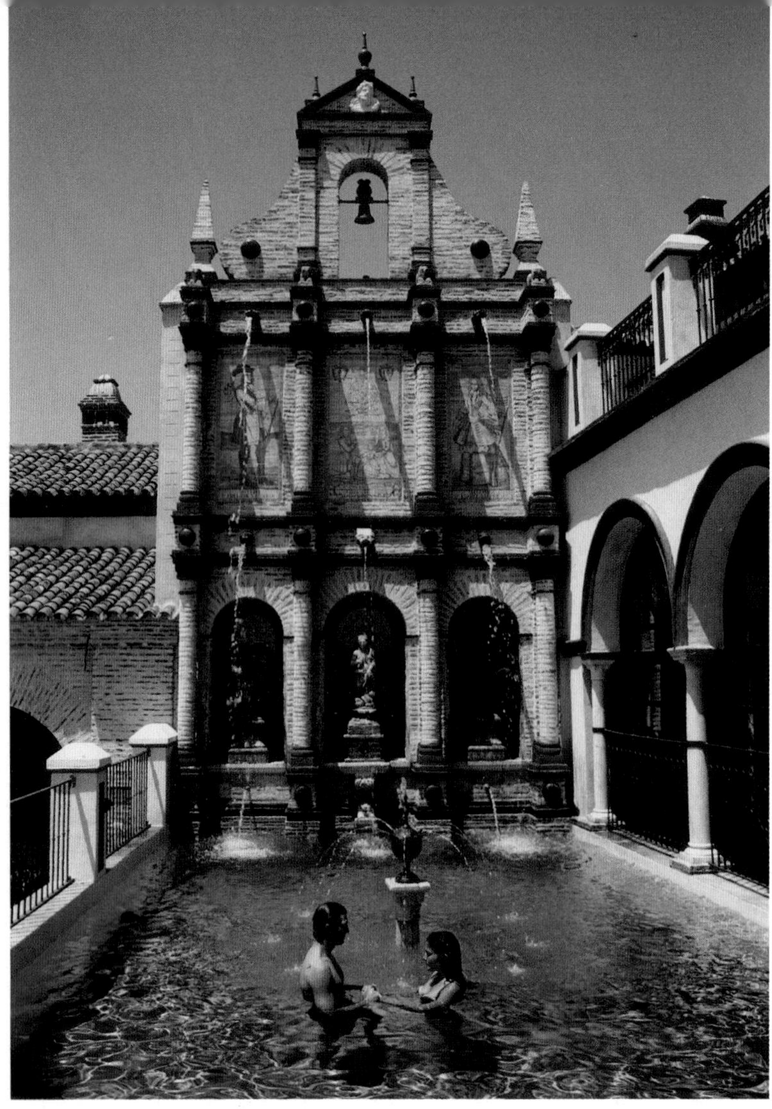

Palacio de San Benito

C/SAN BENITO S/N, 41370 CAZALLA DE LA SIERRA, SEVILLE, SPAIN

Originally a 15th-century church, the hotel was once a stopover for pilgrims and the present owner's family played host to Philip V, the first Bourbon king of Spain. Today its atmosphere is that of a cosy private hunting lodge, filled with exquisite portraits and heirlooms from that period. Unique bedrooms feature Liberty fabrics, fireplaces and tiny patio gardens and there is also a wonderful chapel, dining room and swimming pool that doubles as a fountain.

A l'origine une église du XVe siècle, cet hôtel fut autrefois une étape pour les pèlerins et la famille du propriétaire actuel accueillit Philippe V, premier roi Bourbon d'Espagne. De nos jours, son atmosphère est douillette comme celle d'un pavillon de chasse privé, rempli de délicieux portraits et tableaux de famille d'époque. Les chambres uniques sont décorées en tissus Liberty, et bénéficient de cheminées et petits patios ou jardins; l'hôtel dispose également d'une adorable chapelle, d'une salle de restaurant et d'une piscine qui se présente aussi comme une fontaine.

Dieses Hotel aus dem 15. Jahrhundert war ursprünglich eine Raststätte für Pilger, und die Familie des heutigen Besitzers hieß einst König Philipp V., den ersten Bourbonenkönig Spaniens willkommen. Die Atmosphäre ist die einer gemütlichen privaten Jagdhütte, die mit Portraits und Erbstücken aus jener Zeit gefüllt ist. In den einzigartigen Zimmern findet man Libertystoffe und Kamine, und alle haben Terrassen oder Gärten. Außerdem gibt es hier eine zauberhafte Kapelle, einen schönen Speisesaal und einen Swimmingpool mit Springbrunnen.

***Our inspector loved:** The dreamy individual patio gardens with their antique tiles, fountain and scented flowers.*

Directions: Airport > N-IV for Seville >A431 for Alcala del Rio towards Cantillana > follow the A432 to Cazalla de la Sierra > the hotel is on the right hand side as you enter Cazalla on Paseo del Moro.

Web: www.johansens.com/palaciodesanbenito
Tel: +34 954 88 33 36
Fax: +34 954 88 31 62

Price Guide:
(room only)
single €180
double €210

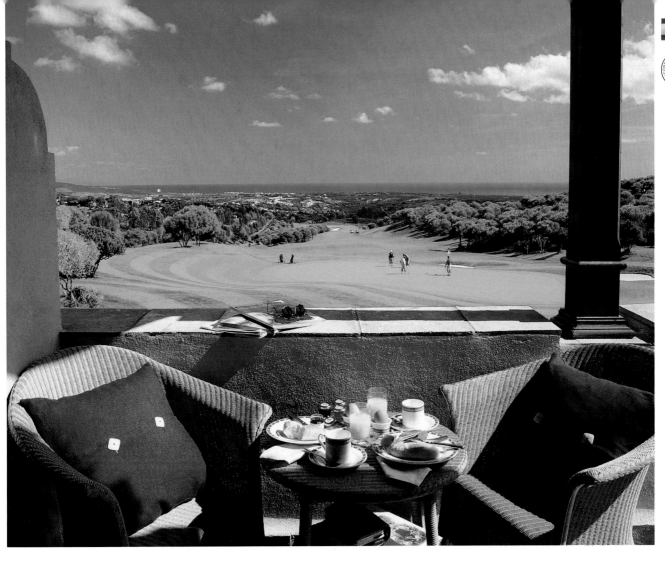

Almenara Golf Hotel & Spa

AVENIDA ALMENARA, 11310 SOTOGRANDE, SPAIN

This exceptional hotel offers stunning views over the countryside to the distant Mediterranean and is surrounded by 4 of Europe's finest golf courses. The bedrooms are tastefully furnished and fitted to the highest standard. Dining is a delight; there are 3 restaurants: the Gaia with its fusion of Spanish and Asian cuisine, the more casual Vein Tee Ocho, and the Cabaña Grill, 3 km away. Guests can tone up in the impressive health club with heated pool, laze around a spectacular outdoor pool or play golf on the hotel's 27-hole course.

Ce magnifique hôtel avec ses vues splendides sur le paysage éloigné de la Méditerranée est entouré par 4 des plus prestigieux parcours de golf d'Europe. Les chambres sont meublées avec goût et pourvues des meilleurs équipements. Les repas sont un ravissement avec le choix entre 3 restaurants: le Gaia mélange de cuisine espagnole et asiatique, le Vein Tee Ocho plus décontracté et le Cabaña Grill à 3 kms. Les visiteurs peuvent faire de l'exercice dans le centre de remise en forme, lézarder autour de la superbe piscine, ou jouer au golf sur le parcours à 27 trous de l'hôtel.

Dieses superbe Hotel bietet herrliche Aussichten auf die Umgebung und das ferne Mittelmeer und ist von 4 der besten Golfplätze Europas umgeben. Die Zimmer sind geschmackvoll und nach höchstem Standard eingerichtet. 3 Restaurants sorgen für kulinarischen Genuss: das spanisch-asiatische Gaia, das weniger formelle Café Vein Tee Ocho und der 3km entfernte Cabaña Grill. Für sportliche Aktivitäten stehen ein eindrucksvolles Fitnesszentrum mit beheiztem Pool, ein prachtvolles Freibad und der hoteleigene 27-Loch Golfplatz zur Verfügung.

Our inspector loved: *The extra details for all occasions like the beach bag with beach towel inside the cupboard alongside the golf umbrella.*

Directions: Málaga to Cádiz coast road E15 > exit 130.

Web: www.johansens.com/almenara
E-mail: nhalmenara@nh-hotels.com
Tel: + 34 956 58 20 00
Fax: +34 956 58 20 01

Price Guide:
single €147–198
double/twin €152–218
suite €222–288

La Parada del Compte

FINCA LA ANTIGUA ESTACIÓN DEL FERROCARRIL, 44597 TORRE DEL COMPTE, TERUEL, SPAIN

Directions: Barcelona Airport > A7 Hospitalet Infante > C304 Mora > N420 to Torre del Compte.

Web: www.johansens.com/laparadadelcompte
Tel: +34 978 76 90 72
Fax: +34 978 76 90 74

Price Guide:
(room only)
single €90
double €100-125
suite €160

Zaragoza
Barcelona
Madrid
M laga

A warm welcome and personal service awaits guests at this converted railway station. Set amidst peaceful surroundings, this is the perfect getaway from the hustle and bustle of everyday life yet well connected to the north/south motorway. Exquisite Aragonese cuisine is served in the El Andén restaurant, situated in the former warehouse, whilst upstairs is a comfortable lounge in which to unwind. Guests can enjoy the new swimming pool or explore numerous medieval villages in the vicinity and may even catch a glimpse of the rare Iberian goat and black vulture that inhabit the area.

Un accueil chaleureux et personnalisé attend les hôtes dans cette station de chemin de fer. Au sein de paysages paisibles, c'est l'échappatoire idéale à la vie de tous les jours, pourtant l'autoroute nord/sud est d'accès facile. Une superbe cuisine aragonaise est servie au restaurant d'El Andén situé dans l'ancien hangar, alors que l'étage supérieur est un salon confortable où se détendre. Les hôtes peuvent profiter de la nouvelle piscine, visiter les nombreux villages médiévaux des entourages et même entrapercevoir la chèvre ibérienne rare et le moine qui habitent dans les environs.

Ein herzlicher Empfang und persönlicher Service erwartet Gäste in dieser umgebauten Bahnhofsstation. Dieses inmitten friedlicher Landschaft gelegene Hotel ist das ideale Versteck vor der Hektik des Alltags. Im Restaurant El Andén in der ehemaligen Lagerhalle werden exquisite Speisen der Region serviert, und im Obergeschoß befindet sich eine gemütliche Lounge. Ein neuer Swimmingpool steht zur Verfügung, und die Gäste können zahlreiche mittelalterliche Dörfer in der Umgebung erkunden. Manchmal sieht man hier sogar die seltene iberische Ziege oder einen schwarzen Geier.

Our inspector loved: *The spacious rooms and warm colour schemes.*

La Torre del Visco

44587 FUENTESPALDA, TERUEL, SPAIN

This beautiful, romantic 15th-century estate house has been superbly restored and is surrounded by lovely gardens and patios with fountains, at the end of a forest track in a remote river valley – the undiscovered "Spanish Provence". The Mediterranean cuisine, for which it is renowned, uses herbs and vegetables, olive oil and truffles from the 220-acre farm, and is complemented by wines from the well-stocked medieval wine cellar. British owners and Spanish staff create a friendly and peaceful atmosphere to be enjoyed all year round.

Ce beau domaine romantique et superbement restauré qui date du XVè siècle est entouré de beaux jardins et terrasses avec fontaines et situé au bout d'un chemin forestier dans une vallée écartée – la "Provence d'Espagne" non découverte. La cuisine méditerranéenne renommée emploie des herbes et légumes, huile d'olive et truffes de la ferme de 90 ha et elle est arrosée de vins de la cave médiévale bien fournie. Les propriétaires britanniques et le personnel espagnol offrent une ambiance accueillante et tranquille tout au long de l'année.

Dieses herrlich restaurierte, romantische Gutshaus aus dem 15. Jahrhundert ist umgeben von hübschen Gärten, Terrassen mit Springbrunnen und liegt am Ende eines Waldwegs in einem abgelegenen Flusstal – die unberührte "Spanische Provence". Die Mittelmeerküche, für die das Hotel berühmt ist, basiert auf Kräutern, Gemüse, Olivenöl und Trüffeln der eigenen 90ha Ländereien und wird von Weinen aus dem gutbestückten mittelalterlichen Keller abgerundet. Britische Besitzer und spanisches Personal schaffen das ganze Jahr über eine freundliche, friedliche Atmosphäre.

Our inspector loved: *The fresh flowers in the rooms and fresh food from the gardens and surrounding farms.*

Directions: The nearest airports are Valencia and Barcelona. From A7 > exit Reus > N420 - Calaceite > Valderrobres - Fuentespalda.

Zaragoza
Barcelona
Madrid
Málaga

Web: www.johansens.com/torredelvisco
E-mail: torredelvisco@torredelvisco.com
Tel: +34 978 76 90 15
Fax: +34 978 76 90 16

Price Guide:
(including dinner)
double €210-255
suite €315

Palacio de Cutre

LA GOLETA S/N VILLAMAYOR, 33583 INFIESTO, ASTURIAS, SPAIN

Built on a hill with incredible views of the surrounding mountains and farmland, this 16th-century farmhouse, with its own chapel, has been recently renovated and has a peaceful and friendly atmosphere. Great attention to detail, antique doll collections and small artefacts make every corner interesting. There is a delicious menu offering the region's seasonal specialities. Outdoor activities include canoeing, rafting, horse riding and hiking.

Construite sur une colline avec une vue imprenable sur les montagnes environnantes et les terres agricoles, cette ferme du XVIe siècle avec sa propre chapelle, a récemment été rénovée et bénéficie d'une atmosphère paisible et amicale. Une attention particulière au détail, des poupées antiques et de petits artefacts en rendent chaque recoin particulièrement intéressant. Un délicieux menu sert des spécialités régionales de saison. Pour activités de plein air, canoë, raft, randonne équestre et marche sont à disposition.

Auf einem Hügel mit herrlicher Sicht auf die umliegenden Berge und Felder liegt dieses kürzlich renovierte Bauernhaus aus dem 16. Jahrhundert mit seiner eigenen Kapelle. Die Atmosphäre ist ruhig und herzlich, und Liebe zum Detail, Sammlungen antiker Puppen und kleine Kunstgegenstände machen jeden Winkel interessant. Die verlockende Speisekarte bietet regionale Spezialitäten, die sich je nach Jahreszeit ändern. Aktivitäten sind z.B. Kanufahren, Rafting, Reiten und Wandern.

Our inspector loved: *The beautifully detailed antique-style bathrooms with soft, ambient lighting.*

Directions: Off the N634 Oviedo–Santander road at Villamayor > direction of Borines/Colunga > signposted.

Web: www.johansens.com/palaciodecutre
E-mail: hotel@palaciodecutre.com
Tel: +34 985 70 80 72
Fax: +34 985 70 80 19

Price Guide:
single €78-85.60
double €108.07-145.52
suite €177.62-204.37

Cas Gasi

APDO. CORREOS 117, 07814 SANTA GERTRUDIS, IBIZA, BALEARIC ISLANDS

Set amidst pretty gardens, almond trees, orchards and olive groves, this former farmhouse has been completely renovated and extended to offer guests an exclusive stay in tranquil surroundings. The beautifully decorated bedrooms provide every modern comfort and are adorned with hand-painted tiles, terracotta floors and beamed ceilings. Guests can explore the countryside on foot or by bicycle and enjoy the beaches and the nightlife of nearby Ibiza town.

Au sein de charmants jardins, d'amandiers, de vergers et d'oliveraies, cet ancien corps de ferme a été complètement rénové et agrandi pour offrir à ses hôtes un séjour exclusif dans un environnement tranquille. Les chambres joliment décorées offrent tout le confort et sont ornées avec des carrelages peints à la main, des sols en terre cuite et des plafonds à poutres apparentes. Les hôtes peuvent explorer la campagne à pied ou bicyclette et profiter des plages et de la vie nocturne d'Ibiza toute proche.

Inmitten von Gärten, Mandelbäumen, Obstgärten und Olivenhainen gelegen, bietet dieses einstige Bauernhaus, das komplett renoviert und erweitert wurde, einen exklusiven Aufenthalt in ruhiger Umgebung. Die hübschen Zimmer haben jeglichen modernen Komfort und sind mit handbemalten Fliesen, Terrakottaböden und Balkendecken geschmückt. Man kann die Umgebung zu Fuß oder mit dem Fahrrad erkunden und die Strände und das Nachtleben der nahegelegenen Stadt Ibiza genießen.

Our inspector loved: *The rustic simplicity combined with comfort and elegance.*

Directions: Santa Gertrudis > San Mateo > turning for San Antonio > hotel on road leading off to the left.

Web: www.johansens.com/casgasi
E-mail: info@casgasi.com
Tel: +34 971 197 700
Fax: +34 971 197 899

Price Guide:
(room only)
double €204–276
suite €330–510

Agroturismo Es Puig Moltó

CTRA. PINA-MONTUIRI, 07230 MONTUIRI, MALLORCA, BALEARIC ISLANDS

Just 30 minutes from the airport and set amidst 35ha of farmland, this charming hotel is one of the oldest documented country estates in the area named "Es Pla" and offers guests a warm welcome and friendly service. The views from the hotel and poolside are simply stunning. All 10 suites, some of which boast large terraces, are tastefully decorated in a contemporary rustic style in pale blue, peach and yellow, and furnished with beautiful antique pieces. The restaurant is open to guests upon request only.

A 30 minutes seulement de l'aéroport et situé au milieu de 35ha de terres cultivées, cet hôtel charmant est un des plus vieilles terres dans la région appelée "Es Pla" et offre aux hôtes un accueil chaleureux et service amical. Les vues depuis l'hôtel et la piscine sont tout simplement magnifiques. Toutes les 10 suites, dont quelques-unes ont une grande terrasse, sont décorées en style rustique en bleu, jaune et pêche pâle, et meublées avec des bels objets d'art. Le restaurant n'est pas ouvert au public, mais sert un menu complet pour les hôtes sur demande.

Nur eine halbe Stunde vom Flughafen entfernt und inmitten von 35ha Land liegt dieses zauberhafte Hotel, einer der ältesten dokumentierten Herrensitze der Region "Es Pla". Geboten wird hier ein herzlicher Empfang, freundlicher Service und eine atemberaubende Sicht auf die Umgebung. Alle 10 Suiten sind geschmackvoll in zeitgenössischem ländlichen Stil in pastellblau, pfirsich und gelb gehalten und mit herrlichen antiken Möbeln eingerichtet. Einige Suiten haben große Terrassen. Das Restaurant ist nicht für die Öffentlichkeit zugänglich, serviert den Gästen aber auf vorherige Anfrage ein volles Menü.

Our inspector loved: *The tasteful décor of this beautifully renovated old house.*

Directions: Palma Mallorca Airport > road to Manacor > at Algaida take Pina Road.

Web: www.johansens.com/puigmolto
E-mail: puigmolto@airtel.net
Tel: +34 971 18 17 58
Fax: +34 971 18 17 58

Price Guide: (per room, excluding tax)
single €90
double €110
junior suite €150-210
family room €200

Ca's Xorc

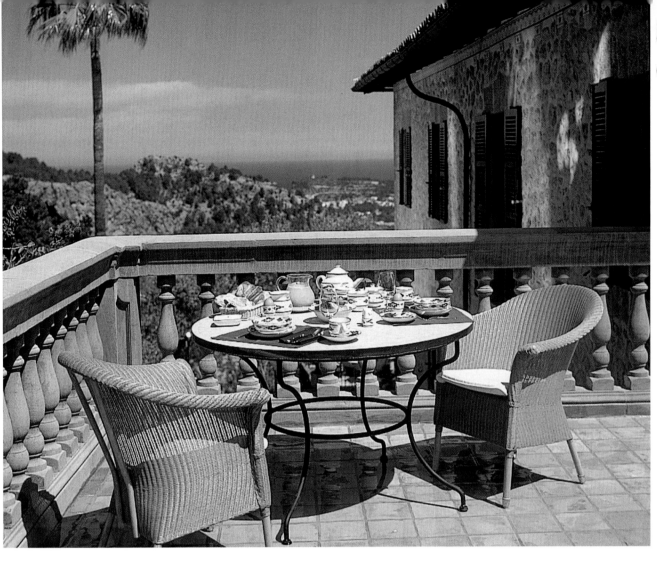

CARRETERA DE DEÍA, KM 56.1, 07100 SOLLER, MALLORCA, BALEARIC ISLANDS

Majorcan tradition and contemporary style have been combined throughout this captivating hotel, which is surrounded by landscaped gardens. Stunning vistas of the Tramuntana mountains and the blue Mediterranean beyond are enjoyed from the terrace, where guests can sample delicacies from a constantly changing menu. Inside, the rooms with their stone floors, exposed beams and white fabrics create an airy and romantic ambience. The hotel's enviable seclusion – 250m above the main road – ensures a peaceful yet invigorating stay.

Tradition majorquine et style contemporain se complètent à merveille dans cet hôtel d'exception, qui est entouré de jardins dessinés. De la terrasse, les visiteurs profitent d'une vue spectaculaire sur la Sierra de Tramuntana et l'étendue azur de la Méditerranée tout en dégustant des mets délicats chaque jour différents. À l'intérieur, les sols dallés, les poutres apparentes et les tissus blancs créent une ambiance claire et romantique. À 250 mètres au-dessus de la route principale, cet endroit retiré offre des séjours paisibles et vivifiants.

Mallorquinische Tradition und Moderne verbinden sich in diesem außergewöhnlichen, von gestalteten Gärten umgebenen Hotel. Auf der Terrasse, von der aus man eine atemberaubende Sicht auf die Tramuntana Berge und das Mittelmeer hat, werden täglich neue Köstlichkeiten serviert. Die Innenräume beeindrucken mit ihren Steinböden, rohen Balken und weißen Stoffen und schaffen eine romantische und luftige Atmosphäre. Die abgeschiedene Lage – 250m oberhalb der Hauptstraße – garantieren einen ruhigen und erholsamen Aufenthalt.

Our inspector loved: *The successful combination of a rustic house with the latest in contemporary interior design.*

Directions: The entrance is marked off Soller - Deía road at milestone 56.1.

Web: www.johansens.com/casxorc
E-mail: stay@casxorc.com
Tel: +34 971 63 82 80
Fax: +34 971 63 29 49

Price Guide:
interior room €155
vista room €175
superior room €210
deluxe room €280

Can Furiós Petit Hotel

CAMI VELL BINIBONA 11, BINIBONA, 07314 CAIMARI, MALLORCA, BALEARIC ISLANDS

Set amidst breathtaking mountain scenery, this enchanting 16th-century villa is the perfect place to unwind and relax. The villa has been carefully converted to provide all modern comforts whilst retaining its original character. The bedrooms are stunning, and the suites have terraces opening onto the landscaped gardens and pool area. Set in the almond press room, which dates back to the 17th century, the Sa Tafoneta restaurant serves exquisite international and Mediterranean cuisine, with seafood being a speciality. Numerous activities to suit every taste can be arranged.

Au sein de beau paysage de montagne, cette villa enchanteur du XVIe siècle est l'endroit rêvé pour se relaxer et se dérouler. La villa a été soigneusement convertie pour offrir tout confort moderne, tout en gardant son caractère original. Les chambres sont fantastiques et les suites ont une terrasse donnant sur les jardins dessinés et la piscine. Situé dans l'ancienne salle de presse, datant du XVIIe siècle et construit en bois d'amande, le restaurant Sa Tafoneta sert une cuisine internationale et méditerranéenne; les fruits de mer étant une spécialité. De nombreuses activités pour correspondre aux goûts de chacun peuvent être organisées.

Inmitten atemberaubender Berglandschaft liegt diese zauberhafte Villa aus dem 16. Jahrhundert - der ideale Erholungsort. Die Villa wurde sorgfältig in ein Hotel mit allen modernen Annehmlichkeiten umgewandelt, wobei der ursprüngliche Charakter erhalten blieb. Die Zimmer sind wundervoll, und die Suiten haben Terrassen mit Zugang zu den Gärten und zum Pool. Das im Mandelpresseraum aus dem 17. Jahrhundert gelegene Sa Tafeta Restaurant serviert internationale und Mittelmeerküche, die Spezialität sind Meeresfrüchte. Zahlreiche Aktivitäten können organisiert werden.

Our inspector loved: *The attention the new owners lavish on their guests.*

Directions: Palma Airport > Inca > Campanet > the hotel is then signposted.

Web: www.johansens.com/canfurios
E-mail: info@can-furios.com
Tel: +34 971 51 57 51
Fax: +34 971 87 53 66

Price Guide:
(room only)
double €100–160
suite €131–240

Menorca
Mallorca
Mahón
Palma
Ibiza
Ibiza
Formentera

La Moraleja Hotel

URBANIZACIÓN LOS ENCINARES S/N, 07469 CALA SAN VICENTE, MALLORCA, BALEARIC ISLANDS

Set on a hill yet only 5 minutes' walk from beautiful sandy beaches, this 5-star hotel has retained the atmosphere of a private home. All bedrooms are large and airy and have their own terraces, whilst the elegant lounges boast antique furniture, bronzes and original paintings. Guests can enjoy the 2 swimming pools, one of which is heated, or visit the showroom with its collection of 25 1950-1970 classic, convertible sports cars. In the evening, the restaurant, Cristal, serves an excellent à la carte menu, and the staff are happy to recommend and organise excursions. Open: 1st May - 30th October.

Situé sur une colline, mais seulement 5 minutes de belles plages de sable, cet hôtel 5 étoiles a gardé son ambiance de maison privée. Les chambres sont grandes et claires avec terrasse, et les salons sont meublés d'antiquités, de bronzes et de tableaux originaux. Les hôtes peuvent profiter des 2 piscines chauffées ou visiter la salle d'exposition avec sa collection de 25 voitures de sport classiques décapotables des années 1950-1970. Un dîner à la carte excellent est servi au restaurant Cristal. Le personnel est heureux de recommander et organiser des excursions. Ouvert du 1 mai au 30 octobre.

Dieses 5-Sterne-Hotel mit der Atmosphäre eines Privathauses liegt auf einem Hügel, nur 5 Minuten von herrlichen Sandstränden entfernt. Die geräumigen Zimmer haben eine eigene Terrasse und die eleganten Aufenthaltsräume sind mit Antiquitäten, Bronzestatuen und Originalgemälden gefüllt. Es gibt 2 Swimmingpools (einer ist beheizt), außerdem kann man einen Schauraum mit 25 klassischen Sportcabriolets der Jahre 1950-1970 bewundern. Im Restaurant Cristal wird abends ein köstliches à la carte Menü serviert. Das Personal kann gute Exkursionen empfehlen und organisieren. Geöffnet vom 1. Mai bis 30. Oktober.

Our inspector loved: *The polite, well-informed staff.*

Directions: Palma Airport > motorway Inca-Pollensa > Cala San Vicente, turning off left. The hotel is on the main entry road. A free airport transfer (e.g. Mercedes or similar) to and from the hotel is available by arrangement.

Web: www.johansens.com/lamoraleja
E-mail: hotel@lamoraleja.net
Tel: +34 971 534 010
Fax: +34 971 533 418

Price Guide:
superior twin €303
suite €338-376

Palacio Ca Sa Galesa

CARRER DE MIRAMAR 8, 07001 PALMA, MALLORCA, BALEARIC ISLANDS

This 16th-century palacio is located in the heart of the Gothic quarter in the centre of Palma and is only a 2-minute walk from the cathedral. Original stained glass, floor tiles, chandeliers and tapestries adorn the beautiful public rooms, whilst the comfortable bedrooms are classically decorated, some with a very cosy feel. At 7pm, guests may enjoy an apéritif in the reading room, which has its own small library filled with books and magazines. The hotel boasts a small spa area complete with sauna and gymnasium; mountain bikes are available for excursions.

Ce palais du XVIe siècle est situé au cœur du quartier gothique de Palma et à deux pas de la cathédrale. Les vitraux originaux, des carreaux, des lustres et des tapisseries ornent les belles salles publiques, alors que les chambres sont décorées de façon classique, quelques-unes avec une ambiance très intime. A 19h, les hôtes peuvent prendre l'apéritif dans la salle de lecture avec sa propre bibliothèque rempli de libres et de magazines. L'hôtel s'enorgueillit d'un petit spa comprenant un sauna et une salle de remise en forme; des VTT sont disponibles pour des excursions.

Dieses Palacio aus dem 16. Jahrhundert liegt mitten im gotischen Viertel von Palma und ist nur 2 Minuten Fußmarsch von der Kathedrale entfernt. Ursprüngliche Details wie Buntglas, Fliesen, Lüster und Wandteppiche zieren die herrlichen Aufenthaltsräume, und die komfortablen Gästezimmer sind klassisch eingerichtet. Einige sind eher klein und gemütlich. Um 19 Uhr trifft man sich zum Apéritif im Lesesaal mit eigener Bibliothek. Das Hotel bietet einen kleinen Wellnessbereich mit Sauna und Fitnessraum. Mountainbikes für Exkursionen stehen ebenfalls zur Verfügung.

Our inspector loved: *The complimentary Harrods' tea and cakes served at 4pm in the Monet kitchen.*

Directions: The nearest airport is Palma. Take the motorway to Port and enter the old town behind the cathedral. At Plaça Santa Eulaka press the button at the police bollard to gain entry to the street.

Web: www.johansens.com/casagalesa
E-mail: reservas@palaciocasagalesa.com
Tel: +34 971 715 400
Fax: +34 971 721 579

Price Guide:
(breakfast €19, excluding VAT)
double €219-278
suite €372-402

Read's

CA'N MORAGUES, 07320 SANTA MARÍA, MALLORCA, BALEARIC ISLANDS

Just 15 minutes from Palma, yet in the country, surrounded by 20,000m² of landscaped gardens, this 500-year-old manor house is a genuine luxury hotel. The spacious interior includes beautiful furniture and stunning frescoes on the walls. There is a 200m² outdoor and 100m² indoor pool, gymnasium, sauna, solarium, Jacuzzi and tennis court. The restaurant, under the auspices of chef Marc Fosh, was recently awarded a Star by a prestigious French guide and is currently No.1 in the Veuve Clicquot Top 10 of luxury restaurants. Open to non-residents; reservations recommended.

Situé à 15 minutes de Palma, mais en pleine campagne, ce manoir vieux de 500 ans qui se dresse dans un parc de 20 000m² est un véritable hôtel de luxe. Il comprend une piscine extérieure de 200m², une couverte de 100m² gymnase, sauna, solarium, Jacuzzi et un court de tennis. Des fresques magnifiques ornent les murs et de beaux meubles agrémentent toutes les pièces. Le restaurant, sous les auspices du chef Marc Fosh, a été attribué 1 étoile par un guide français prestigieux et actuellement il est 1er sur la liste de restaurants de luxe de Veuve Clicquot. Non-résidents sont conseillés de réserver une table en avance.

Dieses prachtvolle Luxushotel ist nur 15 Minuten von Palma entfernt und doch auf dem Land, umgeben von 20,000m² Garten. Es gibt ein 200m² Freibad, 100m² Hallenbad sowie Fitnessraum, Sauna, Solarium, Jacuzzi und Tennisplatz. Das geräumige Interieur ist mit Wandfresken und herrlichen Möbeln geschmückt. Das Restaurant unter Führung von Chefkoch Marc Fosh bekam kürzlich einen Stern von einem angesehenen französischen Restaurantführer und ist derzeit die Nr. 1 der Top 10 der Veuve Clicquot-Luxusrestaurants. Nicht-Gäste sind willkommen, sollten aber reservieren.

***Our inspector loved:** The marvellous indoor pool - big enough for a good swim!*

Directions: From Palma Airport follow directions to Inca. Turn off at Santa María. The hotel is then signposted.

Web: www.johansens.com/reads
E-mail: readshotel@readshotel.com
Tel: +34 971 14 02 62
Fax: +34 971 14 07 62

Price Guide:
double €250–360
suites €320–850

Sa Posada d'Aumallia

CAMINO SON PROHENS 1027, 07200 FELANITX, MALLORCA, BALEARIC ISLANDS

A fine example of Majorcan country architecture, this charming hotel is set amidst beautiful countryside in a secluded and peaceful position. Guests will receive the warmest of welcomes by the owners, the Martí Gomila family, who offer a truly wonderful stay in friendly surroundings. The public rooms are decorated with impeccable taste and boast antique furniture and paintings as well as fresh flowers, whilst the bedrooms are air-conditioned and have all modern amenities. The evenings are filled with fine dining accompanied by piano music played by Andrés Martí.

Un excellent exemple de l'architecture majorquin, ce charmant hôtel est situé en belle campagne dans un endroit retiré et paisible. Les propriétaires, la famille Martí Gomila, font les hôtes se sentir vraiment chez eux, offrant un séjour magnifique dans un cadre accueillant. Les salles communes sont ornées avec le meilleur goût et agrémentées d'antiquités et de tableaux originaux alors que les chambres sont climatisées et disposent de tout confort moderne. Les soirées sont remplies de bonne cuisine accompagnée du piano joué par Andrés Marti.

Dieses reizvolle Hotel ist ein hervorragende Beispiel für mallorquinische Architektur und liegt abgeschieden inmitten herrlicher Landschaft. Gäste erwartet ein herzlicher Empfang von der Familie Martí Gomila, die einen wundervollen Aufenthalt in freundlicher Umgebung bietet. Die geschmackvoll eingerichteten Aufenthaltsräume sind mit antiken Möbeln und Gemälden sowie frischen Blumen geschmückt, und die Gästezimmer sind klimatisiert und bieten jeglichen modernen Komfort. Abends genießt man hervorragende Speisen begleitet von Andrés Martí am Klavier.

Directions: Palma Airport > road to Manacor > Felanitx > Porto Colom. Continue on this road, the hotel is signposted.

Web: www.johansens.com/posadadaumallia
E-mail: aumallia@aumallia.com
Tel: +34 971 58 26 57
Fax: +34 971 58 32 69

Price Guide:
double €120.20–144.31

Our inspector loved: *The nightly piano recitals.*

SPAIN / BALEARIC ISLANDS (MALLORCA)

Sos Ferres d'en Morey

CTRA. MANACOR - COLONIA DE SANT PERE, KM 10.7, 07500 MANACOR, BALEARIC ISLANDS

Nestling in a beautiful position on the grounds of a farm, this impeccably kept small hotel offers a sense of sheer elegance in a rural setting. The interior is held in a contemporary style, with white and cream colour schemes and lamps made by a local designer. Each of the large bedrooms and suites has a spacious terrace and its own bathroom complete with hydromassage bath or shower and high-quality toiletries. There is no restaurant, but lunches and dinners from a set menu are served in the bar area upon prior notice. 5 golf courses and several beaches are within easy reach.

Niché dans le parc d'une ferme, ce petit hôtel bien entretenu offre le sentiment d'élégance dans un cadre rural. L'intérieur est décoré dans un style contemporain, la combinaison de couleurs étant blanche et crème, et des lampes faites par un designer local. Chacune des grandes chambres et suites a sa propre terrasse spacieuse et salle de bain comprenant bain ou douche hydro-massage et des articles de toilette de haute qualité. L'hôtel n'a pas de restaurant mais des déjeuners et dîners peuvent être organisés dans le bar sur demande. 5 parcours de golf et de nombreuses plages sont d'accès facile.

In herrlicher Lage auf dem Gelände eines Bauernhofs liegt dieses wundervoll geführte Hotel, das ein Gefühl purer Eleganz in ländlicher Atmosphäre vermittelt. Das Interieur ist zeitgenössisch in Weiß- und Cremetönen gehalten und mit Lampen eines einheimischen Designers gefüllt. Die Zimmer und Suiten bieten große Terrassen und eigene Bäder mit Hydromassagebad oder -dusche und feinen Kosmetikartikeln. Es gibt kein Restaurant, doch man bekommt auf vorherige Anfrage Mittag- und Abendessen in der Bar. 5 Golfplätze und mehrere Strände liegen in der Nähe.

Our inspector loved: *The view through the spectacular picture window in the suite.*

Directions: Palma Mallorca Airport > Manacor > take the road to Colonia de Sant Pere. The hotel is indicated at km 10.7.

Web: www.johansens.com/sosferres
E-mail: finca@sosferres.com
Tel: +34 971 55 75 75
Fax: +34 971 55 74 74

Price Guide:
single €54.14-68.76
double €84.14-98.76
suite €128.61-225.13

VALLDEMOSSA HOTEL

CTRA. VIEJA DE VALLDEMOSSA S/N, 07170 VALLDEMOSSA, MALLORCA, BALEARIC ISLANDS

Directions: Palma Airport > Valldemossa. The hotel is signposted just before the entrance to the village.

Web: www.johansens.com/valldemossa
E-mail: info@valldemossahotel.com
Tel: +34 971 61 26 26
Fax: +34 971 61 26 25

Price Guide:
single €159
double €244
suite €313.73

Menorca
Mallorca
Mahón
Palma
Ibiza
Ibiza
Formentera

Set in flower-filled gardens on various levels, this romantic stone-built Majorcan house offers spectacular views over the village, the Bay of Palma and the Tramuntana mountain range. Built over 100 years ago, it has been converted into a luxurious hotel with superb facilities. No expense has been spared in the bedrooms, which vary in size and décor and display wonderful touches such as specially made hand-painted lamps. Superb cuisine is served in the Valldemossa restaurant, and there is a large outdoor pool, a small indoor pool and a sauna.

Dans un jardin rempli de fleurs sur plusieurs niveaux, cette maison majorquine romantique construite en pierre offre des vues spectaculaires sur le village, la baie de Palma et les montagnes de Tramuntana. Construite il y a plus de 100 ans, la maison a été convertie en hôtel luxueux avec des facilités superbes. Les chambres opulentes, qui ne manque aucun détail, varient en taille et décor et ont des agréments comme des lampes peintes à la main. Une cuisine superbe est servie dans le restaurant Valldemossa. L'hôtel dispose d'une piscine extérieure, petite piscine couverte et sauna.

In einem mit Blumen gefüllten Garten auf mehreren Ebenen liegt dieses romantische mallorquinische Steingebäude mit Blick auf das Dorf und die Tramuntanaberge. Das über 100 Jahre alte Haus wurde in ein luxuriöses Hotel umgewandelt und bietet hervorragende Einrichtungen. Bei der Ausstattung der unterschiedlich großen und individuell gestalteten Zimmer wurde nicht gespart, man findet zahlreiche Extras wie z.B. handbemalte Lampen. Im Valldemossa wird feinste Küche serviert, und ein großer Pool im Freien, ein kleines Hallenbad und eine Sauna sorgen für Entspannung.

Our inspector loved: *The beautifully laid out gardens, especially the pretty little walled gardens of the suites.*

Elba Palace Golf Hotel

URB. FUERTEVENTURA GOLF CLUB, CTA. DE JANDIA, KM11, 35610 ANTIGUA, FUERTEVENTURA, CANARY ISLANDS

This elegant new hotel is surrounded by a small garden with swimming pool, and beyond, an 18-hole golf course. Décor is sober and elegant combining parquet floors, hand-crafted wooden furniture, doors and ceilings, although the entrance hall does feature a stunning 4-metre chandelier. An basement wine cellar provides meeting space, as do the quiet library and cards room. Other activities include windsurfing, diving, sea fishing and sailing. A gymnasium and beauty centre (reservations required) are also available.

Cet nouvel hôtel élégant est entouré d'un petit jardin avec piscine, et plus loin se trouve un terrain de golf de 18 trous. Le décor est sobre et élégant grâce à une combinaison entre autres de parquets, de meubles, portes et plafonds en bois travaillés à la main. Dans l'entrée se tient un chandelier incroyable de près de quatré mètres. Le cellier à vin souterrain tout comme la bibliothèque tranquille et la salle de jeu, est un endroit agréable où se retrouver. Pour les sportifs, planche à voile, plongée, pêche en mer et voile ainsi qu'un gymnase et centre de beauté (réservation obligatoire) sont disponibles.

Dieses elegante neue Hotel ist von einem kleinen Garten mit Swimmingpool und einem 18-Loch Golfplatz umgeben. Das Décor ist nüchtern-elegant mit Parkettböden und handgefertigten Holzmöbeln und -decken, und die Eingangshalle ziert ein einzigartiger 4m hoher Kronleuchter. Der Weinkeller ist ein beliebter Treffpunkt, ebenso die ruhige Bibliothek und der Spieleraum. Aktivitäten sind Windsurfen, Tauchen, Angeln und Segeln, außerdem stehen ein Fitnessraum und eine Beautyfarm (Reservierung erforderlich) zur Verfügung.

Our inspector loved: *The truly palatial bathrooms in the suites, with outsized baths and massage showers.*

Directions: 8km from Fuerteventura Airport > Caleta de Fuste > hotel is on the right.

Web: www.johansens.com/elbapalacegolfhotel
E-mail: epg@hoteleselba.com
Tel: +34 928 16 39 22
Fax: +34 928 16 39 23

Lanzarote
Arrecife
Tenerife
Santa Cruz
Las Palmas
Puerto del Rosario
Fuerteventura
Gran Canaria

Price Guide:
double €165–335
suite €320–770

Gran Hotel Atlantis Bahia Real

AVENIDA GRANDES PLAYAS, S/N, 35660 CORRALEJO, FUERTEVENTURA, CANARY ISLANDS

Directions: Located on the north coast of the island in the resort of Corralejo. The airport is 35km away.

Web: www.johansens.com/atlantisbahiareal
E-mail: comercial@atlantishotels.com
Tel: +34 928 53 64 44
Fax: +34 928 53 75 75

Price Guide:
single €159.50-257.50
double €213-343
suite €255.50-1,260

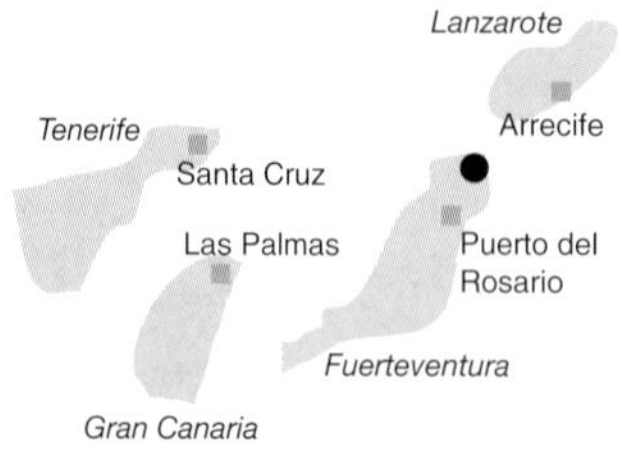

Lanzarote
Arrecife
Tenerife
Santa Cruz
Las Palmas
Puerto del Rosario
Fuerteventura
Gran Canaria

Owned by the reputable Atlantis Hotels and Resorts Group, Gran Hotel Atlantis Bahia Real opens on 1st November 2003. Adjacent to the beach and Las Dunas National Park, this Canarian hotel boasts magnificent views across Lobos Island and Lanzarote. 250 bedrooms have terraces or balconies and pool or sea views, and 7 bars and restaurants serve national, international, Italian and Japanese cuisine whilst live entertainment is held in La Boheme. Bahia Vital Spa offers a wide range of health and beauty treatments, specialising in hydrotherapy.

Gran Hotel Atlantis Bahia Real, qui appartient au groupe bien réputé Atlantis Hotels and Resorts, s'ouvre le 1er novembre 2003. A coté de la plage et du parc national de Las Dunas, cet hôtel canarien offre des vues imprenables sur l'île de Lobos et Lanzarote. Les 250 chambres ont des terrasses ou balcons avec vue sur la piscine ou la mer et les 7 bars et restaurants servent une cuisine nationale, internationale, italienne et japonaise alors qu'il y a des spectacles sur scène à la Boheme. Bahia Vital Spa offre toute une gamme de traitements de beauté et de santé, spécialisant en l'hydrothérapie.

Dieses zur renommierten Gruppe der Atlantis Hotels and Resorts gehörende Hotel eröffnet am 1. November 2003. Direkt am Strand und neben dem Las Dunas Nationapark gelegen, bietet es eine traumhafte Sicht auf die Insel Lobos und Lanzarote. Die 250 Zimmer haben Terrassen oder Balkone mit Blick auf den Pool oder das Meer, und in 7 Bars und Restaurants wird spanische, internationale, italienische und japanische Küche serviert. Im La Boheme finden Live-Unterhaltungsprogramme statt, und das auf Hydrotherapie spezialisierte Bahia Vital Spa bietet Gesundheits und Schönheitsbehandlungen.

Our inspector loved: *The ocean view towards Lobos Island and Lanzarote.*

SPA

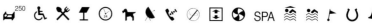

Gran Hotel Costa Meloneras ****

C/MAR MEDITERRÁNEO 1, 35100 MASPALOMAS, GRAN CANARIA, CANARY ISLANDS, SPAIN

Although it has over 1,000 rooms, this hotel retains a sense of individuality and its décor reflects the colonial and Canarian architecture of the island. Spacious public areas filled with exotic furniture and painted tile floors lead to beautifully landscaped gardens, numerous swimming pools and the beach. Activities such as golf and water sports are close at hand, as well as a spa offering a superb variety of water, massage and innovative treatments. A wide selection of restaurants and bars all offer their own distinctive ambience.

Bien qu'il ait plus de 1000 chambres, cet hôtel retient une individualité et ses décors reflètent l'architecture coloniale et canarienne de l'île. Les espaces publiques spacieux emplis de meubles exotiques et aux carrelages peints conduisent à de beaux jardins aménagés, à de nombreuses piscines et à la plage. Des activités telles que golf et sports nautiques sont à potée, ainsi qu'un spa offrant une variété superbe comprenant des traitements innovatifs, d'eau et de massage. Il existe également une vaste sélection de restaurants et bars qui offrent tous leur propre ambiance.

Trotz seiner über 1000 Zimmer hat sich dieses Hotel ein Gefühl der Individualität bewahrt. Das Décor spiegelt die koloniale und kanarische Architektur der Insel wider, die großen Aufenthaltsräume sind mit exotischem Mobiliar gefüllt und die gefliesten Böden führen zu herrlichen Gärten, Swimmingpools und zum Strand. Golf und Wassersport können vor Ort betrieben werden, und es gibt ein Kurbad mit einer großen Auswahl an Wasser-, Massage- und innovativen Behandlungen. Zahlreiche Restaurants und Bars schaffen ein ganz besonderes Ambiente.

Our inspector loved: *The way the hotel's architecture gives a feeling of space and intimacy.*

Directions: Take the motorway south and exit at Pasito Blanco then follow signs to Maspalomas. The nearest airport is (Las Palmas de) Gran Canaria.

Web: www.johansens.com/costameloneras
E-mail: info@ghcmeloneras.com
Tel: +34 928 12 81 00
Fax: +34 928 12 81 22

Price Guide:
single €111–234
double €138–294
suite €210–1,764

       SPA

HESPERIA LANZAROTE HOTEL

URB. CORTIJO VIEJO, PUERTO CALERO, 35570 YAIZA, LANZAROTE, CANARY ISLANDS

Hesperia Lanzarote Hotel is the ideal location from which to explore the island's capital. Whether a family holiday, romantic break or business trip, a wide range of accommodation and facilities are available. Many guest rooms have ocean views and terrace or balcony; 1 buffet and 2 à la carte restaurants and 5 bars offer something for every taste. Activities include 3 swimming pools, a children's pool, spa and wellness centre with fitness centre, steam room and beauty centre, 1 tennis and 1 squash court.

Hesperia Lanzarote est la base idéale pour explorer le capitale de l'île. Que ce soit une vacance en famille ou romantique ou un voyage d'affaires, toute une gamme de logement et de facilités est disponible. Plusieurs chambres ont une vue sur la mer et une terrasse ou un balcon. 1 restaurant aux buffets, 2 restaurants à la carte et 5 bars offrent quelque chose pour les goûts de chacun. Les facilités comprennent 3 piscines, une piscine pour des enfants, un centre de bien-être incluant un centre de remise en forme, hammam et centre de beauté, 1 court de tennis et 1 court de squash.

Dieses Hotel ist der ideale Ausgangsort, um die Inselhauptstadt zu erkunden. Ob Familienurlaub, romantischer Kurzurlaub oder Geschäftsreise – hier findet man eine große Auswahl an Unterkunft und Einrichtungen für jeden Zweck. Viele Zimmer haben Terrasse oder Balkon und Blick aufs Meer. 1 Buffetrestaurant, 2 à la carte Restaurants und 5 Bars bieten etwas für jeden Geschmack. Das Freizeitangebot umfasst 3 Swimmingpools, ein Kinderbecken, ein Wellness-Centre mit Fitness-Centre, Dampfbad und Beautysalon, sowie 1 Tennis- und 1 Squashplatz.

Directions: Located 10 km from the airport, directly on the seafront, adjacent to the exclusive Puerto Calero Yacht Harbour.

Web: www.johansens.com/hespialanzarote
E-mail: hotel@hesperia-lanzarote.com
Tel: +34 828 0808 00
Fax: +34 828 08 08 10

Price Guide:
(room only)
single €168-188
double €168-188
suite €238

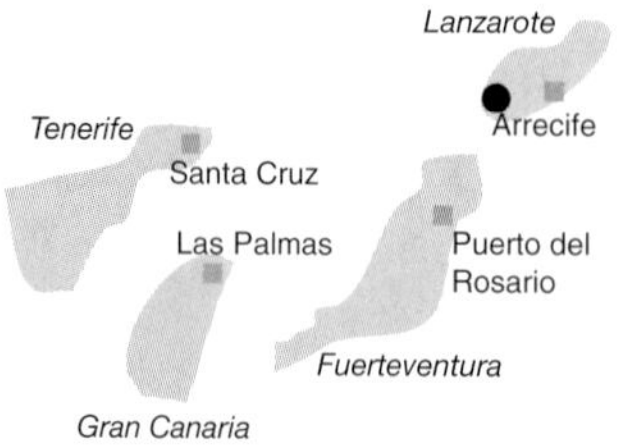

Our inspector loved: *The luxurious amenities and abundance of facilities.*

Gran Hotel Bahía del Duque Resort

38660 ADEJE, COSTA ADEJE, TENERIFE SOUTH, CANARY ISLANDS

This hotel is a private romantic village created on a gentle hill sloping down to the sea. 20 houses in turn-of-the-century Canarian architecture form this prestigious complex in a large estate with sculptured terraces and pools. The furniture has been specially designed, the floors are cool Spanish tiles and the bathrooms are luxurious. Descending towards the coast, guests will find a patio surrounded by 11 restaurants. The newly opened "El Mirador" section, decorated in soft, understated colours, offers its own restaurants and swimming pools.

Cet hôtel est un village romantique privé créé sur une pente douce descendant sur la mer. 20 maisons qui reflètent l'architecture canarienne du début du siècle forment un complexe prestigieux au milieu d'une grande propriété agrémentée de terrasses ornées et de piscines. Les meubles ont été spécialement conçus, les sols sont de céramiques espagnoles et les salles de bain sont luxueuses. En descendant vers la côte, les visiteurs trouveront un patio et 11 restaurants. La nouvelle section "El Mirador" est décorée en couleurs douces et dispose de ses propres restaurants et piscines.

Dieses romantische private Dorf liegt auf einem zum Meer abfallenden Hügel. Die renommierte Anlage besteht aus 20 Häusern im Stil kanarischer Architektur um die Jahrhundertwende, und liegt in einem ausgedehnten Grundstück mit gepflegten Terrassen und Pools. Das Mobiliar wurde eigens für das Hotel entworfen, die Böden sind mit spanischen Fliesen versehen und die Badezimmer sind reiner Luxus. In Richtung Meeresufer liegt ein von 11 Restaurants umrahmter Innenhof. Der neue, in sanften Farben gehaltene "El Mirador" Flügel hat eigene Restaurants und Swimmingpools.

Our inspector loved: *The choices on offer; so many environments in one hotel, more like a fantasy village.*

Directions: Reina Sofia Airport.

Web: www.johansens.com/granhotelbahiadelduque
E-mail: comercial@bahia-duque.com
Tel: +34 922 74 69 00
Fax: +34 922 74 69 16

Price Guide:
single €229–415
double/twin €248–444
suite €452–2,103

Hotel Botánico

AVDA. RICHARD J. YEOWARD 1, URB. BOTÁNICO, 38400 PUERTO DE LA CRUZ, TENERIFE, CANARY ISLANDS

The Botánico stands in extensive gardens filled with tropical plants, lakes, fountains and shady places for those wishing to escape the sun. The lavish rooms provide every possible extra and glamorous bathrooms. Choose between 3 delightful à la carte restaurants offering Spanish, Thai or Italian dishes. The hotel has 2 heated swimming pools as well as an 18-hole putting green. There are special rates at all the local golf courses. A new spa/treatment area has opened including large saunas and steam rooms and showers.

Le Botánico est situé dans un immense jardin orné de plantes tropicales, de lacs, de fontaines et d'endroits ombragés pour ceux souhaitant échapper au soleil. Les chambres somptueuses fournissent tous les agréments possibles et ont des salles de bain séduisantes. Vous pourrez choisir entre 3 délicieux restaurants proposant des barbecues, des plats espagnols, thaïlandais ou italiens. Il y a 2 piscines chauffées ainsi qu'un vert à 18 trous. Tarifs préférentiels dans tous les golfs environnants. Il existe un nouveau spa/coin de traitements, comprenant des grandes saunas et hammams et douches.

Das Botánico liegt inmitten ausgedehnter Gärten voller tropischer Pflanzen, kleinen Seen, Springbrunnen und sonnengeschützten Plätzen. Die großzügigen Zimmer bieten jedes erdenkliche Extra und haben prunkvolle Bäder. Gäste haben die Wahl zwischen 3 zauberhaften Restaurants, die auf Grill-, spanische, thailändische oder italienische Gerichte spezialisiert sind. Das Hotel hat 2 beheizte Pools und ein 18-Loch Putting Green. Alle Golfplätze am Ort bieten Sondertarife. Es gibt einen neuen Spabereich mit Saunen, Dampfbädern, Duschen und einem privaten Wellness-Bereich.

Our inspector loved: *The relaxing poolside bar that overlooks tropical gardens.*

Directions: Tenerife North Airport > motorway to Puerto Cruz > El Botanico > hotel is on the left, past the botanical gardens. Guests can be met at the airport upon request.

Web: www.johansens.com/botanico
E-mail: hotelbotanico@hotelbotanico.com
Tel: +34 922 38 14 00
Fax: +34 922 38 39 93

Price Guide:
single €120.20-234.40
double/twin €156.30-354.60
suite €252.45-3005.10

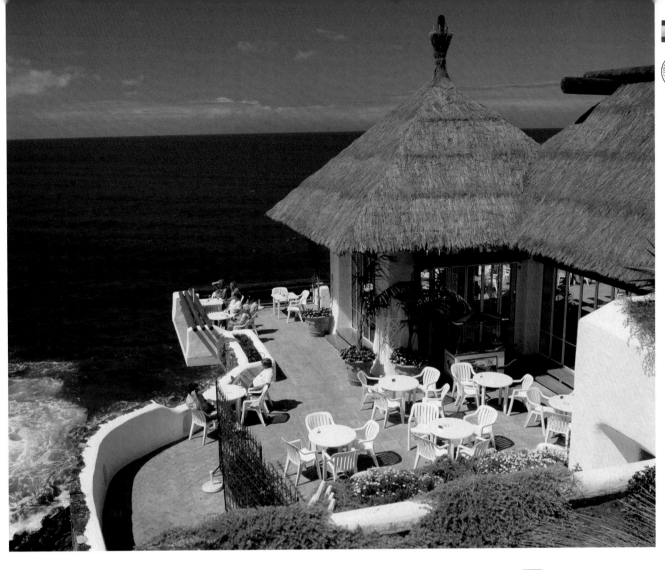

Hotel Jardín Tropical

CALLE GRAN BRETAÑA, 38670 COSTA ADEJE, TENERIFE, CANARY ISLANDS

Built just 14 years ago, this magnificent Moorish palace with its brilliant white walls is enveloped by the exotic green foliage of its subtropical garden interspersed with blue pools and colourful flowers. The interior rooms display cool luxury, and the exclusive Las Adelfas Suites are phenomenal. Guests are spoilt for choice with the cuisine and may enjoy everything from poolside snacks to a gourmet feast in the El Patio restaurant. Beauty treatments are available in the Bio Centre.

Construit il y a tout juste 14 ans, ce magnifique palais mauresque a été embelli par des tours surmontées de dômes. L'hôtel se dresse au milieu d'un jardin exotique parsemé de bassins azur et de fleurs colorées. A l'intérieur, les chambres affichent un luxe sobre et les prestigieuses suites Las Adelfas sont remarquables. Les hôtes sont gâtés au niveau culinaire et pourront se régaler du simple snack au bord de la piscine jusqu'au festin gastronomique au restaurant El Patio. Il y a un "Bio Centre" pour des soins de beauté.

Dieser herrliche, vor 14 Jahren erbaute maurische Palast mit seinen strahlend weißen Wänden ist umgeben von exotischen subtropischen Gärten, leuchtendblauen Pools und bunten Blumen. Die Innenräume spiegeln kühlen Luxus wider, und die exklusiven Las Adelfas Suiten sind einfach prächtig. Was das Essen angeht, haben die Gäste die Qual der Wahl – vom Snack am Pool bis zum Gourmetdinner im El Patio ist alles geboten. Im "Bio Centre" werden Schönheitskuren angeboten.

***Our inspector loved:** The excellent food and service in the à la carte restaurant.*

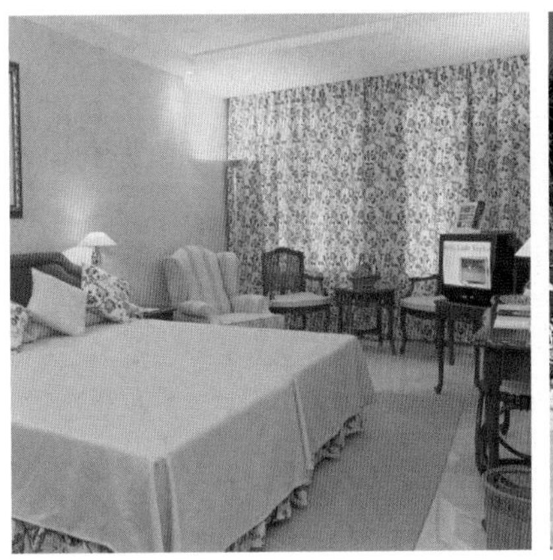

Directions: Airport > Tenerife South > motorway - Playa Americas > exit 29, San Eugenio.

Web: www.johansens.com/jardintropical
E-mail: hotel@jardin-tropical.com
Tel: +34 922 74 60 11/2/3
Fax: +34 922 74 60 14

Price Guide:
single €108.18-330.55
double/twin €150.25-811.36
suite €360.60-961.61

Hotel La Quinta Roja

GLORIETA DE SAN FRANCISCO, 38450 GARACHICO, TENERIFE, CANARY ISLANDS

This historical mansion is a fine example of Baroque architecture, and is set in the attractive town square of Garachico. The original building dates back to the 16th century and the wooden galleries, stone paving and marble fountain all create an atmosphere of a grand bygone era. Each bedroom is individually and tastefully decorated, and The Marquess Dining Room, rustic-style bar and restaurant serve fresh regional cuisine. The fitness club has a Jacuzzi, sauna and solarium.

Situé dans la place du marché de Garachico, ce manoir historique est un excellent exemple de l,architecture baroque. Le bâtiment original date du XVIe siècle et les galeries en bois, le pavé et la fontaine en marbre créent une ambiance d,une époque d,autrefois. Chacune des chambres est ornée avec goût et la salle à manger 'la Marquise', le bar rustique et le restaurant servent une cuisine fraîche et régionale. Il y a un jacuzzi, une sauna et un solarium dans le gymnase.

Dieses historische, am attraktiven Marktplatz der Stadt Garachio gelegene Haus ist ein hervorragendes Beispiel barocker Baukunst. Das ursprüngliche Gebäude stammt aus dem 16. Jahrhundert, und die hölzernen Galerien, der Steinboden und der Marmorbrunnen schaffen eine Atmosphäre vergangener Pracht. Jedes Zimmer ist individuell und geschmackvoll gestaltet, und im Speisesaal der „Marquise", der rustikalen Bar und dem Restaurant werden frische, regionale Köstlichkeiten serviert. Der Fitnessclub bietet Jacuzzi, Sauna und Solarium.

Our inspector loved: *The very young, dynamic staff.*

Directions: From Highway Tenerife North to Puerto de la Crue > continue to Garachico > the hotel is in the village square.

Web: www.johansens.com/quintaroja
E-mail: hotelquintaroja@quintaroja.com
Tel: +34 922 13 33 77
Fax: +34 922 13 33 60

Price Guide:
single €84-132
double €126-180

Lanzarote
Arrecife
Tenerife
Santa Cruz
Las Palmas
Puerto del Rosario
Fuerteventura
Gran Canaria

DES IGN HOT ELS

Hotel San Roque

C/ ESTEBAN DE PONTE 32, 38450 GARACHICO, TENERIFE, CANARY ISLANDS, SPAIN

This 17th-century town house has been carefully restored and converted into a luxurious, family-run small hotel, combining the original construction with the contemporary Bauhaus style. Stone archways guide guests into the generously sized rooms that are decorated in sumptuous colours, featuring dark wooden ceilings and designer furniture. All rooms have Jacuzzi bath tubs and CD players. Fine dishes incorporating fresh fish and locally sourced produce are served.

Cet hôtel particulier du XVIIe siècle a été restauré avec soin et transformé en un petit hôtel de luxe familial remarquable dans lequel l'architecture d'origine se marie au style contemporain de Bauhaus. Des voûtes en pierre s'ouvrent sur des chambres spacieuses, ornées de plafonds en bois foncé et des meubles designer. Toutes les chambres possèdent une baignoire Jacuzzi et des lecteurs CD. De succulents plats sont offerts et combinent du poisson frais et des produits régionaux.

Dieses Stadthaus aus dem 17. Jahrhundert wurde umsichtig restauriert und in ein luxuriöses, kleines familiengeführtes Hotel umgewandelt. Dabei verbindet sich der Originalbau perfekt mit dem zeitgenössischen Bauhausstil. Steinerne Bögen führen in großzügige Räume, die in üppigen Farben gehalten und mit dunklen Holzdecken und Designermöbeln ausgestattet sind. Alle Zimmer haben Jacuzzi-Badewannen und CD-Player. Gäste erfreuen sich an köstlichen Gerichten, die mit frischem Fisch und einheimischen Zutaten zubereitet werden.

Our inspector loved: *The relaxing combination of Jacuzzi baths and CD players (with 300 CDs available) in every room.*

Directions: Motorway > Puerto Cruz > follow the road to Garachico. The nearest airport is Tenerife North.

Web: www.johansens.com/sanroque
E-mail: info@hotelsanroque.com
Tel: +34 922 13 34 35
Fax: +34 922 13 34 06

Price Guide: (exl. VAT)
single €124-155
double/twin €163-230
suites €247-315

El Milano Real

C/TOLEO S/N, HOYOS DEL ESPINO, 05634 ÁVILA, SPAIN

Directions: Madrid > A6 > N110 > Ávila > N502 > Venta Rasquilla > C500.

Web: www.johansens.com/elmilanoreal
E-mail: info@elmilanoreal.com
Tel: +34 920 349 108
Fax: +34 920 349 156

Price Guide:
single €87.74-114.49
double €112.35-142.31
suite €171.20

This welcoming village hotel, surrounded by a beautiful landscaped garden, offers spectacular views of the Gredos mountains and superb bedroom and suite accommodation with elegant furnishings and décor. Some guest rooms have a Jacuzzi, one has a sauna, and many have a terrace for alfresco breakfasts. Guests can relax over an apéritif in the cosy lounge bar before enjoying excellent, creative cuisine in the attractive restaurant.

Au cœur d'un beau jardin aménagé, cet hôtel de village accueillant offre une vue spectaculaire sur les montagnes de Gredos ainsi que des chambres et suites superbes au mobilier et décor élégants. Certaines disposent d'un Jacuzzi, une d'un sauna et la plupart d'une terrasse pour un petit déjeuner "au frais". Les hôtes peuvent se détendre à l'apéritif dans le confortable salon-bar avant de déguster une cuisine excellente et créative dans le charmant restaurant.

Dieses einladende, von einem herrlichen Garten umgebene Dorfhotel bietet eine atemberaubende Sicht auf die Gredos-Berge und elegant eingerichtete Zimmer und Suiten. Einige Zimmer haben einen Jacuzzi, eines bietet eine Sauna, und viele haben eine Terrasse, auf der man frühstücken kann. Die gemütliche Lounge lädt zum Apéritif ein, bevor man sich zu exquisiten und kreativen Speisen im Restaurant niederlässt.

Our inspector loved: *The food, from homemade jams at breakfast to the creative menus at lunch and dinner.*

Hotel Rector

RECTOR ESPERABÉ 10–APARTADO 399, 37008 SALAMANCA, SPAIN

This exclusive hotel stands by the walls of the citadel looking up to the cathedral, a magnificent golden vision at night when floodlit. The interior looks cool and elegant with archways between the spacious reception hall and the welcoming bar. Unique features in the main salon are 2 exquisite modern stained glass windows. There are 13 bedrooms, delightfully furnished with marble bathrooms. Breakfast is served in the hotel, and for dinner, there are numerous restaurants in the vicinity. Salamanca was European City of Culture in 2002.

Cet hôtel exclusif se dresse à côté des remparts de la citadelle; elle même dominée par la cathédrale, qui devient une vision magique lorsqu'illuminée la nuit. L'intérieur est frais et élégant, avec de belles voûtes qui séparent le spacieux hall de réception et le bar accueillant. Le salon principal est orné de 2 ravissants vitraux modernes. L'hôtel compte treize chambres, délicieusement meublées avec salles de bain en marbre. Le petit déjeuner est servi à l'hôtel et de nombreux restaurants sont situés à proximité. En 2002, Salamanca était capitale culturelle de l'Europe.

Dieses exklusive Hotel liegt an einer Zitadelle neben der Kathedrale, die nachts beleuchtet wird und ein herrlich goldenes Spektakel bietet. Das Interieur ist kühl und elegant, mit Bogengängen zwischen der großen Empfangshalle und der einladenden Bar. Hauptanziehungspunkte des Salons sind zweifellos 2 exquisite moderne Buntglasfenster. Die 13 Zimmer sind zauberhaft gestaltet und haben Marmorbäder. Frühstück wird im Hotel serviert, und am Abend locken zahlreiche Restaurants in der Umgebung. 2002 war Salamanca europäische Kulturhauptstadt.

Our inspector loved: *The beautifully embroidered bed linen.*

Directions: Paseo de Rector Esperabé.

Web: www.johansens.com/rector
E-mail: hotelrector@telefonica.net
Tel: +34 923 21 84 82
Fax: +34 923 21 40 08

León
Barcelona
Madrid
Málaga

Price Guide:
(room only, VAT excluded)
single €86
double/twin €108–127
suite €139

Apartments at Hotel Arts

CARRER DE LA MARINA 19-21, 08005 BARCELONA, SPAIN

These stunning duplex apartments offer the very utmost in luxury with the addition of the use of all hotel facilities. Butlers and waiting staff are on hand to attend to guests' every need, including unpacking luggage, organising catering requirements and running mineral salt baths. The hotel chefs will even cook in the apartment kitchens on request. Rooms are elegant, spacious and stylish, boast excellent views from their location above the 34th floor and offer the utmost privacy.

Ces appartements offrent le plus grand luxe ainsi que l'utilisation de toutes les facilités de l'hôtel. Les maîtres d'hôtel sont au service pour répondre au moindre besoin des hôtes; pour aider à défaire les valises, organiser le dîner ou préparer un bain aux sels minéraux. Les chefs de cuisine de l'hôtel même prépareront des plats dans la cuisine de l'appartement sur demande. Les chambres sont élégantes et spacieuses et offrent des vues magnifiques de leur position au 34e étage ainsi qu'une solitude non troublée.

Diese einzigartigen Duplex-Appartements bieten höchsten Luxus und zusätzlich die Möglichkeit, alle Einrichtungen des Hotels zu benutzen. Dienstpersonal steht bereit, um dem Gast jeden Wunsch zu erfüllen, wie z.B. Koffer auszupacken, Mahlzeiten zu organisieren oder auch ein Mineralsalzbad vorzubereiten. Die Hotelköche kochen auf Anfrage sogar in der Appartementküche. Die Zimmer sind geräumig und elegant und bieten traumhafte Ausblicke von ihrer Lage im 34. Stockwerk. Absolut ungestörte Privatsphäre.

Our inspector loved: *The friendly, yet impeccable service; you are made welcome.*

Directions: The nearest airport is Barcelona. The hotel is situated by the marina.

Web: www.johansens.com/hotelarts
E-mail: reservas@rcspain.com
Tel: +34 93 22 11 000
Fax: +34 93 22 11 070

Price Guide:
(room only)
one bedroom €1,200
two bedrooms €1,800
three bedrooms €2,400

Claris Hotel

PAU CLARIS 150, 08009 BARCELONA, SPAIN

This former palace, close to the Paseo de Gracia still retains its graceful Renaissance façade whilst the interior is an example of avant-garde design with marble, glass and rare timbers. Art pieces and 5th-century Roman mosaics abound, and there is a collection of Egyptian art. The bedrooms are contemporary design with antique objets d'art. Creative Mediterranean cuisine and Spanish and French wines can be sampled in the gourmet restaurant and cocktail bar, East 47. There are also 2 other restaurants, La Terraza del Claris and the Claris. Wireless Internet connection available.

Cet ancien palais, près du Paseo de Gracia, conserve toujours sa gracieuse façade Renaissance alors que l'intérieur est un exemple d'avant-garde avec marbre, verre et des bois rares. Des œuvres d'art et des mosaïques romaines du Ve siècle abondent, et il y a une collection d'art égyptien. Les chambres ont un décor contemporain. Une cuisine méditerranéenne originale peut être dégustée au restaurant gourmet et bar-cocktail East 47, accompagnée des vins espagnols et français. Il existe également 2 autres restaurants, La Terraza del Clariset le Claris. Service Internet sans fil disponible.

Dieses einstige Palais nahe des Paseo de Gracia besitzt immer noch seine elegante Renaissancefassade, das Interieur dagegen ist ein Beispiel avantgardistischen Designs mit Marmor, Glas und seltenem Holz. Überall findet man Kunstgegenstände und römische Mosaiken aus dem 5. Jahrhundert, außerdem eine Sammlung ägyptischer Kunst. Die Zimmer sind zeitgenössisch mit antiken Objets d'art eingerichtet. Im Gourmetrestaurant und der Cocktailbar East 47 werden Mittelmeergerichte und spanische und französische Weine serviert, man kann aber auch das La Terraza del Claris oder das Claris besuchen. Drahtloser Internetzugang vorhanden.

Our inspector loved: *The amazing antiquities dotted around the hotel.*

Directions: Pau Claris > Paseo de Gracia > Calle de Valencia. The hotel is in the centre of Barcelona.

Web: www.johansens.com/claris
E-mail: claris@derbyhotels.es
Tel: +34 934 87 62 62
Fax: +34 932 15 79 70

Barcelona
Madrid
Málaga

Price Guide:
(breakfast €19)
single €335
double/twin €372

 124

 150

SPAIN / CATALUÑA (BARCELONA)

GALLERY HOTEL

DESIGN HOTELS

ROSSELLÓ 249, 08008 BARCELONA, SPAIN

Directions: Between Rambla de Catalunya and Paseo de Gracia. Transfers are available from the airport to the hotel.

Web: www.johansens.com/gallery
E-mail: email@galleryhotel.com
Tel: +34 934 15 99 11
Fax: +34 934 15 91 84

Price Guide:
single €232
double €264
suite €310

Visitors to the Gallery Hotel are enveloped by a warm ambience and are treated to a personal service whilst enjoying the fine standards of accommodation. Featuring a stylish blend of modern and classic décor, the bedrooms offer every amenity including fax. The Scotch Bar is ideal for a preprandial drink after which fine cuisine may be enjoyed in the atmospheric Café Del Gallery. A garden terrace, fitness centre and separate saunas offer revitalisation to visitors returning from a day exploring vibrant Barcelona. A business centre is available.

Les visiteurs du Gallery découvrent une atmosphère chaleureuse et un service personalisé, tout en profitant de cet établissement de grand standing. Les chambres, savant mélange d'éléments modernes et classiques, offrent tout le confort possible (incluant fax). Le Scotch Bar est idéal pour prendre l'apéritif à la suite de quoi une excellente cuisine vous est proposée au Café Del Gallery. Une terrasse au jardin, des saunas et un club de remise en forme attendent les visiteurs en quête de revitalisation après une journée de visite de Barcelone. Un centre d'affaires est disponible.

Die Gallery versprüht eine herzliche Atmosphäre, die von persönlichen Service noch verstärkt wird. Die Unterkunft ist erstklassig, und die Zimmer, sowohl modern als auch klassisch gestaltet, bieten jeden erdenklichen Komfort inklusive Fax. Die Scotch Bar ist ideal für einen Apéritif, und danach lässt man sich im charaktervollen Café Del Gallery von erlesenen Speisen verführen. Eine Gartenterrasse, ein Fitnesszentrum und separate Saunen sorgen nach einem langen Tag im lebhaften Barcelona für Entspannung. Ein Business-Zentrum ist vorhanden.

Our inspector loved: *The suites with their sharp, contemporary design.*

Hotel Colón

AVENIDA DE LA CATEDRAL 7, 08002 BARCELONA, SPAIN

Situated in the old Gothic quarter, this hotel offers a combination of fine accommodation, excellent service and friendly staff resulting in a most inviting ambience. Vibrant décor with brightly coloured fabrics features throughout the hotel and the front rooms afford glorious views of the square and the 13th-century cathedral. The suites at the rear boast picturesque terraces. Drinks can be enjoyed in the classic, English-style bar. Seafood is a hotel speciality; with salmon, clams, squid and hake all used to create international and typical Catalan dishes.

Situé dans le vieux quartier gothique, cet hôtel offre un logement raffiné, un service excellent et un personnel amical qui donne une ambiance des plus sympathiques. L'hôtel est paré d'un décor vif avec des tissus de couleurs éclatantes. Les chambres de devant offrent des vues sur la place de la cathédrale du XIIIe siècle, alors que les suites à l'arrière ont des terrasses pittoresques. Les hôtes peuvent prendre un verre au bar classique d'un style anglais, et les fruits de mer sont la spécialité avec saumon, praires, poulpe et colin, tous cuisinés pour créer des plats internationaux et catalans.

Dieses einladende Hotel liegt im Gotischen Viertel und bietet gediegene Unterkunft, exzellenten Service und freundliches Personal. Kräftiges Décor mit bunten Stoffen ziert das gesamte Hotel. Die Zimmer an der Frontseite bieten einen Ausblick auf den Platz und die Kathedrale aus dem 13. Jahrhundert, während die Suiten an der Rückseite malerische Terrassen haben. Drinks kann man in der klassischen englischen Bar genießen, und auf der Speisekarte stehen internationale und katalanische Gerichte, vor allem Fisch und Meeresfrüchte wie Lachs, Muscheln, Tintenfisch und Seehecht.

Our inspector loved: *The spectacular views of the cathedral from the terrace.*

Directions: Located in the Gothic quarter, in the centre of town. The nearest metro station is Jaume I.

Web: www.johansens.com/colon
E-mail: info@hotelcolon.es
Tel: +34 933 01 14 04
Fax: +34 933 17 29 15

Price Guide:
single €155–180
double/twin €220–310
suite €350

Hotel Rigat Park

AV. AMERICA 1, PLAYA DE FENALS, 17310 LLORET DE MAR, COSTA BRAVA, GERONA, SPAIN

Surrounded by lush gardens and pine trees exuding their distinctive aroma, the Hotel Rigat Park is an ideal base for exploring the beaches of Costa Brava and the nearby Catalan towns. The 16 beautiful Mediterranean-style suites have tiled floors and marble bathrooms and 3 have motorised posturing beds. Guests may play billiards, swim in the pool or take advantage of the newly opened spa that offers sauna, Jacuzzi, mineralised water and indoor heated pool.

Entouré de jardins luxuriants et de pins exsudant leur senteur particulière, le Rigat Park Hôtel est une base idéale pour explorer les plages de la Costa Brava et les viles catalanes proches. Les 16 belles suites méditerranéennes ont un sol carrelés et des salles de bain en marbre et 3 ont des lits à position réglable motorisés. Les hôtes peuvent jouer au billard, profiter de la piscine ou des nouveaux Bains avec sauna, jacuzzi, eau minérale et piscine intérieure chauffée.

Dieses von üppigen Gärten und duftenden Pinienbäumen umgebene Hotel mit seiner Landhausatmosphäre ist der ideale Ausgangspunkt für Ausflüge an die Costa Brava und die umliegenden katalonischen Städte. Die 16 zauberhaften Suiten im mediterranen Stil bieten Fliesenböden und Marmorbäder und 3 haben automatisch verstellbare Betten. Man kann Billiard spielen, schwimmen oder das neueröffnete Spa mit Sauna, Jacuzzi, mineralisiertem Wasser und beheiztem Hallenbad besuchen

Our inspector loved: *The private country house atmosphere that has been maintained.*

Directions: A7 > exit 9 > Lloret de Mar > Fenals beach. Barcelona and Gerona Airport are nearby.

Web: www.johansens.com/rigatpark
E-mail: info@rigat.com
Tel: +34 972 36 52 00
Fax: +34 972 37 04 11

Price Guide:
twin €160-280
suite €252-405
presidential suite €800-1,300

SPAIN / CATALUÑA (GERONA)

Mas Falgarona

AVINYONET DE PUIGVENTOS, 17742 GERONA, SPAIN

In this well restored 16th-century farmhouse, décor is contemporary with a mixture of white drapes, terracotta floors, intriguing lighting and original wooden beams. All bathrooms are individually furnished with Mallorcan hand-painted tiles. Care is taken by the owners to offer an attentive and personal service, and dinner menus change daily. The hotel is situated in the open countryside with bicycles provided and golf nearby. Other places of interest include Avinyonet, Figueres and Cadaques.

Dans cette ferme du XVIe siècle joliment restaurée, le décor est contemporain avec un mélange de tentures blanches, des sols terracotta, des lumières fascinantes et poutres d'origine. Toutes les salles de bain sont décorées individuellement avec des carrelages majorquins peints à la main. Les propriétaires prennent soin d'offrir un service personnalisé et attentif, et les menus du dîner changent quotidiennement. L'hôtel est situé en pleine campagne, les bicyclettes sont fournies et le golf est proche. Dans les environs, Avinyonet, Figueres and Cadaques sont à visiter.

Das Décor dieses herrlich restaurierten Bauernhauses aus dem 16. Jahrhundert ist zeitgenössisch mit einer Mischung aus weißen Stoffen, Terrakottaböden, interessanter Beleuchtung und Original-Holzbalkendecken. Alle Bäder sind individuell mit handbemalten mallorquinischen Fliesen gestaltet. Der Service ist aufmerksam und persönlich und die Speisekarte ändert sich täglich. Die ländliche Umgebung lädt zu Fahrradtouren ein, man kann Golf spielen oder Avinyonet, Figueres und Cadaques besuchen.

Our inspector loved: *The attention to detail and the beautifully designed bathrooms.*

Directions: A7 Gerona > France exit 4 > Figueres-Olof > N260.

Web: www.johansens.com/masfalgarona
E-mail: email@masfalgarona.com
Tel: +34 972 54 66 28
Fax: +34 972 54 70 71

Price Guide:
single €116–206
double €145–165
suites €206–249
junior suite €165–185

Romantic Villa - Hotel Vistabella

CALA CANYELLES PETITES, PO BOX 3, 17480 ROSES (GERONA), SPAIN

Overlooking a spectacular sandy beach, this tranquil, unique hotel offers 30 bedrooms, including 8 suites. The Royal Suite features 2 bedrooms. All rooms are individually furnished and most have a sea view. The hotel can organise activities such as scuba diving, water skiing, sky diving and various mountain sports and guests may board the hotel's boat for private excursions. Every Friday and Saturday the gastronomic feasts are not to be missed and with 4 restaurants the hotel serves a sumptuous range of cuisine. The Dali Museum is nearby.

Avec ses vues magnifiques de la plage, cet hôtel tranquille propose 30 chambres, dont 8 sont des suites. La suite royale a 2 chambres. Chaque pièce est meublée de manière individuelle et la plupart ont une vue sur la mer. L'hôtel organise des sports comme la plongée sous-marine, le ski nautique, le parachutisme en chute libre et de divers sports de montagne. Son bateau est à la disposition des clients pour des excursions privées. Le vendredi et samedi il faut déguster la délicieuse cuisine, avec ses 4 restaurants les hôtes ont l'embarras du choix. Le musée Dali n'est pas très loin.

Dieses ruhige, luxuriöse Hotel mit Blick auf einen spektakulären Sandstrand bietet 8 Suiten mit separatem Wohnzimmer, die Royal Suite besitzt 2 Schlafzimmer. Alle Zimmer sind individuell gestaltet, die meisten haben Meerblick. Aktivitäten wie Tauchen, Wasserski, Skydiving und verschiedene Bergsportarten können organisiert werden, und das hoteleigene Boot steht den Gästen für Privatausflüge zur Verfügung. Die Gourmetabende jeden Freitag und Samstag sollte man sich nicht entgehen lassen, und die 4 Restaurants sorgen für kulinarische Vielfalt. In der Nähe befindet sich das Dali Museum.

***Our inspector loved:** The spectacular view and sunset across the Bay of Roses.*

Directions: The nearest airport is Perpignan, France. Alternatively, Gerona or Barcelona International Airports are nearby. Vistabella is 2km past Roses, along the coast road.

Web: www.johansens.com/vistabella
E-mail: info@vistabellahotel.com
Tel: +34 972 25 62 00
Fax: +34 972 25 32 13

Price Guide:
double €96 – 255
suite €258 – 866

Hotel Estela Barcelona

AVDA. PORT D'AIGUADOLÇ 8, 08870 SITGES (BARCELONA), SPAIN

Fusing modern luxury and unique works of art, this hotel pays homage to old masters and contemporary heroes. Upon entering reception guests are greeted by waterfalls, ceramics and a mirror-filled open-top car, whilst outside a wide terrace overlooks 2 pools and sculptures "growing" amongst the scenery. 4 airy bedrooms and suites have been newly added, all with sea views, light beamed ceilings and floors and marble Jacuzzis or huge baths. Soon every room will offer Internet access and DVD player.

Débordant de luxe moderne et d'œuvres d'art uniques, l'hôtel rend hommage aux vieux maîtres et héros contemporains. Dès la réception, les hôtes sont accueillis par des fontaines, céramiques et une voiture décapotable tout en miroirs, alors que dehors une large terrasse surplombe 2 piscines et des sculptures "grimpantes" dans le paysage. 4 chambres et suites ont récemment été ajoutées, toutes avec vue sur la mer, des plafonds et sols à poutrelles et des jacuzzis de marbre ou d'énormes baignoires. Bientôt dans chaque chambre accès à l'internet et DVD seront offerts.

Mit seiner Mischung aus Luxus und einzigartigen Kunstwerken zollt dieses Hotel sowohl den alten Meistern als auch zeitgenössischem Stil Tribut. In der Eingangshalle begrüßen einen Springbrunnen, Keramiken und ein mit Spiegeln gefülltes Cabriolet, die große Außenterrasse blickt auf 2 Pools und Skulpturen. 4 neue Zimmer und Suiten bieten Meerblick, Balkendecken, Holzböden und Marmorjacuzzis oder riesige Badewannen. In Kürze gibt es in jedem Zimmer Internetanschluss und DVD-Player.

Our inspector loved: *The magnificent exhibitions and works of art.*

Directions: Barcelona > A16 > C246 > Sitges north/Aiguadolç.

Web: www.johansens.com/estelabarcelona
E-mail: info@hotelestela.com
Tel: +34 938 11 45 45
Fax: +34 938 11 45 46

Price Guide:
double €93–168
artist room €108–174

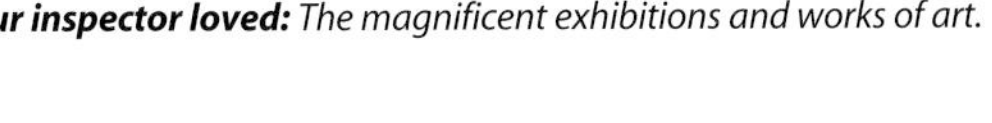

SPAIN / CATALUÑA (SITGES)

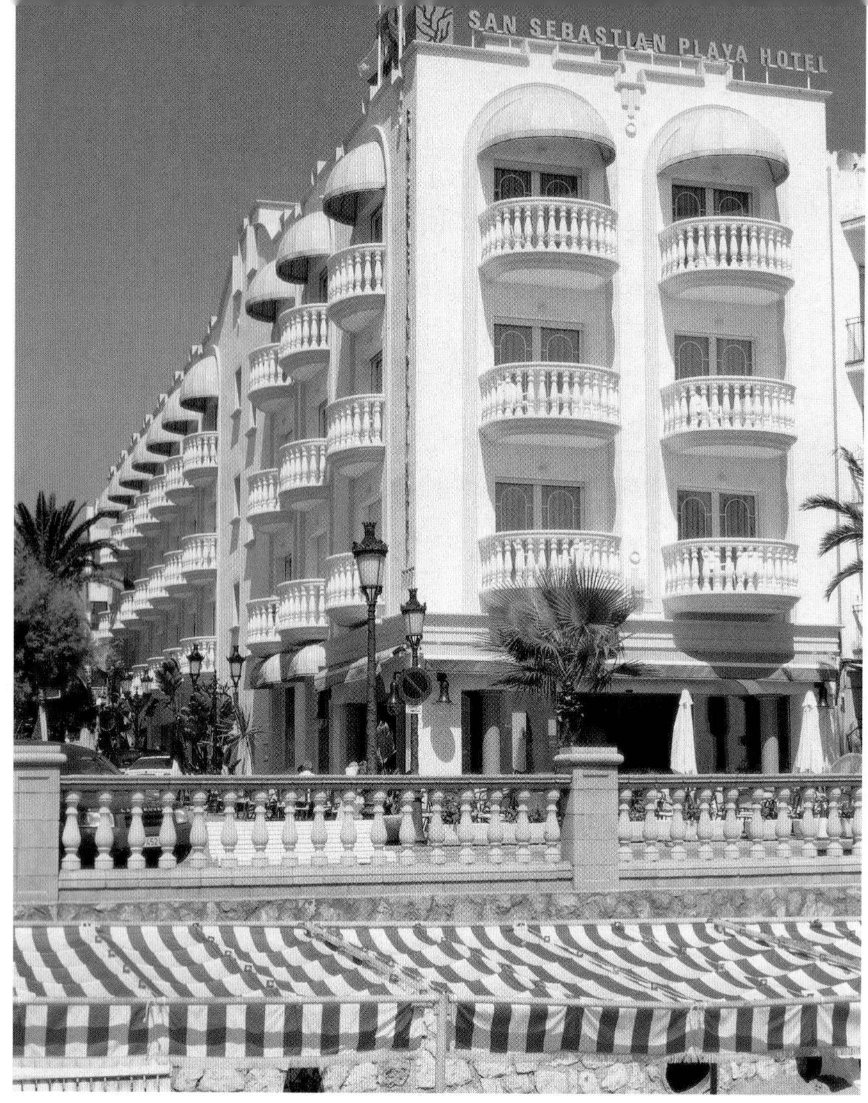

San Sebastian Playa Hotel

CALLE PORT ALEGRE 53, 08870 SITGES (BARCELONA), SPAIN

Located in the cosmopolitan town of Sitges, this hotel offers a sense of peace and tranquillity and extremely friendly Spanish hospitality. 20 minutes from Barcelona Airport and 100m from Sitges town centre, leisurely strolls along the water's edge are a must. The spacious bedrooms have balconies, whilst the bathrooms boast thermostatic showers. La Concha, set directly on the sea, specialises in seafood dishes and uses the finest of local produce. With no less than 17 beaches, an abundance of restaurants and museums, activities for all tastes are catered for.

Situé dans la ville cosmopolite de Sitges à seulement 100 m du centre ville et à 20 minutes de l'aéroport de Barcelone, cet hôtel offre un sentiment de paix et de tranquillité et l'extrêmement amicale hospitalité espagnole. Les balades au bord de l'eau sont incontournables. Chaque chambre est spacieuse et a un balcon, et les salles de bain bénéficient de douches thermostatiques. La Concha, qui donne directement sur la mer, sert poissons et fruits de mer et utilise les meilleurs produits locaux. Avec pas moins de 17 plages, un grand nombre de restaurants et musées, il y a des activités pour tous les goûts.

Dieses nur 20 Minuten von Flughafen von Barcelona und 100m vom Zentrum der kosmopoliten Stadt Sitges gelegene Hotel bietet ein Gefühl von Ruhe und Frieden und freundliche spanische Gastfreundschaft. Gemächliche Spaziergänge an der Uferpromenade entlang sind ein Muss. Die geräumigen Zimmer haben Balkone, und die Bäder sind mit thermostatischen Duschen ausgestattet. Im direkt am Meer gelegenen La Concha wird frischer Fisch und Meeresküche serviert. 17 Strände und eine Fülle von Restaurants und Museen bieten Unterhaltung für jeden Geschmack.

Our inspector loved: *"La Concha" restaurant, overlooking the sea.*

Directions: The hotel is situated on the seafront at San Sebastian beach, Sitges.

Web: www.johansens.com/sebastian
E-mail: hotelsansebastian@hotelsansebastian.com
Tel: +34 93 894 86 76
Fax: +34 93 894 04 30

Price Guide:
(room only)
single €115-€230
double €105-201
suite €195-330

HOTEL MASFERRER

08474 GUALBA, SPAIN

Set at the foothills of the Montseny Park, this beautiful farmhouse dates back to the 13th and 14th centuries. Its large windows, wide entrance halls and landings give it a spacious and tranquil atmosphere, and the bedrooms are decorated in a colourful, simple style exuding minimalist elegance. Simple, first-class cuisine is served in the restaurant. Numerous pretty villages and parks are nearby, and the location is ideal for those who wish to explore the bustle of Barcelona by day and return to peace and quiet at night.

Au pied des collines du parc Montseny, ce beau corps de ferme date du XIIIe et XIVe siècles. Ses grandes fenêtres, ses larges entrées et paliers produisent une ambiance de tranquillité et d'espace, et ses chambres sont décorées dans le style simple et coloré d'un minimalisme chic. Le restaurant sert une cuisine simple mais de 1ère catégorie. Sa situation, toute proche de nombreux jolis villages et de parcs, est idéale pour ceux qui souhaitent profiter de la vie agitée de Barcelone le jour et revenir au calme et à la paix le soir.

Am Fuße des Montseny Parks liegt dieses herrliche Bauernhaus aus dem 13. und 14. Jahrhundert. Große Fenster, weite Eingangshallen und Treppen schaffen eine geräumige und ruhige Atmosphäre, und die in farbenfrohem, klaren Stil gestalteten Zimmer sind von minimalistischer Eleganz. Im Restaurant wird einfache, erstklassige Küche serviert. Zahlreiche hübsche Dörfer und Parks liegen in der Nähe, und das Hotel ist der ideale Ort, um tagsüber das Treiben Barcelonas zu genießen und abends in die Ruhe zurückzukehren.

Our inspector loved: *The tranquil atmosphere of this historic house set in the woods.*

Directions: The nearest airports are Barcelona and Gerona.

Web: www.johansens.com/masferrer
E-mail: hm@hotelmasferrer.com
Tel: +34 93 848 77 05
Fax: +34 93 848 70 84

Price Guide:
(room only)
single €84
double €105-132
suite €146

Duende Rincones Encantados

C/TOMÁS MIRAMBELL 77, PLAYA DE PATOS, PANXÓN, 36340 NIGRÁN, SPAIN

The perfect place to relax and unwind, the Duende consists of 5 completely private, luxurious villas and cottages surrounded by tranquil gardens with a beautiful swimming pool. Each villa has a fully equipped modern kitchen, whilst the exquisite décor ranges from bright modern to classic dark wood. The light, modern loft-style "Galería" apartment can also be used as a meeting room accommodating up to 15. A bar for drinks and snacks is available, and excursions, wine tastings and much more can be arranged. The beach is just 300m away.

L'endroit idéal pour se détendre et se dérouler, Duende Rincones Encantados comprend 5 villas luxueuses complètement privées entouré de jardins tranquilles et une belle piscine. Chaque villa a une cuisine bien équipée, alors que le décor est en styles divers, allant de tons clairs et modernes au bois foncé classique. L'appartement "Galería" en style grenier peut aussi être utilisé comme salle de conférences pour jusqu'à 15 personnes. Un bar servant des boissons et casse-croûtes est disponible et des excursions, dégustations de vin et d'autres activités peuvent être organisés. La plage n'est qu'à 300m.

Der ideale Ort für Entspannung! Das Duende besteht aus 5 völlig privaten Luxusvillen und –cottages inmitten ruhiger Gärten mit einem herrlichen Swimminpool. Jede Villa bietet eine vollausgestattete, moderne Küche und das Décor reicht von hell und bunt bis hin zu klassisch mit dunklem Holz. Das luftige, moderne "Galería"-Appartement dient auch als Konferenzraum für bis zu 15 Personen. Eine Bar für Drinks und Snacks ist vorhanden, und Exkursionen, Weinproben und vieles mehr kann arrangiert werden. Der Strand ist nur 300m entfernt.

Directions: Santiago de Campostela International Airport > A9 > exit Nigrán > signs to Panxón, Playa de Patos.

Web: www.johansens.com/encantados
E-mail: duende@rinconesencantados.com
Tel: +34 986 36 53 38
Fax: +34 986 36 85 30

Price Guide:
house/villa €120-275

Our inspector loved: *This beautifully appointed home with butler service.*

Antiguo Convento

C/ DE LAS MONJAS, S/N BOADILLA DEL MONTE, 28660 MADRID, SPAIN

Dating from the 17th century, this old convent has been beautifully refurbished with modern fittings, antiques and harmonious period details. The former nun cells have been imaginatively decorated as bedrooms and guests can enjoy a stroll through the exquisite ornamental gardens. Impressive skylights and a large covered patio create light and space. The new restaurant offers superb cuisine and extensive business facilities are provided. Madrid is nearby with excellent shopping and tourist attractions.

Ce vieux couvent du XVIIe siècle a été admirablement rénové avec des installations modernes, antiquités et d'harmonieux détails d'époque. La décoration des anciennes cellules des nonnes en chambres est originale et les hôtes peuvent se promener dans les charmants jardins ornementaux. Des lucarnes impressionnantes associées à un grand patio couvert créent lumière et espace. Une cuisine superbe est servie dans le nouveau restaurant, et l'hôtel dispose d'un centre d'affaires. Madrid est proche pour du shopping de qualité et des visites touristiques.

Dieses einstige Kloster aus dem 17. Jahrhundert wurde harmonisch mit modernen und antiken Elementen renoviert. Die ehemaligen Zellen wurden phantasievoll in Schlafzimmer umgewandelt, und die exquisit gestalteten Gärten sind herrlich für Spaziergänge. Eindrucksvolle Deckenfenster und eine große überdachte Terrasse schaffen Licht und Raum. Im neuen Restaurant wird hervorragende Küche serviert. Umfassende Konferenzeinrichtungen sind vorhanden, und Madrid und die Umgebung laden zu Besichtigungen und Einkaufstrips ein.

Our inspector loved: *The discerning cuisine offered by the host in their charming restaurant.*

Directions: M40 out of Madrid towards A Coruña > M511 to Boadilla del Monte.

Web: www.johansens.com/www.elconvento.net
E-mail: informacion@elconvento.net
Tel: + 34 91 632 22 20
Fax: +34 91 633 15 12

Barcelona
Madrid
Málaga

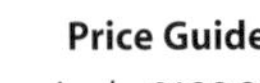

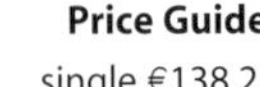

Price Guide:
single €138.23
double €156.26
suite €300.50

Hotel Orfila

C/ORFILA, NO. 6, 28010 MADRID, SPAIN

Located in a quiet residential area and surrounded by stately residences within minutes of the city centre, this 19th-century palace has been converted into a hotel and refurbished to a high standard. Each bedroom is individually decorated with antique pieces and equipped with hydro-massage baths. Guests can savour haute cuisine in the small restaurant, which opens onto a terrace and pretty garden, whilst the cocktails served in the intimate bar are reputed to be amongst the best in Madrid. Guests can enjoy the facilities of a nearby fitness centre with indoor pool.

Situé dans un quartier résidentiel calme et entouré par des résidences majestueuses à quelques minutes du centre ville, ce palais datant du XIXe siècle a été converti en hôtel et remis à neuf. Chaque chambre est ornée de façon individuelle avec des antiquités et équipée avec bain hydro-massage. Les hôtes peuvent savourer la haute cuisine dans le petit restaurant qui donne sur une terrasse et joli jardin, alors que les cocktails servis dans le bar intime sont réputés être parmi les meilleurs à Madrid. Les hôtes peuvent profiter d'un centre de remise en forme avec piscine couverte tout près.

Dieses in ein wundervolles Hotel umgewandelte Palais aus dem 19. Jahrhundert liegt in einer ruhigen Wohngegend, umgeben von herrschaftlichen Häusern nur ein paar Minuten vom Stadtzentrum entfernt. Alle Zimmer sind unterschiedlich gestaltet, mit Antiquitäten gefüllt und bieten Hydromassagebäder. Im kleinen Restaurant mit Terrasse und Garten wird Haute Cuisine serviert, und die Cocktails, die man in der gemütlichen Bar bekommt, gehören bekanntlich zu den besten in Madrid. Ein nahegelegenes Fitnesszentrum mit Hallenbad steht zur Verfügung.

Our inspector loved: *The chic 1920s ambience and the designer cocktails!*

Directions: The hotel is located within minutes of the city centre.

Web: www.johansens.com/orfila
E-mail: inforeservas@hotelorfila.com
Tel: +34 91 702 77 70
Fax: +34 91 702 77 72

Price Guide:
(room only, excluding VAT)
double €297-365
suite €409-1,184

Hotel Quinta de los Cedros

C/ALLENDESALAZAR 4, 28043 MADRID, SPAIN

Surrounded by cedar trees and affording fine views across the city, this charming hotel was built in the elegant style of a Tuscan villa and provides an impeccably high standard of service and the utmost in comfort. Each of its 22 bedrooms and 10 terraced bungalows in the grounds is themed differently and features all modern amenities. The intimate and romantic Los Cedros restaurant serves traditional and modern cuisine with Mediterranean flavours. Guests may enjoy their meals on the terrace overlooking the beautiful gardens. A meeting room is available.

Entouré d'arbres de cèdre avec des vues spectaculaires de la ville, cet hôtel charmant fut construit dans le style élégant d'une villa toscane et offre un excellent niveau de service et confort. Chacune des 22 chambres et 10 pavillons en terrasses est décorée avec un thème différent et équipée avec toutes les facilités modernes. Le restaurant intime et romantique Los Cedros sert des plats traditionnels et modernes avec des saveurs de la Méditerranée. Les hôtes peuvent dîner sur la terrasse donnant sur les beaux jardins. Une salle de réunion est disponible.

Umgeben von Zedern und mit einer herrlichen Sicht auf die Stadt, bietet dieses charmante, im Stil einer eleganten toskanischen Villa erbaute Hotel ein extrem hohes Maß an Service und höchsten Komfort. Alle 22 Zimmer und 10 Bungalows auf dem Gelände sind unterschiedlich gestaltet und mit modernsten Einrichtungen ausgestattet. Im gemütlichen und romantischen Restaurant Los Cedros werden traditionelle und moderne Gerichte mit mediterraner Note serviert, die man auch auf der Terrasse inmitten des herrlichen Gartens genießen kann. Ein Konferenzraum steht zur Verfügung.

Our inspector loved: *The ambience and décor reminiscent of the Tuscan villas of Italy.*

Directions: The hotel is north of Madrid's centre, adjacent to C/Arturo Soria. Close to Chamartin train station and 10km from Madrid Airport.

Web: www.johansens.com/loscedros
E-mail: reservas@quintadeloscedros.com
Tel: +34 91 515 2200
Fax: +34 91 415 2050

Price Guide:
(excluding VAT, breakfast €9)
single €152.90
double €191.40
junior suite €222.20
suite €283.80

Hotel Villa Real

PLAZA DE LAS CORTES 10, 28014 MADRID, SPAIN

Surrounded by cultural attractions, this prestigious hotel offers impeccable service and a palatial interior, filled with wonderful antiques and mirrors, handsome rugs on marble floors, Roman mosaics and Greek ceramics. The newly refurbished Royal and Imperial Suites offer hydro-massage baths; one of the suites has a small sauna. Guests can sample exquisite dishes in the gourmet restaurant Europa or enjoy creative cuisine in the East 47. The hotel boasts a fantastic new fitness centre with separate saunas and relaxation areas for men and women. Wireless Internet connection available.

Entouré des attractions culturelles, ce prestigieux hôtel bénéficie d'un service impeccable et d'un intérieur grandiose, orné des antiquités et des miroirs, de beaux tapis sur des sols de marbre, des mosaïques romaines et céramiques grecques. Les suites Royale et Impériale disposent d'un bain hydro-massage; une a un sauna. Il y a 2 restaurants: le restaurant gastronomique Europa et l'East 47, où une cuisine créative est servie. L'hôtel s'enorgueillit d'un nouveau centre de remise en forme avec sauna et aire de détente séparés pour les hommes et les femmes. Service internet sans fil disponible.

In diesem von kulturellen Attraktionen umgebenen Hotel findet man tadellosen Service und ein palastartiges Interieur gefüllt mit Antiquitäten, Spiegeln, hübschen Teppichen auf Marmorböden, römischen Mosaiken und griechischen Keramiken. Die kürzlich renovierten Royal und Imperial Suiten bieten Hydromassagebäder, eine besitzt sogar eine integrierte Sauna. Im Europa wird Gourmet-, im East 47 kreative Küche serviert. Das Hotel besitzt ein neues Fitnesszentrum mit separaten Saunen und Relaxzonen für Männer und Frauen. Drahtloser Internetzugang vorhanden.

Our inspector loved: *The Roman mosaics and art treasures exhibited around the hotel; one of the finest private collections in Europe.*

Directions: Centre of Madrid.

Web: www.johansens.com/vilareal
E-mail: villareal@derbyhotels.es
Tel: +34 914 20 37 67
Fax: +34 914 20 25 47

Price Guide:
(breakfast €18)
single €301
double/twin €337

HESPERIA ALICANTE GOLF, SPA, HOTEL

AVDA. DE LAS NACIONES, S/N PLAYA DE SAN JUAN, 03540 ALICANTE, SPAIN

This stunning modern hotel is nestled amongst the fairways and greens of a magnificent 18-hole golf course designed by Severiano Ballesteros and is only 5 minutes' walk from many fine sandy beaches. Mediterranean-style décor uses marble, wood, wrought iron and cool pastel shades to create a wonderful atmosphere of light and spaciousness whilst bedrooms are the ultimate in chic comfort with views over the golf course, beautifully tended gardens and pool. The hotel has extensive spa facilities.

Ce superbe hôtel moderne est niché au sein des fairways et greens de ce magnifique golf 18 trous créé par Severiano Ballesteros et est à seulement 5 minutes de marche de nombreuses plages de sable fins. Le décor de style méditerranéen utilise marbre, bois, fers forgés et des tons de couleur pastel pour créer une atmosphère merveilleuse de lumière et d'espace. Les chambres sont ce qui se fait de mieux en confort chic avec vues sur le parcours de golf, les jardins superbement entretenus et la piscine. Cet hôtel dispose également de services de soins.

Dieses eindrucksvolle moderne Hotel liegt inmitten der Fairways und Greens eines herrlichen, von Severiano Ballesteros gestalteten 18-Loch-Golfplatzes und ist nur 5 Minuten zu Fuß von mehreren Sandstränden entfernt. Das Mittelmeerdécor mit Marmor, Holz, Schmiedeeisen und kühlen Pastelltönen schafft eine luftige, geräumige Atmosphäre. Die Zimmer sind höchst elegant und blicken auf den Golfplatz, die wundervollen Gärten und den Pool. Umfassende Kureinrichtungen sind vorhanden.

Our inspector loved: *The light and spacious ambience.*

Directions: Situated 5 minutes from Alicante city centre along the Avenida de las Naciones.

Web: www.johansens.com/hesperiaalicante
E-mail: hotel@hesperia-alicante.com
Tel: +34 965 23 50 00
Fax: +34 965 26 82 42

Price Guide:
(room only)
single €135-176
double €196-220
suite €700

Hotel Sidi San Juan & Spa

PLAYA DE SAN JUAN, 03540 ALICANTE, SPAIN

This excellent hotel is situated on a long, sandy beach near Cabo de Las Huertas and is only 10 minutes away from Alicante, renowned for its cultural activities and sights. With 8,000m² of beautiful gardens filled with over 250 palm trees, this is just the place for a long relaxing stroll. All rooms and suites have magnificent views of the sea. The restaurant, Grill Sant Joan, offers a wide range of international specialities, healthy Mediterranean cuisine and exquisite wines. The hotel has 1 indoor and 1 outdoor swimming pool, 5 tennis and 2 paddle courts as well as a spa.

Cet excellent hôtel est situé sur une longue plage de sable près de Cabo de Las Huertas, à 10 minutes d'Alicante, célèbre pour ses attractions culturelles. Avec ses 8000m² de jardins merveilleux remplis de plus de 250 palmiers, c'est un endroit parfait pour des longues promenades relaxantes. Toutes les chambres et suites ont des vues sur la mer. Le restaurant, Grill Sant Joan, offre des specialités internationales, une cuisine méditerranéenne saine et des vins exquis. L'hôtel dispose d'une piscine couverte, une en plein air, 5 courts de tennis et 2 de paddle ainsi qu'un spa.

Dieses exzellente Hotel liegt in bevorzugter Lage direkt an einem etwa 5km langen Sandstrand in unmittelbarer Nähe vom Cabo de Las Huertas. Alicante mit seinen kulturellen Sehenswürdigkeiten ist in 10 Minuten zu erreichen. Ein 8000m² großer Garten mit über 250 Palmen lädt zum Verweilen ein. Alle Zimmer und Suiten verfügen über Blick aufs Meer. Wahrhafte Genüsse bietet das Restaurant Grill Sant Joan: internationale Spezialitäten, ausgewogene Mittelmeerküche und erlesene Weine. Ein Hallenbad, Swimmingpool, 5 Tennis- und 2 Paddleplätze sowie ein Spa stehen für Wellness pur.

Our inspector loved: *The sea views from the sauna, indoor pool and hydro-massage pool. What a way to relax!*

Directions: From Alicante follow the signs to Playa San Juan. 5km from the city centre the hotel is on the beachfront.

Web: www.johansens.com/sanjuan
E-mail: reservas@sanjuan.hotelessidi.es
Tel: +34 96 516 13 00
Fax: +34 96 516 33 46

Price Guide:
(excluding VAT)
single €143-166
double €177-206
suite €300-350

SPA

Torre La Mina

C/ La Regenta 1, 12539 Alquerias-Castellón, Spain

This 19th-century mansion, set amidst extensive landscaped grounds featuring sculptures created by the acclaimed local artist Juan Ripolles, has the sophisticated ambience of a private stately home. Stone, marble, ceramic tiles and exposed beams create a sleek décor and the 8 individually styled bedrooms provide hydromassage. Regional and Mediterranean cuisine is served in the restaurant, where candle-lit banquets with live jazz in the gardens takes place every Friday evening during summer. A large conference building is available. Special offers available.

De cette demeure du XIXe siècle, au cœur d'un grand parc où se dressent des sculptures créées par l'artiste local Juan Ripolles, émane l'atmosphère sophistiquée d'une propriété aristocratique. Pierres, marbre, carrelages et poutres apparentes créent un décor soigné et les 8 chambres aménagées individuellement disposent d'hydromassage. Une cuisine régionale et méditerranéenne est servie au restaurant, où des banquets aux chandelles avec du jazz dans les jardins se tiennent les vendredis soirs en été. Un bâtiment pour les conférences ainsi que des offres spéciales sont disponibles.

Diese Residenz aus dem 19. Jahrhundert befindet sich in großen, mit Skulpturen des gefeierten einheimischen Künstlers Juan Ripolles gefüllten Gärten und besitzt das Ambiente eines Privathauses. Stein, Marmor, Keramikfliesen und freigelegte Balken schaffen ein edles, frisches Décor und die 8 individuell gestalteten Zimmer bieten Hydromassage. Regionale und Mittelmeerküche wird im Restaurant serviert, wo im Sommer jeden Freitagabend Bankette bei Kerzenschein und Live-Jazz im Garten stattfinden. Ein großes Konferenzgebäude steht zur Verfügung. Sondertarife vorhanden.

Our inspector loved: *The artistic décor and period restoration.*

Directions: From Valencia > A7 north > exit Burriana/Villa Real > follow signs to Alquerias.

Web: www.johansens.com/torrelamina
E-mail: info@torrelamina.com
Tel: +34 964 571 746
Fax: +34 964 570 199

Price Guide:
(excluding 7% VAT)
single €150
double €150
suite €210

Hotel Restaurante Buenavista

PARTIDA TOSSALET 82, LA XARA, 03709 DÉNIA, ALICANTE, SPAIN

Situated between the foothills of the Montgó Massif and the coastal town of Dénia, this cosy hotel captures the essence of the Mediterranean lifestyle with private landscaped gardens, cool pastel tones and natural materials. The superb restaurant offers mouth-watering cuisine, exemplary of the local gastronomy. Dénia Castle and the Natural Park of El Montgó are interesting to visit and outdoor enthusiasts will enjoy golf, watersports, walking and cycling.

Situé entre les contreforts du massif de Montgó et la ville côtière de Dénia, cet hôtel confortable a capturé l'essence du mode de vie méditerranéen, avec ses jardins privés aménagés, ses tons pastels frais et ses matériaux naturels. Le superbe restaurant offre une cuisine alléchante, exemplaire de la gastronomie locale. Le château de Dénia et le Parc Naturel d'El Montgó sont à visiter et les amoureux des activités de plein air pourront profiter du golf, de sports nautiques, randonnées pédestres et cyclistes.

Dieses zwischen den unteren Hängen des Montgó Massifs und der Küstenstadt Dénia gelegene kleine Hotel spiegelt mit seinen herrlich gestalteten Gärten, kühlen Pastelltönen und natürlichen Materialien den typischen Mittelmeercharakter wider. Im ausgezeichneten Restaurant genießt man köstliche, einheimische Küche. Die Burg von Dénia und der Naturpark von El Montgó sind hervorragende Ausflugsziele und aktive Gäste können Golf und Wassersport betreiben, wandern oder Rad fahren.

Our inspector loved: *The exquisite epicurean experience.*

Directions: Alicante > A7 > Dénia > follow signs to Dénia > turn right at sign for La Xara.

Web: www.johansens.com/www.hotel-buenavista.com
E-mail: hotelbuenavista@alc.servicom.es
Tel: +34 965 78 79 95
Fax: +34 966 42 71 70

Price Guide:
(excluding VAT)
single €99
double €165-198
suite €231–364

La Posada del Mar

PLAÇA DE LES DRASSANES, S/N 03700 DÉNIA, SPAIN

La Posada del Mar is situated opposite the marina in the midst of the bustling cosmopolitan town of Dénia. With the magnificent fortified mount of the town to its rear, this charming hotel dates back over 800 years and perfectly combines period features with luxurious contemporary comfort. Beautiful bedrooms enjoy marvellous views and are decorated with terracotta, wood and marble for a cool and comfortable feel. Guests will enjoy the abundance of excellent restaurants and shops in the vicinity.

La Posada del Mar est située en face de la marina au cœur de la ville bruyante et cosmopolite de Dénia. Avec la vielle ville fortifiée à son arrière, cet hôtel charmant date de plus de 800 ans et combine parfaitement des décors d'époque avec un confort luxueux contemporain. De belles chambres offrent des vues magnifiques et sont ornées en terracotta, en bois et en marbre pour créer une ambiance fraîche et confortable. Les hôtes peuvent profiter de l'abondance de très bons restaurants et magasins qui sont tout près.

Die Posada del Mar liegt direkt gegenüber dem Hafen inmitten der lebendigen, kosmopoliten Stadt Dénia, und im Hintergrund befindet sich die herrliche, auf einer Anhöhe gelegene Festung der Stadt. Dieses zauberhafte Hotel, dessen Geschichte bis über 800 Jahre zurückgeht, bietet heute eine perfekte Kombination aus Details vergangener Zeiten und luxuriösem modernen Komfort. Die hübschen Zimmer haben traumhafte Ausblicke, und Terrakotta, Holz und Marmor sorgen für eine angenehm kühle, gemütliche Atmosphäre. Zahlreiche hervorragende Restaurants und Geschäfte liegen in nächster Nähe.

Our inspector loved: *The views by day and night of the marina and seafront promenade.*

Directions: The hotel is situated in Dénia midway between Alicante and Valencia. Take the A7 and turn off at the Dénia exit.

Web: www.johansens.com/posadardelmar
E-mail: info@laposadadelmar.com
Tel: +34 96 643 29 66
Fax: +34 96 642 01 55

Price Guide:
(room only, excluding VAT)
single €133.75
double €178-233.75
suite €181.50-332.75

Hotel Sidi Saler & Spa

PLAYA EL SALER, 46012 VALENCIA, SPAIN

Directions: From Valencia take the coastal road and follow signs to El Saler. The hotel is 12km further on.

Web: www.johansens.com/saler
E-mail: reservas@saler.hotelssidi.es
Tel: +34 961 61 04 11
Fax: +34 961 61 08 38

Price Guide:
(excluding VAT)
single €147-174
double €212-236
suite €294-346

This 5-star hotel is situated on the long sandy beach of El Saler, within the Albufera Nature Park, which features a beautiful lake and habitat for all kinds of birds. All rooms and suites enjoy magnificent views of the Mediterranean. The Les Dunes à la carte restaurant offers a wide range of regional and international dishes accompanied by live jazz, blues and country music. Whether it is a ride on a mountain bike or a swim in either the outdoor or the indoor swimming pool, a game of tennis or a session in the beauty salon, there is always some form of exercise or relaxation on offer.

Cet hôtel 5 étoiles est situé sur la longue plage de sable de El Saler, au parc naturel d'Albufera avec sa grande variété d'oiseaux et son lac magnifique. Toutes les chambres et suites ont des vues merveilleuses de la Méditerranée. Le restaurant Les Dunes offre un menu à la carte de plats régionaux et internationaux accompagnés de musique sur scène de jazz, blues et country. Les hôtes peuvent faire du VTT, nager dans la piscine couverte ou en plein air, jouer au tennis ou se dorloter au salon de beauté – il y a toujours des possibilités d'activité ou de détente.

Die Lage dieses 5-Sterne Hotels ist unübertreffbar: direkt an einem langen Sandstrand und im Bereich des Albufera-Naturparks, ein Vogelparadies mit einem herrlichen See. Von allen Zimmern und Suiten aus hat man einen wunderschönen Blick auf das Mittelmeer. Das à-la-carte Restaurant Les Dunes bietet neben höchsten regionalen und internationalen Genüssen auch Live-Jazz, Blues und Country-Musik. Ob mit dem Mountainbike oder im Hallenbad bzw. Swimmingpool, auf den Tennisplätzen oder im Beauty-und Wellnesscenter, überall ist eine aktive Erholung möglich.

***Our inspector loved:** The setting within a natural park, with the gardens leading out onto the dunes and beach.*

      SPA  

Hotel Mont Sant

SUBIDA AL CASTILLO, S/N XÀTIVA, 46800 VALENCIA, SPAIN

Originally a Moorish palace on whose foundations a monastery was built, this hotel has stunning views over wooded mountains and a majestic floodlit castle. Extensive gardens overlook the valley and are surrounded by ancient city walls. Careful attention to detail and rustic décor have created a cosy ambience whilst superb international and Mediterranean cuisine is served in the hotel's attractive restaurant. There is an abundance of walking and sightseeing in the area.

A l'origine un palais maure sur les fondations duquel un monastère fût construit, cet hôtel a une vue superbe sur les montagnes boisées et un majestueux château illuminé. De grands jardins surplombent la vallée et sont entourés par les anciens murs de la ville. Une attention particulière pour le détail et un décor rustique ont créé une ambiance chaleureuse alors qu'une délicieuse cuisine internationale et méditerranéenne est servie dans l'élégant restaurant. Les possibilités de randonnées et visites sont nombreuses dans la région.

Dieses Hotel mit seiner traumhaften Sicht auf bewaldete Berge und eine majestätische Burg war einst ein maurischer Palast, auf dessen Fundament ein Kloster erbaut wurde. Die großen Gärten mit Blick auf das Tal sind von alten Stadtmauern umgeben. Liebe zum Detail und rustikales Décor schaffen eine gemütliche Atmosphäre, und im Hotelrestaurant werden internationale und mediterrane Köstlichkeiten serviert. Die Umgebung ist ideal für Ausflüge und Wanderungen.

Our inspector loved: *The ambience; a truly Mediterranean experience.*

Directions: Valencia > Albacete >interior auto via N340> turn off for Xàtiva.

Web: www.johansens.com/montsant
E-mail: montsant@servidex.com
Tel: +34 962 27 50 81
Fax: +34 962 28 19 05

Price Guide:
(excluding breakfast and VAT)
single €109
double €130.84

SWEDEN

Hotel location shown in red (hotel) or purple (spa hotel) with page number

HALLTORPS GÄSTGIVERI

38792 BORGHOLM, SWEDEN

The Halltorps Inn is one of the oldest manors recorded on the Viking Island of Öland and it was only in 1975 that it became a hotel. The position is superb, overlooking the spectacular Kalmar Sound. The 10 guest rooms in the original mansion are romantic and traditional, but the hotel is also very proud of its 25 rooms in the extension, each personalised by designers from different Swedish provinces. Gourmet guests will enjoy the local cuisine and extensive selection of wines in the intimate dining room.

Le Halltorps est l'un des plus vieux manoirs de l'île viking l'Öland et c'est en 1975 qu'il devînt un hôtel. Sa localisation est exceptionnelle et offre des vues spectaculaires sur le détroit de Kalmar. Les 10 chambres dans le manoir principal sont romantiques et traditionnelles, mais l'hôtel est aussi fier des 25 chambres de l'annexe, toutes aménagées de manière individuelle par des décorateurs de diverses provinces suédoises. Les fins gourmets apprécieront la cuisine locale et la liste impressionante de vins.

Der Gasthof Halltorps ist eines der ältesten Herrenhäuser auf der Wikinger-Insel Öland und wurde erst 1975 als Hotel eröffnet. Er befindet sich in fantastischer Lage und bietet Ausblick auf den spektakulären Kalmar-Sund. Die 10 Zimmer sind romantisch und traditionell eingerichtet, und auch die 25 Zimmer im Anbau sind ausgesprochen stilvoll, jedes einzelne von einem anderen schwedischen Designer geprägt. Im gemütlichen Speisesaal werden einheimische Gerichte und eine große Auswahl an Weinen serviert.

Our inspector loved: *The fine dining experience in Halltorps' intimate restaurant.*

Directions: E22 > country road 136.

Web: www.johansens.com/halltorpsgastgiveri
E-mail: info@halltorpsgastgiveri.se
Tel: +46 485 85000
Fax: +46 485 85001

Price Guide:
(per person)
single SEK950–1,050
double/twin SEK1,180–1,390
suite SEK1,400–1,700

Hestravikens Wärdshus

VIK, 33027, HESTRA, SMÅLAND, SWEDEN

Behind the traditional yellow country house façade lie 7 immaculately maintained suites, tastefully decorated with contemporary designer furnishings. Some include Jacuzzi baths and fireplaces, whilst all have terraces or balconies. A small relaxation room offers guests the perfect end to the day having taken advantage of Småland's wealth of outdoor pursuits, from walking in the National Park to canoeing in the Nissan river running alongside the Hotel. Excellent cuisine and a generous Scandinavian breakfast is served in the adjacent restaurant and conservatory.

Derrière la traditionnelle façade jaune de cette maison de campagne se tiennent 7 suites immaculées, décorées avec goût dans un mobilier contemporain de designer. Certaines contiennent un jacuzzi et une cheminée, et toutes disposent d'une terrasse ou d'un balcon. Une petite pièce de relaxation offre une fin de journée parfaite aux hôtes qui ont profité de la myriade d'activités en plein air offerte à Småland, des randonnées dans le Park National au canoë sur la rivière Nissan qui coule le long de l'hôtel. Une cuisine excellente et un petit-déjeuner scandinave copieux sont servis dans le restaurant adjacent et la serre.

Hinter der traditionellen gelben Landhausfassade verstecken sich 7 makellose Suiten, die geschmackvoll in zeitgenössischem Design eingerichtet sind. Einige haben Whirlpoolbäder und Kamine, alle bieten Terrassen oder Balkone. In einem kleinen Entspannungsraum kann man den Tag ausklingen lassen, nachdem man Smålands riesiges Freizeitangebot von Wanderungen im Nationalpark bis hin zu Kanufahrten auf dem am Hotel vorbeifließenden Nissan genutzt hat. Hervorragende Küche und ein großzügiges Frühstück werden im Restaurant und Wintergarten serviert.

Our inspector loved: *The comfort of Suite 47 with its spacious bathroom.*

Directions: Jönköping > 26 > Hestra.

Web: www.johansens.com/hestravikenswardshus
E-mail: info@hestraviken.se
Tel: +46 370 33 68 00
Fax: +46 370 33 62 90

Price Guide:
double SEK1,340–1,540
suite SEK1,740–2,640

Romantik Hotel Åkerblads

793/70 Tällberg, Sweden

Sweden's King Carl Gustav has stayed at this outstanding traditional farmhouse, which has been the home of the Åkerblad family since the 15th century. Situated on a hillside in the village of Tällberg, this charming hotel has spectacular views over the Siljan Lake. The traditional dining room offers a wonderful array of Smörgasbord and a delicious evening menu based on grandmother's cooking! Guests can go for sleigh rides and skiing in winter, and take boat trips on the lake in summer.

Le Roi Carl Gustav de Suède a séjourné dans cette superbe ferme traditionnelle qui est la demeure de la famille Åkerblad depuis le XVe siècle. Située sur une colline du village de Tällberg, cet hôtel charmant a une vue imprenable sur le lac de Siljan. La salle à manger traditionnelle offre un merveilleux choix de Smörgasbord et d'un menu qui, le soir, est inspiré des recettes de grand-mère! Les visiteurs pourront faire des tours de traineau et du ski en hiver, et des tours en bateau sur le lac l'été.

Schwedens König Carl Gustaf war bereits Gast in diesem einzigartigen landestypischen Hof, der seit dem 15. Jahrhundert im Besitz der Familie Åkerblad ist. An einem Hang des Dorfs Tällberg gelegen bietet es wundervolle Aussichten über den Siljansee. Der traditionelle Speisesaal bietet ein verlockendes Smörgasbord und köstliche Abendmenues – inspiriert von "Großmutters Küche"! Unternehmungen wie Schlittenfahrten und Skilaufen im Winter und Bootsausflüge auf dem See im Sommer stehen ebenfalls auf dem Programm.

Our inspector loved: *A most enjoyable breakfast on the peaceful veranda after a refreshing early morning swim.*

Directions: Stockholm > E70 > Tällberg.

Web: www.johansens.com/akerblads
E-mail: info@akerblad-tallberg.se
Tel: +46 247 50800
Fax: +46 247 50652

Price Guide:
single SEK695
double/twin SEK1,190–1,290
suite SEK1,590–2,190

Switzerland

Hotel location shown in red (hotel) or purple (spa hotel) with page number

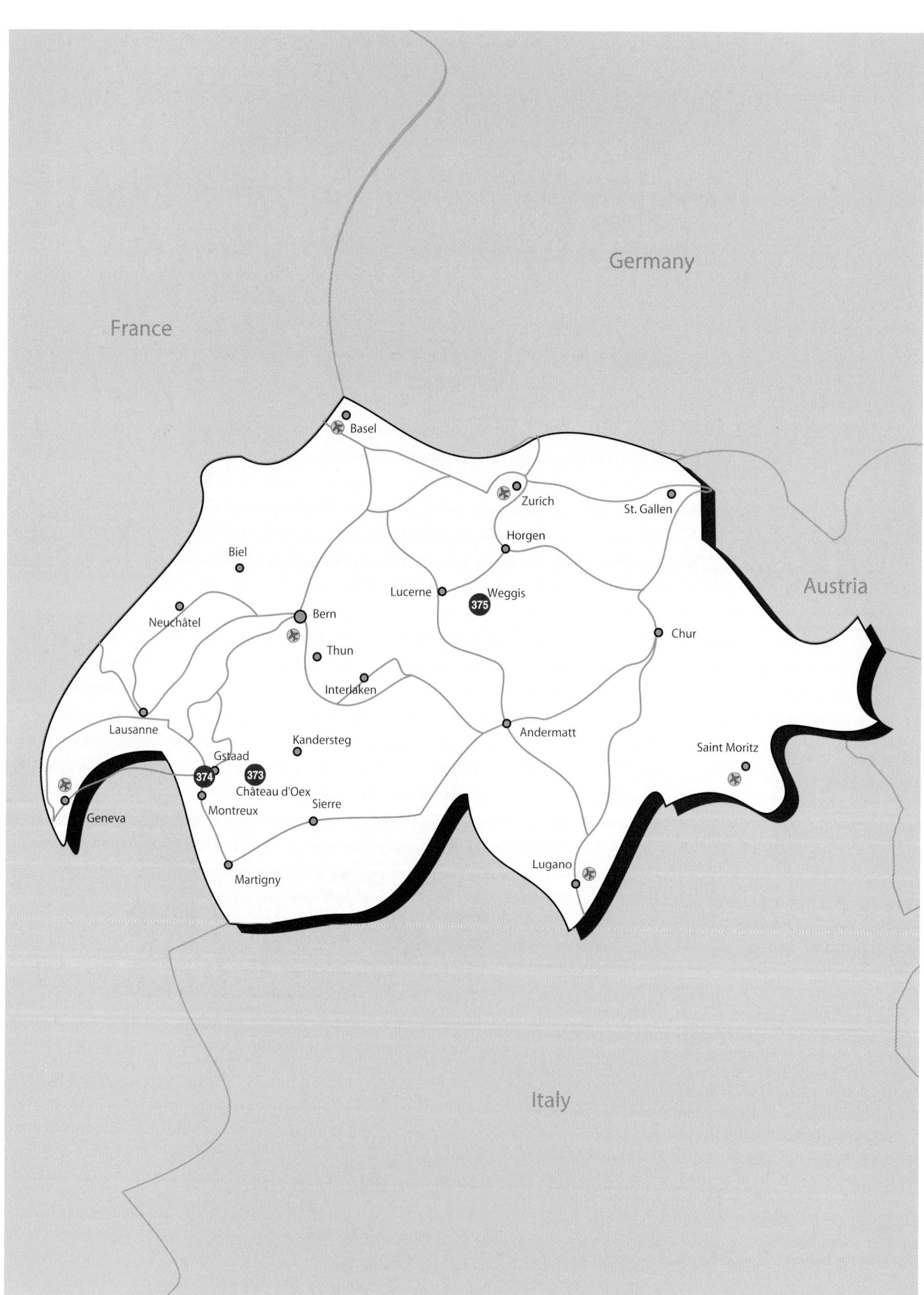

Hostellerie Bon Accueil

1837 CHÂTEAU D'OEX, SWITZERLAND

In the picturesque valley known as Pays d'Enhaut, at an altitude of 1000m, stands the charming Hostellerie Bon Accueil, a typical 18th-century chalet on the outskirts of Château d'Oex. The bedrooms are delightfully decorated in pretty floral fabrics. The cuisine is of the highest standard, enjoyed in the romantic candle-lit dining room. The visitor will enjoy the numerous winter and summer sports and leisure activities.

Ce chalet du XVIIIe siècle, transformé en hôtel, est situé au dessus de Château d'Oex, dans la pittoresque vallée du Pays d'Enhaut, à une altitude de 1000 m. Les chambres typiques sont aménagées avec beaucoup de goût. La cuisine est raffinée, servie dans un cadre chaleureux. Le visiteur trouvera une large palette d'activités sportives en hiver comme en été.

Dieses Hotel in einem Chalet aus dem 18. Jahrhundert liegt oberhalb von Château d'Oex im Pays d'Enhaut, einem malerischen Tal auf 1000 Meter Höhe. Die Zimmer sind hübsch im Chaletstil eingerichtet. Eine raffinierte Küche wird in einem Restaurant mit viel Ambiente serviert. Den Besucher erwartet im Sommer wie auch im Winter ein mannigfaltiges Angebot an Sportmöglichkeiten.

Our inspector loved: *The fantastic setting and welcoming atmosphere.*

Directions: E27 > Bulle or Aigle > Château d'Oex > left > cross railway track.

Web: www.johansens.com/bonaccueil
E-mail: host-bon-accueil@bluewin.ch
Tel: +41 26 924 6320
Fax: +41 26 924 5126

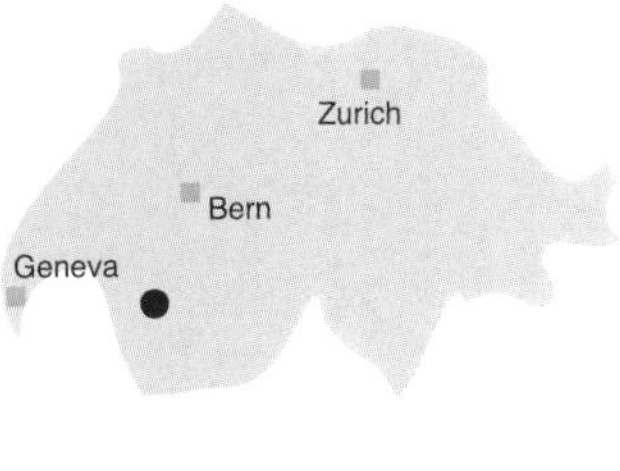

Zurich
Bern
Geneva

Price Guide:
single SF115–150
double/twin SF150–225

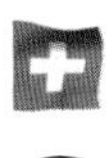

Le Grand Chalet

NEUERETSTRASSE, 3780 GSTAAD, SWITZERLAND

Directions: 220 km from Zurich, 160 km from Geneva.

Web: www.johansens.com/legrandchalet
E-mail: hotel@grandchalet.ch
Tel: +41 33 748 7676
Fax: +41 33 748 7677

Price Guide:
single €116–286
double/twin €176–350
suite €249–445

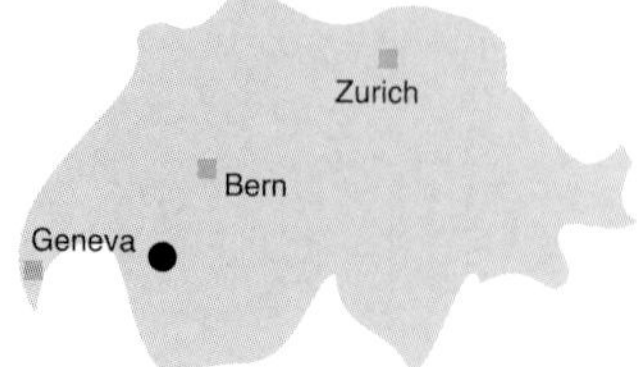

Located a mere 10 minutes from the charming hamlet of Gstaad, this is an idyllic retreat offering magnificent views of the surrounding mountains. Befitting a modern chalet, the bedrooms and reception rooms are all bright and airy, and boast stunning pine furniture and open log fires. Ideal for sports lovers, Le Chalet has an outdoor swimming pool, steam bath and sauna, as well as a golf course 15 minutes away. Its Bagatelle Restaurant is one of the best in the vicinity.

Situé à 10 minutes seulement du charmant village de Gstaad, cet hôtel idyllique est un havre de paix offrant des vues spectaculaires sur les montagnes environnantes. Les chambres et les salles de réception de ce chalet moderne sont toutes claires, spacieuses et agrémentées de beaux meubles en pin et de cheminées. Idéal pour les sportifs, l'établissement compte une piscine à ciel ouvert, un bain de vapeur et un sauna et un terrain de golf à 15 minutes. Le restaurant Bagatelle est l'un des meilleurs des environs.

Nur 10 Minuten vom Zentrum des Dorfes Gstaad entfernt, liegt dieses zauberhafte Chalet mit seiner atemberaubenden Sicht auf die umgebenden Berge. Die modernen Zimmer und Empfangsräume sind alle hell, luftig, mit herrlichen Kiefernmöbeln eingerichtet und haben offenes Kaminfeuer. Le Chalet ist ideal für Sportler: es gibt Freibad, Dampfbad und Sauna und einen 15 Minuten entfernten Goflplatz. Das Bagatelle ist eines der besten Restaurants in der Umgebung.

Our inspector loved: *The steam bath and sauna - perfect for relaxing after a busy day exploring.*

Park Hotel Weggis

HERTENSTEINSTRASSE 34, CH - 6353 WEGGIS, SWITZERLAND

Set in magnificent parkland with a private beach and breathtaking views over Lake Lucerne and the Alps, this unique hotel blends traditional charm and elegance with modern flair. Emphasis is on relaxation, and the 6 private SPA-Cottages offer a full range of beauty and massage treatments. The award-winning Annex restaurant serves imaginative Italian and Mediterranean cuisine, whilst the bedrooms and suites are stylishly decorated with Designers Guild fabrics, Philippe Starck lighting and Molteni furniture.

Situé dans un magnifique parc avec une plage privée et des vues imprenables sur le lac Lucerne et les Alpes, cet hôtel unique marie à merveille le charme et l'élégance traditionnels avec un style moderne. L'accent est sur la détente, et les 6 villas-SPA offrent un choix complet de soins et traitements de beauté et massage. Une cuisine imaginative italienne et méditerranéenne est servie au restaurant primé Annex. Les chambres et suites élégantes sont ornées avec goût avec des tissus de Designers Guild, lampes de Philippe Starck et meubles de Molteni.

Inmitten eines herrlichen Parks mit eigenem Strand und herrlicher Sicht auf den Vierwaldstätter See und die Alpen bietet dieses einzigartige Hotel traditionelle Eleganz mit modernem Flair. Die Betonung liegt auf Entspannung, und in den 6 SPA-Cottages erhält man umfassende Beauty- und Massagebehandlungen. Im preisgekrönten Annex Restaurant werden einfallsreiche Speisen der italienischen und Mittelmeerküche serviert, und die Zimmer und Suiten sind stilvoll mit Stoffen von Designers Guild, Philippe Starck-Lampen und Molteni-Möbeln eingerichtet.

Our inspector loved: *The Bonsai trees in the Japanese meditation garden and the Rachmaninoff Suite.*

Directions: 60 minutes by car from Zurich Airport. The hotel is in the resort town of Weggis, on the shores of Lake Lucerne.

Web: www.johansens.com/weggis
E-mail: info@phw.ch
Tel: +41 41 392 05 05
Fax: +41 41 392 05 28

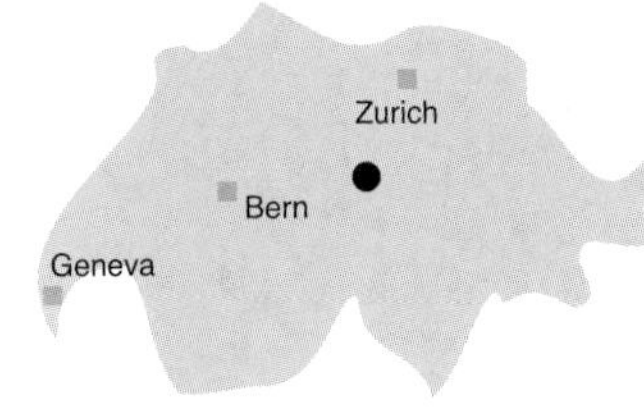

Price Guide:
(per person)
single €163-203
double €110-199
suite €190-390

TURKEY

Hotel location shown in red (hotel) or purple (spa hotel) with page number

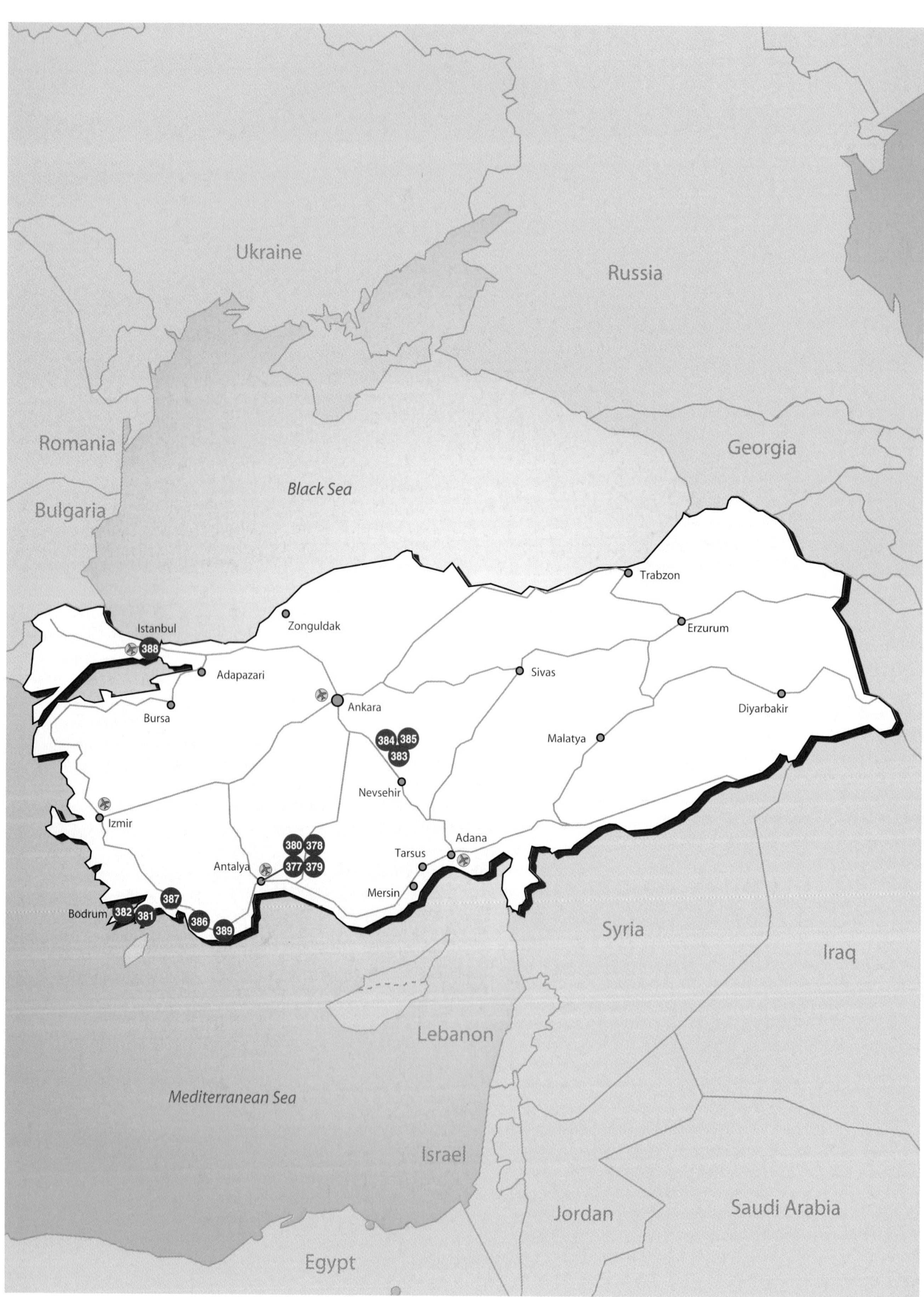

Divan Antalya Talya

FEVZI ÇAKMAK CADDESI NO. 30, 07100 ANTALYA, TURKEY

This impressive 5-star luxury hotel stands on the cliffs overlooking the Gulf of Antalya, in one of Turkey's most beautiful resorts. The 204 en-suite bedrooms are all air-conditioned and have balconies offering views over the Mediterranean or the snow-capped Taurus Mountains. Talya's award-winning kitchen offers the best of traditional Turkish and international cuisine. Snacks are served throughout the day at the poolside's Pub Talya or the beach Snack Bar. The hotel offers a range of watersport facilities as well as a health and fitness and beauty centre.

Cet impressionnant hôtel 5 étoiles se tient sur les falaises et surplombe le Golfe d'Antalya, l'une des plus belles stations de Turquie. Les 204 chambres avec salle de bain ont l'air conditionné et ont des balcons avec vue sur la Méditerranée ou les montagnes au sommets enneigés du Taurus. La cuisine primée de Talya offre le meilleur des cuisines turque et internationale. Des en-cas sont servis toute la journée au pub Talya bordant la piscine ou au Snack Bar de la plage. L'hôtel dispose de diverses installations de sports nautiques ainsi que d'un centre de remise en forme et centre de beauté.

Dieses eindrucksvolle 5-Sterne-Luxushotel liegt auf den Klippen über dem Golf von Antalya in einem der schönsten Resorts der Türkei. Die 204 Zimmer haben Bad, Klimaanlage und Balkon mit Blick auf das Mittelmeer oder die schneebedeckten Taurusberge. Die preisgekrönte Küche bietet traditionelle türkische und internationale Köstlichkeiten, Snacks werden tagsüber im Pub Talya am Pool oder in der Snackbar am Strand serviert. Das Hotel bietet zahlreiche Wassersportmöglichkeiten, außerdem gibt es ein Gesundheits-, Schönheits- und Fitnesszentrum.

Our inspector loved: *The character and style of this 5-star hotel, with its glorious views over the Mediterranean.*

Directions: 15-minute drive from the airport.

Web: www.johansens.com/talya
E-mail: talya@talya.com.tr
Tel: +90 242 248 6800
Fax: +90 242 241 5400

Price Guide:
single US$135
double US$190
suite US$305–475

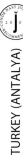

RENAISSANCE ANTALYA BEACH RESORT & SPA

PO BOX 654, 07004 BELDIBI - KEMER, ANTALYA, TURKEY

Directions: Antalya towards Kemer > after 30km turn left at Bedibi 2 exit.

Web: www.johansens.com/antalyaresort
E-mail: info@renaissanceantalya.com
Tel: +90 242 824 84 31
Fax: +90 242 824 84 30

Price Guide:
single US$90–200
double $130–250
suite US$145–1,000

Surrounded by spectacular scenery and set in its own extensive gardens, this resort offers various types of accommodation from generously sized rooms with first-class amenities to self-catering units in the garden. Service is excellent, and guests may enjoy a drink in the Piano Bar or by the pool before sampling delicious Turkish and international cuisine in one of the 4 restaurants. There is an extensive range of sports and leisure facilities including the brand new $950m^2$ spa complex Harmonia Rebirth Wellness and Spa Centre, where "Kneipp" treatments are offered.

Entouré de paysages extraordinaires et situé dans des grands jardins, ce centre de séjour offre divers types de logements dans des grandes pièces avec des équipements de qualité, y compris des unités de cuisine dans le jardin. Le service est excellent et les hôtes peuvent prendre un verre au Piano Bar ou au bord de la piscine avant de déguster la délicieuse cuisine turque et internationale de l'un des 4 restaurants. Pour les sportifs, le choix est étendu, et il y a un nouveau spa de $950m^2$, le Harmonia Rebirth Wellness and Spa Centre, avec des traitements "Kneipp".

Umgeben von atemberaubender Landschaft und ausgedehnten Gärten bietet dieses Resort alles von großzügigen Zimmern mit erstklassigen Einrichtungen bis hin zu Appartements im Garten. Der Service ist hervorragend, und nach einem Drink in der Pianobar oder am Pool kann man in 4 Restaurants türkische oder internationale Köstlichkeiten genießen. Das Sport- und Freizeitangebot ist riesig, und ein brandneuer $950m^2$ großer Spa-Komplex, das Harmonia Rebirth Wellness and Spa Centre, bietet Kneipp-Kuren.

Our inspector loved: *The elegance of this hotel, where quality and nature are in perfect harmony.*

TEKELI KONAKLARI

DIZDAR HASAN SOKAK, KALEICI, ANTALYA, TURKEY

Situated in the heart of the award-winning city of Antalya, just minutes away from the Marina, these 6 restored mansions, dating back to the Ottoman Empire, comprise 8 beautifully appointed spacious rooms overlooking 2 courtyards. All rooms recreate 18th-century Ottoman wealth and the à la carte restaurant and patisserie are both excellent. A friendly and professional personal touch of the management gives a cosy, homely atmosphere to the hotel making guests feel special.

Situées au cœur de la ville primée d'Antalya, à quelques minutes seulement de la marina, ces 6 demeures datant de l'empire ottoman, offrent 8 belles chambres spacieuses surplombant 2 cours. Toutes les chambres recréent l'abondance ottomane et le restaurant à la carte et la pâtisserie sont tous deux excellents. Les hôtes se sentent spéciaux grâce à l'atmosphère chaleureuse procurée par une direction très amicale et professionnelle.

Mitten im Herzen der preisgekrönten Stadt Antalya und nur ein paar Schritte von der Uferpromenade entfernt befinden sich diese 6 restaurierten Häuser, die aus der Zeit des Ottomanischen Reiches stammen. Die 8 zauberhaft eingerichteten, großen Zimmer bieten Blick auf 2 Innenhöfe, und alle spiegeln die Opulenz des 18. Jahrhunderts wider. Das á la carte Restaurant und die Patisserie sind hervorragend, und der freundliche, persönliche Service sorgt für eine heimelige Atmosphäre.

Our inspector loved: *This charming and very homely hotel.*

Directions: Old city > Bell Tower > turn right at end of road > hotel is situated 20m along.

Web: www.johansens.com/tekelikonaklari
E-mail: mirya@superonline.com
Tel: +90 242 244 54 65
Fax: +90 242 242 67 14

Istanbul
Ankara
Antalya

Price Guide:
single US$90-120
double US$110-140

Tuvana Residence

TUZCULAR MAHALLESI, KARANLIK SOKAK 7, 07100 KALEIÇI - ANTALYA, TURKEY

Set in Kaleiçi, Antalya's old quarter, this is the newest of the 3 distinct Tuvana hotels. All rooms are beautifully decorated and offer all modern amenities, and wooden floors and ceilings create a warm and cosy atmosphere. Delightful Turkish cuisine can be sampled in one of the 3 restaurants, and guests have full use of the swimming pool and gardens of the Tuvana Hotel across the road. The historic parts of Antalya such as the old harbour as well as numerous shops, restaurants and beaches are within easy reach.

Situé à Kaleiçi, le vieux quartier d'Antalya, celui-ci est le plus récent des 3 différents hôtels Tuvana. Toutes les chambres sont superbement décorées et offrent toutes les facilités modernes. Planchers et plafonds en bois créent une atmosphère chaleureuse et douillette. Une délicieuse cuisine turque peut être dégustée dans l'un des 3 restaurants et les hôtes peuvent utiliser la piscine et les jardins de l'hôtel Tuvana de l'autre côte de la route. Les quartiers historiques d'Antalya tel que le vieux port, ainsi que de nombreux magasins, restaurants et plages sont d'accès facile

Dieses in Antalyas Altstadt Kaleiçi gelegene Hotel ist das neueste der 3 Tuvana Hotels. Alle Zimmer sind hübsch eingerichtet und bieten jeden modernen Komfort, Holzböden und -decken schaffen ein warmes Ambiente. In 3 Restaurants wird köstliche türkische Küche serviert, und die Gäste haben Zugang zum Swimmingpool und Garten im gegenüberliegenden Tuvana Hotel. Die historischen Teile Antalyas wie der alte Hafen, sowie zahlreiche Geschäfte, Restaurants und Strände liegen in nächster Nähe.

Our inspector loved: *The beautiful courtyard.*

Directions: From the clock tower turn left > left again after 200 metres.

Web: www.johansens.com/tuvanaresidence
E-mail: tuvanaotel@superonline.com
Tel: +90 242 247 60 15
Fax: +90 242 241 19 81

Price Guide:
single US$50–125
double US$70–150

Ada Hotel

BAGARASI MAHALLESI, TEPECIK CADDESI, NO. 128, PO BOX 350, GÖL - TÜRKBÜKÜ, BODRUM - MUGLA, TURKEY

Situated on a slope overlooking Göl-Türbükü bay, this charming and luxurious hotel offers its guests a magical experience. The 14 bedrooms and suites are well-appointed and include a Penthouse Suite and a Presidential Suite, both sharing a private pool and sun terrace. Guests can enjoy a candle-lit dinner and exquisite wines at the exclusive Mahzen restaurant or choose the hotel's beach club, which is a 10-minute walk or a shuttle ride away. The hotel's 2-level health centre boasts a swimming pool, Jumbo Jacuzzi and a magnificent Turkish bath.

Situé sur une colline surplombant la baie de Göl-Türbükü, ce charmant hôtel luxueux offre une expérience magique à ses hôtes. Les 14 chambres et suites sont bien équipées, et la Penthouse Suite et Presidential Suite partagent une piscine et une terrasse privée. On peut savourer un dîner aux chandelles et des vins fins au restaurant exclusif Mahzen, alors que la plage privée est seulement 10 minutes à pied ou quelques minutes avec la navette. L'hôtel dispose d'un centre de remise en forme en deux étages avec piscine, Jumbo Jacuzzi et un bain turc merveilleux.

Auf einem Hügel mit Blick auf die Bucht von Göl-Türbükü gelegen, bietet dieses zauberhafte Luxushotel seinen Gästen einen märchenhaften Aufenthalt. Es gibt 14 Zimmer und Suiten, darunter die Penthouse und die Presidential Suite, die einen Pool und eine Sonnenterrasse teilen. Man kann im exklusiven Mahzen Restaurant bei Kerzenschein feinste Küche und Weine genießen oder den Beach Club besuchen, der in 10 Minuten zu Fuß oder mit dem Shuttle zu erreichen ist. Der zweistöckige Health Club bietet Swimmingpool, Jumbo-Jacuzzi und ein herrliches Türkisches Bad.

Directions: From Milas-Bodrum Airport head towards Bodrum, then right at the junction of Güvercinlik/Yalikavak after 11km. Turn right at Türkbükü and follow signs to hotel.

Web: www.johansens.com/ada
E-mail: info@adahotel.com
Tel: +90 252 377 5915
Fax: +90 252 377 5379

Price Guide:
double US$245-310
suite US$285-545

Our inspector loved: *The elegance and dreamy atmosphere.*

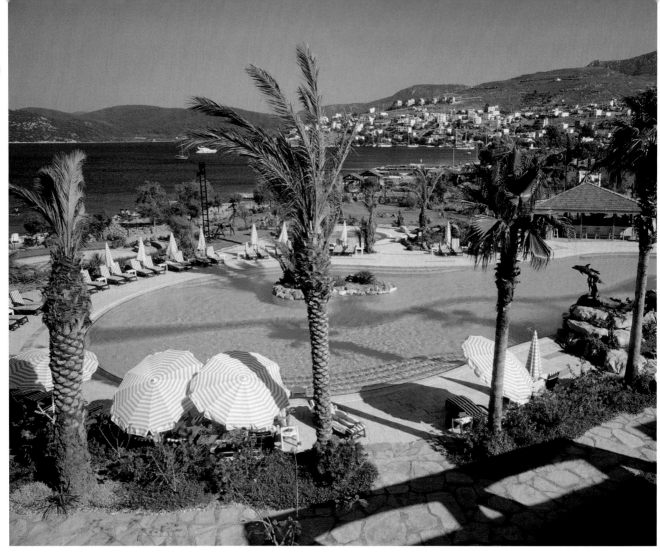

Divan Bodrum Palmira

KELESHARIM CADDESI 6, 48483 TÜRKBÜKÜ – BODRUM, TURKEY

Directions: Bodrum-Milas Airport > follow signs for Türkbükü > follow signs for Divan Palmira towards beach.

Web: www.johansens.com/divanpalmira
Tel: +90 252 377 5601
Fax: +90 252 377 5952

Price Guide:
single US$160–250
double US$185–295
suite US$300–500

Stone walls and wooden balconies give real charm to this wonderful beachfront hotel, which has a lovely colourful garden and a bright lobby with eye-catching paintings. The comfortable rooms are spacious and beautifully decorated; some have sea views. Tasty Mediterranean cuisine is served either al fresco by the swimming pool or in the cosy restaurant. Guests can take advantage of the excellent fitness facilities, water sports, tennis, snooker and basketball or explore the many historical sights nearby.

Des murs de pierre et balcons en bois ajoutent au charme de ce merveilleux hôtel de bord de plage, qui a un ravissant jardin coloré et un hall clair avec des tableaux accrocheurs. Les chambres douillettes sont spacieuses et joliement décorées; certaines ont vue sur la mer. Une cuisine méditerranéenne délicieuse est servie au frais au bord de la piscine ou dans le confortable restaurant. Les hôtes peuvent profiter des excellents équipements de remise en forme, des sports nautiques, tennis, billard et basket ou explorer les sites historiques proches.

Steinwände und hölzerne Balkone sorgen für zusätzlichen Charme in diesem zauberhaften Strandhotel mit seinem farbenfrohen Garten und mit interessanten Bildern geschmückten Empfangsraum. Die attraktiven Zimmer sind komfortabel und geräumig und einige haben Sicht auf das Meer. Köstliche Mittelmeerküche wird am Pool oder im gemütlichen Restaurant serviert. Hervorragende Fitnesseinrichtungen stehen zur Verfügung, Wassersport, Tennis, Billiard und Basketball sind möglich und zahlreiche historische Stätten liegen in der Nähe.

***Our inspector loved:** The relaxing atmosphere and sipping a cocktail at the beach bar.*

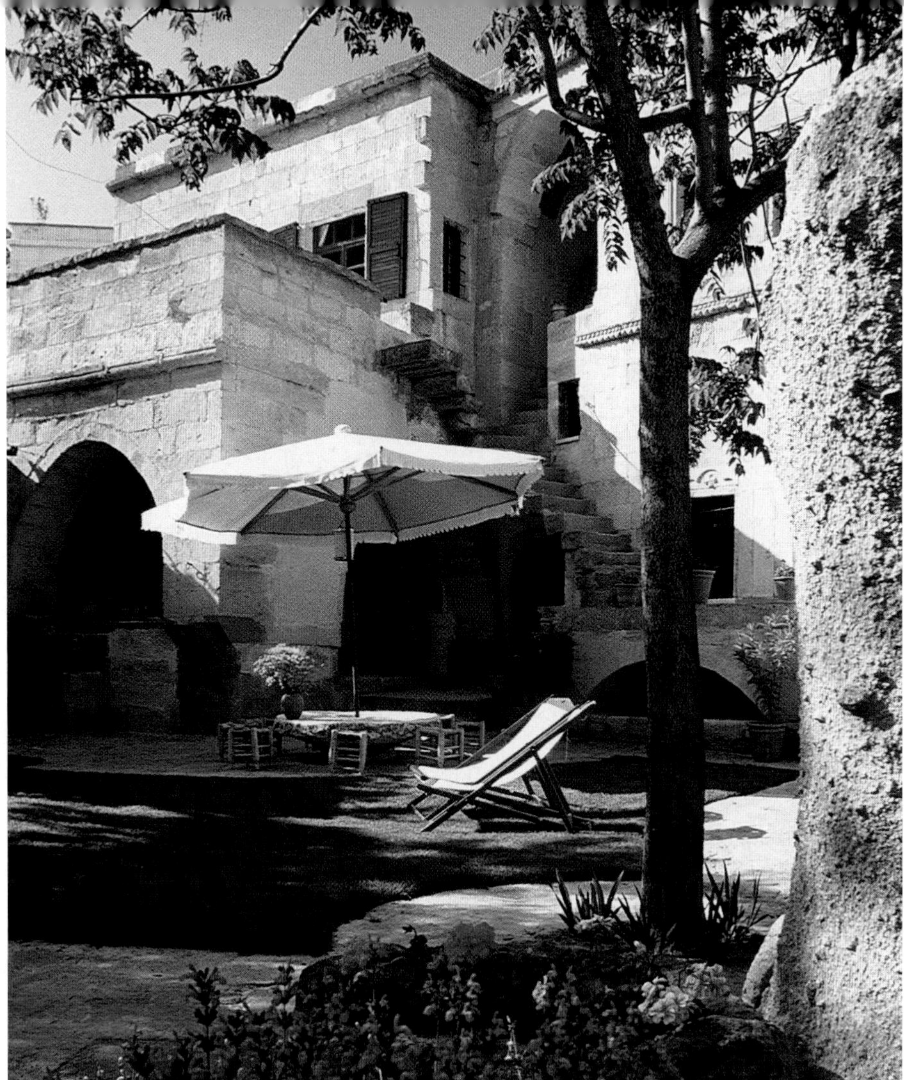

LES MAISONS DE CAPPADOCE

BELEDIYE MEYDANI, PO BOX 28, UÇHISAR, NEVSEHIR, TURKEY

This amazing residence consists of 12 "houses", painstakingly restored and individually decorated. Each offers a spectacular view over the beautiful surroundings, as well as cave extensions, fully equipped kitchens, a dining area and spacious bedrooms. Each room is accessorised with carefully selected local artefacts. Most of the stone houses have central heating and all have open fireplaces. Guests can choose the self-catering option, but food can be served to the houses on request.

Cette résidence incroyable consiste en 12 "maisons", soigneusement restaurées et décorées individuellement. Chacune offre une vue spectaculaire sur les environs magnifiques, ainsi que des extensions en troglodytes, une cuisine bien équipée, un coin dîner et des chambres spacieuses. La plupart des maisons a le chauffage central et toutes ont des foyers ouverts. Les hôtes peuvent choisir l'option nuitée seulement, mais des repas peuvent être servis aux maisons à la demande.

Diese eindrucksvolle Residenz besteht aus 12 sorgfältig restaurierten und individuell gestalteten "Häusern", ein jedes mit atemberaubender Sicht auf die herrliche Umgebung, sowie Höhlenanbauten, voll ausgestatteter Küche, Speisezimmer und geräumigem Schlafzimmer. Jeder Raum ist mit sorgfältig ausgewählten ortstypischen Kunstgegenständen gefüllt. Die meisten der Steinhäuser bieten Zentralheizung, alle haben offene Kamine. Gäste haben die Wahl zwischen Selbstversorgung oder Zimmerservice auf Anfrage.

Our inspector loved: *The peaceful atmosphere and the house with amazing garden.*

Directions: Upon request.

Web: www.johansens.com/cappadoce
E-mail: info@cappadoce.com
Tel: +90 384 219 28 13
Fax: +90 384 219 27 82

Price Guide:
(room only)
US$110-210
US$230-320

Museum Hotel

TEKELLI MAHALESI 1, UÇHISAR - NEVSEHIR, TURKEY

Directions: Nevsehir > 6km towards Uçhisar > the hotel is behind the castle. Kayseri is the nearest airport.

Web: www.johansens.com/museum
E-mail: info@museum-hotel.com
Tel: +90 384 219 22 20
Fax: +90 384 219 24 44

Price Guide:
double US$80–150
suite US$150–450

Set in a wonderfully unique historic location, the elegant Museum Hotel offers a breathtaking panoramic vista of the beautiful Cappadocian valleys and towns. Spacious bedrooms are carved into caves and decorated in a traditional style with all modern amenities. There are local artefacts and antiques on display to create a mystical atmosphere. The café bar on the terrace and the new restaurant are the perfect places to relax.

Dans un lieu historique unique, l'élégant Muséum Hotel offre une vue panoramique à couper le souffle sur les vallées et villes de Cappadoce. Les chambres spacieuses sont creusées dans les caves et décorées dans le style traditionnel et avec toutes les facilités modernes. Des rares objets façonnés et antiques sont en présentation pour créer une atmosphère mystique. Le café-bar situé sur la terrasse et le nouveau restaurant sont des lieux parfaits pour la détente.

Mit seiner einzigartigen historischen Lage bietet das elegante Museum Hotel atemberaubende Panoramablicke auf die traumhaften Täler und Städte der Cappadociaregion. Geräumige, im traditionellen Stil eingerichtete Zimmer sind in die Höhlenwände gehauen und bieten jeglichen modernen Komfort. Überall findet man einheimische Kunstgegenstände und Antiquitäten, die eine mystische Atmosphäre schaffen, und die Cafébar auf der Terrasse und das neue Restaurant sind perfekte Orte zur Entspannung.

Our inspector loved: *The fantastic lobby lounge.*

TURKEY (CAPPADOCIA - ÜRGÜP)

ÜRGÜP EVI

ESBELLI MAHALLESI 54, 50400 ÜRGÜP-NEVSEHIR, TURKEY

Situated in the old district of charming Ürgüp, this lovingly restored, intimate cave hotel is a gem. Bedrooms have wooden floors, cave-carved cupboards, handmade furniture and modern bathrooms, most have sun-drenched terraces to enjoy the view over the town. Gorgeous meals are served in the terrace restaurant and guests will enjoy the friendly informal atmosphere of the hotel.

Situé dans le vieux district du charmant Ürgüp, cet intime et joliment restauré hôtel-cave est un joyau. Les chambres ont des planchers, des penderies creusées dans les caves, des meubles faits main et des salles de bain modernes; la plupart disposent également de terrasses inondées de soleil d'où apprécier la vue sur la ville. De superbes repas sont servis sur le restaurant en terrasse et les hôtes peuvent profiter de l'atmosphère amicale et informelle de l'hôtel.

Dieses liebevoll restaurierte, gemütliche Höhlenhotel liegt in der Altstadt des zauberhaften Ürgüp und ist ein wahres Juwel. Die Zimmer sind mit Holzböden, in den Felsen gehauenen Schränken, handgefertigtem Mobiliar und modernen Bädern ausgestattet, und die meisten bieten sonnige Terrassen, von denen man auf die Stadt blickt. Die Gäste können im Terrassenrestaurant köstliche Mahlzeiten genießen und sich in der freundlichen und ungezwungenen Atmosphäre wunderbar entspannen.

Our inspector loved: *The new cave restaurant.*

Directions: Neveshir > Urgup Main Road > left to Esbelli Quartes.

Web: www.johansens.com/urgupevi
E-mail: faruk@urgupevi.com.tr
Tel: +90 384 341 3173
Fax: +90 384 341 6269

Price Guide:
single US$50–70
double US$60–90
suite US$150–200

GUEST HOUSE 12

Ece Saray Marina & Resort

1 KARAGÖZLER MEVKII, 48300 FETHIYE, MUGLA, TURKEY

Directions: The nearest airport is Dalaman. From Fethiye centre head towards the marina, pass the junction then take first road on the right.

Web: www.johansens.com/ecesaray
E-mail: info@ecesaray.net
Tel: +90 252 612 5005
Fax: +90 252 614 7205

Price Guide:
single US$80-120
double US$120-180
suite US$200-300

This elegant and luxurious hotel will impress even the most demanding traveller. The bedrooms and suites are well-appointed and have all modern amenities as well as pretty balconies offering wonderful views of the sea. Mouth-watering Mediterranean and international cuisine is served by the seaside or in the Terrace restaurant with its stunning views over the bay of Fethiye. Guests can relax by the swimming pool or make use of the hotel's Spa Centre with fitness extension and Turkish bath. Meeting facilities are available.

Même le visiteur le plus exigeant sera impressionné par cet hôtel élégant et luxueux. Les chambres et suites sont bien équipées et offrent tout le confort moderne ainsi que des balcons jolis avec vue sur la mer. Une cuisine méditerranéenne et internationale est servie près de la mer ou au restaurant en terrasse avec vue splendide sur la baie de Fethiye. Les hôtes peuvent se détendre autour de la piscine ou profiter du Spa avec des équipements de remise en forme et bain turc. L'hôtel dispose de salles de conférences.

Dieses elegante Luxushotel wird selbst den anspruchsvollsten Gast beeindrucken. Die Zimmer und Suiten bieten jeglichen modernen Komfort und haben hübsche Balkone mit Blick aufs Meer. Mediterrane und internationale Köstlichkeiten werden direkt am Meer oder im Terrassenrestaurant serviert, von dem man eine herrliche Sicht auf die Bucht von Fethiye hat. Gäste können am Pool entspannen oder das Spa Centre mit Fitnesszentrum und Türkischem Bad besuchen. Konferenzeinrichtungen sind vorhanden.

Our inspector loved: *The restaurant and the wonderful food.*

Monte Negro

GÖKGEOVACIK KÖYÜ, ZEYTINLIK MAHALLESI, GÖCEK, FETHIYE, TURKEY

Situated 10 minutes down a dirt track on the slopes of the Taurus mountains, this small but charming guest house is an idyllic and relaxing haven, where the fragrance of wild herbs and flowers is carried by the breeze as guests relax by the delightful swimming pool or lazy hammock. Breakfast and dinner are prepared using the freshest of ingredients and locally produced olive oil, and are served wherever guests request - on the patio, in the garden or even by the pool.

Situé au bout d'un chemin non macadamisé sur les flancs des montagnes de Taurus, cette petite pension charmante est dans un endroit idyllique et détendu, où l'air est rempli du parfum d'herbes et de fleurs et les hôtes se détendent auprès de la piscine magnifique ou dans un hamac. Le petit déjeuner et le dîner sont préparés avec les ingrédients les plus frais et l'huile d'olives produite dans la région, et sont servis là où les hôtes le désirent - à la terrasse, dans le jardin ou même près de la piscine.

Nur 10 Minuten entlang einer ungepflasterten Straße in den Hügeln der Taurusberge liegt diese kleine, zauberhafte Pension, ein idyllischer Ort mit entspannter Atmosphäre, an dem der Duft von Kräutern und Blumen ständig in der Luft liegt. Die Gäste genießen den hübschen Swimmingpool oder ruhen sich in einer Hängematte aus, und Frühstück und Abendessen werden mit frischesten Zutaten und einheimischem Olivenöl zubereitet und serviert, wo auch immer der Gast möchte - auf der Terrasse, im Garten oder auch direkt am Pool.

Our inspector loved: *Being in the middle of stunning nature; just fantastic!*

Directions: Dalaman Airport is a 35-minute drive. From Dalaman drive towards Göcek and continue for 2 km. Turn left to Gökgeovacik village and take the first right after the village.

Web: www.johansens.com/montenegro
E-mail: selim.karadag@teklan.com.tr
Tel: +90 252 644 0181
Fax: +90 252 644 0182

Price Guide:
double US$80-100
villa US$130-160

Conrad - Istanbul

YILDIZ CADDESI, BESIKTAS, 80700 ISTANBUL, TURKEY

With breathtaking views over the city and the Marmara Sea, the stunning Conrad hotel offers a delightful combination of understated elegance and quiet, contemporary design. Courteous and attentive staff offer a warm welcome typical of Turkish hospitality. The bedrooms, many of which have spectacular views, are the ultimate in comfort. The finest international cuisine is available, and the rooftop terrace on the 14th floor is a treat. The hotel's central location makes it ideal for exploring Istanbul.

Avec des vues imprenables sur la ville et la mer de Marmara, le Conrad offre une combinaison excellente d'élégance et de design calme et contemporain. Le personnel courtois et attentif offre un accueil chaleureux et typique de l'hospitalité turque. Les chambres, dont plusieurs ont des vues magnifiques, sont le nec-plus-ultra du confort. Le restaurant sert une cuisine raffinée internationale, et la terrasse sur le toit au 14e étage est spectaculaire. La situation centrale de l'hôtel le rend parfait pour explorer la ville d'Istanbul.

Mit atemberaubender Sicht auf die Stadt und das Marmarameer bietet das eindrucksvolle Hotel Conrad eine wundervolle Mischung aus zurückhaltender Eleganz und ruhigem zeitgenössischen Design. Das höfliche, aufmerksame Personal sorgt für einen für die Türkei so typischen besonders herzlichen Empfang. Die Zimmer, zahlreiche mit herrlichen Ausblicken, bieten höchsten Komfort. Beste internationale Küche wird serviert, und die Dachterrasse im 14. Stock ist einfach einmalig. Die zentrale Lage macht dieses Hotel zum idealen Ausgangspunkt, um Istanbul zu erkunden.

Our inspector loved: *The stunning views of Istanbul from the rooms.*

Directions: From Atatürk Airport follow, via the coast, signs to the city centre and Besiktas. From Besiktas main square turn left for 500m then turn right at Yildiz Street.

Web: www.johansens.com/conradistanbul
E-mail: istanbulinfo@conradhotels.com
Tel: +90 212 227 3000
Fax: +90 212 259 6667

Price Guide:
single US$180-400
suite US$500-3,000

Hotel Villa Mahal

P.K. 4 KALKAN, 07960 ANTALYA, TURKEY

This intimate hotel stands on a hillside, overlooking the spectacular bay of Kalkan, and is surrounded by olive trees. Stone steps plunge to the villa's own beach platforms, and the pool suite has a private swimming pool and terrace. The bright and airy bedrooms, all with seaview, accommodate a maximum of 26 guests, and the ambience is more like that of a private house than a hotel. Breakfast is a delicious buffet enjoyed on the rooftop terrace, and the Beach Restaurant serves succulent Turkish specialities for lunch and dinner.

Cet hôtel intime, entouré d'oliviers et perché sur une colline, surplombe la baie spectaculaire de Kalkan. Un escalier donne accès à la plage privée (plate-formes), et la suite piscine possède une terrasse et une piscine privée. Les chambres spacieuses et lumineuses, pouvant accueillir jusqu'à 26 hôtes, ont toutes vue sur la mer et l'ambiance ressemble plus à celle d'une maison particulière qu'à celle d'un hôtel. Le petit-déjeuner est un superbe buffet servi sur la terrasse du toit et le restaurant de la plage propose des spécialités turques pour le déjeuner et le dîner.

Dieses kleine, von Olivenbäumen umgebene Hotel liegt auf einem Hügel mit Blick über die spektakuläre Bucht von Kalkan. Eine Treppe führt von der Villa hinunter zum Privatsteg. Die Pool Suite bietet einen privaten Pool und Terrasse, und die hellen und luftigen Zimmer haben Meerblick und beherbergen maximal 26 Gäste. Das Ambiente ähnelt eher einem privaten Haus als einem Hotel. Zum Frühstück gibt es ein köstliches Buffet auf der Dachterrasse, und mittags und abends können die Gäste im Strandrestaurant türkische Spezialitäten genießen.

Our inspector loved: *This hotel as a honeymoon paradise or a place to propose.*

Directions: Dalaman Airport > Kas > Kalkan sign > left > beach.

Web: www.johansens.com/villamahal
E-mail: info@villamahal.com
Tel: +90 242 844 32 68
Fax: +90 242 844 21 22

Price Guide:
single US$113
double/twin US$125–160
suite US$160–200

Mini Listings Great Britain & Ireland

Condé Nast Johansens are delighted to recommend over 660 properties across Great Britain and Ireland. These properties can be found in *Recommended Hotels - GB & Ireland 2004* and *Recommended Country Houses, Small Hotels & Inns - GB & Ireland 2004.* Call +44 208 655 7810 or see the order forms on page 421 to order Guides.

Recommended Hotels Great Britain & Ireland 2004

England

The Bath Priory Hotel And Restaurant	Bath & NE Somerset	+44 (0)1225 331922
The Bath Spa Hotel	Bath & NE Somerset	+44 (0)1225 444424
Combe Grove Manor Hotel & Country Club	Bath & NE Somerset	+44 (0)1225 834644
The Francis Hotel	Bath & NE Somerset	+44 (0)1225 424105
Homewood Park	Bath & NE Somerset	+44 (0)1225 723731
Hunstrete House	Bath & NE Somerset	+44 (0)1761 490490
The Queensberry	Bath & NE Somerset	+44 (0)1225 447928
The Royal Crescent Hotel	Bath & NE Somerset	+44 (0)1225 823333
The Windsor Hotel	Bath & NE Somerset	+44 (0)1225 422100
Flitwick Manor	Bedfordshire	+44 (0)1525 712242
Moore Place Hotel	Bedfordshire	+44 (0)1908 282000
Cliveden	Berkshire	+44 (0)1628 668561
Donnington Valley Hotel & Golf Club	Berkshire	+44 (0)1635 551199
Fredrick's Hotel & Restaurant	Berkshire	+44 (0)1628 581000
The French Horn	Berkshire	+44 (0)1189 692204
Monkey Island Hotel	Berkshire	+44 (0)1628 623400
The Regency Park Hotel	Berkshire	+44 (0)1635 871555
Sir Christopher Wren's House Hotel	Berkshire	+44 (0)1753 861354
The Swan At Streatley	Berkshire	+44 (0)1491 878800
The Vineyard At Stockcross	Berkshire	+44 (0)1635 528770
Hotel Du Vin & Bistro	Birmingham	+44 (0)121 200 0600
New Hall	Birmingham	+44 (0)121 378 2442
Hotel Du Vin & Bistro	Bristol	+44 (0)117 925 5577
Danesfield House Hotel And Spa	Buckinghamshire	+44 (0)1628 891010
Hartwell House	Buckinghamshire	+44 (0)1296 747444
Stoke Park Club	Buckinghamshire	+44 (0)1753 717171
Taplow House Hotel	Buckinghamshire	+44 (0)1628 670056
Great Northern Hotel	Cambridgeshire	+44 (0)1733 552331
The Haycock	Cambridgeshire	+44 (0)1780 782223
Hotel Felix	Cambridgeshire	+44 (0)1223 277977
The Alderley Edge Hotel	Cheshire	+44 (0)1625 583033
The Chester Crabwall Manor	Cheshire	+44 (0)1244 851666
Crewe Hall	Cheshire	+44 (0)1270 253333
Green Bough Hotel	Cheshire	+44 (0)1244 326241
Hillbark Hotel	Cheshire	+44 (0)151 625 2400
Mere Court Hotel	Cheshire	+44 (0)1565 831000
Nunsmere Hall	Cheshire	+44 (0)1606 889100
Rowton Hall Hotel	Cheshire	+44 (0)1244 335262
The Stanneylands Hotel	Cheshire	+44 (0)1625 525225
Alverton Manor	Cornwall	+44 (0)1872 276633
Budock Vean - The Hotel On The River	Cornwall	+44 (0)1326 252100
Fowey Hall Hotel & Restaurant	Cornwall	+44 (0)1726 833866
The Garrack Hotel & Restaurant	Cornwall	+44 (0)1736 796199
The Greenbank Hotel	Cornwall	+44 (0)1326 312440
Hell Bay	Cornwall	+44 (0)1720 422947
The Lugger Hotel	Cornwall	+44 (0)1872 501322
Meudon Hotel	Cornwall	+44 (0)1326 250541
The Nare Hotel	Cornwall	+44 (0)1872 501111
Rose-In-Vale Country House Hotel	Cornwall	+44 (0)1872 552202
The Rosevine Hotel	Cornwall	+44 (0)1872 580206
St Martin's On The Isle	Cornwall	+44 (0)1720 422090
Talland Bay Hotel	Cornwall	+44 (0)1503 272667
Trenython Manor Hotel & Spa	Cornwall	+44 (0)1726 814797
The Well House	Cornwall	+44 (0)1579 342001
Appleby Manor Country House Hotel	Cumbria	+44 (0)17683 51571
Armathwaite Hall Hotel	Cumbria	+44 (0)17687 76551
The Borrowdale Gates Country House Hotel	Cumbria	+44 (0)17687 77204
The Derwentwater Hotel	Cumbria	+44 (0)17687 72538
Farlam Hall Hotel	Cumbria	+44 (0)16977 46234
Gilpin Lodge	Cumbria	+44 (0)15394 88818
Holbeck Ghyll Country House Hotel	Cumbria	+44 (0)15394 32375
The Inn on the Lake	Cumbria	+44 (0)17684 82444
Lakeside Hotel On Lake Windermere	Cumbria	+44 (0)1539 530001
Langdale Chase	Cumbria	+44 (0)15394 32201
Linthwaite House Hotel	Cumbria	+44 (0)15394 88600
Lovelady Shield Country House Hotel	Cumbria	+44 (0)1434 381203
Miller Howe Hotel & Restaurant	Cumbria	+44 (0)15394 42536
Netherwood Hotel	Cumbria	+44 (0)15395 32552
Rampsbeck Country House Hotel	Cumbria	+44 (0)17684 86442
Rothay Manor	Cumbria	+44 (0)15394 33605
The Samling	Cumbria	+44 (0)15394 31922

▼

Sharrow Bay Country House Hotel	**Cumbria**	**+44 (0)17684 86301**
Storrs Hall	Cumbria	+44 (0)15394 47111
Tufton Arms Hotel	Cumbria	+44 (0)17683 51593
Callow Hall	Derbyshire	+44 (0)1335 300900
Cavendish Hotel	Derbyshire	+44 (0)1246 582311
East Lodge Country House Hotel	Derbyshire	+44 (0)1629 734474
Fischer's	Derbyshire	+44 (0)1246 583259
The George At Hathersage	Derbyshire	+44 (0)1433 650436
Hassop Hall	Derbyshire	+44 (0)1629 640488
The Izaak Walton Hotel	Derbyshire	+44 (0)1335 350555
Riber Hall	Derbyshire	+44 (0)1629 582795
Ringwood Hall Hotel	Derbyshire	+44 (0)1246 280077
Risley Hall	Derbyshire	+44 (0)115 939 9000
Riverside House	Derbyshire	+44 (0)1629 814275
The Arundell Arms	Devon	+44 (0)1566 784666
Buckland-Tout-Saints	Devon	+44 (0)1548 853055
Combe House Hotel & Restaurant	Devon	+44 (0)1404 540400
Fairwater Head Country House Hotel	Devon	+44 (0)1297 678349
Gidleigh Park	Devon	+44 (0)1647 432367
Hotel Riviera	Devon	+44 (0)1395 515201
Ilsington Country House Hotel	Devon	+44 (0)1364 661452
Kitley House Hotel & Restaurant	Devon	+44 (0)1752 881555
Langdon Court Hotel & Restaurant	Devon	+44 (0)1752 862358
Lewtrenchard Manor	Devon	+44 (0)1566 783222
Mill End	Devon	+44 (0)1647 432282
Northcote Manor Country House Hotel	Devon	+44 (0)1769 560501
Orestone Manor Hotel & Restaurant	Devon	+44 (0)1803 328098
The Osborne Hotel & Langtry's Restaurant	Devon	+44 (0)1803 213311
The Palace Hotel	Devon	+44 (0)1803 200200
Percy's Country Hotel & Restaurant	Devon	+44 (0)1409 211236
Soar Mill Cove Hotel	Devon	+44 (0)1548 561566
The Tides Reach Hotel	Devon	+44 (0)1548 843466
Watersmeet Hotel	Devon	+44 (0)1271 870333
Woolacombe Bay Hotel	Devon	+44 (0)1271 870388
Bridge House Hotel	Dorset	+44 (0)1308 862200
The Dormy	Dorset	+44 (0)1202 872121
The Haven	Dorset	+44 (0)1202 707333
Langtry Manor	Dorset	+44 (0)1202 553887
Moonfleet Manor	Dorset	+44 (0)1305 786948
Norfolk Royale Hotel	Dorset	+44 (0)1202 551521

MINI LISTINGS GREAT BRITAIN & IRELAND

Condé Nast Johansens are delighted to recommend over 660 properties across Great Britain and Ireland.
These properties can be found in *Recommended Hotels - GB & Ireland 2004* and *Recommended Country Houses, Small Hotels & Inns - GB & Ireland 2004.*
Call +44 208 655 7810 or see the order forms on page 421 to order Guides.

Plumber Manor	Dorset	+44 (0)1258 472507
The Priory Hotel	Dorset	+44 (0)1929 551666
Summer Lodge	Dorset	+44 (0)1935 83424
Headlam Hall	Durham	+44 (0)1325 730238
Seaham Hall Hotel & Serenity Spa	Durham	+44 (0)191 516 1400
Five Lakes Resort	Essex	+44 (0)1621 868888
Greenwoods Estate	Essex	+44 (0)1277 829990
Maison Talbooth	Essex	+44 (0)1206 322367
The Bear Of Rodborough	Gloucestershire	+44 (0)1453 878522
Burleigh Court	Gloucestershire	+44 (0)1453 883804
Calcot Manor	Gloucestershire	+44 (0)1666 890391
Charingworth Manor	Gloucestershire	+44 (0)1386 593555
The Close Hotel	Gloucestershire	+44 (0)1666 502272
Corse Lawn House Hotel	Gloucestershire	+44 (0)1452 780479
Cotswold House Hotel	Gloucestershire	+44 (0)1386 840330
The Grapevine Hotel	Gloucestershire	+44 (0)1451 830344
The Greenway	Gloucestershire	+44 (0)1242 862352
Hatton Court	Gloucestershire	+44 (0)1452 617412
Hotel On The Park	Gloucestershire	+44 (0)1242 518898
Lords Of The Manor Hotel	Gloucestershire	+44 (0)1451 820243
Lower Slaughter Manor	Gloucestershire	+44 (0)1451 820456
The Manor House Hotel	Gloucestershire	+44 (0)1608 650501
The Noel Arms Hotel	Gloucestershire	+44 (0)1386 840317
The Painswick Hotel	Gloucestershire	+44 (0)1452 812160
The Swan Hotel At Bibury	Gloucestershire	+44 (0)1285 740695
The Unicorn Hotel	Gloucestershire	+44 (0)1451 830257
Washbourne Court Hotel	Gloucestershire	+44 (0)1451 822143
Wyck Hill House	Gloucestershire	+44 (0)1451 831936
Thornbury Castle	South Gloucestershire	+44 (0)1454 281182
Careys Manor Hotel	Hampshire	+44 (0)1590 623551
Chewton Glen	Hampshire	+44 (0)1425 275341
Esseborne Manor	Hampshire	+44 (0)1264 736444
Grand Harbour	Hampshire	+44 (0)23 8063 3033
Hotel Du Vin & Bistro	Hampshire	+44 (0)1962 841414
Le Poussin At Parkhill	Hampshire	+44 (0)23 8028 2944
The Montagu Arms Hotel	Hampshire	+44 (0)1590 612324
New Park Manor	Hampshire	+44 (0)1590 623467
Old Thorns Hotel, Golf & Country Club	Hampshire	+44 (0)1428 724555
Passford House Hotel	Hampshire	+44 (0)1590 682398
Tylney Hall	Hampshire	+44 (0)1256 764881
Allt-Yr-Ynys Hotel	Herefordshire	+44 (0)1873 890307
The Chase Hotel	Herefordshire	+44 (0)1989 763161
Down Hall Country House Hotel	Hertfordshire	+44 (0)1279 731441
The Grove Hotel	Hertfordshire	+44 (0)1923 807807
The Manor of Groves	Hertfordshire	+44 (0)1279 600777
Pendley Manor Hotel & Conference Centre	Hertfordshire	+44 (0)1442 891891
Sopwell House Hotel, Country Club & Spa	Hertfordshire	+44 (0)1727 864477
St Michael's Manor	Hertfordshire	+44 (0)1727 864444
The Priory Bay Hotel	Isle of Wight	+44 (0)1983 613146
Brandshatch Place Hotel	Kent	+44 (0)1474 875000
Chilston Park	Kent	+44 (0)1622 859803
Eastwell Manor	Kent	+44 (0)1233 213000
Hotel Du Vin & Bistro	Kent	+44 (0)1892 526455
Rowhill Grange Hotel And Spa	Kent	+44 (0)1322 615136
The Spa Hotel	Kent	+44 (0)1892 520331
Astley Bank Hotel & Conference Centre	Lancashire	+44 (0)1254 777700
The Gibbon Bridge Hotel	Lancashire	+44 (0)1995 61456
Northcote Manor	Lancashire	+44 (0)1254 240555
Champneys Springs	Leicestershire	+44 (0)1530 273873
Kilworth House Hotel	Leicestershire	+44 (0)1858 880058
Quorn Country Hotel	Leicestershire	+44 (0)1509 415050
Stapleford Park Hotel, Spa, Golf & Sporting Estate	Leicestershire	+44 (0)1572 787 522
The Angel and Royal Hotel	Lincolnshire	+44 (0)1476 565816
The George Of Stamford	Lincolnshire	+44 (0)1780 750750
51 Buckingham Gate	London	+44 (0)20 7769 7766
The Academy, The Bloomsbury Town House	London	+44 (0)20 7631 4115
The Athenaeum Hotel & Apartments	London	+44 (0)20 7499 3464
The Beaufort	London	+44 (0)20 7584 5252
Beaufort House	London	+44 (0)20 7584 2600
Cannizaro House	London	+44 (0)208 879 1464
The Colonnade, The Little Venice Town House	London	+44 (0)20 7286 1052
The Cranley	London	+44 (0)20 7373 0123
Dolphin Square Hotel	London	+44 (0)20 7834 3800
The Dorchester	London	+44 (0)20 7629 8888
Dorset Square Hotel	London	+44 (0)20 7723 7874
The Draycott Hotel	London	+44 (0)20 7730 6466
Draycott House Apartments	London	+44 (0)20 7584 4659
The Gallery	London	+44 (0)20 7915 0000
Great Eastern Hotel	London	+44 (0)20 7618 5000
The Halkin	London	+44 (0)20 7333 1000
Hotel St James	London	+44 (0)20 7747 2200
Kensington House Hotel	London	+44 (0)20 7937 2345
The Leonard	London	+44 (0)20 7935 2010
The Mayflower Hotel	London	+44 (0)20 7370 0991
Number Eleven Cadogan Gardens	London	+44 (0)20 7730 7000
Number Sixteen	London	+44 (0)20 7589 5232
Pembridge Court Hotel	London	+44 (0)20 7229 9977
The Petersham	London	+44 (0)20 8940 7471
The Richmond Gate Hotel And Restaurant	London	+44 (0)20 8940 0061
Threadneedles	London	+44 (0)20 7657 8080
Twenty Nevern Square	London	+44 (0)20 7565 9555
Warren House	London	+44 (0)20 8547 1777
West Lodge Park Country House Hotel	London	+44 (0)20 8216 3900
Didsbury House	Greater Manchester	+44 (0)161 448 2200
Etrop Grange	Greater Manchester	+44 (0)161 499 0500
Hotel Rossetti	Greater Manchester	+44 (0)161 247 7744
Congham Hall	Norfolk	+44 (0)1485 600250
Park Farm Country Hotel & Leisure	Norfolk	+44 (0)1603 810264
Fawsley Hall	Northamptonshire	+44 (0)1327 892000
Whittlebury Hall	Northamptonshire	+44 (0)1327 857857
Linden Hall	Northumberland	+44 (0)1670 50 00 00
Marshall Meadows Country House Hotel	Northumberland	+44 (0)1289 331133
Matfen Hall	Northumberland	+44 (0)1661 886500
Tillmouth Park	Northumberland	+44 (0)1890 882255
Langar Hall	Nottinghamshire	+44 (0)1949 860559
The Bay Tree Hotel	Oxfordshire	+44 (0)1993 822791
Bignell Park Hotel & Restaurant	Oxfordshire	+44 (0)1869 326550
The Cotswold Lodge Hotel	Oxfordshire	+44 (0)1865 512121
Fallowfields	Oxfordshire	+44 (0)1865 820416
The Feathers Hotel	Oxfordshire	+44 (0)1993 812291
Hawkwell House	Oxfordshire	+44 (0)1865 749988
Le Manoir Aux Quat' Saisons	Oxfordshire	+44 (0)1844 278881
Phyllis Court Club	Oxfordshire	+44 (0)1491 570500
The Spread Eagle Hotel	Oxfordshire	+44 (0)1844 213661

▼

The Springs Hotel & Golf Club	**Oxfordshire**	**+44 (0)1491 836687**
Studley Priory	Oxfordshire	+44 (0)1865 351203
Weston Manor	Oxfordshire	+44 (0)1869 350621

Mini Listings Great Britain & Ireland

Condé Nast Johansens are delighted to recommend over 660 properties across Great Britain and Ireland.
These properties can be found in *Recommended Hotels - GB & Ireland 2004* and *Recommended Country Houses, Small Hotels & Inns - GB & Ireland 2004.*
Call +44 208 655 7810 or see the order forms on page 421 to order Guides.

Barnsdale Lodge	Rutland	+44 (0)1572 724678
Hambleton Hall	Rutland	+44 (0)1572 756991
The Lake Isle	Rutland	+44 (0)1572 822951
Dinham Hall	Shropshire	+44 (0)1584 876464
Madeley Court	Shropshire	+44 (0)1952 680068
Daneswood House Hotel	Somerset	+44 (0)1934 843145
Holbrook House Hotel & Spa	Somerset	+44 (0)1963 32377
Mount Somerset Country House Hotel	Somerset	+44 (0)1823 442500
Ston Easton Park	Somerset	+44 (0)1761 241631
The Swan Hotel	Somerset	+44 (0)1749 836300

▼

Hoar Cross Hall Health Spa Resort	**Staffordshire**	**+44 (0)1283 575671**
Swinfen Hall Hotel	Staffordshire	+44 (0)1543 481494
Angel Hotel	Suffolk	+44 (0)1284 714000
Black Lion Hotel & Restaurant	Suffolk	+44 (0)1787 312356
Brudenell Hotel	Suffolk	+44 (0)1728 452071
Hintlesham Hall	Suffolk	+44 (0)1473 652334
The Ickworth Hotel	Suffolk	+44 (0)1284 735350
Ravenwood Hall Country Hotel & Restaurant	Suffolk	+44 (0)1359 270345
The Rutland Arms Hotel	Suffolk	+44 (0)1638 664251
Salthouse Harbour Hotel	Suffolk	+44 (0)1473 226789
Seckford Hall	Suffolk	+44 (0)1394 385678
The Swan Hotel	Suffolk	+44 (0)1502 722186
Swynford Paddocks Hotel And Restaurant	Suffolk	+44 (0)1638 570234
The Angel Posting House And Livery	Surrey	+44 (0)1483 564555
Foxhills	Surrey	+44 (0)1932 704500
Great Fosters	Surrey	+44 (0)1784 433822
Langshott Manor	Surrey	+44 (0)1293 786680
Lythe Hill Hotel & Spa	Surrey	+44 (0)1428 651251
Nutfield Priory	Surrey	+44 (0)1737 824400
Oatlands Park Hotel	Surrey	+44 (0)1932 847242
Ashdown Park Hotel And Country Club	East Sussex	+44 (0)1342 824988
Dale Hill	East Sussex	+44 (0)1580 200112
The Grand Hotel	East Sussex	+44 (0)1323 412345
Horsted Place Country House Hotel	East Sussex	+44 (0)1825 750581
Hotel Du Vin & Bistro	East Sussex	+44 (0)1273 718588
Hotel Seattle	East Sussex	+44 (0)1273 679799
Newick Park	East Sussex	+44 (0)1825 723633
The PowderMills	East Sussex	+44 (0)1424 775511
White Lodge Country House Hotel	East Sussex	+44 (0)1323 870265
Alexander House Hotel	West Sussex	+44 (0)1342 714914
Amberley Castle	West Sussex	+44 (0)1798 831992
Bailiffscourt	West Sussex	+44 (0)1903 723511
Gravetye Manor	West Sussex	+44 (0)1342 810567
The Millstream Hotel	West Sussex	+44 (0)1243 573234
Ockenden Manor	West Sussex	+44 (0)1444 416111
The Spread Eagle Hotel & Health Spa	West Sussex	+44 (0)1730 816911
The Vermont Hotel	Tyne & Wear	+44 (0)191 233 1010
Alveston Manor	Warwickshire	+44 (0)1789 205478
Ardencote Manor Hotel, Country Club & Spa	Warwickshire	+44 (0)1926 843111
Billesley Manor	Warwickshire	+44 (0)1789 279955
Ettington Park	Warwickshire	+44 (0)1789 450123
The Glebe At Barford	Warwickshire	+44 (0)1926 624218
Mallory Court	Warwickshire	+44 (0)1926 330214
Nailcote Hall	Warwickshire	+44 (0)2476 466174
Nuthurst Grange	Warwickshire	+44 (0)1564 783972
The Welcombe Hotel And Golf Course	Warwickshire	+44 (0)1789 295252
Wroxall Abbey Estate	Warwickshire	+44 (0)1926 484470
Bishopstrow House	Wiltshire	+44 (0)1985 212312
Howard's House	Wiltshire	+44 (0)1722 716392
Lucknam Park, Bath	Wiltshire	+44 (0)1225 742777
The Old Bell	Wiltshire	+44 (0)1666 822344
The Pear Tree At Purton	Wiltshire	+44 (0)1793 772100
Whatley Manor	Wiltshire	+44 (0)1666 822888
Woolley Grange	Wiltshire	+44 (0)1225 864705
The Broadway Hotel	Worcestershire	+44 (0)1386 852401
Brockencote Hall	Worcestershire	+44 (0)1562 777876
Buckland Manor	Worcestershire	+44 (0)1386 852626
The Cottage In The Wood	Worcestershire	+44 (0)1684 575859
Dormy House	Worcestershire	+44 (0)1386 852711
The Elms	Worcestershire	+44 (0)1299 896666
The Evesham Hotel	Worcestershire	+44 (0)1386 765566
The Lygon Arms	Worcestershire	+44 (0)1386 852255
Wood Norton Hall	Worcestershire	+44 (0)1386 425780
Willerby Manor Hotel	East Riding Of Yorkshire	+44 (0)1482 652616
Aldwark Manor	North Yorkshire	+44 (0)1347 838146
The Balmoral Hotel	North Yorkshire	+44 (0)1423 508208
The Boar's Head Hotel	North Yorkshire	+44 (0)1423 771888
The Devonshire Arms Country House Hotel	North Yorkshire	+44 (0)1756 718111
The Grange Hotel	North Yorkshire	+44 (0)1904 644744
Grants Hotel	North Yorkshire	+44 (0)1423 560666
Hackness Grange	North Yorkshire	+44 (0)1723 882345
Hazlewood Castle Hotel	North Yorkshire	+44 (0)1937 535353
Hob Green Hotel And Restaurant	North Yorkshire	+44 (0)1423 770031
Hotel Du Vin & Bistro	North Yorkshire	+44 (0)1423 856800
Judges Country House Hotel	North Yorkshire	+44 (0)1642 789000
Middlethorpe Hall	North Yorkshire	+44 (0)1904 641241
Monk Fryston Hall Hotel	North Yorkshire	+44 (0)1977 682369
The Pheasant	North Yorkshire	+44 (0)1439 771241
Rudding Park Hotel & Golf	North Yorkshire	+44 (0)1423 871350
Simonstone Hall	North Yorkshire	+44 (0)1969 667255
Swinton Park	North Yorkshire	+44 (0)1765 680900
The Worsley Arms Hotel	North Yorkshire	+44 (0)1653 628234
Wrea Head Country Hotel	North Yorkshire	+44 (0)1723 378211
Charnwood Hotel	South Yorkshire	+44 (0)114 258 9411
Hellaby Hall Hotel	South Yorkshire	+44 (0)1709 702701
Whitley Hall Hotel	South Yorkshire	+44 (0)114 245 4444
42 The Calls	West Yorkshire	+44 (0)113 244 0099
Chevin Country Park Hotel	West Yorkshire	+44 (0)1943 467818
Haley's Hotel & Restaurant	West Yorkshire	+44 (0)113 278 4446
Holdsworth House Hotel & Restaurant	West Yorkshire	+44 (0)1422 240024
Quebecs, The Leeds Town House	West Yorkshire	+44 (0)113 244 8989

Channel Islands

The Atlantic Hotel	Channel Islands	+44 (0)1534 744101
Château La Chaire	Channel Islands	+44 (0)1534 863354
La Frégate Hotel and Restaurant	Channel Islands	+44 (0)1481 724624
Longueville Manor	Channel Islands	+44 (0)1534 725501

Ireland

Dromoland Castle	Clare	+353 61 368144
The Fitzwilliam Hotel	Dublin	+353 1 478 7000
Merrion Hall	Dublin	+353 1 668 1426
The Merrion Hotel	Dublin	+353 1 603 0600
Renvyle House Hotel	Galway	+353 95 43511
Sheen Falls Lodge	Kerry	+353 64 41600
Killashee House Hotel	Kildare	+353 45 879277
Mount Juliet Conrad	Kilkenny	+353 56 777 3000

Mini Listings Great Britain & Ireland

Condé Nast Johansens are delighted to recommend over 660 properties across Great Britain and Ireland.

These properties can be found in *Recommended Hotels - GB & Ireland 2004* and *Recommended Country Houses, Small Hotels & Inns - GB & Ireland 2004.*

Call +44 208 655 7810 or see the order forms on page 421 to order Guides.

Glin Castle	Limerick	+353 68 34173
Ashford Castle	Mayo	+353 94 95 46003
Knockranny House Hotel	Mayo	+353 98 28600
Nuremore Hotel And Country Club	Monaghan	+353 42 9661438
Dunbrody Country House & Restaurant	Wexford	+353 51 389 600
Kelly's Resort Hotel	Wexford	+353 53 32114
Marlfield House	Wexford	+353 55 21124
The Brooklodge Hotel	Wicklow	+353 402 36444

Scotland

Darroch Learg Hotel	Aberdeenshire	+44 (0)13397 55443
Airds Hotel	Argyll & Bute	+44 (0)1631 730236
Ardanaiseig	Argyll & Bute	+44 (0)1866 833333
Cameron House	Argyll & Bute	+44 (0)1389 755565
Loch Melfort Hotel & Restaurant	Argyll & Bute	+44 (0)1852 200233
MV Hebridean Princess	Argyll & Bute	+44 (0)1756 704794
Stonefield Castle	Argyll & Bute	+44 (0)1880 820836
Western Isles Hotel	Argyll & Bute	+44 (0)1688 302012
Balcary Bay Hotel	Dumfries & Galloway	+44 (0)1556 640217

▼

Cally Palace Hotel	**Dumfries & Galloway**	**+44 (0)1557 814341**
Kirroughtree House	Dumfries & Galloway	+44 (0)1671 402141
Knockinaam Lodge	Dumfries & Galloway	+44 (0)1776 810471
The Bonham	Edinburgh	+44 (0)131 623 6060
Bruntsfield Hotel	Edinburgh	+44 (0)131 229 1393
Channings	Edinburgh	+44 (0)131 332 3232
The Edinburgh Residence	Edinburgh	+44 (0)131 622 5080
The Glasshouse	Edinburgh	+44 (0)131 525 8200
The Howard	Edinburgh	+44 (0)131 315 2220
The Roxburghe	Edinburgh	+44 (0)131 240 5500
One Devonshire Gardens	Glasgow	+44 (0)141 3392001
Bunchrew House Hotel	Highland	+44 (0)1463 234917
Cuillin Hills Hotel	Highland	+44 (0)1478 612003
Culloden House	Highland	+44 (0)1463 790461
Glen Mhor Hotel	highland	+44 (0)1463 234308
The Glenmoriston Town House Hotel	Highland	+44 (0)1463 223777
The Golf View Hotel & Leisure Club	Highland	+44 (0)1667 458800
Loch Torridon Country House Hotel	Highland	+44 (0)1445 791242
Muckrach Lodge Hotel & Restaurant	Highland	+44 (0)1479 851257
The Royal Golf Hotel	Highland	+44 (0)1667 458800
Royal Marine Hotel	Highland	+44 (0)1408 621252
Borthwick Castle	Midlothian	+44 (0)1875 820514
Dalhousie Castle And Spa	Midlothian	+44 (0)1875 820153
Knockomie Hotel	Moray	+44 (0)1309 673146
Ballathie House Hotel	Perth & Kinross	+44 (0)1250 883268
Cromlix House	Perth & Kinross	+44 (0)1786 822125
Dalmunzie House	Perth & Kinross	+44 (0)1250 885224
Gleneagles	Perth & Kinross	+44 (0)1764 662231
Kinfauns Castle	Perth & Kinross	+44 (0)1738 620777
Kinnaird	Perth & Kinross	+44 (0)1796 482440
The Royal Hotel	Perth & Kinross	+44 (0)1764 679200
Gleddoch House Hotel & Country Estate	Renfrewshire	+44 (0)1475 540711
Castle Venlaw	Scottish Borders	+44 (0)1721 720384
Ednam House Hotel	Scottish Borders	+44 (0)1573 224168
The Roxburghe Hotel & Golf Course	Scottish Borders	+44 (0)1573 450331
Enterkine House	South Ayrshire	+44 (0)1292 520580
Glenapp Castle	South Ayrshire	+44 (0)1465 831212
Crutherland House Hotel	South Lanarkshire	+44 (0)1355 577000

Wales

Llechwen Hall	Cardiff	+44 (0)1443 742050
Ynyshir Hall	Ceredigion	+44 (0)1654 781209
St Tudno Hotel & Restauarant	Conwy	+44 (0)1492 874411
Wild Pheasant Hotel	Denbighshire	+44 (0)1978 860629
Palé Hall	Gwynedd	+44 (0)1678 530285
Penmaenuchaf Hall	Gwynedd	+44 (0)1341 422129
The Trearddur Bay Hotel	Isle of Anglesey	+44 (0)1407 860301
Llansantffraed Court Hotel	Monmouthshire	+44 (0)1873 840678
Lamphey Court Hotel	Pembrokeshire	+44 (0)1646 672273
Penally Abbey	Pembrokeshire	+44 (0)1834 843033
Warpool Court Hotel	Pembrokeshire	+44 (0)1437 720300
Gliffaes Country House Hotel	Powys	+44 (0)1874 730371
The Lake Country House	Powys	+44 (0)1591 620202
Lake Vyrnwy Hotel	Powys	+44 (0)1691 870 692
Llangoed Hall	Powys	+44 (0)1874 754525
Nant Ddu Lodge Hotel	Powys	+44 (0)1685 379111
Morgans	Swansea	+44 (0)1792 484848

Recommended Country Houses, Small Hotels & Inns Great Britain & Ireland 2004

England

The County Hotel	Bath & NE Somerset	+44 (0)1225 425003
Dorian House	Bath & NE Somerset	+44 (0)1225 426336
Oldfields	Bath & NE Somerset	+44 (0)1225 317984
The Ring O' Roses	Bath & NE Somerset	+44 (0)1761 232478
Mill House Hotel & Restaurant	Bedfordshire	+44 (0)1234 781678
Cantley House	Berkshire	+44 (0)118 978 9912
The Cottage Inn	Berkshire	+44 (0)1344 882242
The Inn on the Green	Berkshire	+44 (0)1628 482638
The Leatherne Bottel Riverside Restaurant	Berkshire	+44 (0)1491 872667
Stirrups	Berkshire	+44 (0)1344 882284
The Greyhound	Buckinghamshire	+44 (0)1455 553307
The Ivy House	Buckinghamshire	+44 (0)1672 515333
The Nags Head	Buckinghamshire	+44 (0)1494 862945
Crown Lodge Hotel	Cambridgeshire	+44 (0)1945 773391
The Meadowcroft Hotel	Cambridgeshire	+44 (0)1223 346120
Melbourn Bury	Cambridgeshire	+44 (0)1763 261151
Broxton Hall Country House Hotel	Cheshire	+44 (0)1829 782321
Willington Hall Hotel	Cheshire	+44 (0)1829 752321
Cormorant On The River, Hotel & Restaurant	Cornwall	+44 (0)1726 833426
Mount Haven Hotel & Restaurant	Cornwall	+44 (0)1736 710249
The Old Quay House Hotel	Cornwall	+44 (0)1726 833302
St. Georges Country Hotel	Cornwall	+44 (0)1872 572184
Stenhill House	Cornwall	+44 (0)1566 785686
Tredethy House	Cornwall	+44 (0)1208 841262
Trehaven Manor Hotel	Cornwall	+44 (0)1503 262028
Trehellas House Hotel & Restaurant	Cornwall	+44 (0)1208 72700
Trelawne Hotel - The Hutches Restaurant	Cornwall	+44 (0)1326 250226
Trevalsa Court Hotel	Cornwall	+44 (0)1726 842468
Wisteria Lodge	Cornwall	+44 (0)1726 810800

Mini Listings Great Britain & Ireland

Condé Nast Johansens are delighted to recommend over 660 properties across Great Britain and Ireland.

These properties can be found in *Recommended Hotels - GB & Ireland 2004* and *Recommended Country Houses, Small Hotels & Inns - GB & Ireland 2004.*

Call +44 208 655 7810 or see the order forms on page 421 to order Guides.

Broadoaks Country House	Cumbria	+44 (0)1539 445566
Crosby Lodge Country House Hotel	Cumbria	+44 (0)1228 573618
Dale Head Hall Lakeside Hotel	Cumbria	+44 (0)17687 72478
Fayrer Garden House Hotel	Cumbria	+44 (0)15394 88195
Grey Friar Lodge	Cumbria	+44 (0)15394 33158
The Leathes Head	Cumbria	+44 (0)17687 77247
Linthwaite House Hotel	Cumbria	+44 (0)15394 88600
The Pheasant	Cumbria	+44 (0)17687 76234
The Queen's Head Hotel	Cumbria	+44 (0)15394 36271
Sawrey House Country Hotel & Restaurant	Cumbria	+44 (0)15394 36387
Temple Sowerby House Hotel	Cumbria	+44 (0)17683 61578
Underwood	Cumbria	+44 (0)1229 771116
Blenheim House	Derbyshire	+44 (0)1283 732254
Boar's Head Hotel	Derbyshire	+44 (0)1283 820344
Buckingham's Hotel & Restaurant With One Table	Derbyshire	+44 (0)1246 201041
The Chequers Inn	Derbyshire	+44 (0)1433 630231
Dannah Farm Country House	Derbyshire	+44 (0)1773 550273
Donington Manor Hotel	Derbyshire	+44 (0)1332 810253
Kegworth House	Derbyshire	+44 (0)1509 672575
Littleover Lodge Hotel	Derbyshire	+44 (0)1332 510161
The Maynard Arms	Derbyshire	+44 (0)1433 630321
The Peacock At Rowsley	Derbyshire	+44 (0)1629 733518
The Plough Inn	Derbyshire	+44 (0)1433 650319
The Wind In The Willows	Derbyshire	+44 (0)1457 868001
Browns Hotel, Wine Bar & Brasserie	Devon	+44 (0)1822 618686
Combe House Hotel & Restaurant	Devon	+44 (0)1404 540400
The Edgemoor	Devon	+44 (0)1626 832466
Hewitt's - Villa Spaldi	Devon	+44 (0)1598 752293
Home Farm Hotel	Devon	+44 (0)1404 831278
Ilsington Country House Hotel	Devon	+44 (0)1364 661452
Kingston House	Devon	+44 (0)1803 762 235
The Lord Haldon Country Hotel	Devon	+44 (0)1392 832483
The New Inn	Devon	+44 (0)1363 84242
Percy's Country Hotel & Restaurant	Devon	+44 (0)1409 211236
The Sea Trout Inn	Devon	+44 (0)1803 762274
Yeoldon House Hotel	Devon	+44 (0)1237 474400
The Eastbury Hotel	Dorset	+44 (0)1935 813131
The Grange At Oborne	Dorset	+44 (0)1935 813463

▼

Kemps Country Hotel & Restaurant	**Dorset**	**+44 (0)1929 462563**
The Manor Hotel	Dorset	+44 (0)1308 897616
Mortons House Hotel	Dorset	+44 (0)1929 480988
Yalbury Cottage Hotel	Dorset	+44 (0)1305 262382
Grove House	Durham	+44 (0)1388 488203
Horsley Hall	Durham	+44 (0)1388 517239
The Crown House	Essex	+44 (0)1799 530515
De Vere Arms	Essex	+44 (0)1787 223353
Prested Hall	Essex	+44 (0)1376 573399
The Pump House Apartment	Essex	+44 (0)1277 656579
Bibury Court	Gloucestershire	+44 (0)1285 740337
Charlton Kings Hotel	Gloucestershire	+44 (0)1242 231061
The Malt House	Gloucestershire	+44 (0)1386 840295
New Inn At Coln	Gloucestershire	+44 (0)1285 750651
Three Choirs Vineyards Estate	Gloucestershire	+44 (0)1531 890223
Tudor Farmhouse Hotel & Restaurant	Gloucestershire	+44 (0)1594 833046
The White Hart Inn	Gloucestershire	+44 (0)1242 602359
The Wild Duck Inn	Gloucestershire	+44 (0)1285 770310
Langrish House	Hampshire	+44 (0)1730 266941
The Mill At Gordleton	Hampshire	+44 (0)1590 682219
The Nurse's Cottage	Hampshire	+44 (0)1590 683402
Thatched Cottage Hotel & Restaurant	Hampshire	+44 (0)1590 623090
Westover Hall	Hampshire	+44 (0)1590 643044
Whitley Ridge Country House Hotel	Hampshire	+44 (0)1590 622354
The Feathers Hotel	Herefordshire	+44 (0)1531 635266
Ford Abbey	Herefordshire	+44 (0)1568 760700
Glewstone Court	Herefordshire	+44 (0)1989 770367
Rhydspence Inn	Herefordshire	+44 (0)1497 831262
The Steppes	Herefordshire	+44 (0)1432 820424
Wilton Court Hotel	Herefordshire	+44 (0)1989 562569
Redcoats Farmhouse Hotel And Restaurant	Hertfordshire	+44 (0)1438 729500
Rylstone Manor	Isle of Wight	+44 (0)1983 862806
The George Hotel	Kent	+44 (0)1580 713348
Hempstead House	Kent	+44 (0)1795 428020
Ringlestone Inn and Farmhouse Hotel	Kent	+44 (0)1622 859900
Romney Bay House	Kent	+44 (0)1797 364747
Wallett's Court Hotel & Spa	Kent	+44 (0)1304 852424
The Inn At Whitewell	Lancashire	+44 (0)1200 448222
Tree Tops Country House Restaurant & Hotel	Lancashire	+44 (0)1704 572430
Abbots Oak Country House	Leicestershire	+44 (0)1530 832 328
Quenby Hall	Leicestershire	+44 (0)116 2595224
The Crown Hotel	Lincolnshire	+44 (0)1780 763136
The Lea Gate Inn	Lincolnshire	+44 (0)1526 342370
Washingborough Hall	Lincolnshire	+44 (0)1522 790340
Oak Lodge Hotel	London	+44 (0)20 8360 7082
The White Hart Inn	Greater Manchester	+44 (0)1457 872566
The Abbey Hotel	Norfolk	+44 (0)1953 602148
The Beeches Hotel And Victorian Gardens	Norfolk	+44 (0)1603 621167
Beechwood Hotel	Norfolk	+44 (0)1692 403231
Broom Hall Country Hotel	Norfolk	+44 (0)1953 882125
Brovey Lair	Norfolk	+44 (0)1953 882706
Elderton Lodge Hotel & Langtry Restaurant	Norfolk	+44 (0)1263 833547
Felbrigg Lodge	Norfolk	+44 (0)1263 837588
The Great Escape Holiday Company	Norfolk	+44 (0)1485 518717
Idyllic Cottages At Vere Lodge	Norfolk	+44 (0)1328 838261
The Manor House	Norfolk	+44 (0)1328 820597
The Norfolk Mead Hotel	Norfolk	+44 (0)1603 737531
The Old Rectory	Norfolk	+44 (0)1603 700772
Petersfield House Hotel	Norfolk	+44 (0)1692 630741
The Stower Grange	Norfolk	+44 (0)1603 860210
The White Horse	Norfolk	+44 (0)1485 210262
The Falcon Hotel	Northamptonshire	+44 (0)1604 696200
The Otterburn Tower	Northumberland	+44 (0)1830 520620
Waren House Hotel	Northumberland	+44 (0)1668 214581
Cockliffe Country House Hotel	Nottinghamshire	+44 (0)1159 680179
Langar Hall	Nottinghamshire	+44 (0)1949 860559
Duke Of Marlborough Country Inn	Oxfordshire	+44 (0)1993 811460
Fallowfields	Oxfordshire	+44 (0)1865 820416
The Flying Pig At The Stonor Hotel	Oxfordshire	+44 (0)1491 638345
The George Hotel	Oxfordshire	+44 (0)1865 340404
The Kings Head Inn & Restaurant	Oxfordshire	+44 (0)1608 658365
The Lamb Inn	Oxfordshire	+44 (0)1993 823155
The Plough At Clanfield	Oxfordshire	+44 (0)1367 810222
The Shaven Crown Hotel	Oxfordshire	+44 (0)1993 830330
Barnsdale Lodge	Rutland	+44 (0)1572 724678
The Hundred House Hotel	Shropshire	+44 (0)1952 730353
Mynd House Hotel	Shropshire	+44 (0)1694 722212
The Old Vicarage Hotel	Shropshire	+44 (0)1746 716497
Overton Grange Hotel	Shropshire	+44 (0)1584 873500
Pen-Y-Dyffryn Hall Hotel	Shropshire	+44 (0)1691 653700
Soulton Hall	Shropshire	+44 (0)1939 232786
Ashwick Country House Hotel	Somerset	+44 (0)1398 323868
Beryl	Somerset	+44 (0)1749 678738

Mini Listings Great Britain & Ireland

Condé Nast Johansens are delighted to recommend over 660 properties across Great Britain and Ireland.
These properties can be found in *Recommended Hotels - GB & Ireland 2004* and *Recommended Country Houses, Small Hotels & Inns - GB & Ireland 2004.*
Call +44 208 655 7810 or see the order forms on page 421 to order Guides.

Chestnut House	Somerset	+44 (0)1278 683658
Farthings Hotel & Restaurant	Somerset	+44 (0)1823 480664
Glencot House	Somerset	+44 (0)1749 677160
Karslake House Hotel & Restaurant	Somerset	+44 (0)1643 851242
Porlock Vale House	Somerset	+44 (0)1643 862338
Three Acres Country House	Somerset	+44 (0)1398 323730
Oak Tree Farm	Staffordshire	+44 (0)1827 56807
Somerford Hall	Staffordshire	+44 (0)1902 850108
Clarice House	Suffolk	+44 (0)1284 705550
The George	Suffolk	+44 (0)1787 280248
Thornham Hall & Restaurant	Suffolk	+44 (0)1379 783314
Worlington Hall Country House Hotel	Suffolk	+44 (0)1638 712237
Chase Lodge	Surrey	+44 (0)20 8943 1862
Stanhill Court Hotel	Surrey	+44 (0)1293 862166
Hooke Hall	East Sussex	+44 (0)1825 761578
The Hope Anchor Hotel	East Sussex	+44 (0)1797 222216
The Chequers At Slaugham	West Sussex	+44 (0)1444 400239
Chequers Hotel	West Sussex	+44 (0)1798 872486
Crouchers Country Hotel & Restaurant	West Sussex	+44 (0)1243 784995
Forge Hotel	West Sussex	+44 (0)1243 535333
The Mill House Hotel	West Sussex	+44 (0)1903 892426
The Old Tollgate Restaurant And Hotel	West Sussex	+44 (0)1903 879494
The Royal Oak Inn	West Sussex	+44 (0)1243 527434
Clarendon House	Warwickshire	+44 (0)1926 857668
The George Inn	Wiltshire	+44 (0)1985 840396
Hinton Grange	Wiltshire	+44 (0)117 937 2916
The Old Manor Hotel	Wiltshire	+44 (0)1225 777393
Rudloe Hall	Wiltshire	+44 (0)1225 810555
Stanton Manor	Wiltshire	+44 (0)1666 837552
Widbrook Grange	Wiltshire	+44 (0)1225 864750
Colwall Park	Worcestershire	+44 (0)1684 540000
The Old Rectory	Worcestershire	+44 (0)1527 523000
The Old Windmill	Worcestershire	+44 (0)1386 792801
The White Lion Hotel	Worcestershire	+44 (0)1684 592551
The Austwick Traddock	North Yorkshire	+44 (0)15242 51224
The Blue Lion	North Yorkshire	+44 (0)1969 624273
The Boar's Head Hotel	North Yorkshire	+44 (0)1423 771888
Dunsley Hall	North Yorkshire	+44 (0)1947 893437
Hob Green Hotel And Restaurant	North Yorkshire	+44 (0)1423 770031
The Kings Head Hotel	North Yorkshire	+44 (0)1748 850220
The Red Lion	North Yorkshire	+44 (0)1756 720204
Rookhurst Country House Hotel	North Yorkshire	+44 (0)1969 667454
Stow House Hotel	North Yorkshire	+44 (0)1969 663635
Hey Green Country House Hotel	West Yorkshire	+44 (0)1484 844235
The Rock Inn Hotel	West Yorkshire	+44 (0)1422 379721

Channel Islands

Aval du Creux Hotel	Channel Islands	+44 (0)1481 832036
Eulah Country House	Channel Islands	+44 (0)1534 626626
La Favorita Hotel	Channel Islands	+44 (0)1481 235666
La Sablonnerie	Channel Islands	+44 (0)1481 832061
The White House	Channel Islands	+44 (0)1481 722159

Ireland

Gregans Castle	Clare	+353 6 57077 005
Ross Lake House Hotel	Galway	+353 91 550109
Zetland Country House Hotel	Galway	+353 9 531111
Caragh Lodge	Kerry	+353 66 9769115
Carrig House	Kerry	+353 66 9769100
Emlagh House	Kerry	+353 66 915 2345
Gorman's Clifftop House & Restaurant	Kerry	+353 66 9155162
Killarney Royal Hotel	Kerry	+353 64 31853
Coopershill House	Sligo	+353 71 9165108
Kilmokea Country Manor & Gardens	Wexford	+353 51 388109

Scotland

Maryculter House Hotel	Abderdeenshire	+44 (0)1224 732124
Balgonie Country House	Aberdeenshire	+44 (0)13397 55482
Castleton House Hotel	Angus	+44 (0)1307 840340
Ballachulish House	Argyll & Bute	+44 (0)1855 811266
Enmore Hotel	Argyll & Bute	+44 (0)1369 702230
The Frog At Port Dunstaffnage	Argyll & Bute	+44 (0)1631 567005
Highland Cottage	Argyll & bute	+44 (0)1688 302030
The Royal At Tighnabruaich	Argyll & Bute	+44 (0)1700 811239
Fernhill Hotel	Dumfries & Galloway	+44 (0)1776 810220
Trigony House Hotel	Dumfries & Galloway	+44 (0)1848 331211
Culduthel Lodge	Highland	+44 (0)1463 240089
Hotel Eilean Iarmain	Highland	+44 (0)1471 833332
The Lodge On The Loch	Highland	+44 (0)1855 821237
The Steadings Hotel	Highland	+44 (0)1808 521314
Castle Campbell Hotel	Perth & Kinross	+44 (0)1259 742519
The Four Seasons Hotel	Perth & Kinross	+44 (0)1764 685333
Knockendarroch House	Perth & Kinross	+44 (0)1796 473473
The Lake Hotel	Perth & Kinross	+44 (0)1877 385258
Monachyle Mhor	Perth & Kinross	+44 (0)1877 384622
Bowfield Hotel & Country Club	Renfrewshire	+44 (0)1505 705225
Ettrickshaws Country House Hotel	Scottish Borders	+44 (0)1750 52229
Traquair House	Scottish Borders	+44 (0)1896 830323

▼
Culzean Castle – The Eisenhower Apartment ......South Ayrshire ....+44 (0)1655 884455

Wales

The Great House	Bridgend	+44 (0)1656 657644
The Inn At The Elm Tree	Cardiff	+44 (0)1633 680225
Conrah Country House Hotel	Ceredigion	+44 (0)1970 617941
Falcondale Mansion	Ceredigion	+44 (0)1570 422910
Castle Hotel	Conwy	+44 (0)1492 582 800
The Old Rectory Country House	Conwy	+44 (0)1492 580611
Sychnant Pass House	Conwy	+44 (0)1492 596868
Tan-Y-Foel	Conwy	+44 (0)1690 710507
Bae Abermaw	Gwynedd	+44 (0)1341 280550
Llwyndu Farmhouse	Gwynedd	+44 (0)1341 280144
Plas Dolmelynllyn	Gwynedd	+44 (0)1341 440273
Porth Tocyn Country House Hotel	Gwynedd	+44 (0)1758 713303
Ye Olde Bull's Head	Isle of Anglesey	+44 (0)1248 810329
The Bell At Skenfrith	Monmouthshire	+44 (0)1600 750235
The Newbridge On Usk	Monmouthshire	+44 (0)1633 451000
Parva Farmhouse And Restaurant	Monmouthshire	+44 (0)1291 689411
The Gower Hotel & Orangery Restaurant	Pembrokeshire	+44 (0)1834 813452
Stone Hall Hotel & Restaurant	Pembrokeshire	+44 (0)1348 840212
Wolfscastle Country House & Restaurant	Pembrokeshire	+44 (0)1437 741225
Glangrwyney Court	Powys	+44 (0)1873 811288
Norton House Hotel And Restaurant	Swansea	+44 (0)1792 404891
Egerton Grey	Vale Of Glamorgan	+44 (0)1446 711666

Historic Houses, Castles & Gardens

Incorporating Museums & Galleries

We are pleased to feature over 200 places to visit during your stay at a Condé Nast Johansens recommended hotel.

England

Bedfordshire

John Bunyan Museum - Mill Street, Bedford, Bedfordshire MK40 3EU. Tel: 01234 213722

Woburn Abbey - Woburn, Bedfordshire MK17 9WA. Tel: 01525 290666

Berkshire

Savill Garden - Windsor Great Park, Wick Lane, Nr Windsor, Berkshire SL4 2HT. Tel: 01753 847518

Taplow Court - Berry Hill, Taplow, Nr Maidenhead, Berkshire SL6 0ER. Tel: 01628 591209

Buckinghamshire

Hughenden Manor - High Wycombe, Buckinghamshire HP14 4LA. Tel: 01494 755573

Stowe Landscape Gardens - Stowe, Buckingham, Buckinghamshire MK18 5EH. Tel: 01280 822850

Waddesdon Manor - Nr Aylesbury, Buckinghamshire HP18 0JH. Tel: 01296 653226

Cambridgeshire

The Manor of Green Knowe - The Manor, Hemingford Grey, Cambridgeshire PE28 9BN. Tel: 01480 463134

Cheshire

Adlington Hall - Adlington, Macclesfield, Cheshire SK10 4LF. Tel: 01625 820201

Dorfold Hall - Nantwich, Cheshire CW5 8LD. Tel: 01270 625245

Dunham Massey: Hall, Park & Garden - Dunham, Altrincham, Cheshire WA14 4SJ. Tel: 0161 9411025

Norton Priory Museum & Gardens - Tudor Road, Manor Park, Runcorn, Cheshire WA7 1SX. Tel: 01928 569895

Tabley House Stately Home - Knutsford, Cheshire WA16 0HB. Tel: 01565 750151

Co Durham

Raby Castle - Staindrop, Darlington, Co Durham DL2 3AH. Tel: 01833 660202

Cornwall

Mount Edgcumbe House & Country Park - Cremyll Torpoint, Cornwall PL10 1HZ. Tel: 01752 822236

Royal Cornwall Museum - River Street, Truro, Cornwall TR1 2SJ. Tel: 01872 272205

Trebah Garden Trust - Mawnan Smith, Nr Falmouth, Cornwall TR11 5JZ. Tel: 01326 250448

Truro Cathedral - 14 St Mary's Street, Truro, Cornwall TR1 2AF.

Cumbria

Dove Cottage & The Wordsworth Museum - Grasmere, Cumbria LA22 9SH. Tel: 015394 35544

Isel Hall - Cockermouth, Cumbria CA13 0QG. Tel: 01900 821778

Levens Hall & Gardens - Kendal, Cumbria LA8 0PD. Tel: 01539 560321

Mirehouse Historic House & Gardens - Mirehouse, Keswick, Cumbria CA12 4QE. Tel: 01768 772287

Wordsworth House - Main Street, Cockermouth, Cumbria CA13 9RX. Tel: 01900 824805

Derbyshire

Chatsworth - Bakewell, Derbyshire DE45 1PP. Tel: 01246 565300

Haddon Hall - Bakewell, Derbyshire DE45 1LA. Tel: 01629 812855

Melbourne Hall & Gardens - Melbourne, Derbyshire DE73 1EN. Tel: 01332 862502

Devon

Downes - Downes, Crediton, Devon EX17 3PL. Tel: 01392 680059

Ugbrooke Park - Ugbrooke, Chudleigh, Devon TQ13 0AD. Tel: 01626 852179

Dorset

Abbotsbury Sub Tropical Gardens - Bullers Way, Abbotsbury, Nr Weymouth, Dorset DT3 4LA. Tel: 01305 871387

Chiffchaffs - Chaffeymoor, Bourton, Gillingham, Dorset SP8 5BY. Tel: 01747 840841

Cranborne Manor Garden - Cranborne, Wimborne, Dorset BH21 5PP. Tel: 01725 517248

Deans Court Garden - Deans Court, Wimborne, Dorset BH21 1EE. Tel: 01202 886116

Mapperton - Mapperton, Beaminster, Dorset DT8 3Nr Tel: 01308 862645

Russell-Cotes Art Gallery & Museum - East Cliff, Bournemouth, Dorset BH1 3AA. Tel: 01202 451800

Essex

The Gardens of Easton Lodge - Warwick House, Easton Lodge, Great Dunmow, Essex CM6 2BB. Tel: 01371 876979

Ingatestone Hall - Hall Lane, Ingatestone, Essex CM4 9Nr Tel: 01277 353010

Gloucestershire

Cheltenham Art Gallery & Museum - Clarence Street, Cheltenham, Gloucestershire GL50 3JT. Tel: 01242 237431

Frampton Court - Frampton-on-Severn, Gloucestershire GL2 7EP. Tel: 01452 740267

Hardwicke Court - Nr Gloucester, Gloucestershire GL2 4RS. Tel: 01452 720212

Kelmscott Manor - Kelmscott, Nr Lechlade, Gloucestershire GL7 3HJ. Tel: 01367 253348

Old Campden House - Chipping Campden, Gloucestershire GL55 . Tel: 01628 825920

Rodmarton Manor Garden - Cirencester, Gloucestershire GL7 6PF. Tel: 01285 841253

Sezincote - Moreton-in-Marsh, Gloucestershire GL56 9AW. Tel: 01386 700444

Hampshire

Avington Park - Winchester, Hampshire SO21 1DB. Tel: 01962 779260

Beaulieu - Montagu Ventures Ltd., John Montagu Building, Beaulieu, Hampshire SO42 7ZN. Tel: 01590 612345

Beaulieu Vineyard and Gardens - Montagu Ventures Ltd., John Montagu Building, Beaulieu, Hampshire SO42 7ZN. Tel: 01590 612345

Breamore House & Museum - Breamore, Nr Fordingbridge, Hampshire SP6 2DF. Tel: 01725 512468

Broadlands - Romsey, Hampshire SO51 9ZE. Tel: 01794 505055

Gilbert White's House and The Oates Museum - Selborne, Hampshire GU34 3JH. Tel: 01420 511275

Greywell Hill House - Greywell, Hook, Hampshire RG29 1DG.

Hall Farm - Bentworth, Alton, Hampshire GU34 5JU. Tel: 01420 564010

Mottisfont Abbey and Garden - Mottisfont, Nr Romsey, Hampshire SO51 0LP. Tel: 01794 340757

Pylewell House - Pylewell Park Estate, Lymington, Hampshire SO41 5SJ. Tel: 01590 673010

Uppark - The National Trust, Uppark, South Harting, Petersfield, Hampshire GU31 5QR. Tel: 01730 825415

Herefordshire

Eastnor Castle - Eastnor, Ledbury, Herefordshire HR8 1RL. Tel: 01531 633160

Moccas Court - Moccas, Herefordshire HR2 9LH. Tel: 01981 500019

Historic Houses, Castles & Gardens

Incorporating Museums & Galleries

www.historichouses.co.uk

Hertfordshire

Ashridge - Berkhamsted, Hertfordshire HP4 1NS. Tel: 01442 843491

Gorhambury - St Albans, Hertfordshire AL3 6AH. Tel: 01727 855000

Hatfield House, Park & Gardens - Hatfield, Hertfordshire AL9 5NQ. Tel: 01707 287010

Isle of Wight

Deacons Nursery - Moor View, Godshill, Isle of Wight PO38 3HW. Tel: 01983 840750

Kent

Cobham Hall - Cobham, Kent DA12 3BL. Tel: 01474 823371

Dickens House Museum - 2 Victoria Parade, Broadstairs, Kent CT10 1JT. Tel: 01843 861232

Finchcocks, Living Museum of Music - Goudhurst, Kent TN17 1HH. Tel: 01580 211702

Graham Clarke Up the Garden Studio - Green Lane, Boughton Monchelsea, Maidstone, Kent ME17 4LF. Tel: 01622 743938

Groombridge Place Gardens & Enchanted Forest - Groombridge, Nr Tunbridge Wells, Kent TN3 9QG. Tel: 01892 863999

▼

Hever Castle & Gardens - Edenbridge, Kent TN8 7NG. Tel: 01732 861701

Leeds Castle - Maidstone, Kent ME17 1PL. Tel: 01622 765400

Mount Ephraim Gardens - Hernhill, Nr Faversham, Kent ME13 9TX. Tel: 01227 751496

The New College of Cobham - Cobhambury Road, Cobham, Nr Gravesend, Kent DA12 3BG. Tel: 01474 812503

Penshurst Place & Gardens - Penshurst, Nr Tonbridge, Kent TN11 8DG. Tel: 01892 870307

Scotney Castle, Garden & Estate - Lamberhurst, Kent TN3 8JN. Tel: 01892 891081

Smallhythe Place - Smallhythe, Tenterden, Kent TN30 7NG. Tel: 01580 762334

Lancashire

Astley Hall Museum & Art Gallery - Astley Park, off Hallgate, Chorley, Lancashire PR7 1NP. Tel: 01257 515555

Stonyhurst College - Stonyhurst, Clitheroe, Lancashire BB7 9PZ. Tel: 01254 826345

Townhead House - Slaidburn, Via Clitheroe, Lancashire BBY 3AG.

London

Dulwich Picture Gallery - Gallery Road, London SE21 7AD. Tel: 0208 6935254

Handel House Museum - 25 Brook Street, London W1K 4HB. Tel: 0207 4951685

Kensington Palace State Apartments - Kensington, London W8 4PX. Tel: 0870 7515170

Leighton House Museum - 12 Holland Park Road, London W14 8LZ. Tel: 020 7602 3316

National Portrait Gallery - St Martin's Place, London WC2H 0HE. Tel: 0207 3060055

Pitzhanger Manor House - Walpole Park, Ealing, London W5 5EQ. Tel: 020 85671227

Royal Institution Michael Faraday Museum - 21 Albemarle Street, London W1S 4BS. Tel: 020 74092992

Sir John Soane's Museum - 13 Lincoln's Inn Fields, London WC2A 3BP. Tel: 0207 4052107

Somerset House - Strand, London WC2R 1LA. Tel: 0207 8454600

Strawberry Hill House - St Mary's University College, Strawberry Hill, Waldegrave Road, Twickenham, London TW1 4SX. Tel: 020 8270 4114

Syon Park - Brentford, Middlesex TW8 8JF. Tel: 0208 5600882

Tower of London - Tower Hill, London EC3N 4AB. Tel: 0870 7566060

Greater Manchester

Heaton Hall - Heaton Park, Prestwich, Manchester, Greater Manchester M25 5SW. Tel: 0161 7731231

Salford Museums & Art Gallery - Peel Park, The Crescent, Salford, Greater Manchester M5 4WU. Tel: 0161 7362649

Norfolk

Hoveton Hall Gardens - Hoveton, Wroxham, Norfolk NR12 8RJ. Tel: 01603 782798

Sandringham - The Estate Office, Sandringham, Norfolk PE35 6EN. Tel: 01553 772675

Walsingham Abbey Grounds - c/o The Estate Office, Little Walsingham, Norfolk NR22 6BP. Tel: 01328 820259

Wolterton and Mannington Estate - Mannington Hall, Norwich, Norfolk NR11 7BB. Tel: 01263 584175

Northamptonshire

Althorp - Northampton, Northamptonshire NN7 4HQ. Tel: 01604 770107

Cottesbrooke Hall and Gardens - Cottesbrooke, Northampton, Northamptonshire NN6 8PF. Tel: 01604 505808

Haddonstone Show Garden - The Forge House, Church Lane, East Haddon, Northamptonshire NN6 8DB. Tel: 01604 770711

Holdenby House Gardens & Falconry Centre - Holdenby, Northampton, Northamptonshire NN6 8DJ. Tel: 01604 770074

Kelmarsh Hall & Gardens - Kelmarsh, Northampton, Northamptonshire NN6 9LT. Tel: 01604 686543

Northumberland

Alnwick Castle - Alnwick, Northumberland NE66 1NQ. Tel: 01665 510777

Chillingham Castle - Chillingham, Northumberland NE66 5NJ. Tel: 01668 215390

Chipchase Castle - Chipchase, Wark on Tyne, Hexham, Northumberland NE48 3NT. Tel: 01434 230203

Paxton House & Country Park - Paxton, Berwick-upon-Tweed, Northumberland TD15 1SZ. Tel: 01289 386291

Seaton Delaval Hall - Seaton Sluice, Whitley Bay, Northumberland NE26 4QR. Tel: 0191 2371493

Oxfordshire

Blenheim Palace - Woodstock, Oxfordshire OX20 1PX. Tel: 01993 811325

Ditchley Park - Enstone, Chipping Norton, Oxfordshire OX7 4ER. Tel: 01608 677346

Kingston Bagpuize House - Kingston Bagpuize, Abingdon, Oxfordshire OX13 5AX. Tel: 01865 820259

Mapledurham House - Mapledurham, Nr Reading, Oxfordshire RG4 7TR. Tel: 01189 723350

▼

River & Rowing Museum - Mill Meadows, Henley-on-Thames, Oxfordshire RG9 1BF. Tel: 01491 415600

Wallingford Castle Gardens - Castle Street, Wallingford, Oxfordshire. Tel: 01491 835373

Shropshire

Burford House Gardens - Tenbury Wells, Shropshire WR15 8HQ. Tel: 01584 810777

The Dorothy Clive Garden - Willoughbridge, Market Drayton, Shropshire, (Staffordshire Border) TF9 4EU. Tel: 01630 647237

Hawkstone Park & Follies - Weston-under-Redcastle, Shrewsbury, Shropshire SY4 5UY. Tel: 01939 200611

Hodnet Hall Gardens - Hodnet, Market Drayton, Shropshire TF9 3NN. Tel: 01630 685786

Royal Air force Museum - Cosford, Shifnal, Shropshire TF11 8UP. Tel: 01902 376200

Weston Park - Weston-under-Lizard, Nr Shifnal, Shropshire TF11 8LE. Tel: 01952 852100

Somerset

The Bishop's Palace - Wells, Somerset BA5 2PD. Tel: 01749 678691

HISTORIC HOUSES, CASTLES & GARDENS

Incorporating Museums & Galleries

www.historichouses.co.uk

Cothay Manor & Gardens - Greenham, Wellington, Somerset TA21 0JR. Tel: 01823 672283

Great House Farm - Wells Road, Theale, Wedmore, Somerset BS28 4SJ. Tel: 01934 713133

Hunstrete House Hotel - Hunstrete, Pensford, Bath, Somerset BS39 4NS. Tel: 01761 490490

Museum of Costume & Assembly Rooms - Bennett Street, Bath, Somerset BA1 2QH. Tel: 01225 477785

Orchard Wyndham - Williton, Taunton, Somerset TA4 4HH. Tel: 01984 632309

Roman Baths & Pump Room - Pump Room, Stall Street, Bath, Somerset BA1 1LZ. Tel: 01225 477785

Staffordshire

Ford Green Hall - Ford Green Road, Smallthorne, Stoke-on-Trent, Staffordshire ST6 1NG. Tel: 01782 233195

Sandon Hall - Sandon, Staffordshire ST18 0BZ. Tel: 01889 508004

Whitmore Hall - Whitmore, Newcastle-under-Lyme, Staffordshire ST5 5HW. Tel: 01782 680478

Suffolk

Ancient House - Clare, Suffolk CO10 8NY. Tel: 01628 825920

Hengrave Hall - Bury St Edmunds, Suffolk IP28 6LZ. Tel: 01284 701561

Newbourne Hall - Newbourne, Woodbridge, Suffolk IP12 4NP. Tel: 01473 736764

Shrubland Park Gardens - Shrubland Park, Coddenham, Ipswich, Suffolk IP6 9QQ. Tel: 01473 830221

Surrey

Claremont House - Claremont Drive, Esher, Surrey KT10 9LY. Tel: 01372 467841

Farnham Castle - Farnham, Surrey GU4 0AG. Tel: 01252 721194

Goddards - Abinger Common, Dorking, Surrey RH5 6JH. Tel: 01628 825920

Great Fosters - Stroude Road, Egham, Surrey TW20 9UR. Tel: 01784 433822

Hampton Court Palace - East Molesey, Surrey KT8 9AU. Tel: Info: 0870 752777 Sales: 0870 7537777

Loseley Park - Guildford, Surrey GU3 1HS. Tel: 01483 304440

▼
Painshill Park - Portsmouth Road, Cobham, Surrey KT11 1JE. Tel: 01932 868113

East Sussex

Bentley Wildfowl & Motor Museum - Halland, Nr Lewes, East Sussex BN8 5AF. Tel: 01825 840573

Firle Place - Firle, Lewes, East Sussex BN8 6LP. Tel: 01273 858307

Garden and Grounds of Herstmonceux Castle - Hailsham, East Sussex BN27 1RN. Tel: 01323 833816

Merriments Gardens - Hawkhurst Road, Hurst Green, East Sussex TN19 7RA. Tel: 01580 860666

Pashley Manor Gardens - Ticehurst, East Sussex TN5 7HE. Tel: 01580 200888

Wilmington Priory - Wilmington, Nr Eastbourne, East Sussex BN26 5SW. Tel: 01628 825920

West Sussex

Arundel Castle - Arundel, West Sussex BN18 9AB. Tel: 01903 883136

Denmans Garden - Clock House, Denmans, Fontwell, West Sussex BN18 0SU. Tel: 01243 542808

Goodwood House - Goodwood, Chichester, West Sussex PO18 0PX. Tel: 01243 755000

High Beeches Woodland & Water Gardens - High Beeches, Handcross, West Sussex RH17 6HQ. Tel: 01444 400589

Leonardslee - Lakes & Gardens - Lower Beeding, Horsham, West Sussex RH13 6PP. Tel: 01403 891212

Weald and Downland Open Air Museum - Singleton, Chichester, West Sussex PO18 0EU. Tel: 01243 811348

West Dean Gardens - West Dean, Chichester, West Sussex PO18 0QZ. Tel: 01243 818210

Worthing Museum & Art Gallery - Chapel Road, Worthing, West Sussex BN11 1HP. Tel: 01903 221150

Warwickshire

Arbury Hall - Nuneaton, Warwickshire CV10 7PT. Tel: 024 7638 2804

Coughton Court - Alcester, Warwickshire B49 5JA. Tel: 01789 400702

Ragley Hall - Alcester, Warwickshire B49 5NJ. Tel: 01789 762090

Shakespeare Houses - The Shakespeare Centre, Henley Street, Stratford-upon-Avon, Warwickshire CV37 6QW. Tel: 01789 204016

Stoneleigh Abbey - Kenilworth, Warwickshire CV8 2LF. Tel: 01926 858585

West Midlands

The Birmingham Botanical Gardens and Glasshouses - Westbourne Road, Edgbaston, Birmingham, West Midlands B15 3TR. Tel: 0121 4541860

Barber Institute of Fine Arts - University of Birmingham, Edgbaston, Birmingham, West Midlands B15 2TS. Tel: 0121 4147333

Castle Bromwich Hall Gardens - Chester Road, Castle Bromwich, Birmingham, West Midlands B36 9BT. Tel: 01217 494100

Coventry Cathedral - Priory Street, Coventry, West Midlands CV1 5ES. Tel: 024 76521200

Wiltshire

Charlton Park House - Charlton, Malmesbury, Wiltshire SN16 9DG.

Hamptworth Lodge - Hamptworth, Salisbury, Wiltshire SP5 2EA. Tel: 01794 390215

▼
Longleat - Warminster, Wiltshire BA12 7NW. Tel: 01985 844400

Sheldon Manor - Chippenham, Wiltshire SN14 0RG. Tel: 01249 653120

Stourhead - Stourton, Warminster, Wiltshire BA12 6QD. Tel: 01747 841152

Worcestershire

Hagley Hall - Hagley, Worcestershire DY9 9LG. Tel: 01562 882408

Hartlebury Castle - Nr Kidderminster, Worcestershire DY11 7XX. Tel: 01299 250410 (state rooms sec) Tel: 01299 250416 (museum)

Harvington Hall - Harvington, Kidderminister, Worcester DY10 4LR. Tel: 01562 777846

Little Malvern Court - Nr Malvern, Worcestershire WR14 4JN. Tel: 01684 892988

Spetchley Park Gardens - Spetchley Park, Worcester, Worcestershire WR5 1RS. Tel: 01453 810303

East Riding of Yorkshire

Burton Agnes Hall & Gardens - Burton Agnes, Driffield, East Yorkshire YO25 4NB. Tel: 01262 490324

North Yorkshire

Castle Howard - York, North Yorkshire YO6 7DA. Tel: 01653 648333

Duncombe Park - Helmsley, York, North Yorkshire YO62 5EB. Tel: 01439 770213

The Forbidden Corner - Tupgill Park Estate, Coverham, Nr Middleham, North Yorkshire DL8 4TJ. Tel: 01969 640638

Kiplin Hall - Nr Scorton, Richmond, North Yorkshire DL10 6AT. Tel: 01748 818178

Newby Hall & Gardens - Ripon, North Yorkshire HG4 5AE. Tel: 0845 4504068

Ripley Castle - Ripley Castle Estate, Harrogate, North Yorkshire HG3 3AY. Tel: 01423 770152

Skipton Castle - Skipton, North Yorkshire BD23 1AQ. Tel: 01756 792442

Thorp Perrow Arboretum & The Falcons of Thorp Perrow - Bedale, North Yorkshire DL8 2PR. Tel: 01677 425323

Historic Houses, Castles & Gardens

Incorporating Museums & Galleries

www.historichouses.co.uk

West Yorkshire

Bronte Parsonage Museum - Church Street, Haworth, Keighley, West Yorkshire BD22 8DR. Tel: 01535 642323

Harewood House - The Harewood House Trust, Moorhouse, Harewood, Leeds, West Yorkshire LS17 9LQ. Tel: 0113 2181010

Ledston Hall - Hall Lane, Ledstone, Castleford, West Yorkshire WF10 2BB. Tel: 01423 523423

Northern Ireland

Co Down

Seaforde Gardens - Seaforde, Downpatrick, Co Down BT30 8PG. Tel: 028 44811225

Ireland

Co Cork

Bantry House & Gardens - Bantry, Co Cork. Tel: + 353 2 750 047

Co Galway

Kylemore Abbey & Garden - Kylemore, Connemara, Co Galway. Tel: +353 95 41146

Co Kildare

Japanese Gardens & St Fiachra's Garden - Tully, Kildare Town, Co Kildare. Tel: +353 45 521617

Co Offaly

Birr Castle Demesne - Birr, Co Offaly. Tel: +353 509 20336

Co Wicklow

Mount Usher Gardens - Ashford, Co Wicklow. Tel: +353 404 40205

Scotland

Aberdeenshire

Craigston Castle - Turriff, Aberdeenshire AB53 5PX. Tel: 01888 551228

Argyll

Inveraray Castle - Cherry Park, Inveraray, Argyll PA32 8XE. Tel: 01499 302203

Ayrshire

Auchinleck House - Ochiltree, Ayrshire KA18 2LR. Tel: 01628 825920

Blairquhan - Straiton, Maybole, Ayrshire KA19 7LZ. Tel: 01655 770239

Kelburn Castle and Country Centre - Fairlie, Ayrshire KA29 0BE. Tel: 01475 568685

Maybole Castle - High Street, Maybole, Ayrshire KA19 7BX. Tel: 01655 883765

Sorn Castle - Sorn, Mauchline, Ayrshire KA5 6HR. Tel: 0141 9426460

Dumfriesshire

▼ **Drumlanrig Castle, Gardens and Country Park - Nr Thornhill, Dumfriesshire DG3 4AQ. Tel: 01848 330248**

Fife

Culross Palace, Town House & Study - Royal Burch of Culross, Fife KY12 8JH. Tel: 01383 880359

Isle of Skye

Armadale Castle, Gardens & Museum of the Isles - Armadale, Sleat, Isle of Skye IV45 8RS. Tel: 01471 844305

Orkney Islands

Balfour Castle - Shapinsay, Orkney Islands KW17 2DY. Tel: 01856 711282

Scottish Borders

Bowhill House & Country Park - Bowhill, Selkirk, Scottish Borders TD7 5ET. Tel: 01750 22204

Traquair House - Innerleithen, Peebles EH44 6PW. Tel: 01896 830323

South Lanarkshire

New Lanark World Heritage Site - New Lanark, South Lanarkshire ML11 9DB. Tel: 01555 661345

West Lothian

Hopetoun House - South Queensferry, Nr Edinburgh, West Lothian EH30 9SL. Tel: 0131 3312451

Wigtownshire

Ardwell Gardens - Ardwell House, Stranraer, Wigtownshire DG9 9LY. Tel: 01776 860227

Wales

Flintshire

Golden Grove - Llanasa, Nr Holywell, Flintshire CH8 9NA. Tel: 01745 854452

Newport

Fourteen Locks Canal Centre - High Cross, Newport NP10 9GN. Tel: 01633 894802

Newport Museum and Art Gallery - John Frost Square, Newport NP20 1PA. Tel: 01633 840064

Newport Transporter Bridge - Usk Way, Newport, South Wales NP20 2JT. Tel: 01633 250322

Tredegar House & Park - Newport NP10 8YW. Tel: 01633 815880

Pembrokeshire

Carew Castle & Tidal Mill - Carew, Tenby, Pembrokeshire SA70 8SL. Tel: 01646 651782

St Davids Cathedral - The Close, St David's, Pembrokeshire SA62 6RH. Tel: 01437 720199

Powys

The Judge's Lodging - Broad Street, Presteigne, Powys LD8 2AD. Tel: 01544 260650

Continental Europe

France

Château de Chenonceau - 37150 Chenonceaux, France. Tel: +33 2 47 23 90 07

Château Royal d'Amboise - B.P. 371, 37403 Amboise, France. Tel: +33 2 47 57 00 98

Fondation Claude Monet - 27620 Giverny, France. Tel: +33 2 32 51 28 21

Château de Thoiry - 78770 Thoiry, Yvelines, France. Tel: +33 1 34 87 53 65

The Netherlands

Paleis Het Loo National Museum - Koninklijk Park 1, 7315 JA Apeldoorn, Holland. Tel: +31 55 577 24 00

Mini Listings North America

Condé Nast Johansens are delighted to recommend over 190 properties across North America, Bermuda, The Caribbean, Mexico, The Pacific. Call +44 208 655 7810 or see the order forms on page 421 to order guides.

ARIZONA - SEDONA

Canyon Villa Bed & Breakfast Inn
125 Canyon Circle Drive, Sedona, Arizona 86351
Tel: 1 928 284 1226
Fax: 1 928 284 2114

ARIZONA - SEDONA

Casa Sedona
55 Hozoni Drive, Sedona, Arizona 86336
Tel: 1 928 282 2938

ARIZONA - SEDONA

The Lodge at Sedona - A Luxury Bed & Breakfast Inn
125 Kallof Place, Sedona, Arizona 86336
Tel: 1 928 204 1942
Fax: 1 928 204 2128

ARIZONA - TUCSON

Arizona Inn
2200 East Elm Street, Tucson, Arizona 85719
Tel: 1 520 325 1541
Fax: 1 520 881 5830

ARIZONA - TUCSON

Tanque Verde Ranch
14301 East Speedway, Tucson, Arizona 85748
Tel: 1 520 296 6275
Fax: 1 520 721 9426

ARIZONA - TUCSON

White Stallion Ranch
9251 West Twin Peaks Road, Tucson, Arizona 85743
Tel: 1 520 297 0252
Fax: 1 520 744 2786

CALIFORNIA - BORREGO SPRINGS

La Casa del Zorro Desert Resort
3845 Yaqui Pass Road, Borrego Springs, California 92004
Tel: 1 760 767 5323
Fax: 1 760 767 5963

CALIFORNIA - FERNDALE

Gingerbread Mansion Inn
P.O. Box 40, 400 Berding Street, Ferndale, California 95536
Tel: 1 707 786 4000
Fax: 1 707 786 4381

CALIFORNIA - LA JOLLA

The Bed & Breakfast Inn At La Jolla
7753 Draper Avenue, La Jolla, California 92037
Tel: 1 858 456 2066
Fax: 1 858 456 1510

CALIFORNIA - LODI

Wine & Roses Hotel
2505 Turner Road, Lodi, California 95242
Tel: 1 209 334 6988
Fax: 1 209 371 6049

CALIFORNIA - MILL VALLEY

Mill Valley Inn
165 Throckmorton Avenue, Mill Valley, California 94941
Tel: 1 415 389 6608
Fax: 1 415 389 5051

CALIFORNIA - PALM SPRINGS

Caliente Tropics Resort
411 East Palm Canyon Drive, Palm Springs, California 92264
Tel: 1 760 327 1391
Fax: 1 760 318 1883

CALIFORNIA - PALM SPRINGS

The Willows
412 West Tahquitz Canyon Way, Palm Springs, California 92262
Tel: 1 760 320 0771
Fax: 1 760 320 0780

CALIFORNIA - RANCHO SANTA FE

The Inn at Rancho Santa Fe
5951 Linea del Cielo, Rancho Santa Fe, California 92067
Tel: 1 858 756 1131
Fax: 1 858 759 1604

CALIFORNIA - SAN FRANCISCO

Hotel Drisco
2901 Pacific Avenue, San Francisco, California 94115
Tel: 1 415 346 2880
Fax: 1 415 567 5537

CALIFORNIA - SAN FRANCISCO

Nob Hill Lambourne
725 Pine Street, San Francisco, California 94108
Tel: 1 415 433 2287
Fax: 1 415 433 0975

CALIFORNIA - SAN FRANCISCO

The Union Street Inn
2229 Union Street, San Francisco, California 94123
Tel: 1 415 346 0424
Fax: 1 415 922 8046

CALIFORNIA - SAN FRANCISCO BAY AREA

Gerstle Park Inn
34 Grove Street, San Rafael, California 94901
Tel: 1 415 721 7611
Fax: 1 415 721 7600

Mini Listings North America

Condé Nast Johansens are delighted to recommend over 190 properties across North America, Bermuda, The Caribbean, Mexico, The Pacific.

Call +44 208 655 7810 or see the order forms on page 421 to order guides.

CALIFORNIA - SANTA MONICA

Georgian Hotel

1415 Ocean Avenue, Santa Monica, California 90405
Tel: 1 310 395 9945
Fax: 1 310 451 3374

CALIFORNIA - TIBURON

Waters Edge Hotel

25 Main Street, Tiburon, California 94920
Tel: 1 415 789 5999
Fax: 1 415 789 5888

COLORADO - BEAVER CREEK

The Inn at Beaver Creek

10 Elk Track Lane, Beaver Creek Resort, Colorado, 81620
Tel: 1 970 845 5990
Fax: 1 970 845 6204

COLORADO - DENVER

Castle Marne

1572 Race Street, Denver, Colorado 80206
Tel: 1 303 331 0621
Fax: 1 303 331 0623

COLORADO - ESTES PARK

Taharaa Lodge

3110 So. Street Urain, PO Box 2586, Estes Park, Colorado 80517
Tel: 1 970 577 0098
Fax: 1 970 577 0819

COLORADO - MANITOU SPRINGS

The Cliff House at Pikes Peak

306 Cañon Avenue, Manitou Springs, Colorado 80829
Tel: 1 719 685 3000
Fax: 1 719 685 3913

COLORADO - STEAMBOAT SPRINGS

The Antlers at Christie Base

2085 Ski Time Square Drive, Steamboat Springs, Colorado 80487
Tel: 1 970 879 8000
Fax: 1 970 879 8060

COLORADO - STEAMBOAT SPRINGS

Canyon Creek at Eagle Ridge

2720 Eagle Ridge Circle, Steamboat Springs, Colorado 80487
Tel: 1 970 879 8000
Fax: 1 970 879 8060

COLORADO - STEAMBOAT SPRINGS

Vista Verde Guest Ranch

PO Box 770465, Steamboat Springs, Colorado 80477
Tel: 1 970 879 3858
Fax: 1 970 879 1413

COLORADO - VAIL

Hotel Gasthof Gramshammer

231 East Gore Creek Drive, Vail, Colorado 81657
Tel: 1 970 476 5626
Fax: 1 970 476 8816

COLORADO - VAIL

Savory Inn & Cooking School of Vail

2405 Elliott Road, Vail, Colorado 81657
Tel: 1 970 476 1304
Fax: 1 970 476 0433

DELAWARE - REHOBOTH BEACH

Boardwalk Plaza Hotel

Olive Avenue & The Boardwalk, Rehoboth Beach, Delaware 19971
Tel: 1 302 227 7169
Fax: 1 302 227 0561

FLORIDA - KEY WEST

Simonton Court Historic Inn & Cottages

320 Simonton Street, Key West, Florida 33040
Tel: 1 305 294 6386
Fax: 1 305 293 8446

FLORIDA - MIAMI BEACH

The Inn At Fisher Island

One Fisher Island Drive, Miami Beach, Florida 33109
Tel: 1 305 535 6080
Fax: 1 305 535 6003

FLORIDA - MIAMI BEACH

The Tides

1220 Ocean Drive, South Beach, Miami, Florida 33139
Tel: 1 305 604 5070
Fax: 1 305 604 5180

FLORIDA - NAPLES

Hotel Escalante

290 Fifth Avenue South, Naples, Florida 34102
Tel: 1 239 659 3466
Fax: 1 239 262 8748

FLORIDA - PALM BEACH

The Brazilian Court

301 Australian Avenue, Palm Beach, Florida 33480
Tel: 1 561 655 7740
Fax: 1 561 655 0801

GEORGIA - LITTLE ST SIMONS ISLAND

The Lodge on Little St Simons Island

PO Box 21078, Little St Simons Island, Georgia 31522 – 0578
Tel: 1 912 638 7472
Fax: 1 912 634 1811

Mini Listings North America

Condé Nast Johansens are delighted to recommend over 190 properties across North America, Bermuda, The Caribbean, Mexico, The Pacific.
Call +44 208 655 7810 or see the order forms on page 421 to order guides.

GEORGIA - PERRY

Henderson Village

125 South Langston Circle, Perry, Georgia 31069
Tel: 1 478 988 8696
Fax: 1 478 988 9009

GEORGIA - SAVANNAH

The Eliza Thompson House

5 West Jones Street, Savannah, Georgia 31401
Tel: 1 912 236 3620
Fax: 1 912 238 1920

GEORGIA - SAVANNAH

Granite Steps

126 East Gaston Street, Savannah, Georgia 31401

GEORGIA - SAVANNAH

The President's Quarters

225 East President Street, Savannah, Georgia 31401
Tel: 1 912 233 1600
Fax: 1 912 238 0849

ILLINOIS - CHICAGO

Fitzpatrick - Chicago - Hotel

166 East Superior Street, Chicago, Illinois 60611
Tel: 1 312 787 6000
Fax: 1 312 787 6133

ILLINOIS - CHICAGO

The Sutton Place Hotel

21 East Bellevue Place, Chicago, Illinois 60611
Tel: 1 312 266 2100
Fax: 1 312 266 2103

LOUISIANA - NAPOLEANVILLE

Madewood Plantation House

4250 Highway 308, Napoleanville,Louisiana 70390
Tel: 1 985 369 7151
Fax: 1 985 369 9848

LOUISIANA - NEW ORLEANS

Hotel Maison De Ville

727 Rue Toulouse, New Orleans, Louisiana 70130
Tel: 1 504 561 5858
Fax: 1 504 528 9939

MARYLAND - ANNAPOLIS

The Annapolis Inn

144 Prince George Street, Annapolis, Maryland 21401-1723
Tel: 1 410 295 5200
Fax: 1 410 295 5201

MARYLAND - FROSTBURG

Savage River Lodge

1600 Mt. Aetna Road, Frostburg, Maryland 21536
Tel: 1 301 689 3200
Fax: 1 301 689 2746

MARYLAND - TANEYTOWN

Antrim 1844

30 Trevanion Rd, Taneytown, Maryland 21787
Tel: 1 410 756 6812
Fax: 1 410 756 2744

MISSISSIPPI - JACKSON

Fairview Inn

734 Fairview Street, Jackson, Mississippi 39202
Tel: 1 601 948 3429
Fax: 1 601 948 1203

MISSISSIPPI - NATCHEZ

Dunleith Plantation

84 Homochitto Street, Natchez, Mississippi 39120
Tel: 1 601 446 8500
Fax: 1 601 446 8554

MISSISSIPPI - NATCHEZ

Monmouth Plantation

36 Melrose Avenue At John A. Quitman Parkway, Natchez, Mississippi 39120
Tel: 1 601 442 5852
Fax: 1 601 446 7762

MISSISSIPPI - VICKSBURG

Anchuca Historic Mansion & Inn

1010 First East Street, Vicksburg, Mississippi 39183
Tel: 1 601 661 0111
Fax: 1 601 661 0111

MISSISSIPPI - VICKSBURG

The Duff Green Mansion

1114 First East Street, Vicksburg, Mississippi 39180
Tel: 1 601 636 6968
Fax: 1 601 661 0069

MISSOURI - ST LOUIS

The Chase Park Plaza

212-232 North Kingshighway Boulevard, St Louis, Missouri 63108
Tel: 1 314 633 3000
Fax: 1 314 633 1144

NEW ENGLAND / CONNECTICUT - ESSEX

Copper Beech Inn

46 Main Street, Ivoryton, Connecticut 06442
Tel: 1 860 767 0330
Fax: 1 860 767 7840

Mini Listings North America

Condé Nast Johansens are delighted to recommend over 190 properties across North America, Bermuda, The Caribbean, Mexico, The Pacific.
Call +44 208 655 7810 or see the order forms on page 421 to order guides.

NEW ENGLAND / CONNECTICUT - GREENWICH

Delamar

500 Steamboat Road, Greenwich, Connecticut 06830
Tel: 1 203 661 9800
Fax: 1 203 661 2513

NEW ENGLAND / CONNECTICUT - NEW PRESTON

The Boulders Inn

East Shore Road, Route 45, New Preston, Connecticut 06777
Tel: 1 860 868 0541
Fax: 1 860 868 1925

NEW ENGLAND / CONNECTICUT - RIDGEFIELD

West Lane Inn

22 West Lane, Ridgefield, Connecticut 06877
Tel: 1 203 438 7323
Fax: 1 203 438 7325

NEW ENGLAND / MAINE - BOOTHBAY HARBOR

Spruce Point Inn

PO Box 237, Boothbay Harbor, Maine 04538
Tel: 1 207 633 4152
Fax: 1 207 633 7138

NEW ENGLAND / MAINE - CAMDEN

Camden Maine Stay

22 High Street, Camden, Maine 04843
Tel: 1 207 236 9636
Fax: 1 207 236 0621

NEW ENGLAND / MAINE - CAMDEN

The Inns at Blackberry Common

82 Elm Street, Camden, Maine 04843
Tel: 1 207 236 6060
Fax: 1 207 236 9032

NEW ENGLAND / MAINE - GREENVILLE

Greenville Inn

Po Box 1194, Norris Street, Greenville, Maine 04441
Tel: 1 207 695 2206
Fax: 1 207 695 0335

NEW ENGLAND / MAINE - GREENVILLE

The Lodge At Moosehead Lake

Upon Lily Bay Road, Box 1167, Greenville, Maine 04441
Tel: 1 207 695 4400
Fax: 1 207 695 2281

NEW ENGLAND / MAINE - KENNEBUNKPORT

The Captain Lord Mansion

6 Pleasant Street, Kennebunkport, Maine 04046-0800
Tel: 1 207 967 3141

NEW ENGLAND / MAINE - NEWCASTLE

The Newcastle Inn

60 River Road, Newcastle, Maine 04553
Tel: 1 207 563 5685
Fax: 1 207 563 6877

NEW ENGLAND / MASSACHUSETTS - BOSTON

The Charles Street Inn

94 Charles Street, Boston, Massachusetts 02114–4643
Tel: 1 617 314 8900
Fax: 1 617 371 0009

NEW ENGLAND / MASSACHUSETTS - BOSTON

The Lenox Hotel

710 Boylston Street, Boston, Massachusetts 02116-2699
Tel: 1 617 536 5300
Fax: 1 617 267 1237

NEW ENGLAND / MASSACHUSETTS - CAMBRIDGE

A Cambridge House

2218 Massachusetts Avenue, Cambridge, Massachusetts 02140–1836
Tel: 1 617 491 6300
Fax: 1 617 868 2848

NEW ENGLAND / MASSACHUSETTS - CAPE COD

The Captain's House Inn

369–377 Old Harbor Road, Chatham, Cape Cod, Massachusetts 02633
Tel: 1 508 945 0127
Fax: 1 508 945 0866

NEW ENGLAND / MASSACHUSETTS - CAPE COD

The Whalewalk Inn

220 Bridge Road, Eastham (Cape Cod), Massachusetts 02642
Tel: 1 508 255 0617
Fax: 1 508 240 0017

NEW ENGLAND / MASSACHUSETTS - LENOX

Cranwell Resort, Spa & Golf Club

55 Lee Road, Route 20, Lenox, Massachusetts 01240
Tel: 1 413 637 1364
Fax: 1 413 637 4364

NEW ENGLAND / MASSACHUSETTS - MARBLEHEAD

The Harbor Light Inn

58 Washington Street, Marblehead, Massachusetts 01945
Tel: 1 781 631 2186
Fax: 1 781 631 2216

NEW ENGLAND / MASSACHUSETTS - MARTHA'S VINEYARD

Hob Knob Inn

128 Main Street, po box 239, Edgartown, Massachusetts 02539
Tel: 1 508 627 9510
Fax: 1 508 627 4560

Mini Listings North America

Condé Nast Johansens are delighted to recommend over 190 properties across North America, Bermuda, The Caribbean, Mexico, The Pacific.
Call +44 208 655 7810 or see the order forms on page 421 to order guides.

NEW ENGLAND / MASSACHUSETTS - MARTHA'S VINEYARD

Thorncroft Inn
460 Main Street, PO Box 1022, Vineyard Haven, Massachusetts 02568
Tel: 1 508 693 3333
Fax: 1 508 693 5419

NEW ENGLAND / MASSACHUSETTS - MARTHA'S VINEYARD

The Victorian Inn
24 South Water Street, Edgartown, Massachusetts 02539
Tel: 1 508 627 4784

NEW ENGLAND / MASSACHUSETTS - MARTHA'S VINEYARD

The Winnetu Inn & Resort at South Beach
31 Dunes Road, Edgartown, Massachusetts 02539
Tel: 1 978 443 1733
Fax: 1 978 443 0479

NEW ENGLAND / MASSACHUSETTS - NANTUCKET

The Pineapple Inn
10 Hussey Street, Nantucket, Massachusetts 02554
Tel: 1 508 228 9992
Fax: 1 508 325 6051

NEW ENGLAND / MASSACHUSETTS - ROCKPORT

Seacrest Manor
99 Marmion Way, Rockport, Massachusetts 01966
Tel: 1 978 546 2211

NEW ENGLAND / NEW HAMPSHIRE - ASHLAND

The Glynn House Inn
59 Highland Street, Ashland, New Hampshire 03217
Tel: 1 800 637 9599/1 603 968 3775
Fax: 1 603 968 9415

NEW ENGLAND / NEW HAMPSHIRE - JACKSON

The Inn at Thorn Hill
Thorn Hill Road, Jackson Village, New Hampshire 03846
Tel: 1 603 383 4242
Fax: 1 603 383 8062

NEW ENGLAND / NEW HAMPSHIRE - JACKSON

The Wentworth
Jackson Village, New Hampshire 03846
Tel: 1 603 383 9700
Fax: 1 603 383 4265

NEW ENGLAND / RHODE ISLAND - BLOCK ISLAND

The Atlantic Inn
Po Box 1788, Block Island, Rhode Island 02807
Tel: 1 401 466 5883
Fax: 1 401 466 5678

NEW ENGLAND / RHODE ISLAND - NEWPORT

The Agincourt Inn
120 Miantonomi Avenue, Newport, Rhode Island 02842
Tel: 1 401 847 0902
Fax: 1 401 848 6529

NEW ENGLAND / RHODE ISLAND - NEWPORT

The Francis Malbone House
392 Thames Street, Newport, Rhode Island 02840
Tel: 1 401 846 0392
Fax: 1 401 848 5956

NEW ENGLAND / VERMONT - CHITTENDEN

Fox Creek Inn
49 Dam Road, Chittenden, Vermont 05737
Tel: 1 802 483 6213
Fax: 1 802 483 2623

NEW ENGLAND / VERMONT - CHITTENDEN

Mountain Top Inn & Resort
195 Mountain Top Road, Chittenden, Vermont 05737
Tel: 1 802 483 2311
Fax: 1 802 483 6373

NEW ENGLAND / VERMONT - LOWER WATERFORD

Rabbit Hill Inn
48 Lower Waterford Road, Lower Waterford, Vermont 05848
Tel: 1 802 748 5168
Fax: 1 802 748 8342

NEW ENGLAND / VERMONT - MANCHESTER VILLAGE

1811 House
PO Box 39, Route 7A, Manchester Village, Vermont 05254
Tel: 1 802 362 1811
Fax: 1 802 362 2443

NEW ENGLAND / VERMONT - NEWFANE

Four Columns Inn
PO Box 278, Newfane, Vermont 05345
Tel: 1 802 365 7713

NEW ENGLAND / VERMONT - STOWE

The Green Mountain Inn
18 Main Street, Stowe, Vermont 05672
Tel: 1 802 253 7301
Fax: 1 802 253 5096

NEW ENGLAND / VERMONT - STOWE

The Mountain Road Resort At Stowe
PO Box 8, 1007 Mountain Road, Stowe, Vermont 05672
Tel: 1 802 253 4566
Fax: 1 802 253 7397

Mini Listings North America

Condé Nast Johansens are delighted to recommend over 190 properties across North America, Bermuda, The Caribbean, Mexico, The Pacific.
Call +44 208 655 7810 or see the order forms on page 421 to order guides.

NEW ENGLAND / VERMONT - WEST TOWNSHEND

Windham Hill Inn

West Townshend, Vermont 05359
Tel: 1 802 874 4080
Fax: 1 802 874 4702

NEW ENGLAND / VERMONT - WOODSTOCK

Woodstock Inn & Resort

Fourteen The Green, Woodstock, Vermont 05091-1298
Tel: 1 802 457 1100
Fax: 1 802 457 6699

NEW MEXICO - SANTA FE

The Bishop's Lodge Resort & Spa

PO Box 2367, Santa Fe, New Mexico 87504
Tel: 1 505 983 6377
Fax: 1 505 989 8739

NEW MEXICO - SANTA FE

Hotel St Francis

210 Don Gaspar Avenue, Santa Fe, New Mexico 87501
Tel: 1 505 983 5700
Fax: 1 505 989 7690

NEW MEXICO - SANTA FE

Inn of the Turquoise Bear

342 E. Buena Vista Street, Santa Fe,
New Mexico 87505-2623
Tel: 1 505 983 0798
Fax: 1 505 988 4225

NEW MEXICO - TAOS

Fechin Inn

227 Paseo del Pueblo Norte, Taos, New Mexico 87571
Tel: 1 505 751 1000
Fax: 1 505 751 7338

NEW YORK - CAZENOVIA

The Brewster Inn

6 Ledyard Avenue, Cazenovia, New York 13035
Tel: 1 315 655 9232
Fax: 1 315 655 2130

NEW YORK - CHESTERTOWN

Friends Lake Inn

963 Friends Lake Road, Chestertown, New York 12817
Tel: 1 518 494 4751
Fax: 1 518 494 4616

NEW YORK - EAST AURORA

Roycroft Inn

40 South Grove Street, East Aurora, New York 14052
Tel: 1 716 652 5552
Fax: 1 716 655 5345

NEW YORK - GENEVA

Geneva On The Lake

1001 Lochland Road (Route 14 South), Geneva,
New York 14456
Tel: 1 315 789 7190
Fax: 1 315 789 0322

NEW YORK - LONG ISLAND

Inn at Great Neck

30 Cutter Mill Road, Greak Neck, New York 11021
Tel: 1 516 773 2000
Fax: 1 516 773 2020

NEW YORK - MT TREMPER

The Emerson Inn & Spa

146 Mount Pleasant Road, Mount Tremper,
New York 12457
Tel: 1 845 688 7900
Fax: 1 845 688 2789

NEW YORK - NEW YORK CITY

The Inn at Irving Place

56 Irving Place, New York, New York 10003
Tel: 1 212 533 4600
Fax: 1 212 533 4611

NEW YORK - NEW YORK CITY

The Kitano New York

66 Park Avenue New York, New York City,
New York 10016
Tel: 1 212 885 7000
Fax: 1 212 885 7100

NEW YORK - NORTHERN CATSKILL MOUNTAINS

Albergo Allegria

#43 Route 296, Windham, New York 12496
Tel: 1 518 734 5560
Fax: 1 518 734 5570

NEW YORK - SARATOGA SPRINGS

Saratoga Arms

497 Broadway, Saratoga Springs, New York 12866
Tel: 1 518 584 1775
Fax: 1 518 581 4064

NORTH CAROLINA - ASHEVILLE

The Wright Inn & Carriage House

235 Pearson Drive, Asheville, North Carolina 28801
Tel: 1 828 251 0789
Fax: 1 828 251 0929

NORTH CAROLINA - BEAUFORT

The Cedars Inn

305 Front Street, Beaufort, North Carolina 28516
Tel: 1 252 728 7036
Fax: 1 252 728 1685

Mini Listings North America

Condé Nast Johansens are delighted to recommend over 190 properties across North America, Bermuda, The Caribbean, Mexico, The Pacific.
Call +44 208 655 7810 or see the order forms on page 421 to order guides.

NORTH CAROLINA - BLOWING ROCK

Chetola Resort

PO Box 17, North Main Street, Blowing Rock,
North Carolina 28605
Tel: 1 828 295 5500
Fax: 1 828 295 5529

NORTH CAROLINA - BLOWING ROCK

Gideon Ridge Inn

PO Box 1929, Blowing Rock, North Carolina 28605
Tel: 1 828 295 3644
Fax: 1 828 295 4586

NORTH CAROLINA - CASHIERS

Millstone Inn

119 Lodge Lane, Hwy 64 West, Cashiers,
North Carolina 28717
Tel: 1 828 743 2737
Fax: 1 828 743 0208

NORTH CAROLINA - CHARLOTTE

Ballantyne Resort

10000 Ballantyne Commons Parkway, Charlotte,
North Carolina 28277
Tel: 1 704 248 4000
Fax: 1 704 248 4005

NORTH CAROLINA - CHARLOTTE

The Park

2200 Rexford Road, Charlotte, North Carolina 28211
Tel: 1 704 364 8220
Fax: 1 704 365 4712

NORTH CAROLINA - DURHAM

Morehead Manor Bed & Breakfast

914 Vickers Avenue, Durham, North Carolina 27701
Tel: 1 919 687 4366
Fax: 1 919 687 4245

NORTH CAROLINA - HENDERSONVILLE

Claddagh Inn

755 North Main Street, Hendersonville,
North Carolina 28792
Tel: 1 828 697 7778

NORTH CAROLINA - HIGHLANDS

Inn at Half Mile Farm

PO Box 2769, 214 Half Mile Drive, Highlands,
North Carolina 28741
Tel: 1 828 526 8170
Fax: 1 828 526 2625

NORTH CAROLINA - MANTEO

The White Doe Inn & Whispering Bay

PO Box 1029, 319 Sir Walter Raleigh Street, Manteo,
North Carolina 27954
Tel: 1 252 473 9851
Fax: 1 252 473 4708

NORTH CAROLINA - RALEIGH - DURHAM

The Siena Hotel

1505 E Franklin Street, Chapel Hill,
North Carolina 27514
Tel: 1 919 929 4000
Fax: 1 919 968 8527

NORTH CAROLINA - ROBBINSVILLE

Snowbird Mountain Lodge

275 Santeetlah Road, Robbinsville,
North Carolina 28771
Tel: 1 828 479 3433
Fax: 1 828 479 3473

NORTH CAROLINA - TRYON

Pine Crest Inn

85 Pine Crest Lane, Tryon, North Carolina 28782
Tel: 1 828 859 9135
Fax: 1 828 859 9135

NORTH CAROLINA - WILMINGTON

Graystone Inn

100 South Third Street, Wilmington,
North Carolina 28401
Tel: 1 910 763 2000
Fax: 1 910 763 5555

NORTH CAROLINA - WINSTON-SALEM

Augustus T. Zevely Inn

803 South Main Street, Winston-Salem,
North Carolina 27101
Tel: 1 336 748 9299
Fax: 1 336 721 2211

PENNSYLVANIA - HANOVER

Sheppard Mansion

117 Frederick Street, Hanover, Pennsylvania 17331
Tel: 1 717 633 8075
Fax: 1 717 633 8074

PENNSYLVANIA - LEOLA

Leola Village Inn & Suites

38 Deborah Srive, Route 23, Leola, Pennsylvania 17540
Tel: 1 717 656 7002
Fax: 1 717 656 7648

PENNSYLVANIA - NEW BERLIN

The Inn at New Berlin

321 Market Street, New Berlin,
Pennsylvania 17855-0390
Tel: 1 570 966 0321
Fax: 1 570 966 9557

PENNSYLVANIA - PHILADELPHIA

Rittenhouse Square European Boutique Hotel

1715 Rittenhouse Square, Philadelphia,
Pennsylvania 19103
Tel: 1 215 546 6500
Fax: 1 215 546 8787

Mini Listings North America

Condé Nast Johansens are delighted to recommend over 190 properties across North America, Bermuda, The Caribbean, Mexico, The Pacific.
Call +44 208 655 7810 or see the order forms on page 421 to order guides.

PENNSYLVANIA - PHILADELPHIA

The Thomas Bond House

129 South 2nd Street, Philadelphia, Pennsylvania 19106
Tel: 1 215 923 8523
Fax: 1 215 923 8504

SOUTH CAROLINA - CHARLESTON

Ansonborough Inn

21 Hasell Street, Charleston, South Carolina 29401
Tel: 1 843 723 1655
Fax: 1 843 577 6668

SOUTH CAROLINA - CHARLESTON

Vendue Inn

19 Vendue Range, Charleston, South Carolina 29401
Tel: 1 843 577 7970
Fax: 1 843 577 2913

SOUTH CAROLINA - NORTH AUGUSTA

Rosemary & Lookaway Inn

804 Carolina Avenue, North Augusta, South Carolina 29841
Tel: 1 803 278 6222
Fax: 1 803 649 2404

SOUTH CAROLINA - PAWLEYS ISLAND

Litchfield Plantation

Kings River Road, Box 290, Pawleys Island, South Carolina 29585
Tel: 1 843 237 9121
Fax: 1 843 237 1041

SOUTH CAROLINA - TRAVELERS REST

La Bastide

10 Road Of Vines, Travelers Rest, South Carolina 29690
Tel: 1 864 836 8463
Fax: 1 864 836 4820

TENNESSEE - KINGSTON

Whitestone Country Inn

1200 Paint Rock Road, Kingston, Tennessee 37763
Tel: 1 865 376 0113
Fax: 1 865 376 4454

TEXAS - BOERNE

Ye Kendall Inn

128 West Blanco, Boerne, Texas 78006
Tel: 1 830 249 2138
Fax: 1 830 249 7371

TEXAS - GLEN ROSE

Rough Creek Lodge

PO Box 2400, Glen Rose, Texas 76043
Tel: 1 254 965 3700
Fax: 1 254 918 2570

TEXAS - SAN ANTONIO

Havana River Walk Inn

1015 Navarro, San Antonio, Texas 78205
Tel: 1 210 222 2008
Fax: 1 210 222 2717

VIRGINIA - CHARLOTTESVILLE

200 South Street Inn

200 South Street, Charlottesville, Virginia 22902
Tel: 1 434 979 0200
Fax: 1 434 979 4403

VIRGINIA - CHARLOTTESVILLE

Clifton - The Country Inn & Estate

1296 Clifton Inn Drive, Charlottesville, Virginia 22911
Tel: 1 434 971 1800
Fax: 1 434 971 7098

VIRGINIA - CULPEPER

Prince Michel Restaurant & Suites

Prince Michel de Virginia, HCR 4, Box 77, Leon, Virginia 22725
Tel: 1 540 547 9720
Fax: 1 540 547 3088

VIRGINIA - MIDDLEBURG

The Goodstone Inn & Estate

36205 Snake Hill Road, Middleburg, Virginia 20117
Tel: 1 540 687 4645
Fax: 1 540 687 6115

VIRGINIA - STAUNTON

Frederick House

28 North New Street, Staunton, Virginia 24401
Tel: 1 540 885 4220
Fax: 1 540 885 5180

VIRGINIA - WILLIAMSBURG

Legacy of Williamsburg Inn

930 Jamestown Road, Williamsburg, Virginia 23185-3917
Tel: 1 757 220 0524
Fax: 1 757 220 2211

WYOMING - CHEYENNE

Nagle Warren Mansion

222 East 17Th Street, Cheyenne, Wyoming 82001
Tel: 1 307 637 3333
Fax: 1 307 638 6879

MEXICO - BAJA CALIFORNIA

Casa Natalia

Blvd Mijares 4, San Jose Del Cabo, Baja California Sur 23400
Tel: 52 624 14 251 00
Fax: 52 624 14251 10

MINI LISTINGS NORTH AMERICA

Condé Nast Johansens are delighted to recommend over 190 properties across North America, Bermuda, The Caribbean, Mexico, The Pacific. Call +44 208 655 7810 or see the order forms on page 421 to order guides.

MEXICO - CANCUN

Villas Tacul Boutique Hotel

Boulevard Kukulkan, KM 5.5, Cancun, Quintana Roo 77500, Mexico
Tel: 52 998 883 00 00
Fax: 52 998 849 70 70

MEXICO - GUANAJUATO

Casa de Sierra Nevada Quinta Real

Hospicio 35, San Miguel de Allende, Guanajuato 37700, Mexico
Tel: 52 415 152 7040
Fax: 52 415 152 1436

MEXICO - ISLA MUJERES

Secreto

Sección Rocas, Lote 11, Punta Norte, Isla Mujeres, Quintana Roo, 77400 Mexico
Tel: 52 998 877 1039
Fax: 52 998 877 1048

MEXICO - ISLA MUJERES

Villa Rolandi

Fracc. Laguna Mar SM 7, MZA 75 Lotes, Isla Mujeres, C.P. 77400, Quintana Roo, Mexico
Tel: 52 987 7 07 00
Fax: 52 987 7 01 00

MEXICO - MERIDA

Hacienda Xcanatun Casa de Piedra

Km 12 Carretera Mérida-Progreso, Mérida, Yucatán, Mexico 97300
Tel: 52 999 941 0273
Fax: 52 999 941 0319

MEXICO - NUEVO VALLARTA

Grand Velas All Suites & Spa Resort

Av. Cocoteros 98 Sur, C.P. 63735, Nuevo Vallarta, Nayarit, Mexico
Tel: 52 322 226 8000
Fax: 52 322 297 2005

MEXICO - OAXACA

Hacienda Los Laureles

Hildago No. 21, San Felipe del Agua, Oaxaca, Oax. Mexico c.p. 68020
Tel: 52 951 501 5300
Fax: 52 951 520 0890

MEXICO - PUERTO VALLARTA

El Careyes Beach Resort

km 53.5, Carretera barra de Navada, Puerto Vallarta, Costa Careyes, Jalisco 48970, Mexico
Tel: 52 315 351 0000
Fax: 52 315 351 0100

MEXICO - PUERTO VALLARTA

El Tamarindo Golf Resort

km 7.5 Carretera, Nelaque, Puerto Vallarta, Cihation, Jalisco 18970, Mexico
Tel: 52 315 351 0000
Fax: 52 315 351 0100

MEXICO - PUERTO VALLARTA

Las Alamandas Resort

km 83.5 Carr, Barra de Navidad, Puerto Vallarta, Jalisco 48980, Mexico
Tel: 52 322 285 5500
Fax: 52 322 285 5027

MEXICO - ZIHUATANEJO

Hotel Villa Del Sol

Playa La Ropa S/N, PO Box 84, Zihuatanejo 40880, Mexico
Tel: 52 755 555 5500
Fax: 52 755 554 2758

BERMUDA - DEVONSHIRE

Ariel Sands

34 South Shore Road, Devonshire, Bermuda
Tel: 1 441 236 1010
Fax: 1 441 236 0087

BERMUDA - HAMILTON

Rosedon Hotel

PO Box Hm 290, Hamilton Hmax, Bermuda
Tel: 1 441 295 1640
Fax: 1 441 295 5904

BERMUDA - PAGET

Fourways Inn

PO Box Pg 294, Paget Pg Bx, Bermuda
Tel: 1 441 236 6517
Fax: 1 441 236 5528

BERMUDA - SOMERSET

Cambridge Beaches

Kings Point, Somerset, MA02 Bermuda
Tel: 1 441 234 0331
Fax: 1 441 234 3352

BERMUDA - SOUTHAMPTON

The Reefs

56 South Shore Road, Southampton, SN02 Bermuda
Tel: 1 441 238 0222
Fax: 1 441 238 8372

BERMUDA - WARWICK

Surf Side Beach Club

90 South Shore Road, Warwick, Bermuda
Tel: 1 441 236 7100
Fax: 1 441 236 9765

CARIBBEAN - ANGUILLA

Frangipani Beach Club

PO Box 1378, Meads Bay, Anguilla, West Indies
Tel: 1 264 497 6442/6444
Fax: 1 264 497 6440

Mini Listings North America

Condé Nast Johansens are delighted to recommend over 190 properties across North America, Bermuda, The Caribbean, Mexico, The Pacific.
Call +44 208 655 7810 or see the order forms on page 421 to order guides.

CARIBBEAN - ANTIGUA

Blue Waters
PO Box 256, St. John's, Antigua, West Indies
Tel: 1 268 462 0290
Fax: 1 268 462 0293

CARIBBEAN - ANTIGUA

Curtain Bluff
PO Box 288, Antigua, West Indies
Tel: 1 268 462 8400
Fax: 1 268 462 8409

CARIBBEAN - ANTIGUA

Galley Bay
Five Islands, PO Box 305, St John's, Antigua, West Indies
Tel: 1 268 462 0302
Fax: 1 268 462 4551

CARIBBEAN - ANTIGUA

The Inn at English Harbour
Po Box 187, St Johns, Antigua, West Indies
Tel: 1 268 460 1014
Fax: 1 268 460 1603

CARIBBEAN - BARBADOS

Coral Reef Club
St. James, Barbados, West Indies
Tel: 1 246 422 2372
Fax: 1 246 422 1776

CARIBBEAN - BARBADOS

The Sandpiper
Holetown, St James, Barbados, West Indies
Tel: 1 246 422 2251
Fax: 1 246 422 0900

CARIBBEAN - CURAÇAO

Avila Beach Hotel
Penstraat 130, Willemstad, Curaçao, Netherlands Antilles, West Indies
Tel: 599 9 461 4377
Fax: 599 9 461 1493

CARIBBEAN - GRENADA

Spice Island Beach Resort
Grand Anse Beach, Box 6, St George's, Grenada, West Indies
Tel: 1 473 444 4423/4258
Fax: 1 473 444 4807

CARIBBEAN - JAMAICA

Half Moon
Montego Bay, Jamaica, West Indies
Tel: 1 876 953 2211
Fax: 1 876 953 2731

CARIBBEAN - JAMAICA

The Tryall Club
PO Box 1206, Montego Bay, Jamaica, West Indies
Tel: 1 800 238 5290
Fax: 1 876 956 5673

CARIBBEAN - JAMAICA

Grand Lido Negril
Norman Manley Boulevard, PO Box 88, Negril, Jamaica, West Indies
Tel: 1 876 957 5010/8
Fax: 1 876 957 5517

CARIBBEAN - JAMAICA

Sans Souci Resort & Spa
PO Box 103, Ocho Rios, St Ann, Jamaica, West Indies
Tel: 1 876 994 1206
Fax: 1 876 994 1544

CARIBBEAN - NEVIS

The Hermitage
Nevis, West Indies
Tel: 1 869 469 3477
Fax: 1 869 469 2481

CARIBBEAN - NEVIS

Montpelier Plantation Inn
Montpelier Estate, PO Box 474, Nevis, West Indies
Tel: 1 869 469 3462
Fax: 1 869 469 2932

CARIBBEAN - NEVIS

Nisbet Plantation Beach Club
St James Parish, Nevis, West Indies
Tel: 1 869 469 9325
Fax: 1 869 469 9864

CARIBBEAN - ST KITTS

The Golden Lemon
Dieppe Bay, St Kitts, West Indies
Tel: 1 869 465 7260
Fax: 1 869 465 4019

CARIBBEAN - ST KITTS

Ottley's Plantation Inn
Po Box 345, Basseterre, St Kitts, West Indies
Tel: 1 869 465 7234
Fax: 1 869 465 4760

CARIBBEAN - ST LUCIA

Anse Chastanet
PO Box 7000, Soufriere, St Lucia, West Indies
Tel: 1 758 459 7000
Fax: 1 758 459 7700

North America

Condé Nast Johansens are delighted to recommend over 190 properties across North America, Bermuda, The Caribbean, Mexico, The Pacific.

CARIBBEAN - ST LUCIA

Windjammer Landing

Labrelotte Bay, P.O.Box 1504, Castries, St Lucia, West Indies
Tel: 1 758 452 0913
Fax: 1 758 452 9454

CARIBBEAN - THE GRENADINES

Palm Island

St Vincent & The Grenadines, West Indies
Tel: 1 954 481 8787
Fax: 1 954 481 1661

CARIBBEAN - TOBAGO

Being - Villa Experience

Arnol Vale, Tobago, West Indies
Tel: 1 868 625 4443
Fax: 1 868 625 4420

CARIBBEAN - TURKS & CAICOS

The Sands at Grace Bay

PO Box 681, Providenciales, Turks & Caicos Islands, British West Indies
Tel: 1 649 946 5199
Fax: 1 649 946 5198

CARIBBEAN - TURKS & CAICOS

Turks & Caicos Club

PO Box 687, Providenciales, Turks & Caicos, British West Indies
Tel: 1 649 946 5800
Fax: 1 649 946 5858

CARIBBEAN - TURKS & CAICOS

Point Grace

PO Box 700, Providenciales, Turks and Caicos Islands, British west indies
Tel: 1 649 946 5096
Fax: 1 649 946 5097

PACIFIC - FIJI ISLANDS (LABASA)

Nukubati Island

PO Box 1928, Labasa, Fiji Islands
Tel: 61 2 93888 196
Fax: 61 2 93888 204

PACIFIC - FIJI ISLANDS (LAUTOKA)

Blue Lagoon Cruises

183 Vitogo Parade, Lautoka, Fiji Islands
Tel: 679 6661 622
Fax: 679 6664 098

PACIFIC - FIJI ISLANDS (SAVU SAVU)

Jean-Michel Cousteau Fiji Islands Resort

Lesiaceva Point, Savu Savu, Fiji Islands
Tel: 679 885 0188
Fax: 679 885 0340

PACIFIC - FIJI ISLANDS (TOBERUA ISLAND)

Toberua Island Resort

PO Box 3332, Nausori, Fiji Islands
Tel: 679 347 2777
Fax: 679 347 2888

PACIFIC - FIJI ISLANDS (YASAWA ISLAND)

Turtle Island

Yasawa Islands, Po Box 9317, Nadi Airport, Nadi, Fiji Islands
Tel: 61 3 9823 8300
Fax: 61 3 9823 8383

PACIFIC - FIJI ISLANDS (YASAWA ISLAND)

Yasawa Island Resort

PO Box 10128, Nadi Airport, Nadi, Fiji Islands
Tel: 679 666 3364
Fax: 679 666 5044

PACIFIC - HAWAII (HILO)

Shipman House

131 Ka'iulani Street, Hilo, Hawaii 96720
Tel: 1 808 934 8002
Fax: 1 808 934 8002

PACIFIC - HAWAII (HONOMU)

The Palms Cliff House

28-3514 Mamalahoa Highway 19, P.O. Box 189, Honomu, Hawaii 96728-0189
Tel: 1 808 963 6076
Fax: 1 808 963 6316

PACIFIC - HAWAII (KAMUELA)

The Jacaranda Inn

65-1444 Kawaihae Road, Kamuela, Hawaii 96743
Tel: 1 808 885 8813
Fax: 1 808 885 6096

PACIFIC - HAWAII (LAHAINA)

Lahaina Inn

127 Lahainaluna Road, Lahaina, Maui, Hawaii 96761
Tel: 1 808 661 0577
Fax: 1 808 667 9480

PACIFIC - HAWAII (LAHAINA)

The Plantation Inn

174 Lahainaluna Road, Lahaina, Maui, Hawaii 96761, USA
Tel: 1 808 667 9225
Fax: 1 808 667 9293

PACIFIC - HAWAII (WAILUKU)

Old Wailuku Inn at Ulupono

2199 Kaho'okele Street, Wailuku, Maui, Hawaii 96793
Tel: 1 808 244 5897
Fax: 1 808 242 9600

PACIFIC - SAMOA (APIA)

Aggie Grey's Hotel

PO Box 67, Apia, Samoa
Tel: 685 228 80
Fax: 685 236 26 or 685 23203

Index by Property

Andorra

Austria

Belgium

Croatia

Czech Republic

Denmark

Estonia

France

▼

INDEX BY PROPERTY

Germany

Great Britain & Ireland

Greece

▼

Index by Property

Hungary

Italy

Luxembourg

Monaco

The Netherlands

Norway

Index by Property

Portugal

Spain

Sweden

Switzerland

Turkey

INDEX BY ACTIVITY

Hotels with heated indoor swimming pool

▼

Outdoor pool

▼

▼

Tennis

Index by Activity

Skiing

Shooting

Golf course on-site

Fishing on-site

SPA Dedicated Spa on-site

▼

M[100] Conference facilities for 100 delegates or more

▼

Index by Activity

Licensed for wedding ceremonies

▼

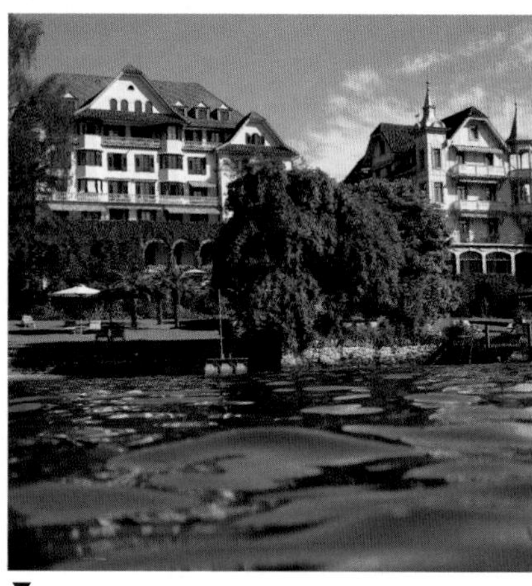

▼

Grand Heritage members

CONDÉ NAST JOHANSENS

ORDER FORM

Choose from our wide range of titles below

Order 2 Guides get €8 off • Order 3 Guides get €15 off • Order 4 Guides get €30 off

Order the Chairman's Collection worth over €140 for just €100

Simply complete the form below, total the cost and then deduct the appropriate discount. State your preferred method of payment and mail to Condé Nast Johansens Ltd, c/o Yale Press, Delga House, Carmichael Road, Norwood, London SE25 5LY, UK. Fax orders welcome on +44 20 8655 7817

ALTERNATIVELY YOU CAN ORDER IMMEDIATELY BY PHONE ON +44 208 655 7810, please quote ref: E008

Hotels
Great Britain & Ireland
410 Recommendations

I wish to order

QUANTITY

copy/ies at €29.95 each.
Total cost

€

Country Houses
Great Britain & Ireland
255 Recommendations

I wish to order

QUANTITY

copy/ies at €26.95 each.
Total cost

€

Hotels & Spas
Europe & Mediterranean
350 Recommendations

I wish to order

QUANTITY

copy/ies at €26.95 each.
Total cost

€

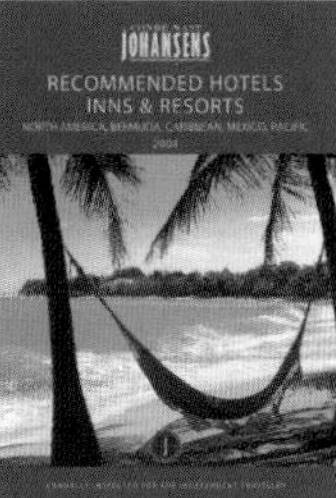

Hotels, Inns & Resorts
N America, Caribbean
200 Recommendations

I wish to order

QUANTITY

copy/ies at €21.95 each.
Total cost

€

Business Venues
230 Recommendations
(published Feb 2004)

I wish to order

QUANTITY

copy/ies at €38.00 each.
Total cost

€

Condé Nast Johansens
Gold Blocked Slip Case
priced at €8 each

Condé Nast Johansens
Luxury Luggage Tag
priced at
€23 each

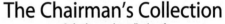

To order these items please fill in the appropriate section below

The Chairman's Collection

Order the complete collection of
Condé Nast Johansens Recommended Guides for only €100

***PLUS FREE Luxury Luggage Tag** worth €23*

***PLUS FREE Slip Case** worth €8*

The Chairman's Collection contains all five titles pictured above. The Recommended Venues guide will be dispatched separately on publication in February 2004.

Now please complete your order and payment details

	tick	
I have ordered 2 titles - **€8** off		–€8.00
I have ordered 3 titles - **€15** off		–€15.00
I have ordered 4 titles - **€30** off		–€30.00
Total cost of books ordered minus discount (excluding the Chairman's Collection)	€	
Luxury Luggage Tag at **€23** Quantity and total cost:		€
Gold Blocked Slip Case at **€8** Quantity and total cost:		€
I wish to order the Chairman's Collection at **€100** Quantity and total cost:		€
Packing & delivery:		
All orders outside UK add **€9** per Guide	☐	€
or for Chairman's Collection add **€38.00**	☐	
GRAND TOTAL	€	

I have chosen my Condé Nast Johansens Guides and (please tick)

Please debit my credit/charge card account ☐

☐ MasterCard ☐ Visa ☐ Switch (Issue Number)

Card Holders Name (Mr/Mrs/Miss)

Address

Country

Telephone

E-mail

Card No. Exp Date

Signature

NOW send to
Condé Nast Johansens Ltd, c/o Yale Press, Delga House, Carmichael Road, Norwood, London SE25 5LY, UK
Fax orders welcome on +44 20 8655 7817

The details provided may be used to keep you informed of future products and special offers provided by Condé Nast Johansens and other carefully selected third parties. If you do not wish to receive such information, please tick this box ☐.
(Your phone number will only be used to ensure the fast and safe delivery of your order)

Guest Survey Report

Evaluate your stay in a Condé Nast Johansens Recommendation

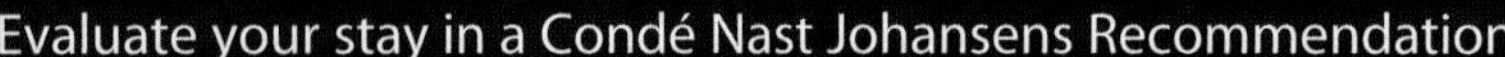

Dear Guest,

Following your stay in a Condé Nast Johansens Recommendation, please spare a moment to complete this Guest Survey Report. This is an important source of information for Johansens, to maintain the highest standards for our Recommendations and to support the work of our team of inspectors.

It is also the prime source of nominations for Condé Nast Johansens Awards for Excellence, which are made annually to those properties worldwide that represent the finest standards and best value for money in luxury, independent travel.

Thank you for your time and I hope that when choosing future accommodation Condé Nast Johansens will be your guide.

Yours faithfully,

Tim Sinclair

Sales & Marketing Director, Condé Nast Johansens

p.s. Guest Survey Reports may also be completed online at www.johansens.com

1. Your details

Your name: ....

Your address: ....

....

....

Postcode: ....

Telephone: ....

E-mail: ....

2. Hotel details

Name of hotel: ....

....

Location: ....

Date of visit: ....

3. Your rating of the hotel

Please tick one box in each category below (as applicable)

	Excellent	Good	Disappointing	Poor
Bedrooms	❍	❍	❍	❍
Public Rooms	❍	❍	❍	❍
Food/Restaurant	❍	❍	❍	❍
Service	❍	❍	❍	❍
Welcome/Friendliness	❍	❍	❍	❍
Value For Money	❍	❍	❍	❍

4. Any other comments

If you wish to make additional comments, please write separately to the Publisher, Condé Nast Johansens Ltd, 6-8 Old Bond Street, London W1S 4PH, UK

....

....

....

....

....

The details provided may be used to keep you informed of future products and special offers provided by Condé Nast Johansens and other carefully selected third parties. If you do not wish to receive such information, please tick this box ☐.

Please return completed form to:
Condé Nast Johansens Ltd, c/o Yale Press, Delga House, Carmichael Road, Norwood, London SE25 5LY, UK
Alternatively send by fax to +44 (0)20 8655 7817

CONDÉ NAST JOHANSENS

BON DE COMMANDE

Commandez 2 Guides & économisez €8 • Commandez 3 Guides & économisez €15 • Commandez 4 Guides & économisez €30

ou commandez la "Collection du Président" valeur €140 pour seulement €100

Completez le coupon ci-après, additionnez les montants et déduisez la remise applicable. Indiquez vos détails de carte de crédit et envoyez le tout à Condé Nast Johansens Ltd, c/o Yale Press, Delga House, Carmichael Road, Norwood, London SE25 5LY, Grande-Bretagne ou par fax au +44 208 655 7817

Si vous le préférez, vous pouvez commander directement au +44 208 655 7810, (donnez la référence: E008)

Hotels
Great Britain & Ireland
410 Recommandations

Je souhaite commander

copie(s) à €29.95 chacune.
Coût total

€

Country Houses
Great Britain & Ireland
255 Recommandations

Je souhaite commander

copie(s) à €26.95 chacune.
Coût total

€

Hotels & Spas
Europe & Mediterranean
350 Recommandations

Je souhaite commander

copie(s) à €26.95 chacune.
Coût total

€

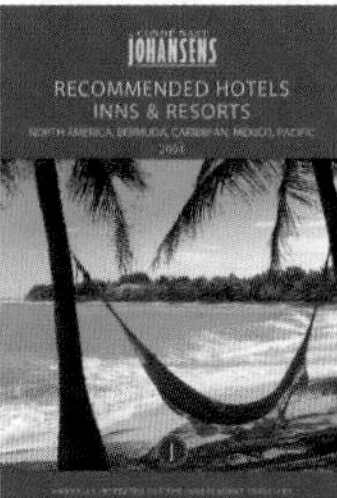

Hotels, Inns & Resorts
N America, Caribbean
200 Recommandations

Je souhaite commander

copie(s) à €21.95 chacune.
Coût total

€

Business Venues
230 Recommandations
(publié le 2004 Février)

Je souhaite commander

copie(s) à €38.00 chacune.
Coût total

€

Etui gravé "Condé Nast Johansens" pour conserver vos guides à €8 chacun.

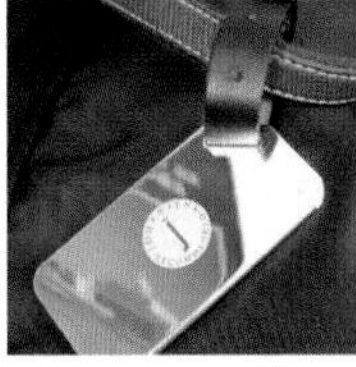

Marque bagage de luxe "Condé Nast Johansens" à €23 chacune

Pour commander ces éléments, complétez s'il vous plait la section appropriée ci-dessous

La Collection du Président

Commandez l'ensemble des guides Condé Nast Johansens pour seulement €100
et recevez gratuitement
***la marque bagage** d'une valeur de €23*
***ainsi que l'étui gravé** d'une valeur de €8*

Incluit tous guides montrés.
Recommended Venues - le guide sera envoyé sur publication février 2004.

Merci de compléter votre commande et indiquer les détails de paiement

	tick	
J'ai commandé 2 guides - remise de €8		−€8.00
J'ai commandé 3 guides - remise de €15		−€15.00
J'ai commandé 4 guides - remise de €30		−€30.00
Coût total des guides commandés moins remise (non applicable pour la Collection du Président)	€	
Marque bagage à €23 Quantité et coût total:		€
Etui gravé Johansens à €8 Quantité et coût total:		€
Je souhaite commander la Collection du Président à €100 Quantité et coût total:		€
Frais d'Envoi: (hors UK) plus €9 par guide	☐	€
Collection du Président ajoutez €38	☐	
TOTAL	€	

☐ MasterCard ☐ Visa

Titulaire de la carte (M/Mme/Melle)

Adresse

Pays

Téléphone

E-mail

CB No. Expire le

Signature

Merci de renvoyer ce bon de commande à
Condé Nast Johansens Ltd, c/o Yale Press, Delga House,
Carmichael Road, Norwood, London SE25 5LY, Grande-Bretagne
ou par fax au +44 20 8655 7817

Les détails fournis pourront être utilisés pour vous informer de futurs produits et offres spéciales de Johansens ou d'autres compagnies soigneusement sélectionnées. Merci de cocher cette case si vous ne souhaitez pas recevoir d'autres informations: ☐.
(Votre numéro de téléphone sera exclusivement utilisé pour livraison de votre commande)

Enquête de Satisfaction

Évaluez votre visite à une Condé Nast Johansens Recommendations

Cher client,

Nous espérons que vous avez apprécié votre séjour dans cet établissement recommandé par Johansens. Merci de nous accorder un peu de votre temps pour compléter le questionnaire d'évaluation ci-joint. Ce document est essentiel pour Johansens, non seulement afin de maintenir les standards de qualité de nos Recommandations, mais également afin d'aider le travail de nos inspecteurs.

C'est aussi la meilleure source pour les nominations aux Prix d'Excellence que remet chaque année Johansens aux établissements qui représentent les meilleurs standards et valeurs de l'hébergement indépendant de luxe à travers le monde.

Merci pour votre aide et j'espère que la prochaine fois que vous choisirez un établissement de qualité en Grande-Bretagne, en Irelande, en Europe, en Amérique du Nord, aux Bermudes, aux Caraïbes ou au Pacifique, vous laisserez Johansens être votre guide.

Cordialement,

Tim Sinclair
Sales & Marketing Director, Condé Nast Johansens

P.S. Vous pouvez également compléter ce questionnaire en tapant sur www.johansens.com

1. Vos détails

Votre nom: ....

Votre adresse: ....

....

Code Postal: ....

Pays: ....

Téléphone: ....

E-mail: ....

2. Détails de l'hôtel

Nom de l'hôtel: ....

....

Ville/Lieu: ....

Date de séjour: ....

3. Votre évaluation de l'hotel

Une seule croix par catégorie:

	Excellent	Bon	Décevant	Médiocre
Chambres	❍	❍	❍	❍
Lieux publiques	❍	❍	❍	❍
Cuisine/Restaurant	❍	❍	❍	❍
Service	❍	❍	❍	❍
Accueil	❍	❍	❍	❍
Rapport qualité prix	❍	❍	❍	❍

4. Commentaires

Pour de plus amples commentaires, merci de nous écrire séparément à
Condé Nast Johansens Ltd, 6-8 Old Bond Street, London W1S 4PH, Grande-Bretagne

....

....

....

....

....

Les détails fournis pourront être utilisés pour vous informer de futurs produits et offres spéciales de Johansens ou d'autres compagnies soigneusement sélectionnées.
Merci de cocher cette case si vous ne souhaitez pas recevoir d'autres informations: ☐.

Merci de compléter et d'envoyer ce coupon à:
Condé Nast Johansens Ltd, c/o Yale Press, Delga House, Carmichael Road, Norwood, London SE25 5LY, UK
ou par fax au 020 8655 7817

CONDÉ NAST JOHANSENS

BESTELLFORMULAR

Bestellen Sie **2** Guides → **€8 Rabatt** • Bestellen Sie **3** Guides → **€15 Rabatt** • Bestellen Sie **4** Guides → **€30 Rabatt**

oder bestellen Sie die Chairmans's Collection (Wert: €140) für nur **€100**

Füllen Sie einfach das untenstehende Formular aus, errechnen Sie den Gesamtbetrag und ziehen Sie den entsprechenden Rabatt ab. Geben Sie Ihre Kreditkartendetails an und senden Sie alles frankiert an Condé Nast Johansens Ltd, c/o Yale Press, Delga House, Carmichael Road, Norwood, London SE25 5LY, Großbritannien. Natürlich können Sie auch per Fax unter +44 208 655 7817 bestellen.

SIE KÖNNEN AUCH TELEFONISCH UNTER +44 208 655 7810 bestellen (bitte Ref.-Nr.E008 angeben).

Hotels
Great Britain & Ireland
410 Empfehlungen

Ich bestelle

QUANTITY

Exemplar/e zum Preis von je €29.95

Gesamtbetrag

€

Country Houses
Great Britain & Ireland
255 Empfehlungen

Ich bestelle

QUANTITY

Exemplar/e zum Preis von je €26.95

Gesamtbetrag

€

Hotels & Spas
Europe & Mediterranean
350 Empfehlungen

Ich bestelle

QUANTITY

Exemplar/e zum Preis von je €26.95

Gesamtbetrag

€

Hotels, Inns & Resorts
N America, Caribbean
200 Empfehlungen

Ich bestelle

QUANTITY

Exemplar/e zum Preis von je €21.95

Gesamtbetrag

€

Business Venues
230 Empfehlungen
(Erscheint im Februar 2004)

Ich bestelle

QUANTITY

Exemplar/e zum Preis von je €38.00

Gesamtbetrag

€

Condé Nast Johansens Mappe mit Goldbuchstaben zum Preis von €8

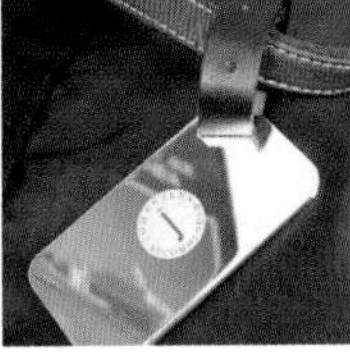

Condé Nast Johansens Luxus-Gepäckanhänger zum Preis von €23

Wenn Sie diese Produkte bestellen möchten, füllen Sie bitte das untenstehende Feld aus.

Die Chairman's Collection

Bestellen Sie die gesamte Condé Nast Johansens-Kollektion für nur €100

***PLUS GRATIS Luxus-Gepäckanhänger** im Wert von €23*

***PLUS GRATIS Mappe** im Wert von €8*

Schließt alle 6 Guides mit ein.

Recommended Venues - wird nach Erscheinen im Februar 2004 versandt.

Bitte füllen Sie Ihren Bestellschein aus und geben Sie Ihre Kreditkartendetails an

	tick	
Ich bestelle 2 Hotelguides - €8 Rabatt	☐	−€8.00
Ich bestelle 3 Hotelguides - €15 Rabatt	☐	−€15.00
Ich bestelle 4 Hotelguides - €30 Rabatt	☐	−€30.00
Gesamtpreis der Guides abzügl. Rabatt (gilt nicht für die Chairman's Collection)		€
Luxus-Gepäckanhänger €23 Menge und Gesamtpreis:		€
Mappe mit Goldbuchstaben €8 Menge und Gesamtpreis:		€
Ich möchte die Chairman's Collection zum Preis von €100 bestellen Menge und Gesamtpreis:		€
Verpackung & Versand: (Außerhalb UK) plus €9 pro Guide oder Chairman's Collection plus €38	☐ ☐	€
Gesamtbetrag		€

☐ MasterCard ☐ Visa

Kredit-karten-inhaber **(Herr/Frau)**

Adresse

PLZ/Ort **Land**

Telefon

E-mail

Kartennr. **Gültig bis**

Unterschrift

Bitte senden Sie dieses Formular frankiert an:
Condé Nast Johansens Ltd, c/o Yale Press, Delga House,
Carmichael Road, Norwood, London SE25 5LY, Großbritannien

Faxbestellungen unter +44 20 8655 7817

Diese Angaben können verwendet werden, um Sie über zukünftige Produkte und Sonderangebote von Johansens und anderen speziell ausgewählten Firmen zu informieren. Sollten Sie vorziehen, solche Informationen nicht zu erhalten, kreuzen Sie bitte dieses Kästchen an: ☐.
(Ihre Telefonnummer wird nur zur Garantie der schnellen und sicheren Lieferung verwendet)

Gastbericht

Lieber Gast,

Ich hoffe, Sie haben Ihren Aufenthalt in diesem von Johansens empfohlenen Hotel genossen. Bitte nehmen Sie sich einen Moment Zeit, diesen Gastbericht auszufüllen. Er stellt eine äußerst wichtige Informationsquelle dar und ist entscheidend dafür, dass wir das hohe Niveau der von uns empfohlenen Hotels aufrechterhalten und unser Team von Inspektoren bei ihrer Arbeit unterstützen können.

Außerdem bildet dieser Bericht die Basis für die "Johansens Awards for Excellence" (Auszeichnungen für besondere Qualität), die jährlich weltweit an die Hotels vergeben werden, die höchste Exklusivität und das beste Preis-Leistungs-Verhältnis für unabhängige Luxusreisen repräsentieren.

Vielen Dank für Ihre Zeit. Ich hoffe, dass Sie sich, wenn Sie zukünftig nach erstklassiger Unterkunft in Großbritannien, Irland, Europa, Nordamerika, Bermuda, der Karibik und dem Pazifikraum suchen, von Johansens beraten lassen.

Mit freundlichen Grüßen,

Tim Sinclair

Sales & Marketing Director, Condé Nast Johansens

P.S. Sie können den Gastbericht auch online ausfüllen: www.johansens.com

1. Angaben zu Ihrer Person

Ihr Name: ....

Ihre Adresse: ....

....

Postleitzahl/Ort: ....

Land: ....

Telefon: ....

E-mail: ....

Diese Angaben können verwendet werden, um Sie über zukünftige Produkte und Sonderangebote von Johansens und anderen speziell ausgewählten Firmen zu informieren. Sollten Sie vorziehen, solche Informationen nicht zu erhalten, kreuzen Sie bitte dieses Kästchen an: ☐.

2. Angaben zum Hotel

Name des Hotels: ....

....

Ort: ....

Datum des Aufenthalts: ....

3. Ihre Hotelbenotung

Kreuzen Sie bitte ein Kästchen in jeder Kategorie an:

	Hervorragend	Gut	Enttäuschend	Schlecht
Gästezimmer	❍	❍	❍	❍
Aufenthaltsräume	❍	❍	❍	❍
Küche/Restaurant	❍	❍	❍	❍
Bedienung/Service	❍	❍	❍	❍
Empfang/Freundlichkeit	❍	❍	❍	❍
Preis-Leistg.-Verhältnis	❍	❍	❍	❍

4. Anmerkungen

Wenn Sie noch weitere Anmerkungen machen möchten, senden Sie diese bitte separat an Condé Nast Johansens Ltd, 6-8 Old Bond Street, London W1S 4PH, Großbritannien

....

....

....

....

....

Bitte senden Sie das ausgefüllte Formular an
Condé Nast Johansens Ltd, c/o Yale Press, Delga House, Carmichael Road, Norwood, London SE25 5LY, Großbritannien
oder per Fax an +44 20 8655 7817

ORDER FORM

Choose from our wide range of titles below

Order 2 Guides get €8 off • Order 3 Guides get €15 off • Order 4 Guides get €30 off

Order the Chairman's Collection worth over €140 for just €100

Simply complete the form below, total the cost and then deduct the appropriate discount. State your preferred method of payment and mail to Condé Nast Johansens Ltd, c/o Yale Press, Delga House, Carmichael Road, Norwood, London SE25 5LY, UK. Fax orders welcome on +44 20 8655 7817

ALTERNATIVELY YOU CAN ORDER IMMEDIATELY BY PHONE ON +44 208 655 7810, please quote ref: E008

Hotels
Great Britain & Ireland
410 Recommendations

I wish to order

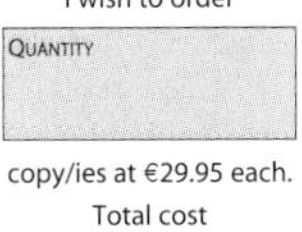

QUANTITY

copy/ies at €29.95 each.
Total cost
€

Country Houses
Great Britain & Ireland
255 Recommendations

I wish to order

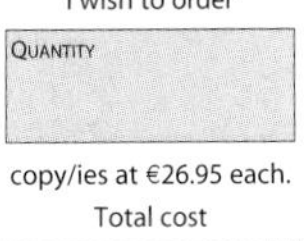

QUANTITY

copy/ies at €26.95 each.
Total cost
€

Hotels & Spas
Europe & Mediterranean
350 Recommendations

I wish to order

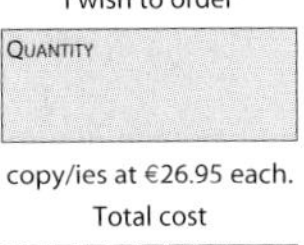

QUANTITY

copy/ies at €26.95 each.
Total cost
€

Hotels, Inns & Resorts
N America, Caribbean
200 Recommendations

I wish to order

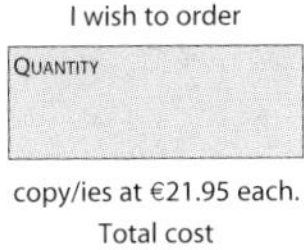

QUANTITY

copy/ies at €21.95 each.
Total cost
€

Business Venues
230 Recommendations
(published Feb 2004)

I wish to order

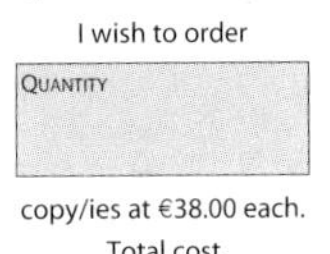

QUANTITY

copy/ies at €38.00 each.
Total cost
€

Condé Nast Johansens
Gold Blocked Slip Case
priced at €8 each

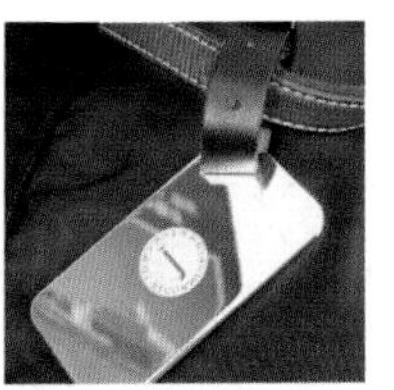

Condé Nast Johansens
Luxury Luggage Tag
priced at
€23 each

To order these items please fill in the appropriate section below

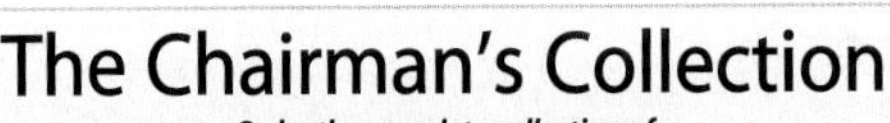

The Chairman's Collection

Order the complete collection of
Condé Nast Johansens Recommended Guides for only €100
PLUS FREE Luxury Luggage Tag worth €23
PLUS FREE Slip Case worth €8

The Chairman's Collection contains all five titles pictured above. The Recommended Venues guide will be dispatched separately on publication in February 2004.

Now please complete your order and payment details

	tick	
I have ordered 2 titles - **€8** off		–€8.00
I have ordered 3 titles - **€15** off		–€15.00
I have ordered 4 titles - **€30** off		–€30.00
Total cost of books ordered minus discount (excluding the Chairman's Collection)		€
Luxury Luggage Tag at **€23** Quantity and total cost:		€
Gold Blocked Slip Case at **€8** Quantity and total cost:		€
I wish to order the Chairman's Collection at **€100** Quantity and total cost:		€

Packing & delivery:

All orders outside UK add **€9** per Guide ☐
or for Chairman's Collection add **€38.00** ☐ €

GRAND TOTAL €

I have chosen my Condé Nast Johansens Guides and (please tick)

Please debit my credit/charge card account ☐

☐ MasterCard ☐ Visa ☐ Switch (Issue Number)

Card Holders Name (Mr/Mrs/Miss)

Address

Country

Telephone

E-mail

Card No. **Exp Date**

Signature

NOW send to
Condé Nast Johansens Ltd, c/o Yale Press, Delga House, Carmichael Road, Norwood, London SE25 5LY, UK
Fax orders welcome on +44 20 8655 7817

The details provided may be used to keep you informed of future products and special offers provided by Condé Nast Johansens and other carefully selected third parties. If you do not wish to receive such information, please tick this box ☐.
(Your phone number will only be used to ensure the fast and safe delivery of your order)

Hotel Brochure Request

Find out further information on the hotels of your choice

Condé Nast Johansens

The Condé Nast Johansens Hotel Brochure Request Service has been established to give guests the opportunity to obtain more information about a Recommendation, additional to that contained within the Johansens Guide.

Condé Nast Johansens will pass your request to the Recommendation specified who will directly send you a brochure.

Hotel name(s) and location(s) (BLOCK CAPITALS)	Page in guide
1	
2	
3	
4	
5	

The recommendation(s) you have chosen will send their brochures directly to the address below

Your name:

Your address:

Postcode:

Telephone: E-mail:

The details provided may be used to keep you informed of future products and special offers provided by Condé Nast Johansens and other carefully selected third parties. If you do not wish to receive such information, please tick this box ☐.

Please return completed form to Condé Nast Johansens Ltd, c/o Yale Press, Delga House, Carmichael Road, Norwood, London SE25 5LY, Great Britain. Alternatively send by fax to +44 20 8655 7817

Hotel Brochure Request

Find out further information on the hotels of your choice

Condé Nast Johansens

The Condé Nast Johansens Hotel Brochure Request Service has been established to give guests the opportunity to obtain more information about a Recommendation, additional to that contained within the Johansens Guide.

Condé Nast Johansens will pass your request to the Recommendation specified who will directly send you a brochure.

Hotel name(s) and location(s) (BLOCK CAPITALS)	Page in guide
1	
2	
3	
4	
5	

The recommendation(s) you have chosen will send their brochures directly to the address below

Your name:

Your address:

Postcode:

Telephone: E-mail:

The details provided may be used to keep you informed of future products and special offers provided by Condé Nast Johansens and other carefully selected third parties. If you do not wish to receive such information, please tick this box ☐.

Please return completed form to Condé Nast Johansens Ltd, c/o Yale Press, Delga House, Carmichael Road, Norwood, London SE25 5LY, Great Britain. Alternatively send by fax to +44 20 8655 7817

BON DE COMMANDE

Commandez **2** Guides & économisez **€8** • Commandez **3** Guides & économisez **€15** • Commandez **4** Guides & économisez **€30**

ou commandez la "Collection du Président" valeur €140 pour seulement **€100**

Completez le coupon ci-après, additionnez les montants et déduisez la remise applicable. Indiquez vos détails de carte de crédit et envoyez le tout à Condé Nast Johansens Ltd, c/o Yale Press, Delga House, Carmichael Road, Norwood, London SE25 5LY, Grande-Bretagne ou par fax au +44 208 655 7817

Si vous le préférez, vous pouvez commander directement au +44 208 655 7810, (donnez la référence: E008)

Hotels
Great Britain & Ireland
410 Recommandations

Je souhaite commander QUANTITÉ copie(s) à €29.95 chacune.
Coût total €

Country Houses
Great Britain & Ireland
255 Recommandations

Je souhaite commander QUANTITÉ copie(s) à €26.95 chacune.
Coût total €

Hotels & Spas
Europe & Mediterranean
350 Recommandations

Je souhaite commander QUANTITÉ copie(s) à €26.95 chacune.
Coût total €

Hotels, Inns & Resorts
N America, Caribbean
200 Recommandations

Je souhaite commander QUANTITÉ copie(s) à €21.95 chacune.
Coût total €

Business Venues
230 Recommandations
(publié le 2004 Février)

Je souhaite commander QUANTITÉ copie(s) à €38.00 chacune.
Coût total €

Etui gravé "Condé Nast Johansens" pour conserver vos guides à €8 chacun.

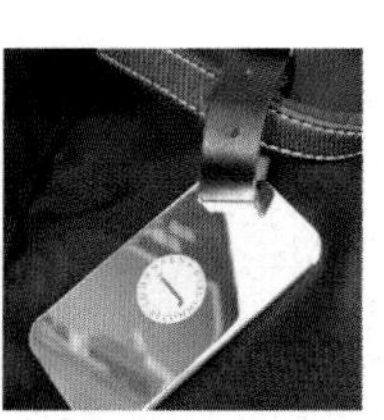

Marque bagage de luxe "Condé Nast Johansens" à €23 chacune

Pour commander ces éléments, complétez s'il vous plaît la section appropriée ci-dessous

La Collection du Président

Commandez l'ensemble des guides Condé Nast Johansens pour seulement €100
et recevez gratuitement
***la marque bagage** d'une valeur de €23*
***ainsi que l'étui gravé** d'une valeur de €8*

Incluit tous guides montrés.
Recommended Venues - le guide sera envoyé sur publication février 2004.

Merci de compléter votre commande et indiquer les détails de paiement

	tick	
J'ai commandé 2 guides - remise de €8		–€8.00
J'ai commandé 3 guides - remise de €15		–€15.00
J'ai commandé 4 guides - remise de €30		–€30.00
Coût total des guides commandés moins remise (non applicable pour la Collection du Président)		€
Marque bagage à €23 Quantité et coût total:		€
Etui gravé Johansens à €8 Quantité et coût total:		€
Je souhaite commander la Collection du Président à €100 Quantité et coût total:		€
Frais d'Envoi: (hors UK) plus €9 par guide / Collection du Président ajoutez €38	☐ ☐	€
TOTAL		€

☐ MasterCard ☐ Visa

Titulaire de la carte (M/Mme/Melle)

Adresse

Pays

Téléphone

E-mail

CB No. Expire le

Signature

Merci de renvoyer ce bon de commande à
Condé Nast Johansens Ltd, c/o Yale Press, Delga House,
Carmichael Road, Norwood, London SE25 5LY, Grande-Bretagne
ou par fax au +44 20 8655 7817

Les détails fournis pourront être utilisés pour vous informer de futurs produits et offres spéciales de Johansens ou d'autres compagnies soigneusement sélectionnées. Merci de cocher cette case si vous ne souhaitez pas recevoir d'autres informations:☐.
(Votre numéro de téléphone sera exclusivement utilisé pour livraison de votre commande)

Demande de Brochures

Le service de demande de brochures de Condé Nast Johansens a été mis en place afin de permettre aux lecteurs d'obtenir de plus amples informations sur une ou plusieurs Recommandations (informations autres que celles contenues dans le Guide Condé Nast Johansens).

Condé Nast Johansens transmettra votre demande à l'établissement spécifié qui vous adressera directement sa brochure.

Nom de l'Hôtel(s) et emplacement(s) (LETTRES MAJUSCULES) Page dans le guide

1 ....

2 ....

3 ....

4 ....

5 ....

La/les Recommandation(s) séléctionnée(s) vous enverront leur brochure directement à l'adresse ci-dessous.

Votre nom: ....

Votre adresse: ....

Code postal/Ville: .... Pays: ....

Téléphone: .... E-mail: ....

Les détails fournis pourront être utilisés pour vous informer de futurs produits et offres spéciales de Johansens ou d'autres compagnies soigneusement sélectionnées. Merci de cocher cette case si vous ne souhaitez pas recevoir d'autres informations: ☐.

Merci de compléter et d'envoyer ce coupon à Condé Nast Johansens Ltd, c/o Yale Press, Delga House, Carmichael Road, Norwood, London SE25 5LY, Grande-Bretagne, ou par fax au +44 20 8655 7817

Demande de Brochures

Le service de demande de brochures de Condé Nast Johansens a été mis en place afin de permettre aux lecteurs d'obtenir de plus amples informations sur une ou plusieurs Recommandations (informations autres que celles contenues dans le Guide Condé Nast Johansens).

Condé Nast Johansens transmettra votre demande à l'établissement spécifié qui vous adressera directement sa brochure.

Nom de l'Hôtel(s) et emplacement(s) (LETTRES MAJUSCULES) Page dans le guide

1 ....

2 ....

3 ....

4 ....

5 ....

La/les Recommandation(s) séléctionnée(s) vous enverront leur brochure directement à l'adresse ci-dessous.

Votre nom: ....

Votre adresse: ....

Code postal/Ville: .... Pays: ....

Téléphone: .... E-mail: ....

Les détails fournis pourront être utilisés pour vous informer de futurs produits et offres spéciales de Johansens ou d'autres compagnies soigneusement sélectionnées. Merci de cocher cette case si vous ne souhaitez pas recevoir d'autres informations: ☐.

Merci de compléter et d'envoyer ce coupon à Condé Nast Johansens Ltd, c/o Yale Press, Delga House, Carmichael Road, Norwood, London SE25 5LY, Grande-Bretagne, ou par fax au +44 20 8655 7817

BESTELLFORMULAR

Bestellen Sie **2** Guides → **€8 Rabatt** • Bestellen Sie **3** Guides → **€15 Rabatt** • Bestellen Sie **4** Guides → **€30 Rabatt**

oder bestellen Sie die Chairmans's Collection (Wert: €140) für nur **€100**

Füllen Sie einfach das untenstehende Formular aus, errechnen Sie den Gesamtbetrag und ziehen Sie den entsprechenden Rabatt ab. Geben Sie Ihre Kreditkartendetails an und senden Sie alles frankiert an Condé Nast Johansens Ltd, c/o Yale Press, Delga House, Carmichael Road, Norwood, London SE25 5LY, Großbritannien. Natürlich können Sie auch per Fax unter +44 208 655 7817 bestellen.

SIE KÖNNEN AUCH TELEFONISCH UNTER +44 208 655 7810 bestellen (bitte Ref.-Nr.E008 angeben).

Hotels
Great Britain & Ireland
410 Empfehlungen

Ich bestelle [QUANTITY] Exemplar/e zum Preis von je €29.95
Gesamtbetrag €

Country Houses
Great Britain & Ireland
255 Empfehlungen

Ich bestelle
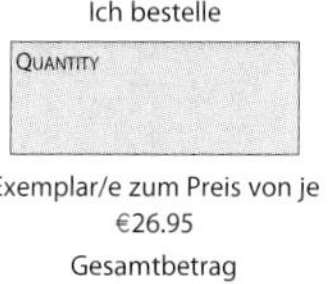
Exemplar/e zum Preis von je €26.95
Gesamtbetrag €

Hotels & Spas
Europe & Mediterranean
350 Empfehlungen

Ich bestelle
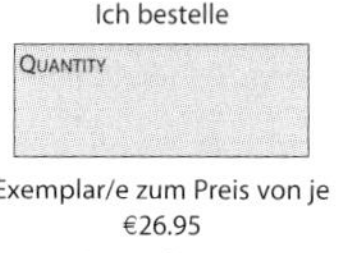
Exemplar/e zum Preis von je €26.95
Gesamtbetrag

Hotels, Inns & Resorts
N America, Caribbean
200 Empfehlungen

Ich bestelle
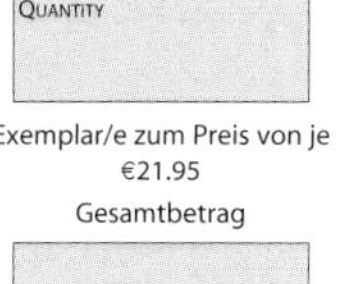
Exemplar/e zum Preis von je €21.95
Gesamtbetrag €

Business Venues
230 Empfehlungen
(Erscheint im Februar 2004)

Ich bestelle [QUANTITY] Exemplar/e zum Preis von je €38.00
Gesamtbetrag €

Condé Nast Johansens Mappe mit Goldbuchstaben zum Preis von €8

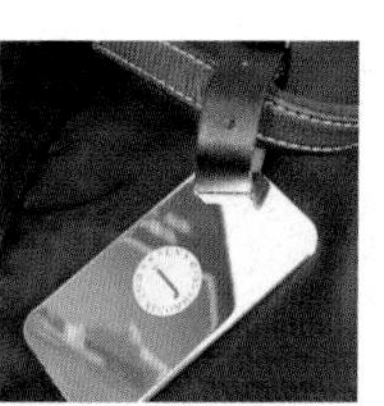

Condé Nast Johansens Luxus-Gepäckanhänger zum Preis von €23

Wenn Sie diese Produkte bestellen möchten, füllen Sie bitte das untenstehende Feld aus.

Die Chairman's Collection

Bestellen Sie die gesamte Condé Nast Johansens-Kollektion für nur €100

***PLUS GRATIS Luxus-Gepäckanhänger** im Wert von €23*

***PLUS GRATIS Mappe** im Wert von €8*

Schließt alle 6 Guides mit ein.
Recommended Venues - wird nach Erscheinen im Februar 2004 versandt.

Bitte füllen Sie Ihren Bestellschein aus und geben Sie Ihre Kreditkartendetails an

	tick	
Ich bestelle 2 Hotelguides - €8 Rabatt		–€8.00
Ich bestelle 3 Hotelguides - €15 Rabatt		–€15.00
Ich bestelle 4 Hotelguides - €30 Rabatt		–€30.00
Gesamtpreis der Guides abzügl. Rabatt (gilt nicht für die Chairman's Collection)		€
Luxus-Gepäckanhänger €23 Menge und Gesamtpreis:		€
Mappe mit Goldbuchstaben €8 Menge und Gesamtpreis:		€
Ich möchte die Chairman's Collection zum Preis von €100 bestellen Menge und Gesamtpreis:		€
Verpackung & Versand: (Außerhalb UK) plus €9 pro Guide oder Chairman's Collection plus €38	☐ ☐	€
Gesamtbetrag		€

☐ MasterCard ☐ Visa

Kredit-karten-inhaber (Herr/Frau)

Adresse

PLZ/Ort Land

Telefon

E-mail

Kartennr. Gültig bis

Unterschrift

Bitte senden Sie dieses Formular frankiert an:
Condé Nast Johansens Ltd, c/o Yale Press, Delga House,
Carmichael Road, Norwood, London SE25 5LY, Großbritannien
Faxbestellungen unter +44 20 8655 7817

Diese Angaben können verwendet werden, um Sie über zukünftige Produkte und Sonderangebote von Johansens und anderen speziell ausgewählten Firmen zu informieren. Sollten Sie vorziehen, solche Informationen nicht zu erhalten, kreuzen Sie bitte dieses Kästchen an: ☐.
(Ihre Telefonnummer wird nur zur Garantie der schnellen und sicheren Lieferung verwendet)

Anforderung von Hotelbroschüren

Dieser Broschürenanforderungsservice wurde eingeführt, um unseren Gästen die Möglichkeit zu geben, sich weitere Informationen über ein von Johansens empfohlenes Hotel zu beschaffen, zusätzlich zu denen im Johansens-Guide.

Johansens wird Ihre Anforderung an das Hotel weiterleiten, das Ihnen dann direkt eine Broschüre zusendet.

Name und Ort des/der Hotels (in GROSSBUCHSTABEN)	Seite im Hotelführer
1	
2	
3	
4	
5	

Die von Ihnen ausgewählten Hotels werden ihre Broschüren direkt an die untenstehende Adresse senden.

Ihr Name:

Ihre Adresse:

Postleitzahl/Ort: Land:

Telefon: E-mail:

Diese Angaben können verwendet werden, um Sie über zukünftige Produkte und Sonderangebote von Johansens und anderen speziell ausgewählten Firmen zu informieren. Sollten Sie vorziehen, solche Informationen nicht zu erhalten, kreuzen Sie bitte dieses Kästchen an ☐.

Bitte senden Sie das ausgefüllte Formular an Condé Nast Johansens Ltd, c/o Yale Press, Delga House, Carmichael Road, Norwood, London SE25 5LY, Großbritannien, oder per Fax an +44 20 8655 7817

Anforderung von Hotelbroschüren

Dieser Broschürenanforderungsservice wurde eingeführt, um unseren Gästen die Möglichkeit zu geben, sich weitere Informationen über ein von Johansens empfohlenes Hotel zu beschaffen, zusätzlich zu denen im Johansens-Guide.

Johansens wird Ihre Anforderung an das Hotel weiterleiten, das Ihnen dann direkt eine Broschüre zusendet.

Name und Ort des/der Hotels (in GROSSBUCHSTABEN)	Seite im Hotelführer
1	
2	
3	
4	
5	

Die von Ihnen ausgewählten Hotels werden ihre Broschüren direkt an die untenstehende Adresse senden.

Ihr Name:

Ihre Adresse:

Postleitzahl/Ort: Land:

Telefon: E-mail:

Diese Angaben können verwendet werden, um Sie über zukünftige Produkte und Sonderangebote von Johansens und anderen speziell ausgewählten Firmen zu informieren. Sollten Sie vorziehen, solche Informationen nicht zu erhalten, kreuzen Sie bitte dieses Kästchen an ☐.

Bitte senden Sie das ausgefüllte Formular an Condé Nast Johansens Ltd, c/o Yale Press, Delga House, Carmichael Road, Norwood, London SE25 5LY, Großbritannien, oder per Fax an +44 20 8655 7817